WALK–DON'T RUN

THE STORY OF

by

Del Halterman

with
Josie Wilson
Bob Bogle
Don Wilson

50 YEARS OF ROCK & ROLL!

Halterman, Del
Walk-Don't Run – The Story of The Ventures
Includes bibliographical references and index
ISBN   978-0-557-04051-3

2nd Edition

ISBN 978-0-557-04051-3

Copyright © 2009 by Del Halterman
All Rights Reserved

Dedicated to the memory of
Josie Wilson
Bob Bogle
Mel Taylor
Howie Johnson
R. "Bob" Reisdorff
Sonia "Sonny" Rivera

Josie Linnea Wilson

Josie Wilson passed away at the age of ninety-one years on February 19, 2007. Her strict business acumen matched with much love and a keen sense of humor, will be sorely missed by countless relatives, friends, and associates. At Josie's funeral, her production of "Softly As I Leave You" by The Nordic Trio was fittingly played for those in attendance. During the reception, a collection of Josie's favorite Ventures recordings accompanied a photo-history of her life.

The Ventures

Bob Bogle

Acknowledgements

My heartfelt thanks to the following people, first The Ventures and close associates, followed alphabetically by the many others whose advice, stories, photographs, and help with such things as book mechanics and language translations made completion of this book possible.

Bob & Yumi Bogle, Don & Dory Wilson, Josie Wilson, Nokie & Judy Edwards, Gerry McGee, Mel Taylor, Fiona Taylor, Leon Taylor, Bob Spalding, and John Durrill.

Bob Adkins, Paul Benbow, Kirk Bjornsgaard, Hal Blaine, Virginia Boles, Steve Bonilla, Dave Burke, Chris Celebrezze, Stephane Chatain, Gordon Close, Dennis Coté, George Creswick, Ray Dahl, Jan Davis, Russ Deck, Jack DeFranco, Ken Dresher, Bettejean Fawver, Dan Forte, Kanad Ghose, Enzo Giobbé, Rolland Grande, Butch Hamblin, Judd Hamilton, Dennis Hite, Bob Hover, Tony Hunt, Sanae Huston, Keith John, Richard Kaplan, Carol Kaye, Barry Keen, Roger Kelly, Mike Kuhn, Stuart Leech, James P. LeGros, Thomas Long, Don Markham, Peter Malski, Art Mineo, Kiyoshi Mochizuki, Gene Moles, Chris Monk, Andy Moseley, Loretta Moseley, Martin Neff, Jason Odd, Davy Peckett, Michel Périllard, Arild Pettersson, Fran Pray, Chidambaram 'Raga' Raghavan, Bob Reisdorff, Aleks Rosenburg, Joe Rosignolo, Glenn Sadin, Judy Sadowsky, Dennis Sanders, Ed Sanner, Paul Selier, Milt Soong, Budd Stidom, Mahiro Tada, Mike Tarno, Joe Tate, Alan Taylor, Keith Thompson, Byron Tietjen, Marty Tippens, Sherri Trujillo, Arnold Van Beverhoudt Jr., Biff Vincent, Stan Wagner, Harvey Wicklund, Bruce Wilson, Staci Layne Wilson, Tim Wilson, George Weir, Gerald Woodage, Donnie K. Wright, Hiroshi Yamachika, Seiji Yamashiro, and Gloria Yuke.

Special thanks to Bruce Smith for his tireless help in editing.

Special thanks also to my wife Emi, who has endured my passion and obsession with The Ventures and their music for over forty-five years, since back before we were married, and also with my submersion into this book project for the past ten years. Without her support and encouragement, the work would have never have been completed.

PREFACE

The Ventures are essentially, in alphabetical order, Bob Bogle and Don Wilson. They founded the group as a duo and performed as such until they could see their way clear to expand, form a band, and make recordings. Throughout half a century, The Ventures group has consisted of many more musicians than most fans would imagine, but essentially, Bob and Don have always been there. The phenomenon of an instrumental group enjoying such longevity was no accident or twist of fate. It was a combination of sheer ambition, persistence, and natural talent that kept the group going. Of the many others who held positions in the band and its management, first and foremost was Don's mother, Josie, a woman who has been described by her business partner as "shy, but filled with determination."

Much has been written about The Ventures with facts being distorted or omitted. Although aging memories are not always reliable, immense effort has been made to verify the information presented here. Various accounts from personal interviews with band members, their families and associates, have been compared with each other along with my own document collecting of forty-seven years. Regardless of any missing or erroneous data here, statisticians, record companies, and broadcasters everywhere concur that The Ventures remain

"The Number One Instrumental Group in the World."
Cash Box – December, 1966

"*Only the truly talented are able to produce work so consistently good that the public awaits each new effort.*"

Phyl Garland

Contents

Acknowledgements		5
Preface		6
Chapter One	The Sixties	9
Chapter Two	The Seventies	184
Chapter Three	The Eighties	237
Chapter Four	The Nineties	301
Chapter Five	Ventures Forever	326
Appendix 1	Recording Sessions	372
Appendix 2	Alternate recording titles	376
	Index	379 - 1
	References	383 - 7

Early Wilson Family Photos

CHAPTER ONE
The Sixties

It looked like the beginning of another boring evening as Don Wilson returned to his job after supper. He knew everything about the fifty-some vehicles in his father's used-car lot, having tinkered with, tested, and cleaned every one of them during his days on the job, only to return at 6:00 p.m. as a salesman wearing a necktie. Most of the cars were in excellent shape, but there were a few, priced accordingly, that teetered on the brink of reliability. Business was slow and as darkness fell, Don switched on the floodlights. Peering outside, he could see that it was happening again. Someone was inspecting the blue '54 Ford that burned nearly as much oil as it did gasoline. Like Don, the smartly dressed fellow that had been strolling through the lot appeared to be in his mid-twenties. Don decided to approach him, but not until *Rebel Rouser* by Duane Eddy and the Rebels had finished playing on the radio.

The body and tires looked good to Bob Bogle as he raised the hood of a good-looking prospect. Having prided himself on driving attractive and fairly new cars since the age of sixteen, he was looking for something clean, reliable, and slightly out of the ordinary. The engine in this car was as clean as a whistle, and the oil on its dipstick showed no discoloration. As Bob considered the vehicle as being his next, a young salesman approached him. At that moment, history took a turn.

DON WILSON

Donald Leroy Wilson was born February 10, 1933 in Tacoma, Washington to Josie and Woodrow "Woody" Wilson. At the time, the couple had a daughter, two-year-old Jacqueline. Five years later, a second daughter, Sally, was born.

When Don was eight, his mother began teaching him to chord on a stringed instrument called a "tiple" [pronounced "tipple" or "tip-lay"], which she had owned since her teenage years. As Josie remembers: "The tiple was somewhat like a ukulele but slightly larger, and with similar tuning of its four main strings. There were six more strings tuned in octaves, which were merely to give more ring to the instrument. The tiple is not well known anymore, but was fairly common around 1930 when sold by Sears-Roebuck. Don would strum chords and sing for relatives, and they always encouraged him. As he grew older, he developed an admiration for big bands like Tommy Dorsey's, but mostly he enjoyed the popular country and western singers.

"While Don was in grade school, he wanted to take trombone lessons, but his father was making less than fifteen dollars a week working in a factory that made battery separators. Our rent then was very close to a week's pay. Don paid for the lessons and bought his own instrument with the money he earned on his newspaper route."

Don stayed with the horn, but in junior high school he met a boy with the unlikely name of Bud Costello, who owned a guitar. They became friends, and soon Bud and Don were singing in harmony while playing the guitar and tiple. Being invited to entertain at a party gave them encouragement to enter a few talent contests. Don remembers experimenting with Bud's guitar in order to obtain a louder, resonating sound by holding it against the oven of his mother's stove. He never imagined that he would someday make a career of playing and coaxing new sounds from such an instrument. Later, Don gained a little more guitar-playing experience with Marty Pettit, another friend that owned a guitar and lived in an apartment next-door.

Being active in sports while attending Lincoln High School, Don put the trombone aside in favor of wrestling classes. In time, he was awarded a school letter and the State Championship in his weight class. During summer breaks, he found a job on the railroad, first as a carpenter's helper, and later as a full-fledged bridge-carpenter. After finishing high school, he worked for a while in a lumber mill. Then, instead of waiting to be drafted, Don decided to volunteer. On February 5, 1953, a few days before his 20th birthday, he was inducted into the U.S. Army for a two-year term. After basic training at Fort Lewis, near his home, the Army sent Don to West Germany to be stationed in Monteith Barracks at Fürth, north of Nuremberg. Further training included a signaling course at an Army school in Augsburg. There, he met a fellow from California who was stationed at Nuremberg. The two became friends, but after the Signals course, Don would not see Mike Gutierrez again for over ten years.

Back in Fürth, Don applied his trombone talent in the Special Services by joining the 39th Infantry Regimental Band, and was soon also touring the area with an Army dance combo. His interest in music revived, Don wrote home and asked his mother to send the old tiple overseas so that he could improve his playing while stationed in the barracks. Josie obliged and immediately sent the old relic to Germany. Don spent much of his free time on the tiple until the day that a barracks buddy approached him with a sad tale. Jack had a date with a girl that night, but he was nearly out of money. He offered his guitar to Don for a hundred marks [then about twenty-five dollars]. Emptying his pockets, Don counter-offered eighty-seven marks plus the tiple. The deal was sealed and as Don recalls, he too fell in love; "I simply could not put that guitar down for more than five minutes. I heard later that Jack married that girl, and in a way, you could say that I've been going steady with guitars ever since. A recruit that played the glockenspiel on parade offered to teach me some chords. I was surprised he knew the guitar until he said that he'd played professional jazz guitar in the late forties with the famous Page Cavanaugh Trio. He showed me how to chord, and pretty soon I was playing for the guys in the barracks, trying to sound like Hank Williams."

As for the tiple, Josie regrets: "I sometimes wish I hadn't sent it away to Germany, but I hardly ever said 'no' to my kids if they really wanted something. I would like to have kept the tiple because I haven't seen or heard of one since that time. As a teenager I had a girlfriend who also had a tiple. In the summer we would play and sing together outdoors to the neighbors sitting out on their porches."

In August of 1954, Don was promoted to the rank of Corporal. He was honorably discharged six months later, shortly before his 22nd birthday. When he returned to the U.S., his parents had moved to Seattle, and he took a job in his father's used-car lot on the corner of Dravus Street and 15th Avenue West in the Interbay neighborhood of the city. Along the way, he married a lovely girl named Karen, and the couple began raising a family.

By now, Don could sing and play several popular country hits. The 'twangy guitar' of Duane Eddy hit the airwaves then, and at the age of twenty-five, Don became an instant rock 'n' roll fan.

BOB BOGLE

Robert Lenard Bogle was born January 16, 1934 on a small farm near Tulsa, Oklahoma. Rural midwives were common then, and a neighboring lady assisted with Bob's birth. Bob was the second born of four boys and a girl.

During the 1930s, some half-million migrants headed west to escape the ravages of the Dust Bowl, but the Bogles held out until 1940. Bob was six when the family sold everything and struck out to settle in California. In the ensuing search for employment, the family proceeded up and down the West Coast, with father and sons hiring out for any and all kinds of farm work. During school months, the boys worked in the mornings and again in the evenings. Finally, Bob's father found work in an Oregon sawmill and settled in the Portland district near the village of Forest Grove. Here, the last of the children and Bob's only sister, Sybil, was born. Around this time, Bob's older brother, Clarence, bought a lap-steel guitar. Even in the hands of a beginner it sounded good because of its open chord tuning. Bob learned to move a small steel bar along the strings to change chords, and by the age of twelve, he could sing and chord to a few country songs while dreaming of becoming a movie star.

Later, younger brother, Dennis, got a regular guitar, but when he joined the Air Force, he left the instrument behind. Bob then took an interest in the guitar, and could soon play simple songs while simultaneously chording.

In reminiscing, Bob recalls his first mistake in life; "At the age of fifteen, I decided to quit grade nine and go to work. Persuading my parents wasn't easy, but they finally gave in. I began in the lumber industry, first as a logger, then as a tractor operator, before getting an inside job at a plywood plant. Later, I found work at my uncle's Southwestern Waterproofing Company. I thought it was a good setup, living with my aunt and uncle while learning a trade. My uncle's business involved the restoration and repair of brick buildings. I started by working high on scaffolding that was suspended by ropes. At first I was a hod carrier, taking wet cement up a ladder to the bricklayers. I must have put in a thousand miles up and down that ladder. The foreman probably saw that I was getting bow-legged, as he promoted me to apprentice bricklayer. I got pretty good at that, and soon I was a journeyman. In those days, the trade unions were strong and strict, so I had to join. Being a teenager, I was the youngest journeyman in the union. Some of the apprentices were older than I was. I learned a lot about the repair of brick buildings, but the hard work and long hours eventually made me realize my mistake in quitting school, so I enrolled in night-classes at Benson Polytechnic in Portland."

While working eight to eleven hours a day on the job, Bob continued with his education. Jobs were still scarce, so he stayed with the job at hand. Before long, he was being assigned big projects in the outlying area that took weeks or months to complete.

THE MEETING

Bob was eighteen when the Seattle based Sahara Waterproofing Company secured a contract to restore a building in Vancouver, Washington. They put out a notice that they were hiring workers for $4.85 an hour. This was considered a decent wage at the time, and Bob decided to better himself. Sahara hired him on the spot, and when the Vancouver job was finished, the company offered him permanent employment if he would relocate to Seattle. Bob accepted and made the move.

As Bob recalls, with better wages and big city living, destiny soon prevailed; "After living in Seattle for a couple of years, I started thinking about changing automobiles and looking around the used-car lots after supper. One evening, I was looking around a place called The Bargain Spot. As soon as I became interested in a particular used car, a salesman walked up and introduced himself as Don Wilson. Don quickly told me that the car I was looking at was not in very good condition, and he showed me a unique looking '55 Hudson that he said was in fine condition. I checked it out and decided to buy it. One of my first cars had been a '52 Hudson Hornet. It was fairly luxurious, and when I showed up at a drive-in or a ball game, some of the guys I had gone to school with wouldn't believe that this wasn't my dad's car.

Don Wilson and Bob Bogle

"While Don was doing the paperwork, I told him that he was really too honest to be a good used-car salesman. He could have sold me the lemon and his boss would have been happy. Don laughed and said that he was the owner's son, but he hated to sell a vehicle that wasn't in top condition. We became pretty good friends that day, and later on we found that we had a lot of the same interests."

Metaphorically, while Don could appreciate the simplicity and efficiency of a mousetrap, Bob would contemplate building a better one for half the cost. While Don was talkative and very outgoing, Bob was more quiet and reserved. This wide difference in personalities may well be why the two hit it off so well. Bob continues; "After that, I often stopped by The Bargain Spot to visit or to go for lunch with Don. As we talked, the topic often drifted to his discontent with cleaning vehicles and performing minor repairs by day with hopes of selling them in the evenings on a commission basis. After I'd worked several months in the Seattle area, my immediate supervisor, Rod Eggerling, left Sahara to start his own business, The Pioneer Waterproofing Company. This left an opening at Sahara, and I was promoted to foreman. I then bought a house in a Seattle suburb called Mountlake Terrace. One of the first places I visited was a store called Joos Music, run by a fellow named Art Joos."

Upon learning of Bob's promotion, Don asked him if there might be an opening at Sahara for an apprentice. Bob spoke to *his* boss and within a month, Don was hired as a hod carrier and placed with a local Seattle crew. After three months, a contract came up where Don and Bob were on the same job, with Bob as the foreman. The work at hand involved removing and replacing old mortar on brick buildings. One day, Don had car trouble and took the bus to work. After work, while waiting at a bus stop he was offered a ride home in Bob's Hudson. When Don noticed a beat-up guitar case on the backseat, he remarked that he, too, had been playing around with a guitar since his Army days. A jam session was arranged for Sunday, where they procured the idea of playing together in their off-duty hours. Thinking back, Bob recalls: "We usually rode together, traveling by car and sharing a low-cost hotel room. Our guitar sessions soon became a relaxing diversion from the drudgery of construction work, and after buying a couple of chord books we made some rather pleasing sounds. After a few weeks on those old sun-warped artifacts, we wondered what our music would sound like on electric guitars. Incidentally, it wasn't too long after that when I traded the Hudson back to Woody Wilson for a '58 Chevy Impala. The car was so attractive that people on the street stopped to look and walk around it. This was the year that American automobiles switched from having two large headlights to four smaller ones."

Browsing pawnshops after work resulted in Don and Bob purchasing two electric guitars. According to Don, the cost was around ten dollars each for his Harmony guitar and Bob's Kay. The guitars were hard to play by modern standards, but the boys found them to be much better than their old ones. At the same time they obtained a small amplifier with dual inputs, allowing both to play through it at once. Excited with this new equipment, they practiced even more while thinking how wonderful it would be to have a career in music. The long hours of dirty, strenuous work brought dreams of escaping into the world of recording and live entertainment.

Don could read music written in the bass clef, as this is how trombone music is printed, like the left-hand lines of a piano score. Guitar music, however, is presented in treble clef notation, and is difficult to read for a person trained in the bass clef. Thus, Don and Bob relied solely on chord books, their ears, and the talent with which they were born. Fondly, Bob remembers: "I enjoyed practicing so much that I would play late into the night without the amplifier until I suddenly realized that it was after two in the morning. It wasn't a problem on weekends, but I was sleepy some days at work. When Don and I got together on the weekends, we would play *really* late, with the amplifier turned on. Sometimes we had complaints from neighbors about the noise we made.

"Part of the job in restoring a brick building involves grinding out old mortar from between the bricks to a depth of about a half inch. The space is then filled with fresh mortar mix. The procedure is called tuck-pointing. The grinding was done with a power saw fitted with an abrasive blade. Don and I had to wear goggles and respirators as the air was filled with choking cement dust. Sometimes we worked on a scaffold, swinging 300 feet above ground. Every day, after only a few minutes of this kind of work, we were too dusty to be even recognizable. When the tuck-pointing was done, we usually had to sandblast the brick surface to remove weather stains and moss. Sandblasting was another dirty job that required hundred-pound bags of sand to be hoisted onto the roof. This was usually accomplished by pulling the bags hand over hand with a rope up the side of the building. During lunch break one day, while eating cold sandwiches in the basement of the building we were working on, Don looked at me and said, 'I can't wait until we get to the point where the heaviest thing we will have to pick up is a guitar.' I was tired, cold, and miserable, but I was still able to laugh. I'm still not sure what the biggest motivation to play my guitar was; success in the music business or getting away from hell."

FAST FRIENDLY FRETS

By the fall of 1958, the boys were thinking seriously about entertaining on the local front. Realizing they were struggling with inferior equipment, they decided to take the plunge into some top line professional instruments. As Bob recalls, they went to Joos Music, near his home; "We selected two Fender guitars and a Fender 'Twin' amplifier. As it turned out, the Jazzmaster was not yet available in Seattle, so I got a Stratocaster and Don ended up with a single pickup model called the Musicmaster. I was making more money at the time, so I carried the debt for the purchase. Immediately, we found playing to be much easier and exciting, as the necks were straight and the strings were low. Not only did the beauty and feel of the new guitars excite us; gone were the sore fingertips that stung every time we put our hands in water. We also started collecting as many guitar records as we could find.

"When we bought the guitars, Art Joos said that the Stratocaster came with free lessons in his guitar school for the first six months. I was happy with the deal, but we ran into a snag on the very first lesson. He laid out the music for 'Mary Had A Little Lamb' and started showing me where the notes were so I could pick out the tune. I showed Art that I could pick out that, or any song I knew, and stated that I wanted to learn chords. Art obliged, and wrote out words to familiar songs, placing the chord names above them and drawing finger charts for each. After six weeks of this, he told me, 'You must be practicing a lot because you've mastered all the chords I know! It's time we move on to some other subjects in your lessons.' I said that I would now stop with the lessons, having found what I was looking for. With that, Art advised that if I was thinking of trying to make money in music, I should forget it and play guitar as a hobby. Art considered himself a very good guitarist, but he had concluded that it was impossible to make a living at it."

Luckily for Bob, Don, and millions of record buyers, Art's advice fell on deaf ears that day. Bob did not visit Art Joos again for almost two years, but when he did, the two had a good laugh. Up on the wall above the counter was a photo of Bob with the added caption; "I Taught This Man How To Play." As Bob admits, it was not all that implausible; "Actually, Art Joos taught me ninety percent of the guitar chords that I would ever use."

Having always liked to sing, Don now had the chance to get serious about his talent. With Bob's encouragement, Don began learning more vocals to add to their growing list of instrumentals. Practice mixed with eager enthusiasm brought the twosome to the point where they began looking for chances to let someone else hear what they could do. With a repertoire of some twenty tunes, they carried their guitars and amplifier in the car at all times, ready to set up and play for anyone with the slightest interest. One day, they stopped by a car lot where Calvin, a friend of Don's worked. It was not long before the subject of their musical obsession became the topic. Business on the lot was slow, and Calvin anxiously called for a demonstration in the office. When he saw the beautiful Fender equipment and heard Bob and Don perform, Calvin nearly burst with honest excitement. His enthusiasm was such a confidence booster that Bob and Don began telling their friends that they were available for parties, and even weddings, for absolutely no charge. Then, some neighbors living a couple blocks from Don asked them to entertain and play dance music for what Bob later described as a "big, full-blown party where everyone was having a *real* good time. Everything we played was followed by huge applause and sincere compliments. One happy guest spouted: 'You guys are going to be famous some day, and *we* will be able to say we knew you before you made it big'." But then, as Bob thinks back, the party was marred by the abundance of alcohol; "After about two hours, an attractive lady that had obviously been drinking came up to talk to us while we were in the middle of a song. We kept on playing while she talked, telling us how great we were and how impressed she was with the rhythm. A guy who was apparently her husband became jealous and told her that he wanted to leave. When she insisted on staying until the music ended, he said, 'I'll fix that. I'll end it right now.' He grabbed the neck of Don's guitar, holding the strings down and muting the sound. Big mistake. Suddenly he was on the floor holding his mouth. He had a cracked lip and Don had barely skipped a beat. That's when I realized how serious Don was about our music."

The pair received invitations to play for more parties, and they accepted whenever their work schedule permitted. The way they played worked well, each taking turns on lead guitar while the other provided rhythmic backing. In time, Bob played more and more lead, while Don perfected his percussive method for rhythm.

Early in 1959, work at Sahara Waterproofing slowed to a crawl. Bob and Don then contracted themselves to Pioneer Construction, the company owned by Bob's old boss. Pioneer had secured a lengthy job about 300 miles from Seattle, in Pullman, Washington, for repair work on the state's college (now WSU) campus buildings. The population of Pullman was then around 6,000, but due to the college it nearly doubled when school was in session. About once a month during the job, Don and Bob would drive home on Friday night, and return to Pullman on Sunday evening. The five-hour drive always passed very quickly as they fantasized about appearing on radio, television, and making hit records.

While the union scale for out of town work allowed a daily subsistence of only seven dollars, the boys recall that it was enough for them to live on. Arriving to begin the job, they checked into the Washington Hotel, an old establishment with tiny rooms and a "community" bathroom off the hall. Rooms were five dollars per night, and as they were making payments on two guitars and an amplifier, Bob and Don shared a room.

The hotel was owned and operated by a couple with three sons and a daughter, all of whom rotated shifts on the front desk. As regular customers, Don and Bob soon became friends with the family. Noticing a large banquet room that seemed seldom used, the two thought it would be a much better place to practice than in their room next to other hotel guests. Stressing this fact to the owner, regular evening sessions ensued that lasted until well after midnight. When the alarm clock rang at six in the morning, the boys were tempted to throw it out of the window, but resisting this urge, Bob and Don always arrived at work on time.

During the evenings, college students passing by would hear music and come in to see what was happening. The audience grew larger each night, which was just fine with Don and Bob. A local student of dentistry, Jack Lilywhite, soon befriended them with an invitation to play for a Friday night record hop at the college. No pay was involved, but the duo was thrilled at being asked to perform and they hastily learned as many top-forty rock 'n' roll songs as possible.

Jack Lilywhite was also a budding guitarist, and after a couple of immensely successful Friday night dances, he offered the use of some recording equipment that was set up in his father's basement in case Bob and Don wished to make a demo tape.

A few weeks later, Bob and Don heard about Saturday night dances at the Elks Lodge in nearby Moscow, just across the state line in Idaho. Apparently, the music was from someone's record collection and mostly older couples patronized the dances. Bob spoke to the manager and obtained what they consider their first professional booking for the sum of twenty dollars each. A few days later, a local newspaper advertised; "DANCE TO THE MUSIC OF THE BOB BOGLE BAND." While laughing at this, the boys wondered how they would be received as only two guitarists. Then, another concern arose regarding their repertoire. Knowing the Elks Club to be an older crowd, Don and Bob immediately began learning several ballads and "old standards." The twosome worked hard to make up for the lack of drums and bass, striving for as "full" a sound as possible. Don hit the chords fairly hard on the up-tempo numbers, while Bob worked at playing lead over the chords. Their amplifier had a tremolo effect that worked for a few numbers, but the throbbing volume became tiresome. Bob found that he preferred the true vibrato effect obtained by holding the guitar's pitch-bending bar while picking or strumming. That sound, backed with Don's driving rhythm, produced a unique blend that would become one of their keys to success.

At this time, the pair also began thinking about their stage presence. Bob, being clothes-conscious by nature and considered by most as a "snappy dresser," had no trouble convincing Don that matching jackets and ties would improve their image in the eyes of "the Elks crowd." Their clean-cut appearance was indeed important, but it was Bob and Don's music that brought the Elks dances to life. The mixture of upbeat pop songs and older "big band" tunes was a huge hit with the mature audience as they danced to two-guitar arrangements of oldies like *Hawaiian War Chant*, *Blue Tango*, and *Yellow Bird*. The crowd also seemed to enjoy some of the modern "teen hits," perhaps making them feel younger. A few good laughs were also had when Don introduced a few numbers with an uncanny impersonation of TV's popular variety show host, Ed Sullivan.

WALK-DON'T RUN

Along with buying and learning all of the hit singles, Don and Bob collected instrumental albums to learn songs for their play list. They tried some Les Paul tunes, but his dexterity and multi-track recording techniques prevented the boys from copying his style. They listened extensively to Chet Atkins and picked up many tunes from his albums, but again, Chet's finger-style picking was much too advanced for them to copy. They did, however, manage to glean some songs from the recordings of Duane Eddy, finding it easy to imitate his sound and style. They loved Duane's sound and the new popularity of that sound also delighted their audiences.

Bob and Don's fascination with Chet Atkins had led to a growing collection of his recordings. Of these, their favorite was the 1957 album owned by Bob, *Hi-Fi In Focus*. Among the great old tunes like *Lullaby of the Leaves*, *Tara's Theme*, and *El Cumbanchero*, Chet played a difficult sounding tune called *Walk-Don't Run*. It had been written and recorded in 1956 by guitarist Johnny Smith, popular at the time for working with Stan Getz, a most respected alto sax artist in the jazz community. Bob and Don had not heard Johnny's recording, but gradually, they were able to simplify the chord pattern of Chet's version and give *Walk-Don't Run* a danceable, swinging upbeat. Don remembers their fascination with the tune; "Chet's version was a complicated semi-jazz thing that he played finger-style. We tried playing along with it, but we couldn't even come close. It was far too advanced for us, but for some odd reason, we kept going back to it. In about three months we had it completely rearranged into a rock style that we were satisfied with. We didn't think it was a big deal or anything, but after adding the number to our repertoire, we noticed a new excitement from our audience. Each time we played in public, we were swamped with requests to play *Walk-Don't Run*, sometimes up to five or six times!" As Bob recalls; "It was Don who came up with the arrangement. I thought it was strange at first, but it just kept getting better and better."

More practice and playing for dances brought Don and Bob many new friends. As their fan following grew, a rousing cheer would accompany the familiar A–G–F–E chord progression that introduced *Walk-Don't Run*. According to Bob, their confidence was soon given another boost; "A fellow introducing himself as Gary Andrews asked if we would come to Spokane and play for a party on the following Sunday. We were happy to oblige, and after a two-hour drive north from Pullman, we spent the rest of the day and evening playing for over twenty of Gary's friends. We received so many great compliments that we felt like stardom had already happened to us. We woke up to reality the next morning when we found ourselves on the business end of a sandblasting hose."

After months of nightly practicing and playing for dances each week, Don and Bob started thinking about recording. They stopped booking dances in Pullman in favor of returning home to Seattle on weekends. In nearby Tacoma, Don's sister, Jacqueline, had a nice home where she graciously welcomed them to rehearse on weekends. As Don remembers, he bought a used tape recorder and began recording the repertoire of the two would-be pop stars; "We set that little recorder with its mike on a chair, and taped a half-dozen of our best songs, including *Walk-Don't Run*. It was a real pain because the tape would snap during rewind, and we were always splicing it back together. Just Bob and I were on it, with no bass or drums."

Don played the tape for his mother, forty-five-year-old Josie Wilson. Josie had always encouraged Don's musical interests because she, too, was a talented songwriter and poet. With full confidence in her son and his friend, she spared no energy or expense in helping the pair break into the record business. First, she called C&C Distributors, a company that circulated records for independent northwest labels. The folks there referred Josie to thirty-nine-year-old Bob Reisdorff, who had been their promotion manager before going into partnership with his boss, Lou Lavinthal in January 1959 to form Dolphin Records. By now called Dolton Records, the fledgling Seattle company was known for the huge Fleetwoods hit, *Come Softly To Me* [Dolphin 1].

The label was formed after Reisdorff heard a tape from some Olympia, Washington high-school students calling themselves Two Girls And A Guy. Recognizing the trio's highly marketable talent, Reisdorff and Lavinthal set about managing the group while realizing they needed someone knowledgeable about recording. Around this time, Reisdorff was getting ukulele lessons from a man named Paul Tutmarc. As luck would have it, Paul's thirty-five-year-old wife was a superb singer and competent guitarist who had made over a dozen records under the name of Bonnie Guitar. Bonnie's Dark Moon and Mister Fire Eyes had been major hits for the Dot label in 1957. Knowing she had gained extensive experience in the recording studios of Los Angeles, Reisdorff and Lavinthal offered Bonnie a third of their new company if she would be their recording director. Bonnie accepted, and her soft guitar was soon accompanying Come Softly to Me as sung by Two Girls And A Guy. Meanwhile, Reisdorff began his part in managing by suggesting the trio find a new name. According to lead singer Gretchen Christopher, they took that name from Fleetwood, the local Olympia telephone exchange. Lou Lavinthal remembers that time in early 1959; "Bonnie took The Fleetwoods into a recording studio in West Seattle run by a fellow named Joe Boles. Then, Bob took 'Come Softly' to Hollywood for some enhancement and mixing at Liberty Records. He returned with pressings and started promoting the song locally while I sent it out to friends who owned distributorships like ours around the country. In Philly, a distributor friend of mine took it to a local disc jockey. When he played it, there was a lot of immediate reaction and we received our first large order. The song hit the top of the charts in April, and in May we got a legal notice from Doubleday in the New York area, claiming the name of Dolphin Records was under their ownership. It was very small and not popular in the business, so that's probably why we missed it during our search for a name."

Bob Reisdorff, Bonnie Guitar, and The Fleetwoods

The label name was changed to the meaningless "Dolton," but its artsy image of three dolphins remained. Soon, the company had a number one hit on its hands and Bob contracted Liberty Records to handle the huge distribution job. Seven months later The Fleetwoods' third release, *Mr. Blue* [Dolton 4], also went to the top, distinguishing them as the first artists in the world to top the charts twice in one year. Dolphin/Dolton operations had begun in C&C Distributors' south Seattle warehouse, but after more hits from the Fleetwoods, Reisdorff set up office space for Dolton at 622 Union Street. The new promo man at C&C was Jerry Dennon of Portland, Oregon.

Bonnie Guitar recorded *Candy Apple Red* [Dolton 10] in 1959. When it charted at #97 in December, it was scheduled for re-release on Dolton 19. However, after disputes over whom or what should be recorded, Bonnie left Dolton with Jerry Dennon to form Seattle's Jerden Records, and Dolton 19 never surfaced. For the next twenty years, Bonnie enjoyed success as a prolific and popular country artist.

As Josie recalls; "Bob Reisdorff had an uncanny gift for recognizing a hit song. It's amazing that five of the first six Dolton records where on the national charts in 1959, and two of them made Number One!"

The two chart toppers were, of course, the aforementioned Fleetwoods tunes on Dolton 1 and 5. The Frantics made 91 and 93 in Billboard with *Straight Flush* [Dolton 2] and *Fog Cutter* [Dolton 6], while *I Love An Angel* by Little Bill And The Bluenotes [Dolton 4] reached number 66. In addition, *You Mean Everything To Me* (the flip side of *Mr. Blue*) was a number 84 hit for The Fleetwoods.

Josie's call to Reisdorff ended with his consent to an audition, and at the appointed time, Don and Bob took their homemade tape to the office at 622 Union Street. After listening to the recording, Reisdorff kindly told the duo that although they were good guitar players, this was not what he was looking for. He had already signed a Seattle based instrumental group whose records had been mildly accepted, but the demand for their music did not seem overly great. Don and Bob were well aware of The Frantics, whose sound, in addition to guitar, bass, and drums, included organ and saxophone.

Reisdorff advised further that the pair compose some original tunes, as finding the right material was an important part of getting a hit record. He went on to say how they would have to totally immerse themselves if they hoped for even a small chance at breaking into the field of top forty hits. For starters, he suggested they visit some record distributors and radio stations, and while there, get to know some key people in the music business, especially managers and disc jockeys. These were the folks who could supply invaluable pointers on how the industry worked. Reisdorff also suggested that the two try to learn something from Ron Peterson, guitarist for The Frantics who gave lessons on the side. Bob gave it a try, but quit after three sessions with Peterson, feeling it was a waste of time and money.

Josie Wilson in 1956

Bob and Don were disappointed, but not discouraged. Following Reisdorff's advice, they started with a visit to Seattle's popular AM radio station, KJR. There they met music director John Stone, who welcomed them but did not offer much encouragement. The next stop was C&C Record Distributors, where the eager pair mentioned Bob Reisdorff's name in order to talk to top executive, Lou Lavinthal. Lavinthal treated the pair well, granting them a long and enlightening conversation. Once more, they obtained valuable, but discouraging advice as Lou expounded on the record business as exceedingly difficult to break into, especially in the Northwest, far from the mainstreams of Hollywood or New York. Don and Bob heard again how the odds were stacked against them with literally hundreds of musicians striving for hits. Many of these acts were associated with major companies that had financing and promotion by the big labels, but still failed to score in this viciously competitive profession. There were just too few hours in the day for program managers to even listen to the number of records being released, much less add them to their play list. And with radio time being so valuable, a "catch 22" situation existed where the smaller stations would only play the current hits for fear of sinking ratings. Some might participate in breaking a new record, but would not play it in prime time until it appeared on the national charts.

Undaunted, Don and Bob used their new knowledge to formulate a plan. Being quite good at impressions, Don had learned to imitate several movie stars since doing his Ed Sullivan bit for the Elks Hall dances in Idaho. While collecting various hats, the two worked up a musical comedy routine to the tune of Because of You. As Don mimicked one voice after another, he would put on a different hat. Besides Ed Sullivan, he mimicked Walter Brennan, James Cagney, Lionel Barrymore, James Stewart, Edward G. Robinson, Jack Benny, Lawrence Welk, and Bela Lugosi as Dracula. Audience response to this was so good that the twosome formulated a "Plan B." If they could not get a hit record, they would develop a lounge act and strive to establish themselves in Las Vegas.

The boys' next plan was to enter every talent contest where they qualified. In the fifties, many radio stations sponsored weekly talent contests, but upon inquiring, Bob and Don learned that these were merely "popularity polls." With prizes awarded according to applause, the contestant bringing along the most friends was usually the winner. The pair knew they could not win that way, but they still entered, just for the experience. To their delight, they won two contests in a row without knowing anyone in the audience. Relishing in victory, they decided they needed a stage name. Pondering their livelihoods, they supposed: "We know a trade in construction. We sing, do impersonations, and we can trade off on lead and rhythm guitar." The word versatile suddenly came to mind, and they named themselves "The Versatones."

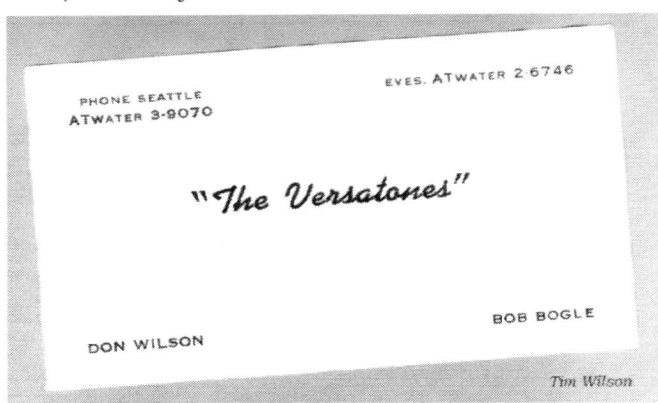

Bill Wiley and Grover Jackson were a popular entertainment team that hosted a TV show on Tacoma's KTNT. Grover picked finger-style guitar, while Bill sang and strummed rhythm. They also played for weekend dances at the Belfair Barn, some twenty miles northwest of Tacoma. As Don and Bob admired anyone that could play like Chet Atkins, they watched Bill and Grover's Variety Show at every opportunity. On one such occasion, a talent contest was announced for the following week at a nightclub called The Circle. The winner would get to perform live on the Bill and Grover Show. On Saturday afternoon, Don and Bob left home early to find the Circle. When they located it, they found themselves down on Tacoma's Pacific Avenue in the sleazy part of town. They placed their entry, and sat in the audience enjoying the live music prelude to the contest. As they watched, their attention focused on an impressive guitarist. Standing at least six feet tall, he was rather quiet and unassuming, until he played a solo. Then, his blond Fender Telecaster poured out crisp and intricate melodies, attracting everyone's attention to fingers that literally danced about the strings. Nudging Bob as the tall musician played, Don said; "I saw this guy on TV. He's the best guitar player I've ever seen."

They watched him so closely that he soon noticed and smiled back. The forty-five minute set passed quickly, and suddenly it was time for the contest. When The Versatones were called to the stage, they played *Walk-Don't Run*. After the final act, the contestants were called back up for the voting by audience applause. The Circle, now full to capacity, held about 200 people. Grover walked behind the line of performers, and when he held his hand above Don and Bob's heads, the applause was the loudest by far. The boys would play next Saturday morning's television variety show in front of a live studio audience. Before leaving, Bob mentioned the tall guitarist in the stage band. Bill and Grover then raved about the fellow known as "Nokie" Edwards. They said that he was the best guitarist in town, and a member of the house band at a drinking establishment called The Seaport, next-door and upstairs above another tavern called the Britannia.

Arriving home from work on Friday, Don found a telegram. Opening it, he read,

TO THE VERSATONES. WISHING YOU GOOD LUCK AND SUCCESS
ON YOUR FIRST TV APPEARANCE.   WITH LOVE, MOM.

On Saturday morning, Don showed Bob the telegram. Suddenly realizing the importance of the step they were about to take, the pair felt very excited.

NOKIE EDWARDS

When Don and Bob arrived at the Channel 11 TV station, they sat down in the audience to wait for their turn on stage. Fairly soon, Nokie came in and sat down beside them. They started talking, and while getting to know each other, Bob and Don learned that Nokie was twenty-four years old and that he was proud to be fifty percent Cherokee on his mother's side.

Nokie was born May 9, 1935 in Lahoma, Oklahoma, the state in which folks were lovingly referred to as "Okies." He mentioned that his name was actually "Nole," but that his father, Elbert, had combined Nole with Okie and dubbed him Nokie. He told the pair how at the age of five he had begun learning to play stringed instruments owned by various family members. There had been twelve children in the family, all of whom had musical talent, so he had the opportunity to try his hand at banjo, violin, mandolin, steel guitar, and the standup bass. Music was a big part of family get-togethers and at one of these, he had found it necessary to stand on a chair to play the huge string bass. At the age of nine, his interest had focused on the acoustic guitar, and at the age of eleven he had won first prize in a talent contest. Two years later, he performed on an Idaho radio station with brother Ira, and in another three years, he got his first electric guitar. In high school, due to his size, he was coerced into playing the tuba, but it was not to his liking.

Bob asked how Nokie, having roots in Oklahoma, had come to be in Washington. Nokie related a frightening story regarding the last will and testament of his grandmother. When she passed away, a large piece of farmland was left to Nokie's mother, Nannie, stipulating that the land be kept in the family, and not to be sold. One night, after many offers to buy had been turned down, Elbert Edwards was coming home from his railroad construction job, driving a team of horses used for hauling railroad ties. On a lonely stretch of road, some dangerous looking men stopped him in his tracks. They threatened Elbert and the lives of his family if the land was not given up for sale. Rather than give in, the family moved away from Oklahoma, settling in Washington slightly east of Tacoma in a town called Puyallup [pew-al-up]. There, while attending high school, he worked in a packing plant for a dollar thirty-five an hour. He later found better paying jobs doing farm work and roofing, but as Nokie recalls, an offer to play guitar paid even more, and he jumped at the chance; "I started getting paid to play in the early fifties when I was seventeen. I had my first electric then, a Guild, I think. Me and this other guy got a job playing in a big dance club in Oregon, but when he started leaving the stage, I would be up there playing all by myself. It was an adult joint with a bar, so I couldn't get off the bandstand, except to go through the kitchen to the washroom or whatever. I ended up doing a lot of entertaining without him before I finally quit. When I did, they offered me $300 a week to come back, about four times what most people were making at the time. The guy that owned the club also had a small plane, and he even flew me home once a week to keep me from quitting. In my late teens I joined the Army Reserves and I was sent to California and then Texas for training. After that, I went back and started playing in Tacoma taverns."

Nole "Nokie" Floyd Edwards – early 1950s

In January of 1958, a country songwriter and guitar picker by the name of Johnny "Buck" Owens had come to Puyallup from California. Among Buck's first recordings were a couple of 1956 attempts to get a rock and roll hit under the name of Corky Jones. Released later as a Buck Owens single [Pep 45107], *Hot Dog* seemed to have potential, whereas the flip side, *Rhythm and Booze*, sounded suspiciously like an attempt to impersonate Gene Vincent.

Buck had also been lead guitarist for the Orange Blossom Playboys, the house band at the Blackboard Club in Bakersfield, California. Renowned fiddler Bill Woods led this group, comprised of future stars such as Don Rich, Red Simpson, and Don Markham. Markham was master of several instruments, but primarily played the saxophone. Another guitarist, Gene Moles, cut four tracks on Buck's first studio session for Capitol Records, and remembered Markham for playing the bass while also playing the trumpet "by hammering the strings on his Fender bass with the volume turned way up."

Having relocated to Washington as part owner of Puyallup radio KAYE, Buck Owens was a very busy man. In addition to disc jockey duties and selling radio time, Owens had formed a lively country combo to work in Tacoma's Britannia nitery. In the Seaport, which was upstairs in the same building, Nokie played in the house band. Whenever the group took a break, Nokie would, at Buck's invitation, run downstairs and sit in with the Britannia group. At times, Nokie would then appear as lead guitarist on KTNT TV with the Bar-K Gang in which Buck sang with Don Rich playing fiddle, Ray "Shotgun Red" Hildreth on upright bass, and Donald "Dusty" Rhodes on steel. Owens developed a high regard for Nokie's talent, as evidenced in late 1958 when *The Grand Ole Opry* tour landed in Tacoma and put out an emergency call for a proficient substitute guitarist. Buck sent Nokie to the armory, where he backed artists such as Ferlin Husky and Lefty Frizzell.

Bob and Don were amazed, for they now played the Britannia on Monday nights when Buck Owens was off with no idea that Nokie was playing on the floor just above. Bob then disclosed their ambitions and asked if Nokie played any rock and roll music. Nokie laughed as he related how he had learned what rock was all about when the music was in its infancy. When this blending of rhythm-and-blues with country had erupted, it seemed so important to young people that Nokie had gone out and bought the top-ten singles and learned to play along with them. Some of it did not make sense, so he went out and bought another ten records. Soon, the music not only made sense, it seemed quite easy to play. He said that it had been fun and was now paying off, as the gap between country and rock was growing smaller, particularly when working with Buck Owens. At this point, Bob and Don enticed Nokie to play bass with them on the TV appearance they had won on the KTNT talent contest.

Something that amazed Don and Bob was how Nokie was able to bend the strings so far when he played his guitar. Ultra light "rock & roll" type strings were still a few years away, but as Nokie explained; "I threw out the two heavier strings from a standard set and I shifted everything over. Then I used two banjo strings for the high E and B strings. I could bend everything pretty easy after that. I knew of some guys who used one banjo string, but I used two."

At this time Nokie also introduced Bob and Don to drummer Skip Moore, who was also game to play with them. So, on March 20, 1959, The Versatones took their next big step, a live audience television appearance with the help of a drummer and the hottest guitarist in the state on bass.

NANCY CLAIRE

Another guest on the TV show was a cute teenager named Nancy Claire. Nancy strummed a guitar and sang cowboy songs under the watchful eye of her mother. When the TV show ended, the mother introduced herself to Don and Bob as Nancy's manager and described a problem that she hoped they could help to solve.

As winner of a talent contest, Nancy had her own fifteen-minute radio show on country station KAYE in Puyallup, but her limited ability on guitar restricted the number of songs she was able to sing. Impressed with The Versatones, mother Claire proposed that they back Nancy on her show. There would be no pay, but Mrs. Claire would bill the act as "Nancy Claire and The Versatones." Radio exposure being valuable and not easily obtainable, the pair readily accepted.

On the next Saturday, when Don and Bob appeared at the radio station to perform the first show, they again met Nokie Edwards, as he and his brothers had their own show just prior to Nancy's. Through more conversation, Bob and Don learned that Nokie too was a great admirer of Chet Atkins and Les Paul, the original multi-tracking recording artist. Nokie related a funny story regarding his struggle to duplicate Paul's lightning finger work. Without realizing that the solos were recorded at slow speed and played back at normal speed, Nokie worked on songs like *Nola* and *How High The Moon* until he could play them just like the records. He was surprised much later when he read about Les Paul's studio trickery.

An increase in out-of-town masonry restoration soon prevented Don and Bob from adhering to the regular schedule of the radio show. After only two months, they were forced to abandon their support for Nancy Claire. Nancy was soon singing in a Seattle combo called The Adventurers, and The Versatones didn't hear of her until five later when her single record, *Baby Blues* b/w *I'm Burning My Diary* was released on the Pacific Jazz label (acquired that year [1964] by Liberty). In the meantime, Nancy shared the stage with a good many more of the Puget Sound area groups, including The Checkers, The Casuals, The Viceroys, The Dynamics, and The Exotics. Ten years later, in recalling her experience with Bob and Don, Nancy told Northwest rock historian R. Bruce Smith; "When I sang with Bob and Don, I considered them 'old married men' because they were in their twenties and I was only fifteen. But I noticed that after they hit with *Walk-Don't Run*, every band in the country was trying to sound like them."

As Nancy grew a little older, she sang with The Frantics for a while, and later toured with some famous country acts. Eventually, she became an award-winning blues singer, enjoying popularity in the Seattle area through the turn of the century.

Nancy Claire and The Versatones on the air at KAYE

(Bob with his Stratocaster, Don with his Musicmaster)

As Bob explains, it was not long before he and Don got more work at the Britannia; "We had started out playing there on Mondays, which was Buck's off night. Buck also became successful with Saturday night barn dances out at Bressman's Park, so Don and I started playing the Britannia on Saturdays as well. We played from noon 'til five and after two-hours, we would go on again from seven until midnight. When Nokie was on a break at the Seaport upstairs, we got him to come down and sit in with us."

Regarding the work on Pacific Avenue, Don adds; "None of these places deserved to be called 'clubs.' The Circle, Britannia, and the Seaport were all down there on 'skid row' and the guys who patronized those places were animals! There were at least five brawls every night, and the cops would sometimes park their paddy wagon on the street ahead of time because they knew they would be hauling a bunch of troublemakers and drunks away before the night was through."

The job at the Britannia became very tiring, and the boys soon put it behind them, deciding it just did not pay enough for the long hours worked. In a short time, the duo was offered some work in a tiny tavern called the Java Jive, situated on Highway 99. It was (and remains) a concrete landmark in the shape of a coffee pot on what is now South Tacoma Way. The bar and small dance floor left little room for more than a single entertainer. To draw more customers with a live band, proprietor Bob Radonich splurged and built a special stage for the Versatones, but it was still so cramped that the pair soon opted out. Nearly fifty years later, proprietor Danette Staatz informed any interested customers that this was where her father gave The Ventures their start.

The Java Jive - 26 feet in diameter at ground level

Rid of tavern work and the Nancy Claire job, The Versatones concentrated on their goal of making a hit record. First on their agenda was to find players to fill out the group. Skip Moore was usually available for talent shows, but when it came to the longer jobs, he was busy with his regular group. Bob and Don admired and envied Tacoma's popular five-man group, The Wailers. They thought this was the way to go, but available musicians with reasonable talent were very scarce. One day, while discussing their predicament with Don's sister, Jackie, she suggested the boy next door, who she heard practicing. As Jackie had a party planned for the weekend, she offered to invite young George Babbitt to bring his drums. Josie tells what happened; "In April of 1959, my family decided to give me a birthday party on the patio of my daughter Jacqueline's home. Don and Bob brought their guitars, and they asked George to set up his drums. We were having a great time dancing and enjoying the music when the doorbell rang. I expected to see some late arrivals on the front porch, but to my surprise, there stood two burly policemen, one of which said, 'We've had some complaints about the noise, so please tone down the music.' We did of course, but I often think of the irony, because our 'noise makers' soon had a nationwide hit on the radio. I'm sure that later, some of the complainers happily paid for tickets to see this group in concert!"

George Babbitt had been learning drums at school, where an excellent music program provided marching band, concert, and jazz ensemble experience. At seventeen, and in his tenth year of drumming, George really knew what he was doing. Don and Bob were so impressed that they invited George to join up with them. With no idea that his youth might become a problem, George immediately accepted.

During the week, while Don and Bob were back in Pullman, they talked to Jack Lilywhite about using his home studio for a better quality demo recording. Jack agreed, and introduced them to Buddy Dumas, a college friend that owned drums and could play them. They rehearsed with Buddy in Pullman for the demo recordings, and on weekends they would return to Tacoma to rehearse with George Babbitt. Thanks to an earlier suggestion from Nancy Claire, they also found Earl Herbert, a bass player who was a friend of hers. This is also when Don took over Bob's Stratocaster, and Bob traded in the Musicmaster guitar for the Jazzmaster that he had always admired. As he recalls; "The dealer said that this was the very first Fender Jazzmaster to arrive in Seattle, and likely the first to be sold in the Pacific Northwest."

Two weeks later, the group recorded a second demo tape in Pullman. In addition to the instrumentals, Don sang a variety of numbers that included Guy Mitchell's *Singin' The Blues,* a nice impersonation of Elvis doing *Treat Me Nice,* plus a couple of aging classics, *Remember Me (When The Candle Lights Are Gleaming)* and *The Kentucky Waltz.* Pleased with the results, the guys felt ready to cut their first record.

THE BLUE HORIZON VENTURE

Since Dolton had already turned them down, Don and Bob faced a dilemma. They were squeamish about re-approaching Bob Reisdorff, and time off from their work was too limited to record in another city. Fortunately, Josie came to their rescue. Her words have been well documented in many magazines and liner notes; "If the established companies don't want to listen, we'll just have to start our own production company." Although having no experience in such matters, Josie reckoned that if she succeeded, the guys could record on a weekend and send the tape to a pressing outfit without missing even one day of work. This was important, as Don and Bob had families to feed and could not risk losing their jobs. While spending some of their "music income" on equipment, they had saved the remainder for making a recording.

Josie began by obtaining a local distributor's advice on the mechanics of starting a record label. The procedure included registering a label, a publishing company, and the name of the artist. Proceeding quickly, and knowing that Don and Bob had saved hard for a recording session, she generously paid the up-front fees. For the label name, Josie submitted Blue Horizon as her first choice, while selecting the publishing name of Electron Music so as to collect songwriting and performance royalties for original compositions. Upon learning that both names were available, Josie suddenly had her own record label. She was not so lucky, however, when registering the artist name. A New York group was already registered as the Versatones [*Tight Skirt & Sweater* b/w *Bila* - All Star 501, 1958]. The pair then named themselves The Impacts, but in less than three weeks, they learned of a doo-wop group that recorded under that name. When Don suggested The Adventurers, Josie then reasoned; "Since you are 'venturing' into a new career, why not make that The Ventures?" They readily agreed, and a mark in history was made. With Josie, Don, and Bob as equal partners, The Ventures were duly registered.

Upon hearing that J.F. Boles Custom Recording was the best studio in the entire Northwest, Josie booked a session for The Ventures on a Sunday when they were off work. Indeed, it was the studio where, in February, Bob Reisdorff had recorded The Fleetwoods, who by then had charted four singles and released the first Dolton album, *Mr. Blue* [BLP-8001].

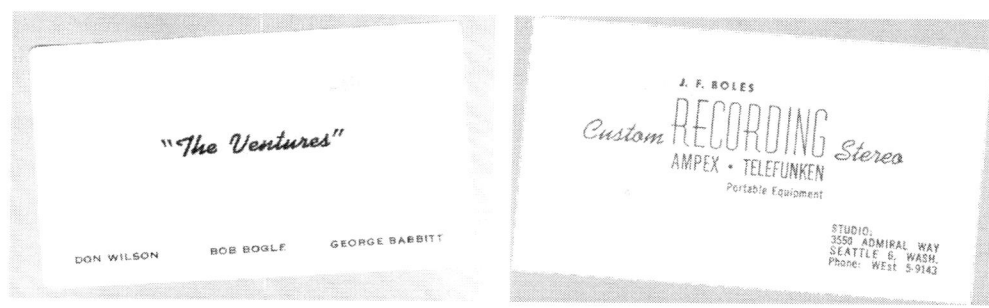

Located in the basement of Joe and Virginia Boles' home in West Seattle, the studio centered on an Ampex model 351-2 tape recorder, the "2" designating two-track stereo capability. As Virginia recalls, the recorder was a very busy machine in its time; "For years, Joe ran a boat service in Puget Sound while recording music as a hobby. When he saw the need for a studio in Seattle, he bought some good equipment and went into business. His Ampex 351-2 was the first ever to be brought into the Northwest, and it became the workhorse for mastering almost all of the historic records from this area."

Unknown to Virginia and Joe, this recorder would remain a classic machine into the twenty-first century, with many digitally equipped recording studios advertising inclusion of an Ampex 351 two-track analog deck in their gear line-up. More songs have been recorded on this model than possibly any other piece of equipment.

Arriving at the Boles' home, The Ventures carried their equipment down into the basement studio. After setting up, they relied completely on Joe Boles to guide them as they were inexperienced and had no producer other than Josie to help them get a balanced sound. The group found, as did other musicians who were customers there, that Joe and Virginia Boles were hospitable, understanding, and patient. When Virginia asked Josie to sign a guest book that she kept in the studio, Josie read praises from numerous musicians and groups including the Wailers, Julius Wechter of the Martin Denny Group, The Four Freshmen, along with The Fleetwoods, Bonnie Guitar, and Dolton's high-school guitar band, The Frantics. There was also a message from Bobby Darin, who, after recently performing in Seattle with The Frantics, had the band back him on a demo for his next single. The Frantics brought Bobby to Boles Custom Recording, and by June, *Dream Lover* was in the Top Ten of both the pop and r&b charts.

Another message, written in April by Donald Blocker of Liberty Records alleged; "The best studios in Hollywood can do no better or, in many cases, [not] as good." Turning to a new page, Josie wrote;

> Something new on the Blue Horizon. The Ventures - Sept.20-1959
>
> Bob Bogle – Guitar, Don Wilson – Guitar – Vocal, George Babbitt - Drums
>
> Joe, with you at the controls, our first record is sure to be a hit!
>
> Jo Wilson Blue Horizon Label "Cookies & Coke" - "The Real McCoy"

Joe Boles set up The Ventures with instruments on one track and Don's vocal on the other. At this point Don and Bob had still not made the decision to become an instrumental act, as roughly half of their repertoire was singing. For their first professional recording, they chose two vocal numbers. The first was an original composition with teen-appealing lyrics by Josie, entitled *Cookies and Coke*.

Joe at the Ampex 351-2 transport   Joe and Virginia Boles

During a few takes, the guys added handclaps and increased the tempo until they were satisfied. The flip-side bore a humorous number they had written with a melody based on the opening riff in a recent top-ten hit called *I've Had It* by The Bell Notes [Time 1004, 1959]. *The Real McCoy* spoofed a current TV sit-com, *The Real McCoys*, starring the humorous character actor, Walter Brennan. Don's excellent Brennan imitation depicted the geezer protesting being coaxed to dance like the teenagers did. By now, Don even looked the part on stage, in a hat with the brim turned down while pulling his arms into his jacket sleeves to give the garment an "oversized" look.

When the tapes were ready, Josie sent them to United Recording Studios in Hollywood where engineer Bunny Robine mixed the tracks to monaural before pressing a set of test recordings to be mailed back to Seattle. In the meantime, Josie had an amateur artist design a label. The simple design had gold lettering on a royal blue background with a few hand-drawn stars and a wavy line under the name. The first release on this label would be numbered 100.

Next, Josie sent the recordings and the label to a pressing plant in Los Angeles with an order for 500 singles. At this time, a clever plan struck her; "After I sent *The Real McCoy* tape to be mastered in California, I sent a note to Pat O'Day at radio station KJR in Seattle, and in large print I simply wrote, 'THE REAL McCOY IS COMING!' A few days later, I mailed this message again. After a few more days, I sent Pat a letter saying, 'THE REAL McCOY IS ON ITS WAY!' and a second and third letter with the same message. Just before the record was delivered, I wrote, 'THE REAL McCOY IS HERE!' This time I signed it 'Josie.' Later, Pat told me he had been nearly driven crazy trying to determine the source of the messages and what they might mean. It seems they had done the job intended, as he quickly recognized the title when the record arrived."

As it happened, Don and Bob delivered the record to KJR, where Pat O'Day told them that, had he not recognized the title from Josie's provocative letters, it is unlikely the pair would have made it past the front desk. O'Day remembered Bob and Don as they delivered their record, saying that he would surely put *The Real McCoy* on the air.

Blue Horizon 100   Pat O'Day

Following Don and Bob's visit to KJR, Josie continued with the legwork, taking the recording to the other stations while the boys were at work on their day jobs; "I was determined to present the record personally, although I remember thinking, 'I wonder what the DJ's will think of an old lady trying to get a rock and roll record played on the air?' I was forty-five then, and already the grandmother of three!"

Most of the stations welcomed Josie's approach, including one in Moscow, Idaho, where *The Real McCoy* climbed the local popularity chart until it reached the Top Ten. In Tacoma, the record was also in good company, sharing space on the local chart with *Torquay* by the Fireballs, *In the Mood* by the Ernie Fields Orchestra, and a two-sided instrumental by The Wailers, *Shanghied* and *Wailin'*. As Bob recalled; "There were no sales of our record yet, as copies were not to be found in the stores, but we were just thrilled to have our music on an actual record."

Encouraged by the interest shown in the Pullman-Moscow area, Josie went around to the other stations in Seattle. Although they said they would try to work the recording into their play list, it never seemed to happen. The record, in fact, did not even get much play at KJR, but it *had* served to introduce The Ventures to the Pacific Northwest.

Back at the Washington Hotel in Pullman, the owner's son expressed disbelief and major disappointment that The Ventures had not recorded the captivating instrumental that he considered to be their best number, *Walk-Don't Run*. The boys paid attention, noting that instrumental combos seemed to be increasing in popularity. Following Duane Eddy's *Movin' and Groovin'* and *Rebel Rouser*, hits were being made by Link Wray And His Ray Men, Johnny And The Hurricanes, The Fireballs, and again, The Wailers, whose progress Don and Bob watched very closely. By mid-summer this group had hit the top forty with *Tall Cool One*; secured a show on Tacoma's KTNT radio; and signed up with a New York label for an album.

THE FABULOUS WAILERS significantly influenced The Ventures

Rich Dangel, Mike Burk, Mark Marush, Kent Morrill, John Greek

While expanding their repertoire, Bob and Don found it easy and fun to arrange their own versions of the hits. Without a saxophone or organ, considerable skill was required to compose a full sounding guitar version without too much repetition. Of course, rock 'n' roll instrumentals were not new when *Rebel Rouser* arrived. The Champs had hit high with *Tequila*, and Bill Justis was very successful with *Raunchy*. Both tunes were on Bob and Don's song list from the beginning. Realizing rock instrumentals to be more than mere novelty tunes, the two began improving their version of *Walk-Don't Run*, making small changes or additions each time they practiced.

BLUE MOON

After completing the college job in Pullman, Don and Bob resumed their jobs at Sahara Waterproofing. Their first assignment after rejoining the company was at Fort Lewis, near Tacoma. As they now spent much of their time in Tacoma with music and their day job, the two men decided to relocate there and find extra work at night. As Bob recalls, it was then that he and Don made an attempt at improving their presentation; "A Tacoma nightspot hosted a weekly half-hour TV show on which dance lessons were taught by Margie Millar. She was known for having been a regular dancer on ABC TV's *Ray Bolger Show*. When we retained her to learn some stage presence, she soon had us doing simply ridiculous choreography. She started us doing twirls and turns, and then wanted us to hop and skip, and lie on the floor while playing the guitar. For publicity photos, she took us to Tacoma's Narrows Bridge and had us put on swimsuits and wade in the water with our guitars in hand. She also wrote some ridiculous dialog for our act. When Don mentioned his impressions, she wanted him to come on stage in a cowboy hat, holding a gun, and say, 'I'm Bat Masterson and I shoot 'em down.' We quickly decided we were wasting our time and money, and we said goodbye to Margie Millar."

~~~

In pursuit of more experience and cash to finance recording costs, Don and Bob began soliciting local nightclub owners for stage work. Bob remembers Ralph, the owner of a nitery in southeast Tacoma called the Blue Moon; "Ralph told us right off that he didn't hire live bands because he couldn't afford them. When we told him there were just two of us and could entertain very well for a wage that wouldn't be outrageous, he hired us for four nights a week. We would play 9:00 p.m. until 1:00 a.m. from Wednesday to Saturday for the union scale of fourteen dollars each per night. On Thursdays and Fridays, after getting to bed around two in the morning, we had to rise at six to go to work in construction.

"After a couple of weeks at the Blue Moon, we began noticing many familiar faces in the audience as well as a lot of new ones. As the audience was steadily growing, we thought it was a good time to ask Ralph if we could hire a drummer and bass player. Ralph was quick to squash that idea, but said that if we were not happy as a two-piece band, *he* would sit in on drums. He was the boss, so we had no choice but to accept. The following night, we arrived to find Ralph's drums set up on stage, but he told us to start without him, as he would be busy for a while. We waited in vain for him to get on those drums, but he was always busy tending bar or conversing with his friends. We were lucky if we had a drummer for more than two numbers per night, and sometimes he didn't play at all.

"One night, about a month later, we saw Nokie Edwards come in through the front door with a guitar case and sit down at a table. When it was time for our break, we went and sat with him and he showed us a Fender Precision bass with a sunburst finish and gold anodized pickguard. It looked almost new, but Nokie said that he had got it for $125 in a pawnshop. He said he would be happy to sit in for a while on bass with us. Nokie played bass for the whole set and when it was time for our break, he asked if I would trade with him on the next set. I said, 'OK, but I don't know anything about playing the bass'. Nokie said, 'It's easy! The four strings on the bass are the same as the bottom four strings on your guitar, only an octave lower. Just play one note instead of a chord.' That sounded good to me and I gave it try. Nokie played the bass with a pick and told me to do the same. There I was, playing bass for the very first time in front of a live audience while Nokie played my Jazzmaster."

Nokie came into the Blue Moon several times after that, and on one of these nights, he mentioned being worried about his regular job with country music renegade, Buck Owens. The occasional gigs didn't provide much income, and Nokie, like Don and Bob, was supporting a young family. The money had been steady while Buck was in Tacoma, but he had begun making trips to California to record for Capitol. This is when he had added a sensational young fiddler named Don Ulrich, who also played a respectable guitar. Ulrich, who became a good friend of Nokie, eventually streamlined his name to Don Rich. Nokie's concern was realized when Buck's *Under Your Spell Again* charted at number four in July of 1959. Buck began cutting ties in Tacoma so as to return to Bakersfield, the city north of L.A. soon to be known as "Nashville West" to many in the music business. Don Rich was the first to follow, becoming Buck's lifelong friend and one of his key musicians, both on violin and guitar.

Don Markham with Buck Owens

Don Markham soon followed, but Nokie had no interest in relocating. Bob Bogle continues; "He found a weekly job at another nightclub, but when the manager announced that he was going out of business, Nokie was happy to start playing steady with Don and I. Although Ralph wouldn't spend another cent on entertainment, he didn't object to a trio if we divided our existing pay between the three of us. We were not thrilled with this decision, but in the interest of better music, we decided to go along if it was OK with Nokie. The more I played the bass, the more interesting and enjoyable I found it. After Nokie joined us at the Blue Moon, we divided the twenty-eight dollars between the three of us. I really liked the bass and I became quite comfortable with it."

Don and Bob still had their day jobs, but Nokie depended on the music. For added income, he played as many jobs as possible. As he recalls, he also sold his Stratocaster; "I liked almost everything about the Strat, but the middle pickup used to get in the way and I was always hitting it with the pick. I still had my Telecaster, and I started using it for everything."

Each night thereafter, Nokie and Bob traded instruments several times while Don, in response to delighted customers, performed his impersonations. One night during a break, Ralph commanded Don to repeat the comedy routine for some friends that had just arrived. Not wanting to repeat the routine so soon in front of the same audience, Don suggested the friends come back another night. Immediately, Ralph grew angry and said; "Well, if you refuse, you're fired. Pack you're things and git!" And so they did.

After completing the restoration at Fort Lewis, Don and Bob learned that there would be a fairly long lapse before work on any new contracts would start. Hearing this, they informed Pioneer Construction that they were available for masonry restoration. Immediately, Pioneer assigned them to the college in Moscow, Idaho. Luckily for Nokie, he was again needed at the Seaport Club in downtown Tacoma.

While working in Moscow, the two Ventures continued to practice and play for parties. In a few weeks, Harold "Butch" Hamblin joined Pioneer Construction as an apprentice. A friend of Don's since grade school, Butch had been unhappy doing civil service work and had taken an extended sabbatical so that he could work with Don and Bob. When Butch saw how well the two had learned to play their guitars and entertain an audience, he became a permanent Ventures fan.

MOONIE'S

After finishing the Moscow job, Don and Bob returned to Sahara Waterproofing. They had just resumed contact with Nokie when Sahara assigned the tuck-pointers to a big renovation job on the State Capitol Building in Olympia. Upon hearing this, Nokie remembered that the owner of Moonie's nightclub was looking for a small entertainment group on weekends. Once settled in Olympia, Bob and Don looked him up. Within minutes, the three were booked to play Saturday nights for fifteen dollars each. As Bob recalls; "Moonie was really happy with the increase in business, so after a month we asked him for a raise. Again, we heard a definite 'NO' followed by 'You musicians are a dime a dozen.' From then on, his general attitude became unacceptable."

As winter of 1959 approached, Bob and Don met with their old friends Bill and Grover, who now owned a tavern in Bremerton, just ten miles from Tacoma. While relating their recent bad luck, the pair mentioned being ready to record *Walk-Don't Run*. Bill and Grover agreed that it should be recorded, and told of a friend named Art Mineo, who had been helpful in connecting The Wailers to Golden Crest Records in New York. Don had bought *The Fabulous Wailers* album, having all but worn it out while he and Bob learned to play several of its cuts.

Art Mineo's large Tacoma nightclub would be a perfect setting for recording, and with their own equipment, Bill and Grover could tape *Walk-Don't Run* during the day while the club was closed. Bill called Art, and in minutes had arranged for a session. Unfortunately, Bill was either not much of an engineer or the equipment was substandard, for the results did not impress The Ventures.

Art Mineo was born in Brooklyn, hence the name of his nightclub, The New Yorker. His early love of music eventually led to his position as pianist with the renowned Paul Whiteman Orchestra for several years. In his eighties, he recalled The Ventures' audition at the New Yorker; "I really liked The Ventures and thought they played well, and I especially liked *Walk-Don't Run*. But when they left, I put the tape in my desk and forgot about it."

One positive note arose from Bob and Don's final meeting with Bill and Grover. The boys were booked for a Saturday rock 'n' roll extravaganza at the Tacoma Armory on November 14, 1959, along with other popular groups including The Wailers, The Princetons, The Del Gatos, The Majestics, and The Searchers. While Don and Bob were happy to finally meet the Wailers, musicians Richard Dangel and Johnny Greek had no idea that they would soon be receiving royalties from their songs as played by The Ventures. Nor did vocalist Kent Morrill imagine that fifty years later, his Wailers would collaborate with The Ventures on a historic CD album [*Two Car Garage* - Blue Horizon].

At the last minute, Tacoma's first rock 'n' roll group, The Bluenotes, was added to the Armory roll. Led by guitar man Bill Engelhart, and boasting dual saxophones, the group became known as Little Bill and the Bluenotes, making the Hot 100 with *I Love An Angel* [Dolton 4]. Gradually evolving from rock to a classic blues group, the band's longevity would nearly parallel that of The Ventures.

Near the end of 1959, The Ventures landed a New Year's Eve dance at the Fort Lewis Community Center. Knowing an available saxophonist, bassist Earl Herbert brought Keith Schumacher along. With five Ventures on stage, the New Year's Eve job brought more jobs. One of these was at the Spanish Castle, a popular ballroom between Seattle and Tacoma. The place had featured big-band music until 1959 when Pat O'Day booked the Wailers there for a teen dance. Soon, it was *the* place to go, with top rock bands throughout the Pacific Northwest being booked, as well as touring artists like Gene Vincent, Jerry Lee Lewis, and The Beach Boys.

Keith Schumacher - George Babbitt – Don & Bob - Earl Herbert

Although the recent events were good publicity for The Ventures, their music was not bringing in much money. Even for 1959, $1.25 was a small admission fee, and Bob and Don were slowly sinking further into debt while planning to make a recording. Relief in the form of a loan came from Don's friend and co-worker, Butch Hamblin. Butch had faith in Don and Bob's musical ability, so when he learned they needed funding for a recording session, he offered a sum from his Civil Service pension payout. Pledging to more than make it up to him, the boys excitedly accepted. Stating one condition, Butch said; "When you get a hit, I want to be your road manager." Laughingly, the two promised to comply. The very next evening, Don and Bob stopped by the club where Nokie was working to discuss his playing bass on the recording. While there, they signed up Skip Moore, with whom they had played at nearly a dozen talent contests. Don offered the twenty-one-year-old drummer an equal share of the record's sales revenue, but with no faith in percentage deals, Skip signed for the current three-hour session rate of twenty-five dollars.

Together, the quartet played a few dates in the area before informing Josie that they were ready to record. True to her word, Josie booked another session at Joe Boles' Studio for March 22, 1960.

Don Wilson

A simplified melody (played with vibrato bar in hand) and a refreshing up-tempo were among elements giving The Ventures' arrangement of *Walk-Don't Run* its wide appeal, but it was their ingenious intro with a four-beat drum roll accented by powerful rim-shots that immediately caught the listener's ear. Unlike the "press-roll" used by most drummers, Skip played a unique single-stroke-roll, followed by two bars of basic rock beat. Bob and Don then decided to build the introduction, one man at a time until all were playing, much like school children do with *Row, Row, Row Your Boat*. Don followed Skip's intro with four chords and Nokie echoed with four bass notes. As Don repeated the chords, Bob came in with the melody. Happy with their final arrangement, the four practiced *Walk-Don't Run* to perfection.

On March 22, the group arrived at the Boles' home with three amplifiers, (Fender models Vibrolux and Bassman, and a Gibson GA-40). Joe Boles placed an RCA 44 microphone in front of Nokie's Bassman and a Telefunken U47 microphone in front of Skip's drums. The two guitar amps were recorded with Electro-Voice 666 and Altec 639 microphones.

With four microphones feeding the Ampex tape deck, Joe channeled both guitars on one track with drums and bass on the other. As Bob recalls; "With two-track equipment, there was not much chance of overdubbing, so the final take had to be perfect from start to finish. After about ten takes, we had one that seemed alright, but it wasn't good enough. We recorded about a dozen more takes until we had done the best that we could. For the flip side, we chose *Home*, a romantic number popularized by Gracie Fields in 1959, and which we often played for dances."

Once more, Josie sent a tape reel to Bunny Robine with an order for a test pressing. As Don recalls; "When the pressing arrived back in Seattle, we decided that the highs on *Walk-Don't Run* were too prominent. We asked Robine for a remix that wasn't so 'trebly' and when his second attempt arrived, it was exactly what we were aiming for. Mom sent that test pressing to be duplicated, along with a box of labels. After getting burned with 500 copies of *Cookies & Coke*, we trimmed our order for *Walk-Don't Run* down to just 300 copies."

Near the end of May, Josie delivered a copy of *Walk-Don't Run* to every DJ she could find. Although they seemed enthusiastic, there was no guarantee of airplay, but at KJR, Pat O'Day assured Josie that he would air the record. Josie explains how this was accomplished; "It was on the Memorial Day weekend in May, 1960. As the kids were out of school, they were able to call in to the station. The first few bars of the recording were played just before the hourly news, and this was called a 'news kicker.' After playing a few bars of *Walk-Don't Run* just a couple of times, the newscaster announced 'Please don't call the station. Our lines are flooded! Following the *News*, we *will* play the full recording!' It wasn't only kids calling in, but also many grownups! In fact, once I had moved to Hollywood and started The Ventures' fan club, I received a letter from a boy whose parents had said they enjoyed The Ventures because it didn't sound like they were beating on pots and pans! And so, with exposure through the 'news kicker' The Ventures' career was born!"

With such a response, Pat O'Day had no trouble adding *Walk-Don't Run* to his regular play list. Bob recalls the first time he heard their record on the radio; "Don, Nokie, Smitty, and I were playing at the Britannia when we heard that KJR was using our song for a news kicker. We arranged to take our breaks at five minutes to the hour, and we ran out to the car. When we heard them play *Walk-Don't* Run, we could hardly believe it. We did it three times that night."

Don recollects having purchased one of the new 'transistor' portable radios around that time and taking it to work with him in Olympia; "I took the radio up on the roof of the Capitol building as I knew our record would be on before the news. I was working with another guy that day, and when *Walk-Don't Run* came on, I took the radio over to him and said, 'Hey Walt, this is the record that Bob and I made!' Walt said, 'Sure, sure kid, as if you would still be up here doing roofing.' It took a little explaining, but I was finally able to convince him that it was us on the radio."

Fondly recalling his own experience, Bob relates: "I didn't really think I could quit my job, even though *Walk-Don't Run* was on the radio nearly every morning on my way to work. One day in Olympia, I was repairing some masonry on the Capitol building, cutting away old mortar with a power saw. I looked a mess, completely covered with cement dust. A bunch of office girls came out and asked me for my autograph. I really felt dumb in those dirty old clothes, trying not to get their papers all grimy."

Blue Horizon 101 in good condition commands upwards of $1000

While Don and Bob enjoyed local airplay of their single, someone else was also paying close attention. Bob Reisdorff heard *Walk-Don't Run* on his car radio, but ironically did not recognize it as the tune he had given the "thumbs down" treatment. Of course, it was then played on a small recorder with no bass or drums, and with a milder beat. In recalling, Reisdorff relates; "I heard the entire recording on KJR, and while it sounded good, the notes were continually bending both flat and sharp, but in such a way that it was really exciting! After hearing it again the following day, I called KJR to ask about it. I remember thinking, 'This instrumental will really go!' Pat O'Day said it was on a private label called Blue Horizon, and he gave me a phone number. Within minutes, I was on the phone with Josie Wilson, who updated me on the progress of her son and his friend that had played their earlier version for me as The Versatones. I could hardly believe it."

Josie also remembers that day; "Bob was truly amazed at how the song had developed. Without involving Dolton at all, he offered to pass it directly to Liberty Records in Hollywood where our record would receive international promotion and distribution."

Shortly after forwarding the Blue Horizon master to Hollywood, Reisdorff received a shocking response from Liberty president Alvin S. Bennett; "He listened to *Walk-Don't Run* twice and then called me to say the tune didn't have any sales potential. I couldn't believe it and I said, 'Al, this thing is a hit. It's already climbing the charts in Seattle!' He replied, 'But we don't like it. How many has it sold on Blue Horizon?' I said it hadn't sold any because it was only distributed to disc jockeys in our area. Bennett said, 'If you think so highly of this thing, why not put it out on Dolton?' That was all I needed to hear! I believed the record to be pure guitar genius and I proceeded to buy the master from Blue Horizon and sign The Ventures as exclusive Dolton recording artists."

As new friends, Bob Reisdorff and Josie met for lunch one Friday in late June to celebrate Bob's birthday. As Josie recalls; "Conversation led to The Ventures recording, and I asked, 'Bob, do you really feel that this will be a national hit?' He replied, 'Josie, here's how much I believe in it. Liberty has refused to take the record, but I'll give you $10,000 for half of Blue Horizon.' This was a huge sum of money in 1960, when a three-piece meal at Kentucky Fried Chicken® cost only a dollar. Suddenly, I had a partner. Bob was so sure of himself that he borrowed from his mother for this venture. A three-year contract was drawn up with Reisdorff and I holding forty percent apiece while Don and Bob received ten percent each. Bob Reisdorff didn't know us well then, nor did we know him. Although the label was mine, I had an Assignment of Share drawn up where Don and Bob gave up all interest in Blue Horizon to me for the sum of one dollar. This was to protect Reisdorff from a future claim or lawsuit by Don and Bob. After we moved to Hollywood and The Ventures were being recorded on Dolton, Bob Reisdorff and I retained the name Blue Horizon for our new company, Blue Horizon Productions."

Two weeks later, as airplay for *Walk-Don't Run* expanded past Washington and Oregon, Dolton 25 appeared as the "record to watch" in Billboard, the recording industry bible for music dealers and disc jockeys.

In just over a week, *Walk-Don't Run* was the number one hit across the U.S. Pacific Northwest. To say that The Ventures and their families were excited would be putting it mildly. The very thought that music lovers were rushing out to buy their record, and that it could be heard several times a day on every pop radio station in the region, was almost unbelievable. While the guys talked more about quitting their construction work, Bob returned to Woody Wilson's car lot and traded his Chevy Impala in for a shiny new 1959 Oldsmobile.

DRUMMER WANTED

Equally amazed was Nole Floyd Edwards. With years of musical experience, and known as THE hotshot guitarist in the area, his best bid at fame and fortune was not for playing the guitar; but for playing the bass!

Another facet of the Blue Horizon partnership was that Bob Reisdorff became the predominant producer of The Ventures. Recalling events that followed, he added; "About a week later, when popularity of *Walk-Don't Run* reached California, Al Bennett called me and said, 'OK Bob, I was wrong. Get that record!' I told him that I had it on Dolton, and the contract was finalized. This is possibly what triggered the eventual buyout of Dolton by Liberty Records."

According to Art Mineo, RCA producers Hugo Peretti and Luigi Creatore had offered $10,000 for rights to distribute *Walk-Don't Run*. Upon learning of this offer over forty years later, Josie commented; "I sometimes wondered how Bob Reisdorff came up with that figure when he bought into Blue Horizon. His encounter with RCA is likely the answer."

Bob Reisdorff had other reasons to be excited. Instead of being in debt over his partnership loan if *Walk-Don't Run* failed, he was already profiting from it. Second; formerly doubting Al Bennett was now slapping him on the back. But, as Josie booked another session at Boles Custom Recording, Reisdorff felt a sudden discomfort. It seems he was not on good terms with Joe Boles after a dispute that erupted a year earlier. Recalling how Little Bill and the Bluenotes came to him with a new song, Bob relates; "Bonnie (Guitar) and I really liked *I Love an Angel* and we sent the group to Joe's Custom Recording to make a demo. Joe recorded the group, but then tried to sign them up for himself, claiming to have discovered them. Joe and a fellow named Tom Ogilvy had started their own label called Bolo. We were devastated because up to then, Joe had recorded our Fleetwoods and Frantics with no problems at all. When I said I would give him a penny a record on the Little Bill release, he had been fairly resentful so we hadn't used his studio for almost a year. Little Bill's song was huge in the area and it made the national charts [#66] as well, so I hoped Joe was satisfied. We started working with Kearney Barton, who had Northwest Recorders in the same building on Union Street where we worked. Much like Phil Spector, Barton became legendary in the Pacific Northwest as a producer and engineer. I wanted to continue recording there, but when The Ventures expressed how comfortable they felt with Joe, I agreed to work with him again."

With a hit on their hands, The Ventures needed a permanent drummer. Skip Moore told the group that he could not work steadily with them he had to operate the family-run service station. As Don recalls, their drummer problem suddenly evaporated; "While we were playing all over the place at talent contests and in bars, no one took us seriously or wanted to stick with us. We had a list of drummers we would call, mostly guys that Nokie knew, such as Howie Johnson or Smitty that would sit in with us if they weren't busy. After *Walk-Don't Run* hit, we could choose most anyone we wanted to be our drummer, and the one we picked was Howie."

Twenty-seven-year-old Howie Johnson was a native of Washington State, born in city of Everett on September 23, 1932. After learning the drums as a teenager, he settled in Tacoma where he became a truck driver. Ironically, a car accident after a dance job nearly took his life in the fall of 1957. The crash occurred at night, and hours passed before Howie was found beneath the vehicle. He suffered a broken neck that was a source of discomfort for the next several years. When he met with Bob and Don, Howie still wore a neck support, but he showed them that he was fully able to play the drums.

Howard Austin Johnson Jr. in 1960

After only a month, the first 200,000 copies of *Walk-Don't Run* available in the U.S. market were sold out, demanding a second pressing. Reisdorff then suggested changing the mellow B-side to a rousing Ventures original. The group was horrified at the thought of tampering with their hit record but they were quickly convinced when Reisdorff explained that an original would bring them songwriting royalties. Revisiting their first release, *The Real McCoy*, The Ventures dropped the comedy vocal and recorded it as a crackling instrumental, simply titled *The McCoy*. Pressings of Dolton 25 would now be Dolton 25X, although a few of the old labels without the "X" were used, creating a rarity for future collectors. Due to Josie and Bob Reisdorff's partnership, publishing credit for *The McCoy* went to Electron-Cornerstone on this single. As Cornerstone belonged to Reisdorff, a bit of revenue was steered in his direction.

It was unusual for a record company to distribute internationally before a group had completely proven itself, but Liberty Records now licensed *Walk-Don't Run* to Canada's Reo label and then to Top Rank in Europe and Australia.

NATIONAL RADIO

It was truly a hectic time for The Ventures as requests poured in from booking agents, radio stations, and college graduation committees. The popularity of *Walk-Don't Run* put the foursome on the cover of *DJ*, Seattle's hit-parade weekly periodical. Inside, a diagramed introduction to the wonder of stereo sound preceded a two-page article predicting big things to come for the band. It was an odd time for Howie, becoming famous and sharing the publicity while not (yet) having played on a record.

On August 29, *Walk-Don't Run* peaked at number two across the nation as every kid with a guitar worked on playing the melody. What *Wildwood Flower* had done for an earlier generation of young country music fans, *Walk-Don't Run* now did for the rock 'n' roll crowd. It was a hectic time for Don and Bob, trying to function on their day jobs while envisioning the next steps in a musical career. The future arrived very suddenly when Reisdorff called and said; "You must quit your jobs immediately. The producers at ABC have requested you to play on Dick Clark's TV show." The booking was for *Dick Clark's Saturday Night Show*, based in New York City and sponsored by Beechnut Chewing Gum.

This event, along with Reisdorff offering them monthly salaries of $300, was the signal Don and Bob needed to quit their jobs. Don was gone in a flash, but Bob had a problem. As a crew foreman, he hated to leave without giving the proper two-week notice. His supervisor understood, however, telling Bob to go ahead and not to worry about the job. Still, Bob felt so guilty that he never went back to collect his final paycheck.

While Reisdorff arranged their flight to New York, Josie took the boys to Penney's department store in Tacoma. They bought red blazers, black pants, and white buck shoes; the outfits seen first on North American television, and later around the world on a famous long-play album (and on our cover).

Upon arrival at New York City's Little Theater, the group learned that most performing artists on this show did not really perform. Singers lip-synced to their hit records, and The Ventures were no exception, even if they could play *Walk-Don't Run* without a glitch. This was network television, where engineers, not rank musicians, controlled the sound. On the set, The Ventures were honored to meet Lloyd Price [*Personality*], Fabian [*Tiger*], and Jamie Horton [*My Little Marine*], whose recent hits had also charted well.

The Dick Clark Saturday Night Show

The show's producers asked each of The Ventures to stand on a pedestal and do the dance steps popularized by groups like The Fendermen and The Fireballs. Even after some practice, The Ventures found that dancing on a circular pedestal while smiling and pretending to play guitars required heavy concentration. During the second drum break, Bob, Don, and Nokie stepped down from their pedestals and walked around in front of Howie, where they resumed swaying and kicking to finish the song. Howie had a different problem. While pretending to drum over Skip Moore's performance on the record, he completely missed the drum roll at the halfway point. However, the footage was shown August 12, 1960 on an *American Bandstand* special, celebrating the show's third anniversary. The Ventures shared this broadcast, with Elvis Presley, Brenda Lee, Roy Orbison, and Fats Domino. On August 27, The Ventures' performance was repeated on *The Dick Clark Saturday Night Show*.

While in the "Big Apple," the boys met Harvey Gold, Liberty's Eastern division promotion man. Harvey became a familiar face in New York, chauffeuring the band to various radio stations for on-air interviews on this and future visits to the city. It was much too soon for The Ventures to imagine that someday Harvey would be working for *them*.

Around this time, another recording artist was enjoying his second attempt at fame and fortune on the other side of the USA. Ernest Evans was his name, but with his cover of Hank Ballard's *The Twist*, he became known around the world as Chubby Checker. The dance craze had already hit Dick Clark's *American Bandstand*, giving Chubby's rendition more fuel to propel it to the top.

When *Walk-Don't Run* broke the National Top Ten at number seven, Brian Highland's *Itsy Bitsy, Teeny Weeny, Yellow Polka Dot Bikini* was enjoying Number One above Brenda Lee's *I'm Sorry*. Others ahead of The Ventures were Roy Orbison's *Only The Lonely*, *Alley Oop* by the Hollywood Argyles, and *Image Of A Girl* by the Safaris. The Ventures would soon overtake all but Elvis Presley, just back from Germany after two years in the army, and sitting at number three with *It's Now or Never*. The following week, *Walk-Don't Run* hit number five while Elvis went to number one, pushing Brian Highland down to number two. Soon, The Ventures were at number three below Elvis and Brian Highland, and just above Chubby Checker's *The Twist*. The following week, *Walk-Don't Run* was in second place, but Elvis commanded the top spot for another two weeks. Meanwhile, *The Twist* rose to number two, and finally to the top, as *Walk-Don't Run* began its descent. By late fall, The Ventures had disappeared from the charts after an eighteen week ride, nine of which were in the Top Ten. To this day, the only guitar instrumental to top Billboard's chart was in 1959 when Santo and Johnny's *Sleepwalk* held Number One for two weeks.

The Cash Box charts were much the same as in Billboard, *Walk-Don't Run* rising to number three in one month and remaining for another before slowly descending. The classic instrumental was gone in the week ending November 26, by which time the next Ventures single was on the rise.

Recalling her recording's success and a sad event that followed, Josie summates; "My husband, Woody died in late 1960, but not before he heard *Walk-Don't Run* played on nearly every radio station. With a complete change of heart, Woody proudly told one and all, 'That's my son's record!' "

While the Cash Box chart was less flattering to The Ventures, the opposite was true in Canada. *Walk-Don't Run* remained on the Canadian Top Fifty list for fourteen weeks, during which time it held the Number One spot two weeks and remained at Number Two for another *three* weeks.

TRANS-ATLANTIC COINCIDENCE

A few months after *Walk-Don't Run* had become a smash hit, Skip Moore lawyer threatened a lawsuit, attempting to obtain a quarter of the record's sales revenue. Again, it was Josie's proper business sense that prevented this bluff from going any further. Before the recording session, Skip had knowingly signed away his right to anything more than the standard fee. A simple letter from Josie's lawyer was enough to settle the issue. The Ventures never heard from Skip again, but his mother called Don a few years later. The news was both shocking and sad, as Skip had succumbed fairly quickly to cancer. Skip Moore would never know how many people around the world would repeatedly hear his performance on every record medium to come for the next several decades.

Another drummer was actually devastated to hear *Walk-Don't Run* played repeatedly on the air. George Babbitt, now a retired U.S. Air Force General, laughingly recalls his dismay; "I was feeling crushed for quite a while when *Walk-Don't Run* hit number one in Seattle and The Ventures went on *Dick Clark's* TV show. It was nearly a year since I'd played with them, having been let go because of my age. As for *Cookies and Coke* and *The Real McCoy*, I still have my copy of that awful record hanging on the wall in my office."

Awful or not, a good copy of Blue Horizon 100 fetched upwards of $800 at auction in 2002, even though the market had become contaminated in the mid-seventies by a number of bootleg copies. Some experts reported the source of these to be in the UK, while others put the blame on Richard Minor, part of a notorious bootlegging ring indicted in 1981 for making illegal Elvis recordings. Thirty years later, the shiny copies appeared on eBay, touted to be the real thing. Although they perfectly matched the original, they could be distinguished by etchings in the vinyl near the edge of the label.

Markings on the original release say "Blue Horizon 100-1 3224P," whereas the bootleg reproductions state "45-BH-100-1" and "RE" (Re-issued Edition?).

While The Ventures enjoyed the chart status of *Walk-Don't Run*, a band in the UK was experiencing an uncanny parallel. The Shadows, former backers for pop crooner Cliff Richard, had parted with the singer and become an instrumental quartet. Like The Ventures, The Shadows had bombed in 1959 with their first recording. Likewise again, they now enjoyed the fruits of their second attempt, as *Apache* [Columbia DB 4484] became a huge hit on their home turf. The coincidence goes even further. While *Walk-Don't Run* climbed several foreign charts, it stopped at Number 8 in the UK when the John Barry Seven covered of the tune. Although Barry's version only made Number 11, it seemed to have significantly dampened The Ventures' UK sales.

When Danish guitar stylist, Jorgen Ingmann's version of *Apache* [Atco 6184] was released in America, it soared to number two while The Shadows version was totally ignored. The Shadows never did gain a foothold in America. By the same token, in nearly fifty years of world touring, The Ventures never performed on British soil, a fact sadly lamented by many dedicated Ventures fans in the UK. Considering this, Bob Bogle surmised; "I'm certain it was John Barry's recording of *Walk-Don't Run* that prevented the mass popularity we experienced everywhere else from reaching the United Kingdom. There have always been a number of loyal Ventures fans there, but never enough to support a tour. The Shadows may have been a factor, but there were good guitar bands in most other countries, and that didn't seem to affect us."

1960 Sheet music

Among The Ventures' British admirers was seventeen-year-old Stuart Leech of Gorleston-On-Sea. As the first fan to start his own Ventures club, he became known to Josie and the band as the "Day One Man." Later a thriving businessman, guitar-collector, and grandfather of two, Stuart recalled; "As a teenager in 1960, I was keen on

American guitarists such as Duane Eddy, the String-a-Longs, and others whose records were available in the UK. The pure sound and presentation of The Ventures stood out from the rest, and I decided to help in promoting them over here by forming a fan club. For our single-sheet bulletin, I derived what scarce information was available from magazines such as Billboard. I also queried Liberty's London office on Mortimer Street, but with our own UK pop boom happening, they were not much help. I received much better response from the company's American office."

Although The Ventures were very busy performing in the fall of 1960, they spent several days in the studio with Joe Boles. Over twenty tunes were recorded, and because editing was not yet possible, each song required several takes due to flubs or the guys making changes to their arrangements. Joe liked to use little tricks that were novel at the time, like placing the lead guitar on one track and adding echo for it on the opposite track. An example of this can be heard on *My Own True Love*, from the first album, on which Don played lead guitar. As Don recalls; "Joe Boles had some really good ideas, and that's why we went back to him when the time came for albums. There were times when he put a microphone right by our hands so as to get the 'pick' sound on the record. Another thing he did was put a microphone in the shower to get a little echo. That was before commercial reverb units were available."

Eventually, there were more than enough songs "in the can" to make a Ventures album. There were even a half-dozen of Don's vocals recorded. Often, at the end of a session, Don would go to a microphone and record romantic ballads such as *You'll Never Walk Alone*. He was never satisfied with that one enough to put it on vinyl, nor with *Dear Miss Lonely Hearts*, a song Josie had written about someone writing to a "lonely hearts" columnist in search of a mate. However, Don and Bob kept experimenting with this song until they created a stirring instrumental entitled *Lonely Heart* that would later appear on a single and their third album. The romantic melody and tempo remained the same, but Don underscored it with a heavy, busy rhythm that would become his career trademark.

Howie Johnson, Nokie Edwards, and Bob Bogle – 1960

TAPING AND TOURING

Knowing that promotional touring was a great booster of record sales, Bob Reisdorff registered The Ventures with Star's Personal Management. The tour agency responded quickly, giving the band little time to rest upon arriving back from New York. Immediately, another tour with current vocal star, Jimmy Clanton [*Just a* Dream] was launched. For The Ventures, it was an honor to open for Jimmy and then back him up in concert. Nearly two-dozen shows through the western States filled up August and half of September.

Although *Walk-Don't Run* did not hit the top in Billboard, the magazine's poll-results revealed America's disk jockeys having voted the tune Best Instrumental, and The Ventures as <u>the</u> Top Instrumental Group in the country. When total world sales surpassed a million copies, Liberty presented each band member with a Gold Record Award. In the next forty years, countless re-issues pushed sales of *Walk-Don't Run* well past ten million.

Blue Horizon Productions wasted no time in releasing another Ventures single. Early in their friendship, Bob and Don learned to play *Perfidia*, a big-band hit for Xavier Cugat, Jimmy Dorsey, Benny Goodman, Glenn Miller, and Gene Krupa. Finally, in 1952, a harmonious vocal version by the Four Aces had achieved top-ten status. By 1960, Bob and Don's arrangement was a driving, up-tempo dance number in the style of *Walk-Don't Run*. At a session with Joe Boles on August 8, the band made a bold entry in the studio's *Friends of Ours* log book that included the signatures of Nokie, Howie, Bob, and Don, with the footnote, "The Ventures (Perfidia Session)."

For the flip side, a driving rocker based on pianist Floyd Cramer's 1958 single called *Flip, Flop and Bop* was chosen. The Ventures named their arrangement "No Trespassing" after a sign posted in someone's yard. For many guitar enthusiasts, both sides of this record were equally enjoyable, an aspect that became the norm with most Ventures' singles. In 1962, Floyd Cramer's second version of this tune and charted at number 63 with the title, *Hot Pepper*. Tacoma's Wailers also had a version of the tune back then, but it wasn't released on a recording until 1998 [Norton EP-085].

Unknown to fans for years, *No Trespassing* featured Nokie on lead guitar. By then, the big man was playing rock 'n roll with a vengeance, using a technique where practically every note of a solo was hit on the "wrong" fret and the string(s) pushed or pulled up to the correct pitch. The method became a challenge to guitarists of all skill levels, with only the best coming close to mastering it.

The Joe Boles sessions produced the first of many movie themes to be recorded by The Ventures. Delving into the Chet Atkins *Hi-Fi In Focus* album, the guys played *Tara's Theme* from *Gone With the Wind*. Having been a Top Forty hit for Jimmy Clanton in 1959 as *My Own True Love*, this title was retained by The Ventures. It was one of the few times when Don was recorded playing lead guitar while Nokie played rhythm and chord fills.

CALIFORNIA DREAMIN'

Soon after the release of *Perfidia*, Decca realized the power of instrumental rock, releasing a Bill Haley and His Comets album entitled *Strictly Instrumental* [Decca DL 78964]. At the same time, Bob Reisdorff moved to Hollywood, near the headquarters of Liberty Records, and it was not long before he beckoned Josie and The Ventures to move south. Before moving, Josie issued one more Blue Horizon record from Seattle. In a San Francisco nightclub, she had discovered a fine young singer from the UK named Douglas Longley. At the end of their chat, Josie had asked him to look her up if he ever came to Seattle. This he did, and when she recorded him at Boles' studio, she also convinced him that "Scott Douglas" as a better name for a new singing star. The Ventures provided backing for his two vocals, *Hold Me Thrill Me Kiss Me* and *No Next Time*. However, the artist listing on Blue Horizon 102 specified "Scott Douglas And The Venture Quintet." Some forty years later, Josie reflected; "The Ventures played that session as a favor to me, knowing I was short on money and didn't know any other musicians. They had just made a name as an instrumental group, and did not want to be known for backing a singer. Not wanting to tell an outright lie, we decided on a 'little white one' and inserted the word 'quintet.' Anyway, the record didn't sell very well, likely because Scott Douglas was a crooner with a style that was no longer very popular."

~ ~ ~

Once *Walk-Don't Run* reached the top-ten across the continent, Bob Reisdorff took the Ventures' master tape to Los Angeles. After renting a luxurious apartment, he began coaxing Josie and The Ventures to follow. Before anyone moved, however, there was one more request for their services that The Ventures would not turn down. It was an invitation to perform at the prestigious Evergreen Ballroom near Lacey, now a suburb of nearby Olympia. In past years, the Evergreen had hosted dances played by the best of the big bands. Louis Armstrong, Benny Goodman, and Duke Ellington had played there, but as times changed, management lured younger crowds by booking r&b groups like Little Richard, Fats Domino, James Brown, and Ray Charles. Drummer Howie Johnson was especially eager to accept the job, knowing family and friends would come to see him play where the likes of Count Basie and Woody Herman had performed. A large, appreciative audience made the night one of The Ventures' fondest memories of 1960. For years, the Evergreen Ballroom hosted acts ranging from Jimi Hendrix to the best country and hip-hop bands. Sadly, in July of 2000, the building was completely destroyed in a spectacular fire.

One reason for Bob Reisdorff's relocation to Hollywood was that Al Bennett had suggested the move; "Later, I realized that what Al really had in mind was getting his hands on Dolton." In 1958, Bennett had left Dot Records to become Liberty's vice president, and in February 1960, stockholders elected him to be president. While the company's profits had then increased, lately they had begun to sag, causing Al to smack his lips at the thought of acquiring Dolton's top stars, The Fleetwoods and The Ventures.

For the next few months, The Ventures were on the road. Between tours, they checked into Hollywood's Orange Motel for a few days, recorded several songs before hitting the road once more. Instead of relocating, Nokie and Howie decided to commute to Hollywood for recording sessions. Howie was especially skeptical about moving, having started a young family again after the collapse of a first marriage that began when he was just seventeen years old.

Page 40

Al Bennett Elected President Of Liberty Records

AL BENNETT

LOS ANGELES—Alvin S. Bennett has been elected president of Liberty Records, stepping up from his post of executive vice president, it was announced following the annual board of directors meeting in Los Angeles on February 15.

Simon R. Waronker moves from president to chairman of the board in Liberty's executive realignment. Among his management responsibilities as the company's senior executive officer, Waronker will continue to head Liberty's expanding A&R division.

Re-elected at the stockholders' meeting were Hal Linick, vice-president and treasurer; Seymour Zucker, secretary and director; and Raymond C. Sandler, assistant secretary and director.

Additionally, the board was increased to seven members including the five officers named above and two additional to be appointed.

A native of Joiner, Ark., Bennett started out in the record business in Memphis, Tennessee, as a salesman for Decca Records in 1948, moving on to Gallatin, Tenn., as a National Sales Manager for Dot. Liberty's new president next moved to L. A. for Dot in 1956, and joined Hart Distributing as general manager shortly later.

Bennett assumed the post of vice president and general manager of Liberty early in 1958, bringing in a new management team.

When The Ventures arrived in Hollywood, Reisdorff took them to Liberty's headquarters on the musically rich Sunset Strip. The boys learned that the modern building had recently been purchased from America's most successful singing cowboy, Gene Autry. Imperial Records had then moved into Liberty's previous building nearby. Liberty retained their studio there, and because it was an addition to the older building, it was referred to by most as "the annex."

From this point, Liberty attracted a variety of recording artists ranging from the Martin Denny Orchestra to Bobby Vee. Much of the company's success was attributed to Al Bennett, whose reputation varied from "music business wizard" to "conniving manipulator." Taking over as president, he began running Liberty like the head of a large, (and usually) happy family.

A young A&R [Artists and Repertoire] man was introduced to The Ventures as "Snuff" Garrett. According to Bob Reisdorff, Tommy Garrett had been nicknamed "Snuff" in high school after the American Tobacco Company's eminent product "Garrett Snuff." Garrett seemed, in the eyes of Bob and Don, to have considerable influence at Liberty, where he was affectionately called "Snuffy." Reisdorff told the boys that while Snuffy only twenty-two, he had impressed the company with his knack of finding just the right songs for artists like Johnny Burnette [*You're Sixteen*], Gene McDaniels [*A Hundred Pounds of Clay*] and Bobby Vee [*Rubber Ball*]. In fact, it was Garrett who had signed Bobby Vee to the Liberty label in the fall of 1959.

Don Wilson recalls his first impression of Reisdorff's office; "Upstairs at the right rear corner of the Liberty building, we saw a room that had been the broadcast studio for Gene Autry's radio show from the time when I was a small child. It was now Bob Reisdorff's office, and it looked pretty impressive."

The two Ventures noticed tape recorders in some of the offices as well as turntables and speakers, and when their tour was finished, Don said; "We were hoping to see the recording studios." Bob Reisdorff replied; "They do auditions and demos in a small studio over at the 'annex,' but most everyone records up the street at Western or the new United Recorders. They are across the street from each other, further up on Sunset. You'll be seeing a *lot* of those places soon enough."

Liberty Records in 1960 - 6920 Sunset Blvd.

ON THE ROAD

With *Walk-Don't Run* still in the top 100 and *Perfidia* beginning to slide, Reisdorff contacted a tour agency called ZEE to arrange a Ventures promotional tour. As Don remembers, the first booking was not far from Hollywood; "Our first job in California was on the outskirts of L.A. at the El Monte Legion Stadium. There were other bands like The Fendermen on the same program, and The Platters closed the show. We felt pretty honored to be on the same stage as them."

ZEE arranged a string of one-night stands that lasted close to Christmas. Booking was an easy task as The Ventures were in high demand. A widespread belief that Liberty/Dolton financed such tours was not the case. The group alone was responsible for expenses and collecting payment while on the road. Sometimes the guys were given a check that upon deposit, was found to be bad, and Josie would spend hours acquiring the payment. The band asked for cash whenever possible, but the request was not always welcome.

While preparing for the road, the idea occurred to add some variety to their sound by taking saxophonist Don Markham on the tour. Josie and Reisdorff deemed the extra expense to be minimal, and Markham, who was usually in high demand, was able and willing to join The Ventures for a short tour.

Winter promo-photo 1960

If there was ever any questions regarding The Ventures' rise to fame without having "paid their dues," touring in the extremely cold winter of '60-61 that saw much more snow than usual would put them to rest. Pulling a rental trailer behind a station wagon, the six (including Butch Hamblin), set out to appear in thirty-six cities across the U.S.A. The heater in the Pontiac barely kept them from freezing, and sometimes they got lost and had to backtrack several miles in a snowstorm. When arriving at a venue, the equipment needed warming before it would work properly, and several times a night, the guitars needed tuning.

Sleep was another problem. Every night in a different hotel was bad enough, but the worst was when they had to sleep in the car while traveling, sometimes going three days without seeing bed. Most jobs paid two or three hundred dollars, but after meals, gasoline, and vehicle repairs, there was not much left. Near the end of the tour, The Ventures called Josie for help. She wired them funds to get back, so they were home for Christmas and a well-deserved rest.

Don Markham said he had traveled enough for a lifetime, so he went back to Bakersfield to join up with Buck Owens and become the leader of the Bakersfield Brass, which appeared on the early "Hee Haw" television shows. Later in the sixties, Markham played with several San Francisco groups, most notably Sly And The Family Stone. Don did not play at *Woodstock* with Sly, but is heard on the group's studio recording of *Stand*. In the early seventies, Markham worked with Johnny Paycheck before joining Merle Haggard in 1974. Thirty years later, Don Markham was still blowing trumpet and sax with Merle Haggard and the Strangers, playing what Merle termed "country jazz."

By Christmas *Perfidia* had peaked at a respectable 15 in Billboard. The song hit number 7 in Canada while in Britain it climbed to number 5. When Cash Box named The Ventures "the most currently played instrumental group," radio broadcasters everywhere knew they had more than a one-hit-wonder on their hands. As sales of *Perfidia* soared, it was re-issued in a sleeve bearing the photo shown on our cover.

At this time, Liberty licensed *Walk-Don't Run* and *Home* to the Victor of Japan (now JVC). This record [Rank 1075] was packaged in a "teens around a jukebox" picture-sleeve. Because sales there were light, the record eventually became a valuable rarity. Once Toshiba licensed The Ventures' recordings, the country saw an endless string of singles, always in colorful picture sleeves.

Don and Bob subscribed early to the principle of "The show must go on." Whenever someone was unavailable for a job proposal, they arranged for a substitute. This sometimes caused confusion for fans at a dance, recognizing just three or perhaps only two of the musicians on stage. There had been times when Don and Nokie had performed with drum and bass players borrowed from local bands such as Walla Walla's Gems or Portland's Sandy and the Beaumonts, and other times when Bob and Nokie toured with comedian George Hopkins playing his drums while Chuck Sedacca handled rhythm guitar. In the coming years, George worked with The Ventures more than once, but good friend Chuck's career soon ended tragically in a horrible highway accident. Apparently, his Volkswagen bus was trapped between two large trucks that crashed and burned, taking the lives of Chuck, his wife, and their two young children. As Bob recalls; "Chuck was an amazing musician, highly trained in music and proficient on the piano, guitar, and bass."

Nokie Edwards, George Hopkins, Bob Bogle, and Chuck Sedacca

In his short lifetime, Chuck cut two records; *A-Hopin' and A-Prayin'* / *You'll Never Know* – [Donna 1350] and *I Don't Wanna Know* / *Busy* [Smash-1773]. Both are purported to be rarities.

Although the Gems played many Ventures tunes and had backed notables including country singer Bobby Bare and teen idol, Donny Brooks, they came to Seattle from Walla Walla, Washington to record original material at Joe Boles' studio. In the winter of

1960, Don and Bob recruited Gems' bassist Ron Overman and drummer Larry Loney for backup on a tour of the West Coast. Later, while Bob was setting up his own new record label, Don and Nokie commandeered the two again for a pair of Northwest tours that averaged around one month each. Overman tells of numerous fans voicing discontent when they saw only two of the real Ventures on stage, but quickly forgetting about it once they saw Nokie's dazzling guitar work.

The list of musicians working with Bob and Don grew through the decades, some being the subject of fascinating or funny stories that the guys remember to this day. Not all of the tales concerned musicians, as the band employed several "roadies" along the way. One of Butch Hamblin's last tours with the group found him driving in circles. Although he felt sheepish at the time, Butch now laughingly recalls; "We finished our job one night and took off immediately after, wanting to make sure we got to the next one on time. It was about 500 miles from Winona, Minnesota to Green Bay, Wisconsin. After driving for around four hours, the sun started to rise. I stopped the car and checked my map, but when it didn't seem to make sense, I stopped at the next service station. I told the guy there that we were on our way to Green Bay and I asked if he could tell us where we were. He said 'Where'd you come from?' I said 'Winona, Minnesota.' Then he said, 'Well, see those lights across the river there? That's Winona!'"

Bob Bogle continues; "Butch came back to the car and he was laughing. When he told us that we had made a big loop and were only two or three miles from where we started, we were pretty downhearted. We had been trying to sleep in the car without much success, and now we had to drive all day and play the job that night without any real rest."

Recalling that era, Don adds; "We ran into some real hooligans on one trip. This venue in New Mexico had a balcony, and a few guys up there found they could reach outside and get snow off the roof. Every so often they pelted us with a snowball. Everyone thought it was funny to see us dodging snowballs while trying to play. That wasn't so bad, but later, when we were on our way to the next place, the same guys tried to run us into the ditch by passing us and pulling right in front. It was snowing and we slid all over the icy road when we slammed on the brakes. They're lucky we never caught up with those ruffians."

While the group toured, Bob Reisdorff called Josie in Seattle to say that an apartment was for rent across the courtyard from his, and that he had taken out an option on it for her at $250 per month. Josie remembers her first reaction; "Exorbitant! How could I ever afford it? Nevertheless, I left for Hollywood near the end of October. When I arrived at the Liberty building, I encountered no hostility, but I was not greeted with open arms. This business having been the domain of men only from Beethoven to Bacharach, it must have come as quite a surprise to have a woman record producer among them!

"Shortly after becoming settled in my new apartment, I decided to explore the street on both sides of Hollywood Boulevard. Eventually, I came upon the famous Music City Records shop at Hollywood and Vine. I went in to see if they were selling our Ventures hit record, and of course, there it was! It was quite a thrill to see my own produced record being sold in Hollywood. While browsing around the store, I overheard a lady mention to the clerk that she was a songwriter. Although not yet completely 'with it' about the recording business, I did realize that a hit song made all the difference to the success of an artist. So I approached her, thinking she just might have a hit instrumental up her sleeve for my guys. I had barely begun to ask her when the clerk scowled and loudly said to me, 'Hey, lady! I'm trying to make a living here!' I was so embarrassed that I quickly left the store. After thinking about this encounter for a few days, I decided to go back and apologize to the clerk for interrupting while he was making a sale, even though it was he that had been rude. With 'hat in hand' so to speak, I approached him to say I was sorry for having interrupted. I also mentioned the reason, saying I was the producer of The Ventures' record, *Walk-Don't Run*. He quickly apologized for embarrassing me and I learned that his name was Christian Wilde. He was also a songwriter who occasionally lent his talents as an arranger for singers. After we became friends, he often stopped by for dinner and insisted on making the salad. Chris has written many beautiful melodies to which I have suggested he add lyrics for a stage production." The Ventures didn't meet Christian Wilde for several months, but once they did, he became a good friend plus a significant contributor to their repertoire.

When it was time for Josie and Reisdorff to plan The Ventures' first album, there were around thirty songs from which to choose the standard twelve. As a matter of course, *Walk-Don't Run, Home*, and *The McCoy* were selected. Another original, noted for the melody switching twice to a "Tequila" beat was appropriately titled *The Switch*. The album would also contain *My Own True Love*, one of the few tracks on which Don had the distinction of playing lead guitar. Josie recalls her hand in selecting material: "As my partner, Bob strongly supported me in all the choices I made, from the songs to be recorded to LP cover concepts. In return, I respected his knowledge of music and uncanny business acumen. We were truly a team! As he has mentioned many times since, The Ventures were a joy to work with. They were a team also, with no inflated egos getting in the way of recording the best possible music. How fortunate it was that the six of us had such camaraderie."

The final selections were a careful mix of fast and slow numbers, mostly well-known songs, but with a couple of driving Ventures' originals thrown in.

 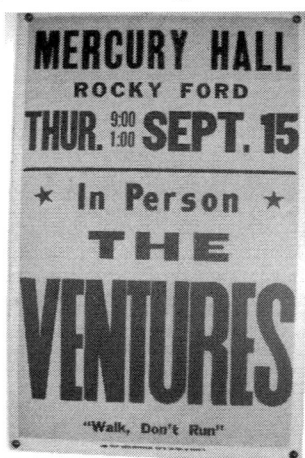 

September 1960 – New Mexico, Colorado, and Nebraska

As The Ventures continued touring, a crisis was building back at the offices of Liberty's long-time cover artists, Pate/Francis and Associates. *Walk Don't Run* albums were being pressed in the thousands while the company's art designers searched for a color photograph to front The Ventures' record jacket. As the band was out on tour, the designers opted for stand-ins. Some drums and electric guitars were rented, a lovely model hired, and four stockroom employees were posed haphazardly on the floor, as if in a tizzy over Miss Barbara Grimes. The Liberty folks thought no one would notice the difference, especially with a striking model in a tight blouse at the forefront.

When the first shipment of *Walk Don't Run* arrived at Liberty, someone noticed how much the stockroom boys on the cover differed in appearance from the real Ventures shown on the back cover. An artist quickly solved the dilemma by replacing the photo with offset tracings of it on a sheet of opaque "onion skin" paper. The result looked rather artsy, and attracted little attention until many years later when record collectors discovered the existence of the rare "first run" cover with an actual photo of The Ventures clad in their hound's-tooth sports jackets.

Another quirk on the stereo issue of this album was the two tracks from the first single, *Walk-Don't Run* and *Home*, appearing in monaural format. There had been such a rush to release the LP that the single version was used instead of obtaining the original tape from Joe Boles. Even ten years later, when mono records became history, re-issues of the album did not have these tracks in stereo. After twenty years went by, a stereo take of *Walk-Don't Run* appeared on compact disc, but *Home* in this format has never been found. If a stereo tape of *Home* ever existed, it was likely erased and overwritten. During the recording of *Walk-Don't Run*, no one had imagined it would become a hit and subsequently part of an album.

Had sales of the *Walk Don't Run* album reached 500,000 in the United States, the band would have received a Gold Record from the Recording Industry Association of

America (RIAA). However (as with their hit single), it was *worldwide* sales of the album that eventually reached one million, earning the band a Gold Album award from Liberty Records.

The Ventures' next step also consumed a goodly amount of their time. As their fame grew and they began touring, disc jockeys and journalists hounded them for interviews. At first, it was Don and/or Bob who were interrogated, but later, the others joined in. When interviews with Nokie finally appeared, surprised readers learned of his playing lead guitar on several tracks of the first album. After decades, the exact tracks are still undetermined, but both Nokie and Bob agree on Nokie's having led *No Trespassing*, *Raunchy*, and *Night Train*.

A DREAM FULFILLED

A fall booking landed The Ventures in the city of Wenatchee in central Washington on a bill with Bobby Vee (*Rubber Ball*) and Jimmy Jones (*Handy Man*). While organizing the show, local DJ Don Bernier had also booked a local group called The Furys as an opening act. Earlier, during a Junior College talent show, Bernier had noticed a young singer-guitarist named Judd Hamilton, and convinced him to record with The Furys at a Spokane radio studio. Singing his own *Little Lost Angel* and *I'm Not Around Anymore* [Julian 101], Judd's single was soon available locally. Subsequently, Judd Hamilton and The Furys opened for The Ventures and Bobby Vee in Wenatchee's D&D Roller Rink.

Entering the dressing room, which was actually the rink's Men's Room, Judd found The Ventures and Vee waiting to go on stage. Judd remembers being rather star-struck as he worked up the nerve to ask Bob Bogle for some advice on getting started making records. When he did, Bob advised Judd to send some demo tapes to the A&R department of a few record companies. As their chat ended, Bob wished Judd good luck and said; "If you're ever down in Hollywood, look us up."

Judd Hamilton

Bob never expected to hear from the young man again, but as Judd remembers, he became obsessed; "To eighteen-year-old ears, that was the ultimate compliment, the ultimate invitation! I continued in college for two more semesters, but I couldn't get that conversation with Bob Bogle out of my mind. I just *had* to go to Hollywood. I had been doing well in college, so I faced a lot of resistance from the dean as well as my parents when I dropped out. Luckily, my father could see my determination and, as a first step, he got me a job in Seattle, working for a friend who manufactured ski jackets. My employer soon saw that I was unhappy, my mind being on Hollywood and a career in music. In an act of mercy, he searched out the phone number and called The Ventures' office. After talking to Josie and obtaining the address where I should go when I reached Hollywood, he produced a box of ten surplus ski jackets. He gave them to me at below cost, instructing me to sell them to my schoolmates in back in Wenatchee, to finance my trek to Hollywood. I went home, sold the jackets, and in the spring of 1961 I said goodbye to my parents and fourteen-year-old brother, Danny. Arriving at Liberty records in Hollywood, Josie welcomed me with a tour of the facilities and directions to find Bob Bogle. Meanwhile my money ran out and I started sleeping in my car. By the time I got up the nerve to go and see Bob Bogle, I was getting very hungry.

"At the time, Bob shared a suite with Bobby Vee. Bob had found another apartment for himself, but had been too busy to make the move. He was very surprised when I showed up at his door. When he learned that I had been sleeping in my car and had barely eaten for two days, he invited me out for supper and offered me his couch to sleep on. During this the next week, I hung around Bob in the studio, learning everything I could about the music production. When it was time for another Ventures tour, Bob saw a chance for me to make a little money. Butch Hamblin had been handling most of the "roadie" chores, but wasn't available for every tour, especially those for with short notice. I pledged to be The Ventures' road manager, any time they wished.

"Upon returning to Hollywood, I couldn't believe my luck! Bob set me up in his unoccupied apartment to look after it. Now I had a place to live and would be paid for being there. I stayed three or four months until I found a day job parking cars."

~ ~ ~

Following the Holiday season, the boys enjoyed another hit single while assembling album number two. As Bob Reisdorff recalls; "There were several tracks on tape from the last Seattle recording session and I took them to Hollywood for remixing by engineer Henry Lewy. He operated the studio in the annex of the Liberty building, and we brought the Johnny Mann Singers in for a couple of the romantic ballads. For the related single, we picked a tune revived by Bill Doggett. The writers back in the forties had their own way of spelling 'Rambunctious,' so we were stuck with the tongue-twister, 'Ram-Bunk-Shush'. This one made it to 29 in Billboard."

A PICTURE WORTH A THOUSAND GUITARS

When the album entitled *The Ventures* [Dolton BLP-8004] was released, the mere sight of it made it sell. If any budding guitarists had passed up the *Walk Don't Run* album, they simply could not resist the full-size color picture on the front of this one (again, see our cover). They would stare at it and daydream for hours about being part of this group. The Ventures had proven that it was all right to play guitars and drums without singing, and this album cover defined what such a group should look like. The smart matching outfits and shiny Fender guitars stirred the imagination of teenage boys, first across North America, and then around the world. It did not matter that the album contained no original compositions, the creative cover versions having vastly more youth-appeal than the originals. So delightful was the sound that first-time Ventures buyers immediately ran out to get the previous album. Garage bands were not new, but their numbers increased by the thousands as young musicians joined together to imitate The Ventures. By midsummer, the album charted at 39 in Billboard, and soon after, Don Randall at Fender Musical Instruments offered to replace all of The Ventures' equipment with shiny new product. All that Don, Bob, and Nokie had to do was to bring in their used equipment. The boys complied, but as Bob Bogle relates; "I'm sure we could have left our old stuff at home and still got the new equipment. We were so naive and innocent back then. I would love have my old *Walk-Don't Run* Jazzmaster. I don't know what they did with those guitars, but by now they would have some real value."

The publicity given by the album to the Stratocaster, Jazzmaster, and the Precision bass was priceless to the company. Founder Leo Fender later claimed that The Ventures had likely heavily influenced the acceptability of the electric bass. In realizing this fact, Fender extended the offer by telling the guys that if they were ever in need, to come in and get anything they wished.

A little later in 1961, The Ventures were invited to appear on Hollywood's *Top Ten Dance Party* at KCOP TV, hosted by the legendary Wink Martindale. When asked to appear, The Ventures went shopping at downtown costume shop known for its stock of show business garments. While being fitted for a set of matching gold lamé jackets, they were recognized by another customer. Upon introducing himself, Gene Davis said that he played guitar and was leader of the Palomino Riders at the Palomino Club. The boys knew this North Hollywood club as a hotbed of top musicians. More chat revealed session artists like Glen Campbell and James Burton often sat in when a member of the Palomino Riders was out doing studio work. The conversation ended with Gene inviting the boys to drop into the club that night and see what they thought of his group. The Ventures said that they would.

At the Wink Martindale Show, Don, Bob, and Nokie finally met Duane Eddy, who also performed that night. Howie, eager to be back with his young wife, was already on the road back to Washington.

Attired in their flashy new jackets, the three went in and watched the band over a drink. It was not long before Gene Davis pointed out The Ventures in the audience. With records on the charts, the boys received a rousing cheer from the crowd, including calls to go on stage and play. Gene beckoned to the boys, but Bob declined, saying their drummer had not come along. That is when Gene's drummer, Mel Taylor, spoke up; "That's no excuse. I know your stuff." Obligingly, the boys retrieved their guitars from the trunk of the car.

On stage, Don sang a couple of country vocals before signaling Mel to start *Walk-Don't Run*. Bob recalls their surprise; "Mel was so good that it could have been Howie or Skip Moore behind us. After finding out that he had our records and knew our arrangements, we played for almost an hour. We knew that Howie would not relocate and he did not like commuting, so when the set was over and we had time to chat, I asked Mel if he would do some studio work with us. He agreed and gave us his phone number. After about six months, we called him."

THE ROAD TAKES A TOLL

As The Ventures' second album was being pressed, their agency booked a January tour covering several eastern U.S. cities and two in Canada. The all-star package included Bobby Vee, The Ventures, Buddy Knox [*Party Doll*], Dion [*The Wanderer*] and Ersel Hickey [*Blue Birds Over the Mountain*]. The Ventures were to provide backing music for all except Buddy Knox, who worked with his own trio. Upon calling Howie in Tacoma, The Ventures were shocked to hear that the drummer would no longer do roadwork. Howie said he did not want another divorce, and that the low pay was not worth the time away from his family. Don and Bob had barely started looking for a drummer when Nokie also announced that he would not be touring. He said he was not getting rich on the road and he wanted to pursue some musical projects of his own. It was a serious blow to The Ventures, and they wondered if they were destined to remain a two-man group forever. Quick collaboration with Josie and Reisdorff resulted in a whole new arrangement. In order to fuel record sales, they would tour with a hired bassist and drummer. Later, for recording sessions, Howie and Nokie would be retained on a per-session basis. As both Howie and Nokie agreed, Reisdorff and Josie arranged for a new promotional photo depicting The Ventures as a duo.

Anyone reading the fine print on Dolton 32, *Ram-Bunk-Shush* might not have realized its significance. "Dolton Records, A Division of Liberty Records" indicated Al Bennett was now the owner of the Dolton label. Bob Reisdorff and his partners at C&C Distributors had sold the company and paid out some remaining shares to Bonnie Guitar. Bob would continue as head of the Dolton division and also as co-producer and manager of The Ventures. At this point, the label was still light blue, but would soon be changed to dark blue with a slightly different drawing of the three dolphins. To commemorate the acquisition, Liberty issued *Teensville* (LX-5503) a special album containing three songs each by Liberty's Bobby Vee and Johnny Burnette along with Dolton's Fleetwoods and The Ventures. The Ventures' tracks were *No Trespassing*, *Ram-Bunk-Shush*, and *Rawhide*. Further indicating their current group status, a liner note described The Ventures as the most "exciting instrumental twosome as you are likely to hear." The twosome was pictured on the cover clad in what Mel Taylor described many years later as "those peacock jackets."

Josie with Don and Bob

As head of Liberty's new Dolton division, Bob Reisdorff had requested a secretary. Al Bennett then had his own secretary, Miss Arlene Biedenkopf, place a classified in the newspapers. One of the applicants was a twenty-nine-year-old Puerto Rican woman, Sonia Rivera, who had, with her husband Ray, moved to California from New York in 1955. Arlene was familiar with Sonia's work and highly recommended her to Bob. Sonia was hired and quickly persuaded everyone to call her "Sonny."

Sonia "Sonny" Rivera – 1961

Josie recalls; "For some reason, she did not care for her first name, but I thought it was beautiful. I was surprised that she spelled her nickname 'Sonny' rather than 'Sunny', but I suppose it was because of the letter 'o' in Sonia. Although she was Bob Reisdorff's Dolton secretary, she did plenty of work for Blue Horizon Productions, and we became dear friends."

At this time, television producers in New York invited The Ventures to appear on a TV variety program for a Billboard award presentation. As the appearance was just before the eastern tour, Bob and Don had to head for New York a couple of days early. On the way to pick up Butch Hamblin as road manager in Bob's new Thunderbird, a garbage truck hit the T-bird broadside. With a severely damaged passenger-side door and fender, the threesome proceeded in the mangled vehicle. A day or two later, Bobby Vee drove his Volkswagen "beetle," straight to Canada's capital city of Ottawa where the tour would begin before looping down through several eastern U.S. cities. The tour would finish back in Canada for the All Star Dance Party at the huge Palais Du Commerce in Montreal.

In New York, Don and Bob appeared on NBC's *Saturday Prom*, where they played their latest hit. After they performed *Ram-Bunk-Shush*, host Merv Griffin presented them with *two* awards resulting from Billboard's Thirteenth Annual Disc Jockey Poll.

For this tour, The Ventures borrowed a local drummer in each city, but were accompanied throughout by saxophonist Paddy Sevin and his bassist, who traveled in a Volkswagen mini-bus. When Don and Bob met with the pair in New York, the weather was bitterly cold. Driving northward towards Canada, they spent the night in a village called Madrid, about ten miles from the St. Lawrence River border crossing. Bob remembers being very cold that night; "I doubt if a thousand people lived in the town, and I think we were the first customers the archaic hotel had seen in months. There was absolutely no heat in the rooms and we nearly froze. I got into bed with all of my clothes on, including my shoes, but I couldn't get warm. I even put the floor rug on top of the bed, but it wasn't much help. Sometimes I wonder how we survived."

The next day, they were in Ottawa where the icy, humid air bit right through their clothing. Meeting up with the two New Yorkers and their VW mini-van, Paddy Sevin remarked; "We hope you guys enjoy riding in that posh T-Bird. The only way *we* could keep warm in this microbus was to pick up hitchhikers and use them for firewood!"

Billboard awards captured by The Ventures

Recalling some of the performances, Bob relates; "Later, when we backed up Ersel Hickey, he kept telling us to play loud because he didn't think he sounded very good. He was right. His records sounded good, but for some reason his voice would drift off-key on stage. We obliged, and played a little louder to help cover him up." As Don recalls; "The drummer we had in Montreal was actually a local teen-idol singer by the name of Michel Louvain. Everyone was surprised to see him play drums with us."

When the Ottawa-Montreal shows were completed, Bob volunteered to help Bobby Vee with his long drive back to California, leaving Don and Butch to come back in the Thunderbird. They arrived home just as *Perfidia* had slipped off the charts and *Ram-Bunk-Shush* had peaked at 29 in the March 6 issue of Billboard. The single didn't do as well as *Perfidia*, but its Top Thirty status was very encouraging.

In searching for new material, Bob and Don adapted many older popular songs to their style. Bob Reisdorff encouraged the pair to write more songs, although he realized this was difficult owing to their hectic schedule. During a phone conversation with one of his UK contacts, Reisdorff learned of an exciting instrumental recorded by British guitarist Bert Weedon. Seeing an opportunity for The Ventures, he quickly obtained a copy of *Ginchy*. When the 45 arrived, he gave it to Bob Bogle, who quickly went to work with Don on an arrangement. At their next rehearsal with Nokie and Howie, *Ginchy* was so good that it was slated for release while *Ram-Bunk-Shush* was still on the pop charts.

Striving for more smash hits, The Ventures converted another jazz arrangement from the Chet Atkins *Hi-Fi In Focus* album. Reiterating their famous *Walk-Don't Run* intro, they arranged a brilliant pop version of George Olsen's 1932 hit, *Lullaby of The Leaves*. The three-channel mix featured Bob's lead on one side, Don's rhythm on the other, with Nokie's bass and Howie's drumming in the middle. The record was released in April '61 with *Ginchy* on the flip side [Dolton 41]. When *Lullaby of The Leaves* placed 69 on Billboard's national chart, the guys had no idea that fifty years later, they would still be performing it in medley along with *Perfidia* and *Walk-Don't Run*.

With Bobby Vee - Cobblestone Ballroom, Storm Lake, Iowa

The next tour was for two weeks in April in the western states, again with seventeen-year-old Bobby Vee headlining. Other groups sharing the tour were Washington's Checkers (whose bassist and drummer backed Don and Bob) and Little Bill And The Bluenotes. Both from Tacoma and early Dolton artists, The Ventures and "Little Bill" Engelhart became lifelong friends. Forty years later, in his book, *Next Stop, Bakersfield*, he credited Bob Reisdorff with renaming The Bluenotes to Little Bill And The Bluenotes after learning that Bill's grandmother called him "Little Bill." Bill also wrote of being influenced by Nokie's brother Ira in the early 1950s, and later considering himself a one-hit failure until being enlightened by Don during an evening at the Wilson kitchen table in 1994. Don argued that Bill, having maintained a career in the work he loved; made several wonderful blues recordings; and sustained a thirty-year marriage with two wonderful children, could look back on his life with pride. His self-esteem boosted, Bill ended his book with this account and a picture of himself with Don and Bob.

One stop on this tour was Denver, Colorado, where a call came to the hotel from Johnny Smith, the original composer of *Walk-Don't Run*. By this time, The Ventures' version of *Walk-Don't Run* had been recorded by instrumental groups everywhere, from guitar driven surf groups like The Challengers and The String-A-Longs to orchestras such as The Tijuana Brass and Count Basie's big band. Even the legendary Billy Vaughn did a version, dousing his signature saxophones for an all-guitar arrangement. Thanking the Ventures for making his song a hit that was paying royalties unheard of in jazz circles, Johnny invited the guys to his home for dinner, where over an hour was spent in conversation and Johnny playing some guitar for them. When they asked about the title of his song, Johnny said he had seen a safety sign near the subway one night while playing jazz clubs in New York City.

Another detail that Don and Bob learned was that while the Chet Atkins' *Walk-Don't Run* began with the A-G-F-E chord sequence, Johnny's began with D-C-Bb-A. This stirred an interesting but chilling thought. If Chet had not adapted the simpler key signature, Bob and Don might not have attempted playing the tune and would still be sandblasting mortar and laying bricks.

Johnny Smith 1961   *Gibson*

Through Bobby Vee (real name, Robert Velline), The Ventures had met Bill Velline, Bobby's brother and competent lead guitarist. As Bill was available for the tour that followed, he became a Venture, along with a drummer from another group. By now it was not uncommon for Bob or Don to play bass, rhythm, or lead, and on some numbers, Bob and Bill would share lead duties while Don played rhythm and sang. This tour penetrated central Washington with a stop in Wenatchee. As this was Judd Hamilton's hometown, he arranged for Bob and Don to have dinner at his parents' home. Laughingly, Judd relates a surprising discovery; "Here I was, coming home having made it. I was the roadie for The Ventures! In the discussion after dinner, Dad said to Bob and Don, 'I think you should hear Judd's brother play the guitar'. I thought, 'Huh? What does my little brother know about playing guitar?' Danny was shy and hesitated, but Dad brought out the guitar. I had no idea that Danny even had a guitar. He was only fourteen, and although we'd always been close, he was just 'my little brother. Well, Danny played Ventures' stuff, and he was better at it than I was!"

DON DIXON SINGS

Don Wilson began life in Hollywood by living with Josie in her large apartment. As Don and Bob would be touring and recording much of the time, their families had opted to remain in Washington with the guys coming home when time permitted. Josie now had her own office near that of Bob Reisdorff in the Liberty Records building. The offices and studio were accessible from the parking lot by an outside staircase.

Having settled in Hollywood, Don thought he should try for a vocal hit. He was recording the tender love ballads, *I Love You, Yes I Do* and *For Your Love*, plus his rendition of Frankie Laine's top hit from 1950, *Cry of the Wild Goose* when Liberty president Al Bennett dropped by. After hearing a few takes, he said to Don; "I see you are doing some vocal tracks here. They're good, but you guys have made quite an impact as an instrumental group and that's what the public expect to hear. It never pays to rock a successful boat." The band respected Bennett and took his advice to heart until Josie thought of a way for Don to release his songs. Don liked the idea, and soon the first single by "Don Dixon" was in the works on a newly re-designed Blue Horizon label. The Ventures were now realizing some decent income for their records, so in addition to enjoying new living quarters, a new Thunderbird for Bob and a Cadillac for Don, they went "all out" on the production of Don's record by hiring background singers plus Ernie Freeman for keyboard work. Ernie, with his orchestra, was known for the instrumental hit, *Jivin' Around*, and a 1957 cover of *Raunchy* that did almost as well as the Bill Justis original. Recently, Freeman had joined with several studio musicians to accompany Ernie Fields for some instrumental rock recordings of which *In The Mood* was a hit [Rendezvous 110]. Like many session musicians trying for a hit of their own, Ernie would issue several organ instrumentals, including his version of the soon-to-explode dance craze, *The Twist*.

Unfortunately, the "Don Dixon" experiment did not begin at a very good time, as Blue Horizon Productions was busy with tours, Ventures recordings, and the infinite quest for new material. The few demo copies in existence were mostly located by collectors searching storage boxes and dusty shelves in radio stations.

The new Blue Horizon label – flip side, *For Your Love*

Up to now, most of The Ventures' bookings had been for dances or teen hops in skating arenas or armory halls. They were usually four-hour jobs having three short intermissions. In the spring of 1961, as *Lullaby of the Leaves* hit the airwaves, an opportunity arose for a proper concert tour. In mid-April, Bob, Don, and Bobby Vee joined a two-week package deal that took them to Australia, New Zealand, and Hawaii with headliner Connie Francis (*Everybody's Somebody's Fool* - MGM 12899), Johnny Burnette (*Dreamin'* – Liberty 55258), and Donnie Brooks who had just hit big in America with *Mission Bell* [Era 3018]. Arranged by Lee Gordon, known for bringing the hottest American acts to teens "down-under," the show was opened by Australia's Colin "Col" Joye And The Joy Boys who had recorded their own string of fine rock instrumentals. The tour kicked off with two nights at Sydney Stadium, followed by two shows nightly in Melbourne and Adelaide before hopping over to Auckland, New Zealand for two evening shows. It wasn't long before versions of *Walk-Don't Run* were available on records by the Joy Boys and New Zealand's own Supersonics.

The entourage then flew to Honolulu for two evening concerts under the stars. During the long flight home, as Don and Bob reflected on the exuberant crowds and luxurious accommodations, they envisioned worldwide touring.

GENE MOLES

While Bob and Don adapted to life in sunny California, Nokie remained in Washington, thinking that if *Walk-Don't Run* could do so well, he and an accomplished guitarist friend named Gene Moles should be able to get a hit.

When Gene, who played on the first Capitol recordings of Buck Owens, was age 31 and just getting started in the Tacoma nightclub scene, he met Nokie Edwards. Recalling their meeting after forty years, Gene relates; "I moved to Tacoma in January of 1960 to play at the Britannia Tavern with Dusty Rhodes. One night I was an hour late to a delay in driving back from Bakersfield, where I had lived. When I arrived, the band had hired Nokie to sit in for me. We hit it off real well and became good friends, even before we discovered we were both from Oklahoma. One day I went out to Nokie's place in Puyallup to jam with him. When he asked if I had any ideas for a new song, I started playing this thing that goes [hums the melody of *Scratch*], and then Nokie came in with a bridge part. That's when we started writing together. Later that year, Nokie suggested I come up to Seattle to a recording studio. We picked up a drummer named Bill Graham and we cut *Scratch* and *Night Run* right there in Joe Boles' basement. I played lead on *Scratch* and Nokie played bass. We were the only ones on that take. We stole *Hybrid Corn* off an old Chet Atkins single [RCA 48-0500, 1951], gave it a rock 'n' roll beat, and called it *Night Run*. Nokie played lead on it and I played rhythm. Later, he added a bass track to it and I added some hand clapping to both songs. When we put them on a record, we called ourselves The Marksmen. Nokie may have picked up the name from Don Markham, who used it back in the fifties. We got real excited when Dick Clark played *Night Run* on *American Bandstand*. We thought, 'Hey, it's gonna be a hit!' but it didn't catch on for us."

Bob Reisdorff and Josie were barely settled in Los Angeles when they put the Marksmen versions of *Night Run* and *Scratch* on Blue Horizon 6052 and distributed it to radio stations. At the time, Nokie and Gene had no idea they were delving into the realm of classical music, Chet Atkins having taken *Hybrid Corn* from the Johannes Brahms classic, *Hungarian Dance No.5*.

It seems almost a wonder that *Scratch*, the lively B-side did not become a hit. But it's also unsettling to imagine what "might have been" if Josie (with her talent for such things) had renamed the song and it had been widely promoted. Major success of *Scratch* might have swept Nokie up and away from any future work with The Ventures.

Once *Night Run* had received airplay on the *Dick Clark* show, Nokie and Gene wrote another pair of tunes recalled by Gene; "We were so excited about these tunes that we never thought to name them. Bob Reisdorff named them *Gringo* and *Sunny River*. For years, I never knew that he named that one after his secretary, Sonny Rivera."

As Nokie and Gene spent more time in the studio, their funds were gradually diminished, so when *Sunny River* and *Gringo* eventually appeared on Ventures records, as did *Night Run* and *Scratch*, they greatly appreciated the royalties.

Gene Moles and the Marksmen "45"

In addition to various surf and drag recordings, Gene made some rare singles in 1963, including one of special interest to Ventures fans; "We did one called *Kaha Huna, Goddess of Surfing* [Garpax 44176] on Gary Paxton's label, and another with Mel Taylor on a session at Henry Russell's H&R Studios down on Melrose [Avenue]. It was a hot new version of *Raunchy* [Three Star 4304], and Mel really went to town on those drums. It was the pick of the week on KAFE here in Bakersfield, just a few days before President Kennedy was shot. When that happened, everyone forgot about music or we might have had a hit on our hands."

Eventually, Gene went into repairing guitars, which led to him becoming widely known as respected luthier. As "The Doctor of Guitars," he remained in high demand to the age of seventy-three before succumbing to lung problems in April, 2002.

Gene's mention of "Don Markham and the Marksmen" refers to two early singles recorded on the Donna label. Don Markham explains; "I never really had a group called the Marksmen. I just worked with some studio musicians, Gary Paxton and his friends who recorded as Skip & Flip as well as The Hollywood Argyles." The records were *The*

Shuck b/w *Hully Gully Trumpets* [Donna 1323] led by Don's deep-throated tenor sax, and *Goose* [*Parts 1 and 2*, Donna 1325] on which Don also played flute in *Part 2*. The Ventures kicked off their second album with Markham and Paxton's *The Shuck*, which worked amazingly well with a guitar in place of the saxophone.

Another Blue Horizon record was distributed to L.A. radio stations in 1961 after Scott Douglas (a.k.a. Douglas Longley) approached Josie to produce him on another recording. Josie accepted the job, although she now felt that Scott's style was too outdated for the youth-driven market. By this time, dancing the twist was so popular that Bob and Don portrayed themselves to interviewers as being "a twist group." Scott's *A Hundred Thousand Ways* [Blue Horizon 6053], became another "Ventures rarity" when future collectors learned that Bob (and possibly Don) had added guitar backing on the flip side, *Pretending*. Older fan club members obtaining this record may have recognized Charlie Vance as the writer of *Pretending*, but they would not have known about "Longley," who shared writing credits with Don and Bob for *A Hundred Thousand Ways*.

Although Josie was right about Douglas' singing style, he managed to stay in the music business albeit a mere office job at Liberty. Josie remembers taking him in; "When Scott decided to stay in Hollywood and seek his fortune, I offered him a room in my large apartment. There was plenty of space and he helped pay my rent. As it turned out, his association with The Ventures wasn't quite finished."

ALONG CAME DAN

By mid-1961, Judd Hamilton had made several friends in Hollywood, his best buddy being teen heartthrob, Jack Chaplain. Jack's girlfriend, Ginger Blake, sang in a trio called The Honeys, along with along with Brian's future wife, Marilyn Rovell and her sister, Diane. They were all friends living south of Los Angeles in Hawthorne, where Brian worked with brothers Carl and Dennis after making their first recording as the Beach Boys.

Jack Chaplain - Aug. 1961

As Judd recalls; "I heard that the group was unhappy with Dave, the kid that played bass, so I said, 'Hey guys, you should hear my brother! He is an amazing kid when it comes to playing stuff like this!' Serious about their music, the Wilson's quickly arranged to fly Danny in from Wenatchee. They were impressed with Danny's bass playing, but then Dave's parents threatened to sue the Beach Boys if Danny replaced their son. As Danny was only fifteen, he stayed with me and hung around the studios, making himself useful as possible, all the while improving his musical skills."

Jack Chaplain's career was mostly in TV, but after being cast in current top programs like *Gunsmoke* and *Bonanza*, he was given the leading role in a Disney-style doggie movie entitled *Git!* Through his connections, he helped Judd break into the movie industry.

~ ~ ~

Back from the South Pacific tour, Bob and Don summoned Howie and Nokie after hearing Josie and Reisdorff's plan for album number three. The guys recall being continually pressured by Reisdorff to compose more tunes, not only for the additional revenue, but also to provide more album material. This time, they presented a delightful tune in honor of Josie, and added the The String-a-Longs' current number 3 hit, *Wheels* [Warwick M603]. Nokie had worked up a stinging version of Link Wray's *Rawhide* and was also ready to record *Bulldog* by the Fireballs. The Ventures' arrangement of *Bulldog* provided Don with another chance to use the driving rhythm he popularized on *No Trespassing*. For the next single, Reisdorff and Josie had selected *Lullaby of the Leaves* and *Lonely Heart*, which would also appear on the album along with *Ginchy* and more tunes by Chet Atkins and Floyd Cramer. The album began with Don playing lead guitar on *Ghost Riders in the Sky*.

Around this time, The Ventures played one of the most prestigious concerts of their career. The Alan Freed Rock 'n' Roll Show was an exciting prospect, even if was to end on a sour note. The good news was that no traveling was required, the event taking place at the Hollywood Bowl. Sharing the bill with Jerry Lee Lewis, Chuck Berry, and the Everly Brothers, The Ventures gave the sold-out crowd a truly great plug for instrumental rock. The bad news hit when the whole thing was over. Alan Freed was in trouble over a payola scandal, and with the ensuing confusion concerning service charges and entertainer's fees, payment for The Ventures' appearance apparently fell through the cracks. Phone calls and letters to Freed's office brought nothing. Months turned into years, and when the Grand Jury was finished with Freed, he was ruined and died shortly thereafter. As Bob Bogle lamented later; "We're still waiting to get paid for that one. It's one of the few times we had that happen in forty-five years. $500 was big money for us in those days. Most jobs paid half that or three hundred at the most. We saw a few bad checks in our day, but they were usually resolved in a short time."

Recalling this incident reminded Don of an unscrupulous club owner that pulled a dirty trick on The Ventures in the early sixties; "This guy asked us if we would go on stage earlier than we had been scheduled to play. We did as he asked, but when it was time to collect our money, he refused to pay us because we hadn't followed the terms of our contract. After that, we followed every contract to the letter, but it happened to us again several years later. We had played the night before in a town that was forty-seven miles up the road. After we played the next night, the guy informed us that we were not getting paid because the fine print in his contract said we couldn't play within a fifty-mile radius of his club. I wonder how many times he pulled that one on his entertainers."

One day between tours, Don worriedly mentioned to Bob Reisdorff that they were running out of material to record. Don says Reisdorff's answer still rings in his ears; "Don, don't worry! There are a lot more sounds in your guitars than you can ever imagine. Keep on experimenting."

Confident in his prediction, Reisdorff scheduled a studio session for The Ventures with composer/arranger, Hank Levine. His idea was to add orchestral backing to a Ventures tune. Levine had written a song entitled *Silver City*, which, although never used as a movie theme, may have been inspired by *Silver City* starring Edmond O'Brien and Yvonne de Carlo. Paul Sawtell, composer of over 200 movie scores through the forties, fifties, and sixties wrote the music for that 1951 movie. Bogle clearly recalls playing lead on The Ventures' version of Hank's *Silver City*, [Dolton 44].

Levine, who had been working with producer-guitarist Dick Glasser, also provided orchestral backing for the single's B-side, *Bluer Than Blue*, a song Glasser had co-written with western swing guitarist Tommy Allsup. While working at Imperial Records, Allsup and Glasser became friends, and began composing guitar instrumentals. Hank's string section added rich accompaniment to *Bluer Than Blue*, creating a western feel in the vein of his *Silver City*. Josie and Bob Reisdorff liked the sound so much that they contracted Levine to put strings on a number of instrumentals, one of which was a lovely Wilson-Bogle original that Reisdorff named *Josie*. Others included Floyd Cramer's *Last Date* and Bill Pitman's *Beyond the Reef*, which was enhanced with studio-created ocean waves and seabird calls.

Drawing from their record collection, *Meet Mr. Callahan* (sic) was given The Ventures' treatment, having been recorded as *Meet Mr. Callaghan* in 1952 by both Chet Atkins and Les Paul. As Bob recalls; "I was playing that one at parties and dances even before we started playing *Walk-Don't Run*."

The back photo on *Another Smash* [Dolton BLP-8006] portrayed Bob and Don only, with a short revelation that they alone were The Ventures. Record dealers had received this news in the mid-May issue of Cash Box when the magazine featured photos of the Liberty Records executives and the company's star performers. Don and Bob knew this would be disconcerting to their fans, but in light of the recent developments, it seemed the only reasonable procedure. Fortunately, concern of their fans was somewhat quelled when the disc was played and a dozen more delightful instros were heard. Those receiving a club bulletin were further comforted to see the message from Josie; "We would like to explain that Don Wilson and Bob Bogle are joint leaders of The Ventures as well as the lead and rhythm guitarists, and the ones who create the special Ventures sound. The other two members do not perform with them on road tours or in concert, but they do record with them."

A COLORFUL CONCEPT

As a single, *Silver City* peaked at 83 in September, indicating its considerable airplay and appearance in North American jukeboxes. Oddly, the song was enjoyed even more in Australia, where it reached 11 in Adelaide. Again, it seemed that while Ventures singles paid for themselves, each one was less successful than its forerunner. More singles would be made, but the best selling Ventures recordings were their albums. Searching for more album material, Bob Reisdorff came up with an idea; "It occurred to me that both sides of The Ventures' last single had colors in their title [*Silver City* and *Bluer Than Blue*], and I wondered if an entire album could be made like that. I sat down with Josie and the group, and I asked everyone to think of as many songs about color that they could. It wasn't long before we had about twenty titles. The recent hit by The Marcels was mentioned, and the guys' arranged *Blue Moon* so well that we decided it should be the next single. *Lady of Spain* was on tape from a previous session, so we used it for the B-side" [Dolton 47].

Regarding *Blue Moon*, Don Wilson laments; "Bob and I had been doing our arrangement of that song since 1960, but we never dreamed it had any hit power. When The Marcels made it a chart-topping doo-wopper, we were kicking ourselves for weeks!"

The oddity in the final selection of tunes for *The Colorful Ventures* [BLP-8008] was one suggested by Josie. It was an old Lionel Hampton tune called *Red Top*. Although written by Hampton's associate, Ben Kynard, credit on The Ventures' recording went erroneously to Woody Herman, who was actually responsible for an entirely different melody titled *(My Little) Red Top*.

Easily making *Red Top* a swinging guitar instrumental, The Ventures retained the cut in preference to other "color" tunes they had tried like *Mr. Blue*, *Golden Earrings*, *Blue Hawaii*, and *Deep Purple*. While recording *Yellow Bird*, Liberty crooner Vic Dana was in the studio and was, as Josie relates, the first, if not the only, musician to not be paid for working on a Ventures session; "At a recording session of *The Colorful Ventures* album, we were not quite satisfied with the sound on *Yellow Bird*. I had just finished an ice cream 'Dixie Cup,' and rinsed the container to have a drink of water from it. I set the empty cup down, and when Vic Dana picked it up and began tapping it on the bottom, inspiration struck! I said, 'Let's try to add that.' So, what you hear on *Yellow Bird* is Vic Dana playing Dixie Cup! There are absolutely no drums or any other percussion on it!"

Continuing on *The Colorful Ventures*, Bob Reisdorff mused; "At the time, I bought a pair of very colorful shirts that I got Bob and Don to wear for the cover photo. Don wishes I still had the shirts, but they were so loud that I donated them to a charity store. I still wonder if *The Colorful Ventures* was the first rock 'n' roll concept album."

In Japan, The Ventures' *Walk-Don't Run* had appeared only as a single release, prompting Toshiba to break the "colorful" concept of this new album. Consequently, in that country's 1962 edition of *The Colorful Ventures* [Liberty Japan LBY-1007], *Bluer Than Blue* was deleted in favor of *Walk-Don't Run*.

Japan's 1962 *Colorful Ventures* features "Walk-Don't Run"

In America, the album outsold *Another Smash*, squeezing into the Top 100 at 94. The album cover showed Bob and Don holding their guitars from Fender's swap offer, while the back included a thank-you to Nokie and Howie for their help. While the message was upsetting to fans, the music soon erased their concern.

The *Blue Moon* single topped out at 54 in late November. Some who bought both the single *and* the album noticed that *Blue Moon* had different endings. Bob Reisdorff explained that it was cheaper to record a separate mono version than to mix down a stereo take to mono. With several takes on a tape, it was common for a single to vary slightly from its album counterpart, and sometimes differ in length by several seconds.

Following the *Colorful Ventures* sessions at Liberty Custom Recorders, Judd Hamilton borrowed Nokie's Fender Precision bass for a live performance. Nokie tended to not lend his instruments, but sometimes kindness outweighed his reluctance. After the job, Judd left the instrument in his car, intending to return it the following morning. Even in 1961, the outcome was inevitable. Late in the night, someone smashed the window and took the Fender bass. Judd was unable to replace it, so Fender absorbed the loss. While obtaining his replacement, Nokie also picked up a Jazzmaster guitar. He still liked his Telecaster, but after using Bob's guitar he decided he needed one with a vibrato bar.

Late in 1961, Don tackled another vocal project. He had written a novelty tune merging the twist with the stomp into a new dance called the "Twomp." For the flip side, he sang an up-tempo ballad by Josie, Bob, and himself called *Heart on my Sleeve* [Blue Horizon 6054]. *The Twomp* was a take-off on the "Stomp," a dance popularized at beach clubs and weekend dances by Southern California surfers. *Surfer's Stomp* by The Mar-Kets was Liberty's first single for 1962, produced by one Joe Saraceno. Although the surf music movement was spreading like wildfire, no one suspected that the surfing genre would enjoy such longevity, and a seemingly unending number of revivals.

The Ventures had been exploited to this point due to inexperience. An instrumental group that would back up several singing acts was a virtual goldmine for booking agents. Following their opening of a show, the guys would obligingly provide background music for the headliners while receiving no supplement to their already meager pay. Soon, Don and Bob looked at other facets of the music business to increase their income. The guys tried many of these, from songwriting and backing others in the studio to launching a new publishing company and then selling it. When they learned of Josie's sale of 'Electron' to Lawrence Welk, they too, created and sold publishing companies, one after another. Some names that fans may recognize include their Longbow Music, DoBo [Don-Bob], Quadron, Red Box, Lenroy [Lenard-Leroy], and Paulcrest, named for the street where Don lived in the mid-sixties. Later, Bob owned Euphony Publishing. The latest, at the time of this writing, was called Ventures Two Thousand Music.

A "TWIST" OF FATE

To many, the next pair of albums became the most loved of over thirty Ventures LPs from the sixties. By 1962, the twist had grown from a teen fad to a craze that captivated dancers of all ages. Nearly two years after its inception, the time was ripe for a Ventures twist album. Single releases were suspended as Reisdorff and Josie produced albums as fast as possible. This increased an already hectic pace for the guys, under pressure to write songs while playing concerts for publicity. Writing was difficult, but they adapted a clever approach to obtain new material. The idea may have come from Johnny and the Hurricanes, who turned *Red River Valley* and *Blue Tail Fly* into delightful rock instrumentals. Reworking traditional and public domain songs allowed musicians to receive royalty credits on the arrangements. The Ventures adaptations were *My Bonnie Lies*, *Swanee River Twist*, *Dark Eyes Twist*, and *Red Wing Twist* as well as fresh arrangements of *Blue Tail Fly* and *Bumble Bee Rock*. An improved version of *The Twomp* included sparkling new guitar work from Nokie.

It took time and careful selection to come up with enough tracks for the first *Twist* album, and as fall gave way to winter, friends were called upon for help. Additional complications arose when Howie was unable to attend recording sessions in August and September, forcing Josie and Bob Reisdorff to fill the void with studio drummers.

Twist With The Ventures [Dolton BST-8010] all but stunned the group's fans. A Ventures album that didn't slow down from beginning to end was just too good to be true. It quickly outsold all their preceding albums except *Walk Don't Run*, ultimately reaching 24 on the Billboard LP chart. Although every track was a winner, there was a crowning jewel at the very beginning of this exciting collection. Amongst the covered hits, rearranged classics, and half-dozen originals, Bob, Don, and Nokie had authored *Driving Guitars,* a tune that remained a favorite of fans for decades. This perfect instrumental rocker, with its equally perfect name, especially delighted students of the guitar, being almost, but not quite within their reach to play it.

Even in 1962, listeners (unless they had attended a live performance) had no idea that Nokie played the lead on any of Ventures records. Cover art for *Twist With The Ventures* as well as its sequel appeared without group-photography or any informative text. If the actual proceedings that occurred during the making of these early albums had graced the liner notes, they would have indeed made interesting reading.

SESSION MUSICIANS

Nothing has fascinated avid Ventures fans more than the quest to learn "who played on what." Hired session musicians were common, but frequently in the early sixties, many were engaged to record as a group under an assumed name. Much has been written about them, but specific session details are sparse. A most notorious group was the Mar-Kets (later the Marketts after a dispute with the Mar-Keys). Producer Joe Saraceno became infamous for assembling L.A. session musicians to produce a string of instrumentals like *Surfer's Stomp* in 1962 and huge the number 3 hit *Out of Limits* in 1964. The same musicians, more or less, recorded as The Routers for *Let's Go,* and The T-Bones on *No Matter What Shape (You're Stomach's In),* all produced by Saraceno.

Existing in Hollywood was a pool of some 300 freelance studio musicians from which a "clique" emerged of roughly sixty top players. One was drummer Hal Blaine who, in adapting the context of Detroit's Motown session group, the Funk Brothers, dubbed Hollywood's group "The Wrecking Crew." One "crew" member was drummer Sandy Nelson, who brought drums to the fore on pop recordings in 1959. Sandy was a top hit celebrity with *Teen Beat* [Original Sound 5], but he was not above "sitting in" on tour with The Ventures for nearly six months in 1962. Later, he shuddered at the thought of that winter grind; "I'd hit with *Teen Beat* by then, but I hadn't made a lot of money from it. All I got was a songwriter's contract. I did a lot of thinking on those long treks between towns with The Ventures. I'd never seen so much snow. I hated the road and I decided to work on another hit and make sure I would get paid for it. The Ventures brought along a sax player on that tour, and what a character he was! His name was Paul Vincent, and when he wasn't asleep or playing his sax, he took our minds off the cold with his crazy antics. With Butch the roadie, we were three in the front and three in the back, but it was still freezing in that station wagon. The heater in those cars had just one vent *away* up under the dashboard. As soon as we got back to Los Angeles, I did *Let There Be Drums* and it made the Top Ten."

Don also recalls the sax man's antics; "Paul Vincent was a good player, but he was really goofy. He was always telling us how he wanted to be black. He was only with us for about two weeks, but that was plenty. One night, he locked Sandy out of the room. Sandy pounded on the door, but Paul wouldn't let him in. Sandy finally came and stayed in my room for the night. I think Vincent had a girl in the room, and he didn't want us to know about it. We were glad to be rid of him after that tour."

Sandy had more hits and played on several albums, but for years, record marketing managers ensured that only the main performers were mentioned in the liner notes. Many top studio musicians went unknown until 1973 when engineer-turned-producer,

Dayton "Bones" Howe instigated the Musician's Union to insist that session players be included in album documentation. The record companies may have seen this coming, as Ventures album jackets began showing this information over a year before the law was passed. Soon, as listeners scrutinized album covers and read periodicals like *Guitar Player* and *Modern Drummer*, names surfaced like Tommy Tedesco, Hal Blaine, Don Randi, and Earl Palmer. One of these musicians was Carol Kaye, a guitarist and top bassist on thousands of recordings including movie and television soundtracks. In answer to a query regarding The Ventures, Carol volunteered; "A lot of pop artists never ever played on their records. Sometimes we cut a hit album in six hours, and then the record company would hire some cute guys to do a promotional tour as the band. The labels were careful not to mention that studio players were involved. I did meet The Ventures, but they played so well that any added studio musicians were simply used to enhance their recordings."

In his book, *Hal Blaine And The Wrecking Crew*, much is revealed about the use of studio musicians, but details for the sixties sessions has depended mostly on the faded memories of those involved. With The Ventures, the problem becomes greater, given their longevity and abundance of recorded material. For the *Let's Go!* album, Hal Blaine recalled working with session drummer Frank Capp on The Ventures' first *Wipe Out* session. For many ardent fans, this was a welcome revelation, they having always been suspicious of the drumming on that track. The versions on live albums and at concerts were considered far superior to the one heard on their *Let's Go!* LP [Dolton BST-8024].

Hal Blaine

The above studio photo of Hal Blaine with tambourine beside Mel at the drums is included in Hal's book. Hal informed us that it was shot during a Ventures session.

According to session sheets obtained by *Pipeline Instrumental Review* editor, Dave Burke, *More* and *Wipe Out* were recorded with Tommy Tedesco and Billy Strange on guitar, David Gates on bass, Leon Russell and Bud Coleman on keyboards, along with drummers Blaine and Capp. Such substitution had been done a year earlier in 1962 when The Ventures were short handed due to Bob Reisdorff's rush to finish the next album. Reisdorff remembered the group being upset with cuts on their albums in which they had no part, and with Al Bennett telling the guys that music is business, and if they were to succeed, business had to be taken care of. Fortunately, Reisdorff never found it necessary to use such tactics again, at least to the degree on *Let's Go!* Session sidemen were still recruited, but only to work alongside The Ventures.

As years passed and consumer knowledge increased, rumors and speculation spread through fan clubs wanting to know more about who actually played on what. By this time, The Ventures had recorded so many albums that it was impossible for them to remember. Bob Bogle sums it up fairly well; "The Union rules allowed no more than four songs to be cut at a session. It was likely a good rule because we were so gung-ho that we would have cut a whole album in a day. Our playing quality could have slowly declined and we may not have noticed until playing it back much later. It's really a factory when we get in the studio. Sometimes, by the end of a session, we couldn't remember what we recorded earlier that day."

One compelling mystery involves the two Marksmen tunes composed by Gene Moles and Nokie on the album, *Twist With The Ventures*. Gene recalled playing both tunes for the album, whereas Bob and Don don't remember Gene playing on any of their sessions. The editors of *Pipeline Instrumental Review* have now determined that the Marksmen sessions took place in the same time frame as The Ventures' twist sessions, which may be a clue or else add to the confusion. Other issues regarding this album include works credited to Tommy Allsup and Jerry Allison, who became session sidemen after working with Buddy Holly. Tommy often told of how he and drummer Allison came to Reisdorff's aid on several tracks of *The Ventures' Twist* album when the group had lost its drummer and lead guitarist. Plus, he remembered working with Mr. Bob Bogle. Allison does not remember this, and with good reason. Dave Burke, co-editor of *Pipeline Instrumental Review*, has generously shared session records procured from Capitol/EMI while compiling the Ace Records CD series, *Ventures In The Vaults*. The data includes a 1961 sheet dated September 6, revealing that Bob, Don, and Nokie recorded *Road Runner*, *Movin' & Groovin'*, *Shanghied*, and *Lady of Spain* with drummer Milton "Muddy" Berry. A month later, Howie is shown on drums for *Moon Dawg*, *Driving Guitars*, and *Bumble Bee*. *Blue Tail Fly* was also recorded on this session, and shelved until the second volume of twist tunes was compiled. Allsup and Allison are not named.

In the spring of 2001, Gene Moles recalled his part on the album; "Shortly after Nokie moved down to Ventura, me and my wife, Joy, and our two boys moved there and stayed with Nokie and Jean for a couple of weeks. One day, Josie called while Nokie and Jean were out Christmas shopping. Josie said, 'Gene, we've got to get going on this *Twist* album and we're short on tracks! Do you know if Nokie has any songs in mind?' I said, 'I would think he has one or two.' Then Josie says, 'what about you? Do you have any?' I said, 'Yeah, I've probably got a couple you could use. The next thing I know, Bob Reisdorff has us scheduled for a session upstairs in the Liberty building. I remember Tommy Allsup playing *Guitar Twist* and Muddy Berry on drums. Between us, we cut four or five tracks. I went into the control room and had a listen to the others that The Ventures already had on tape. Bob Reisdorff said, 'What do you think, Gene?' I said, 'Man, you're the one that knows this stuff.' and Bob said, 'I don't want to hear that! I want to know what *you* think!' I always admired his attitude because he never came off as being a know-it-all."

Of course, the tunes brought to this session by Gene were *Sunny River* and *Gringo*, while Tommy Allsup contributed his *Opus Twist* and *Guitar Twist*. The *Pipeline* editors reckoned that *Opus 1* and *Opus 2* from an August session were *Opus Twist* and *Guitar*

Twist played by Bob, Don, Nokie, and session drummer Edward "Sharkey" Hall, but the timing and account by Gene Moles suggests that the word "opus" was being used literally to describe other works yet to be named. Either way, Gene's memory does not put Jerry Allison in the studio, nor do any of the available session sheets.

Tommy Allsup and Dick Glasser shared writing credits for *Guitar Twist*, as they had done on *Bluer Than Blue*, which Allsup remembers playing for The Ventures' *Colorful* album. Thus, with Reisdorff and Josie contracting filler songs while The Ventures were out on tour, it is small wonder that many such events are impossible for Don, Bob, or Nokie recall. Details can become hazy after such a long time, but talking with Bob Reisdorff sheds some light on what transpired; "Sure, I used session musicians. Sometimes The Ventures would be touring and I needed a song or two to complete an album. Rather than wait for their return, I could get guys like Muddy Berry, Glen Campbell, or Billy Strange to do the work. That's the music business as it was, and no one knew the difference. Recorded music is a product, and to ensure success, the product has to be delivered. Session musicians are an important part of studio work, and the fact is no longer a secret. Lists of participants can now fill an entire page of a CD booklet, but nobody cares as long as they enjoy the music. I did try, however, to include at least two of the guys on every track." Of course, Reisdorff had no way of knowing that The Ventures would last for five decades, and that "the difference" would be detected by multitudes of obsessed fans.

Young guitarists thrilled to every tune on *Twist With The Ventures*, but *Driving Guitars* remained the ultimate anthem to many for a lifetime. It was harder to play than *Walk-Don't Run*, but with dedicated practice, a decent showing was possible. One can only speculate how this tune would have fared as a Dolton single, but it's very likely that it would have been a chart topper. Unfortunately, The Ventures had manpower problems at the time, and American singles from their twist sessions are non-existent. The album, however, was like a Christmas gift to the fans, who pushed it up to 24 in Billboard by the middle of 1962.

1962 concert posters for California

Although liner notes were sparse, a tiny logo and a message on the back *Twist With The Ventures* informed buyers of the band's International Fan Club at the address of Liberty Records. How did that famous logo originate? Josie has the answer; "I had been on a trip to Tacoma when Bob [Reisdorff] moved my office from La Brea Avenue to the Liberty building on Sunset. When I returned, all was ready, although I was disappointed to find that all of my recordings were gone! I even lost my few first pressings of *Walk-Don't Run*. After I settled in, Scott Douglas [a.k.a. Douglas Longley] began coming up for occasional visits. During one of these, he was doodling on a piece of paper and came up with The Ventures logo in the staggered lettering that they have used ever since. You might say it is their trademark. A few logos having different styles were tried through the years, but the guys have always reverted to that first one."

The font that Scott used for his logo was almost certainly lifted from *DIG*, a popular teen magazine that carried ads for the latest Liberty releases as well as an occasional article on The Ventures. As shown here, the style of the monthly's header in its letters-to-the-editor section would appear very familiar to any ardent Ventures fan.

Font comparison - Several copies of DIG inhabited the offices at Liberty Records

Scott made more attempts at a hit record, his next being a novel dig at the hairstyles of a new combo from the UK. Produced by GRAMMY® winning songwriter David Hess [*I Got Stung* Elvis Presley, *Speedy Gonzalez* Pat Boone], Scott sang *The Beatles' Barber* b/w *The Wall Paper Song* [Apogee 105] in 1964. The following year, Scott made his last recording, this time with Ernie Freeman arranging and conducting his orchestra. Appearing on Tollie [T-9048], *Miss You* b/w *Hold My Hand* was widely distributed, but never made the charts. Scott Douglas may not have shaken the world with his voice, but his doodling became imprinted in the minds of millions in nearly every country in the world. Through the years, new logos with arrowed letters and later, stylish, rounded lettering were tried, but ultimately, Scott's Ventures logo is the one that prevails.

This alternate logo was introduced on the 1966 Dolton album, *Go With The Ventures*

MEL TAYLOR

On September 24, 1933, Melvyn Taylor was born in Brooklyn New York to Grace and Lawrence Taylor. Mel's mother was of Euro-Russian Jewish descent while his father claimed German, Dutch, and Cherokee roots. From age five, Mel grew up in his father's birthplace, Johnson City Tennessee. There, Mel was close to musical uncles and a grandfather, all of which played banjo, guitar, or both. In June, 1942, brother Samuel Lawrence Taylor was born, by which time Mel was nine and joining family jam sessions by chording on a guitar.

In high school, Mel played band drums until age seventeen, when he joined the Navy. There, he honed percussive skills in a drum and bugle corps known as the Fabian Melodeers. When the Navy stint was over, Mel found various jobs around Tennessee, pumping gas, driving truck, and briefly, selling life insurance. Forming a five-piece country band, Mel strummed his guitar and sang backup alongside banjo, violin, steel guitar, and upright bass players. After some radio exposure on Johnson City's WJHL, Mel Taylor And The Twilight Ramblers found plenty of work in the station's local area.

Now in his teens Brother Larry returned from a trip to California with an electric guitar. He impressed Mel with one song he had learned to play, *The Poor People of Paris* (Billboard's top instrumental for 1956). Knowing the basic guitar chords, Mel taught him to play rhythm in three or four keys before Larry went back to California.

A musician that played with Mel was steel-guitarist Roger Kelly. With a keen memory and a rare photo, Roger provides interesting details; "Mel and I played country music together in several bands from 1955 to 1957, doing early morning radio shows on WJHL, WBEJ, WEMB, and a daily two-hour afternoon show on WCYB radio out of Bristol, Virginia. That one was called *Farm and Fun Time*, and it covered five states. The most memorable group we played with was 'Red' Malone and The Smoky Mountaineers. Mel played rhythm guitar and helped with the vocals on duets and trios. He also picked a little Merle Travis style on hymns, and he was very good at it, too. We also did some television work, appearing twice a week for half-hour shows on WCYB. Back then, everything on TV was broadcast live. During the week, we played up to four shows a day on radio plus square dances on Friday and Saturday nights.

"While Mel and I were with the Smoky Mountaineers, we played package shows with Jimmy Dickens, Mother Maybelle and the Carter Family, Charlie Monroe, The Stanley Brothers, Doc Watson, Jimmy Martin and the Southern Mountain Boys, to name a few. In 1956, rock 'n' roll was becoming popular, and we talked about adding a drummer. Mel had drummed in his teens and said he would give it a try. He was good, and we became one of the first country bands with a drummer. We kept trying to make it playing music here in East Tennessee, riding and sleeping six-to-a-car to save on expenses. We played in little mountain school houses and anywhere else we could make a few bucks, but by summer of 1957, bookings were much harder to get, and the Smoky Mountaineers disbanded."

Although Mel lived in Johnson City, Tennessee, he preferred the popular Bristol Virginia radio station. One day, he drove to Bristol hoping to see some of the newer groups in action. He wandered into the studio and sat down at a small drum set while a bluegrass group called the Clinch Mountain Boys rehearsed during a station break. Without thinking, Mel picked up the brushes and quietly played along to the music. Waiting in the wings were Joe Franklin And His Mimosa Boys. Liking what they heard, they invited Mel to play on their broadcast. Over the years, Mel repeatedly wondered if he might have been the very first drummer to play in a bluegrass band.

Red Malone and the Smoky Mountaineers

Doug Morris, bass, Mel Taylor, rhythm guitar (and later, drums), "Red" Malone, singer, guitar, Jackie Miller, lead guitar, John Holt, manager. Seated - Roger Kelly, steel guitar.

Subsequently, Joe Franklin hired Mel for a road trip. At that point, he moved to Virginia, where, after a few months, the group was booked on the *Ed Sullivan Show*. Mel informed his family, and on the designated Sunday evening, relatives from Tennessee to California watched their TV sets. Panning between the fiddling acrobatics of Jimmy Buchanan, Joe Franklin's banjo, and the other exciting string men, the camera never focused on the drummer. All viewers saw of Mel was his arm. If Mel thought that his proverbial "ten minutes of fame" had evaporated, he need not have worried. He would just have to wait a while longer.

Mel drummed for more groups like Franklin's, notably that of Gordon Terry, one of the period's finest fiddlers in bluegrass. Mel, however, was now twenty-three with a young family and the need to earn more money. In 1958, attracted by a bustling music industry, Mel and wife Thelma, along with daughters Rita and Sylvia, sons Leon (who was nearly three) and newly born Michael, moved to Los Angeles.

Among the skills Mel had acquired in Tennessee was that of a meat cutter, which landed him a job in L.A. By chance, he met a successful songwriter that invited him to an audition where the needed of a drummer. Being immediately hired, Mel borrowed from his mother to buy a set of blue Ludwig drums. Working three nights a week led to a job country star Little Jimmy Dickens, Mel was hired for session work with other recording stars, including a young Buck Owens.

Mel's next steady job in music was house drummer at L.A.'s Lariat Club. In late 1959, he auditioned with Gene Davis for the same position at North Hollywood's prestigious Palomino Club. Easily qualifying, Mel was able to quit his meat-cutting job. Fairly soon, the Palomino Riders were hired to back Johnny Cash and Patsy Cline at the first country music show presented at the Hollywood Bowl. Now consisting of Gene Davis (guitar-vocals), Ernie Ball (pedal steel), Delaney Bramlett (bass-vocals), Glen D. Hardin (piano), and Mel on drums, the group backed other rising acts like Mac Davis and Roger Miller. After Ernie Ball moved on, the band welcomed a new steel guitarist from Illinois on New Year's Eve of 1960. Orville J. Rhodes, quickly nicknamed "Red," was one of Hollywood's most popular studio musicians. Later that year, Mel teamed with some of the Palomino Riders to record a single as Mel Taylor and the Darts. *That's It*, written by Mel, Gene Davis, and Red Rhodes was backed with a Glen Garrison tune called *Drum Fever* [Toppa 1054]. In the vein of Sandy Nelson's *Teen Beat*, Mel's drums were intensely featured on both sides of the record.

Mel's flamboyant style garnered more studio work, drumming with pop groups assembled and produced by Gary Paxton and partner Clyde Battin. Among those recordings was *Cherry Pie* [Brent 7010] as Skip 'n Flip. In 1962, Paxton produced Bobby "Boris" Pickett and the Crypt-Kickers doing the novelty hit *Monster Mash* [Garpax 44167], with Mel on drums, and Leon Russell at the organ.

To avoid contract disputes with the Brent label, Paxton released several singles as The Hollywood Argyles. Although some biographies have stated that Mel played on that group's *Alley Oop* [Lute 5905], Sandy Nelson especially recalls doing that session and contributing to the vocal content with a few screams. The instrumental work consisted mainly of tambourine, piano, and bass, although a guitar in the background was credited to a young session man named Jerry McGee.

Original Sound Records was owned by a Los Angeles DJ name Art Laboe. Art was the first to compile "oldies" albums, using artist cuts from various labels. Laboe coined the title *Oldies But Goodies* in 1959 for an Original Sound album [LPM-5001] that remained on Billboard's Top 100 chart for over *three years*, encouraging another fourteen volumes. Following his lucrative production of Sandy Nelson's 1959 smash hit *Teen Beat* [OS-5], Laboe also began producing guitar instrumentals by session men billed as The Teen Beats. A 1961 Teen Beats session found Mel recording his own composition of *Night Surfing* [OS-16] with brother Larry on bass. Larry (and possibly Mel) backed similar music on another label called Last Chance. With only the opening sound effect changed from ocean waves to a bubbling sound, the recording of *Night Surfing* was re-released as *Atlantis* by the Blue Bells [Last Chance 1].

More fine Teen Beats singles followed, including *Big Bad Boss Beat* b/w *Down Below* [OS-46], and *Swimmin' Part One* b/w *Swimmin' Part Two* [OS-49]. An interesting feature of Original Sound labels was the printed strobe pattern, allowing the user to precisely check turntable speed at 45 rpm.

Collaboration with other sidemen led to another Mel Taylor single. At Rendezvous Records, he met and became a lifelong friend of guitarist Jan Davis, who first recorded as Jan Davis And The Ricco Shays. As Jan recalls; "In '61 and '62, Rendezvous was recording a lot of singles by B. Bumble and The Stingers with Mel and I on several of them. When some of us started recording individually, Mel decided to do the same. I produced two Mel Taylor instrumentals with his drums in front titled *Big Bad Pogo* and *Drumstick* [Rendezvous R-187]. On the record, you will see writing credit for Taylor, Roberts, and Bird. At the time, 'the Bird' was my nickname. I'm playing bass, Bob Roberts is on the organ, and of course, Mel is on drums. My friend Bob Roberts was co-writer on many Rendezvous jobs, including much of the B. Bumble catalog with Ernie Freeman on organ, John 'Plas' Johnson on tenor sax, and Red Callender on bass. Earl Palmer played drums and Rene Hall, who was my mentor and like a second father to me, played guitar. They were the main guys in The Stingers at the time, but Mel and I were on a few tracks as well."

Some of the work that came Mel's way became controversial in later years, including a 1962 job for Herb Alpert's recording of *The Lonely Bull* on which Mel recalled working on "the single version." In a discussion for this book, drummer Hal Blaine mused; "It's entirely possible, but I was with the Tijuana Brass from day one, and generally, the single cut was the same one as on an album. I often get stories like this. There are at least four drummers that claim they did *These Boots Are Made For Walkin'* with Nancy Sinatra. I have pictures of Warner Brothers handing me my Gold Record for *Boots* and I have a tape of Nancy announcing on the *Ed Sullivan Show* how instrumental I was in the making of that record. Same thing happens with other drummers; everyone in the business knows that Jimmy Gordon played with Mason Williams for *Classical Gas*, and yet there are three or four drummers that say they were on that. It's ridiculous!"

More recent research reveals that once *The Lonely Bull* became a hit, Albert and his A&M people simulated a stereo version for the album by placing the mono mix in one channel while adding a trumpet track to the other. Critics deemed the result rather odd, the second track exhibiting dead silence during the intro and also during the two guitar parts. Today, computer waveform analysis confirms that the same drumming track, played by whomever, appears on both versions.

TWISTING TO A DIFFERENT DRUMMER

Twist With The Ventures outsold every previous Ventures album but *Walk Don't Run*. Immediately, Bob Reisdorff and Josie hurried to cash in on the craze before it faded. With *Blue Tail Fly* already on tape from the 1961 sessions, the "twist beat" was applied to more old songs like *Red Wing*, *Dark Eyes*, and even *My Bonny Lies (Over the Ocean)*. Perhaps the most ingenious twist adaptation came from *Bésame Mucho*, a hit for crooner Andy Russell and a Number 1 for the Jimmy Dorsey Orchestra in 1944. Nokie created a fine twister called *Instant Guitars* by rearranging a 1953 Chet Atkins single called *City Slicker* [RCA 47-5484].

While enjoying the freedom to improvise on the bass, Bob had not given up the guitar. With royalties in mind, he came up with a tune of his own which he called *Counterpoint*. Some tracks contained extra guitar tracks, tambourine, and handclaps that made some young listeners wonder just how many Ventures there were. Overdubbing was the answer, as session sheets for this album show no extra musicians. The sheet for February 5, however, lists one recording that did not make the album. The aging folk tune, (*Listen to the*) *Mockingbird* remained "in the can" for almost three years before its release as *Candy Apple Racer* on a Japanese single [LR-1199]. The song was also available in America, but only to alert fans such as John Magee of Indianapolis; "I remember buying a 'various artists' album, *Shut Downs and Hill Climbs* [Liberty LST-7366] around 1965, just to get The Ventures' cut of *Candy Apple Racer*."

~ ~ ~

Early in 1962, while discussing a drummer replacement for Howie, Don and Bob remembered when Mel Taylor had offered to sit in. A call was made and the next day, Mel came into the studio to work with Don, Bob, and Nokie. Bob Reisdorff and Josie were surprised and relieved at seeing this brand-new drummer who was ready, willing, and *very* able.

Years later, when the fact was disclosed that two different drummers appeared on *Twist Party Vol.2* [Dolton 8014], many fans tried to determine which drummer played on each track. Some judged the sound while others, usually drummers, listened to the beat count. This method indicated Howie playing on tracks two, three, five, nine, eleven, and twelve, while Mel did the other six. Mel apparently placed heavily accented quarter notes on beats two and four of each bar, while Howie played double eighth notes on the second beat of each bar and accented the fourth. Skip Moore played this way on *Walk-Don't Run*, and Howie duplicated the style on songs like *No Trespassing* and *Bulldog*. This method of distinguishing the drummers works fine, as long as one does not carry it too far into later recordings. Otherwise, one may come to the absurd conclusion that Howie returned for *Walk-Don't Run '64* and *Journey to the Stars*, to name just two. Moreover, while the session sheets acquired by Dave Burke conform to most of this theory, Mel is clearly shown working on *Red Wing,* which became track twelve. *Bogie's tune*, assumed to be Bob's *Counterpoint*, was recorded with Howie in October and then with Mel in the following February. If the listening method is reliable, then the take with Howie ended up on the album as track nine. Furthermore, if *Original 4* and *Original 5* from the same session are deemed to be *Kicking Around* and *Bluebird*, then Mel is also the drummer for track ten and eleven (Ventures fans have *so* much fun!).

When the recordings were done, The Ventures asked Mel if he would join the group. Mel said that he had a thing going at the Palomino Club and did not want to take any chances, but that he was available for more recording sessions if needed.

Around this time, Mel and Don dropped into a Hollywood nightclub to hear Mel's twenty-year-old brother on the Fender bass. Larry Taylor had already distinguished his short career, having toured with Jerry Lee Lewis almost two years earlier. During a break, Larry introduced drummer Bill Lewis and guitarist "Jerry" McGee to the visitors. At the time, none of this trio known as The Cajuns imagined that each would spend some part of their careers working with The Ventures.

During one of the last *Twist* sessions, sad news from Seattle reached Josie and The Ventures. Joe Boles, their first recording engineer and hospitable friend, had suffered a fatal heart attack on February 16, 1962. Virginia Boles remained in Seattle, living in the same house that had contained the studio. In the year 2000, she would donate several photos and other memorabilia, including the studio log book, to Seattle's Experience Music Project, a monumental museum illustrating the area's contribution to rock music. Weakened by a stroke, she died on January 13, 2007 at the age of ninety-five.

CONQUERING THE ORIENT

In the spring of '62, Don's dream of seeing the orient became a reality. He had always wanted to visit Japan, and now there was a tour of U.S. military bases being organized for the month of May. Album sessions had begun with Nokie and Mel, but as Bob recalls, The Ventures were still a twosome; "We hadn't signed Mel as our drummer yet, as he still worked nights at the Palomino. Nokie was also doing his own thing, and it was all we could do to get him to a session. We just continued, filling the void with pick-up musicians." To this, Don added; "We would have taken the whole group on that tour, but it was being paid for by the General Artists Corporation and they could only afford to send the two of us. Some people think Liberty Records had something to do with that, but it was the G.A.C. Around then I turned in my Stratocaster for a new Jazzmaster. We really liked the look of those matching instruments."

Publicity photo for two-man Ventures tour

The first stop was for ten days in the Philippines to play in Manila's Araneta Coliseum and two American Air Force bases. Although the country seemed generally poor, the Araneta was the world's largest domed stadium. As Bob recalls; "The facilities for musicians at that stadium were like a high-class hotel. And we had continuous crowds there of around 15,000 people."

At the Coliseum, The Ventures borrowed bassist Alan Austria and drummer Bernie Evangelista from a local combo, RJ and The Riots led by seventeen-year-old guitarist, Ramon Jacinto. Ramon's father was Don Fernando Jacinto, founding father of the Philippines' steel industry.

As Bob recalls, it was a surprise when Ramon invited them to lunch, but the sight of the family's estate, was a real eye-opener; "The place was surrounded by a high fence with barbed wire on top, and the gate was manned by armed guards. Inside, it was a mansion, complete with swimming pool and *two* Rolls Royce sedans. Ramon had his own radio station right there on the property.

"We heard how the Jacintos had vacationed in Boston a year earlier, and how Ramon had begged his mother to buy a red Gretsch guitar. When he couldn't get a "Ventures sound" from it, he coaxed his mother into ordering a complete set of Fender guitars for his band, the same as on the cover of our second album."

The young Filipino, known as "RJ," became a good friend and a huge fan of The Ventures, citing them as the instigators of a massive guitar boom in the Philippines. More than once, The Ventures would meet RJ again.

Don, Bob, and Bobby Vee with "RJ And The Riots "   *"Rollie" Grande*

Next was a stint in Hong Kong for two "packed to the walls" evening shows. The show opened with an Armed Forces doo-wop sextet called the Fabulous Echoes, followed by Kon Ling, a pretty Chinese singer who had a hit record after being discovered in America by radio host, Arthur Godfrey. The Ventures were next, aided by the army's bassist and drummer, followed by Jo Ann Campbell and Bobby Vee. The first night's show was recorded for broadcast on Armed Forces Radio. Following the second night's performance, The Ventures were guests of honor at a party hosted by The Ventures Fan Club of Hong Kong.

The next stop was the town of Tachikawa in Japan. Sitting in the audience for the first show was fifteen-year-old Robert Eugene Spalding, whose memories of that day are still vivid; "My dad was assigned to USAF HQ at Fuchu Air Station. The closest air base was Tachikawa AFB, and the show was in one of the U.S. housing communities. Besides Jo Ann Campbell, The Ventures, and Bobby Vee, there was an orchestra with a horn section, piano, drums, and a standup bass. Jo Ann Campbell opened with a couple of her songs, but walked off the stage in her third number when the band didn't know the song. She still got a nice applause. Next were Don and Bob, whose amps were set up on chairs. They came out with their guitars, plugged in, and played *Walk-Don't Run*. Luckily, the standup bass and drummer were not 'miked' as they tried to keep up, but even with that distraction, the crowd's response was great. Don excused the lack of coordination by saying, '...sorry for the sound, but we can't hear them and they can't hear us.' Next, they played *Yellow Bird* and *Runaway*, finishing up with *The McCoy*. The crowd called them back and they played *Perfidia*. Bobby Vee then sang about five songs with great response as well. We followed them to the Officer's Club where they had dinner and we had two of our albums autographed. I remember thinking, 'that's really what I want to do, play in a band like The Ventures'."

While fully enthralled with the music, young Robert never imagined that twenty years later he would be joining The Ventures' on stage, or that in forty-four years, he would begin tenure as a full-time "Venture," there on a stage in Tachikawa.

In late May, the tour opened in Tokyo. Shows for the two days were sold out at the Shinjuku Koma Theater, which seated 2,000 people. Posters publicized Bobby Vee, with no mention of Jo Ann Campbell or The Ventures. By then, Don and Bob had noticed that the electric guitar was not popular in Japan, and the Fender bass was completely unknown. Also, as Don remembers; 'When we arrived at the theater, we recruited the bass player and drummer from a local Hawaiian-style band, but we soon asked them not to play, as they were completely unfamiliar with the rock 'n' roll beat."

The media had not given much attention to the tour, but entertainment agent, Tatsuji "Tats" Nagashima, had arranged for a TV appearance. Long-time Ventures fan, Mahiro Tada, remembers the event well; "At that time, not many in Japan knew of The Ventures. Some friends and I knew of the group through American Forces Radio. On Japanese TV, they did dance steps to their recorded hits without really playing. They did *Walk-Don't Run* swinging their Jazzmasters with much body movement. When playing E on the A-G-F-E intro, they simultaneously stepped forward and bent their knees."

The clean-cut Ventures were mildly accepted, although many adults still believed the rocking electric sound to be nothing less than evil. The guitar was traditionally used for classical and Spanish music in Japan, although country and western hits were gaining popularity due to imported American TV shows.

Rock 'n' roll had penetrated Japan as early as 1958, with imported records by the likes of Jerry Lee Lewis and Little Richard, plus visits from American stars like Gene Vincent and Neil Sedaka. Then, the guitar suffered a setback when reports of wild behavior at a huge Tokyo rockabilly festival hit Japan's news media. Parents and teachers labeled the "eleki guitar" as a device associated with delinquents and school dropouts. So great was their fear, that the instrument was banned in some areas.

Don and Bob had sown a seed in Japan that was fertilized with the release of their music on Toshiba Records. Soon, guitar and amplifier factories blossomed, as did importers of such items. Japan's experience was a bit similar to that in America in the fifties. There was protest, but rock 'n' roll was here to stay.

The fads following the twist were a blessing for The Ventures and other groups. After Dee Dee Sharp's rendition of *Mashed Potato Time*, a plethora of new songs followed. New dances were given names like the wobble, the hully gully, and the Watusi. While working on songs for these dances, The Ventures recorded Don and Bob's composition entitled *Instant Mashed*. Josie remembers the policy adopted by the group around this time regarding the sharing of royalties; "In almost every song that one or more of the group wrote, they decided to share the royalty earnings. Thus followed hundreds of tunes credited to Bogle-Wilson-Edwards-Taylor, or whatever combination existed at any particular time."

While Don and Bob toured the Orient, Bob Reisdorff and Josie had decided to carry on without them. Nokie recalls being involved; "They wanted to release the *Mashed Potatoes* album around the time Bob and Don would be arriving home, so they got Mel and me along with Billy Strange and David Gates to finish it up. Bud Coleman was there too. There might have been a song or two in the can, but we recorded the rest. We needed a couple of originals, so Bud wrote one, and I wrote one that ended up being a surfing song. I think Darlene Love added some backing later."

Available session data reveal only one song "in the can," that being *Venus*, recorded seven months earlier at one of the last sessions with Howie Johnson on drums.

Guitarist Ervan "Bud" Coleman enjoyed writing cowboy songs, but likely profited most from his Tijuana Brass instrumentals, *Mexican Shuffle* and *Tijuana Taxi*. His contribution to The Ventures' *Mashed Potatoes and Gravy* album was *Hot Summer*, which then became *Asian Mashed*.

David Gates was on his way to stardom in the fifties when he backed Chuck Berry with high-school band in Tulsa, Oklahoma. Don Wilson's early memories of David include auditioning the young musician singing several songs on which he hoped for Ventures' backing. Looking back, he regretted having no time to promote young David, who, by the end of the sixties had become a successful record producer and founder of the group, Bread. Gates was proficient on many instruments, but in the last week of May, 1962, he played bass for The Ventures in the studio.

On the *Mashed Potatoes* project, editors for the UK's *Pipeline* magazine provided documentation from the four sessions. From Tuesday to Friday, twelve songs were recorded, from oldies like *Poison Ivy* and *Lucille* to four hits reflecting the current dance craze. Surprise arrangements were *Hernando's Hideaway*, a pre-rock 'n' roll hit from 1954, and George Gershwin's minor-keyed *Summertime*. Four remaining originals included The Marksmen's *Scratch* and Bud Coleman's *Hot Summer*. *Country Gravy*, an original recorded when Bob and Don were present, was scrapped in favor of *Instant Mashed*. Josie named Nokie's new song *Spudnik*, playing on the dance fad and Sputnik, the satellite launched by the Soviet Union in 1957. Josie also recalls naming the album; "It was originally designated *Mashed Potatoes* but I felt that the market would be flooded with recordings by that name. We had recorded a version of Dee Dee Sharp's *Gravy* for the album, so I just added some to the title."

As *Mashed Potatoes And Gravy* [Dolton BST-8016] broke into the Top 50, another California band called The Lively Ones asked permission to use part of *Spudnik* for an instrumental they were recording called *Surf Rider*. As Bob Bogle recalls; "We had no objection, having borrowed musical phrases from other groups ourselves. We were pretty surprised when *Surf Rider* [Del-Fi 4196] became a hit as a note-for-note cover of *Spudnik*. We had no problem with that, as long as they directed the royalties to Nokie."

In June, Bob and Don returned from their tour of the Orient. The next Ventures album release was scheduled for August, but with demand high for public appearances, they decided on two men in the studio and two on tour. This time, Bob and Mel stayed behind to work with Billy Strange and David Gates while Nokie went out with Don on a tour of the Pacific Northwest. As Don recalls; "We had a promo shot of Nokie and I made up by cropping one of our *Dick Clark Show* photos. Wherever we went, we got a bass player and drummer from a local band that opened for us."

With Billy Strange as second guitarist, Bob Bogle led the first recording session for *Going To The Ventures Dance Party* [Dolton 8017]. The first tune recorded was *Lolita Ya Ya* with Mel on drums, Hank Levine on harpsichord and David Gates on bass. As with the previous album, vocal "yeahs" and "wahs" by Darlene Love and the Blossoms were added later to many of the album's tracks. Next, as confirmed in BMI's session data recovered by the editors of *Pipeline Instrumental Review*, Mel, Bob, David Gates and Billy Strange composed *Ya Ya Wobble*.

Going To The Ventures Dance Party was just what the title suggested, catering to every new dance fad from the Locomotion to the Limbo. Among the album's few originals, Nokie's *Night Drive* became a favorite pick for dozens of emerging garage bands. Two more tracks on this album also stood the test of time with guitarists. One was *Mr. Moto*, initially recorded by the Belairs in 1961 [Arvee 5034]. The other was an unreleased Don Wilson original, formerly recorded as *Ventures Stomp*. Don renamed it *Gandy Dancer*, a term he learned while working on a railroad in his high-school days; "I was a bridge carpenter then, and the guys who drove spikes into the ties were called gandy dancers. They had to be in perfect time with each other to keep from getting hurt. 'Gandy' was a Chicago-based company that made our tools."

While reminiscing about writing sessions with The Ventures, Billy Strange recalled that whoever came up with an instrumental pattern would assume the lead guitar part for the new composition. If it sounded good and met the approval of Bob Reisdorff, it was arranged and recorded on the spot. In this way, Billy received credit for *The Intruder* and was also able to include his *Limbo Rock* on the album.

A surprising entry for this collection of dance tunes was the theme from the 1961 movie, *Come September* starring Bobby Darin and Sandra Dee. It was chosen mostly for title strength, as the movie was then a hit with the teen crowd.

Packaging for the album revealed once more that The Ventures was a two-man entity. However, most fans still envisioned the cover of album number two with Howie at the drums and Nokie on bass. The only evidence that Mel Taylor had anything to do with *Dance Party* was his sharing in the writing credits of *Ya Ya Wobble*. His distinctive voice appeared in the background on *Gravy*, *Mashed Potato Time*, and *The Wah-Watusi*, but the public had yet to be informed of Mel's presence.

As Nokie needed work and was ready to resume traveling, Mel signed for a short tour with the group. Upon returning home, Bob asked again if Mel would like to join The Ventures. This time Mel said 'yes.' When meeting Mel's family, Don and Bob understood Mel's hesitation, as sons Michael and Leon were both under age ten.

Although Howie had a sore neck during his early tours with The Ventures, his daughter, Sherri insists that the problem was gone by the time of his exit from the group; "Dad left the band primarily because of financial reasons. Perhaps if he had stayed, things would have got better, but he had six kids from his first marriage and another family started. To him, his future with The Ventures was too uncertain. His car accident happened over three years before he joined The Ventures, so that wasn't a factor. As soon as he quit the band, he resumed his favorite occupation next to music. He drove long haul logging trucks for the forest industry, and his neck was fine. For the rest of his life, he played drums with local groups for Saturday night dances."

Regarding royalty payments, Howie was seldom involved in songwriting. Of the five tunes he co-wrote, only *The Switch* and *No Trespassing* were released on vinyl. For nearly forty years, the arrangements of *Danny Boy*, *Greensleeves* and the rejected *Ventures Stomp* remained hidden in the vaults.

FLIGHT OF THE 2000-POUND BEE

The Ventures' next recording project was an experiment in "fuzztone," a new guitar sound heard widely in 1961 when Marty Robbins topped the country charts and made Number 3 on Billboard's pop chart with *Don't Worry*. The fuzzy sound was the result of an electronic fault which occurred during the recording of Grady Martin's guitar solo. Although Martin found it repulsive, producer Don Law liked it and kept it in the mix.

Although the history of fuzz goes back into the fifties, when Link Wray created the dirtiest sound possible by poking holes in the cone of his loudspeaker. Wray charted at 16 in 1958 with *Rumble* and 23 in 1959 with *Raw-Hide*. In 1960, the first actual fuzz-box was likely heard in *Go On Home* by Sanford Clark [Jamie 1153]. Al Casey played guitar on this one, crediting his deep fuzz-tone to a little box constructed by a radio station technician for producer Lee Hazelwood. Clark, however, had already enjoyed his one and only hit, *The Fool* [a Bob Bogle favorite] in late 1956 [Dot 16481].

In addition to playing pedal steel at the Palomino Club in Los Angeles, session man Orville "Red" Rhodes was also into electronics. Having assembled a small fuzz box with variable distortion and a bypass switch, Red showed it to Billy Strange, who used it on Ann Margret's *I Just Don't Understand* [RCA 47-7894]. This led to The Ventures trying the gadget in the fall of 1962. Paraphrasing the answer to a silly riddle then circulating; (Q: What does a 2000 pound canary sound like? A: CHIRP!!); Don said "Hey, this sounds like a 2000-pound bee!" With the title in hand, it did not take the band long to compose some music for the Red Rhodes fuzz box.

The 2000-Pound Bee encompassed two parts; each on a side of Dolton 67. Composer credits went to Mel for *Part One*, and Don for *Part Two*. While Nokie played some lead on both sides, Billy Strange added fuzz to side one on Thursday, October 4. On October 12, side two was recorded by just the four Ventures. By February, 1963, *Part Two* was at the peak (#91) of a four-week stretch in Billboard's *Top 100 singles sales chart*.

Near the end of October '62, Bob Reisdorff and Josie presented an ambitious project to The Ventures. The concept was an album of hits by other artists to be done with little deviation from the original arrangements. This meant that for some tracks, sidemen were needed for keyboards and brass. Although two late-fifties hits (*Tequila* and *Red River Rock*) were slated, they decided to name the LP *Hits Of The Sixties*. Most of the tunes would be rock, but Josie and Reisdorff added a few songs for "adult appeal" like Lawrence Welk's *Calcutta* and the movie theme from *Never On Sunday*. For this cut, they had Hank Levine play the melody on mandolin from beginning to end. *The Lonely Bull* having made the Top 10, Reisdorff wanted to include it if he could draft a trumpet player. Recalling his embarrassing quest, Bob relates; "I wanted a good bullfight-sounding trumpet and I immediately thought of Herb Alpert, whom I'd met on various sessions. When I approached him to do The Ventures session, he gave me quite a shock. He told me that the original record was his, and that Jerry Moss, [his partner in A&M Records] would not be happy with the idea. I was really embarrassed, as *The Lonely Bull* was huge, and somehow I had missed the fact that it was Herbie's. I apologized and found another trumpet man in a day or two."

According to session sheets retrieved by Dave Burke, Reisdorff recruited two trumpet men for the early November session. One was Al Porcino, a highly respected trumpeter who had played in many 'big bands' in the fifties. Frank Huggins, the other great horn man, had played with Woody Herman and Stan Kenton. Bob Reisdorff continues; "I just got that problem solved, when Don Wilson came to me with this song he was hearing on the radio by a group in England. He was sure it would be a monster hit and he wanted to do it right away for the album. Of course, it was *Telstar* by England's Tornados, on their way to becoming the first British group to hit Number 1 in the U.S.A. It was so good that we decided to use it for the album title. The Telstar satellite had been up for three months and was getting a lot of publicity at the time."

Interviews given years later reveal that Don Wilson was responsible for the opening rocket ship sounds on *Telstar*. Josie relates how the sound was created; "The blast-off sounds at the beginning *Telstar* were made by Don releasing foam from a fire extinguisher. After trying several solutions, one of the engineers laughingly said, 'Pull the fire extinguisher off the wall and try that.' Don did, and lo and behold, it worked!"

Leon Russell, on his way to becoming a renowned Liberty co-producer, arranger, and keyboard musician was responsible for the powerful Hammond organ on *Telstar, Last Night, Percolator,* and *Red River Rock*. The session for these tracks took place at the end of October with Bob Bogle on lead and David Gates on bass. Don's rhythm guitar was particularly important for *Red River Rock*, but it was mixed down to be nearly inaudible. Nothing was done about this until 1992 when the album was digitally remastered and remixed for a special CD in EMI's *Legends of Rock 'n' Roll* series. The original mixing might have been rushed in order to beat the Tornados' album to the record stores, or, as Josie recollects, she may have had a hand (as well as an ear) in the proceedings; "Bob Reisdorff was quite taken by my own ability to predict if a song would be a hit or not. He also said I a *good ear* for music. Little did he know how right he was! As I had learning a lot about studio production, Reisdorff elected to mix the mono records, generally leaving me with the engineers to mix the stereo records. This could take hours, especially on a long-play recording. Can you imagine his chagrin when he finally learned after several months that I really did have 'an ear' for music? Yes, one ear! Since birth I have been totally deaf in my left ear, and he had assigned me to the stereo recordings! To compensate, I stood back and turned my 'good' ear toward one speaker and then to the other. Since the recordings turned out so well, I assume that the engineers thought my constant turning was just an idiosyncrasy!"

The Ventures Play Telstar And The Lonely Bull [Dolton BST-8019] was group's all-time, highest selling album, earning their first RIAA Gold Album award for surpassing a half-million sales in the U.S.A. By the fall of 1965, U.S. sales had reached 600,000. Around the globe, the album sold five million copies. With the title strength of *Telstar* and middle-of-the-road tunes like *Calcutta, Mexico,* and *The Lonely Bull*, the album enticed buyers of all ages and both sexes. Even so, hard-core Ventures fans, most of whom were male and played guitar, were not overjoyed with this collection. To them, with no Ventures originals and so many added instruments, the album seemed like a sellout. As one upset fan club member wrote: "If I had wanted to hear trumpets playing 'Lonely Bull' I would have bought the Tijuana Brass album."

One young man who *was* thrilled with this album was the barely-known Herb Alpert. His single had done well, having peaked at number six, but when the royalties began rolling in from The Ventures' LP recording, Alpert took the trouble to locate the boys and thank them profusely for covering his song.

Of course, the album also generated many new Ventures fans with its marvelous interpretations of The Mar-Keys' *Last Night,* Mel Taylor's tribute to Sandy Nelson, *Let There Be Drums,* and a mighty guitar-driven version of Booker T And The MGs' *Green Onions*. Dozens have testified in writing that *Telstar And The Lonely Bull* was their first in a large collection of Ventures albums. It is little wonder that *Telstar, Tequila,* and *Apache* became imbedded forever in the band's stage repertoire.

Telstar and The Lonely Bull also made a very big splash in Japan. Following its 1963 release on a ten-inch disc, the LP reappeared on regular twelve-inch vinyl in 1965, 1974, 1978, and, most surprisingly, a collector's edition in 1992, three years after its release there on Compact Disc.

The absence any photos on the album left fans with nothing but confusing liner notes. Credit went to Nokie and Bob for lead and bass, and to Don for lead and rhythm. Credit for Mel was the first indication that Howie Johnson was no longer with The Ventures. Finally, members of the fan club were informed by a bulletin in March, 1963. Two months later they received this eight-by-ten glossy found later on countless compilation recordings.

The first photo of The Ventures with drummer Mel Taylor

The Ventures' gold album brought more tours, but they were now different. No longer was the band an opening act, and in some cities, radio stations sponsored an opening band for them. Generally, tours went smoothly, but conditions sometimes made the guys wonder if they were in their right minds, pulling a trailer in wintery weather instead of basking in the California sun. The contrasting climate combined with insufficient sleep in rooms with no humidity, often caused colds and sore throats. As Bob recalls; "We had this agency called ZEE, who seemed to be arranging our tours by throwing darts at a map so that we zigzagged all over the country. They were also insensitive about climate changes. They booked us in the ovens of Arizona and Texas in the summer, and when winter came, we'd be touring around Minnesota and Wisconsin, freezing our tails off."

Traveling in winter was not only cold, but sometimes perilous. One of Don's worst memories is of a moose suddenly appearing on a narrow road while he was driving at night; "There wasn't enough time to stop, and no way to get around him. Just as I braced for a crash, the moose loped into the trees."

An incident that made Bob shudder while talking about it happened one night on the way to an Iowa town of Storm Lake; "I was at the wheel, making my way through a blinding blizzard. Poor visibility was made worse by snow building up on the headlights, in spite of frequent stops to clean them. There were six of us including Don Markham [saxophone] and roadie Butch Hamblin. We were pulling a trailer full of equipment and I couldn't see a thing. Don tried holding a flashlight out of the side window, but that didn't help at all. When the ride started feeling bumpy, I stopped and got out to see if we were still on the road. It's a good thing I did, because there was a curve in the road that I couldn't see, and we were stopped on the edge of a steep cliff. When Don shined his flashlight over the edge, we couldn't see the bottom. That's about the closest we ever came to dying on the road."

Josie especially remembers a comment made by Don after relating that trip to her; "Touring and one-night stands were pretty tough on the guys when they reached their late sixties, but, what tickles me is, when they were touring in the winter of 1960, Don came home and said, 'I sure hope we're not doing this when we get to be forty!'"

NOKIE STICKS HIS 'NECK' OUT

Nokie Edwards was always inventing new guitar licks, but there were times when something he wanted to play was nearly impossible. He thought he might overcome the problem if the neck of his Telecaster was shaved down, allowing faster hand action. Having mentioned the idea to Gene Moles, Nokie later heard from Gene about a fellow who could easily perform the job, although Nokie would have to take the guitar up north into Kern County. Nokie wasted little time in driving to Bakersfield. There he met Gene, and they drove down a country road called Panama Lane to where a man named Semie Moseley was building guitars. Semie was about ten years younger than Gene, but at twenty-seven, he was the same age as Nokie. Although Nokie stood six-foot-two, he had to look up at Semie, who was a good two inches taller. The pair soon found that they had much more in common than being born in Oklahoma. Semie was a guitar player also, and feeling that standard guitar necks were too big for maximum finger-ability, had decided to do something about it when he was in his late teens. Needing money to supplement singing and traveling with a gospel group, he had found a job in Los Angeles at the Rickenbacker guitar factory. While making a dollar an hour, Semie learned everything he could about guitar building from master guitar maker Roger Rossmeisl. After two years, Semie was caught building his own guitar and was dismissed. Back to evangelizing, he traveled with the Reverend Ray Boatright. When the reverend saw the guitar that Semie had made, he provided a shop and tools in his garage for Semie to start building guitars for celebrities. Semie combined Moseley with Boatright to call his guitars "Mosrite." Merle Travis was the first to order an instrument, and then Boatright introduced Semie to Joe Maphis, who wanted a double-necked guitar. As Maphis and Travis were well known locally for their scorching country and bluegrass recordings, Semie's guitars grew in demand from 1954 on.

Following the failure of a too-young marriage, Semie returned to Bakersfield to live with his mother. Outgrowing a shop in her garage, he moved his tools to a friend's tractor barn. The friend that owned the barn was "Jelly" Sanders, a versatile musician who became a mentor to Buck Owens, and Semie's partner until 1962. During this time, Semie built the first Mosrite bass for Jelly, who then ordered a double-neck octave guitar. Unfortunately, Semie became so busy that the double-neck guitar was not completed until 1966.

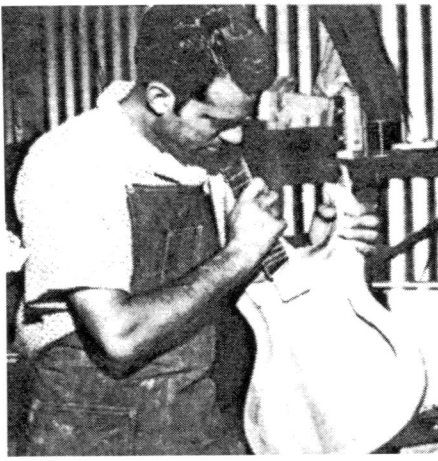

Semie Arbin Moseley in the early 1960s

Another partner of Semie's Semie was his older brother Andy. Regarding the odd name of "Semie," Andy offers; "Semie's first name was in honor of a distant relative, the first Governor of Oklahoma and a Chickasaw Indian named Semion Moseley. My brother was named Semie Arbin Moseley when he was born in the sticks of Oklahoma. I have never seen the name anywhere else. I was named after our two grandfathers. One was part Indian and married a Choctaw-Cherokee. His name was Andy, not Andrew. Our other Grandfather was named Jasper, so I was named Andy Jasper. Semie was two years younger than me, and a true genius as a guitar maker. By age twenty, he had built the famous double-neck guitars for Joe Maphis and Larry Collins. Semie and I got along well and we worked together for a long time."

Nokie and Gene followed Semie around the crowded shop to where the saw a beautiful guitar that had a wonderfully narrow neck and a smooth, vibrato-bridge with an innovative string-muting lever. As it would take some time to modify the Telecaster, Semie made an offer which Nokie remembers; "When Semie said he could shave down the neck on my Telecaster, he asked me to try this Mosrite and see if I liked it. I tried it right there and it felt real good."

When anyone asked or commented on the unusual shape of the guitar's body, Semie usually replied; "All I did at first was to lay a Fender Strat on its face and trace around it. Then I slimmed the middle a bit, rounded the bottom and extended the horns." Next, the body edge was contoured in what Semie called a "German carve," which he had learned from his associates at Rickenbacker. Intentional or not, Semie's guitar had sex appeal, its body resembling the torso of a shapely female.

Supplementing its beautiful body, the guitar featured an ultra-slim neck bound in smooth-edged vinyl and a precision mounted zero-fret to give open string notes equal tone and sustain to that of fretted notes. There were even little fret-marker dots on the side binding, a unique idea at the time. Semie's first patented vibrato tailpiece had a built-in string-muting device, hence the trademark "Vibramute." The muting bar would soon be discontinued, and individual string-rollers would later enhance the bridge, but the Vibramute name remained on the tailpiece for almost two years.

Nokie took the guitar back to Hollywood and began using it for recording sessions as well as taking it on the road. He later commented: "I had never played anything so nice. Semie wanted $300 for it and I bought it right away." Semie has been quoted as charging only $200 for the guitar that bore the serial number 0047, but with Nokie's memory almost as renowned as his musical skills, his version is likely correct.

K. Nagasawa

RIDING THE WAVES

Although The Ventures' huge album appeal was plainly evident, singles were still the only way to get airplay and eventual hits. With this in mind, *El Cumbanchero* b/w *Skip to M' Limbo* [Dolton 68] was recorded in the last half of November for release in the New Year. *El Cumbanchero* seemed to have the makings of another blockbuster and was plugged during radio interviews at almost every stop on The Ventures' 1963 spring tour. *El Cumbanchero* and *Skip to M' Limbo* also appeared in France on a four-track "extended-play" single that also contained *Memphis* and *Tarantella*, the Italian folk dance referred to by Dean Martin in his hit, *That's Amore* [Capitol 2589]. Like polkas, there are dozens of tarantella dance tunes, and as Bob recalls; "The one we played was known as *Sicilian Tarantella*. It was a song that Don had liked since his childhood. The melody on the record was played on the ocarina, or "sweet potato" as it we called it in those days because of its shape and size."

Sicilian Tarantella, written by G. Balsamo, appeared on 78-RPM records in the 1950s, and was soon released on 45 for jukebox play [RCA 447-0208]. The song was an odd choice for The Ventures, which is why, although found in Europe, Brazil, and Australia, it never appeared on American or Japanese vinyl.

~ ~ ~

As popularity of The Ventures' *Telstar* album was rising around the world, Dick Dale released his classic debut album, *Surfer's Choice* [Del-Tone T1886], half of which was guitar-dominated instrumentals. This was enough to get Bob Reisdorff, Josie, and the band thinking about another Ventures theme-album. Josie recalls the strategy; "When we were releasing four LPs per year, no set quota was required by Liberty Records. When it became apparent that fans were ready for a new one, we searched for material to record a surfing album. This turned out to be a continuous pursuit, with singles released in between."

Early '63 brought the release of *Pipeline* [Downey 104] from the Chantays. Although the Beach Boys and Jan and Dean were recording their own impression of surf music, guitar instrumentals were considered the "real thing" by enthusiasts. The Ventures needed some "surf" originals, but they knew very little about the genre and there was limited time before a scheduled March-April tour. The Lively Ones had turned *Spudnik* into a surfing hit, so *Surf Rider* was quickly selected. *Pipeline*, which was rocketing up the charts to become the ultimate surfing anthem song fit The Ventures' style so well that it was chosen to open their album. They picked a couple more tunes from other artists, including *Diamonds* by the UK's Jerry Lordan and J.D. Loudermilk's *Windy And Warm* from a Chet Atkins album. This one had not been a surfing tune, but the title was perfect and they had already recorded it during November's *El Cumbanchero* session. This commonly occurred, where a recorded tune that seemed unsuitable at the time was found to fit nicely some months or even years later. Such was the case with *Matador*, a tune written by Don that seems to be inspired by The Tijuana Brass. By eliminating the trumpets and slowing the tempo slightly, it became *The Lonely Sea*.

On February 21, Nokie's *Surf Rider* and the three more tunes were recorded at Hollywood's Conway Studios. Although the session sheet on the next page shows space for six entries, the Union limited recording to four songs per session. In the two remaining sessions, the band sat in the studio and wrote songs on the fly. Thinking back, Josie remembers her reaction to terms like "Ho-Dad" and "Gremmie," heard in songs from the Surfaris and Dick Dale & his Deltones; "When the Surfaris hit number two on the charts with *Wipe Out*, Blue Horizon Productions hurried to produce a Ventures surfing LP. There was also great haste to get material for the album cover. While The Ventures were in the studio, I headed down the freeway to Dana Point, where an authoritative magazine was published called *The Surfer*. While there, West Coast surfing champion Ilima Kalama gave me an excellent photo and a glossary of terms used by surfers which we used for the album jacket."

For each recording session, a leader had to be designated that would receive twice the amount of union pay. Expenses were high, but at this point, the cost of studio time was no object. Josie remembers the arrangement; "The record company paid the studio *and* the Musician's Union for each session. The Union then paid the musicians, minus Union dues and any other deductions owing."

The Ventures' "*Surfing*" album [Dolton BST-8022] was soon available in countries around the world, although it was not always sold intact. In Brazil, for instance, where it was titled *Pipeline* and displayed a different cover photo, some tracks were replaced with non-surf type songs like *Tarantella* and *Caravan*.

From this point, through the remainder of the sixties, Liberty/Dolton pressed 200,000 domestic copies of any Ventures album upon its release. Never before had any Liberty artist earned such confidence. The records always sold, usually with second pressings required. Huge sales totals were also achieved on the foreign market.

Phonograph Recording Contract Blank
AMERICAN FEDERATION OF MUSICIANS
OF THE UNITED STATES AND CANADA

(Employer's name) 0436
61187

Local Union No. 47

THIS CONTRACT for the personal services of musicians, made this 21 day of February, 1963 between the undersigned employer (hereinafter called the "employer") and Four (4) musician (hereinafter called "employees").

WITNESSETH, That the employer hires the employees as musicians severally on the terms and conditions below, and as further specified on reverse side. The leader represents that the employees already designated have agreed to be bound by said terms and conditions. Each employee yet to be chosen shall be so bound by said terms and conditions upon agreeing to accept his employment. Each employee may enforce this agreement. The employees severally agree to render collectively to the employer services as musicians in the orchestra under the leadership of **Don Wilson** as follows:

Name and Address of Place of Engagement: Conway Recorders, 1441 No. McCadden Pla., Hollywood 28, Calif.

Date(s) and Hours of Employment: 9:30 p.m. to 12:30 p.m. (3 hours) – 2/21/63

Type of Engagement: Recording for phonograph records only
WAGE AGREED UPON $ SCALE

This wage includes expenses agreed to be reimbursed by the employer in accordance with the attached schedule, or a schedule to be furnished the employer on or before the date of engagement.

To be paid WITHIN 15 DAYS

Upon request by the American Federation of Musicians of the United States and Canada (herein called the "Federation") of the local in whose jurisdiction the employees shall perform hereunder, the employer either shall make advance payment hereunder or shall post an appropriate bond.

Employer's name and authorized signature: **BLUE HORIZON PRODUCTIONS** / R. Lewdorff
Street address: Sunset Blvd.,
City/State/Phone: Hollywood 28, California – HO 2-2371

Leader's name: Don Wilson
Leader's signature: Don Wilson
Local No.: 76
Street address: Hollywood Blvd.
City/State: Los Angeles 69, California

(1) Label name: DOLTON

Master no.	No. of minutes	TITLES OF TUNES	Master no.	No. of minutes	TITLES OF TUNES
		"Pipeline"			"Diamonds"
		"Surf Rider"			"Windy & Warm"

(2) Employee's name (Last, First, Initial)	(3) Home address	(4) Local Union no.	(5) Social Security number	(6) Scale wages	(7) Pension contribution
Wilson, Don L. (Leader)	Hollywood Blvd. Los Angeles 69, Calif.	76		$112.00	$8.96
Bogle, Bob L.	Sunset Blvd. Hollywood 28, Calif.	76		56.00	4.48
Edwards, Nole F.	Ruscher Avenue Milton, Washington	117		56.00	4.48
Taylor, Mel	Beck Avenue No. Hollywood, California	47		56.00	4.48

CONTRACT RECEIVED 1963

PAID MAR 5 1963

Courtesy of *Pipeline Instrumental Review*

During editing of *The Ventures Surfing*, a tour put the group on the road for ten days. During that period, the album was pressed and released for distribution. Don was irritated to learn this, as he was unsatisfied with the mixing. Nevertheless, the album made the Top 30 in the States and is considered one of The Ventures' most successful projects. It remained on the charts for seven months, defining surf music to many who would never see a surfboard. Like the *Telstar* album, it was the first Ventures LP in many homes, but likely not the last.

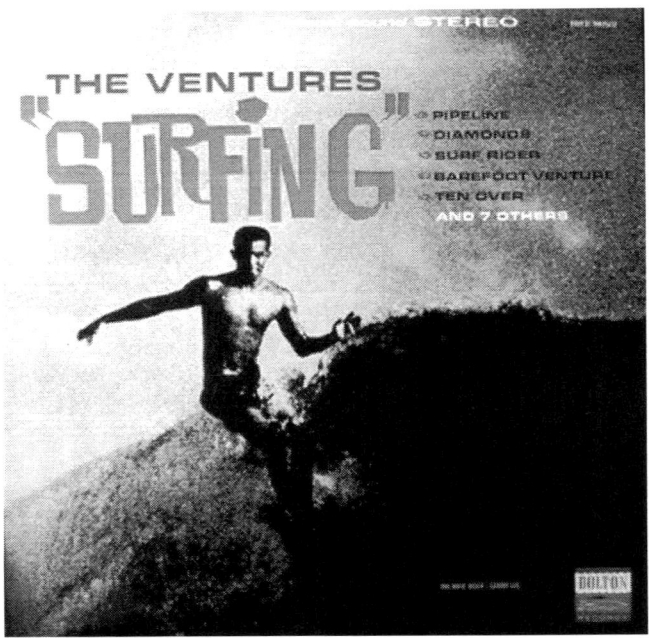

Ilima Kalama adorns The Ventures' tenth album

~ ~ ~

Although The Ventures tried to avoid being typecast, various Radio personalities in decades to come hailed them as an "ahead of their time" surf group, even specifying *Walk-Don't Run* as the first surfing song. The Ventures resisted being labeled until they noticed that a surfing revival erupted every few years. The group then embraced the genre by recording an occasional surfing tune and keeping a few surf classics in their stage presentation. After all, it was fun, and everyone seemed to enjoy it. In an early 1980's discussion about this, Mel Taylor offered; "The real surf music nuts don't consider The Beach Boys or Jan And Dean as surf music. They define a surf band as having two guitars, a bass, and a drummer. That's why we ended up with the tag. The way I classify it is by song titles. I don't consider our first version of *Walk-Don't Run* as surf music, or *Perfidia*, or *Apache*. It should be related to the sport, such as *Pipeline* is. Surfers considered that one to be their national anthem back when surf was the happening thing. I guess you could call *Hawaii Five-0* surf music because [laughing], it came from a TV show that had waves in it."

A prime example of the The Ventures' dilemma appears on *The Awesome Surfing Album*, a 1995 CD from Prime Cuts. Along with classics surf cuts by Jan & Dean, The Marketts, and The Routers, it features Ventures tracks *Perfidia* and *Walk-Don't Run*. With a bit of forethought, the disc could have featured the brilliant surf-adaptation of the latter, *Walk-Don't Run '64*, and their top of the surf line, *Diamond Head*.

MOVIES 'R' HOLLYWOOD

People in Australia loved *The Ninth Wave* [Dolton 78] so much that it reached Number 8 in Sydney. As American listeners seemed more interested in Ventures albums, many missed out on the flip side called *Damaged Goods*. Fan club members, however, were advised early about such releases and were informed by Josie to watch for *Damaged Goods* the movie, for which The Ventures were commissioned to write the soundtrack. As far as Josie and The Ventures knew, it was to be a remake of a 1954 action film called *Forbidden Cargo*, concerning drug smuggling on the high seas. For its theme, the band re-titled *Jaguar*, an unreleased 1962 recording, to *Damaged Goods*, giving writing credits to Bob Bogle's wife, Carol Bedford. During the second *Surfing* session, the tune was freshly recorded along with *The Heavies*, *Ten Over*, and *Barefoot Venture*.

Damaged Goods was released on VHS and eventually DVD

When *Damaged Goods* emerged on film, it was found to be a remake of the 1937 film called *Forbidden Desire*, forewarning the dangers of venereal disease. Built around a frightening U.S. Public Health Service film (included in its entirety), the plot centered on a handsome high-school track star contracting syphilis from a prostitute. Although the film had bombed two years earlier in 1961 under the title of *V.D.*, the new name seemed to give it longevity. The Ventures' recording is heard three times in the film, but Josie recalled that she and the band were not pleased; "To say we were disappointed in the content is putting it mildly. We simply didn't push it any further in the fan club news."

Another Ventures movie was to be titled *Wild Party*, but was soon renamed *Wild Holiday* due to an existing 1956 picture called *Wild Party*. The Ventures were named to star in this 1964 production, but it never came to pass. Bob Bogle remembers; "We spent a lot of money on that one. It was going to be Ventures-produced, with us playing our own music in it. We recorded some more surfing music and we hired Jack Warner Jr. for about six months to coordinate the project. He was on a very good salary for those days, in the range of four grand a month. Eventually, we became so busy with touring and recording that it was impossible for us to work on a full-length feature. As for those surf songs; it's just too long ago to recall if we ever used them or not."

While the fans were left wondering if the picture had been made, it was another five years before the Ventures in a movie was again addressed. When it was, Don and Bob got a taste of acting.

In March 1963, a series of concerts took The Ventures up through the western provinces of Canada, and in April, southward into the northern and central States. No longer clad in the red jackets seen on their two-year-old album cover, The Ventures appeared in blue shirts, buttoned to the neck, with the sleeves shortened just enough to seem fashioned for lightning-speed drumming and strumming. Their shiny sunburst guitars and "piggyback" Fender amplifiers covered in creamy vinyl with dark grille cloth and white knobs, resting on chromed tilt-back legs, created a memorable vision beside Mel's glittering Gretsch drums.

As Don recalls, The Ventures were not always the main attraction during their performance; "Sometimes girls would jump on the stage and start dancing until they were removed by security, but on this tour, we were in Calgary, Alberta when a couple of heavily endowed women started dancing the 'dirty boogie' out on the floor. Suddenly the crowd had completely encircled them, which encouraged them to dance even more suggestively. Here we were [laughing], pounding out the *Bumble Bee Twist*, and not one person was paying any attention to us.

"That trip across western Canada was something I never forgot. We played Edmonton the night after Calgary, and then we were off to Regina, Saskatoon, and Moose Jaw. The land was flat as a pancake and we didn't see a car for hours, and when we did, it was a Mountie wanting to ticket us for speeding. When he saw our California license plates, he was nice enough to let us go with a warning. It was grueling in those days, driving four and five hundred miles and arriving just in time to set up and play four sets and sometimes five. Once, I woke up in the car completely disheveled and all alone with people going by me on the sidewalk. The guys had stopped in a town for breakfast and left me there because I was asleep. Sometimes we would arrive in a place, only to learn that we had been cancelled. If we got the call the night before from our agent, we considered ourselves lucky. Too bad there were no cell phones back then."

1963 provided a few surprises for avid fans attending their first live Ventures concert. To begin with, the man seen as "the bass player" in photographs was doing most of the lead guitar work. Secondly, he had a nameless but beautiful looking guitar with white inlaid binding on the outer rim of the body. This was, of course, Nokie Edwards with his unmarked Mosrite guitar. Tune after tune, The Ventures amazed would-be guitarists and entire garage bands pressing up to the stage. Another surprise was the unrecognizable drummer. Of the first ten Ventures albums, only the second had shown a drummer, that being Howie Johnson. For fans not members of the fan club, this was their first introduction to the dynamic Mel Taylor.

Dancers were still twisting in 1963, but as twist songs became historic, Don rewrote *The Twomp* so that it urged dancers to do *The Swim*. Some fans reportedly heard the song during the band's 1963 spring tour, and The Ventures actually made a recording of it. Unfortunately, the acetate demo of *Let's Do The Swim* was left hiding in a cardboard box for almost fifty years before being rediscovered by this writer. Meanwhile, in 1964, Bobby Freeman hit Number 5 with *C'mon And Swim* [Autumn Records 2].

Home from spring touring, The Ventures learned that Snuff Garrett had negotiated with Bob Reisdorff for a Liberty album to be called *Bobby Vee Meets The Ventures*. A year earlier, Garrett had made a successful album called *Bobby Vee Meets The Crickets*. Reisdorff remembered the deal well; "Snuffy wanted Bobby Vee to sing on every track, but I just couldn't let that happen. The Ventures had just swept the country with *Telstar And The Lonely Bull* and I couldn't insult them by proposing that they back Bobby for the whole album. Snuffy agreed to The Ventures doing one song on each side, so I was satisfied with that."

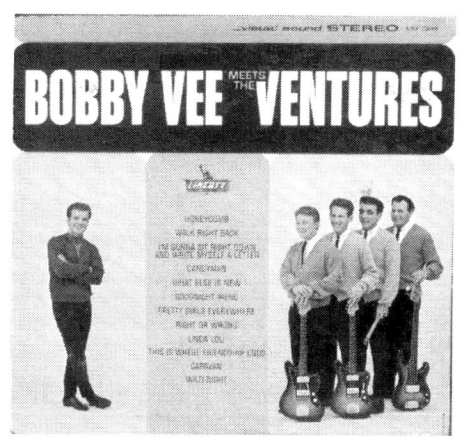

For one Ventures cut, Reisdorff chose *Party in Laguna* from the *Surfing* album, but the name was changed to *Wild Night* (a little trick that Liberty used to sell more albums). The other "Ventures-only" track was an updated version of *Caravan*, described thirty years later by Nokie as his most difficult number. During live performances of *Caravan*, Mel added a drum solo, quite short at first, but longer and more interesting when he tapped out a little solo on the bass strings while Bob fingered the frets. Although the concept originated on a stand-up bass in the recording of *Big Noise From Winnetka* by the Bob Crosby Orchestra, it was also recorded this way by others. As Bob Bogle recalls; "Mel and I worked up the routine after hearing Gene Krupa's version. Mel hit the strings hard, so when my bass began showing dents and the E string actually broke, I started carrying a different bass for this part of the show. Our audience came to expect the number, so we never dropped it." In a short time, *Caravan* with drum solo and bass tattoo became the closing number for thousands of concerts. In the meantime, Nokie continued enhancing his arrangement of the melody with near impossible guitar licks.

Although *Bobby Vee Meets The Ventures* [Liberty LST-7289], showed Nokie with the Fender bass, he had played lead guitar on every track. A similar photo graced the cover of the April 20 Cash Box while the inside story touted the band's recent success with *Telstar and The Lonely Bull*, along with naming The Ventures' *Surfing* album as its "Popular Pick of the Week."

Bobby Vee Meets The Ventures was in the Top 100 for eight weeks, peaking at 91 in the summer of '63. Careful inspection of the album revealed that Liberty was now a subsidiary of Avnet Electronics Corp. To celebrate the coup, the company produced an album of fourteen top Liberty recording artists entitled *Avnet Presents The Sounds of Liberty* [Liberty AV-5877]. Included in the collection was *Walk-Don't Run* by The Ventures. The next move for Avnet was to invest in several small record companies and tighten the budget on its recording artists.

As half-owner of Liberty, Al Bennett reaped a sizable profit and also retained the position of Head of Sales. As time went on, he watched the company's stock value dwindle, and in less than two years, he scooped up Liberty Records for $8,000,000.

I SOLD MY SON

When Liberty released the *Bobby Vee* collaboration, Dolton unleashed *The Ventures Play the Country Classics* [Dolton BLP-8023]. It had been put off earlier in favor of the *Surfing* album. *Country Classics* was near and dear to Nokie's heart, and he relished the chance to improvise the Chet Atkins versions of *San Antonio Rose*, *Wildwood Flower*, and *Steel Guitar Rag*. Don, Bob, and Mel were also comfortable with the project, having musical beginnings in country as well. When the need arose for background singers on several tracks, Josie brought in the Jack Halloran Singers, a group that backed everyone on records from Martin Denny to Ray Charles. The result was a delightful collection of country standards that even rock and rollers enjoyed.

As the fusion of country music and rock 'n' roll had just begun, *The Ventures Play Country Classics* [Dolton BST-8023] was a stroke of genius. Artists like Roger Miller, Don Gibson, Jim Reeves, Boots Randolph, and Patsy Cline were now crossing over to the pop charts. Soon, the term *country-rock*, would be coined, and become the choice of millions. The cover art for *Country Classics* was only drawing, but it was notable for finally depicting Nokie on lead and Bob on the bass. As Josie recalls, this was the last LP that she helped produce; "I began taking many plane trips back to Tacoma where my father was very ill. In a bit of a fog, I became quite detached from the recording business. He left us in less than a year, passing away in 1964."

Knowing she would be away for awhile, Josie found a replacement to run the evergrowing fan club. Some time back, a handsome young songwriter named Charlie Vance had come into her office to promote his songs. After Josie recorded Scott Douglas singing Charlie's *Pretending* [Blue Horizon 6063], Charlie had become such a good friend and huge Ventures fan that she gave him the job. He handled it well, writing exciting monthly bulletins and sending out kits to new members. Intending to stay only until Josie returned, circumstances arose which kept Charlie there indefinitely. When the condition of Josie's father had improved somewhat, she returned to Hollywood in time to help in the production of *Country Classics*. However, with three years having quickly passed, Josie's contract with Bob Reisdorff was about to end. Josie recalls that instead of renewing, Reisdorff had another idea; "Feeling that any artist could only expect a short career, Bob thought it was smart to sell The Ventures' contract while they were still going strong and Liberty Records was ready to buy! We decided to keep our Electron Music publishing company, but we sold The Ventures contract. I must now confess that I sold my son and his friends! Years later, while contemplating a book about my part in the band's success, I was going to call it *I Sold My Son*. After the sale of that contract, Bob Reisdorff moved his office to his lovely home in the Hollywood Hills. Fairly soon, Sonny Rivera went to work there as his employee. She had a young child then, which she brought with her and kept in a playpen."

MOONLIGHTING

After living in Los Angeles for about three years, Bob Bogle felt he had learned enough to start his own record label. In addition to trying for a hit record of his own, Bob wanted to help other musicians to break into popular music. In the fall of 1962, he started Unity Records by obtaining office space in the Liberty annex and designing an emblem depicting a sword-wielding fist on a blue-green background. His first customers were Pat and Lolly Vasquez, a pair of talented Mexican-Native American brothers who had worked as studio musicians after touring with the Jimmy Clanton band. Bob had met Pat in July when he played bass on a Ventures session.

Recording under the surname "Vegas," Pat sang *That Smile* b/w *The Best Girl in the World* [Unity CP-2113]. The Vegas brothers harmonized well, and Lolly played a respectable lead guitar backed by Pat on bass. The record was placed in a few stores, but did not get much action. On their way to fame and fortune, the brothers would encounter The Ventures yet again, and work with Josie as well.

Other Unity singles produced by Bob included Judd Hamilton singing *Till I Found You* b/w *On a Night Like This*. For backing musicians, Bob hired guitarist Pat Vegas, pianist Leon Russell, and bassist David Gates, who was also helpful as an arranger.

Bob also recorded Judd's good friend, Jack Chaplain, singing *Boys Aren't Supposed to Cry*. With Hank Levine arranging and Eddie Bracket engineering, a full orchestra was brought into United Studios for the final take. While Jack Chaplain's record remained a demo, he was soon landing acting roles in popular TV westerns such as *Laramie*, *The Rebel*, and *Wagon Train*.

In the vein of one-name singers like Dion and Fabian, Judd Hamilton sang a pair of romantic ballads billed as "Shane" (after the 1953 western movie hero). He wrote *On a Night Like This*, while *Till I Found You* was co-written by Bob Bogle, wife Carol Bedford, and "Scott" Douglas Longley. Mysteriously, this single [Unity CP-2112] was reproduced years later and issued with a revealing *light*-green label.

Bob had always enjoyed cleverly contrived novelty records, so when he learned how Ross Bagdasarian (a.k.a. David Seville) had solved Liberty's financial troubles with his recordings of *Witch Doctor* and the popular series of Chipmunk records, he decided to try his own hand at record humor. Remembering the 1956 success of Dickie Goodman and Bill Buchanan's wacky *Flying Saucer* singles, Bob and Carol applied the concept to *Project Venus*, presenting a madcap news report of a space alien's visit to Earth by answering a reporter's questions with injected clips from current hits.

For the B-side, Bob laid down an instrumental called *Rockin' Ship*, playing all of the parts himself. Using his given names, he cut the single as Bobby Leonard and the Explorers [Unity CP-2114] and hired Liberty promo man Norm Winter to publicize it. Aware of Buchanan and Goodman's encounter with record companies over copyright infringement, Mr. Winter obtained rights for the song-clips used in *Project Venus*. As Bob recalls; "The whole thing was very expensive, but at the time, I thought *Project Venus* was pretty funny. That's my 'funny' voice on the record. Apparently there was only room for one 'Buchanan and Goodman' in the world. If any copies of my record were sold, I never found out about it."

Although the Bobby Leonard single is among the rarest collectibles for Ventures fans, it occasionally gets airplay on American FM specialty stations. At auction, the record has brought upwards of $150.00 from bidders in the Orient.

As the career of The Ventures gained momentum, side projects fell by the wayside. Bob continues; "After pouring around $20,000 into the Unity thing, I decided it was a hobby that was far too expensive. I left the label to be used by whoever wanted it. As it turned out, Josie was interested in recording some singers, and so was Judd."

A few UNITY singles

Josie recalls that, as an independent producer, one of her clients was James A. Christiansen; "Jim had a beautiful singing voice with an amazing range. We recorded him doing his own song called *Sylvie*, at which time he wished to be billed as Chris Christiansen and the Sundowners [*Sylvie* b/w *Daddy Rollem'* UNITY CP-2116]. We had also recorded him doing a song I had written called *Destiny*, which he backed with *Sylvie* for a later release [Imperial 66062, 1964]. Don had always loved Jim's recordings; saying that I had done a good job, but I guess it was not the right music or the right time. Don finally sang *Destiny* on his own country album with the title changed to *The Wind Blows East*. I'm not sure who made that decision, but I wasn't thrilled about it.

"The next thing I did was to record Don singing his own composition called *Angel*. We had Roy Lanham on guitar for that one. On the flip side, Don sang *Forever and Ever*, an old waltz that he had been singing since he was a teenager." [Unity CP-2117]

Among Don's Unity recordings that never made it to vinyl were versions of *Cindy* and *You'll Never Walk Alone*; a tune called *Shake It Easy* released instrumentally as *Night Stick*; and *The Swim*, an updated version of *The Twomp* with entirely new lyrics.

Now that Blue Horizon Productions was history, Josie became restless. Since she and Charlie Vance had become very close, Josie proposed a partnership; "As Charlie had become very dear to me, he and I formed a recording company in 1962. After several hit records by The Ventures, I fancied myself a full-fledged producer and I rented office space above Western Recorders at 6000 Sunset Blvd. We called our label Regency, having no knowledge of the Regency label carrying Hank Ballard and Little Richard. When a commercial name is chosen in the music business, it is supposedly researched before being registered, but we were never told of the conflict.

"Another idea I had in starting the Regency label was to provide a sort of clearing house where artists could find songs that they would like to record. Artists and writers would belong to this 'club' for a fee, and if they used our label, we would promote them and share in the profits. Christian Wilde joined us in this enterprise, and we called ourselves Regency Producers Group. I believe our first client was Larry Meadows, who had made a record in 1959 that had realized little success. Larry seemed to have great potential, and became a protégé of Charlie's. He had a nice singing voice and was such a handsome young man that *Teen Screen* magazine ran a picture of him in a promotional contest. We recorded him singing two of Charlie's compositions, *Don't Hide Your Love* and *Such A Lonely Boy* [Regency 25].

"We also recorded Larry singing *Couldn't That Just Tear Your Heart Out* backed with another of Charlie's songs, *Pretending*, which Scott Douglas had sung on Blue Horizon. Scott also designed a picture sleeve for this one [Regency 27]. Perhaps it wasn't the right time, but nothing we tried seemed to catch on. We even promoted Larry through The Ventures fan club bulletins with an autographed photo from that picture sleeve. I never knew if it was his wretched home life or the fact that his career didn't take off that prompted Larry to take his own life.

"A wonderful doo-wop group that I recorded and named The Check-Mates, consisted of two white and two young black men that had sung background for Don on *The Twomp*. As one of my first projects, they sang *Shoo-Be-Shoo-Be-Do* and a slow ballad called *What Do You Do* [Regency 26]. After engaging Ernie Freeman to play piano on this one, we hired him many more times, mostly to write scores for sidemen on Ventures recordings. The last that we heard of The Check-Mates, they were enjoying success in the Las Vegas casino lounge circuit."

In the summer of 1963, Josie and Charlie looked for more talent to record. Knowing Judd Hamilton to be making many musical friends, Josie invited him to bring in any prospects that he would like to record. Seizing the opportunity to be an A&R man, Judd assembled an instrumental group. Starting with Pat and Lolly Vegas, he added brother Danny and drummer Gary Leeds. Naming the group The Avantis, Josie formed a company called "Avanti Productions." Asked about the name, Josie said; "For a time, Bob Bogle drove a fancy Corvette around Hollywood. Not to be outdone, Don bought the new Studebaker Avanti from which I 'stole' the name for our recording group!"

With Judd as arranger, several outstanding surf instrumentals written by Pat Vegas were recorded. *Wax 'Em Down* and *Gypsy Surfer* were on Josie's master recording, and published by Electron Music, but they never made it to her Regency label. As Judd recalls, he was chatting with Bob Marcucci, who had made big stars of Frankie Avalon and Fabian on his Chancellor label; "I was trying to promote my brother Danny as a teenage idol, but one thing led to another and I found myself playing the Avantis master tape for Marcucci. When he heard it, he grabbed the phone and made a deal with Josie, right while I was sitting there." Consequently, the single was a local hit on Chancellor [C-1144], attracting enough attention to be bootlegged on the infamous Astra label.

The next Avantis release was a doo-wop single entitled *Surfin' Granny*, written by Pat Vegas and Danny Hamilton. Appearing on Regency 108, it was backed with the same tune minus the vocal, and entitled *Do The Surfin' Granny*. By this time, Josie had sold Electron Music to bandleader Lawrence Welk, so she registered these Avantis tunes under her new publishing company, Voltage Music. Regency 110 quickly followed with the Avantis' version of Little Richard's *Lucille*, and an original instrumental, *Phantom Surfer*. Additional sounds on this production included David Gates on guitar and some heavy B3 organ by Leon Russell. Unfortunately, the records drew little attention until forty years later when they became rare collector's items.

Decades later, a partially labeled acetate demo of *Wax Em Down* fell into the hands of The Ventures' UK Fan Club. Rumors spread through the club that this instrumental gem was unreleased Ventures material. Eventually, a labeled copy of the rare Avantis record surfaced, and the rumor was laid to rest.

Another recording of interest is a Charlie Vance song, *Initials on a Tree* backed with *Flight 103*. The intended artist was western star Ty Hardin of the *Bronco Lane* TV series. However, when Hardin's contract remained unsigned, Josie was not about to waste a pair of romantic ballads. Aware of Judd Hamilton's vocal talent, she invited him to try the songs. Judd sang them well and both were released on Regency 111.

Of all her Regency recordings, the last was most vivid in Josie's memory; "Years earlier, while living in Tacoma, I had been impressed by a trio of boys who attended Pacific Lutheran College. Calling themselves The Nordic Trio, they accompanied themselves on guitar. When I invited these young men to come and make a recording in Hollywood, they were soon on their way. During this time, Chris Wilde and I had become friends, so I proposed that he work with the boys. We rehearsed for days and sometimes into the night, trying to get just the right sound. Unbeknownst to me was the fact that Frank Sinatra kept offices in the same building. I hired studio musicians and we produced a beautiful recording of *Softly, As I Leave You* [Regency 113]. The song had enjoyed former success on Liberty by Matt Monroe, but we thought we could surpass his version. For the flip side, we chose *Young Love*, a pop and country hit for Sonny James in 1956. It had even made Number 3 on the R&B chart. I remember Don congratulating us on producing what he thought would be a hit.

"Just as I got our record pressed, I was astounded to hear *Softly, As I Leave You* on the radio sung by Frank Sinatra! Is it any wonder that I came to a certain conclusion? Ever the optimist, I took my record to Randy Wood, who was having great success with the Dot label. He released the record for me, but not without a warning that I should not expect to top Sinatra. Well, so much for the big record producer! It seems I just couldn't replicate the success I had when producing my guys, The Ventures. I realize now that I was greener than grass, and that the smartest thing I had done was to partner with someone with experience and connections in the music industry."

Looking back, Don recalls his initial warning to Josie about continuing in the record business; "Shortly after Mom came into money by selling The Ventures, I told her, 'You should go back to Tacoma, buy an apartment building, and manage it. If you keep spending your hard-earned money recording unknowns, you will probably end up broke.' And basically, that's what happened."

Josie recalls the final crush; "As for Charlie Vance, he had also written lyrics to The Ventures' recording of *Josie*, but it was never released as a vocal. This is what happens, without that big push and proper representation. Sadly, Charlie died in an automobile accident on a California freeway in the late sixties. Devastated, I soon left Hollywood. Charlie is the subject of my two poems, 'City of Angels' and 'Standing Tall'."

THE VENTURES MODEL IN SPACE

Judd Hamilton wanted a hit record more than anything, but opportunities kept steering him in other directions. With each endeavor he gained more experience, but his next move was, in his words; "the biggest career mistake an aspiring teenage idol can make. I got married!" Soon, a son was born which put Judd's show business endeavors on hold. For the time being, he stuck to parking cars for a steady paycheck and tips.

Bob Reisdorff, now on his own and savoring the colossal success of *Telstar & The Lonely Bull* album, decided to produce The Ventures on another twelve current hits. The Blue Horizon contract having expired, he was able to steer the group a little easier in any direction he pleased. With liberal use of session musicians, the result was *Let's Go!* Darlene Love and The Blossoms were again hired for prominent vocal parts on the tracks, *Hot Pastrami*, *So Fine*, and *Walk Right In*. Male voices were also heard, the collaboration being named The Moon Stones in the liner notes. Reisdorff also produced a Moon Stones single with the group singing the Bogle-Wilson penned *My True Love* and a Dick Glasser song, *Love Call* [Dolton 70]. Years later, when Mel revealed that the male voices on *My True Love* were The Ventures, and that the band also played on that single, it suddenly became a collector's item. After forty years, decent copies of this Blue Horizon production fetch as much as $150 at auction on the Internet. As we shall see, *My True Love* became a Ventures' instrumental the following year, but under a new title.

By mid-September, *Let's Go!* was well on its way to peaking at Number 30 in Billboard, while *Telstar, Surfing, Bobby Vee Meets The Ventures*, and *Country Classics* were in slow descent. Five albums in the Billboard Top 100 at the same time was (and remains to be) an amazing and unique achievement!

Although the record jacket for *Let's Go* presented only a headshot of cover girl, Barbara Bouchet, young men found it very attractive. Barbara launched her movie career a year later, her most famous role being Miss Moneypenny in 1967's James Bond spoof, *Casino Royale*.

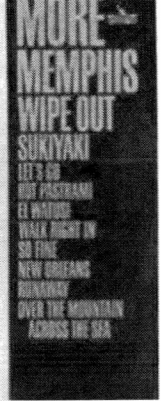

Barbara Bouchet in 1963 and '64

The guitar that Nokie now played brought many questions from concertgoers. Nokie always explained the details of the instrument, referring the serious inquiries to Semie Moseley in Bakersfield. Nokie also revealed that he had used the Mosrite for a few tracks on *Let's Go!* As Nokie recalls, after receiving a couple of orders through such a referral, Semie came up with a deal; "He offered me fifty dollars for every Mosrite that he sold as a result of my using the guitar on tour. I started to get some commission money, and that's when the other guys in the band got interested."

This "interest" hatched a deal to put The Ventures' logo on Moseley's guitars. At the same time, Bob Reisdorff announced that he would be quitting the music business by the end of the year. Also, America having started a communications satellite program, Telstar II was launched in May. Fortunately, Reisdorff was still around for production of the year's final project, a concept album dedicated to space exploration.

In need of someone to handle the business end of the Mosrite deal plus the duties left by Charlie Vance, The Ventures hired thirty-one-year-old Stanley Wagner, a sharp young man they had known as manager and writer for comedian/drummer, George Hopkins. The first task that Wagner tackled was the crowded, upstairs operating space in the Liberty building. The Ventures offices were soon moved to a much larger facility taking up two storefronts at 1213 and 1215 North Highland Avenue, just a few blocks away from Liberty. On July 1, Stan became president of Venture Enterprises. In addition to running the band's publishing company, he assumed operation of the fan club. While working to get the group exposed on TV shows like Ed Sullivan, Merv Griffin, and Johnny Carson, Stan dreamed up promotional projects. Soon needing assistance, he hired pretty Nancy Messenger as his secretary, a position she would hold for the next two years. Stan remembers his next move; "At the time, Nokie's life revolved almost completely around guitars, with one big diversion. The back of The Ventures' first LP said Nokie was into 'stock cars,' but I think it should have said 'slot cars.' Those things were a big fad back then, and Nokie loved them. Anyway, since he had told me that this Mosrite was the best guitar he had ever played, I decided we would price them higher than anything Gibson or Fender had. We were searching for an advertising slogan when Bob Bogle came up with 'Built in Soul.' I still have my original brochure with Bob's slogan and a Rolls Royce behind the guitar. We got our lawyer, Leon Leonian, to draw up a contract that began with our advancing Moseley the sum of $50,000 to relocate and start production."

As Andy Moseley recalls, the loan was for even more; "In '63, brother Semie and I drove from Bakersfield to North Hollywood, discussing the deal we would try to make at a meeting with the Ventures organization. The retail price was already set, but the distributor price needed some debate. The meeting went well, with Semie and I coming away with a verbal contract and a $70,000 line of credit from The Ventures to build the first twenty guitars. As I recall, they had just sold a lucrative publishing company. The Ventures, as Mosrite Distributing Company, would buy our guitars at a distributor's price and profit by selling them to retail music stores."

Elated, twenty-eight-year-old Semie immediately began work on the new guitar. To distinguish the new Ventures design, he began making slight alterations to his Joe Maphis model. First, the wide end of the neck was cut at an angle to match that of the slanted rhythm pickup. The top of the headstock, which had been squared off, was now angled slightly, and the "M" was not cut as deep. The Maphis model had clear plastic control knobs, whereas The Ventures model sported chrome-plated brass knobs. Other changes were more subtle, such as the application of the logos to the headstock *before* the final clear-coat, instead of silk-screening them after.

Don, Nokie and Bob receive their new Ventures models

In the fall of 1963, The Ventures were made several live appearances using guitars from Semie's growing company, but their first TV appearance with the Mosrite was purely by chance. Prior to hosting ABC TV's *Newlywed Game*, Bob Eubanks owned a teenage nightclub in North Hollywood called the Cinnamon Cinder. So popular was the nightspot that The Pastel Six recorded a dance number called *The Cinnamon Cinder* [Zen 102]. When David L. Wolper produced a documentary series called *Teenage Idol*, footage from a Ventures' Cinnamon Cinder performance of *Driving Guitars* was used by NBC. Hosted by movie star Joseph Cotten, the show was aired on the network's *Hollywood and the Stars* program on January 13, 1964. It was one of very few American TV appearances where The Ventures actually played rather than sync to one of their records, and perhaps the only one showing them with their original Mosrites.

Popular hits of the time included *Out of Limits* [Warner Bros. 5391] from Joe Saraceno's Marketts/studio musicians, and *Penetration* [Best 13002] from The Pyramids, a group that shaved their heads in reaction to the invasion of the mop-haired Beatles. This music inspired the Ventures' concept album entitled *(The) Ventures In Space*, which employed various galactic sound effects played on musical instruments.

Interesting trivia involves the themes of two popular TV science-fiction programs, ABC's *The Outer Limits* and Rod Serling's *The Twilight Zone* on CBS. *Outer Limits* was the title of the Marketts' single when it first appeared and ABC TV had no objection, but when Serling noticed that the introductory four-note riff was the exact beginning of the theme from his *Twilight Zone* series, he threatened a lawsuit. Subsequent pressings were entitled *Out of Limits*, although many people (including Don and Bob) still referred to the song by its original title. The publicity generated may have even helped the tune in charting at Number 3, and subsequently being chosen as the perfect opener for *(The) Ventures In Space*. Only one track, *Exploration in Terror*, was explicitly written for this album, although some older originals were revamped and appropriately renamed. A recording session at the time ended with a track that would be lost forever, and a pair of instrumentals never to be heard on an album in their original form. The plan had first been to release an old original called *Monster Monkey* backed with another one called *The Lost Surfer* on single Dolton 85. *Monster Monkey* had also been revamped a year earlier for Don and Bob's *My True Love* as sung by The Moon Stones on Dolton 70. During the *In Space* sessions, *Monster Monkey* was renamed *He Never Came Back*, and yet another unreleased track, *Scotch*, was converted to *Solar Race*. Ironically, *The Lost Surfer* "was" completely and irrevocably "lost" in the shuffle!

Al Bennett awards The Ventures with a Gold Disc for surpassing one million album sales in 1963

Solar Race was then chosen from the *In Space* album for Dolton 85, but instead of the eerie organ ending, racecar sounds were inserted throughout to fit the song's new title, *The Chase*. The flip side of Dolton 85 contained The Ventures' punchy version of The Savage, drawn from the repertoire of the UK's mellower sounding Shadows.

Continuing with *In Space*, the guys converted Don's vocal composition of *Sally* to an exquisite instrumental called *Love Goddess of Venus*. For this new version, Nokie simply overdubbed Don's vocal track with an all-guitar melody.

As Bob Reisdorff recalls, he did some legwork to find additional material; "After shopping around, I found the theme on a single from 'One Step Beyond,' a TV show from around 1960 with [composer] Harry Lubin conducting a symphony orchestra. It was an eerie theme song called *Fear,* and it added a lot to the mysterious element of *The Ventures in Space*. We used more themes, like *The Twilight Zone* and one from a Vincent Price movie called *The Bat*. The guys did a great job converting Alvino Rey's 'big band' swing version to a slow, danceable rocker."

Reisdorff found more material by digging into the singles he had produced before meeting The Ventures. The Frantics' instrumental, *Werewolf* [Dolton 16] fit the album perfectly. Of their many Dolton singles, the Frantics likely had the most fun with this one. Reisdorff had opened the number by mimicking the eerie voice of horror film actor Vincent Price; "*Even a man whose heart is pure and says his prayers at night, can change to a wolf when the wolf bane blooms, and the full moon's shining bright.*" The tune, mixed with assorted snarls and growling by engineer Kearney Barton, ended with a chilling wolf howl from Bonnie Guitar. Charting at 83 nationally, the song remained a favorite of guitar instrumental fans for decades. Creating their own *In Space* sound effects, The Ventures named their version *The Fourth Dimension*.

The Ventures picked up two tunes written by associates Julius Wechter and Danny Hamilton. As a session musician, Wechter, of Tijuana Brass and Baja Marimba Band fame, was brought in to add unusual percussion effects on some of the cuts. The album inspired him, along with his wife, to write track three, which they named *Moon Child*. During the final session, as Danny Hamilton sat in the studio watching his favorite band record, the group had completed eleven songs for the album. While they pondered what to play for the twelfth, Danny told Don Wilson that he had written a tune that just might do the trick. Judd tells what happened next; "When Danny mentioned his song to the group, Don was kind enough to say 'Well, OK' and he handed Danny a guitar. Don knew that Dan could play, having heard him a year ago at our home in Wenatchee, but he didn't realize how much the kid had improved. Danny played this little song and suddenly had the attention of everyone in the room. When he played it again, they all looked at each other and nodded. They started arranging it right there on the spot. Bob Reisdorff said, 'Danny, what do you call this tune?' Recalling a movie that had terrified him when he was twelve, Danny blurted, '*War of the Satellites*!' When I heard what had happened, I almost went into shock. My little brother had written a song that was being recorded by The Ventures!"

THE STRAIGHT MAN

Among the session sheets procured by *Pipeline* magazine's Dave Burke, one from this period shows the curious absence of Bob Bogle. Dated November 22, 1963, David Gates is listed as the bassist along with other prominent helpers including Billy Strange, Leon Russell, Julius Wechter, and Red Rhodes for the final recording of *Twilight Zone, Out of Limits, One Step Beyond* and *War of the Satellites*. Fortunately, Bob and Judd Hamilton were able to provide an answer to the mystery. Apparently, the hiatus between recording sessions and tours was sometimes a little too long for Bob.

Recording sessions for *In Space* were not finished, but by now, able sidemen were available and affordable. While chatting with Stan Wagner, Bob thought of the time they had used George Hopkins on drums following Howie Johnson's exit from the band. At the time, Wagner had been George's manager. Bob also liked George's stand-up comedy spiel, and thought it would be great to work with him in a lounge act. Through Stan, Bob located George and found him to be available. Within a week, the pair worked up a comedy act with Bob as the "straight man." Bob then hired Judd Hamilton as their road manager, and the three assembled a string of musical numbers to break up the comedy routines. With Bob on lead guitar, Judd sang and played rhythm while George backed them on drums. A booking agency sent them on tour across the country, playing clubs all the way to Miami, Florida. From there they went to Chicago where they performed nightly for two solid weeks in *Playboy*'s Bunny Club. Judd remembers Bob's car; "It was late in 1963, and we traveled in Bob's new Mercury 'Turnpike Cruiser'. It had this neat rear window that would roll down at the push of a button. It was just the three of us, with all of our equipment in a 'Nationwide' rental trailer."

(The) Ventures In Space [Dolton 8027] arguably became the most memorable of The Ventures albums, capturing the imagination of all who heard it. Among other celebrities, Keith Moon, the zany drummer of The WHO, stated this to be one of his all-time favorite albums. The liner notes expounded the fact that only musical instruments were used for the sound effects. When Bob Reisdorff was asked about this, he proudly replied; "That is absolutely correct. I've been asked if there was a theremin used, and I always answer that it was the steel guitar of Red Rhodes that made that sound."

The theremin, often heard in science-fiction movie soundtracks, could be called an early synthesizer, worked by moving one's hands above two antennae to control pitch and volume. Nokie's guitar was responsible for several other sounds on the album, including the "creaking door" produced by slowly scratching a muted string with the edge of a plectrum. Nokie recalls this as the time he began using a small box built by Red Rhodes called a compressor, which regulated peaks in the guitar's volume.

When record buyers finished gazing at the intriguing hot-rod cover-photo overlooking Los Angeles at night, they had their first look at the Mosrite guitars pictured on the back. A note at the bottom offered further information from Mosrite Distributing. In spite of the action shot of The Ventures being black and white and not showing the guitars very well, over 3,000 letters poured in from fans and music stores, asking for brochures. By year-end, Mosrite Distributing was swamped with orders for the $400(U.S.) guitar. A Ventures Model bass was offered for ninety dollars less. A full color leaflet was also sent to fan club members around the world, picturing The Ventures with the guitars. A larger picture of the sunburst finished model was a sight to behold with the gorgeous curves of the body and pickguard plus The Ventures logo on the headstock. The instrument came with a padded white leather strap, two vibrato springs (for regular and light gauge strings), and was shipped in a deluxe hard-shell case.

So many people pronounced it "Moss-rite" instead of the correct "Moze-rite" that Semie (at Don Wilson's suggestion) soon placed a dash over the "o" in the company logo.

As Stan Wagner recalls, every opportunity was taken to promote the Mosrite; "During one tour, I took Nokie around to the music stores in every city we hit. The kids were wide-eyed when they saw him and were allowed to hold the guitar that he played, especially when they found that they could wrap their fingers around the neck so easily. The dealers saw that we were onto something, and we got orders of five to eight guitars from twenty-five of the twenty-six stores we visited. We got an order of fifty guitars from a store in New York. By the end of 1965, it seemed that everyone in Japan wanted a Mosrite, so we set up a distributorship through Yamaha. The duties and tariffs were terrible then, but we still sold a lot. Before long, we were selling unbreakable Ventures/Mosrite guitar picks and Ventures-Mosrite strings."

Forty years later, the obsession to own a sixties Mosrite guitar remained in the hearts of thousands of Ventures fans around the world.

June 20, 1964

NO CONTEST

Stan Wagner was a man with many ideas. Soon there was a series of Ventures music books, record discounts to fan club members, and even a contest for composing instrumental songs submitted on demo tapes. The winner would get Don or Bob's Fender Jazzmaster plus his winning song recorded by The Ventures, and a contract to write more tunes for them. Second to fourth runners up would win a quantity of albums, as would winners of an essay contest about their favorite Ventures recording. While the club bulletin indicated both contests as being exclusive to its members, a three-page spread in April's "Special Beatles Issue" of DIG also invited entries.

As no further mention was made in fan club periodicals, members assumed that no prizes were awarded because contest entries were few and inferior. The fact revealed later was that Don and Bob never heard about the contest until years later, after Stan Wagner had become disassociated with them. Don's Jazzmaster could have been won, but Bob had already given his to a close friend, Lynn Kienle. Lynn often said he would never part with it, and decades later, he still had not.

The Ventures appeared on a single in late 1963 that was not a big hit, but is quite a collector's item. Still yearning to make records, Judd Hamilton recorded an up-tempo doo-wop version of Johnny Mercer's sleepy *Dream* with backing by The Ventures. The flip side carried Judd's own teenage-lament, *Your Only Boy*. For background vocals, he commandeered Gary Paxton and friends, known as the Hollywood Argyles of *Alley Oop* fame. Judd knew these singers through his friendship with Mel Taylor, and in turn, Mel's brother, Larry. The recording, now very rare, was released on Dolton 80.

The band closed out the year with a trip to Hawaii just after Christmas for a concert in Honolulu's Civic Auditorium. Milton Soong, a fourteen year-old Ventures fan in 1961, was in attendance; "I remember being surprised to see The Ventures not playing Fender guitars. They were playing Mosrites and there were Mosrite posters all over the auditorium. During the breaks, radio station KORL [later owned and managed by Pat O'Day], sponsored a Battle of the Bands among local high-school groups with The Ventures acting as judges. Most of the bands played Ventures and surf tunes. I was interested in the fuzz box that Nokie used. It was just a plain metal box that appeared to be homemade, but it sure sounded good."

Later that year, The Ventures went along with another of Stan Wagner's ideas. The plan was to train the fellows to gyrate around the stage in time with their music.

Stan hired choreographer Tony Monaco to work with the group for about one month until they could do several dances while playing.

The next live job happened to be a concert shared with the Beach Boys at the Anaheim Convention Center near Disneyland. After the show, the guys felt embarrassed by their choreographed act, and they vowed never to do it again. Around this time, The Ventures discovered their *In Space* album to be rising towards its peak of 27 during an eighteen week ride on the Top 100 Chart.

Early in 1964, Stan Wagner witnessed a side of The Ventures that he had not seen before. When he heard Don's uncanny Walter Brennan impersonation, he quickly asked for more. A comedy writer and promoter himself, Wagner insisted on recording Don's version of *(Gul Durn It) What'd I Say*, and he actually sat down with the group to compose *T'ain't Funny* for the flip side [Imperial 66038].

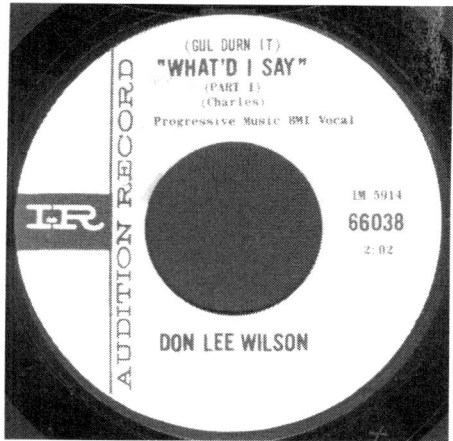

As the sole owner of Liberty Records, Al Bennett began acquiring other labels, the first of which was Imperial with its artists such as Johnny Rivers, Rick Nelson, and Fats Domino. In May of 1964, Imperial added Don Wilson. Not overly fond of "Leroy," and considering it unsuitable for a pop recording artist, Don now recorded as *Don Lee Wilson*. A year later, he moved to the parent label, Liberty, releasing his rendition of *Feel So Fine* in Japan. Below is a chronology of the Don Wilson singles, the first entry being released under the name, Don Dixon.

Cry of the Wild Goose/For Your Love	Blue Horizon	6051	1961
The Twomp / Heart On My Sleeve	Blue Horizon	6054	1961
Angel / Forever and Ever	Unity	CP-2117	1962
T'ain't Funny / What'd I Say	Imperial	66038	1964
Angel / Tell Laura I Love Her	Imperial	66064	1964
Feel So Fine / Angel	Imperial	66091	1965
Feel So Fine / Angel	Liberty-Japan	LR-1436	1965
No Matter What Shape / Angel	Liberty	55862	1966
Don't Avoid Me / Angel	Liberty	55872	1966
Don't Avoid Me / Sally	Liberty	55890	1966
Sally / Kiss Tomorrow Goodbye	Liberty	55946	1967
Behind Stained Glass Windows/Hey There Sunshine	Liberty	55991	1967
Seattle In The Rain / How Can I Help You Girl	L&M	WO-100	1968
Tell Laura I Love Her / Bad Boy	Tridex	101	1981

Note: Don originally recorded *Feel So Fine* at Western Recorders on Bob's UNITY RECORDS label.

In addition to the scarce American releases, many of Don's vocals appeared on Japanese singles in the 1960s and '70s. Always sheathed in a picture sleeve, the Japan singles were also considered valuable to collectors. More of Don's rarities include acetate pressings of songs like *Kentucky Waltz*, *Remember Me*, and a favorite of Josie's, *You'll Never Walk Alone*. Through the kindness of Don, this music and more became available on special cassette tapes sold in support of the band's fan clubs.

GOODBYE BOB – HELLO DICK

Having sold his Dolton label and The Ventures' contract, Bob Reisdorff now pursued other interests. It seems that he had become disillusioned with the recording business; "I was aware of considerable dishonesty in the business, with things going on like royalty skimming and I wanted no part of anything like that. For the next couple of years I wrote a book called *Crossing the Rapids*, but I never got it published." For his replacement, Reisdorff advised Al Bennett that his friend and co-worker, Dick Glasser would be an excellent choice to manage the Dolton division.

As head of publishing for Liberty, twenty-seven-year-old Dick Glasser was also a talented producer, singer, and songwriter that had recorded under the pen name of "Dick Lory" on various labels throughout the fifties, as well as seven singles on Liberty.

Dick Glasser

Jan Davis

Dick was also a guitarist, and having received royalties for a couple of his songs recorded by The Ventures, he was more than willing to produce the band. In the eighteen months he spent at the job, Dick produced four marvelous Ventures albums. The first of these was called *The Fabulous Ventures* [Dolton BST-8029], which was to contain an updated version of *Walk-Don't Run*. One of the best production ideas of the decade came from Dick Glasser after hiring saxophonist Steve Douglas for a part in the song. During the session, Glasser tried recording Steve's soprano saxophone through Leon Russell's rotating Leslie organ speaker. Listeners perceived it as an odd sounding organ until years later during interviews. When finished, the song was so good that Glasser decided to keep it off the album and release it as a summer single. Meanwhile, the effect of the sax through a Leslie organ speaker was used for another track titled *Walkin' with Pluto*, which *was* included on *The Fabulous Ventures* album.

In place of the new *Walk-Don't Run '64*, The Ventures did a perfect cover (complete with barking dogs) of *Fugitive*, an excellent instrumental recorded by Jan Davis. The tune was familiar to Mel Taylor, having recently played drums on the Davis release [A&M 733]. As Davis recalls, it was not Mel who brought the song to The Ventures; "Mel told me many times that he had protested The Ventures covering my *Fugitive*, but it was a decision made by Liberty and the group's producer. The actual 'Benedict Arnold' for that happening was my co-writer, Lou Josie, who was notorious for giving songs to other groups so as to benefit from royalties. He just didn't have faith in our product. It didn't do any good, however, as that was in 1964, when the Beatles emerged and the radio stations wouldn't play anything else. Mel also told me that Nokie had a helluva time mastering the lead on *Fugitive*. I'm sure that it was because I tune my guitar different, which made it a lot easier for me. I started playing as a kid when I found a guitar someone had thrown away and I didn't know how to tune it. I came up with a sort of Hawaiian tuning, and it stuck with me for the rest of my career. It's something like how Jimmy Rodgers played, and Dolly Parton plays with a similar tuning, but as far as I know, I'm the only one to ever play lead like that, especially on Classical and Flamenco music. The others just used it for rhythm."

Having just bought Liberty Records from Avnet Electronics for eight million dollars, Al Bennett may have simply been enjoying a power trip, but when he shunned *Walk-Don't Run '64* as having no sale ability, it was obvious to everyone that he had not learned anything from the 1960 experience. Dick Glasser finally convinced Bennett that *Walk-Don't Run '64* was worth a single release, so it hit the stores in June at almost the same time as *The Fabulous Ventures* LP. The single was an all-time smash hit, peaking at Number 8 in August. In Japan and Hong Kong, it shot up to Number 3. For the next four decades, the tune became an 'essential' at nearly every Ventures concert.

On the charts for nearly three months, *Walk-Don't Run '64* brought the band honors ranging from *Artist of the Week* at San Antonio radio KONO in August, to being videotaped for an episode of Dick Clark's *Where The Action Is*. Many musicians had released remakes of their hits, but none had ever made the Top Ten with *both* versions. Riding on the second wave of *Walk-Don't Run*, other guitarists such as Billy Strange and Glen Campbell quickly added versions of the hit to their own latest albums.

Unknown to most Ventures fans was an obscure single released in late 1964. Produced by Chet Atkins, composer/crooner Tommy Leonetti sang a pleasing version of *Walk-Don't Run* with lyrics by one Dottie Faye [RCA 47-8353].

~ ~ ~

The Ventures had the knack of covering a tune to make it their own, but one track became an amusement to fans when the facts surrounding its recording became known. Prior to this job, Dick Glasser had produced numerous demo records using singers Sharon Sheeley and Jackie DeShannon. Demo records are usually intended for use by known artists who will hopefully make hits of the songs, but some of Jackie's demos were so good that Dick released them on their own merit. *When You Walk In The Room* was one of these, and another was *Needles and Pins*. As Glasser now produced an instrumental group, a bizarre (if not slightly illegal) idea came to him. In place of Jackie's vocal track, Glasser recorded Nokie playing lead guitar over her taped accompaniment for *Needles and Pins*. The musicians were already paid for their work, but an alert union leader could easily have brought some trouble. Forty-one seconds into the opening track on *The Fabulous Ventures* album, Jackie's cry of "hey!" from her original record, emerged with nary a peep of objection from anyone.

Walk-Don't Run '64 inspired the title of the next album, *Walk, Don't Run Vol. 2* [Dolton BST-8031]. In a clever idea to "set the record straight," the band's first album cover was duplicated, this time showing the real Ventures on the cover. When someone suggested that Don's wife would be just as good as a hired model, Nancy agreed to pose. Murray Garrett and Gene Howard of Studio Five photographed Nancy first, and later shot The Ventures sprawled on the floor with their instruments.

Album content followed true to form, mixing covers of the hottest hits with several originals. Playing on the word "rhapsody," Nokie's Marksmen single, *Night Run* was freshly recorded and renamed *Rap City*. As stated earlier, the melody was derived from *Hungarian Dance No.5*, but the title of *Rap City*, was just too good to waste.

Embracing the invasion of British groups, a fine rendition of *House of the Rising Sun* opened *Walk, Don't Run Vol. 2*. Danny Hamilton's *Blue Coral*, now renamed *Diamond Head* followed. A Ventures original called *Pedal Pusher* demonstrated the guitarist's accessory volume-pedal, adapted from electronic organ technology. Again, Leon Russell's organ work embellished every track but two. Although session sheets reveal that Bob and Mel had recorded *Stranger on The Shore* and *Blue Star* in July of 1962, 'Sneaky' Pete Kleinow now added the sweet sound of his pedal-steel guitar on these and others for the new album. *Blue Star* had been a top hit for the Les Baxter Orchestra in 1955 when the song introduced weekly episodes of NBC TV's *Medic*. Delving into a Chet Atkins album from 1960 [*Teensville* – RCA- LSP 2161], the guys converted *One Mint Julep* to one of the most exciting rockers on *Walk-Don't Run Vol. 2*.

BURNING THE DRUMSTICKS AT BOTH ENDS

A session in January found Mel moonlighting for Buck Owens. After getting the top two spots in Billboard's Special Survey of Hot Country Singles, Owens used them for the title of an album; *Buck Owens - Together Again - My Heart Skips A Beat* [Capitol T 2135]. With six different drummers on the twelve tracks, Mel appeared more than the others, playing on *Together Again*, *My Heart Skips A Beat*, and *Ain't It Amazin' Gracie*.

Mel also found time to work with the Norm Raleigh Band at a country and western club called the Lazy X. Norm played bass beside Johnny Meeks on lead guitar, 'Sneaky' Pete Kleinow on steel, and Al Harris on Piano.

As shown in this 1964 poster, Mel drummed for the Norm Raleigh Band, The Ventures, and about thirty other acts at two giant benefit concerts for ex-Cricket, Jerry Naylor. As Jerry's life was in jeopardy with heart problems, the music community rallied to raise funds for medical treatment. Included on the roster were the likes of Jan and Dean, Roger Miller, and Glen Campbell, along with various country stars. From that show, Bob Bogle recalls his impression of another budding guitarist; "Roy Clark was fairly unknown then, and I was amazed at his talent. He was a good singer, but it was his guitar work that was fascinating. I told myself that this guy was going to be famous!"

Naylor recovered and stayed active in music for over forty years. As Ventures tours became longer and more frequent, Mel quit the Norm Raleigh band, but he still found time to squeeze in some "extra-curricular" activities. When he left the Raleigh band, he was replaced by Dewey Martin, known later as the drummer in Buffalo Springfield.

In July, The Ventures exhibited Mosrite guitars at the National Association of Music Merchants [NAMM] trade show in Chicago. Later, on July 29th, the guys caught their TV performance of *Walk-Don't Run '64* on ABC s Sam Riddle Show.

Mel, Nancy Messenger, and Stan Wagner at the Chicago Hilton

The first edition of *Walk, Don't Run Vol. 2* in both America *and* Japan became an odd item for the discerning collector because of an oversight in the cover photo. The picture showed a perspiration blotch under the right arm of Don Wilson's t-shirt as he held his guitar above his head. The haste in releasing Ventures albums allowed the flaw to until the second printing. Some fans joked that Don may have been in a sweat over the beautiful model posing in front of the band. This may have been the case, although Don and Nancy Bacon had met in 1963 and were soon married.

According to Don, the perspiration blotch was not the only problem with the cover art on *Walk, Don't Run Vol. 2*; "When I saw all that eye-makeup and heavy lipstick, I couldn't believe it. They made her look like a streetwalker! An original proof from that photo session is not even close to the album cover, but that's marketing for you."

The "perspiration" cover issue   The "real" Nancy Bacon

As one of The Ventures' most requested songs, *Diamond Head* warranted a single release [Dolton 303]. Peaking at 70 in America, it topped the charts in Japan and became a hit around the globe in countries as unlikely as Iran, where it shared vinyl terrain with The Beatles on an EP recording. When the royalties began pouring in, Danny Hamilton was inspired to write even more for The Ventures. A list of those chosen includes *Escape* (originally titled *Target*), *Wild and Wooly*, *Kandy Koncoctions*, *The Gallop* and *No Exit*, the latter appearing on a Mel Taylor solo project. Danny also wrote an instrumental entitled *Run, Don't Walk*, which, although pleasing to the ear and registered with BMI, never made it past the acetate demo stage.

While *Diamond Head* was The Ventures' nineteenth single in the States, the few singles released in Japan attracted little attention until *Diamond Head*. When it became Japan's first million-seller, Mr. Tats Nagashima sprang into action. Contacting Stan Wagner, he booked a ten-day tour in the coming New Year for The Ventures and The Astronauts, a Colorado group that made the Top 100 in 1963 with *Baja* [RCA 8194]. Picking up on the Japanese electric guitar craze, RCA had released four Astronauts albums and a half-dozen singles in that country.

Diamond Head sold an historic 1,850,000 copies in Japan, to the delight of The Ventures and, of course, Danny Hamilton. While brother Judd had found an affordable apartment in Hollywood, young Danny soon owned a home in the San Fernando Valley.

Based on growing sales in the Orient, Liberty/Dolton had already planned on having The Ventures record some popular Japanese songs to market there in the coming year. With news of a Japan trip, this idea was pushed to the fore with Dick Glasser stretching the one-week schedule into ten days and arranging for studio sessions at Toshiba Records in Tokyo. Airline reservations for early January of 1965 were confirmed, and for the time being, all seemed well.

While Dick Glasser enjoyed success with The Ventures, he admitted that the group did much of its own producing, referring in point to one of their all-time favorite hits. Extracting from Rodgers and Hart's 1936 Broadway musical *On Your Toes* (popularized in 1952 by the Ray Anthony Orchestra), Dick and The Ventures arranged the theme to fit the group's unique style. Amid the near classical melody, the soprano sax of Steve Douglas was again heard through a Leslie organ speaker. It was more easily detected this time, as the recording also included Leon Russell on a genuine organ. The result thrilled listeners beyond anything previously heard from the band, one fan being fourteen-year-old Tom Petty in Florida. Thirty-three years later, he and his band, The Heartbreakers were still playing The Ventures' arrangement of *Slaughter on Tenth Avenue* for enthusiastic crowds at San Francisco's Fillmore West.

As *Slaughter on Tenth Avenue* [Dolton 300] climbed to 35, Dick Clark signed The Ventures for another TV appearance. Having moved the show to Los Angeles made it convenient for the band to tape "Slaughter" and *Walk-Don't Run '64* for the September 26 episode of American Bandstand. The two hits also put The Ventures on an all-star tour in October. Titled *The Johnny Rivers Memphis Special*, it also featured Ronnie and the Daytonas [*Little G.T.O.*], and Chad and Jeremy [*A Summer Song*].

Don's absence on this tour provided a break for Danny Hamilton, now eighteen and able to fill in on rhythm guitar. As Bob Bogle reflects, the tour was unique for another reason; "That was the only time we ever toured the U.S. by bus. It was a chartered Greyhound with no washroom, kitchen facilities, or sleepers like the big touring coaches nowadays. The only extra we got was a bus driver. On that tour, we found out that there really wasn't a Ronnie in The Daytonas. It was a make-up group, put together by a record company. We let them use our Mosrites for part of the tour. One of our stops was in Lake Charles, Louisiana, and that's where Danny Hamilton met a very pretty girl. It wasn't long before they were married." To this, Don adds; "The last show of that tour was at San Bernardino, so I drove up to see how Danny was doing in my place. He did a great job. I ended up sitting in at the autograph session afterwards, which is why some albums and other items out there were signed by both Danny *and* me."

For Stan Wagner and The Ventures, the success Mosrite seemed almost too good to be true, probably, as Bob recalls, because it really *was* too good to be true; "After Mosrite Distributing was fairly well established and we were selling about five-hundred guitars a month, Semie told us that he wasn't realizing enough profit. We said that we weren't either, but there wasn't anything that we could do about it. He said, 'Yes, you can raise the price of the guitar.' We felt it was unwise to put our price higher than Fender, which was far more established in the business than us. Semie then reminded us that we were under a 'perpetual contract' for product distribution, so it was not legal and binding. Therefore, we would simply have to pay more towards his profit, either by raising the price or by absorbing the loss. Stan and the others decided to go along with Semie, but I said we should abandon the whole thing and let Semie carry on by himself. The final result was that they bought me out. I played the instruments for another five years, but I was no longer part of the Mosrite operation."

In the fall of '64, Stan Wagner launched another contest. This time, the prizes were three Ventures model Mosrite guitars. When the contest ended in November, winners announced to the fan club were Dennis Richards of Inglewood, California, Mike Rogala of Syracuse, New York, and Bob Cancasci of Cleveland, Ohio.

Although the "British Invasion" was well underway in 1964, any Ventures fan can testify that North American music stores now stocked the complete catalog of Ventures albums in both mono and stereo. Years later, experts explained this phenomenon by revealing that the UK groups did not affect record sales of The Ventures or any of the Liberty artists like Bobby Vee, Jan and Dean, or Rick Nelson. Instead, the invaders provided new cover material for the established musicians, while crowding out numerous new artists from breaking onto the pop charts.

Near the end of 1964, recording began for the *Ventures Knock Me Out!* [BST-8033]. Amid covers of Everlys, Orbison, and Coasters hits, (plus four originals), the group delivered stinging versions of Manfred Mann's *Sha La La*, and The Zombies' *She's Not There*, both from the UK. In fact, the first sound heard on *Knock Me Out* is that of The Beatles. Again, Dick Glasser dared to clip from another artist's work; this time from the "fab four's" *I Feel Fine*. The song opens with a six-second bass note expanding into feedback that was apparently difficult to mimic, so Glasser had his engineer lift the intro from the original, shorten it to four seconds and splice it in front of The Ventures' version of *I Feel Fine*. Reflecting on this ploy, Don uttered; "Who knows? Maybe we were the first to use the process now known in the music business as 'sampling'."

The Ventures' original *Bird Rockers* was chosen from the album for a single release, backed with a rocked up *Stranger in Paradise*, the giant hit for crooner Tony Bennett back in 1953. On Dolton 308, The Ventures called it *Ten Seconds to Heaven*, but this version appeared in other parts of the world as *The Stranger* [Liberty 308]. Instrumental fans in the United Kingdom were particularly surprised to hear this release, as their countrymen, The Shadows, had recorded their own original entitled *The Stranger* back in 1960, comprised of a totally different melody.

Appearing in India on Liberty 308, *The Stranger* became a rare collector's item due to its 78-RPM format. While the heavy ten-inch platters had become a scratchy memory in most of the world, the number of wind-up phonographs still used in some countries enticed a few record companies to prolong the format. Well over two-dozen different Ventures 78 recordings are known to exist in the Philippines, along with some in India, South America, and South Africa.

~ ~ ~

Having bought a beautiful new home in Encino, Bob now had room for guests. He remembers one being special; "Sometimes the Jacinto family from the Philippines would be in the USA on business. On one occasion, Ramon stayed with me for a week while his parents were in Washington D.C. for a conference with the President. As Ramon still had his rock 'n' roll radio station, he wanted to shop for records, so I offered to chauffeur him around Los Angeles. Fernando, his father, left Ramon the sum of $5000 to do his shopping. After about three days, I got a call from Fernando asking how things were going with his son. When I said everything was fine, he asked to speak to Ramon. The next thing I heard was Ramon saying, 'Well, I'm getting pretty low again. Can you send me another five thousand?' Ramon asked me for my bank account number, and the next morning there was a deposit for five grand. By the time his folks arrived to pick him up, Ramon had spent $10,000 in just one week!"

By 1965, Ramon was twenty years old with a degree in economics and studying law at night school while managing over 2000 employees at one of his father's steel mills. During the years that followed, severe turmoil transpired in his country, but as we shall see, Ramon Jacinto was an amazing survivor, and a dedicated fan of The Ventures.

VENTURE-MANIA

By the end of 1964, The Ventures enjoyed "rock star" status, but as always, remained humble, hard working, and unassuming. Always looking to better themselves, their stage show continuously improved. Mel's drum solo became longer and was highlighted by beating on the low string of the bass while Bob fingered a little tune on the frets. This always brought a nice round of applause before Nokie resumed a flashy new version of *Caravan*. The arrangement had been heard on *Bobby Vee Meets The Ventures*, but had grown in length and excitement. There had been no thought of treating record buyers to such a long track until a call came from Toshiba Musical Industries. Their manager for Western-World Music had completed a schedule for The Ventures' 1965 visit to Japan, but due to the number of shows, there would be no time for studio recording. As 1965 approached, Capitol Records was enjoying success with its "live" recording of the Beach Boys, As such; Mr. Futara asked if Liberty would allow Toshiba to record The Ventures for a similar project. After discussions with Dick Glasser and Al Bennett, Stan Wagner told Futara that they had never considered a live album, but that it was a great idea. Toshiba agreed to record *The Ventures In Japan,* with Liberty covering all of the costs while reserving the right to edit the tapes before Toshiba began pressing. In return, Liberty would receive royalties from Toshiba for album sales while retaining all performance rights. Futara agreed, but then informed Wagner of a vigorous campaign to have the electric guitar banned in Japan in fear of its children becoming dropouts and delinquents. If the crusade were successful, the Government of Japan would likely prohibit The Ventures' tour. However, a few days before Christmas, word arrived from Tats Nagashima that a counter movement had extinguished the campaign. Japan's young people had endured the banning of their music in many of the schools, but when radio, television, and stage performances were attacked, they raised a terrible fuss. Topping off the good news, Nagashima informed The Ventures that tickets were nearly sold out for the three days of extra performances. While Don, Bob, Nokie, and Mel along with Stan Wagner, prepared to leave for Japan, *The Ventures Knock Me Out!* was being pressed in the hundreds of thousands

"Caravan" on Prom Night in Fresno, CA   *George B. Feist*

Before 1965 was one day old, The Ventures were on a Pan American Airways flight to Tokyo to play fourteen concerts in ten days. Their equipment consisted of guitars, drums, and three large Fender amplifiers. Many articles and interviews have told of the huge crowd waiting at Tokyo International Airport. The band had no idea of Japan's enthusiasm for their recent records. For the group's newest member, this phenomenon remained vivid in Mel's mind for the next thirty years; "At first, we looked around at the other passengers, wondering if we hadn't noticed Japan's Emperor or a movie star who was on board. As the plane came to rest, we were amazed to see banners waving that said, 'Welcome Ventures' or 'Ventures Ichiban!' [Number One!] I actually had goose bumps! We'd been flying for hours, and we were all pretty tired, but the sight of that crowd really energized us."

On the ground, the furor resembled the "Beatle-mania" newscasts that the guys had seen on television. The noisy fans pushed against the security guards, hoping for autographs or just an up-close look at the guitar band from Hollywood. The Ventures found it a little frightening until they were safely inside a waiting limousine. On the way to the city, they learned from their hosts that every performance for the duration of their stay had sold-out in advance.

Arriving at the hotel, the bedlam resumed. Still in shock, the group was impressed to see an elaborate, twenty-page souvenir program for their ten-day tour. Nothing quite so grand was printed at home for any rock 'n' roll extravaganza. In addition to several photos and a schedule of their fourteen concerts, the booklet included a discography of

The Ventures' record releases in Japan. Other pages were dedicated to The Astronauts and the Japanese groups that would open each show.

The Tokyo shows opened with a Japanese vocal quartet called The Johnnys, followed by Terry and The Blue Jeans, a group of three guitars, keyboard, bass, and drums backing vocalist, Yuya Uchida. Lead guitarist "Terry" was actually twenty-five-year-old Takeshi Terauchi, Japan's premier guitarist whose own life story would likely make a fascinating book. At age four or five, Takeshi was forced to practice Japan's three-stringed shamisen until his fingers bled and the bones of his fingertips became visible. As he grew older, he took up classical guitar and Japanese folk (known as minyo music), but to the horror of his wealthy father, the boy became obsessed with the *electric* guitar. Before he was ten years old, young Takeshi fashioned a pickup from a telephone receiver and played his guitar over a public address system. He had no idea that he was duplicating the exact experiment America's Les Paul had performed years earlier, leading to development of the electric guitar.

Terauchi's father tried frantically to avert his son from taking up the "eleki" guitar. In exchange for Takeshi's promise to stick to classical guitar, Terauchi senior went so far as to build a college nearby so the boy would not have to leave home for his education. When Takeshi finally broke the promise, the college was immediately bulldozed into the ground. It was the mid-fifties when Takeshi began earning a living as a country picker with Jimmy Tokita and the Mountain Playboys led by singer Keiichi Teramoto, who had by this time appeared on America's Grand Ole Opry. As The Ventures' music penetrated the country, Takeshi founded Terry and the Blue Jeans and began to play rock and roll. In 1964, they released Japan's first surf music album, *Korezo Surfing* (This Is Surfing). Not long after, they recorded a three-disc set entitled *The Blue Jeans Go To The Ventures Melodies*. Terry eventually became a star solo performer in his country. Displaying a strong Nokie Edwards influence, he also played amazing arrangements in his own unique style.

In the distant future, Takeshi Terauchi and Yuya Uchida would become involved with The Ventures, but for now they were just part of an opening act. Takeshi was mesmerized by the band's wonderful guitars, and amazed at the skill of Nokie Edwards. He never learned to speak much English, but with the help of an interpreter, became a good friend of the group. From then on, they always called him Terry.

The Ventures only used their Fender amplifiers for the first concert. The units had sounded good during the sound check rehearsal, but were found to significantly distort when played at concert level. The reason for this became apparent when the guys learned that the AC line voltage in Japan was a nominal 100 volts, fifteen percent lower than in America. Guyatone representatives, having placed a full-page ad in the tour book for their Japan-made equipment, were more than happy to supply replacement amps to further promote their product for the rest of the tour. Several models were tried for Bob's bass before settling on the GA-1200 stereo model with two large seventy-watt speaker cabinets. Nokie and Don chose the two-piece GA-950, similar in style to their Fender Showman units. In time, however, the Guyatone amps became somewhat unreliable under the strain of touring. Occasionally one would cut out or start crackling in the middle of a song. When this happened, Bob or Don cured it temporarily with a sharp kick. At the next opportunity, a road technician quickly exchanged the amplifier.

For a Master of Ceremonies, Toshiba engaged Mr. Bing Concepcion, a multi-lingual Filipino nightclub MC with a great sense of humor. Of thirteen scheduled concerts, nine were in Tokyo and three were in nearby Yokohama, Nagoya, and Osaka. Following the first concert on January 3rd, a second concert took place in a large wrestling arena called the Riki Sports Palace. When the seats were filled, the floor area was opened and hundreds of young people rushed into the standing area. The staff had set up a barrier of chairs in front of the stage, but as the crowd pressed forward, the barrier began to move. Staff members tried to hold the chairs steady, but the pressure soon caused the line to inch forward. As the performers watched, they wondered what would happen if the crowd broke through. Fortunately, the line held. After a successful concert, Nokie often remarked "We got 'em," but on this occasion, Mel Taylor replied; "Yeah, we got 'em, Nokie, but for a while there, I thought they were gonna get us!"

It wasn't long before they did "get them," and they tore Nokie's jacket to shreds. Stan Wagner recalls a time when they got Mel; "After one concert, there was a huge crowd outside and our limousine was waiting about thirty feet from the door. As Nokie, Don, and Bob fought their way through the crowd of kids, they opened a path between to the limo. As Mel hesitated, I told him to walk, don't run, and stop every few steps to bow, first left and then right. He said 'They'll kill me!' I said 'No Mel, they won't touch you.' He did as I said and it worked until about six feet from the car, he broke into a run and the kids leaped at him. When he got inside and closed the door, he found that one of his boots had been yanked right off his foot! I have to admit, that trip was almost an ego trip for me as well. I was never molested, but as the group's manager, I was highly respected and asked several times for my autograph."

On stage in January 1965 with one Fender and two Guyatone amps

M. C. Bing Concepcion

One night before The Ventures went on stage, three young men appeared at their dressing room. Introducing themselves as Mr. Shigehara, Mr. Goto, and Mr. Taguchi, they expressed their desire to purchase the band's Mosrite guitars. At first, the band was suspicious, but with Bing Concepcion's help, they learned that the boys were students who had a band called the Beatniks. It was a bold and clever proposition, and if The Ventures agreed to sell, these beautiful new guitars would be the first Mosrites to be owned by a Japanese band. A deal was set for Haneda, Tokyo's International Airport in about a week. As it turned out, selling the guitars reduced the amount of equipment to be shipped, declared, and inspected when the group returned to the States.

A few days later, more musicians came to the dressing room to ask how Nokie was able to play such extreme string bending licks as seen in several songs. As usual, Bing Concepcion was available for translation duties before and after the concerts. Nokie demonstrated for Narumo-san, and Tsutsumi-san, who were totally in awe of the light-gauge strings on Nokie's guitar. Such strings being yet unavailable in Japan, the two fans were immediately presented with sets as gifts from The Ventures. The boys also wondered about Nokie's strange sounding "behind the bridge" solo in *Bulldog*. Nokie related having first used the technique to open *Pink Panther* and *War of the Satellites*, explaining how this only worked well on a Mosrite guitar with its specially designed tailpiece. In the years to come, the two Japanese fans became well-known Ventures imitators, as they formed bands called The Fingers and The Planets.

During negotiations with Toshiba to record a couple of the Tokyo performances, Mr. Futara was surprised that Mel Taylor represented The Ventures, as Stan Wagner had done most of the talking so far. The men were delighted when Mel agreed to most of their requests until they asked for *Diamond Head*. Although a huge hit in Japan, it had not been heard at any of the concerts so far. Mel explained that they had not played the song on stage, and would need some time to add it to their play list. The Toshiba men still reported The Ventures to be easier to work with than some foreign acts, referring to a scene that Eddie King of King Records had experienced earlier when singers Peter and Gordon [*A World Without Love*] had embarrassed everyone by acting rudely, and loudly dispensing orders.

Two Ventures concerts were recorded using three Sony 37A microphones on high stands feeding a three-channel Ampex. Two gray Guyatone GA-950 amps were set up for Nokie beside a beige one for Don. For Bob used an improved GA-1200, its power head bridged across twin speaker cabinets. Unlike Fender, the Guya amps were not equipped with tilt-back legs for large venues. At one concert, Nokie placed his GA-950 on a chair and tilted it back. At the next show, he and Don were provided with concrete blocks to hold their amps in a tilted position.

GA-950 Guitar Amp   **Guyatone**   GA-1200 Bass Amp

To some, Mel appeared to be seated on a tom-tom drum, as he was given a combination drum-stool and accessory case that closely matched his drums. This "canister throne" harkened back to the days of big band drummers like Gene Krupa and Buddy Rich.

A recent innovation for musicians was the cable curled in the style of a telephone handset cord. The "curly cord" eliminated the guitarist's worry of tangling and damage from being stepped on, but like an over-stretched telephone cord, eventually a wire could break. On January 8, during the recording of *Driving Guitars*, Don suddenly had no sound. He called out the stage technician, who quickly investigated. As Bing Concepcion conveyed a problem with Don's equipment to the audience, the technician pinpointed the bad cord. Jokingly, the M.C. alleged that a Japan-made cord would have been better; " .... dynamic amplifier Guyatone, shin-hatsubai! Oh, cord is bad! America no cord damé, Nihon no cord, ichiban!"

In translation, first an excuse; "Guyatone amplifier is new-product being sold." Then, after the bad cord is found; "Cord from America no good. Japanese cord is number one!" This brought a hearty laugh from the audience. In reality, the American cords were of top quality, but as our heroes often found, even the best equipment could be a source of embarrassment.

Following the concert at Sapporo's Citizen Hall on January 13, The Ventures headed home (minus the guitars sold to the Beatniks). Outside every venue they had been swarmed with autograph hunters, had their clothing ripped and buttons pulled off, had their hair pulled and nearly been suffocated. In addition, Japan had experienced a problem with cockroaches that year; so much so that as hotel guests, The Ventures had been supplied with complementary bug-spray. Although a grueling schedule of three shows a day (Don says; "One day we did five!"), left the guys exhausted, they remained elated and also amazed that Japan was already waiting for their return.

Within a few days, the concert tapes were sent to Liberty for editing while Toshiba selected a jacket photo from several taken at a session in front of Hie Jingu shrine in the Akasaka section of Tokyo. A light snowfall had begun, but it didn't stop a traditionally kimono-clad model from posing with the band.

In a few weeks, Japanese fans were enjoying the ten-track *Ventures In Japan* LP. If ten tracks sound like a puny album, keep in mind that the opener was a clever medley of three early singles as the guys endeavored to add more songs to their concerts without dropping the three compulsory favorites *Walk-Don't Run*, *Perfidia*, and *Lullaby of the Leaves*. This "Ventures Medley" became a trademark concert favorite for the group's entire career. In addition, the stunning encore of *Caravan* featured Mel's dynamic drum solo, extending the track to nearly eight minutes. With member introductions and liberal kidding around by Bing Concepcion, the album's total time filled a respectable thirty-five minutes.

LIBERTY DOES THE HANKY PANKY

Arriving home, The Ventures found an invitation to appear on ABC Television's *SHINDIG!* From 1964 to 1966 the Hollywood teen-hop musical variety show played host weekly to acts ranging from Louis Armstrong to The Beatles and Rolling Stones. The in-house band, known as The Shindogs, had displayed early young talents such as Glen Campbell, Leon Russell, Billy Preston, Delaney Bramlett, and James Burton.

On February 3, host Jimmy O'Neill announced that The Ventures would appear the following week. Sure enough, a week later, which happened to be Don Wilson's 32nd birthday, guitar bands across the continent gathered in front of the TV to watch The Ventures play *Diamond Head* and *Caravan*. The band played pearl-white Mosrites, which, for some reason, did not carry the "Ventures Model" logo. Pat and Lolly Vegas were also on this show, and were delighted when Bob and Don lent them their sparkling new Mosrites to play of *La Bamba* and *Write Me, Baby*.

The Vegas Brothers on SHINDIG!

At the end of March, a statistic was published that made the band humbly pleased and equally amazed. Gilbert Youth Research of New York had polled the America's young people, the results of which put The Ventures ahead of the Beach Boys and second only to The Beatles as the most popular musical group. Although it is hard to imagine our boys ranking that close to the Beatles, they would soon achieve even more remarkable statistics regarding Britain's top group.

Also in March, Dick Glasser decided to bring a "live" Ventures record to the rest of the world, albeit with a bit of skullduggery. In keeping with live TV performances, particularly those of The Beatles, heavy crowd noise was a must. With some tape-loop engineering magic, fake announcers and screaming females were applied to each track. Glasser presented side one of *The Ventures On Stage* [Dolton BST-8035] as a Japan concert, while side two contained tracks purported to originate in the UK. Recalling that week at Western Recorders, Bob iterates; "They told us to come in and cut loose on our songs as if we were doing a concert. We weren't sure what was happening, but when we saw what they did, we were not thrilled at all." Don adds; "That's one album we are still a bit embarrassed over. It seems there was always some guy in a suit with a great idea for us. We were sort of naive and we did whatever they suggested. We were fairly upset when they put that thing out while we were on the road without even discussing it with us or letting us hear what they'd done."

When rumors of the deception leaked out, the "Japan performance" was still thought to be authentic because of the dialog between the band and M.C. Bing Concepcion, as well as his introduction of the numbers. However, in years to follow, not only did the session sheets reveal the entire album to be a studio project, several of the clean, unaltered tracks appeared later for all to enjoy in the fourth disc of the CD series, *The Ventures in The Vaults* [Ace CDCHD 1176].

The crowning glory of *The Ventures On Stage* was *Caravan*. The frantic tempo of the new arrangement was filled with blistering guitar licks played at blinding speed by Nokie until Mel began a lengthy drum solo and his intricate bass tattoo. The version was such a crowd-pleaser that it permanently remained as The Ventures' closing number.

Many fans were not fooled by the LP's canned applause containing certain sounds at regular intervals. Even the authentic "Japan side" contained an incessant whistle from the audience at exact two-second intervals. However, although repeated listening confirmed suspicions of tape-looped crowd noise, the music was so exciting that the album remained a favorite for over forty years. At the time of its release, it showed the world how Mel Taylor really played *Wipe Out*, inspiring thousands of young drummers to play it "Ventures style." The track also raised even more suspicion regarding who played *Wipe Out* on the *Let's Go!* album.

Peaking at 27 in Billboard's album chart, *On Stage* was soon a worldwide hit capturing the imagination of nearly every kid with a guitar or set of drums. Meanwhile, the Japanese agency was busy making arrangements for an additional five week tour.

~ ~ ~

Between their two visits to Japan, recording for an album was scheduled around Ventures concerts in California and a tour stretching east to the Great Lakes. In June, the band was in Texas for the annual Navy Relief Festival at Corpus Christi Naval Air Station. Don and Bob remember playing to nearly 4000 people from Friday to Sunday in a huge airplane hangar that was as hot as an oven. Adding a little variety, Don did his famous Walter Brennan impression.

A feature of that year's festival was an amateur talent contest. On Sunday evening, Don presented a glittering Mosrite guitar to the grand prize winner. Weeks later, the guys were surprised to receive Honorary Naval Aviator certificates for their generous work.

As avid Ventures fan Ken Dresher confirms, technical problems could surface just as easily on home turf; "I had been a Ventures fanatic for about two years when I heard about their 1965 July 1 concert at the Shrine Auditorium in Duluth, Minnesota. To get there, I rode with another fan for over a hundred miles on a scooter in the rain. Another friend arranged for us to sneak a reel-to-reel recorder under the stage in the afternoon. It was pretty impressive when The Ventures strode into that jam-packed hall in matching suits with their Mosrite guitars, but nothing compared to the thrill when they started playing. They started with *Walk-Don't Run* and it was loud! I get goose bumps just thinking about it. During their second set, they were pounding out *Bulldog* when the Fender Bassman amplifier went dead. As Don and Bob tried to locate the problem, Nokie and Mel played on as if nothing had happened. My friend and I were on pins and needles in fear of them finding our tape recorder, but they were only concerned with the amplifier. They couldn't make it work, so Bob played the rest of the show through a Bandmaster amp. It was weaker, but not that bad. We were just happy to hear them and have a tape to remember it by."

The 1965 U.S. summer tour marked the addition of Chuck Berry's *Johnny B. Goode* to Don's vocal repertoire, notable because Don has never [officially] recorded it. He eventually dropped the classic rocker from his song list, but as we shall see, it would return as part of The Ventures' act many times when sung by others.

Arriving home, the band learned that they were again without a producer. Having produced four smash albums for the group the period of a year, Dick Glasser had gained an impressive reputation within the recording industry. Citing Al Bennett as his mentor, Dick was ostensibly attached to Liberty, but not enough to prevent him from trying to better himself. When Warner Brothers asked him to head their A&R department, Dick had cleared out his desk before the end of June.

By now, Capitol Records producer Joe Saraceno's work was familiar to nearly everyone in the music business including the Liberty camp. Promotion head Bob Skaff quickly lured Joe to his staff, specifically to produce The Ventures. For Joe, it was a change to handle an established group that could do their own promotional touring.

GUITAR SCHOOL ON VINYL

Having started with Liberty in the 1950s as head of promotion, Don Blocker was now the vice president. Shortly after Dick Glasser left, Wilbur M. Savidge, a major-appliance salesman from Santa Barbara was ushered into Blocker's office. Also a musician, Savidge had developed a guitar teaching system using recordings and fingering-diagrams that he called Guitar Phonics. Savidge deemed The Ventures to be the perfect vehicle to promote his system. Although Blocker was skeptical, Saraceno and The Ventures liked the idea and the project was launched. The result was better than anyone ever expected. *Play Guitar With The Ventures* [Dolton BLP-16501] was an contained four tunes played slow at first and then at normal tempo with lead, rhythm, or bass parts missing. Verbal instructions prompted the student throughout while playing his own guitar. A large book with fingering diagrams, chord charts, and photographs were part of the gatefold cover. Released in July, the instruction set surprised everyone when it made both Billboard and Cash Box's Top 100 charts in August as over 50,000 would-be Ventures learned to play *Walk-Don't Run, Raunchy, Tequila,* and *Memphis*. An instructional album on the charts was a first for any record company, prompting Don Blocker to wonder if there was a market for more such albums. To research the idea, the company added a questionnaire card to the next thousand copies distributed on the West Coast. Meanwhile, Toshiba licensed the album replacing the dialog with Japanese narration. They also issued *Play Guitar* singles, allowing players in Japan to learn *Pipeline* or *Out of Limits* at minimal expense.

The Ventures A Go-Go [Dolton BLP-8037] was the next Ventures album, and again it was a winner. Following their proven format, five sparkling originals were blended with six upcoming U.S. hits and *Satisfaction* from the Rolling Stones. As Leon Russell was no longer available, one Lincoln Mayorga filled in with exciting B-3 organ work. In 1960, this young session wizard had been part of a novelty instrumental group called The Piltdown Men that made the Billboard Hot 100 with *Brontosaurus Stomp*, and the UK Top 20 with *McDonald's Cave*.

When a harmonica player was needed for the bridge in The Ventures' version of *La Bamba*, Joe Saraceno engaged Tommy Morgan, who had worked in Hollywood since the fifties when he recorded with the Andrews Sisters. Morgan was no stranger to The Ventures, having worked under Bob Reisdorff on the Moon Stones single, *My True Love* plus an unreleased track called *Louisiana*.

Naming original tunes was much easier for The Ventures' twentieth album, simply by prefixing a word with the catch phrase, "A Go-Go." Thus, a tune formerly dubbed *Rim Shot* now became *A Go-Go Guitar*. Of special interest were two titles containing the exact same rhythm pattern and four-bar drum break. This led many listeners to believe that *Night Stick* and *A-Go-Go Dancer* were the same song, other than the former being led by the organ instead of the guitar. Some called the album unique for containing the same song twice, as they failed to distinguish between two completely different melodies.

ENCOR!

Having cut his relationship with Mosrite, Bob Bogle made plans to start a company that would build amplifiers as well as guitars. He began by visiting a small electronics factory in a Los Angeles suburb. Arriving at 7823 Deering Street in Canoga Park, Bob met Mr. George Faith, who was eager to undertake the project. Following negotiations, Bob named his product "Encor." In a few weeks, when it looked as if Encor Manufacturing would be in business by fall, they needed salesmen to solicit dealers to sell their amplifiers. As sales progressed, they would produce a radical new guitar design. Bob had designed a wedge shaped guitar which, when the neck was added, somewhat resembled a spade. He had showed a drawing to some of the Mosrite staff, but as he recalls; "They liked my design, but none of them were interested in building it." A preliminary brochure displayed two guitar models, mainly distinguished by their neck sizes. The Ocelot was for players having small to average sized hands, while the Marlin catered to players like Don with his larger hands. Also shown was the El Toro bass, unique in that it boasted a vibrato bar (erroneously tagged as "tremolo").

Meanwhile, having fallen on hard times, Judd Hamilton was in a desperate situation. Little Judd Jr. (or "Chip" as he was called) had caught pneumonia and very nearly died. With medical bills accumulating and another child on the way, Judd decided that parking cars would never support a family of four. As he recalls; "By then, The Ventures were so busy that I had lost track of Bob Bogle. Eventually, I heard about his guitar company and I hitchhiked out to the factory. Upon finding him, I asked if I could do anything around the place to make some money, even if it was janitor work. Bob said, 'Judd, your timing couldn't be better! I need another salesman and I think you would be a good one."

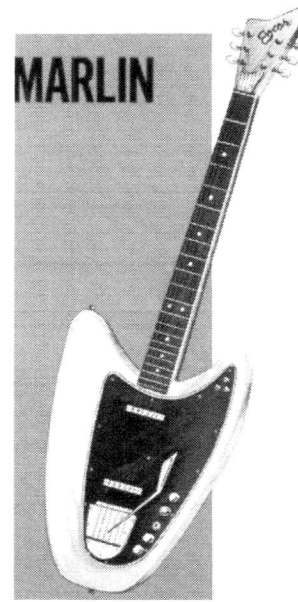

Designed especially for average to large size hands. Contoured solid body with advanced styling. Double deep cutaway. Adjustable truss-rod neck. Fast fingering for larger hands. 4-way adjustable bridge including tremolo (all in one unit). Tone controls (lead & rhythm) give wide variation of treble and bass.

Ultra-high-sensitive pick-ups with individual magnets. (Use either pick-up or both at the same time). Selector switches for activating or combining pick-ups. Attractive shell pick-guard, plated bridge section and rose wood fret board. Choice woods. Richly polished. Arctic Ice Blue, Pearl White, Mustang Red, Ebony Black, Sunburst, Candy Apple Red (metallic).

Bob Bogle's concept of an Encor model from the 1965 advertising brochure

During a recent return flight from the East Coast, The Ventures were waiting for a plane in Denver when Bob met with twenty-six-year-old Gordon Close, who taught guitar at a Denver music store. Gordon still recalls how Bob lured him away from over a hundred paying students; "I had talked with Bob before, as the store where I worked sold Mosrite guitars. Now, he was asking if I would be interested in working for him. It sounded really exciting, especially the Encor amplifier, which, instead of reverb springs, would employ a full-blown tape echo system. I got married soon after, and during our honeymoon we stopped in Los Angeles where I met George Faith for lunch. He painted a great picture of success, so I agreed to cover the Rocky Mountain area from Colorado into Utah and Wyoming. Later, a demonstration amp was sent and I began taking orders from music stores all through the West. The 'Waikiki' had a sixty-watt head and a separate speaker cabinet with two fifteen-inch speakers. With black vinyl covering and a silver grille cloth, it looked like a Bandmaster, but it had solid-state technology, which was fairly new at the time, and a distortion effect labeled 'Buzztone'. In the future, there was to be a hundred-watt model. I got a lot of orders because it was Bob Bogle's company, but the dealers were also intrigued with the innovative echo feature."

The Encor Waikiki

The Encor Newport

When factory had completed another Waikiki model, Bob gave one to Judd for use on the road. As Encor's West Coast spokesman, Judd recalls his assignment; "Bob took me outside behind the building where he had a four-door '65 Cadillac. Having bought a new Thunderbird, he said that the Cadillac would be my sales vehicle. Handing me the keys and $500 for new clothes, he told me to get out there and sell. While The Ventures toured Japan, I drove up and down the Western Seaboard, accumulating orders."

While Bob was in Japan, George Faith had color brochures printed and mailed to a list of music dealers. In addition to the instruments, nine amplifier models were featured with power ratings from 30 to 120 watts. The two top models featured twin speaker enclosures, copied from the three-piece Guyatone that Bob had used in Japan. However, Encor's Newport and Malibu models boasted fasteners allowing the cabinets to be locked together either horizontally or vertically. Supposedly written by Bob, a signed promotional message in the brochure named Faith as the company president. Although Bob did not realize it, his falsely reproduced signature was the first indication that his partner was not to be trusted.

BELOVED INVADERS

On July 21, Japan Airlines took The Ventures to the Far East for the second time in 1965. First on the agenda was an extensive autograph session at Tokyo's Ikebukuro Tobu Department Store. In addition to a huge group of fans, press photographers were also eager to get close, but The Ventures' fear soon waned when, instead of being attacked, the guys were continuously presented with flowers and gifts.

This time, the souvenir booklet featured a full-page photo of each band member. With no opening act specified, the book was entirely dedicated to The Ventures with a page near the back promoting *Play Guitar With The Ventures*. In hopes of reducing the huge demand for autographs, the band's signatures were printed inside the front cover, but if the ploy worked, it wasn't really noticeable. While waiting for a train, autograph hunters were so numerous that The Ventures were nearly pushed onto the tracks. Later, police disbursed over a thousand fans that were overrunning a hotel where the group was staying. After that, police maintained order by organizing fans into rows.

For all fifty-three concerts, the group played pearl-white Ventures model Mosrites. By now, *Diamond Head* was added to their show, Japan sales for the single having reached 300,000. As they had the top single and top album in Japan, it is little wonder it was one of the group's most unforgettable tours.

More Guyatone amplifiers were tried, some with six-foot speaker cabinets. As shown above, the head or "brain" for each amp rested on a metal stand.

The tour began with two concerts in Tokyo's Kosei Nenkin Hall on Saturday, July 24 with two more shows on Sunday. Toshiba recorded both days for the very first Ventures boxed set. Subsequent live albums were mere excerpts on one disc, but *All About The Ventures* encompassed four sides of translucent red vinyl. Also inside this sturdy, brass hinged box was a ten-page photo booklet. There were still a few tracks missing, and to get them, fans had to buy the fifteen-track LP, *Ventures in Japan Vol.2*. Release of both albums was timed for March, the following year, when the Ventures returned once more. This *may* be the source of an error printed decades later in liner notes for the American CD, *Live In Japan '65*. Instead of July, it placed the recording in March.

Thus began a unique system of producing Ventures material in Japan that would continue indefinitely. New albums would be deleted every few months with their content mixed with that from others to create a new compilation. Fronted with large, colorful photos, every package was difficult for a fan to resist. First pressings of live albums on red vinyl became traditional. Fans in America found it hard to obtain these LPs, but those that did consistently reported a higher sound quality. Speculated reasons for this included newer technology and the use of "virgin" vinyl.

Countless singles in attractive picture sleeves also chronicled the band's visits to Japan. Ventures picture sleeves were plentiful in Europe, Australia, Mexico, and Brazil, but never to the extent of that in the Far East. In addition to the dozens of singles, Toshiba Records released a plethora of EP (33 RPM extended-play) recordings, mixing and matching to create endless combinations of The Ventures' music. While most EP records contained four songs, some boasted six or eight selections.

On July 28, 1965, The Ventures were invited to appear on Fuji TV's hour-long *Hit Parade Star* show, along with twenty-nine-year-old Yuzo Kayama and his group, The Launchers. In addition to The Ventures playing several of their hits, Yuzo Kayama played lead guitar on *The McCoy* while Nokie played the bass. Yuzo selected this one, as it was then his "Ventures favorite." Many young people preserved such broadcasts using reel-to-reel tape machines, never imagining that someday there would be home video recorders that would play on their TV sets.

As if sixty performances in forty days were not enough, the guys were even busier after meeting Mr. George Reid on August 26. A movie producer for International Films of Japan, George wished to shoot a Ventures documentary during the final week of their tour. The band was exhausted after five days on the northern island of Hokkaido, but their very own movie sounded so exciting that they were soon being filmed in 70mm Cinemascope. In addition plenty of concert footage, they were seen sampling food and riding a streetcar in Tokyo, relaxing in Kyoto, and sightseeing Osaka and Hiroshima. Commentary was in Japanese, including voice-overs for The Ventures' dialog, both in conversation and a couple of humorous skits.

Like many to come, an outdoor concert at Oiso Beach was broadcast live on radio, with announcers asking The Ventures how long they had been together or how they liked the food. Food was a favorite subject, as it took some time for the guys to become accustomed to several dishes. There was a period when they brought along cases of canned goods and spreads such as peanut butter.

On Stage at Oiso Beach, just south of Tokyo

Standing room only - Oiso Beach wading pool

In November, Don and manager Stan Wagner returned to Japan to view and approve the selected footage. With documentary material added, the movie would be released a year later as *Beloved Invaders*. Although the movie was shown in some Japanese theatres, it was not widely promoted for nearly twenty years until it appeared on videotape and LaserDisc as *Beloved Invaders, The Golden Era Of The Ventures, 1966*. The production then found its way to fans around the globe. With "1966" included in the title, plus the insertion of *Stop Action* from a 1966 album, many viewers believed the stage performances therein to be from that year. *Beloved Invaders*, filmed in black and white with Japanese dialog became the favorite video of nearly every fan that saw it. The tempo of the 1965 performances seemed almost too fast, but as Don commented years later; "We played those songs a lot faster than we should have, but our goal was to make it exciting, and I think we did that."

YUZO KAYAMA

Near the beginning of the guitar boom in Japan, a fine young musician named Toshihiro "Yuzo" Kayama became one of the first and most successful performers to rise above thousands of Venture-loving musicians across the country. Raised by movie-star parents near Tokyo, Yuzo appeared youth oriented movies in 1960, and by the summer of 1965, was seen in twenty-seven pictures. An excellent singer, he also wrote and played guitar instrumentals under the pen name, Dan Kohsaku. Even on his earliest recordings, Yuzo sometimes sang in English. In 1965, he and some friends formed Yuzo Kayama and The Launchers. Heavily influenced by The Ventures, they soon released four singles that included *Black Sand Beach* and the explosive hit, *Yozora no Hoshi* [Starry Night] which won them a Grand-Prix award from Japan's recording industry. Yuzo and the Launchers then played both tunes with Terry Terauchi in the teen movie *Eleki No Wakadaisho* [The Young General's Electric Guitar]. The Ventures' influence shone through clearly when Terry ended *Yozora No Hoshi* with the "tiki tiki tiki" sounding surf run from *Pipeline* and *Walk-Don't Run '64*.

Upon meeting Yuzo on their January tour, The Ventures had heard some of his instrumental works. This time, they were so impressed with Yuzo's music that before leaving, Nokie presented him with his pearl-white Mosrite guitar. That winter, The Ventures released *Yozora No Hoshi* b\w *Kimi to Itsumademo* (Forever with You) [Japan Liberty LR-1500]. Before long, The Launchers were all playing white Mosrites on a string of long-play albums.

Yuzo Kayama in the sixties

While attaining "Frank Sinatra status" in Japan as a musician, movie actor, and painter of scenic art, Yuzo became a lifelong friend of The Ventures. In later years, he would invite the band to appear on many of his musical television specials, at times, the group making a special overseas trip for this purpose.

Following 1965's summer Japan tour, The Ventures stopped in Hawaii on the Labor Day weekend to play two shows at Honolulu's H.I.C. Stadium. Eric Brant, a fan now living in Canada, recalls his excitement; "The Ventures were a big motivating force that started me playing drums. I'll never forget being thirteen years old and seeing them live on that hot summer night in Honolulu. They were, truly – fabulous! The warm-up acts comprised an assortment of styles, from surf-based instrumental (The Impacts), to early 'British Invasion' imitation. But when The Ventures hit the stage, it was pure magic. Unforgettable to this day, and comparable to seeing The Beatles back then. I idolized them then and I still love them today."

Upon arriving home, The Ventures were exhausted but thrilled. However, with two Japan trips in a year plus recording and home concerts still ahead, they were developing a work habit that few, if any, groups would ever match. In late August, *The Ventures A Go-Go* had been released to immediate orders totaling 200,000 units. As they watched the album climb to sixteen in Billboard, they appeared to be on top of the world, but at Encor, shock and disappointment was waiting for Bob.

LOSING FAITH

Judd Hamilton was excited. Music dealers were so enthusiastic over the new Encor amplifiers that Judd recruited older brother John to push the product in Nashville. As a musician, John had spent substantial time in the country music capital and was well acquainted with the music store circuit. The father of a new baby girl, Judd anxiously anticipated his commission on roughly $100,000 worth of amplifier orders. Downing his breakfast, he jumped into the Cadillac, and headed for Canoga Park where he expected to find Bob Bogle.

Arriving just ahead of Judd, and seeing no cars near the building, Bob sensed something was wrong. Upon entry, he found the place deserted with no evidence of work in progress. Two phone calls later, Bob felt both sick and angry. George Faith had withdrawn the company funds and placed Encor into bankruptcy. Entering as Bob hung up the phone, Judd remembers how Bob looked; "I walked in and said 'Hi Bob!' He appeared unhappy as he murmured 'Hello Judd, I'm afraid I've got some awful news for you'. I said, 'What's wrong, Bob?' Slowly my heart sank as he told me how his manager had left him in such a precarious position that he would have to close the company. Then he said, 'Come on Judd, I've got to have the car back so I'll drive you home. I'm really sorry, but I just can't do anything for you right now.'

"Later that afternoon, as I wondered what I was going to do next, Bob called me. He was still reeling from anger and frustration, but he said he had a book he wanted me to read. I thought to myself, 'Book? What kind of book?' Bob came over to the apartment and said 'I'm in a rush, but I just think you need to read this book.' I took the book, and Bob was gone. The book was a self-help book written by Emmett Fox about the power of positive thinking. I wasn't able to sleep that night, so I picked up the book and started to read. It was a small book with less than 200 pages, and pretty soon I had read the whole thing. The message of the book was that you could project your life through your thoughts by concentrating on exactly what you want in order to obtain it, but that it must be done in such a way so as not to adversely affect friends and loved ones. I wanted to believe the book so bad. Recalling that the reason I had come to Hollywood in the first place was to have a hit record, I began saying over and over in my mind that this is what I wanted. 'I believe... I believe...' and I finally fell asleep." A series of events soon followed that caused Judd to never forget Bob's little book.

When Bob left Judd, he went to visit his attorney. Once the lawyer had assessed the situation, Bob considered himself fortunate. Although he had lost his initial investment, it appeared that he would have been worse off had the company succeeded. Apparently, Bob's stock in Encor had been arranged with loop-holes, so that it all belonged to Faith. The accountant showed Bob how lucky he was to be squeezed out of a company that was now bankrupt. Now, Faith alone was responsible for Encor's liabilities.

Back in Denver, salesman Gordon Close was equally distraught; "I was in shock, but I felt sorrier for Bob than for myself. I wish I still had that Encor amplifier. After going back to teaching guitar, I used it in my studio for some time, hoping Encor might come back to life, but after a while I sold the amp to a needy guitar student."

Gordon remained in the music business, opening various music stores and working with Canada's Yorkville Sound, distributing their Traynor amplifiers on the West Coast. With two university degrees, he was later able to combine musical equipment distribution with a successful marketing consulting service.

IF AT FIRST, YOU DON'T SUCCEED...

As Bob Bogle recalls, his idea for a Ventures model amplifier was not dead; "We wanted a Mosrite amp to go along with the guitars, but at the time, Semie didn't have the wherewithal to get into amp building. I found a designer and also a company in Minnesota that would build it, but they insisted on putting *their* brand name on it. We agreed to that and started promoting the Award amplifier near the end of 1966."

Ironically, engineer Howard A. Dumble was already designing an amplifier for Mosrite of California. In the years to come, Dumble started his own company which became known for some of the finest professional amplifiers in the world.

Nokie remembers; "The first thing we did was to find a really good electronics engineer. I wish I could recall his name, but I can't. He had developed a radar system for his car to prevent crashing on the L.A. freeways in the morning fog. He offered to install it in my car, but one of us was always too busy so he never got around to it. He designed us a prototype amp head that we could use with whatever speakers we wanted. He said that Fender claimed to have a 100-watt amp, but he had proven that it averaged only 70 watts. When our amp was built, he showed me that it had full power by connecting a 100-watt light-bulb to the speaker jack and letting me play. When I cranked it up, that bulb glowed real bright."

Stan Wagner was also eager to see a Ventures model amplifier; "The prototype worked great, so I took the design to the best in the business, the J.B. Lansing Company. I wanted them to mass-produce the amp, but they were just not interested."

A company willing to build amplifiers was finally found in Rochester, Minnesota. A maker of home-entertainment products, Waters-Connelly agreed built two models. The 100-watt unit housed two fifteen-inch speakers, while a smaller model delivered 50 watts to a single speaker. Both models employed J.B. Lansing musical instrument speakers and a high-frequency horn. Along with a separate bass channel, the amp featured the current popular effects, including an on-board fuzz circuit borrowed from Mosrite.

Ed Sanner, formerly the Mosrite company's electronics man, also remembers; "We had planned to build amplifiers in 1966, but it took some time before we could start production. The Ventures couldn't wait for us and started looking elsewhere. They found someone, but it took almost a year for their people to come up with the design and build a prototype. As it worked out, we got our first amplifiers into production shortly after they did. Around that time, I had come up with a fuzz-tone pedal for Leo LeBlanc, a friend of mine who played steel guitar. Semie said we should sell it, so we started production of the Fuzzrite. We had shipped around 200 units when Leblanc discovered a problem with the pedal when it was on a cold concrete floor. We then switched to using silicon transistors and a modular network built for us by Sprague Electric."

Both of the Ventures' Award models included Sanner's fuzz circuit. The cabinets were fitted with rolling stands and a plastic Ventures logo mounted on the speaker grille. The Ventures contracted 500 units of each model on a one-time basis to be shipped directly to dealers when the orders started pouring in.

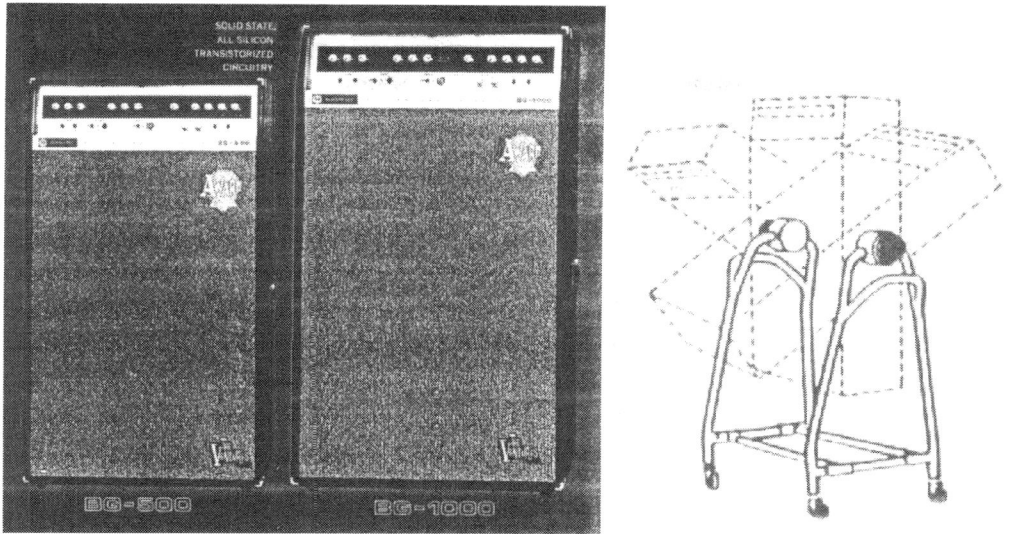
Pictures from the Mosrite Distributing catalog included the "SWINGER STAND"

As Stan Wagner recalls; "Operating as Mosrite Distributing, I obtained a $500,000 line of credit for The Ventures with California's Crocker National Bank [now Wells Fargo] from which we drew loans to cover production costs. I then approached Semie Moseley with another idea to increase sales. Semie agreed and accepted a payment of $5000 for the addition of the Mosrite name on our Award amplifiers, and for the fuzz effect to be labeled 'Fuzzrite'." [Note: Although Andy Moseley had no knowledge of this transaction, Semie confirmed it in separate interviews published by author Tom Wheeler in *American Guitars* (revised edition - HarperCollins Publishers 1992), and in the February 2007 issue of *Vintage Guitar*].

ACTION AND ALKA SELTZER

While Joe Saraceno kept busy with other musicians, he did not forget The Ventures while they were in Japan. Upon returning to America, the band started work on two more concept albums. The first included songs based around Dick Clark's currently popular ABC Television series, *Where The Action Is*. At the same time, they began working on a Christmas album. Composing a half dozen originals for the *Action* album while applying their style to Christmas songs was no small task. A source for one track on the "Action" LP ultimately involved dropping the vocals from a tune which Don had recorded under two different titles. Acetate demos for his *I Want You To Want Me* and *You've Got A Mind of Your Own* were condemned to the vaults when the melody was adapted for *Little Bit Of Action*. Meanwhile, Stan Wagner booked a Northwest college tour in October while contemplating a European tour in early '66. This left little wonder why the guys had no time when Liberty asked for another *Guitar Phonics* album.

A year earlier, Joe Saraceno and associate Dave Pell had launched some studio musician recordings under the name of The T-Bones. *Rail Vette* [Liberty 55677], and *That's Where It's At* [Liberty 55814] were not big hits, but a new single based on an Alka-Seltzer jingle was doing much better. When *No Matter What Shape* [Liberty 55836] hit the Top Ten, Saraceno quickly produced an album while looking for a promotional band that would tour as The T-Bones. Bob Bogle knew who could handle the job and who certainly needed the work when he suggested the Hamilton brothers.

The morning after reading Emmett Fox's self-help book from Bob, Judd Hamilton awoke to the telephone. The call was from Saraceno, known only to Judd as producer of The Ventures. When Joe asked if he could form band and travel as The T-Bones, Judd gave a resounding "Yes!" Within a week, Judd and Danny had a quintet that included Richard Torres on keys and sax, George Rosenthal on bass, and Gene Pello, of Marketts fame, on drums. The brothers also went into debt, each buying a new Pontiac GTO. With rented trailers and *No Matter What Shape* (*Your Stomach's In*) as their anthem, the five hit the road as The T-Bones. Recalling his joy, Judd reflects; "As the weeks passed and we traveled across the country, the instrumental reached Number 3 on the charts, settling under the Beatles' *Eight Days A Week* by and *Barbara Ann* by the Beach Boys. I was riding in the backseat when I remembered *The Sermon On The Mount*, the little book Bob had given me. It just blew my mind remembering what I had wished for and that it was actually happening. Here I was, the leader of a band with a Top Five record!"

While the T-Bones toured, Saraceno released a single based on a Nabisco jingle. When *Sippin' and Chippin'* [Liberty 55867] charted at 62, he produced an album with that name and a photo of five unknown young men on the back (and cover model Barbara Bouchet on the front). The tour band weathered some personnel changes, but *No Matter What Shape* was named the Top Instrumental of 1965. Working the tune's popularity, Saraceno convinced Don Lee Wilson to return to the studio. With Joe as producer, Don came up with some lyrics and assumed a blatant British accent for his own version of *No Matter What Shape* [Liberty 55862]. Sales of the disc were low, but positive response in concert was enough to keep Don singing on records. In the next two years, Joe produced Don on four more Liberty singles, always with hope for that elusive major hit.

Work on the next Ventures album was postponed when Don presented his idea to splice intros from current hits onto popular Christmas songs. Soon one of The Ventures' most enjoyable projects was underway. *Walk-Don't Run* became *Sleigh Ride*, *Memphis* became *Jingle Bell Rock*, the Beatles' *I Feel Fine* became *Rudolph The Red-Nosed Reindeer*, and so on. Not only did *The Ventures Christmas Album* [Dolton BST-8033] make Number 9 on Billboard's Christmas chart, it placed therein for the remainder of the sixties. Having since found its way onto several compact disc labels, selections from the album continue to get shopping mall and radio play every Yuletide season.

In 1990, EMI issued *The Ventures Christmas Album* on CD in which the version of *Rudolph the Red Nosed Reindeer* featured a previously discarded track played by Nokie. The resulting peculiar harmony seemed to steal the attention of disc jockeys away from the other fine tracks on the disc [EMI - CDP 7-94994-2].

The *Christmas Album* also enjoyed longevity in Japan. There were six re-issues between 1965 and 1990, plus a fresh recording in 2001 with *Scrooge* deleted in favor of four additional Christmas favorites.

In September, 1965, while The Ventures worked on their Christmas album, Liberty pressed hard for another instructional LP. Thus, while the band recorded *Sleigh Ride*, *Silver Bells*, and *Frosty the Snowman*, "Wrecking Crew" musicians Tommy Tedesco, Rene Hall, Bill Pitman, Dennis Budimir, and Hal Blaine recorded *Play Guitar with The Ventures Vol. 2* [Dolton BST-16502]. Over the next two years, another five *Guitar Phonics* albums followed, including three *Play With The Ventures* and one each with Chet Atkins and Jimmy Bryant. The last three pictured a Ventures member on the cover, but again, they were absent due to touring.

Always popular, the *Play Guitar* series was issued in the nineties on compact disc in Europe and America. Meanwhile, the old vinyl versions command the highest resale prices of all the group's U.S. LPs. As for Wilbur Savidge, he never had to sell another refrigerator. *Guitar Phonics* gave him a whole new career in the production of guitar instruction publications. His books are found in music stores across the continent with names like *First Scales and How to Use Them* or *Everything About Guitar Chords*. In 1997, the *Play Guitar With The Ventures* series appeared on CD in the UK. See-For-Miles had obtained the rights to press the recordings, but when the instructional pages followed in a tidy unauthorized booklet, Savidge quickly put a stop to its production.

As mentioned, Don returned to Japan with manager Stan Wagner in November '65 to review the movie filmed in August. Other reasons for the mission were to arrange more concert appearances for March '66 and to establish a Ventures fan club in Tokyo. Deemed to be worth the investment, Stan, at the expense of The Ventures, arranged for one Al Avalon to live in Tokyo and operate the club for as long as required. While fan club totals for the U.S. were never disclosed, a 1966 Ventures Japan tour booklet reported Japanese membership had mushroomed above 25,000.

ACTION PLUS

In January 1966, The Ventures were touring the American East Coast when Mel Taylor was asked to hold a drum clinic for high-school students in Glens Falls, New York. Obligingly, Mel set up his drums along with a phonograph in a local hotel. Playing to Ventures records, he demonstrated his technique for 200 spellbound teenagers. That night, The Ventures rocked the local high school with an attendance of nearly 2000.

When Dick Clark launched a second musical TV show, his theme was the stirring *Action*, recorded by Freddie Cannon. Clark also took a line from the song to name his program *Where The Action Is*. The Ventures had chosen this same line for their next album title and opened with "Action" on probably their most energetic package ever. During their January tour, record stores everywhere sold copies of *Where The Action Is* [Dolton BST-8040]. Charting at 33, it became the new "favorite LP" of Ventures lovers around the world. Seven rising hits accompanied five originals, many enhanced by the rocking organ of Evelyn Freeman.

One of the cover songs on *Action* was *Hang On Sloopy* The song had become a worldwide smash for an Indiana group formed in 1963 called The McCoys. Some ten years later, as lead guitarist Rick Derringer rose to fame with The Edgar Winter Group, The Ventures were amused and slightly honored to learn that Rick's first group had taken its name from *The McCoy*, the backing tune for *Walk-Don't Run* on Dolton 25X.

Although *Action Plus* is considered a Ventures original, the tune was extracted from an obscure 45 in Mel's collection of singles. Back when he worked with Art Laboe, an L.A. session group consisting of James Burton on guitar, Larry Taylor on bass and Sandy Nelson drumming, had recorded as The Gamblers. They originated a tune called *Moon Dawg* [World Pacific 815], which was soon covered on the album *Twist With The Ventures*. Mel owned another Gamblers recording, *Teen Machine* [Last Chance 2] featuring Leon Russell on organ. It was a simple matter for The Ventures to improve on the obscure arrangement and rename it *Action Plus*.

With Christmas out of the way, a single of *Secret Agent Man* [Dolton 316] was released in the first week of 1966. In spite of becoming a hit by the end of March, distribution of this popular tune was the source of some aggravation for The Ventures. Prior to recording this theme from the TV series, *Secret Agent*, the band obtained verbal assurance that *Secret Agent Man*, as sung on the show by Johnny Rivers, would not come out on a record. In February, as The Ventures' flashy arrangement climbed the charts, inspiration struck for a concept album based on TV crime series themes. Then, out of the blue, Liberty released the Johnny Rivers version on its Imperial label. Immediately, The Ventures' instro froze at 54 while Johnny's vocal soared to Number 3 in less than a month. The Ventures had nothing against Johnny Rivers, but they never forgave Al Bennett and the company for that breach of trust. Joe Saraceno's explanation fingered Liberty's apathy towards Ventures singles because of the band's heavy LP sales. With so many Ventures albums in the Top 100, the theory was hard to dispute, but The Ventures still felt that if their version had not shown promise, Johnny's version would never have been released. There was, however, some justice for The Ventures when their version became a favorite around the world, including Hong Kong where it reached Number 7. On March 29, while the group was nearing the end of two-weeks in Japan, the guys were seen performing *Secret Agent Man* on Dick Clark's *Where the Action Is*. On April 2, the footage was rebroadcast on *American Bandstand*. As a result, the song was part of The Ventures' concert repertoire for the next forty years.

The next album, titled *The Ventures* but known also as *Batman* [Dolton BST-8042], was based on four popular TV themes like *Secret Agent* plus eight Ventures originals. One was written in hopes of being the theme for a new fall series resurrecting the old radio sleuth, *The Green Hornet*. The Ventures' submission would have been a fine theme for the show, but while the album climbed the charts, the network selected a completely different *Green Hornet Theme* from the pen of Billy May.

During the winter of 1965-'66, Dick Glasser was at Warner Brothers, but still accessible to Mel Taylor. The adoration and respect received from Japanese audiences got Mel thinking about doing more solo work. Drummers Sandy Nelson and Hal Blaine having recently released albums of their own, Mel approached Dick Glasser with the same idea. Sessions with Mel and several studio musicians gave us *Mel Taylor & the Magics In Action* [Warner Bros. WB1624]. Japan pressed the album on red wax with the title *Drums A-Go-Go* [Toshiba BP-7461]. Singles from the album were also released in that country. One, *Watermelon Man/Skokiaan* [Warner Bros. 5675] was issued in America.

Late in 1965, Josie commenced a project unknown to fans for many years. As she recalled; "My intent was to have an album made up of the beautiful and relaxing music tucked away in the first fifteen Ventures albums. Mellow songs were not much in vogue at the time, so I chose twenty-two of my favorites to be pressed in a limited number for use as Christmas gifts to the family and close friends."

Considered "BackGround music," the record was numbered BG-101 at the pressing plant, and simply entitled with the group's logo. The "gem" on BG-101 was a beautiful rendition of Lionel Newman's theme from *Adventures in Paradise*, which ran from 1959 to 1962 on ABC television. In 1960, another version of the theme had been a Top 100 hit for Jerry Byrd, then the country's most influential steel guitarist. Associated with Chet Atkins and renowned for his country and western work, Byrd was also a lover of Hawaiian music. His albums, entitled *Hi-Fi Guitar* [1958] and *Byrd of Paradise* [1961], had inspired The Ventures to play *Beyond the Reef* and *Adventures in Paradise* featuring Bob's smooth and mellow lead over Hank Levine's strings. On the subject of Byrd, Bob surmises; "A lot of people think Don and I were influenced by Chet Atkins, Les Paul, and Duane Eddy, but I don't think that's true. We always admired them, but we never tried to sound like them. We just did what we could with what we had. If anyone influenced my sound, it would have to be Jerry Byrd on his steel guitar. I think his recording of *Moon of Manakoora* was also the reason we put it on one of our early albums. Nokie played lead on that one." The Ventures' version of *Adventures in Paradise* eventually surfaced in the early nineties on cassette tape from the Ventures International Club, and in 2005 on the third *Ventures in the Vaults* CD [Ace Records - CDCHD 1031].

Wishing to share the BG-101 collection with dedicated fans, Josie suggested in a club bulletin that members tape-record their own mellow set from their Ventures vinyl collection. She did not mention the private LP pressing, but listed its contents in sequence from the label while describing her idea. However, she had either forgotten or did not know that *Adventures in Paradise* had never been released, and was completely unknown to the club. Ironically, by the time letters from curious fans arrived, the club had been terminated and Josie had left Hollywood for good. With just forty copies pressed on vinyl, BG-101 is the rarest of all Ventures LP albums. In the years to come, it became known as *The White Album* after a Beatles' record with no title was tagged with that name. Hence, The Ventures' thirty track CD compiled in 2006 for the same purpose was given the title, *The New White Album*.

GROWING PAINS

By the end of 1965, countless young guitarists around the world ached to own a Mosrite guitar. Bands that played matching Ventures Models were popping up everywhere from the United States and Canada to Europe and Japan. The mere sight of such a group seeded plans for other groups to do the same, if only they could afford it. As the choice of The Ventures, the instruments were considered by scores of players to be the "Cadillac of guitars!"

Mosrite instruments now boasted a separate bridge roller for each string, maintaining tuning in spite of vibrato bar use, but gone was the inlaid binding around the body and the side mounted 'jack' or cord-socket. Semie Moseley had redesigned The Ventures Model in order to speed production and lower the cost. The jack was moved to the pick-guard, and the formerly glued-in neck was now screwed into position. The muting device was gone and the sand-cast tailpiece was now die-cast and labeled "Moseley" in place of "Vibramute." When production doubled, more employees were hired in an attempt to quadruple product output. Within a year, international orders piled up, demanding an even larger factory. Busier and making more money than he had ever imagined, Semie made the first of several bad decisions by purchasing the Dobro Company in Gardena, just south of Hollywood. Then he moved that operation into his Bakersfield building and began manufacturing the thunderous Dobro acoustic guitar with its large aluminum resonator under a perforated metal cover.

Semie also thought about producing Mosrite amps, but for time being stuck with ideas such as a twelve-string Ventures Model and a line of semi-acoustic instruments. Additionally, he and brother Andy decided to sink some of their newfound wealth by expanding their Gospel recording company. Mosrite Records primarily recorded country music, but employee Gene Moles managed to get a pair of his early guitar instrumentals onto the label. *Durango* would have made a great theme for a western movie, while the flipside, *Scotish Guitar* (sic) rocked the Scottish folk song, *Loch Lomond*.

At about this time, Don Wilson admitted to being not completely enthralled with the ultra-thin necks of the Mosrite guitars. When he mentioned to Semie that he would like to have a wider neck made available, at least for his own use, Semie's reaction was explosive and negative, insisting that the design was perfect and would never be altered. Don was unsatisfied, but there was no further dispute.

In mid March, 1966, The Ventures returned to Japan for a two-week visit. On this trip they presented a dazzling spectacle with a set of matching red Mosrites. While there, a two-month tour was arranged for the approaching summer. Upon arriving home in early April, they found their so-called *Batman* album peaking at 42.

Bob, Mel, and Don with Japan Tour Manager Charles Comelli and friend

Between the overseas tours, while squeezing in a three-week tour on home ground, the guys recorded two albums. *Go With The Ventures* [Dolton BST-8045] was a surprise release, having not even been announced to the fan clubs. This album had three rocking Ventures originals in addition to Danny Hamilton's rousing *Escape*. As The Mamas and the Papas were hot then, two of their hits were covered, along with Nancy Sinatra's *These Boots Are Made For Walkin'*. More hits of the day were added, but the most important track on *GO* was *Ginza Lights*, written by The Ventures for their Japanese audience. Mention of this track reminds Bob; "We wanted harmonizing lead guitars on *Ginza Lights*, so we brought in Dennis Budimir for the session. I admired a technique he sometimes used, playing the melody on two strings. He would leave one string open and finger the frets for the other one." In time for the Japan summer tour, a Ventures single bearing *Ginza Lights* was ready in July.

As the group toured the central States, *Go With The Ventures* began its climb to 39 on the charts. During the tour, an incident occurred that left a few fans in the State of Iowa with cherished memories for the rest of their lives. One of these was a teenager named Paul Benbow, who recalls; "It was in Fort Madison, during the summer of 1966. Our small local music store known as Rempe's got an urgent call for help from someone associated with the band. As the owner, Harry Rempe was asked if he could supply a good set of drums, some amplifiers, and sound equipment to be used by The Ventures for their appearance at the local high school. As it was to be a dance, I was excited because this would allow us to get up close to the stage. Harry contacted me first, knowing I had a set of pearl white Ludwig drums and that my brother Jeb had a custom-built amplifier with Newcomb sound columns. We volunteered our equipment and were given free tickets in return. I took my drums to the auditorium where the person in charge said that The Ventures always carried their guitars with them, but the drums and sound equipment traveled separately and had somehow gone astray. Sure enough, when the band arrived, they had guitar cases only, and Mel had his sticks. As they set up, I was thrilled and fascinated as Mel adjusted my drums to his liking. That evening, I not only got in free, I watched the entire concert just five feet away from the stage, frequently making eye contact with Mel as I watched him play on my drums. I remember feeling pretty special, having helped make it all possible. I had a brief visit with Mel afterwards as autographs were being given, and found him very gracious and appreciative. He said he was particularly impressed with my chrome snare, and as a special thanks, he signed the head of my floor tom-tom, linking two drummers, as it were. I've been a lifelong Ventures fan ever since."

"We played hundreds of school gymnasiums like this in the sixties" says Don Wilson

Home from the tour, the guys began sessions for *Wild Things* [Dolton BST-8047]. As pop rock became louder and guitars more distorted, The Ventures adapted while keeping their music recognizable and classy sounding. The album title was a take-off on the Troggs' *Wild Thing*, covered in fine style with Don doing a precise and hilarious impersonation of Peter Lorre. Establishing a theme, five originals were given titles containing "Wild," including Danny Hamilton's *Murfreesboro* which the guys renamed *Wild and Wooly*. The group, now in control of their destiny, took the naming of songs less seriously. If they wanted to name a song *How Now Wild Cow*, who could object when they were selling a million albums annually for the fifth year in a row? Actually, *How Now Wild Cow* was jokingly suggested by one of Mel's sons during the recording session, and the guys said; "Why not?"

~ ~ ~

In autumn, the debut of a weekly *Green Hornet* TV series starring Bruce Lee as the Hornet's sidekick, was fast approaching. The Ventures had written a fine Green Hornet song for their *Batman* album, but Joe Saraceno made sure that The Ventures cut Billy May's TV version in time for the show's opening in September. Released in a colorful (and now very rare) picture sleeve, *Green Hornet Theme* [Dolton 323] "bubbled under" the Hot 100, possibly because collectors assumed this excellent rendition to be the same as *Green Hornet '66* on the *Batman* album. A second possibility; with programs like *The Man from U.N.C.L.E., Secret Agent,* and *Get Smart* crowding the channels in prime time, it may have been too late for *The Green Hornet*. In just six months, the series was over after twenty-six episodes.

GETTING SIDETRACKED

Abundant Japanese sales of Mel Taylor's singles prompted Dick Glasser to produce a follow-up album, *Mel Taylor & The Magics In Action* [Warner Bros 1624]. Unfortunately, as Stan Wagner and secretary, Alice Eng never mentioned solo projects in club bulletins, North American fans had no knowledge of Mel's album. The material was an interesting combination of old and new instrumentals, including five heard previously on Ventures albums. One of these, *Escape*, was renamed *Bullseye* which, along with *No Exit* was borrowed from Danny Hamilton's bag of tunes. Fans still belonging to clubs in 1996 were finally able to obtain the album on compact disc from Japan. As a bonus, the CD carried Mel's four 1966 single sides.

In addition to *Secret Agent Man* and *Green Hornet*, four more Ventures singles were issued in 1966. A rocking version of the bluesy Mel Tormé hit *Comin' Home Baby* [Dolton 320] was one of few tunes not included on an album until a re-recording in the eighties. *Wild Thing* [Dolton 325] promoted the *Wild Things* album, and the guys dabbled in motorcycle music for the theme from the current Peter Fonda/Nancy Sinatra movie, *The Wild Angels* [Dolton 327]. Although the remaining single, *Ginza Lights* [Dolton 321] did little at home, it would soon be making sizable waves in Japan.

Because Ventures records were popular in Hong Kong, Taiwan, Korea, Singapore, Thailand, and of course, the Philippines, the group made occasional side trips. In the summer of 1966, they played two evening concerts in Taipei before going to Tokyo to meet their new tour agent. Having either retired or quit the business, Tats Nagashima had passed the group over to one Mr. Ono of TOA Attractions. As Don recalls, this was a step backward regarding the band's comfort on tour; "When Ono was persuading us to go with him, he talked like a big time operator, but we then had to carry all of our equipment; including those big heavy amplifiers, in humid and unbearable heat. Traveling was also unpleasant, as we had to take the 'milk run' buses and trains. However, a highlight for me was meeting Bruce Welch of The Shadows at the Lipo Bar in the old Hilton, now known as the Capitol Tokyu Hotel. We drank to the two of us being the highest paid rhythm guitar players in the world!"

After performing on television, the fifty-eight-concert tour began. While in Tokyo, the guys were surprised to learn that lyrics had been added to their *Ginza Lights*, and the resulting vocal was already a smash hit under the name, *Futari no Ginza* (Two on the Ginza) by Ken Yamauchi and Masako Izumi [Toshiba TP-1346]. It wasn't long before the song became part of a Japanese movie soundtrack called *Futari no Ginza*.

The first Japan artists to sing Ventures' melodies

As in March, Yuzo Kayama performed *Kimi to Itsumademo* (Forever with You) and *Yozora No Hoshi* (Starry Night) with The Ventures at the Tokyo concerts. The fervent reception of these tunes plus and the huge success of *Ginza Lights* inspired The Ventures add both tunes to their instrumental repertoire, and to compose more instrumentals with Japanese melodic structure.

KELLY JON WILSON   1961-1966

Foreign tours had their moments of stress, but the 1966 summer tour had more difficulties than usual. After just two weeks in Japan, devastating news arrived from home. Josie, living in Hollywood at the time, recalls the horrifying incident; "As Don would be touring much of the time, he had left Karen and the children in Tacoma when he went to Hollywood. In July of 1966, Karen's doctor advised that she needed a short vacation. Although reluctant to leave her three children, Karen enrolled them at a guest ranch before leaving to visit her father in Montana. On August 5, I received a tearful call from my daughter Jacqueline, telling me that four-year-old Kelly had died in an accident. I was stunned. Near hysterical, I kept repeating 'No, no! It can't be true! After I became somewhat composed, Jackie explained what had happened. Apparently the children were taken on a horseback ride, although I can't imagine putting a four-year old had never ridden before, on a horse. As we learned later, the two students were not qualified to supervise young children that were not expert riders.

"After calming down, I thought of poor Karen in Montana and of Don, far off in Japan. The thought of Kelly's siblings having seen what happened to their little brother was almost too much to bear. Jill was ten and Tim was only seven.

"Filled with shock and disbelief, Don came home from Japan immediately. The funeral and burial became a blur in my mind, and Karen could not bear to return to the rented house where little Kelly had spent his short, happy life. Jackie and I packed everything and put the furniture in storage. Later, Don bought a home by a lake, and that's where Jill and Tim grew up."

In reviewing Josie's account, Don had difficulty discussing the death of his son, but eventually added; "We were in Yamaguchi City when Mel brought me to a room where the other guys were, and then they broke the news to me. Kelly Jon had been placed on the horse behind a bigger kid whose legs were long enough to reach the stirrups. The horse bolted because the saddle was loose and slid under him. The older child was thrown clear, but Kelly's feet had been tied to leather saddle strings used for securing gear or saddlebags. It's just too horrible to imagine!"

In Don's absence from Japan, the band played as a threesome until they were able to recruit Takeshi Terauchi, now a star in his own right, to play rhythm and sometimes interchange with Nokie on lead guitar. Upon Don's return, the band was complete again, but in less than three weeks, catastrophe struck once more.

On August 30, during a concert at Kushiro, Mel slipped and fell on the stage. Aching some, he finished the show, but by morning, his pain was so severe that a doctor ordered him not to perform that evening. The Ventures had to work without a drummer, but as Bob recalls; "Shortly after we began our concert, a fellow came up from the audience. He said he was a drummer and he was willing to sit in. Mel's drums were set up, so we said 'Sure, come on up.' Well, he got up there and he was terrible. We felt bad, but we just had to ask him to go back and sit down. We finished the concert as a trio that night, and it felt a bit like we had gone back in time to 1959."

Summer 1966 – Pearl white Mosrites and Guyatone amps

The tour ended with three days of concerts at U.S. military bases on the occupied island of Okinawa. Nokie often tells of that time when he and Don switched on their amplifiers and it suddenly became apparent that the base operated under its own 220-volt power system. Following the snap of blowing fuses, a wisp of smoke arose from one amplifier. The Ventures were impressed when competent technicians quickly repaired the amps. A portable generator was set up, and the amps worked fine.

The Ventures' homecoming was just in time to see *Wild Things* peak at 33 on the Billboard chart. They also saw statistics reporting every American family with teenage offspring to own 1.3 Ventures albums, and that their 11.5 percent of the world market share of album sales ran a close second to 13 percent enjoyed by The Beatles.

During the band's summer Japan tour of 1966, Liberty Records created a "budget" label offering previously released material at a discount. Limited to just ten-tracks, Sunset albums were packaged without inner protective covers and pressed on thick polystyrene plastic. Occasionally, Liberty/Dolton put a formerly released song on an album, but with The Ventures' *Runnin' Strong* [Sunset 5116], they went too far. By renaming *every* song on the album, fans believed it was all new material. For example, the title track *Runnin' Strong* was actually *Runnin' Wild* from *The Fabulous Ventures* album. The Ventures were unaware of this maneuver until protests began arriving in their fan mail. An apology appeared in a club bulletin, but in 1978, *Runnin' Strong* was re-released on the Pickwick label, complete with bogus titles and only nine tracks. On a positive note, the Pickwick disc seemed to sound better on some record players. To The Ventures, these budget records were advantageous in that the selected material was nearly one hundred percent original, bringing extra royalty income for their songwriting.

While Ventures fan clubs thrived in America, the UK, and Japan, new clubs formed in Sweden, Mexico, France, and Germany. From the beginning, the Scandinavian bestseller charts indicated a strong group of fans. That is what led young Arild Pettersson to form a club in Malung, Sweden. Beginning in 1966, Arild ran the Ventures Scandinavian Fan Club (V.S.F.C) for over thirty-five years, providing members with news, rare recordings, and hard-to-get material from Japan.

Near the end of September, The Ventures were gearing up for a lengthy U.S. tour when the whole thing was postponed. Stan Wagner remembers what took precedence; "I had a friend named Bob Leonard who was an entertainment agent. He wanted to book us for ten nights in Mexico City at one of the most famous nightclubs in the world, The El Patio. The price of admission there was unbelievable for the sixties. They extracted ten dollars at the door from people who would be spending $100 for dinner and drinks. They were Mexico's elite of the elite coming in with their children to see The Ventures.

"When Leonard said he needed an opening act for The Ventures, I remembered an enormously talented guy by the name of George Hopkins, whom I used to manage. He played several instruments, did impressions, and was an all-round comedian. He could get crazy at times, but he had worked with some of The Ventures before, and they knew him well. There was a problem, however, in that George did not speak Spanish, and most of the audience didn't understand his humor. He tried hard, even swinging out on a rope above the stage, yelling like Tarzan for his entrance, but he knew by the second night that he was bombing."

El Patio Club – Mexico City - October '66

"I still remember a funny thing that happened during that engagement. Unlike a lot of bands, The Ventures had never been interested or involved with drugs. Well, I was in my room one night after the guys had finished performing, when I got a call from George. He said, 'Come over to my room. A couple of girls are here and they have some marijuana.' I couldn't believe what I was hearing. I said, 'Are you crazy? You're trying it out in Mexico City? If you want to get busted, do it in your own country!' He took my advice, and I'm sure that's the closest any of us ever got to the stuff.

"Anyway, Bob Leonard came up with an idea to let George be part of The Ventures' show, playing some percussion instruments and joking around with the band. The Ventures went along with it, and after some rehearsing, they had worked George in quite well. After a couple of good nights, George didn't show up and there was some scrambling to add some numbers to the act. During The Ventures' second set, a very inebriated heckler appeared in the audience, and it was George. No one was laughing, and when the set was finished, George showed up in the dressing room with a girl. After catching hell for showing up drunk, he retorted by calling Don some unflattering names and quickly found himself on the floor with a sore jaw. The Ventures didn't want him in their act anymore, so George went back to doing his opening show. After continuing to bomb, he just stopped in the middle of his act one night and said 'Ladies and Gentlemen, I don't know what in hell I'm doing here' and he walked off the stage. Meanwhile, The Ventures broke every attendance record the El Patio ever had."

In recalling this incident, Don adds; "When I hit George, I was suddenly seeing stars as well. I almost passed out and my head was really sore. The girl that George brought in had hit me over the head with a big stoneware snack tray."

"The El Patio was a great place, but we were a bit uncomfortable during our daily rehearsals because there was dead rats the size of cats lying around the place. We'd see these critters running around outside, but I guess they would come in at night and then get poisoned. Anyway, the place would always be cleaned up before showtime."

Upon their return to Hollywood, the band learned that TV's *Batman* producers were resurrecting cartoon detective *Dick Tracy* and that The Ventures were contracted to write and perform the show's theme song. Airing was not to begin for a year, but the guys had *The Dick Tracy Theme* ready for NBC by mid-November. When low network faith halted filming past the pilot episode, the recorded theme went into storage where it remained for the next thirteen years!

Meanwhile on the big screen, a series of biker-gang movies created a trend in "motorcycle music." *The Wild Angels* (starring Peter Fonda and Nancy Sinatra) was the first of the genre. The Ventures joined the movement by recording the movie's theme. For the flip side, they added appropriate sound effects to *A Go-Go Dancer* and renamed it *Kickstand* [Dolton 327]. *Theme from The Wild Angels* was the last single by anyone to appear on Dolton. Beginning in 1967, all of the label's artists recorded on Liberty.

Perhaps the next album should have been titled *The Industrious Ventures*, as it was finished and released in January 1967. One of five originals on the project was the title song, *Guitar Freakout* [Dolton BST-8050, reissued in 1971 as *Revolving Sounds*]. True to form, a half-dozen rising hits were covered, along with a Glen Campbell original. As Don recalls; "I was attending Glen's birthday party when I invited him to sit in on our next session. His home was only about two blocks from mine, and I remember meeting Rick Nelson at that party. When Glen showed up at the studio, he played on five or six songs. He named his contribution *Cookout Freakout on Lookout Mountain* but he didn't play lead on anything. I think Bob and I gave him a Mosrite guitar. We gave away quite a few guitars around that time."

In his early years as a session musician, Glen recorded "Winkie Doll" b/w "Girls" under the pseudonym,
    Billy Dolton.

Kaybo 617 45 RPM (USA)
Parlophone R 4733 (UK)
1961

Glen Campbell with his 12-string Mosrite

One track on *Guitar Freakout* intrigued listeners for years as they wondered if Bob Bogle had played upright bass on *Wack Wack*, a then current r&b hit for the Young-Holt Trio. Bob said no, it was not him, and later, research by discographer Russ Wapensky proved the artist to be Don Bagley, a busy studio musician who worked with orchestra leaders ranging from Stan Kenton in the fifties to Burt Bacharach in the eighties.

By now, Semie Moseley was producing acoustic guitars, and as The Ventures were the Mosrite distributors, *Guitar Freakout* displayed the hollow-body-electric Celebrity model on the back cover. Watching Semie over-extending his capabilities, Stan Wagner offered a solution; "Semie couldn't produce enough guitars to keep up with the demand, which put *us* behind the eight-ball. I told Al Bennett that if he bought Mosrite, he would already have a million dollars worth of advertising on all those The Ventures records. Bennett was convinced and offered Moseley a million dollars cash and a $50,000 annual salary for Semie to oversee the factory, plus another five million over ten years if the business remained successful. With an aversion to losing the Mosrite name to outsiders, plus the knowledge of the $13,000,000 Fender buyout by CBS, Semie countered with an outrageous cash price of $10,000,000. Fully aware that Mosrite was a minnow among whales compared to Fender, Al upped the cash offer by $1,000,000, but Semie wouldn't budge. Bennett might have offered more, but his accountant was having fits already."

"FOR AN UNPRECIDENTED ONE MILLION ALBUMS SOLD EACH YEAR 1961 – 1966"

Although busy with Mosrite Distributing, Stan Wagner did not neglect the fan clubs. Having placed Al Avalon in Tokyo to run the Japanese club, Stan worked to increase U.S. club membership by offering a discount on previous albums, plus *Guitar Freakout* free to any member that could recruit six new fans. With yearly dues set at just $1.50, the club was soon welcoming many new members.

As Cash Box readers voted The Ventures the Top Instrumental Group for 1966, Bob Reisdorff was beckoned back to the music business; "Al Bennett was telling me how Liberty artists like The Ventures were tremendous hits in Europe and that he wanted to expand to the UK. Back in 1963, when we were recording *The Ventures in Space*, he and Snuffy had flown to London and nearly signed The Beatles while Capitol Records was resisting American exposure of that group. Brian Epstein was ready to sign when Capitol reversed its decision under pressure from [parent company] EMI. The Liberty offer was discarded, but we pondered 'what might have been' for months after that.

"I don't know if Al knew this, but I had fallen in love with England while stationed there during World War II. If he was baiting me, I bit hard when he suggested I open a Liberty office in London. For the next two years, I partied with top artists like The

Beatles and Jimi Hendrix. During my tenure in London, I was pleasantly surprised one day when Stuart Leech, who ran The Ventures' UK fan club, dropped in for a visit. He'd come about a hundred miles, all the way from Norfolk."

Before going to the UK, Bob sought out Sonny Rivera. As Dick Glasser's secretary, she had left Liberty when her boss had defected to Warner in 1965. At home with two children and managing a publishing company for Leon Russell, Sonny was willing to also manage Reisdorff's affairs.

~ ~ ~

After family visits in Florida and Washington, Josie Wilson was; "..missing Don and the boys in California, I bought a beautiful home overlooking the San Fernando Valley. The view at night was a panorama of twinkling lights. Having my own home meant that I could do a bit of entertaining. At one of my parties, I introduced Don and Chris Wilde. Don was surprised that this guy who had been rude to his mother on that first meeting, turned out to be such a nice fellow. They struck a staunch friendship, each appreciating the other's talents."

Fans catch Bob at a train station in Japan - 1966

1967 kicked off with The Ventures' full-page photo heading the International section in a February Cash Box, and in April, gracing the magazine's front cover. This was also the year that California guitarist, teacher, and music dealer Bud Eastman founded *Guitar Player* magazine. Beginning as a bi-monthly of less than fifty pages, this authoritative publication would double in size each decade while inspiring several competitive magazines. *Guitar Player* and its imitators, along with teen-zines like *Hit Parader* and *Teen Screen* would periodically feature The Ventures, but it was the January issue of *Reader's Digest* that exposed the group to an entirely new audience in a four-page article called "Loud The Twang Of The Guitar." Condensed from a 1966 story in Colorado's *Denver Post*, writer Virginia Kelly related how, in 1958, two construction workers playing guitar in their spare time had since sold 18,000,000 record albums, owned a guitar company grossing $1,500,000 in the preceding year, and marketed 375,000 albums teaching people how to play the instrument. She then described a worldwide guitar binge that left the music business stunned. The article went on to imply that The Ventures were $25,000,000 richer after only six years in the business. To that, Don says; "Liberty sold an awful lot of our records, but *we* never saw money like *that*!"

 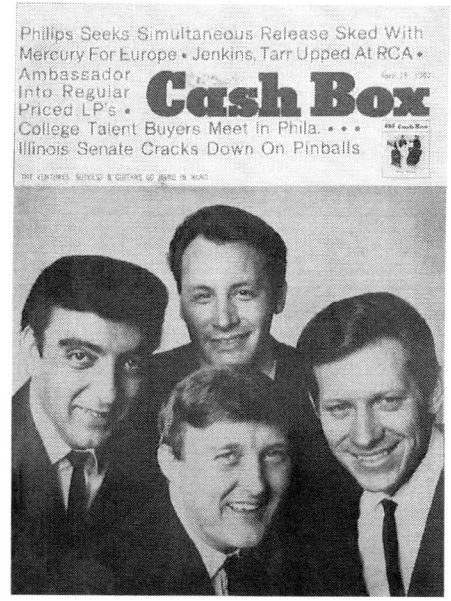

February 25 and April 15 - 1967

At the time, actor Boris Karloff hosted *Tales From the Reader's Digest* with daily readings on syndicated radio. To promote the magazine's current issue, the seventy-nine-year-old actor interviewed Don and Bob on January 16 for use in the closing minutes in two of his quarter-hour programs.

The band spent the next few weeks writing and recording. *Super Psychedelics* [Liberty LST-8052] boasted seven original Ventures tunes plus *Kandy Koncoctions* from good friend Danny Hamilton. "Psychedelic" was not yet in dictionaries, but the term quickly spread after Dr. Timothy Leary spoke out in support of LSD and the drug's hallucinogenic effect on its users. By this time, young people with flowers in their hair were extolling peace and love in protest of America's military involvement in Vietnam. Chanting, "Tune in, turn on, and drop out," the widespread hippy movement generated fear and dismay among parents. Music was changing, as were clothing styles. While the hippies wore baggy garments and blankets cut with head holes, a counter-culture adopted smart new styles from San Francisco's Haight-Ashbury region. Meanwhile, The Ventures kept their clean-cut image, surrendering only slightly to the "mod" look.

Opening *Super Psychedelics* with The Beatles' flower power anthem, The Ventures' version of *Strawberry Fields Forever* was so delightful that it was immediately slated for a single. Added keyboards gave it the sound of the times, with studio wizard Tommy Tedesco adding mandolin to this and the closing track, *Happy Together*. Tedesco reported working on the session for three hours at twenty-seven dollars an hour. Quoting his Studio Log [*Guitar Player* Jan. '87]; "Joe Saraceno sometimes added me to established groups such as The Ventures to give a quality that he felt I had."

Although *Strawberry Fields* was not a big seller, Liberty issued it twice within a few months, backed first with *Endless Dream* [55967], and then with The Ventures' version of the theme from *Endless Summer* [55977], a surfing reality film that *Newsweek* described as "Breathtaking! Sweeping and Exciting!" while *Time* called it "a dazzling ode to sun, sand and surf!" Released on digital medium in the twenty-first century, the film with its soundtrack by The Sandals became a monument to the sport of surfing.

Of particular delight to fans was the packaging of *Super Psychedelics* in a beautiful gatefold jacket containing a dozen color photos of their heroes away from stage and studio. In a fan club bulletin, Josie described the pictures; "From top-left and going down, 1 through 5 and 7 were taken at Don's home, 6 at Mel's home, 8 at a Hollywood hamburger stand, 9 outside the Liberty Records building, 10 and 11 at Bob's home, and 12 at a Los Angeles clothing store."

Josie recalls some memorable times at Don's fabulous home on Paulcrest Drive; "They threw some real Hollywood costume parties in that house! It was there that I met actresses Judy Garland and Hedy Lamarr. Besides her fame for playing opposite Victor Mature in *Samson and Delilah*, Hedy had a hand in the invention of a secret communication system that apparently helped the allies during *World War II*."

Don and Nancy   Mel and Lorraine   Bob R. and Josie

Don recalls a few more celebrities at those parties; "I met Jayne Mansfield and Richard Dawson, and I even shot a game of pool with Rudolph Wanderone, better known as Minnesota Fats. I don't have to tell you who won. We also had authors Henry Miller [*Tropic of Cancer, Tropic of Capricorn*] and Raymond Strait, who wrote a lot of biographies in Hollywood. Other film stars I recall are Andre Philippe and Jack Chaplin [not Bob's friend] who worked together in the TV series, *Mr. Novak*" at the time.

Don, Mel, and Josie

SLAUGHTER ON SUHARTO'S AVENUES

It was now two years since Operation Rolling Thunder, America's massive bombing campaign against North Vietnam. During the war's escalation, The Ventures entertained multitudes in peaceful Japan, barely aware of the unrest just three thousand miles to the southwest. In the fall of 1965, after pursuing increasingly pro-Communist policies, President Ahmed Sukarno was implicated in a Communist-instigated attack on Indonesia's military leaders. An attempted Communist coup triggered an anti-Communist government takeover by the army. With killings in the range of 1,000,000, control of the nation was seized by the brutal and corrupt dictator, General Mohammed Suharto. Rejoining the United Nations in 1966, Suharto's government bolstered public morale by sponsoring concerts by foreign entertainers. The first contract signed was for a two-week tour by The Ventures, beginning in mid-February, 1967.

The Ventures employed an equipment manager for local tours, whereas promoters supplied a man in Japan. Needing a "roadie" for Indonesia, they approached Harvey Gold, the promoter who had ushered them around New York for radio interviews. It had been just over a year since Harvey had been transferred to Los Angeles, and he was quick to accept a one-time job in the East Indies.

On February 10, 1967 Don celebrated his 34th birthday with Bob, Nokie, Mel, and Harvey, sipping wine on a United Airlines flight to the Philippines. From Manila, they flew on Indonesia's Garuda Airlines to the ancient capital of Jakarta. During the flight, the guys learned that Jakarta had a population greater than New York City crammed into seventy percent of the space. Being the first-ever rock group allowed to visit Indonesia, The Ventures felt fairly honored. Just three years earlier, this government's ban on Beatles haircuts had made world news. The guys were not, however, aware of the country's political situation, or of recent violence under its martial rule.

It was 10:00 p.m. and pitch-dark outside when the flight landed at Jakarta. A native introducing himself as Purnomo had been assigned as their translator and tour guide. With a population exceeding 4,000,000, The Ventures were surprised to see few bright lights in Jakarta. Purnomo explained that electricity was quite an expensive luxury.

Wending their way to the Jakarta Hilton, the band noted that the city was supported by an extensive system of canals. They also noticed the presence of armed soldiers everywhere, and no local police. Further into the city, tanks patrolled streets between barbed wire barricaded intersections. Explaining this to be how the government-decreed curfew was enforced, Purnomo warned the guys to stay off the streets at night or they would likely be shot, and if they were still alive, brutally interrogated later. For the rest of the ride, the boys in the band wondered nervously over what surprise was next.

The next day, The Ventures were wined, dined, and treated for nearly four hours, courtesy the government, to an interesting but overly long presentation of native cultural music, bamboo bands, and Balinese dancing. Traveling about the city was increasingly disturbing, as the guys witnessed extreme poverty of most of the citizens. Thousands of people lived on the banks of the huge canal network, in homes consisting of a simple lean-to over some bedding. Lizards crawled everywhere on just about everything. More distressing was the sight of the canals being used for everything from bathing and laundering, to open-air toilets. As Bob recalls; "It's hard to describe all the things we saw. It was like being on another planet. We stayed at the Jakarta Hilton, as we were told it was the only decent hotel in the entire country at the time. We became so afraid that we stayed in our rooms most of the time. Conveniently, our first concert was there in the hotel ballroom. We did a sound check and ran through a few tunes before returning to our hotel rooms. When it was show time, we had just gone down to the dressing room when the power went off and we were in the dark. After sitting there for twenty minutes, we went back up to our rooms. Purnomo taught us a few short phrases for use on stage, and we asked about the power failure. He said it could have been anything from a vehicle hitting a power pole to a generator breakdown, but that the major fear was of another attempted coup. With several generals present for our show, it would be an opportune time for a mass assassination. More than ever, we were wondering what we were doing in such unstable surroundings.

"In about an hour, the power came on and six armed soldiers escorted us from the dressing room. The guards should have made us feel safe, but we found the procedure fairly unsettling. We were even more upset once we were on stage and the curtain went up. As we opened with *Walk-Don't Run*, we saw the front row filled with high-ranking military officials. Next we saw young soldiers lying on their stomachs at each end of the stage, aiming guns toward the crowd, apparently to protect the Generals from any sudden assault. Two or three times during our concert, we heard a commotion in the lobby. We only played about a dozen numbers, but it seemed like the longest concert we had ever played." To this, Don added; "Obviously, we played any and all requests!"

Bob continues; "At the end of our show, we were enjoying a lengthy applause when the military police marched on stage to usher us back to the dressing room. We were just getting used to the soldiers when two young fans approached us for some autographs. Without a word, the guards drove their rifle butts into their faces causing blood to spatter everywhere. We protested and tried to explain that these were our fans, but they just ignored us. Then, when we got back to the dressing room, each guard asked us for our autographs!"

Two days later, the group was off to Surabaya, the second major city on the island of Java. This 500 mile *Garuda Air* flight employed the crudest aircraft that the guys had ever seen. The body had no inner lining, its aluminum skin visibly shaped by the metal frame. For seating, canvas was stretched between steel bars. Purnomo informed the band of a lavatory at the back of the cabin. After a while, Mel decided to use it, but was back in his seat almost immediately. Using a term picked up in Japan, Mel told the others; "Don't bother using the *benjo*, guys. It's nothing but a bucket behind a curtain!" To this, Don added; "Bob and Nokie shouldn't mind. Isn't that what they had back on the farm?" It was one of the few chuckles the boys would have on the tour. As in Jakarta, the Surabaya concerts sold out with around 2,000 attending each show. Unfortunately, the military tension was just as high.

Back in Jakarta, another pair of concerts filled up the week. There was no more sign of bloodshed, but students approaching the band were still manhandled. As Purnomo explained, many students were desperate to see The Ventures, but could not get in because they had no money or the seats were filled. During the week, the Indonesian Security Forces had shot some fans that had become a bit rowdy. Purnomo knew of five students killed while attempting to force their way into one of the concerts. Shocked at first, the guys then felt anger and sadness. That night, they decided to put a stop to the mayhem. With ten concerts left to play, they made Purnomo inform the officials of a Ventures' family emergency. Claiming one of their wives was on her deathbed, the group was taking the next flight out of the country.

Meanwhile at home, the excuse neared reality as Mel's wife had become so ill that she had asked Stan Wagner if Mel could come home early. Stan was about to fulfill her wish when Lorraine began to recover.

As Harvey Gold had business in Japan, he parted company with the band and caught a flight to Tokyo. The next morning, The Ventures boarded a Garuda Airlines 747 bound for Manila. Upon landing, the foursome faced another problem. Their United Airlines reservations were not due for a week, and earlier flights to the U.S.A. were full. In hope of cancellations, United put the band on standby status. Sure enough, some "no-shows" were announced, but there were only three. Bob remembers how they handled it; "We drew straws to see who would stay behind. I remember aching to get back to Hollywood and the sinking feeling when I drew the short straw. I was waving goodbye to Mel, Nokie, and Don as they climbed the steps to the plane when I felt a tap on my shoulder and heard the sweetest sound ever. It was a United employee saying, 'Come on, we have one more seat.' We were so glad to be out of Indonesia that we didn't care that we didn't get paid. After fleeing like that, we didn't even write to the Government for our money. We just tried to erase the whole episode from our minds."

Once back in Hollywood, there was little time for rest. *Guitar Freakout* had peaked at 57 and it was time to compose and record some music with an Oriental flavor. The resultant *Hokkaido Skies* became one of the group's biggest Japanese hits of all time on a single backed with *Tokyo Nights* [Toshiba LR-1722]. Soon, an entire album was ready for summer release. *Pops in Japan* [LP-8161] contained nine popular Japanese songs (including two Yuzo Kayama compositions), both sides of the recent single, and a third Ventures original titled *Yokohama Lights*. Sales of this album earned The Ventures a Gold Record award from Toshiba-EMI, encouraging a few more Japan Pops albums from the band. Reminiscing, Don recalls; "We were told by the president of Toshiba Records that if Japan had been keeping charts since the early sixties, we would have had at least twenty Number 1 hits!"

While summer saw youthful masses focusing on The Monkees and the Beatles, Ventures fans reveled in *Super Psychedelics*. In June 1967, the album reached 69 in Billboard, indicating The Ventures were still a band to contend with. In July, as *Record World* featured The Ventures on its cover, the band received another invite to perform on *American Bandstand* for the July 1 show. With no current big hit, The Ventures began with the familiar notes, A-G-F-E. This time, however, it was not *Walk-Don't Run* or *Surf Rider*, but the intro to *Vibrations*, an original from *Super Psychedelics*. For their second number, The Ventures played their own *Green Hornet '66*.

After the Dick Clark session, Stan Wagner and The Ventures flew to Chicago to promote their line of beautiful guitars at the National Association of Music Merchants (NAMM) trade show. While there, they took time to visit various booths and try some of the new equipment on display. Eventually, Bob came upon a booth for Hallmark Guitars, a company located in Arvin, California, about twenty miles from Bakersfield. Hallmark was run by Joe Hall, a Mosrite employee from the late fifties to 1962 who was involved in developing the Ventures Model. The display made Bob do a double take and wonder if he was dreaming, for there, in splendid reality, were four models of the Encor guitar he had designed, but they were now called the Hallmark "Swept Wing" guitar. One was a bass with the same design. During the ensuing conversation, Bob learned that Hall now had been joined by ex-Mosrite employee Bill Gruggett, who confessed to using Bob's design upon deciding it was just too good to waste. Closer inspection revealed the thin hollow-bodied model to have several Mosrite characteristics, including a zero-fret and a bridge with individual string-rollers. Even the rhythm pickup was mounted at a slight angle. Several of the parts were obviously from Mosrite, including the wood-aluminum tailpiece, the pickups, and the super-thin neck with a Mosrite shaped headstock, [minus the cutaway "M"]. Spectators were told that there would soon be solid-body models in twelve-string and double-neck. Thinking back, Bob reflects; "I knew I had no claim on the design as I had never taken steps to protect my work. All I could do was to chalk it up to another of life's lessons."

Hallmark display at Chicago Hilton - NAMM '67   *Joe Hall*

To promote the radically shaped guitar, Hallmark presented instruments to bands like The Doors, the Grateful Dead, The Mamas and the Papas, The Baja Marimba Band, Jefferson Airplane, and The Association. Apparently ahead of its time, with less than fifty units produced, Hallmark became an icon of American guitar history in less than a year. According to Semie Moseley, Hallmark's downfall stemmed from the inability to build its own guitar necks, considerably raising production costs.

In 1995, the Hallmark was re-introduced on a custom order basis by Front Porch Music of Bakersfield. Later, Hallmark reappeared with the Swept Wing model in the State of Maryland under the direction of guitar collector-luthier Bob Shade, assisted by Joe Hall and Bill Gruggett. By then, most of the Mosrite features had vanished.

~ ~ ~

Arriving home, The Ventures found a set of three completed amplifiers waiting to be tested. The wait had been long, but it proved seemingly worthwhile. Rated at 100 watts of true power, the BG-1000 stood four feet tall. Like the Vox amplifiers used by The Beatles, the cabinet sat in a chromed metal stand and could be tilted back and tightened with locking knobs at the sides. Two pre-amp channels handled a regular guitar with selected effects, or a deep-pitched electric bass. In addition to reverb, the player could choose between tremolo and *true* vibrato! These effects, as well as Fuzzrite overdrive, could be controlled with a three-button footswitch. With high-current silicon transistors driving the heavy-duty speakers, the equipment was slightly ahead of its time. The amplifiers were a handsome sight, although the number of logos was slightly confusing. While the control panel declared it to be a Mosrite amplifier, the neon blue grille-cloth sported a large Award emblem in one corner and a Ventures Model logo near the bottom. Don remembers when they put the amplifiers to the test; "We took those amps on our next tour, and they were absolutely incredible! At the time, they would blow the biggest Fender amp right off the stage."

In July, before leaving for Japan, The Ventures taped another appearance for the Dick Clark show, which led to yet another project. Clark had been contracted by the U.S. Navy to promote recruiting with a series of weekly radio broadcasts. Earlier shows had featured popular heroes like John Wayne, but they were now using trendy teen groups such as The Turtles and Gary Lewis & The Playboys. Entitled "Your Navy Presents," each fifteen-minute radio spot featured dialogue with the band along with three or four musical numbers. Given their abundant repertoire and current popularity,

Clark and company wasted no time creating four broadcasts based around the group's music. The programs, pressed on a pair of long-play platters, made wonderful collector's items because the music was special. Instead of drawing from The Ventures' many records, Clark obtained raw studio recordings, lacking the any enhancements or overdubbed tracks. The songs ranged from the early *Bulldog* to their most recent Monkees' cover, *A Little Bit Me, A Little Bit You*. With just three guitars and drums, the sound was much like a stage performance, but without any reverb or crowd noise. Most noticeable was the missing electronic organ in *House of the Rising Sun*.

Another boon to collectors was the theme song played by The Ventures. The tune is unique to this pair of long-playing albums, and it's title has never been identified.

In the years to come, broadcaster Sam Riddle replaced Dick Clark on the broadcasts. In 1971, four more Ventures shows appeared on two LP discs, by which time the series was called *Sounds Like The Navy*. The music on these consisted of samples from recent Ventures' albums and the classic *Walk-Don't Run '64* as the theme. However, while noting that memory is sometimes poor, Bob Bogle is fairly certain that The Ventures never received payment for their part in any of the Navy projects.

Although the 1967 Japan tour was for just three weeks in July, The Ventures arrived with three powerful BG-1000 amplifiers. For instruments, Bob and Don took Combo model Mosrite guitars finished in sunburst while Nokie took a red Combo and a white solid body twelve-string. For concert material, the guys were surprised to find Japanese lyrics had been written for their *Hokkaido Skies*, and that female pop star Chiyo Okumura had made a hit recording of the song. Toshiba had arranged for Chiyo to perform her vocal with The Ventures at the Tokyo concerts, one of which was recorded for a live album at Kosei Nenkin Hall.

Instrumental rock bands with guitars and drums were still springing up in Japan and America, the difference being in their repertoire. North American groups had several Ventures songs in their play list, whereas their Japanese counterparts played almost nothing *but* Ventures music. One late-sixties survey reported some 300-guitar bands in Tokyo alone. Thirty-five years later, dozens of these "Ventures copy bands" continued to perform, some with their original members, with names like Nikawa Ventures, Tokyo Ventures, Kawada Ventures, Adventures, Apache, and Miserlou. Sometimes The Ventures or Nokie would be invited to judge tournaments in which some of these bands demonstrated an amazing similarity to their mentors, not only in sound, but also in equipment and stage attire. In 1967, the Golden Cups were scheduled to open for The

Ventures, and Bob recalls that there was a slight problem; "We noticed that they were playing all our material. We couldn't have that, and asked the promoter if he could get them to play something else. He said, 'That's all they know,' so we asked if he could arrange for a different group, and the promoter said, 'That's all *any* of them know!' so there wasn't much we could do."

A popular album cover photo showing the band with their BG-1000 amplifiers

A singer in the Golden Cups was Eddie Ban, who returned from a 1965 visit to America with what was likely the very first "fuzz box" in Japan. As we shall see, after another fifteen years, Eddie would sing on a unique single with The Ventures.

The Ventures played their songs loud and fast, thrilling the audience more with each successive number. A speedy rendition of *Wooly Bully* proved that the band did not need a keyboard to play anything from their records. Not only did Nokie play the organ solos faster and with more licks, he also threw in his "behind the bridge" solo introduced in *Bulldog* and later in *Yellow Jacket*. For mellower parts of the program, *Hokkaido Skies* and *Slow Sundown* were selected from *Pops in Japan*, and Nokie played the twelve-string Mosrite on *Blue Chateau*.

A FALLING OUT

As mentioned previously, TOA Attractions had assigned Mr. Ono to promote The Ventures in 1966. Ono-san not only helped organize the tours, but also negotiated contracts. Following the 1967 tour, Mr. Ono revealed a concern he had regarding Al Avalon and the tour contract. Don and Bob then heard how Avalon had obtained twenty-five thousand dollars "on the side" from Ono's company for The Ventures' to return to Japan. Ono also said that Stan Wagner might have sanctioned the deal. The emotions felt by Don and Bob ranged from shock and disappointment to anger, even before they heard the rest of the story. Avalon had also disappointed the fan club by running a contest in which the winner would spend a week with "the Venture of his choice." Response was brisk until the whole thing was cancelled. The Ventures had not heard of the contest, and said that such a thing would never fit into their hectic schedule. As Bob recalls; "Upon being reprimanded, Avalon blurted, 'I don't work for you, I work for Stan Wagner. Anything I did was with his approval.' Don came back with something like, 'Stan works for us, and that means you do too, but not any longer. Consider yourself fired and lucky to escape a term in prison!'"

On the trip home, the guys were feeling violated. They all liked Stan Wagner and could barely believe Avalon's allegations. Opinions were split on what to do next. Don and Mel were adamant that Wagner be fired as soon as they arrived in Los Angeles. While Bob surmised that Stan might not be guilty, Nokie just shook his head.

As The Ventures spent so much time away from home, they employed a personal business manager to handle their affairs. At this time, Mr. Don Gursey, a tough young fellow noted for his high ethics, was handling the job. When Gursey heard about Al Avalon, he concurred that ties with Stan be severed, rather than enter a drawn-out conflict of accusations and denials. The solution was simple, and it would avert the malice that could erupt if charges were pressed. Aware that the band was squeamish about letting Wagner go, Gursey shouldered the task without hesitation.

In fairness, Stan Wagner's account is presented here, forty years after the fact; "I have to say that I was accused of being dishonest because of secondhand information that was untrue and completely void of any proof. Don approached me at about two-thirty one morning, saying he had heard from the promoter about a deal between Al Avalon and me. It was apparently to split some additional money that The Ventures didn't know about. I had absolutely no idea what he was talking about. I had nothing to do with any of it, and I never, ever took a penny that The Ventures didn't know about. I would swear on a Bible or take lie detector tests if it would help them to believe me. I asked Al, 'Why did you tell the promoter that I was part of your deal?' He said something like, 'Well, it was extra cash and I didn't think I was hurting anyone. I told Ono you were involved to make sure that I got paid. I told the same thing to Bob and Don in the panic of trying to save my job.'

"Al had been a good friend for years, but suddenly I had lost my group, and possibly my career. I had always been available for the guys twenty-four hours a day and they knew it. For the amount of money involved, why would I jeopardize such friendship? It was only a few thousand dollars. My main regret is that I was found guilty without any proof. I also wish I still had the Mosrite guitar that Semie gave me during that time. When I left, I was feeling very dejected and I gave it back to him. What would that fetch on eBay now? As the end of 1967 drew near, I felt like a dead man.

"I worked with other groups after that, and in 1970, producer Al Schmitt gave me a group to manage called Redeye. We got a hit that year with *Games* [Petagram PE-204] that was on the charts for ten months. A prominent L.A. disc jockey told us that *Red Eye Blues* was so good that if we put it on a single, he would play the hell out of it. They normally didn't play anything that wasn't already in the top thirty, so we put it on a single in a hurry. It was sitting at 27 with a bullet when radio program directors everywhere received a letter warning that the FCC would be listening for songs with drug-oriented lyrics. Suddenly, having the best agent and public relations people didn't mean a thing. The opening line of the song was 'Can't seem to find that hidden sunshine.' The guy that wrote it was heavily into beer, but in the parlance of drug talk in those days, sunshine turned out to be LSD! Our 'sunshine' had nothing to do with LSD, but the program directors were scared off playing that song and anything else by Redeye. The business was just getting more frustrating for me every year."

With no manager and declining tour activity, The Ventures resumed their pattern of recording for a new album while booking appearances between sessions. Don kept his voice in shape with Del Shannon's *Runaway* and *Hats Off To Larry*, while continuing to record love ballads and pairing them with his older singles. The last of these appeared in 1967 on Liberty. This is not to say that Don ended his pursuit of the elusive hit vocal. After religiously attempting *You'll Never Walk Alone* and being unsatisfied with it, he tried more ballads. While the trend in pop music was now embracing protest and political undertones, Don stuck with lighter and more pleasant material. Friend Christian Wilde also wrote songs which he offered to Don and The Ventures. As Chris was a trained classical tenor, he surprised the guys with some country and western flavored tunes.

The following spring found The Ventures at Hollywood Sound Recorders with Don singing his heart out on *Paliachi Joe*, backed by Red Rhodes on pedal steel. The session also included *How Can I Help You Girl*, *Seattle In The Rain*, and *Transit Man*, all written and produced by Christian Wilde. Chris started to produce an entire album of Don's vocals, but there just never seemed to be time. After nearly thirty years, fan clubs were treated to the project on a 1995 cassette tape. Even later, under the group's new M&I Japan label, CDs of this and some re-recorded versions appeared in 1999 and 2004.

Following Japan Tour '67, the band's morale was restored by some great news from Liberty Records. A series of *Golden Hits* compilations initiated by Snuff Garrett had been so successful that Liberty had decided to create another series of *Golden Greats* albums. Packaged in luxurious gatefold covers that pictured a bikini-clad model dubbed "The Liberty Belle," each set would be an anthology of a popular artist's recordings. The prolific Ventures more than qualified for this series, and their *Golden Greats* compilation arrived hot on the heels of *Super Psychedelics*. Many fans preferred to see The Ventures on the band's album covers, but few objected to the photos of nineteen-year-old Chris Cranston, featured in the center as well as on both outside covers of *Golden Greats* [Liberty LST-8053]. A year later, Miss Cranston's career blossomed when she was seen in the pages of the September '68 *Playboy* in recognition of her appearance as a Ziegfeld girl in the Barbra Streisand movie, *Funny Girl*. In 1971, she appeared again in *Playboy*, this time as April's "Playmate of the Month." Her centerfold pose resembled that on The Ventures' *Golden Greats*, although she had removed her bikini.

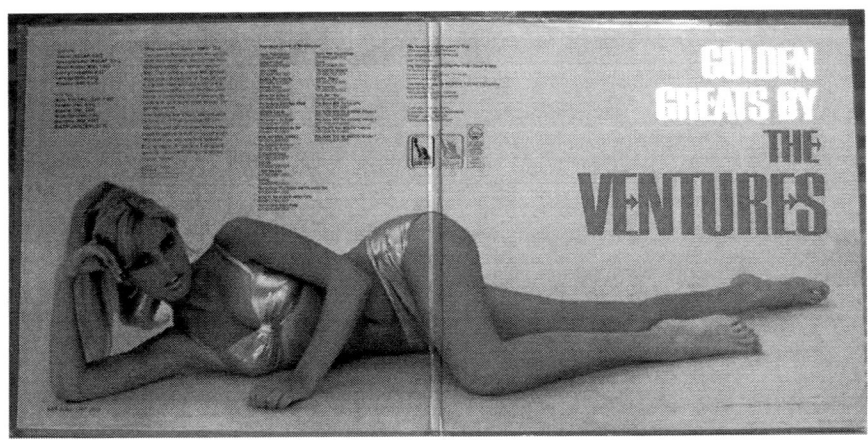

The LP discography and liner notes by Stuart Leech were not readily noticed.

Just in case the stalwart Ventures fan might think of passing up this sampler from past albums, an unreleased cover of the Duane Eddy hit *Rebel Rouser* was added for bait. Unknown for several more years was the fact that Don Wilson played lead guitar on this cut. The album included one more consolation for the Ventures completist, containing what many consider to be a superior cut of *Apache* compared to that on the *Telstar* album. Not only did the version have a brighter, so called "Mosrite sound," it closed with a firm ending rather than an engineered fadeout.

While *Golden Greats* only peaked at 50 in early September, it eventually earned The Ventures their second RIAA Gold award for sales above 500,000 on home ground. Like *Telstar and The Lonely Bull*, this album introduced The Ventures to thousands of homes, where it created a hunger for even more samples of their recorded music.

MIDDLE-OF-THE-ROAD TEST

The last project for 1967 seemed to be an attempt to duplicate the awesome success of *Telstar & Lonely Bull*. Consisting mostly of MOR tunes like *Georgy Girl* and *What Now My Love* and no original compositions, the album was a a slight disappointment for fans of rock 'n' roll. Still, fans quickly pushed *$1,000,000 Weekend* [Liberty LST-8054], up to a respectable 55 in Billboard. Nokie, Don, Bob, and Mel played on all of the tracks, but in true Saraceno form, top session musicians were employed to fill out the sound. Extras included Michel Rubini and John Gallie on keys, Red Rhodes on steel, Bill Pitman on bass, and Gene Pello for some added percussion. The beautiful acoustic rendition of the Beatles' *Yesterday* that topped off *Weekend*, remained a popular solo piece for Nokie.

A tiny message on the back of this and the next several albums stirred the interest and imagination of guitar playing fans for the whole of the following year.

The Ventures Use Award Amplifiers Exclusively - 6565 Sunset Blvd 90028

The announcement brought letters from hundreds of fans, as well as dozens of music dealers recognizing the power of a Ventures endorsement. Each prospective dealer was informed that shipment would begin in a matter of two or three months.

Although the Indonesian experience and the problems with Al Avalon had made 1967 an unforgettable year, more turmoil and triumph lay ahead. 1967 was also the year that Don and Nancy mutually agreed to terminate their marriage and sell their large home on Paulcrest Drive.

Nancy turned to writing as a career, first for Hollywood gossip columns, and later, penning a number of published novels.

THOSE HAMILTON BROTHERS

We left the Hamiltons in 1966, touring as The T-Bones with Danny on lead, Judd on rhythm. As Judd's singing voice developed, they played fewer instrumentals. Plagued by personnel changes, arguments between Judd and Danny became more frequent until one day in New York, Danny quit the group and returned to California. His replacement was Tommy Reynolds, who sang and played several instruments in a group called The Uncalled Four, but wasted no time in joining the famous T-Bones. In a few months, bassist George Rosenthal tired of touring and Judd picked up Joe Frank Carollo from a group called the Bar-Kays. Carollo was an asset to The T-Bones as he could sing while playing the bass. When Richard Torres dropped out, Tommy Reynolds took over keyboards guitar player, Jay Allen was picked up in Chicago.

When The T-Bones landed back in Los Angeles, they were such a hot sounding band that they were invited to play in the company of the Beach Boys, the Righteous Brothers, and Buffalo Springfield for a benefit function at the Aquarius Theater. The five worked so well together that Joe Saraceno brought them into the studio to record the final T-Bones album, *Everyone's Gone To The Moon (And Other Trips)*. Now that The T-Bones were a genuine group, their photo appeared on the back of *Everyone's Gone To The Moon*. The boys covered The Ventures logos on their headstocks with their hands, but a small note near the bottom proudly proclaimed that The T-Bones played Mosrite guitars.

The road version of The T-Bones

Jay Allen, Tommy Reynolds, Judd Hamilton, Gene Pello, Joe Frank Carollo

Eventually, Danny heard the group, and while congratulating Judd on the great sound of the new T-Bones, he expressed a desire to rejoin. When Jay Allen announced he would be returning to Chicago, he was quickly replaced with Danny, and the Hamilton brothers were reunited.

Still in Hollywood, Stan Wagner arranged a Japan tour for these "friends of The Ventures." However, drummer Gene Pello was making good money for session work, so he opted out. His work at the time included Ventures albums *Guitar Freakout* and *$1,000,000 Weekend*. Consequently, Joe Frank Carollo switched from bass to drums and Judd took over the bass. With Danny on guitar and Tommy Reynolds on keyboards, the quartet toured Japan. Upon their return, the T-Bones disbanded. As The Hamilton brothers, Judd and Danny hired a drummer and took a nightclub job at Joanna's Castle. Tommy Reynolds formed a group called Renaissance with Malcolm Evans, Richie Hernandez, and a hot little drummer named Joe Barile.

When Joanna's Castle was destroyed by fire, Judd began working in movies, along with making occasional recordings on various labels. Meanwhile, Danny went to work with Joe Frank Carollo and Tommy Reynolds to record a demo entitled *Don't Pull Your Love*. Thus, the group Hamilton, Joe Frank and Reynolds was born. When the song topped charts across the continent [Number 4 in Billboard], a promo tour followed. As Carollo was back on bass, they now needed a drummer. Having played with Tommy Reynolds in Renaissance, Joe Barile was summoned.

Danny Hamilton

For the B-side of *Don't Pull Your Love*, the trio wrote a funky instrumental called *Funk-In-Wagnal*. This title, cutely playing on encyclopedia publishers Funk and Wagnalls, was coincidentally the name of a Ventures recording (spelled slightly different), and later donated to fan clubs by Don Wilson. Fans were surprised that *Funk 'n' Wagnell* and the other songs on the tape had never been released on vinyl.

JOSIE TO THE RESCUE

1968 began for The Ventures with an invitation from the National Academy of Recording Arts and Sciences to entertain at the Tenth Annual GRAMMY® Awards. As Bob recalls, the event was not shown on television; "Back then, the Grammys were not such a big thing as they are now. The presentation ceremony was only an hour long, and as we sat there, we noticed Pat Boone and Glen Campbell sitting in front of us. We looked around and recognized others like Hal Blaine, Johnny Rivers, and our old engineer, Bones Howe. There was a big party afterwards, and we played in half-hour sets, alternating with Les Brown and His Band of Renown. The whole thing turned out to be a four-hour gig, which was unusually long for us."

Entertaining for the Grammys – Feb. 29, 1968

Album Of The Year (1967) went to the Beatles for *Sgt. Pepper's Lonely Hearts Club Band*, while The Fifth Dimension won Record of The Year for *Up, Up And Away*. The Ventures saw their own favorite guitarist take the Grammy for Best Instrumental Performance with an album entitled *Chet Atkins Picks The Best*. Later at the dinner party, The Ventures played *Up, Up And Away* as part of their show. Clad in tuxedos, Bob, Don, Nokie, and Mel presented a classy appearance with their Combo Mosrites and enormous BG-1000 amplifiers. Of course, Josie was there, wearing a long gown and wrapped in furs, looking equally classy and radiant.

Early 1968 saw The Ventures tackle a new batch of Japanese hits while continuing to record for European and American markets. At home, however, concertgoers had no idea that the band was covering hits from Japan. Sonny Rivera handled fan inquiries and orders for records, but she had no time to write bulletins. When Josie learned of the situation, she immediately resumed command of the club she had started. In February, she announced her comeback by offering records to members at typical "good old days" prices. Liberty albums sold for $3.50, while Sunset albums went for $1.50. Singles were just sixty cents, and in all cases, postage was prepaid.

If Ventures fans worried about the band's direction after hearing the placid music on *$1,000,000 Weekend*, their fears were calmed when *Flights of Fantasy* [Liberty LST-8055] appeared in spring. The music was mostly fast and powerful, with new fun effects such as the guitar through a Leslie speaker on *Innermotion Phase*, a guitar-generated machine gun on *Bonnie and Clyde*, and electronic "phase-shifting" on the title song. This effect had appeared accidentally in an acetate recording of *Psyched Out* on February 2, 1967. It sounded so bad that it was re-recorded for *Super Psychedelics*, but then, Joe Saraceno talked engineer Lanky Lindstrot into refining the phasing error so the track could be used on a future album. Lanky was successful and the song was renamed to become the next LP's title song, *Flights of Fantasy*. Even fans that abhorred Liberty's song recycling tricks welcomed this one with enthusiasm. Lindstrot also applied the phasing trick on one of the album's five new originals, *Fly Away*.

While *Flights of Fantasy* climbed to 169 in Billboard, The Ventures' five-year contract with Mosrite expired. During a scheduled meeting with Semie, Don and Bob received some shocking news. With artists such as Glen Campbell now appearing on album covers with an unendorsed Mosrite, Moseley had decided not to renew, stating that his guitars could now stand on their name alone. As owners of Mosrite Distributing, The Ventures continued to play Mosrite guitars without their logo, but their suspicions that Semie was making a mistake would soon be confirmed.

SHODDY WORKMANSHIP

When The Ventures first heard about dealer claims for refund on Award amplifiers, they thought it was an April fool's joke. Award had begun to make a smaller, BG-500 amplifier, which turned out to be much more popular with music dealers than the expensive BG-1000. The units worked fine for a while, but eventually began to fail. Technicians repaired the simpler problems, but failures followed that indicated serious flaws in the design. It was then discovered that some of these amps were equipped with Jensen speakers instead of the advertised J.B. Lansing units. In June 1968, The Ventures' American fan club bulletin announced, "Due to technical difficulties of which we are uninformed, manufacture [of Award amplifiers] has been suspended." Contracting an unbiased technical firm to analyze the failures, The Ventures had received a five-page report listing design problems. The document concluded that the number of required alterations made the amplifiers unsalvageable. Mere parts replacement would be futile without a complete redesign.

Suggested reasons for the problems ranged from shoddy design to deliberate mischief. Nokie was sure that disgruntled Waters-Connelly employees had sabotaged the units, probably because they desired their own company to market the product. He based his opinion on some of the problems discovered, one of which seemed an obvious failure in crimping a pin, causing the reverb units to eventually fall apart. Another problem involved short-circuiting in the tremolo section.

Mosrite Distributing was now in a squeeze. While attempting to fulfill demands of dealers everywhere, The Ventures' line of credit was soon depleted. To make matters worse, the Crocker Bank called in their loan. For the first time since *Walk-Don't Run*, Bob and Don had serious financial concerns. The incident took nearly a year to resolve, during which time Waters-Connelly Electronics went bankrupt. In 1970, for two cents on the dollar, Minneapolis electronics dealer Stan Clothier bought the remaining Award product line, which included ten BG-1000 and a dozen BG-500 amplifiers, all with rolling stands and vinyl covers. In the spring of '71, Clothier sold the amplifiers, speakers, and a number of empty cabinets to private buyers until nothing was left but a large box of parts, which he junked.

By now, Mosrite was producing its own line of amplifiers along with a stand-alone battery-powered FUZZrite "stomp box." Although Ed Sanner is credited with designing this device, Nokie has suspicions about its internal circuitry; "The transistor fuzz box I had been using for years was designed by Red Rhodes. We had it built into our prototype and the Award amps, and I believe that Mosrite also used Red's design."

A Mosrite echo unit was also introduced, utilizing a small oil drum to create one of three selectable delay times. These Adineko units were made in Los Angeles by Tel-Ray Electronics, and licensed to Fender, Gibson, Rickenbacker, and Vox, amongst others, and eventually to Mosrite. Although the Mosrite unit flaunted a small "Ventures model" logo, Bob and Don say they never had an opportunity to try the device.

The Tel-Ray Echo box with Mosrite and Ventures logos.

Faced with a serious financial bind, The Ventures' only solution was to dissolve their Mosrite Distributing Company. Semie Moseley, now desperate for a distributor, made a deal with California's Thomas Organ Company. The company advanced him some working cash, but seemed far more committed to distributing Vox equipment popularized by the Beatles. With no Ventures' endorsement and little promotion by Thomas, Mosrite of California sank further into debt. Thus, when Valentine's Day arrived in 1969, so did the Internal Revenue Department. With tax arrears in the range of $45,000, Mosrite plunged into receivership. On April 1, a massive auction was held at the Bakersfield plant where all tools, machines, and office equipment were sold. Thirty-five years later, Andy Moseley recalls the proceedings; "We were there all day. It was a very sad time for us. Over a hundred new guitars were sold in lots of ten. Some were in cases, but most were not. I bought some of the guitars and basses along with many other items. The assembly and testing room contained a large stock of guitar parts, and I bought everything in that room."

The Ventures, still troubled with factors regarding Award amplifiers, were in no position (or mood) to bail Semie out of debt. Don recalls his anger; "We had orders outstanding all over the country because Semie couldn't keep up with the demand. Instead of expanding the guitar operation, he started blowing money on Dobro production and cutting records. He *really* blew it by not selling out to Liberty when he had the chance. He could have been a multi-millionaire and making another $50,000 a year to oversee the factory. And that was *huge* money in the sixties! But he ran it into the ground. As the distributor, we had all these guitars out there without our logo on them with hundreds of accounts receivable. Payments slowed when the Award amps crunched, and then retailers quit paying when they heard Mosrite was bankrupt. We were suddenly out by hundreds of thousands of dollars. I get sick thinking about it!"

Sadly, the collapse of Mosrite Guitars and Mosrite Distributing marked the end of an era for The Ventures. It was now apparent to many in the industry that, along with being extremely unlucky, Semie was a terrible businessman. He was down, but not out, and The Ventures would meet Mr. Moseley again.

According to electronics man Ed Sanner, the blame for the company's collapse should not *all* be placed upon Semie; "Another factor in the fall of Mosrite was the internal theft. Often, there were hundreds of parts missing that our inventory showed in stock. Most of the culprits got away with it, but I know of some that didn't. If Andy Moseley is around long enough to finish his book on Mosrite, I hope he names some of those crooks. It wasn't just the plant people. At least one of them wore a suit."

For decades to come, guitar playing fans around the world continued to associate The Ventures with Mosrite. Meanwhile, newer acts such as Iron Butterfly, MC5, The Ramones, Nirvana, Collective Soul, and Smashmouth, played a Mosrite or one of its clones. In 1967, the legendary Jimi Hendrix arrived at the studio with a double-necked Mosrite to record *Spanish Castle Magic* for his *Axis: Bold as Love* album. In addition, The Ventures' prolific back-catalog of albums kept the Mosrite name alive as they were continually re-issued with the guitars shown on the covers. As for the band, their attachment to Mosrite became a bittersweet bond that could never be severed.

TROUBLE IN THE STUDIO

Late in 1967, Mel developed a business relationship with lawyer Leon Leonian. As attorney for The Ventures, Leon lad become so interested in the music business that he and Mel formed Melee Productions with Mel as producer and Leon as engineer. That year, they produced Don Lee Wilson on their own label, singing Christian Wilde's *Seattle In The Rain* b/w *How Can I Help You Girl* [L&M WO-100]. The next year, they recorded a female duo called The Shannons singing *Mister Sunshine Man* b/w *Born Too Late* [L&M S-1003]. It was picked up for national distribution on Liberty [56073], but the girls' fifties style love songs backed with violins did not catch on. Mel and Leonian tried this group again with *Little White Lies* b/w *Are You Sincere* [Liberty 56100], but even with international distribution, the demos went nowhere. As luck would have it, Mel was a close neighbor of recording engineer, Ted Keep. The two had worked together on a 1962 session when Herb Alpert re-recorded Sol Lake's *Twinkle Star*. Backyard chat about the music business led to discussion of a new project in which Ted was involved. Mort Stevens had written the theme for a new CBS TV crime series and would be conducting his orchestra for the soundtrack. The show was to be taped on location in the country's fiftieth state, hence the name, *Hawaii Five-O*, a fictional State police crime unit. Keep felt that a recording of the theme by The Ventures would help launch the program. It was a simple matter for Mel to convince producer Joe Saraceno to record the theme for release in time for the show's fall debut. A session was booked for April 30, 1968.

Over twenty years later, readers of *Pipeline Instrumental Review* were shocked when an aging Joe Saraceno was quoted as saying; "We recorded 'Hawaii Five-O' with Tommy Tedesco while The Ventures were in Japan." However, session dates from Capitol-EMI printed in CD liner notes for *Walk-Don't Run – The Best of The Ventures* [93451], puts the *Hawaii Five-0* session in April 1968, months before the band's July-August Japan tour. When Tommy Tedesco related in his autobiography that he was present on the session, he verified that The Ventures were on the scene, as does Josie; "Playing alongside a twenty-four-piece orchestra was a first for the guys, and Don invited his sister Jackie and myself to the studio to watch the historic session. A problem soon arose when it was discovered that Nokie had only rehearsed the first portion of *Hawaii 5-O* and supposed that what followed would be a repeat. Unbeknownst to him was the fact that there was a modulation in the next portion of the song. Being unable to read the score, Nokie was having difficulty getting it right, so Joe Saraceno had session guitarist Tommy Tedesco come in and play the part for him. Tedesco made a grandstand show of sight-reading the part, but we were more impressed when Nokie then played it perfectly after hearing it only once. Tommy was no longer needed and spent the rest of the session seated beside us, drinking coffee. I have to say, it was not that The Ventures couldn't have learned to read music. The fact is, they never felt the need, being proficient musicians without it."

Don in the studio with Joe Saraceno

The grandstanding recalled by Josie was Tedesco's playing the guitar up behind his head while demonstrating his sight-reading ability. Tommy enjoyed telling the story later, but did not claim to have actually recorded on that session. However, a union record documented four months later as a "sweetening" session confirms Saraceno's memory of Tedesco working alone on *Hawaii Five-0*, just prior to its release. As we shall see, Nokie was unavailable at the time, having parted with the band by then.

In discussing the session for this timeless favorite, Nokie concluded with twinkling eyes and a grin; "I never get tired of playing that one. *Hawaii Five-0* has to be one of the greatest instrumentals ever written. My luck! I wrote *Hawaii Four-0*."

Hollywood apparently agreed with Nokie's regard for *Hawaii Five-O*, keeping The Ventures' version of the theme alive in movies such as Paramount's *A Very Brady Sequel* [1996], and the super-animated 2005 feature from DreamWorks, *Madagascar*.

THE ALBUM THAT NEVER WAS

"We had been doing a lot of traveling up to then, and I was kind of fed up with the music business," recalls Nokie; "I went back up to Washington and built up a stable of around a dozen thoroughbreds. Things were going pretty good when I got a call from The Ventures to go back to Hollywood to do some recording. I couldn't get away at the time and I told them they would have to get somebody else, so that's what they did."

In explaining what transpired, Don relates; "Liberty wanted to do a special album on us with new material to supplement songs on our Telstar album. It was actually for the Columbia Record Club, and they wanted it right away. As 'Record of the Month,' it would be included as a free bonus with new-member packages and we would receive instant royalties the same as if several thousand copies had been sold in the stores. Nokie was up there in Seattle with his racehorses, so I called him. He said he wasn't coming and I got mad. When I said, 'Nokie, you just *have* to get down here!' he said there was no way and to get somebody else. So we let Nokie go and replaced him, but by then it was too late to start recording a bunch of new songs for that record club."

The Columbia Record Club was well acquainted with The Ventures, having included tracks by the group since 1963 on its annual *Headliners* compilation album along with hit makers like Marty Robbins, Ferrante and Teicher, Ray Conniff, and The New Christy Minstrels. When Columbia heard what had happened, they quickly obtained a few uncommon tracks from Liberty for their special Ventures album. With first-time stereo versions of *The 2000-Pound Bee, Skip To M' Limbo, Ten Seconds to Heaven*, and *The Chase*, the album became a trophy for the band's avid fans. Another bonus on *The Versatile Ventures* [Liberty SCR-5] was the band's superb version of *Gemini*, a track heard only in mono on the flip side of their rather scarce *La Bamba* single [Dolton 311, 1965].

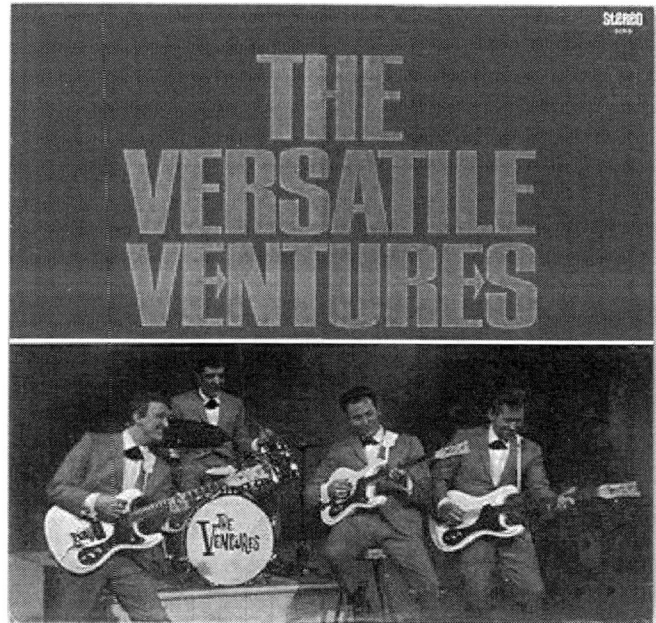

The Ventures' Columbia Record Club album

It was distressing to have dismissed their star picker in the heat of a dispute, but once again, Don and Bob forged ahead. After countering the British invasion with their own invasion of Japan, nothing such as losing a band member could stop them. They knew Nokie was a huge part of their success and that he would not be easily replaced, but like other obstacles, this one could be overcome by careful planning. Wishing Nokie well, The Ventures began looking for his successor. The first guitarist that came to mind was Mel's close friend, Jan Davis. Of those queried, Jan has the clearest recollection of the proceedings; "Mel told me that The Ventures were looking for a lead guitarist, and that I should go to their office on North Highland and talk with Don Wilson. When Don learned that my guitar had to be tuned different than his, he was scared off because he thought I wouldn't be able to play the stuff they were playing. He might have been right, I really don't know, but there are plenty of guitarists that can't play some of the stuff that I do."

Meanwhile, Don was relieved when Mel quickly lined up another audition. After meeting "Jerry" McGee six years earlier in a nightclub, the two had met a few more times and had kept in touch.

GERRY McGEE

On November 17, 1937, Gerald James McGee was born in Eunice, Louisiana. He was one of nineteen children sired by Dennis McGee, a highly revered fiddler who recorded roots Cajun music from 1929 to 1934, and who was still performing in the late eighties at over ninety years of age. Dennis, labeled the Dean of Cajun music by experts, also enjoyed fame in the South as a songwriter. Following a 1994 CD entitled *The Complete Early Recordings of Dennis McGee* [Yazoo 2012], notables such as the Magnolia Sisters and Beausoleil began recording his tunes.

"Cajuns," a slang derivation of "Acadians," denotes the white descendants of eighteenth century French exiles expelled from Acadia (now Nova Scotia, Canada). These isolated folk spoke a unique French dialect, still in use by Gerry's family while he was growing up. Surrounded with music and instruments from birth, Gerry experimented with the harmonica, banjo, and accordion until age fourteen, when he got a guitar. It soon became his instrument of choice for both country and rock music. Gerry especially liked the fingerpicking style of Merle Travis and Chet Atkins. His favorite singers were Hank Williams and Elvis Presley.

Gerry's first guitar was a Dobro-style Regal brand instrument borrowed from a young friend. Before long he had his own acoustic instrument, which he recalls as being a Stella. When Gerry and some friends formed a band, he bought an electric Silvertone guitar from a Sears & Roebuck catalog. Calling themselves the Boogie Kings, the teens played local dances for nearly three years. In 1955, when Gerry was eighteen, he joined the army. More money and the opportunity to play in service clubs with talented friends led to Gerry's upgrading to a Fender Broadcaster and a small Magnatone amplifier.

Gerry McGee

Now considered a rare and valuable find, the Broadcaster was the world's first commercially available solid-body electric guitar. It was not long before the Broadcaster had to be renamed when the Gretsch Company protested, having already registered "Broadkaster" for a new line of drums. Fender's Broadcaster guitar was then renamed as the Telecaster. One of the first rock 'n' roll performers to catch Gerry's attention was Buddy Holly, prompting Gerry to switch from the Broadcaster to a Stratocaster.

In 1957, during his eighteen-month duty in Korea, Gerry had the opportunity to visit Japan. A popular Japanese song of the time stuck in his mind, but he never imagined that he would record his own version of *Shina No Yoru* [China Night], some forty-five years later for a solo album. As he recalls, the military was the launching pad for his career; "An army buddy that happened to be a good singer promised me a job in his band after our discharge. I jumped at the chance since I hadn't played at all while we were in the Orient. It was summer, 1958 when we got out, and the first thing I did was buy a brand new Stratocaster. We didn't make much money in the taverns of Atlanta, but I met great guys like Jerry Reed and Joe South before they got to be big names."

One job led to the next, and after a year, Gerry was working in Shreveport, Louisiana where he met the now legendary James Burton. That job was probably responsible for Gerry developing his identifiable sound. Gerry tells it best; "My move to Shreveport was mainly to back up a professional Johnny Cash type singer. To get the sound of the Johnny Cash records, I put real heavy strings on my Stratocaster, which then required a heavier picking action. I guess it gave my playing a whole different tone. When I met James Burton in 1959, he kidded me about being unable to bend those heavy strings, but I think they were a help in developing my own style of playing."

As happens to many young musicians, Gerry fell on hard times that forced him to give up his Stratocaster for some instant cash and settle for a well-used Telecaster. Then, while discussing their future, James Burton told of how, three years earlier at age sixteen, he had trekked to Hollywood with Bob Luman to film a rock 'n' roll movie called *Carnival Rock*. As it led to a job with Ricky Nelson's band, James declared that the best move he had ever made was his migration to Los Angeles. Already with a childhood desire to be a film actor, Gerry hitched a ride to the West Coast. Landing his first job in a lounge on the east side Los Angeles, he could not believe his luck; "Before I left Shreveport, someone gave me a number to call into L.A. I called and asked the guy if he had a job for a guitar player. He said that the player he had was leaving in three days and to come on over. It was really amazing how fast I got a job. After five months, I was able to buy a cheap car and start scouting around Hollywood for better work."

Later that year (1961), Gerry went to a Hollywood studio and recorded a Latin flavored single with a group called The Bambinos. Although he co-wrote *Andante Amore*, very little guitar was heard over the keyboard melody. With even less guitar on the B side, *Algiers* featured nothing but the saxophone [Dot 16238].

From this group, a trio consisting of Gerry, Larry Taylor, and drummer Bill Lewis was formed. As The Cajuns, they became the house band at The Seawitch, a favorite L.A. watering hole for people in the music business. Here, Gerry met David Gates, Leon Russell, and the now legendary producer, Jimmie Haskell. After meeting Haskell, Gerry landed the lead guitar job on a recording session with Bobby Darin, who by this time had charted fourteen singles including his piano instrumental, *Beachcomber*. At least six songs were recorded on the session, but the Bobby Darin track that spurred Gerry's career was *You Must Have Been a Beautiful Baby* [Atco 6206]. Gerry was more than a little nervous when he found himself surrounded by professional sidemen, but he need not have worried. Even though his guitar was mixed well below the level of the heavy rhythm section, his distinctive style and tone were already evident. Charting at Number 5, the million-seller put Gerry in demand for several years. A session for doo-wop stars Little Anthony and the Imperials led to another job for Jerry McGee and the Cajuns, backing fifties rock 'n roll icon Teddy Randazzo [*The Way of a Clown* - ABC-Paramount 10,088] at a Las Vegas Strip hotel. A few years later, Teddy would be a key connection for both Gerry McGee and Larry Taylor.

Another patron at the Seawitch was popular orchestra leader, Don Costa, who was also a producer. Impressed with the Cajuns, he gave them some recording experience with three instrumental singles issued in two years on the Reprise label. Gerry recalls; "Don Costa was returning to New York and invited us to send him some tapes of our originals. When we did, he produced them and put them out on Frank Sinatra's Reprise label. It was also through Costa that I got some session work with Trini Lopez. By that time, I had quit correcting everyone who spelled my name with a 'J' and I just let it go."

The first two releases with the Cajuns were McGee originals, *Walkin'* b/w *Blues Train* [R-20057], and *Solitude* b/w *Jam Up* [R-20098]. The last was *Unknown Soldier* and a version of Floyd Cramer's *On the Rebound* [R-20156].

Early Gerry McGee singles with both spellings of his name

Two years later, in 1965, producer Jerry Fuller brought a New Jersey "Beatle-type" group called The Knickerbockers to Los Angeles where they recorded their solitary hit *Lies* [Challenge 59321] with session musicians Louie Shelton on lead guitar and Jerry McGee on rhythm. In the same year, a pair of singles appeared from Gerry as a solo artist. *Twilight Zone* and the flipside, *I Wonder* [Pacemaker 236], introduced Gerry's vocal talent. Later that year, Gerry returned to instrumentals with *Moonlight Surfin* b/w *Cajun Guitar* [A&M 711]. On this one, the record company got the spelling of his name right.

After the Trini Lopez sessions, Gerry backed artists such as Elvis Presley, Herb Alpert, Linda Ronstadt, The Everlys, and Nancy Sinatra. While working with Sandy Nelson, Gerry performed some great blues guitar in his two-part composition, *Mr. John Lee* on the mock live LP, *Sandy Nelson, Live In Las Vegas* [Imperial 12272, 1964]. In 1966, Gerry replaced James Burton in a Rick Nelson recording session. The following year, he played on Sandy Nelson's *The Drums Go On* [Imperial 66246] and a track called *Mystery Boogaloo* [Imperial LP-12367, *Boogaloo Beat*].

Recalling 1962, Gerry recalls meeting two musicians that would later change his life; "I had worked at the Seawitch for over a year with Larry Taylor when his brother, Mel, came in one night with Don Wilson. I was aware of The Ventures, but I never thought the day would come when they would ask me to play with them."

When The Monkees were created for television, Gerry's former association with Teddy Randazzo began to pay off. One of Randazzo's backup singers had become a writer for The Monkees, and through Teddy's friends (producers Tommy Boyce and

Bobby Hart), the Cajuns were put to work on the Monkees' first two albums, and Gerry composed the familiar introduction to (*Theme from*) *The Monkees*. He worked alongside guitarist Louie Shelton, who was also part of the Monkees' crew. In the November 2000 issue of *Guitar Player*, Louie Shelton claimed the opening riff on *Last Train to Clarksville* had launched his career. When asked about this, Gerry replied; "Louie Shelton only ever gives credit to Louie Shelton. I came up with that lick and played it for the first couple of takes. For some reason or other, the producer didn't like the tone of my guitar and asked Louis to try it. So yeah, it's him on the record, but I wrote it and I played it at least a hundred times on the tour that followed."

After touring with the Monkees, Gerry and the Cajuns became the Boyce and Hart Band when Tommy Boyce and Bobby Hart toured the country to promote their records. Gerry then hit the road in 1967 with Frank Zappa's protégé and high-school friend, Captain Beefheart, replacing nineteen-year-old Ry Cooder who left after recording the psychedelic album *Safe As Milk* [Buddah BDM-1001]. Uncomfortable with Beefheart's bizarre Zappa-esque influence, Gerry quit at the first opportunity.

Gerry McGee (2nd from left) with "Captain Beefheart"   *Michael Ochs*

Of the various studio sessions on which Gerry played, one of note generated a hit for the ever-changing Grass Roots combo. In February of 1971, *Temptation Eyes* [Dunhill D-4263] hit Number 15 in Billboard. In 1975, Gerry played on an album for Canadian folk legend, Valdy [*See How The Years Have Gone By* – A&M 4538].

Asked what happened next, Gerry replied; "There were dozens more sessions before I did an album for Delaney and Bonnie [*Accept No Substitute* Elektra EKS-74039]. They were expecting me to play on the follow-up tour when Mel Taylor called and asked me to join The Ventures. I had seen them in San Francisco, so I knew what they were into. All I had to do was talk to them for a while and play *Walk-Don't Run* for Don. I was married and raising a family by then, and The Ventures' offer was decent. Touring Japan sounded great too, so I accepted the job. I had been Japan and I loved it. Soon after going there with The Ventures, I was getting my own fan base. The Japanese are fantastic fans, and they want to know everything. Not just the exact settings of every knob on our equipment, or the number of millimeters between the guitar neck and my strings. They want to know what size shoes and clothes I wear! One fan has my discography on the Internet. It's pretty good, but it's probably not complete."

NEW IMAGE, NEW SOUND

When the news of Nokie's replacement reached Japan, East Asian Attractions sent an agent to Los Angeles to ensure that would be ready for the August Japan tour. In the meantime, between recording sessions for a new Ventures album, Gerry worked on nearly fifty songs from tapes supplied by Don. He was also furnished with a gleaming Mosrite Combo guitar which he still remembers; "The Mosrite was a great sounding guitar alright, but I found the neck hard to get used to after playing Fenders. I stuck with it because that's what the band was into then. I used it for touring and I was getting pretty used to the neck by the time we switched to other guitars."

The fall album was entitled *The Horse* [Liberty LST-8057], after the brass-heavy instrumental hit by Cliff Nobles & Company. Along with news of the new album, fan club members received a virtual bomb in their mail when Josie wrote; "It is with regret that we must inform all of his wonderful fans that Nokie has temporarily suspended his career with The Ventures to devote his time to things dear to his heart. As you know, the entertainment business is a fulltime job, and one rarely has time for outside interests. We will keep you posted on Nokie's activities from time to time. Although we will surely miss Nokie, The Ventures take pride in adding the talents of Jerry McGee as the newest member of their group. Blond hair, blue-eyed Jerry, stands 6 feet, weighs 160 pounds, and handles a lead guitar with a skill that defies the fact that he has only played guitar for eleven years. Jerry is a self-taught musician with great feeling, who also writes songs. The combination of his endless talents has made him a very sought-after young man by the top recording groups in the world."

Regarding the spelling of his name, Gerry explains; "When I came west, everyone spelled my name with a "J." I got tired of correcting them so I just accepted it. I got contracts and checks with the J spelling, which I had to sign that way, and I even started autographing that way for fans."

If Josie's announcement was not enough to send dedicated Nokie fans into depression, the enclosed photo made certain of it. The formerly clean-cut Ventures not only posed in "mod" clothing, but had let their hair grow long and Don flaunted a moustache and beard. Most fans who wrote in were appalled, urging the guys to get a shave and haircut. One writer jokingly asked Josie if their drycleaners had mistakenly mixed up The Ventures' clothing with that of the Beatles!

Having learned the importance of image in show business, The Ventures were keeping up with the times. New stage outfits included silver embroidered Nehru jackets and chained medallions, worn in new publicity glossies and on the cover of *The Horse*. It was nice to have an album fronted with a photo of the band, but the contents were also "something else." Hardly considered rock, the title tune and *Licking Stick-Licking Stick* seemed based on repetitious soul-flavored riffs. *Crazy Horse* and *Grazing in the Grass* demonstrated Gerry's expertise on the guitar, but again, not being prime Ventures-style selections, the sound took some time to be accepted by many of the group's fans.

Here Comes The Judge really hit the target with its delicious B-3 organ backing and humorous vocal injections from Mel and Don, built upon a series of skits from *Rowan and Martin's Laugh-In* TV series. Long-time fans found another enjoyable track, especially if they had not heard the latest Ventures single of *Walk-Don't Run* in medley with *Land of a Thousand Dances* [Liberty 56044], soaked in fuzz and backed with a cheering crowd. If they still held any reservations about Gerry McGee fitting in with The Ventures, they simply had to turn up the volume for the band's refreshing versions of *Jumpin' Jack Flash* and *Choo Choo Train*.

Mel Taylor   Bob Bogle   THE VENTURES   Don Wilson   Jerry McGee

1968 promotional photo introducing Gerry to the Fan Club

At this time of change, new material not taken from current chart-climbers was drawn from The Ventures' musical friends, Danny Hamilton and Christian Wilde. Danny's final contribution was *The Gallop*, a funky, danceable tune with Gerry exhibiting his 'chicken pickin' technique. In addition to clever liner notes for this album, Chris Wilde wrote *Soul Breeze*, extracting the melody from his *How Can I Help You Girl* written for Don's recent single release [L&M WO-100]. So pleasing was the result that it was chosen to back the *Hawaii Five-O* single, released at almost the same time as *The Horse*. Chris also wrote the brass-backed rocker, *Horse Power*, featuring an electric sitar solo by Gerry.

The final track on *The Horse* left many listeners blinking in disbelief. When the eccentric character known as Tiny Tim made a Top Twenty hit with *Tip-Toe Thru' The Tulips With Me* [Reprise 0679], he was publicized on TV variety shows as well as *Rowan And Martin's Laugh-In*. The recording obtained cult status in America, while making Tim somewhat of a phenomenon around the world. The Ventures' tongue-in-cheek rendition featured exaggerated vibrato and fuzz, a few out-of-tune notes, and an amusing impersonation by Don of Tiny Tim's impersonation of Porky Pig. This bit of comic relief gave most Ventures fans a genial chuckle, although some reported feeling little more than nausea. However *The Horse* LP topped Billboard's chart at 128 in August of 1968.

ON THE ROAD AGAIN

At a time when three guitars with drums were becoming dated, The Ventures began rehearsing with Sandy Lee Gornicki, a competent organist who was also a singer. A two-week return visit to Mexico City was deemed as the perfect induction for Gerry and Sandy Lee into the hectic pace of The VenturesAs Gerry remembers, he was a bit uneasy near the beginning; "When I first joined The Ventures, I was nervous and a little apprehensive. I had big shoes to fill and a lot of music to memorize, but everyone in the group was really good to me. One thing that was hard to get used to was the ultra-slim neck on those Mosrites."

The highlight was a free *Sunday in the Park* charity concert shared with Creedence Clearwater and Canned Heat. An audience of well over 20,000 was a new experience for Gerry, and his palms became sweaty on the skinny Mosrite neck as he imagined he had forgotten every tune on the set list. He never knew if it was mind-over-matter or a bottle of Seven-Up that settled his stomach, but he soon felt better and the concert was a huge success. The Ventures were a quintet now, and ready for the Far East.

Sandy Lee on keys and Gerry using a BG-1000 Ventures Model amplifier in Mexico

While The Ventures found it impossible to stay at the top of the ever-changing world of rock and pop music in America, Orientals could not get enough of the group. When July arrived, several stops were scheduled ahead of the ten-city Japan tour. Hong Kong was first, followed by Andersen Air Force Base on the tiny island of Guam. From there, The Ventures went to Thailand for a dinner performance at Bangkok's Café de Paris. The guys were busy the next afternoon, performing at the Bangkok NCO Club and an evening show at Chulalongkorn, Thailand's premier university founded in 1917 and named for the reigning monarch. At each venue, the group's fans were surprised to see a new lead guitarist. Similar astonishment was expressed in Japan, where a free concert for American servicemen had been arranged in the huge Thew Gymnasium at Yokosuka Naval Base, but it did not take long for Gerry to impress the fans expecting to see Nokie. With huge Japanese audiences yet to be faced, Gerry recalls the encouragement he received from Mel Taylor; "The first time I played to the Japanese fans, I was feeling fairly nervous, but as each number was being introduced, I would turn and glance at Mel. He would wink and smile, which was very comforting and it gave me a lot of confidence."

This Far East tour was the last time The Ventures were seen with Mosrite guitars. Also on this trip, Don sang the title song from the current motion picture, *Born Free*. In retrospect, Don says; "What were we thinking? I suppose we thought we should do more of a lounge act in this type of venue. I wasn't really thrilled that *Born Free* ended up on our live recording."

The Ventures played thirteen concerts from July 29 to August 7. Their program combined tunes from new and old recordings plus Sandy Lee's vocal of *Ode to Billy Joe* and a showcase of Gerry's fingerpicking skill on the Flatt and Scruggs hoedown, *Flint Hill Special*. With licks usually heard on a five-string banjo leading to a high-speed climax, the fans were literally dazzled. They also liked Gerry's renditions of *Walk-Don't Run*, *Pipeline*, and *Wipe Out*, but another surprise came with his approach to The Ventures' arrangement of *Caravan*. Rather than copying Nokie, Gerry attacked the song with wild abandon in a style that was all his own.

The Ventures looked very "mod" in their satin Nehru jackets, and some fans wondered if Nokie could ever have been induced to wear such bold-fashioned attire. This historic change in the appearance and sound of The Ventures was preserved on an album released in December called *The Ventures In Tokyo '68* [Liberty LP-8542]. It was Bing Concepcion's last time to act as M.C. before he returned to his native Philippines.

Nehru jacketed Ventures with Sandy Lee Gornicki

RUMBLINGS AT LIBERTY

The Ventures arrived home to find Al Bennett dealing with insurance conglomerate, Transamerica Corporation. Having fallen into the recording business with its 1967 acquisition of United Artists, Transamerica was now closing a thirty-eight million deal for Liberty. At first, it seemed of little consequence, but in time, Liberty's management, staff, and recording artists would be reeling from the effects of the takeover.

Due to an incident at the Mexican border, Don and Bob let Sandy Lee Gornicki go after the Japan tour. It turned out that she was into marijuana, and upon returning to California, she was caught by U.S. Customs officials and detained along with Gerry and Bob. As Bob recalls; "They tore open the lining of our luggage, and when they found nothing, we were then strip-searched. They even slit the hems of our boxer shorts. We had already contracted Sandy for the Japan tour, but once that was over, we let her go." Several years later, the group was shocked and saddened when Bob got a call from Sandy's daughter, informing them that pretty Sandy Lee had taken her own life.

Gerry McGee now had little time for side jobs, but as he recalls, an opportunity arose which he simply could not refuse; "In October, I was asked to work on the soundtrack for an Elvis Presley movie. It was called *The Trouble With Girls* and we did the sessions for M.G.M. at United Recorders. I felt lucky to meet Elvis because he was protected from everybody quite a bit. The studio was closed up tight while he was there, unlike a lot of sessions where spectators were allowed." Gerry's outstanding Dobro work is easily recognizable during Presley's performance of *Clean Up Your Own Backyard*.

In December 1968, The Ventures covered hits by Steppenwolf, Cream, Janis Joplin, The Band, and The Doors in an album titled *Underground Fire* [Liberty LST-8059]. On side two, Christian Wilde collaborated on original tunes. As Don's name was absent from the credits, some fans believed he was using "Christian Wilde" as a 'nom de plume.'

The Ventures still remember a humorous incident during a 1968 concert when they were playing the Cream hit, *Sunshine of Your Love*. At the end, Don kept going on rhythm, not feeling that this was where it ended. Bob and Mel quickly joined back in, and Gerry played another verse. At the end of that verse, they were not exactly sure how to end the song, as the ending on their record had been a "fade-out." With some heavy concentration and a lot of eye contact, they finally finished the number together.

A month or two later, an amusing thing happened to Bob. Among other items, he had stored a radio-phonograph console in a friend's garage. Having moved into a new apartment, he brought the unit home, plugged it in and put on a record. As he recalls; "The platter rotated, but the stylus arm seemed to be caught on something underneath. When I removed the rear panel, I backed away in a hurry. A large snake, about six-feet long came out and slithered along the floor. I phoned the police and in a few minutes, two officers arrived with a large bag. When they opened the bag in front of the snake, it crawled right in and curled up. They said it was a boa constrictor, and that it wasn't dangerous. They said that they were used to such calls as pet snakes were a current fad and a lot of them were escaping. The press must have been monitoring police reports because the story was soon in newspapers as far away as the east coast."

During fourteen weeks on the charts, *Underground Fire* peaked at 157 in Billboard. By then, Don and Bob had made a lot of friends in Hollywood, one being TV actor Fletcher Fist of *COMBAT*, a series about a U.S. Army platoon during WW II. After three seasons, Fist withdrew from the series to try his hand at producing. In January 1969, as both producer and director, Fletcher approached Don and Bob to star in his first movie project. Republic International Films would shoot *The Mountain Men* in Arizona, where the film's investors were located. After some deliberation, Don and Bob decided it might be fun to grow beards and try their hands at acting, so they stayed away from the barber for over a month. By the end of February, they were on location in Arizona, filming first in Old Tucson where the weather was warm and they were "attacked by Indians," and then in Flagstaff and Prescott in snow and freezing temperatures for trapping scenes in the bush. Josie remembers enjoying some of the action during the filming; "I was invited to Arizona to watch the movie being filmed in Old Tucson, a western town "prop" for filming cowboy movies. I saw a few scenes taken in a typical old-time bar, and some with Don and Bob riding horses in the snow covered hills. As neither of them had any movie experience, I wondered if it would be a very good movie."

Don on the set for *The Mountain Men*

Meanwhile, as the February issue of *Playboy* hit the newsstands, The Ventures themselves voted among the top performers in the reader's jazz and pop poll. However, a bigger and more lucrative surprise was to come in just a few short weeks.

BOOK 'EM DANNO!

Hawaii Five-O was among the new TV programs introduced in the fall of 1968. After three months, the novel crime series was getting poor ratings because of (according to December's *TV Guide*) unrealistic plot writing. Nine weeks into 1969, almost a year after it was recorded, The Ventures' *Hawaii Five-O* theme was released [Liberty 56068]. Still shooting *The Mountain Men*, Don and Bob received an astonishing call came from Liberty/UA, but this time the news was good. Apparently, talk of canceling the *Hawaii Five-O* series had spurred CBS to promote the show on radio and hire new scriptwriters. The ratings improved slightly, but did not begin to soar until Honolulu disc jockey Prince Aku-Aku decided to enhance the radio ads with The Ventures recording. Over the next week, the switchboard overflowed with inquiries about the record, causing stores to be swamped with orders for it. Don remembers getting the news; "Our record sales had dropped to the point where I had returned my Mercedes Benz to the dealer and started driving an old beater Lincoln. When we heard about our sales in Hawaii, we personally hired promo-man, Mike Borchetta to break the record on the mainland. After he got a breakout in Sacramento, it was easy for him to get a lot of other big stations involved."

Meanwhile, twelve thousand copies were sold in Hawaii, surpassing the island's record of ten thousand for native Don Ho's *Tiny Bubbles*. *Hawaii-Five-O* was soon heard on stations from coast to coast, sparking huge orders from Liberty. In May, sales of the theme pushed *Hawaii-Five-O* up to Number 4 in the USA and Number 2 in Canada. As the guys have often told interviewers since; "It was *Walk-Don't Run* all over again!"

On May 17, 19 The Ventures were seen once more on American Bandstand, playing *Hawaii Five-O* and *Theme from A Summer Place*. Copies of the record were soon being sold around the globe. Later in the year, the band was caught by surprise with a Record of The Year award from the Dominican Republic. Total sales soon passed one million, bringing the guys their second Gold Record Single from Liberty Records.

After shooting for only a month, expenses for *The Mountain Men* had soared past the targeted budget, and the backers withheld the financing needed to finish the picture.

When Don and Bob returned to Hollywood, they found Mel at work with Mort Stevens, acting as producer for a *Hawaii Five-0* soundtrack album with Liberty engineer, Ted Keep handling the sound equipment. Released on Capitol ST-410, the *Hawaii Five-0 TV Soundtrack* became a collector's item for Ventures fans when they learned of the cut on which Mel, Gerry, and Bob had played. Stevens took credit for the writing, but Mel later revealed that when the directors requested a bluesy background melody for part of an episode, Gerry came up with a tune on the spur of the moment. His style and guitar tone are easily recognizable on *Blues Trip*.

~

The next Ventures album was to be a second volume of *Golden Greats*, following the enormous success of the first issue two years earlier. While *Golden Greats* had introduced only one new track, *More Golden Greats* would share new and old material equally. The new tracks included Gerry McGee's triumphant rendition of *Classical Gas*, which became so impressive that it remained part of the group's stage act for the next thirty years.

More Golden Greats [Liberty LST-8060] was about to be released in America when it was shelved due to the rocketing success of *Hawaii Five-O*. The theme still high on the charts, it became the centerpiece for an entirely new album. Although completed in only six weeks, *Hawaii Five-O* [Liberty LST-8061] shot up to Number 11 in Billboard. The only Ventures album to ever do better was *Telstar & The Lonely Bull*, reaching Number 8 in 1963. Once again, the writing was on the wall. Albums covering well-known "middle of the road" material sold better than concepts such as *Surfing* or dance fads like the twist. The *Hawaii Five-O* album flourished for over a year, bringing The Ventures their third and final RIAA Gold Album award.

America's luxury cars having been equipped with eight-track players in 1967, under-dash players were so common in 1969 that all Ventures albums were released on the cartridge format. With technology still on the march, *Hawaii Five-O* appeared on both stereo and "Quadrasonic" cartridges. Within two years, Liberty/UA declared tape to account for over a third of their sales. When total sales of tape and vinyl copies breached the one million mark, *Hawaii Five-O* brought The Ventures another Gold Record award from Liberty Records.

JOHN DURRILL

Being heavily in demand at home, The Ventures opted out of a 1969 Japan tour. It also gave them time to initiate another keyboard player, should they be lucky enough to find one. By coincidence, a young singer-songwriter-keyboardist was having tough luck finding work after three years of prosperity as a member of The Five Americans. Born in Houston, Texas on August 20, 1941, John Robert Durrill played trumpet, flute, and drums in high school, but was self-taught on piano and organ. Upon earning his BA degree, in 1962 John taught high-school English in Oklahoma. Then, as a member of The Mutineers, he relocated to Dallas where the band became The Five Americans. In 1965, John wrote and sang on the group's first top-ten hit, *I See The Light* [Abnak 109]. Two years later, their *Western Union* [Abnak 118] was a Top-Ten hit, enticing The Ventures to play *Western Union* on their *Super Psychedelics* album. As keyboard man in

The Five Americans, John was honored; "Back when we started, Mike Rabon, *Walk-Don't Run* was one of the first things we learned. When The Ventures recorded *Western Union*, we were on top of the world; just to think that they would cut one of our songs. Nobody could talk to us for a while after that!"

The Five Americans enjoyed two more Top Forty hits, but when their popularity began to fade, John left the group.

Seeking his fortune in Los Angeles, the future was looking bleak; "I came to the West Coast with some demos I had written, but nobody wanted them unless The Five Americans were included. Luckily, I knew singer Vic Dana, who said I should give Bobby Vee a call. I called up Bobby to see if he knew of any bands that needed someone. As it turned out, Bobby had just been talking to Mel Taylor and learned that The Ventures were looking for a keyboard player. When I called Mel, he invited me to United Artists for an audition. They asked me to play the brass parts in *Hawaii Five-O* on my keyboard. I got the job, which paid a retainer of $150 a week and a lot more when touring. When we went to Japan, I found that I could live on *that* pay for the rest of the year."

John Durrill

In June, The Ventures welcomed Bob Reisdorff back after a five-year absence, and rehired him as their manager. Publishing would be covered by their new Tridex Music Company for any new "Ventures originals." While The Ventures re-focused on albums, Liberty released another single in 1969. The dreamy *Theme From A Summer Place* from the *Hawaii Five-O* album was backed with a Ventures-original pulled from the archives. With Nokie on lead guitar, *A Summer Love* was also very mellow, a surprise to most fans who expected at least one side of a Ventures 45 to rock. Settling in at 83 in mid-July, *Theme From A Summer Place* [Liberty 56115] was the last Ventures single to make the Billboard Hot 100.

The Ventures now entered a period where they used various makes of guitars. Don opted for a Gibson SG Standard, while Bob obtained a German-made Hofner bass like Paul McCartney used. Gerry simply made alternate selections from his Fender and Gibson collection.

In early June, The Ventures made a commercial video to promote *Hawaii Five-O*. It was not the first for the group, having made their debut in this field a year earlier with Nokie, when a video presentation of *Flights of Fantasy* was made using hollow body

Mosrites. That special production was taped for legendary disc jockey Hy Lit, who hosted Philadelphia's *Hy Lit* TV show from 1965 to 1971.

For the videotaping of *Hawaii Five-O*, a parched California lakebed was chosen near Palmdale, on the Mojave Desert. For props, The Ventures loaded a truck with their new Sunn sound equipment that included five amplifier tops and seven matching speaker cabinets. Don played the Gibson SG and Bob used his lightweight Hofner viola bass, but for this video, Gerry brought his seldom-seen Telecaster. Mel took a standard drum kit, and Johnny set up his portable Farfisa keyboard. Like any music video, the guys faked playing to the sound of their record. Josie recalls an incident following the filming; "On returning to Los Angeles, the truck driver turned a little too sharp on the freeway exit ramp. The truck rolled over three times, with amplifiers, guitars, and drums tumbling all about. The driver was not seriously hurt, and amazingly, the equipment suffered minimal damage. The Ventures and film crew were following close behind, but they managed to stop in time."

On August 2, The *Hawaii Five-0* video was aired on ABC's *Happening '69*, a rock music series by Dick Clark Productions and co-hosted by Paul Revere and Mark Lindsay of Paul Revere And The Raiders.

Don with the Gibson SG, and Gerry with a late 60s Gibson Firebird I

Summer touring took the quintet into Canada for a sellout concert in the Winnipeg Auditorium where upwards of a thousand people flocked to hear The Ventures. Several eastern U.S. dates followed, ending with two nights shared with Jefferson Airplane and The Dillards at Chicago's prestigious Aragon Ballroom. This date, as Don recalls, was *not* one his best memories; "The place reeked of marijuana and the hippie-types seemed indifferent to us. Then, when we went to get our money, the club owner said, 'You don't get paid for the second night.' When we asked why, he quoted a part of our contract that said we couldn't play the next day within a radius of fifty miles. He said, 'You're playing only forty-eight miles away tomorrow, so you don't get paid for tonight.' Technically, he was right, but c'mon man... only two miles?"

While Jefferson Airplane continued on towards Woodstock, The Ventures wound their way back through Melodyland, Disneyland, and the Sacramento State Fair. The tour ended at Brigham Young University in Utah with an estimated crowd of seven thousand people.

Next, it was back to Hollywood for five-nights at America's first discotheque. Upon mention of the Whiskey-a-Go-Go, Don offered; "About five years earlier, we were booked at the Whiskey for an all-night Sock Hop. It was going to be a big splash with a half-dozen Liberty recording artists booked. I know that one was Johnny Rivers. Matter of fact, I still have the socks that they gave out with all our names printed on them. Just before we were to go on, the lights went out. We sat there for hours and they just couldn't fix it. There must have been a major burnout somewhere. We've seen our share of power problems, but that one was really unusual."

While news from Woodstock was mesmerizing teens (and outraging parents), The Ventures worked with Bob Reisdorff on a concept album called *Swamp Rock*, combining the classic sound of Louisiana's bayou country with Ventures style rock. The album mixed current hits fitting the theme with originals by each member of the band. When Gerry suggested that *Swamp Rock* [Liberty LST-8062] needed accordion and harmonica for maximum Cajun effect, Don knew the people to call. Tommy Morgan was the best around the studios and had worked with The Ventures in 1962. Accordion players were scarce, but Don knew one that owned a club called The Baked Potato near Universal Studios. Although Don Randi was a jazz pianist at heart, he played all styles of music and was proficient on the accordion. He was also part of the infamous Hollywood "wrecking crew," performing on countless pop records, soundtracks, and commercials.

Randi and Morgan's appearance added greatly to the feel to of *Swamp Rock*, which became a veritable Gerry McGee showcase. In addition to baring his roots with delightful guitar sounds, Gerry established his songwriting aptitude on *Gumbo* and proficient Dobro skill on *Catfish Mud Dance* and *Proud Mary*.

Topping it all off, John Durrill's tasty Hammond organ on *Suspicious Minds* and his piano on the other cuts was so good that Bob and Don said they wished that they had found him ten years earlier.

Bob with his Hofner bass

As Bob Reisdorff recalls, they needed one more extra for *Swamp Rock*; "We just couldn't have an album of Cajun music without a fiddle player. Back then, the best in Los Angeles was a fellow named Byron Berline. He played on dozens of albums for many top artists, and we got him for *Swamp Rock*." As Gerry recalls, the album was all but finished when it was time for a tour; "We had just headed out towards Utah and Idaho when Bob Reisdorff got the idea to put some sitar on a couple of the songs. It wasn't any big deal, because anyone who plays a guitar can play one of those. They got James Burton to come in and add a really nice sitar track for *Suspicious Minds* because he had played on it with Elvis. They also had him do something on [Gerry's composition] *Plaquemines Parish*. I named that song after a county in Louisiana where the Mississippi runs into the ocean."

Swamp Rock hit the stores in December 1969, and two weeks later was sitting at 81 in Billboard. For many, The Ventures' arrangement of Hank Williams' 1952 hit, *Jambalaya*, set to crackling washboard percussion, was the album's masterpiece. As ever-loving fans repeatedly played their latest "Ventures fix," Gerry McGee became increasingly endeared to them.

Meanwhile, in their quest for new sounds, The Ventures found a novel use for tremolo in *Pandora's Box*, an unreleased tune by the UK's ex-Tornado, Alan Caddy. After Gerry's jazzy syncopated guitar intro, John Durrill took the lead on his Farfisa organ in old-time waltz tempo. While electronic keyboards had always featured a true vibrato effect, the Farfisa was recorded through a Fender amp set on deep tremolo. Appearing only in Japan and Western Europe, this eerie melody remained virtually unheard in North America for over two decades.

BOOTLEGGERS

As The Ventures marked their ninth year in the music business, the task of counting their album output was becoming difficult. *Swamp Rock* was their 33rd regular U.S. release, but adding the PLAY GUITAR series, Columbia Record Club's *Versatile Ventures*, three Sunset compilations, two Japan Pops albums and six Japan live sets, brought the total closer to fifty. From these, many more albums were compiled in other countries. While many were licensed, some were bootleg creations that contained titles never recorded by The Ventures. An example of such skullduggery appeared on an album supposedly from First Records of Taiwan called *The Golden Hits In 70*. This so-called Ventures album contained *Squad Car* and *I Want To Hold Your Hand* played by an Asian group. Another contained *Please, Please Me*, *Living Doll*, and *King of the Surf Guitar*, titles that The Ventures had never recorded. The lack of copyright laws in many Asian countries made it possible for anyone to walk into a shop and have a record duplicated on a "while you wait" basis. The people doing this also had no fear of copying cover art. Albums appeared in Korea, some alleged to be "live" performances, using photos from Japanese record jackets. Many of these included tracks never recorded by The Ventures, such as *My Blue Heaven, Django, Summer Wine,* and *Tragic Wind*. Others contained simplistic versions of *Twisted, Red Nose Reindeer, Gonzares* (sic) and, of all things, *Auld Lang Syne*. The label of one album overlapped the grooves of its final track so as to prevent *Auld Lang Syne* from being played! Of course, *Tragic Wind* was a Chantays release, *My Blue Heaven* was the String-A-Longs' arrangement, and *Gonzales* was an early song from The Shadows. *Django*, originally from Denmark's Cliffters, could have come from any one of a dozen covers, but not from the repertoire of The Ventures.

Another blatant bootleg album, *Let's Go Monkey*, came from Taiwan on the Liming label with few if any real Ventures performances. As late as 2001, Koreans were offered thirty-one tracks on The Ventures Gold compact disc [Soodo Media SDCD-3192] with songs entitled Jango, Wayward Nile, My Blue Heaven, and When Maggie Was Young. Not only had The Ventures never recorded these songs, the remaining twenty-seven tracks were not The Ventures' renditions at all. However, some Korean labels such as First Records have issued first-rate Ventures albums with heavy, textured jackets and attractive artwork rivaling that in Japan.

Some of the distorted titles are good for a laugh if nothing else. One song on a Korean album [Go-Go and Twist Korea '75 - Daihan ORG-24] that brought some smiles in America was *Love Potion #9* written as "Love Position #9".

Near the end of 1969, alert Ventures fans in North America were treated to a Ventures appearance on network television. During the summer, Screen Gems had taped the group, along with Liberty singing artist Nancy Ames on a Trini Lopez variety TV special. Nancy had enjoyed a Top 100 hit in 1966 with her answer to Staff Sgt. Barry Sadler's Ballad of the Green Berets when she sang *He Wore the Green Beret*.

On the special, Trini Lopez sang a dozen of his favorites, including his 1963 smash, *If I Had A Hammer*. The Ventures provided backup for Trini and Nancy on *Twenty-Five Miles, Land of a Thousand Dances*, and *Light My Fire*, but they mimed *Hawaii Five-O* to their recording.

Viewers that had lost track of The Ventures were surprised, not only by seeing Gerry McGee on lead guitar and John Durrill on organ, but also with the absence of Mosrite guitars. Mel surprised the hardcore fans with his set of double bass drums.

Later, a soundtrack album of The Trini Lopez Show became another unique find for Ventures collectors [LP Reprise 6361; CD Collectables Records COL 6766].

Trini Lopez and The Ventures at NBC Studios in Burbank   - *Fabine*

The Ventures had learned much in the sixties, but with music being ever-changing, their future became increasingly uncertain. After celebrating ten years in the business, could they find their way along the rocky road of the seventies? To answer this, we quote Bob Bogle as he regards a fascinating fact about the busy bumblebee; "With so much body weight in proportion to its size, the laws of physics say that flight is impossible. The bee doesn't know that, so he flies just fine."

CHAPTER TWO
The Seventies

The Ventures wanted to commemorate their tenth anniversary with a special recording, but it seemed there was never enough time. To begin with, Japan was eager to see them after being bypassed in 1969. Also, as sales in Japan were high for their *Golden Pops* album, it was obvious that music written expressly for Japan was a valuable commodity. From this album, *Kyoto Doll* became one of the biggest selling singles in the Orient, amassing sales exceeding 4,500,000. The song also became a long-standing favorite as *Kyoto no Koi* (Love of Kyoto) when pretty Yuko Nagisa applied Japanese lyrics. A top hit for eleven weeks, it was one of Japan's best for 1970. Within two months, the band's own *Reflections in a Palace Lake* was a popular Japanese single, as was the unique flip side, *Swan Lake*, adapted from the Tchaikovsky ballet.

To celebrate 1970's World's Fair, The Ventures released *Kyoto Doll* in America and the rest of the world as *Expo Seven-O*, with *Swan Lake* on the flip side [Liberty 56153]. In time, Japanese lyrics were written for *Reflections in a Palace Lake*, giving Yuko Nagisa another big hit when she sang it as *Kyoto Bojo* [Kyoto Splendor]. She would repeat this feat later by making The Ventures' composition, *Nagasaki Memories* another vocal hit.

Kyoto Doll (aka *Expo Seven-O*) was the last Ventures music produced by Bob Reisdorff. Decidedly tired of the music business, he set about creating a long-envisioned Broadway play. When his father passed away, Reisdorff moved to New York, again leaving Sonny Rivera out of work. After closing out his father's business, Reisdorff partnered with his brother to run New York's illustrious Broome Street Bar.

When Reisdorff left, Mel Taylor took over the group's business affairs. He had learned much about the record business, and the experience now paid off. Also, from this point on, The Ventures began self-producing nearly all of their material. Regarding producers, Bob Bogle explains some of the discrepancies on album jackets; "In those days, they would print production credits on an album without even checking to see if anything had changed. Being so busy doing our jobs, we didn't pay much attention to such things. Months or years later, someone would ask us about a producer named on some album, and it was news to us."

Early in the year, *More Golden Greats* was released in North America, a full year after its UK debut. Content was slightly altered, however, *Theme From A Summer Place* giving way to *Hawaii Five-0*. Although die-hard Ventures collectors were surprised and delighted to find new versions of *Torquay* and *Raunchy* along with the four new songs, sales of the album were far less than the first *Golden Greats*. The LP was, however, chosen by *Michigan Record Review* as their "Album of the Week" [of Feb. 16, 1970].

Around this time, Bob noticed a sale bulletin for a 1968 Fender Jazzmaster posted at the Musicians Union office for $250. Although the neck was slightly bowed, it turned out to be a great buy; "I didn't have the right equipment, so I put the guitar on a couch with the neck sticking out over the end. I hung a weight on the neck, and each day I slightly adjusted the truss rod that runs through the neck. After about a week, it was perfectly straight. This was just before my second wife, Carol [Bedford] passed away unexpectedly. It was near the end of February, the 26th as I remember. She was only thirty-three and it was a terrible time for me. I didn't think I would never be married again and I never liked talking about it for quite a few years."

1970 being the tenth anniversary of their first hit, The Ventures spared no expense in creating a double album of current popular music. Don remembers the project; "We really wanted it to be something special. A lot of the songs had big arrangements that were pretty complicated, and being a double album, it took us over three months of rehearsing before we were ready to go into the studio."

Supported by strings and brass, Gerry McGee played everything from the latest "wah-wah" sounds to wonderful acoustic and sitar work. Along with Gerry's delicious guitar-through-Leslie solo on The Beatles' *Let It Be*, John Durrill excelled throughout on organ, piano, and harpsichord. Perhaps the biggest challenge for The Ventures was playing *Hey Jude* as an instrumental. Running over seven minutes, The Beatles had set the record for the longest-ever Number One hit. The Ventures trimmed it to five minutes, wherein the final few seconds, careful listening reveals a bit of vocalizing by Mel.

For Bob Bogle, the time had finally come to play the bass strings with his fingers. He remembered leaving the pick in his pocket for nearly every cut on the two-disc album.

Originally, the double disc album was to be titled *A Decade Of Hits*, but the name was scrapped upon discovery that Liberty/U.A.'s Sunset division was releasing a budget package of ten Ventures originals titled of *A Decade With The Ventures*.

This mail sticker was obsolete when it was printed

While recording the *10th Anniversary Album* [Liberty LST-35000], the band experienced a major theft that sealed the end of their Award amplifier forever. Don explains; "Those first Award amps had worked so well that we used them on records. We did a lot of recording at Liberty's studios on Third Street, and one day we went in and someone had stolen the amps. That killed any future attempt to copy them if we had wanted to. The theft included our prototype and the two speaker cabinets we used with it. It was about a $10,000 heist. By that time we were using even bigger equipment on the road. We had bought all new Sunn amps with extra speaker cabinets. They had some real big ones out by then" [to which Bob adds] "We liked those Sunn amps so much that we took the heads with us on our next trip to Japan."

When the *10th Anniversary* project was completed, the guys felt that it was the best work they had ever done. Later, they knew that their goal for something special had been reached when a congratulatory letter arrived from Frank Sinatra. Their final reward came several months later when sales triggered the group's fifth Gold Album, presented by Liberty Records for worldwide sales exceeding 1,000,000. For the next few decades, interview queries as to their favorite work were usually answered with "Our *10th Anniversary Album*!"

E.J. Auzins

Japan tour '70 was a rather short one, squeezing sixteen concerts in the last two weeks of July, plus a stop in Thailand. While Japanese fans were surprised to see and hear John Durrill, The Ventures were also surprised to meet their new Master of Ceremonies. He appeared to be Japanese, but with the name of Jimmy Allen and speaking very good English, The Ventures assumed him to be Japanese American. The band never forgot how Jimmy would introduce a musical number to the audience followed by a raucous "Let's go, boys!"

Japan had not seen the band for two years, but with songstress Yuko Nagisa having made two top hits using their melodies, the country was still very Ventures conscious. Early in the tour, the band was presented with Japan's Composer of the Year award in recognition of their outstanding songwriting for Japanese singers. It was the first time ever that a foreign group received such an honor.

Anniversaries being big in Japan, Toshiba-EMI also joined in, awarding The Ventures their sixth (and final) Gold Album for their first LP made expressly for that country, *Pops in Japan* [LP-8161, 1967]. The group also received a Gold award for an eight-track tape cartridge [*Golden Best 20; This Is The Ventures, Vol. 3*].

The tour included two appearances at Osaka's Festival Plaza. Equipped with computerized stage facilities, this venue was the performing arts center for the current World's Fair. Running from March 15 to September 13, Expo '70 broke all records for the number of participating nations, admissions in a day (over 800,000), and total attendance of 64,000,000. The guys had little time to enjoy the attractions, but they managed to visit a few of the 110 pavilions. Then it was off to Thailand for a pair of concerts on the way home.

Back in the States, the *Hawaii Five-0* phenomenon continued with spin-off action in the form of a new TV series premiering in the fall. CBS Television contracted The Ventures to play the theme, penned by *Hawaii Five-0* writer, Mort Stevens. *Storefront Lawyers*, starring Robert Foxworth and A. Martinez, chronicled a firm of young lawyers helping the needy in Los Angeles. Liberty/UA released the orchestral-backed *Storefront Lawyers* [Liberty 56189] to coincide with the series premier in September. Although the theme and its flip-side (John Durrill's country flavored *Kern County Line*) enjoyed moderate sales in America, neither cut appeared in Japan until a "rarities" album included them ten years later [*Rare Collections* King K18P12-13].

Storefront Lawyers was telecast on Wednesday nights for a year, although in 1971, the title was changed to *Men at Law*. But for the last few months of 1970, Ventures fanatics tuned in weekly, just to hear their idols pound out the theme and to watch the closing credits pay homage to the band.

Following the *Storefront Lawyers* session, journalist Leonard Ferris dropped in to interview Don, Bob, and Gerry for *Guitar Player* magazine. Being published eight times a year, the fifty-page periodical had gained popularity and respect around the world. Headlined "Still Going Strong," Ferris lauded the band for its longevity of more than a decade while still amassing new fans. When the short article appeared in 1971's February issue, the amount of photos stretched it to nearly three pages.

1970 was also the year that Bill Cosby recorded Christian Wilde's lament to the Vietnam G.I, *(Private) Grover Henson Feels Forgotten* [UNI 55223]. The record hit 13 on the national Easy Listening chart, 70 in Billboard's Top 100 chart, and was second runner up for a GRAMMY in the category for Best Spoken Word Recordings.

Following a rest from Japan tour '70, The Ventures accepted a November booking for U.S. military bases in Germany. While there, the band was surprised to meet fan club president Stuart Leech, who had come from the UK to meet his heroes in person. Recalling the time spent with his idols, Stuart offered; "As club members, we always harbored a pipe-dream of meeting The Ventures when they would one day visit these shores to give us a concert. Our hopes waned as the seventies approached, as we did not expect the group's career to last much longer. When I learned that they were going to play at some army bases in Germany, I saw the chance of a lifetime and eagerly headed to Baden-Baden. Checking into the Rex Hotel, I asked the desk clerk to ring the boys and let them know I had arrived. It was only seven o'clock in the evening, but I was told that they were all sleeping. While waiting in the foyer for over two hours, a call came to the desk from one of The Ventures asking for fresh towels. Offering to deliver them, I was soon introducing myself to a bleary-eyed Bob Bogle. When the band had freshened up, we shared a meal in a place that cooked pizzas on an open fire. I felt good when they thanked me for sticking with them from 'day one,' and I was even more delighted when Don asked me to be their road manager for the next few days. It was a truly unique experience that provided me with everlasting memories."

Before the tour was finished, The Ventures accepted an additional booking in Naples for a huge military base comprised of Army, Navy, and Marine Corps. It was the one and only time for the band to visit Italy.

CONSOLIDATING

Touring finished for the year, The Ventures arrived home to find their *10th Anniversary Album* on Billboard's Hot 100 list. While Liberty/UA threw a banquet in their honor, Billboard ran a twelve-page Ventures section in its September 19 issue, filled with photographs, stories, and *"Thank You, Ventures"* ads from record companies in Singapore, Sweden, Mexico, Australia-New Zealand, Canada, U.S.A. and Japan. The section ended with a full page signed by Mel, Don, Bob, Gerry, and John... "Thank you everyone, for making these first ten years golden ones."

While the Billboard ads expressed appreciation from the record companies publicly, The Ventures received more permanent gratitude in the form of trophies they could proudly display alongside the gold records in their homes. An outstanding Grand Prix plaque from Japan bestowed honors best described as a Hall of Fame award for composers. Other trophies from Mexico and Japan included a Toshiba plaque for mammoth sales of tape cassettes.

As The Ventures were celebrating, all hell broke loose at Liberty. Having discovered that Liberty was not worth what they had paid for it, Transamerica Corporation executives decided to merge their two record companies. A major shuffle in management resulted in Al Bennett and many of his staff being fired on the spot. A stern character named Mike Stewart replaced Bennett, and The Ventures felt suddenly abandoned. Don remembers how they were treated; "Liberty had been like a big happy family that we had been part of for ten years. Suddenly we were orphans. We always had the run of the place, but now we needed an appointment to get in! Out of the blue, there was a security guard at the door who had to know who we were, and what our business was!" When United Artists began dropping their Liberty artists, The Ventures were saved due to their substantial Far East record sales.

Following their *10th Anniversary Album*, the group stepped bravely into the realm of Santana and Led Zeppelin, along with that of George Harrison, Tom Jones, and Cat Stevens. This time, assuming the role of co-producer and engineer, Lanky Lindstrot accompanied the band to four different studios before the album was completed. As plenty of Latin percussion was needed for the *Santana* and similar tracks, two significant extras were hired for the sessions. The first was Mike Gutierrez a friend of Sonny's husband, Ray Rivera, and who Don had known at Army Signals School in Augsburg, Germany. The reunion resulted in Mike playing congas and doing a little vocalizing in the studio for The Ventures' new album project, *New Testament* [UAS 6796].

Requiring one more percussionist, Don remembered Diana Biggins and her capable drummer fiancé, Joe Barile (pronounced Barilly). Sometime earlier, Diana had invited Don and Bob to hear Joe and his group, Renaissance, playing at The Copa in Glendale. Friendships developed, and on occasional revisits, Don or Bob sat in with the band.

JOE BARILE

Joe Barile was born on an Italian island on July 9, 1947. When he was nine years old, his family immigrated to New York. Joe owned a set of bongos as a teenager, but he was not serious about drums until 1959 when he heard Sandy Nelson's *Teen Beat*. The following year, the drums on *Walk-Don't Run* by The Ventures further influenced him.

Joe was still a teenager when the family moved to San Pedro, California. After school, he worked in his father's bakery, where constant beating on tables led his father to enroll him for drum lessons. By 1961, Joe was drumming in a group called the Cyclones. At age twenty, with friends Malcolm Evans, Richie Hernandez, and Tommy Reynolds, Joe formed a group called Renaissance. Working five nights a week allowed Joe to quit the bakery and work on his music during daytime, which included learning to play an old Fender Esquire guitar. It wasn't long before Joe met Diana Lee Biggins, the girl he would marry. When Diana introduced him to her friends, The Ventures, Joe was soon socializing with Don and Bob over billiard games at their homes, and on occasional club dates, Joe had them sit on rhythm or bass with Renaissance.

Joe Barile

When Renaissance was about ready to record, they discovered an English folk-rock band with the same name, so they renamed themselves Shango. After some moderately successful recordings and a couple of personnel changes, the band became Hamilton, Joe Frank & Reynolds with Joe Barile on drums. Joe toured with this group for a year before going into studio session work. Almost immediately, he was asked to play timbales on several tracks for The Ventures' *New Testament*.

Among the album's excellent originals was a tune that came from songwriter Norman Ezell, who had left The Five Americans with Johnny Durrill. The five-minute *Good Mornin' Captain* really surprised Ventures enthusiasts when Don and Johnny began to sing! Fans had not heard the band openly vocalize on a recording since they stomped and finger-popped their way through *The Twomp* back in the twist era. Had there been a single released, or any promotion at all, *Good Mornin' Captain* would have easily been a top contender on the numerous "album rock" stations quickly filling the FM radio band. The album may then have ensnared a whole new generation of fans. Sadly, United Artists considered The Ventures only worth promoting in Japan, even though *New Testament* was distributed in countries as diverse as Turkey. When the album bubbled under the top 200, it was little wonder that The Ventures became disenchanted with touring anywhere other than Japan.

Another disappointment was the sleeve artwork on this and a few other albums, as explained by Don; "New Testament was scrawled across the front of that album to be almost unreadable! Whenever I look at it, I see 'News Gestamert.'" And what about *Rock and Roll Forever*? It had that dumb cartoon on the front and 'Ooh Poo Pah-Doo.' That song isn't on the album and we've never played *Ooh Poo Pah-Doo*! In hindsight, we should have taken control of our album art and titles, but we left that in supposedly capable hands."

In Japan, New Testament showed an updated group photo

Following *New Testament*, the seventies became a confusing time for American Ventures fans. Until then, many had kept up with the band's activities while happily ordering pennants, key tags, and six-for-a-dollar bumper stickers from Josie. But in the summer of 1971, the club bulletins ceased. On the one or two albums surfacing each year, the group's sound was good, but it did not always fit the style or concept in which fans envisioned their idols. The Ventures realized this, but they knew that to survive, they must be progressive. However, without faithful support from their Japan audience, it is likely they would have fallen into obscurity along with the sixties' surf groups.

~ ~ ~

While touring in the U.S.A. had ground to a halt, Japan remained a huge event for The Ventures. In 1971, they performed fifty-eight times from mid-July to the end of August. Their repertoire, mainly from the sixties, had only one track, *Free*, from *New Testament*. Japanese titles were also essential, with renowned songstress Yuko Nagisa performing *Kyoto no Koi* (Love of Kyoto) and *Kyoto Bojo* (Kyoto Splendor). These were the songs mainly responsible for The Ventures being crowned Composers of the Year for a second time. Accomplishing this for two years in succession put the band in the country's All-Time Top Ten Composers list, and they became the first foreign inductees to Japan's Conservatory of Music.

Other concert highlights included extended organ and guitar solos in the near seven-minute *Light My Fire*, Gerry McGee's sizzling lead in *Walk-Don't Run*, and of course, Mel's embryonic drum solo in the nine-minute *Caravan* finale. Gerry refreshed the lengthy closer (as he now did on many of the group's past hits), by adding his own bluesy style to the music. *On Stage '71* [Liberty LP-93019B] was soon available to Japanese fans in stereo as well as in a condensed "4-Channel" format.

In America, United Artists delved into the band's history with an album of twenty past hits simply titled *The Ventures* [UXS-80]. As a sticker on the shrink-wrap declared the double-disc album to be a "Super-Pak," the compilation became known to collectors as *Superpak*. The tape cassette and cartridge versions of UXS 80 actually bore this title.

The SuperPak gatefold double LP package

JOIN THE CLUB

Back home in America, as many original fans joined the workforce and started families, club membership dwindled. Josie closed it down, but not before passing a members list to a pair of young men who were starting their own club in the eastern states. George Galey and Jeff Keyser called their club The Ventures' Resurgence. Other clubs still existed in Sweden, Germany, and the UK, so Josie felt safe in leaving Hollywood to address personal concerns; "I came back to Tacoma in 1971 to be near my mom, whose health was failing. With Sally in Florida and Don in Los Angeles, I came back to be of as much help as I could. I'm very glad that I did, as Mother passed away in 1974."

Meanwhile, paid up members in North America were delighted to receive Ventures news through the mail from the Pennsylvania Resurgence boys. Over in the UK, as "Day-One Man" Stuart Leech recalls, changes in club management also occurred; "By the mid-seventies, my lifestyle was changing rapidly. Along with raising two young children, I was proceeding rather ambitiously to advance my career. Due to increasing commitments, I put out a call for someone to pick up the reins. Membership was around the 200 mark when I handed the club over to Keith Gleeson."

Keith Gleeson was the young man who, in years gone by, had bombarded local newspapers with letters expounding his views on current guitarists. Perhaps his most controversial tirade being; "My craze for the sound of the electric guitar drove me to see Hendrix and Clapton 'live.' I have never seen or heard such distasteful use of an electric guitar. The sound was good to the extent that the electric guitar was used, but ninety percent of the tune and tone was *pure bluff.* I have seen the American group, The Ventures in Japan while I was in the Navy, and honestly and truthfully just cannot put Hendrix and Clapton in their class."

Under Keith's leadership, the UK organization was also named *Ventures Resurgence*. The club changed leaders and names a few more times, but each time, the bulletins became bigger, better, and more attainable. *Ginza* was next, followed by *Pedal Pusher*, both under the pen of Dave Peckett, who also published an instrumental rock periodical, *Gandy Dancer*. Eventually, Dave merged both publications into a fifty-page *New Gandy Dancer* that carried commercial and classified advertising. In 1978, the typewriter gave way to commercial printers, and the glossy, photo abundant quarterly became the rock instrumental fan's dream magazine.

Other clubs came and went in various parts of the world with the exception of the Ventures Scandinavian Fan Club. Instrumental rock remained so popular in Sweden, Norway, Finland, and Denmark that by the year 2001, Arild Pettersson was celebrating thirty-five years of publishing his *V.S.F.C. Hot Line*.

During the great resurgence of the eighties, British fans would again feel the need for a Ventures periodical of their own. While continuing his magazine dedicated to instrumental rock, Davy Peckett passed the reigns of the Ventures club to long-time fan and fervent collector, Gerald Woodage. Resurrecting the title *Ventures Resurgence*, Gerald operated The Official Ventures International Club from 1984 to the end of 2008.

~ ~ ~

By late '71, hard core Ventures addicts in the Americas, the Orient, Europe, or Australasia would buy anything released by The Ventures. Japan was their biggest market, to which they fed periodic singles with titles such like, *Stranger in Midosuji*, *Nagoya Express*, and *Naruto*. As Japan welcomed periodic solo singles from Don and Mel, John Durrill soon sampled this market. Seated at his piano in front of the Tokyo Symphony, John recorded *Love Knot Machine* b/w *Summer of '42* [Dan VA-6]. Moderate success prompted John to follow six months later with two more self-penned instrumentals, *Black Friday* b/w *Shadow of Peking* [Dan VA-12].

Undaunted by poor sales of *New Testament*, the Ventures forged ahead with another album for America. Leading off with Isaac Hayes' Oscar winning movie theme and its scratchy new guitar lick, they recorded *Theme From Shaft* [UAS 5547]. With selected hits from Cat Stevens, The Spencer Davis Group, Cher, and The Grass Roots, the band added contemporary styled originals like *Indian Sun*, and *Cherries Jubilee*. Joe Barile was again drafted for extra percussion, along with "Red" Rhodes on steel guitar. Fans enjoying the vocals on *New Testament* were impressed once more as Don and John harmonized on *Deep, Deep in the Water*. Getting used to the "McGee sound" by now, fans accepted the album, enough to place it at 195 in a January 1972 Billboard.

CLASSIC EXAMPLE

Early in the year, a group called Apollo 100 hit Number 6 with an instrumental adapted from Bach's *Jesu, Joy of Man's Desiring* [Mega 615-0050 *Joy*]. The Ventures were quick to record *Joy* as a John Durrill keyboard solo with full orchestral backing. A single was quickly released in North America [UA 50872]. It came out in Japan [Liberty LR-2984] with their original, *Squaw Man* on the flip side. Peculiar for a Native American premise, *Squaw Man* was recorded completely without drums.

Gerry McGee had made many contacts in his pre-Ventures days while building a reputation on guitar, Dobro, and sitar. Still known to the music world as "Jerry," he was in considerable demand as a studio musician. As a free agent, he played on sessions with luminaries such as Ry Cooder and Emmylou Harris. From 1969 to 1971, Jerry's name appeared on albums by Nancy Sinatra, Henry Gross, Rita Coolidge, Marc Benno, Southern Fried, Booker T. Jones, and Delaney & Bonnie.

In November 1970, John Mayall was nearly finished recording his *Back to the Roots* album [Polydor 25-3002] when Harvey Mandel quit the group. At once, Gerry was recruited to play on the cuts entitled *Blue Fox* and *Devil's Tricks*. Being in the right place at the right time also brought Gerry a ten-second solo spot on The Grass Roots' recording of *Temptation Eyes* [ABC Dunhill D-4263]. The song peaked at 15 as The Ventures' Japan Tour '71 was approaching, but Gerry still found time to do the complete lead work on an album with Mayall and Larry Taylor, late of Canned Heat. None of the tracks on *Memories* [Polydor PD-5012] had drums or percussion, save for handclaps and tambourine on the rousing, five-minute finale, *Play the Harp*.

While recording *Shaft* with The Ventures, Gerry had also begun sessions with Delaney Bramlett for the album, *Something's Coming* [Columbia 31631]. *Shaft* was finished before Christmas of 1971, so when Delaney arranged a promotional tour, Gerry was ready to go. Following the tour, the Everly Brothers summoned Gerry and Delaney to work on one of the last albums. Gerry's slide work on *Stories We Could Tell* [RCA 4620] complemented that of two more great musicians, Buddy Emmons and again, Ry Cooder.

As for The Ventures, Bob Bogle recalls the situation in early '72; "We didn't have much going just then, so we had no objection to Gerry leaving. We had a Japan tour scheduled in the fall, and we thought he would be back. We had no idea he would be out of the picture for over ten years."

As fate interceded, 1972 saw even more changes within the group. The Ventures' recording of *Joy* had inspired an entire album of classics. Such adaptations were nothing new, The Ventures having reworked Rimsky-Korsakov's *Flight of the Bumble Bee*, Tchaikovsky's *Nutcracker Suite*, and *Hungarian Dance No.5* by Brahms, but this time, the music adhered to the original melodies and tempos.

Gerry being absent, Bob embraced the Jazzmaster he had obtained via the Musicians' Union poster for lead guitar duties. Mel drafted brother Larry for bass, and George Tipton was contracted for orchestral backing. Building on *Joy* and *Swan Lake*, the group added ten more tracks that would please even the original composers. Bob's guitar work was enhanced with a Leslie speaker on *Mozart's Minuet* and Prokofiev's *Peter and the Wolf* while the album's gleaming bass work proved Larry Taylor's talent to extend far beyond the realm of boogie and blues. Later, as Don and Bob recalled, the sweet mandolin in Puccini's *One Fine Day* came from one of George Tipton's musicians.

The star of *Joy - The Ventures Play the Classics* [UAS 5575] had to be John Durrill, whose keyboards dominated every number. Sadly, but unknown at the time, John's musical genius would soon be absent from the band.

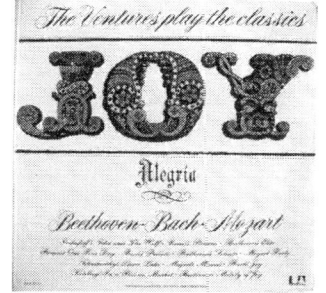  

The JOY album as it appeared in Peru, New Zealand, and on 8-track cartridge in America

During the last few recording sessions, the paperwork required in The Ventures office had fallen sufficiently behind to require assistance. Sonny Rivera was re-hired for three days a week, working from an office in Bob's home in Encino. This worked for nearly a year until Sonny was hospitalized. During her recovery from surgery, the office was relocated to her home in Burbank and became a full-time job. For the next sixteen years, mail for The Ventures was addressed to P.O. Box 1646, Burbank CA, 91507.

Having ascended from fifties rock 'n' roll to conquer surf, acid, and soul in an industry where everything changes but change itself, once again The Ventures had embraced another musical genre. While scoring 146 in Billboard's album chart *Joy – The Ventures Play The Classics* became an important part of every fan's collection around the world. Regarding the chart status, Don states; "Other than the routine ad in a few trade magazines, we received almost no promotion at all. United Artists had their own artists that they promoted, and they just took us for granted along with our success in Japan." To this, Bob added; "Every time we went in, we met with people who didn't know us and wouldn't listen. Everyone from top executives down to the mailroom was on a fixed salary with no vested interest in the success of recorded music. They didn't know who or what they should promote, and all we could do was watch while they threw away millions of dollars."

MEANWHILE, BACK IN TACOMA

A line of fine print on the back of the *Joy* album read; "The Ventures Worldwide Fan Club - 605 East 56th Street, Tacoma WA, 98404." Although it was Josie's new address, the listing surprised even her; "When I returned to Tacoma in fall of 1971, I immediately bought a house. As I had talked about continuing the fan club, Don and Bob put my address on the *Joy* album, but as it turned out, I let Jeff Keyser and George Galey take care of that job."

Buried among the production details, Josie's address brought few applications. Those received were promptly forwarded to *The Ventures Resurgence – Box 36 – Roslyn, Pennsylvania*. Sparse news from an ancient mimeograph machine trickled out to fans from these enthusiastic students who charged nothing for their efforts. Then, in 1973 as Jeff Keyser and George Galey took their separate paths in life, the club ran aground. At that time, a nineteen-year-old club member in New Jersey began contributing Ventures news to the UK fan club whenever possible. His name was Michael Kuhn.

By now, Josie was a young fifty-seven; "At the end of 1971, a couple invited me to a party at the local Veterans' Hall. Feeling that New Year's Eve was really for couples to celebrate, I declined, saying I didn't want to be a 'third wheel.' As they wouldn't take 'no' for an answer, I was ready to go when they arrived.

"I was about to pay for my ticket when the man in the booth said, 'You're in luck! Someone turned in a ticket, so you don't have to buy one!' The hall was packed, but we were able to find a table. Before long, a good-looking man came up and asked me to dance. He was a great dancer and we danced together several times. During one number, he took me to his table to meet his sister and her husband. I thought it odd that he was there with them, and I said as much to him. He explained that something had happened at the last minute to prevent his date from coming, and he had turned in her ticket at the door. Not only did I get her ticket, but I also got her man! Don Nephew and I were married in June of 1972."

~ ~ ~

The fact that The Ventures were missing Gerry McGee did not bother producer Joe Saraceno at all. He simply convinced Don, Bob, and Mel to record an album of *Greatest Hits* with Art Munson on lead guitar. Within a short time they had recorded a dozen past hits ranging from *Walk-Don't Run* to *Caravan*. However, several of the tunes, notably *Slaughter on Tenth Avenue* and *Joy* were completely keyboard dominated, while *Batman* had a saxophone lead. Upon hearing the result, the guys decided that while the production was too diverse from The Ventures' sound. The tapes were shelved indefinitely, but apparently not forgotten. As we shall see, more than ten years would pass before Joe Saraceno found a way to have the cuts released.

DYNAMIC CHANGES

When Mel proposed doing a solo project for Japan, Don and Bob were happy to assist with the production. In fact, when a song was needed to fill *James Bond 007* [Dan VC-7501], they helped Mel compose *Bondolero*. Bob and Don handled the guitar work, but Mel also wanted some orchestral backing. When Lanky Lindstrot heard of this, he introduced The Ventures to David Carr, a talented arranger having recently settled in Los Angeles. Dave wasted no time in drafting horns and strings for Mel's album, and when a song called *Morning Glory* needed keyboard work, Dave played electric piano.

John Durrill had co-written three of the tunes, but as he explains, he was no longer with The Ventures; "I had known Snuff Garrett since the days of the Five Americans when he was producing Bobby Vee. In 1971, I spent a week in Snuffy's office playing my songs for him. Later, while touring Japan with The Ventures, I got an idea for a song, and I was so excited about it that I telegraphed some of the lyrics to Snuff. It was about a woman who discovers that her fortuneteller is involved with her man [*Dark Lady*]. Snuff sent a reply to me, and he ended it by saying 'Make sure the bitch kills him,' so I sat down in the Tokyo Hilton one night and wrote;

> 'So I sneaked back and caught her with my man,
>
> Laughing and kissing 'till they saw the gun in my hand.
>
> The next thing I knew they were dead on the floor.
>
> *Dark Lady* would never turn a card up anymore.'

"Pretty soon, Garrett got me connected with people like Frank Sinatra, Jim Nabors, Phil Everly, Merle Haggard, and Cher. She did *Dark Lady* and it became a Number 1 hit.

"Everything began happening for me after that, including *The Only Couple On The Floor*, which Sinatra did, and five more of my songs recorded by Cher. Since then I've been involved in projects totaling 60,000,000 record sales. I never got into high-tech stuff like MIDI, but I played some synthesizer on Chicago's Christmas album [*Chicago 25*]. I delved into computers a bit, but it really cut into my writing time. I do my writing at home with my piano and a little cassette recorder in a room with a hardwood floor. When I'm ready, I go into a studio and make a proper recording."

Working with Snuff Garrett, John made some major movie music. He worked on five Burt Reynolds pictures, including music for Peggy Lee and Sarah Vaughan in *Sharkey's Machine*. Of four Clint Eastwood movies to which he contributed, John's *Misery And Gin*, written for *Bronco Billy*, became a Number 1 song for Merle Haggard. In addition to writing four songs for *Any Which Way You Can*, John also appeared on screen; "In that one, I was the bandleader wearing a cowboy hat and playing a guitar with Sondra Locke at the Palomino Club. In another scene, I introduce Fats Domino and later I play piano for my song, *The Good Guys And The Bad Guys* when the bar fight breaks out."

Besides composing hits for Roger Williams, Vicki Lawrence, and the Statler Brothers, John released a nice set of ballads and love songs entitled *Just For The Record* [UA LA824-G]. From this album, a single was extracted containing the tracks, *Changin'* b/w *I Think My Heart Is Gonna Let Me Stay* [United Artists XW-1141].

JUST FOR THE RECORD

In the late eighties, John reconnected with Trini Lopez, writing and harmonizing on *Tijuana Radio* for Trini's *25th Anniversary Album*. Having reached age sixty, John said; "I'm busy as ever, thanks to the loyalty of Snuffy Garrett. I can't say enough about him. He was very smart, with an acute sense for a hit song. God only knows how many Number 1 songs he's produced. I wrote for over eighty acts with him. He was tough, but if you worked hard and he was behind you, you did well."

"I loved all of The Ventures and I really miss Mel, who was always so good to me. But there was one time when he was, along with everyone in the band, fairly upset with me. It was in 1971 on my second trip to Japan. We were in Hokkaido, and after the late show, we stayed out even later to relax at a supper club. The next morning, Mel called my room and said to hurry up, as they were all down in the lobby, ready to catch the plane back to Tokyo. I must have been really wiped out because I fell back to sleep. Mel called again and wanted to know what was taking so long. He was yelling by then, so I hustled down there as fast as I could, but it was too late. We missed our flight and had to ride this dawdling farm train that had goats and chickens on it, making about fifty stops during the 500-mile trip. We laugh about it now, but at the time I was very unpopular with them for several days."

DAVE CARR

David John Carr was born near London on August 4, 1943. His mother being a choir singer and his father a church organist, David began piano lessons at the age of five, but started playing by ear during his school years. By age nineteen, Dave was a member of the Fortunes, a group well on its way to making hit records.

In October of 1965, *You've Got Your Troubles* [Press 9773] hit Number 7 in the USA, bringing the Fortunes to New York for a tour early '66. Dave stayed with the Fortunes for three years, but by the early '70s, he was expanding his career to producing, writing, and arranging in California, as well as playing keyboard on Mel Taylor's *James Bond 007* album for Japan. More Mel Taylor albums featured Dave on keyboards, and once The Ventures discovered him, Dave remained in their demand for well over thirty years.

The Fortunes – 1967

David Carr

After moderate success with his *James Bond* album, Mel teamed brother Larry with David Carr and friends for two brilliant albums called *Sun Sea and Love* [Dan VC-7503] and *Mel Taylor in Japan* [Dan VC-7506]. The friends were John Mayall, Artie Munson, and Larry's former Canned Heat bandmate, Harvey Mandel, who later wrote in his biography; "There were no Hendrixes or Claptons when I started playing. You couldn't go down to your local record store and get the real blues-rock stuff, so my original bible was The Ventures."

The A Side of Mel's albums contained six Bogle-Wilson-Taylor writings, the B-sides covering mellow Japanese songs. Artie Munson played rhythm while John Mayall and Larry Taylor shared the bass duties. On the back of *Mel Taylor in Japan*, a small but ominous logo heralded "Mel Taylor & The Dynamics."

It is likely that the album *Sun Sea and Love* was to be named after the track <u>Sand Sea and Love</u> on the album, before suffering alteration during translation to Japanese. Also, because the words "Mel Taylor – Dynamite" appear on the cover drawing of a bass drum, *Dynamite* was the title used by some English-speaking owners of the album.

By July, 1972, United Artists was ready for more Ventures product, but in the face of personnel shortage, Bob, Don, and Mel had taken up producing. If the musician credits on the *Joy* album seemed strange, the next album was even more confusing. With Harvey Mandel, Larry Taylor, and David Carr having worked well together on Mel's albums, the idea blossomed to have this group join Mel as The Ventures to record several past favorites. Linking Mandel's bluesy guitar with Carr's growling Hammond organ created a heavy blues-rock sensation on every track.

Larry Taylor and Harvey Mandel

Remembering his delight with Harvey, Bob recalls; Harvey fed his guitar through an Echoplex tape delay into a compressor and then into his 'miked' amplifier for a smooth 'late fifties' sound. Don and I were producing and switching back and forth on rhythm, but I played the straight lead part in *Guitar Boogie Shuffle*, and Harvey came in later."

Another heavy contributor to this new "Ventures sound" was veteran sax man, Jackie Kelso. Renowned for his work with Gene Vincent as far back as 1958, Kelso had since recorded with artists diverse as Neil Sedaka and Steely Dan.

When *Rock And Roll Forever* [United Artists UAS-5649] appeared in September, fans' emotions were mixed. Kelso's raspy sax and Mandel's blues guitar were superb, but this was not something Ventures lovers associated with their idols. Nevertheless, the album brought few complaints because it was so downright enjoyable. According to many fan club letters, it was one of the finest Ventures albums to date.

THE RETURN OF THE KING

After losing his place in The Ventures, Nokie sought the services of lawyer Norton Karno. Retained at the time by Semie Moseley, Karno later became prominent as the Will executor for Church of Scientology founder, L. Ron Hubbard following that multi-millionaire's questionable demise. Nokie's lawsuit netted him a $100,000 cash settlement, but in return, lost his sixties songwriting royalties from future Ventures record sales. This included songs previously credited to Nokie alone, such as *Orange Fire, Bluebird,* and *Surf Rider*. Investment in horses and racing along with other expenses (including a new Corvette) soon ate up the settlement, and as Nokie recalls, 1970 was a year that left him with more than one unpleasant memory; "I had fifteen Mosrite guitars in hard-shell cases that I was saving for a retirement nest egg. They were all new except for the prototype that I bought from Semie in 1963. In 1970, they were all stolen from my home near Tacoma. Somebody broke in when no one was at home. To make matters worse, I went through a divorce and had to sell my horses, so I went back to playing music for a living."

One of Nokie's first moves was to book a session at Wiley's Sound Studio in Tacoma. The owner was Bill Wiley, formerly of the *Bill and Grover Show* on which Don and Bob had made their TV debut. Wiley's low-budget studio had most of its releases mounted on a wall, including some early cuts by The Wailers and The Sonics going back to when the place was known as Wiley Griffith Studios. Country guitarist Big Bill Griffith had now left the business, but Wiley was ready and willing to record Nokie's pop single that united gentle acoustic sounds with wild electric wah-wah solos. Recalling the ill fate of his recording, Nokie said; "I recorded Bobby Goldsboro's *Muddy Mississippi Line* and backed it with *Land of 1,000 Dances* [Wasp WR-123]. I ordered 300 pressings, but before I could get there to pick them up, Bill Wiley died in a car accident. He was on a freeway ramp when his door came open and he fell out of the car. When I got to Wiley's place, it was cleaned out and up for sale. His widow had disposed of everything and she didn't know anything about my records. I never knew if the pressing was completed, or where the records ended up. I met a guy in Japan who had paid a couple hundred dollars for one, so there must be a few of them out there."

Indeed there are, for in a few months after Nokie's above declaration, a California record dealer placed his copy of WR-123 up for auction. By then, aggressive Japanese collectors having discovered eBay, Nokie's record brought $820.

Nokie's next move was to the Ventura area, northeast of Los Angeles, where he renewed his acquaintance with Al Bennett. Since leaving Liberty/UA Records, Bennett had established a record label named Cream. Working with Bennett's son who managed the label, Nokie covered a dozen current hits and a couple of movie themes. When asked about the accompanying musicians on the album, Nokie said; "I wish I could, but my chances of remembering their names are about the same as winning the State lottery."

Allan Lavinger, another casualty of Transamerica's housecleaning, wrote the liner notes for *NOKIE!* [Cream CR9006]. As Liberty's merchandising director since the fifties, Lavinger added the final touch to what should have been a very classy album. However, in addition to bland production, there was a problem with the vinyl. For the American release, Bennett seemingly took the cheap route, having *NOKIE!* pressed in an upstart economy plant. Many of the records were deemed defective from the beginning, and the rest reportedly wore rapidly and became noisy or warped. At home, distribution was minimal, providing a rather feeble introduction to Nokie's solo career. It seemed that marketing was aimed at Japan, where much higher quality pressings appeared. Copies of this red vinyl rarity were quick to sell out, and *NOKIE!* was soon re-issued on Japan's Stateside label [SOSL-10104].

Meanwhile, being in demand as producers for young Japanese artists, Don and Bob formed B&W Productions. In 1972, they flew to Tokyo early to spend almost a week working with ex-Golden Cups singer, Mamoru Manu. The result was a popular single on Liberty containing the Bogle-Wilson compositions *All The Children* and *Running To Nowhere* with lyrics by Keisuke Yamakawa.

Bob and Don with Mamoru Manu   Liberty single LTP-2694

Adapted for Japan, *All The Children* became *Futari no Hodo* [Two on the Road] and *Running to Nowhere* became *Yoake no Highway* [Highway at Dawn].

Other Japanese artists produced by B&W included Juran Lee, Riki Akira, and Mika Hayashi. With lyrics added to a Ventures' melody called *House Of Tomorrow*, Mika recorded *Mousugu Kokiyo* (Homeland Soon). In the years to come, this single became a valued rarity in Japan [Teichiku SN-1269].

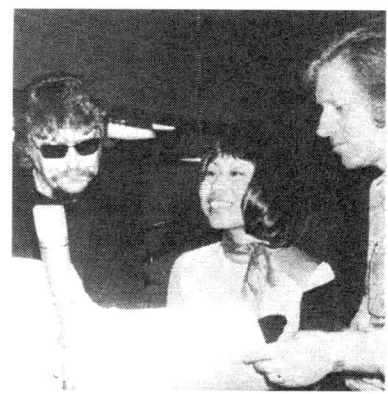

Producing Juran Lee on "The One (I Love) in Sapporo" (tune "Bondolero") Dan VA-7

In the same year [1972], Nokie recorded an album with B&W Productions entitled *Nokie Again!* Backing musicians on this one were David Carr, Artie Munson, David Vaught, and Joe Barile. In addition to a few Japanese titles, the album featured a cleverly accelerated *House of The Rising Sun*. The album appeared on Cream ISP 80546 in both Japan and America with no problems at all in production or vinyl quality.

At this time, Stan Wagner ended his tenure with the Redeye band. As he recalls, his days in the music business were numbered; "Nokie was on his own now, and he asked me to manage him. We released some singles in Japan from the album and Nokie had a huge hit there with the *Love Theme from The Godfather* [Cream ISR 10091]. In a year or so, I quit the music business. Since 1974 I've been fundraising for the Southern Christian Leadership Conference (SCLC) founded by Dr. Martin Luther King."

After two more Nokie singles, the Cream label vanished and his last Japanese 45 appeared on Stateside. Years later, Nokie was surprised to learn that one of his Cream singles was part of a movie soundtrack. Although filmed in Japan, *The Little Adventurer* was a British movie starring young Mark Lester, famed at age nine for the starring role in 1968's *Oliver Twist*. The songs extracted from *Nokie Again!* for the soundtrack single were *Sapporo Summer* and *Summer Affair* [Cream ISR-10239].

With Gerry away on tour and Nokie under contract as an "individual performer and recording artist," it was almost natural for Don and Bob to recruit him for their 1972 Far East tour. A few rehearsals ly were all that was needed to prepare the big surprise for Japanese Ventures fans. When the posters went up in July showing their guitar god Nokie having returned, anticipation and excitement ran high.

In Japan, Don and Bob appeared again with the Gibson SG guitar and Hofner bass, but it was the first year for the fans to see Nokie on stage with something other than a Mosrite. After leaving The Ventures, Nokie had returned to his 1952 Fender Telecaster. In preparation for Japan Tour '72, Nokie gave the guitar a coat of candy-apple red paint.

It was around this time that Kustom Electronics of Chanute, Kansas announced their becoming exclusive distributors of Mosrite guitars. Kustom was then famous for its powerful solid-state amplifiers enclosed in "tuck and roll" upholstered cabinets. The company advanced Moseley more than $100,000 to resume work in the Bakersfield factory, but Semie's comeback was cut short when Kustom underwent a change of ownership. They called in the loan, and Semie was out of business once again.

Semie Moseley and Charles A. Ross at NAMM '72

Meanwhile in Japan, fans reveled in The Ventures mix of ten-year-old hits with modern tunes such as *Gimme Some Lovin'* and *I'm A Man*. Like McGee's rapid absorption of the group's 1968 repertoire, Nokie had promptly mastered *Kyoto Doll*, *Paint It Black*, *Aquarius*, and *Manchurian Beat*. In turn The Ventures' backed Nokie on *Love Theme From The Godfather*. Combining Nokie's version of *Proud Mary* with that from The Ventures on *Swamp Rock*, a version was now heard with Nokie adding an expert demonstration of "chicken pickin'." Further on, his Telecaster having no vibrato mechanism, Nokie used the E-string tuning key for the deep bend ending on *Driving Guitars*, always to great applause. Another delight was his wild wah-wah pedal solo during *Bulldog*. He used the pedal again with a scratchy "chika-chaka" effect on *Gimme Some Lovin'* and *I'm A Man* from The Ventures' *Shaft* album.

Memorabilia hunters received a bonus when both TOA Attractions *and* Toshiba Records produced large souvenir tour books for 1972. Tokyo and Osaka patrons were also treated to the vocalizing of Fifi Ohyan, the lovely Taiwanese wife of Japan's famous racing driver, Shikiba Sokichi. Fifi's popular hit version of *Ame No Midosuji* (composed by The Ventures as *Stranger in Midosuji*), established her among Japan's top female vocalists. Traditionally, Fifi performed this song with The Ventures for many more years.

On August 1, The Ventures were in Osaka when Mel met an attractive English girl in the hotel lobby. Introductions revealed Fiona Miles to be a troupe dancer based in Singapore, and now in Japan to visit a friend; "Mel invited me to a performance, and the next day, I saw my first thrilling Ventures concert at Osaka Festival Hall. I'll never forget the audience reaction to Mel's drum solo on *Caravan*. He radiated so much power and energy that I was completely enthralled!

"At the time, I was traveling all over the world with various modern dance groups. Although based mostly in Paris and Monte Carlo, I was born and grew up in Bournemouth in the South of England. This was where I obtained my diploma for classical ballet in 1963.

"After crossing each other's paths for the next three weeks, Mel and I became friends and began going out to the few nightspots frequented by English speaking people. One night, when Mel said he was going to meet with a fellow named Reid, an amazing coincidence happened. I said, 'Would that be George Reid?' Mel said, 'Why yes! He filmed us in 1965 for a movie called *Beloved Invaders*. It really is a small world! When Mel went back to the States, we kept in touch by writing letters."

On this tour, The Ventures performed an unprecedented 100 concerts plus nine TV appearances in the seventy-six days from July 17 to September 30. With Nokie billed as "Special Guest," every concert sold out in advance. In recalling the pace on such tours, Bob remarked; "On days when we played only one concert, it was like having a day off."

A live album usually commemorated The Ventures' Japan visits, and 1972 was no exception. On the final night at the Shibuya Public Concert Hall, Nokie's return was archived on vinyl with *The Ventures - On Stage '72* [Liberty 93101B]. Planning for 1973, the group arranged storage at Tokyo's Imperial Hotel to avoid the bother and expense of shipping the bulk of their equipment (a decision later be deemed to be a mistake).

At this time, an important development took place when The Ventures decided to abandon Mr. Ono and his TOA Attractions in favor of an agency called Kyodo Tokyo. Their new contact was Mr. J. Uchino, who immediately pointed out a recent statistic claiming instrumental rock bands to have ninety percent *male* audience appeal. Uchino then suggested adding a female singer, a possibility which Don and Bob agreed to explore. It was around this time that the band learned of Japan's law stating that if a foreign performing entity changed touring agencies, they must wait one full year before returning to Japan. This caused them a little stress until Mr. Uchino told Bob and Don not to be concerned, as it was an old law that was not enforced. Unfortunately, Mel was not present when this last piece of information was delivered.

FINDING A NICHE

In the seventies, younger fans were harder to win, their fascination being with new guitar heroes like Eric Clapton, Jimi Hendrix, and Jeff Beck. Mel Taylor was aware of this and he did not like the fact that with Nokie's return to the group, many older hits were being revived for the concert repertoire. It was done to please the audience, but Mel was less than eager to be part of a nostalgia act. As winter 1972 approached, he saw an opportunity that was too good to resist. Armed with knowledge of "the law" prohibiting The Ventures from touring Japan until 1974, he decided to start a band of his own. Under his own name, this new group would record for Japan and follow with a summer tour. In 1973 he was able to recruit Gerry McGee and Johnny Durrill. Mel also had a rhythm player in mind, but he did not know an available bassist. Gerry solved the problem by suggesting his session bassist friend, twenty-seven-year-old Bill Lincoln.

In the early sixties, William D. Lincoln played on records by The Strangers, The Bushmen, The War Babies, Nobody Cares, and The Word. He was also an original member of Euphoria, which followed their 1966 single [*Hungry Women/ No Me Tomorrow* [Mainstream 655] with 1969's ambitious fifteen-track album, *A Gift From Euphoria* [Capitol SKAO-363]. This Beatles-inspired compilation remained in the shadows of psychedelic rock, country, and bluegrass until 1996 when a CD from See-For-Miles revealed Bill as having played guitar and bass as well as being a singer. In 1970, Bill collaborated with Hollywood guitarist Bernie Schwartz on an album called *The Wheel* [Coburt 1001]. As session work was not heavy at the time, Bill welcomed the chance to join Mel Taylor and friends on an LP record and a promotional tour in Japan.

During a 1971 session at United Sound studios for his *James Bond 007* album, Mel had met and become friends with producer Dennis Ganim. In fact, Dennis became the new owner of a beloved sports car when Mel decided to sell it. Ganim produced a band for United Artists called Sweet Pain, and knowing lead guitarist Bob Spalding to be a devout Ventures fan, introduced him to Mel. When Spalding told Mel of being awestruck by The Ventures at age fifteen while living in Japan, and of his delight at meeting Nokie in a Tacoma nightclub in 1970, Mel knew he had his rhythm guitarist.

BOB SPALDING

Robert Eugene Spalding was born in San Bernardino, California on February 10, 1947. Coincidentally, this was the same day that a teenager named Don Wilson was celebrating his fourteenth birthday in Tacoma, Washington.

As Bob grew up, he followed in his brother's footsteps by taking up the guitar at the age of twelve. At the time, Ricky Nelson and Elvis Presley were popular, but Bob paid more attention to their respective guitarists, James Burton and Scotty Moore. At fifteen, Bob was following instrumental performers like Johnny and the Hurricanes and Duane Eddy when he heard The Ventures for the first time. The Spaldings were an Air Force family, which meant relocating upon demand from headquarters. A three-year station in Japan allowed Bob to attend a 1962 concert that featured The Ventures opening for Jo Ann Campbell and Bobby Vee. As Bob recalls; "I never forgot the sound of those driving guitars, and I was soon collecting albums. A most memorable joy of my youth was perusing the racks for a new Ventures LP and actually finding one every three or four months. When we moved back to the States, it wasn't long before I got a guitar group going in Austin with my brother on the drums. We were called the Nomads."

After high school and a year of college, Bob completed his military duty, first in Vietnam, and then in Fort Lewis near Don Wilson's hometown of Tacoma. During this time, Bob married his girlfriend, Artie. He then began playing guitar with Dwight Bement, who had played saxophone with Gary Puckett and the Union Gap [*Young Girl*]. One evening, Bob and Dwight attended a show at Tacoma's Circle nightclub, where they heard Nokie Edwards perform and were later able to chat with him.

Released from the army in 1968, Bob joined the six-man combo, Sweet Pain. With a sound somewhere between Santana and Strawberry Alarm Clock, they produced an album and a pair of singles for United Artists. During session work at United Sound, Bob Spalding met and became friends with Mel Taylor.

Sweet Pain's music was good enough that, in addition to an attractively packaged vinyl album in a textured, gatefold cover, *Sweet Pain* [United Artists UAS 6793] was also released on eight-track and cassette tape. Unfortunately, heavy competition from similar bands at the time prevented the album and its two related singles from selling well, and Bob returned to San Bernardino to complete his college degree. He honed his musical talent during that time doing session work and backing stage acts such as Chuck Berry.

When Mel Taylor's *Diamonds Are Forever* b/w *Bondolero* appeared on Avalanche 36008, Sweet Pain released a single on Avalanche 36009, *Diego* b/w *The Witness* under the name of Dolphin Market. As Bob recalls; "We got into jamming during a show in San Diego that evolved into a twenty-minute instrumental. We named it *Diego* and added it to our repertoire. As J.C. Phillips and David Riordan of Sweet Pain had penned *Green Eyed Lady* for Sugarloaf, they had some leverage with United Artists. Our producer, Dennis Ganim, was a real proponent of *Diego*, and he used his leverage to have UA produce an edited-down version for release on Avalanche. It was released during the summer of 1972, with hopes that it would be a hit and The Ventures would record it."

 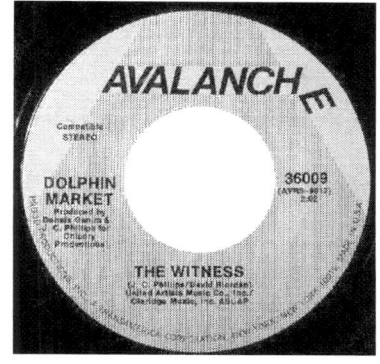

Bob Spalding (top left) on UA album 6793   Flip side of "Diego" on U.A.'s auxiliary label

Although Sweet Pain dissolved, Bob's music career did not. Early '73 found him in the promotion department of San Bernardino's radio station KMEN, when an invitation to play rhythm in The Dynamics came from Mel Taylor. Mel had already inquired if a Japan tour was OK with Artie Spalding, then an expectant mother. The baby was due before the tour, so Bob was free to go. Packing his beloved Gibson, and with Hollywood just an hour away, Bob was soon cutting an album with Gerry, John, Bill, and Mel.

Mel's next move was to confirm the dates for his Japan tour. Contacting Mr. Ono of TOA Attractions was a simple matter, and the tour was set to begin in late July. He would soon have to inform Don and Bob of his project, but as it happened, they "heard it through the grapevine." As Don remembers, he received the shock during a long-distance call to Japan; "Bob and I were wrapping up some business dealings with someone at Toshiba. During our talk, he asked us why three of us had been replaced with other musicians working with Mel on the next tour. We didn't understand, and asked him for details. He laid out the whole thing, naming Gerry, John, Bob Spalding, and Bill Lincoln as Mel's bandmates. We didn't know anything about that, but after pondering for awhile, Bob and I decided to call Mel over for a coffee and see what was going on. Mel arrived in about ten minutes, and I told him that we had heard a strange story, and if it were true, I would fall right off the couch I was on. After relating what we had just heard, Mel hesitated for a bit, and then he said, 'Go ahead and fall off the couch Don. It's true.' When we asked him why he would do such a thing, he said that he was under the impression that The Ventures couldn't perform in Japan for a year, and that he had seen a niche for himself. We were naturally very angry with him, as he had made a commitment that he couldn't get out of. We had just gotten Nokie back, and now we would have to hire a new drummer for Japan Tour '73!"

~ ~ ~

When touring in North America seemed all but over for The Ventures, a contract was signed for some concerts in the Canadian city of Montreal in early 1973. As this was the only venue, air travel was elected, with guitars being the only equipment taken along. Drums were rented from Steve's Music in Montreal, along with large, Canadian-made Traynor amplifiers boasting "musician-preferred" vacuum-tube technology. After more than ten years since Don and Bob had played Montreal with Bobby Vee, The Ventures discovered they were popular there as ever. Unknown to fans at these shows, all was not well with the band, as Mel's upcoming Japan tour was not resting well with the group. By Saturday, February 24, they were barely on speaking terms while the unsuspecting crowds at La Salle Maisonneuve de la Place des Arts hollered and cheered to music at the sold-out shows. The set-list included *Honky Tonk*, which had recently peaked at 11 on Montreal's Hit Parade after The Ventures' Harvey Mandel version was released on a French Canadian labeled single [United Artists UA 50925].

The Ventures using Traynor amplifiers in Montreal – February 1973

HOT SUMMER ROCK 'N' ROLL

Adding four Taylor-McGee-Durrill originals to various popular hits, Mel's new album took the name of its "oldies" selection, *Roll Over Beethoven*. This Chuck Berry gem had recently enjoyed a makeover by The Electric Light Orchestra, and it was this complex version that Mel and his group covered. Although John Durrill would play organ on the upcoming Japan tour, he played with wild abandon on a grand piano in the studio. The original cuts were published under Jermeljon (Jerry-Mel-John) Music; a company later renamed Quadron Music under Mel's sole ownership. *Roll Over Beethoven* [DAN VC-7510] was released in Japan in July.

While Mel and his group were recording, so were The Ventures. Taking Mel's departure in stride, they quickly recruited Joe Barile, who had recently assisted on Nokie's *Again* album. Their first project was a collection of hits entitled *Pops In Japan '73* [Liberty LP-80801]. Half of the fourteen tracks were well-known Japanese works, the remainder being Ventures originals. The masters were shipped to Japan where the album's release coincided with the July to October summer tour.

United Artists began 1973 by re-issuing singles of The Ventures' big hits from the sixties. As part of their *Silver Spotlight Series*, they released *Walk-Don't Run*, *Perfidia*, and *Hawaii Five-O*, backed with equally popular tracks such as *Ram-Bunk-Shush*, *Telstar*, and *Walk-Don't Run '64*. There were earlier UA singles, but *Last Tango in Paris* [UA XW207], is significant for containing Bob Bogle's first recorded "vocal." The background moaning in this theme from the Marlon Brando movie did not sound much like Bob, but he definitely remembered doing it. Confirmation later came when a session list for the track was released, indicating Nokie on lead, Don on Rhythm, Bob on bass and "moaning vocal," Dave Carr on keyboards, Joe Barile on drums, and Jackie Kelso on saxophone. Although the movie score won a GRAMMY, there were so many recordings of the haunting theme that none earned hit status. Besides the original soundtrack and a vocal by Andy Williams, there were instrumentals by Herb Alpert, Andre Kostelanetz, and Roger Williams. In fact, Ventures fans were more enamored by the original tune on the flip side. *Prima Vera* was a snappy Latin melody from *Pops in Japan '73*, an album obscured to most fans outside Japan for the next twenty years.

Having contracted songwriter Manny Freiser to write English lyrics for *Kyoto Doll* and *Stranger in Midosuji*, The Ventures began auditioning female singers. Don and Bob were becoming desperate when one Susan Schreiber applied for the job. Not only did she outperform all others, she was willing to go to Japan at the end of June. By the time they took off for Japan, Susan had recorded the two vocals for a Toshiba/Liberty single. Upon checking into Tokyo's Imperial Hotel, The Ventures were greeted with a disappointing surprise. Not only was their storage room completely empty, the hotel staff knew nothing about the equipment stored there after the previous year's tour. Among the missing gear was Bob's Hofner bass. He had hoped to be using the lightweight "Beatle bass" on the ninety concert tour, but it was gone and there was nothing like it available. For a replacement, Bob was furnished with a heavy Precision bass, which he shouldered for the entire fourteen-week trip.

Susan Schreiber and her 45 rpm single.

Since Bob was again playing some lead guitar, he had brought along his Jazzmaster to do the medley that Nokie had played in the sixties, combining *Walk-Don't Run*, *Perfidia*, and *Lullaby of the Leaves*. As it turned out, the medley was seldom performed once Susan Schreiber's numbers were added to the itinerary.

Early in the tour, Don set his Gibson SG aside and began using Bob's Jazzmaster. The guitar felt good and played so well that Don never went back to the Gibson. When Bob played the medley, he used Nokie's Telecaster. Thirty years later, Bob laughingly recalled; "Don fell in love with that guitar. He played it so much that I finally told him it was his. He's tried other Jazzmasters, but they just aren't the same as that '68 model."

The Ventures spent the first week of Japan Tour '73 on the island of Hokkaido. As usual, about half of the program was different from that of the previous year. *Walk-Don't Run*, *Bulldog* and *Ginza Lights* were replaced with *California Dreamin'*, *Classical Gas*, and Don's vocal treatment of *Jambalaya*. This year, the group was provided with master of ceremonies, Yoshiyuki Kohno. Yoshi spoke English fairly well, and gradually became a good friend of the group.

The audience heartily accepted Susan Schreiber's English renditions of *Now Good-Bye* and *Streets of the City*, but as Bob remembers, he and Don were not happy; "When Susan came on stage, we wondered what we had heard during that audition. Both her pitch and voice quality seemed to have simply deteriorated." To this, Don added; "Needless to say, Susan was only with us for that summer. We decided that if Uchino wanted a female singer on the next year's tour, we would start auditioning much earlier. We tried to help Susan by producing her on a single, but it wasn't much of a success."

If fans were surprised to see a girl singing with The Ventures, they were astounded at the performance of Joe Barile, especially in the larger venues where he employed a huge trap set. Although dwarfed behind two bass drums and six finely tuned rack-toms, Joe's power and skill were soon evident as he played in tune with the melody, and adding flourishes and fills on nearly every number. In songs like *Diamond Head* and *Pipeline*, Joe echoed Don's "tiki-tiki-tiki" sound by rolling across the tom-rack. He closed each concert with an exhaustive *Wipe Out* followed by *Caravan* with an enduring drum solo and delicate bass tattoo. Like Mel, Joe could keep a drum solo interesting for all of fifteen minutes. Early in the tour, he celebrated his 26th birthday. As the other Ventures were now pushing 40, Joe was most popular with the girls in the audience.

A new era begins as Don, Nokie, and Bob are joined by Joe Barile

On most Japan tours, The Ventures performed in Tokyo at least twice. Occasionally, after a TV or radio show, the group had time in the evening for relaxation and nightclub entertainment. During one such outing they saw Italian singer Bobby Solo, known in Europe as "The Italian Elvis Presley." Several club patrons recognized The Ventures, and it wasn't long before the stage performers learned of the band's presence. Soon, lead guitarist Marco Carlieri introduced himself and said that he had been influenced by The Ventures as a teenager in Rome. When The Ventures learned that Marco yearned to visit America, they assured him that if he came to Los Angeles, they would help him find work in the music business. Marco welcomed their offer, never dreaming that he would eventually go on tour and record in the studio with The Ventures.

During August, a performance at Yubin-Chokin Hall was once again recorded for Toshiba Records. A two-record set, *The Ventures On Stage '73* [Liberty LP-93101B] was available in two or four-channel stereo, commemorating the tour theme selected by the agency, "Hot Summer Rock 'n' Roll."

Sadly, while Ventures-lovers were again being thrilled in Japan, most North American fans knew nothing of the band's activities. Few were aware that the group was still intact, let alone that Nokie was back and Mel was out. For these fans, hope was restored in October when *The Venture's Only Hits* [United Artists LA147G] appeared in record stores. Released on vinyl, eight track, and cassette ("Quadrasonic" mode optional), the album was also the band's last to appear in the seven-inch reel-to-reel format. The misplaced apostrophe in the title may have irritated a few grammar freaks, but it was the album's content that confused the bulk of Ventures fans. While the music on this two-disc set was pleasing and up-to-date, again it sounded very little like The Ventures. It seemed that United Artists did not realize or did not care that Ventures fans knew the difference between session musicians and the sound of their idols. By the time the band returned from Japan, the work was nearly completed, most notably by Mr. Ben Benay in the role of arranger. A redeeming feature was the doublewide inner photo divulging Nokie's return and the addition of Joe Barile.

Two-disc vinyl set

Twin cartridge eight-track set

While Don and Bob expressed irritation with producers and record companies attempting to fool the public in this way, Josie wondered how they got away with it. The answer seemed that, as long as there was some actual "Ventures content," it could be classified as a Ventures album. In this case, it was the *Last Tango in Paris* cut.

After a published interview confirming Joe Barile to have no part in *Only Hits*, information slowly leaked out that Gene Pello was the drummer and Richard Bennett had done much of the guitar work alongside Mike Henderson on sax, Tom Hensley on piano, Ray Pohlman on bass. Later, some of these names became associated with records produced by Joe Saraceno under the name, The New Marketts.

Unsure of what was happening with The Ventures, most fans listened to *Only Hits* a few times before filing it at the back of their collections. One can only speculate how wonderful it might have been if instead, United Artists had obtained the live-in-Japan masters from this period for release in the Western world.

1997 Compact Disc *Bad News Records BNCY-29*

Three weeks into The Ventures' 1973 Japan tour, Mel and the Dynamics began *their* thirty-six-show tour. Gerry used the gold Gibson Les Paul Standard he had used in 1969, but the guitar was now fitted with a pair of Bigsby palm pedals. The guitar Bob Spalding used was also special; "It was a Gibson ES-150DC [Double Cutaway], a rare variation of the ES-150SC from the late sixties. I obtained it as part of the deal with UA/Liberty when I was with Sweet Pain in 1970-71. I had a Bigsby tailpiece added at the time of purchase. It was a great guitar, but I eventually wore it out."

Mel, Gerry McGee, and even John Durrill had a faithful following in Japan, so the concerts were well received. It is little wonder that some Japanese fans remember 1973 as the summer of "two Ventures visiting," for as it turned out; over half of The Dynamics' set list was part of The Ventures' repertoire. *Slaughter on Tenth Avenue* was included, along with *Caravan*, wherein Mel expanded his celebrated tattoo by moving from the bass to a guitar for a fascinating interlude of chording with his drumsticks.

In August, The Dynamics were featured on Japan's TBS TV show, *Ginza Now*. The highlights of the Dynamics' show were two high-energy Chuck Berry numbers, *Rock and Roll Music* and *Roll Over Beethoven*, each containing exhilarating McGee solo work. Although the guys sang in English, audience response was exuberant. Their final concert being taped for an album, The Dynamics finished in their seventh week, well before The Ventures went home. Although Miss Toshiko Sudou had sung two vocals at some Dynamics' concerts, she was omitted from their album. Also missing was dialog by Master of Ceremonies, Yusaku Hayano.

During the tour, the studio album, *Roll Over Beethoven* was sold, but *Live in Japan '73* [shown above] was not (officially) released for over twenty-three years!

CHANGING CAREERS

The Dynamics' tour ended sourly when the sponsoring company held back on the agreed amount of money because The Ventures were also on tour. According to Mel, he paid off the band while taking a severe personal loss. On a more positive note, Mel had maintained contact with Fiona through the mail until the tour ended in September. Fiona recalls the next phase of their relationship; "After the last performance of The Dynamics, Mel invited me to come to the States. By January of 1974, I was back in the UK where I completed a business and secretarial course. In July, I came to California where we lived together and were eventually married."

Upon returning home, Mel explored various musical enterprises. Ten months later, Fiona arrived; "When I first came to America, I worked for a biochemist who had recently sold his own company and started a small business importing and exporting blood products. As his personal assistant, I learned the business from the inside. The company expanded and was eventually sold to an organization based in Florida. After eighteen months, my former boss and I formed a partnership. Along with two others, we started a new company."

Mel and Fiona

Following the Dynamics' Japan tour, John Durrill continued singing and writing songs while doing session work for established artists like Brenda Lee. In 1978, he recorded the fine country-pop album previously mentioned, *Just For The Record*. In 1980, the Clint Eastwood movie, *Any Which Way You Can* appeared with Johnny singing *The Good Guys and the Bad Guys* during the closing credits. John had written most of the movie's soundtrack, co-writing some tracks with Snuff Garrett and one with Phil Everly. A single was then issued with John singing *The Good Guys and the Bad Guys* b/w *Orangutan Hall Of Fame* [Warner Bros. 49673]. Since that time, John's songs have appeared on many soundtracks and albums, performed by a plethora of popular artists. Besides *Dark Lady*, Cher recorded five more of his songs, and Sarah Vaughan received an Academy Award nomination for singing John's *Before You* in the Burt Reynolds movie, *Sharkey's Machine*.

Gerry McGee went back to Hollywood and resumed studio work in a variety of genres along with various screen appearances. Distinguished artists he backed included Jimmy Buffett, T-Bone Burnett, Mac Davis, Gene Clark, Linda Ronstadt, and Rosanne Cash. He also worked with blues legends Brownie McGhee and Sonny Terry. Near the end of

1975, Gerry appeared on stage with Eric Clapton in San Bernardino. He also performed on several Rita Coolidge albums, which led to work with her husband, Kris Kristofferson. Between 1973 and 1979, Gerry played a variety of instruments on five Kristofferson albums. Billy Swan (*I Can Help*) also worked extensively with Kristofferson, and when Billy went solo, he had Gerry play on his 1978 album, *Your Ok I'm Ok* with Kris and Rita on background vocals [Pickwick SPC-3743].

Working with Kris Kristofferson opened a door for Gerry at the Screen Actors Guild when Kris got him a musical part in one of the top grossing films of 1976, *A Star Is Born*. Gerry played in the band alongside *Green Onions* organist Booker T. Jones, who was now married to Rita's sister, Priscilla. Gerry was cast in more movies, including Sam Peckinpah's *Convoy* [1978] and Michael Cimino's *Heaven's Gate* [1981], both starring Kristofferson. While writing and recording with Tanya Tucker, "Jerry" wrote a help book for aspiring musicians titled *Dynamite Guitar Licks* [Lucky Publishing 1979]. It was released again in 1987 by Alfred Publishing.

After rejoining The Ventures in 1973, Nokie challenged some heavy UK rock music on his solo recordings. His *King of Guitars* LP [Stateside ISP 80859] offered the surprise tracks, *Easy Livin'* from Uriah Heep and two Deep Purple rockers, *Black Knight* and *Highway Star*. In contrast to the metallic thundering of the British groups, Nokie presented "laid back" versions that were hopefully more appealing to his fans.

Nokie's *King of Guitars* added to Mel's Dynamics records plus that of The Ventures (along with simultaneous tours by all) truly gave Japan a summer of "Hot Rock 'n' Roll."

King of Guitars centerfold   Glorious Guitarist, a.k.a. *Beloved Old Hits*

Nokie's next album was titled exclusively in Japanese, and then only on the *back* of the cover. This time, it was entitled *Glorious Guitarist* [Stateside ISP 97019]. Arriving in 1974, this set moved back in time with a dozen country and fifties rock 'n' roll favorites. Again, if the album had been available outside Japan, there would have been many more happy fans. For some reason, the few English-speaking fans lucky enough to get a copy of this album referred to it as *Beloved Old Hits*. Regarding this and his other albums from the period, Nokie commented; "I never knew what they were going to call my albums or put on the covers. Some were only titled in Japanese. I just supplied the track list and they did the rest."

In America, a hot new daytime TV series had adapted *Nadia's Theme* as its theme song. In their constant quest for another hit single, The Ventures gave the theme their own treatment. Bob did the lead guitar work on this late '73 release, and while there were no spectacular results for *Theme from the Young and the Restless* [UA-XW369], collectors had another gem for their collection of "45's." The record re-appeared in February '74 in a rare "picture sleeve" envelope [UA-XW392]. Fans of the "soap," were doubly lucky as the back cover pictured over a dozen of the show's original cast. A *Young and The Restless* music video was also produced on which Bob played the lead. The TV show's producers may have been impressed with the package, as Ventures music was occasionally heard in poolside or party scenes for the next twenty years.

As The Ventures pondered ideas for their next album, inspiration came through a tragic event that struck America's top-forty music realm. In September 1973, popular folk-rocker Jim Croce and four others had perished in a plane crash. The entire Croce catalog then became best-selling material. Changing times had left little in the way of pop-rock music fitting the style of The Ventures, but the Jim Croce craze opened their door for The Ventures' *Jim Croce Songbook* [United Artists LA217G].

For this album, Dave Carr was both keyboardist and arranger. Nokie played acoustic guitar, along with some Dobro and sitar. Bob Bogle remembers their approach to the project; "We were really interested in producing by then, and Don spent more and more time in the booth. I played a lot of rhythm, and we got Armando Compean to play bass on several songs. He's known more for jazz and blues work, but he's a pro that can play anything. We did the same thing on the next album with all those Carpenters songs."

In spring of '74, the band was well into recording *The Ventures Play The Carpenters* [United Artists LA231G]. More mellow music here, but now girls as well as guys were listening. Later, recalling his use of the "Red Rhodes" compressor box with its single control knob, Nokie cited the Carpenters tribute as his favorite work with the band.

Although the Croce album was a memorial to Jim, The Ventures never expected some fans to later consider their Carpenters set to be a posthumous tribute. Another nine years went by before Karen Carpenter's tragic passing from anorexia in 1983.

Japan issue of The Carpenters tribute album

LIVING IT UP

Having halted touring on home ground, The Ventures found more time for leisure and outside interests. In fact, it was a nightclub where they had met Joe Barile and a host of other new friends. Now past age forty, they enjoyed luxurious living in the San Fernando Valley. Don had settled in Sherman Oaks, a short distance east of Bob's home in Encino. Both guitarists owned Rolls Royce automobiles at some point, both for enjoyment and as investments. According to Don, his Rolls had a bit of history; "We were all like part of a family at Liberty, and when Al Bennett decided to sell his 'Forest Green' Rolls, I decided to keep it in the family. Actually, I bought it from his son, and Al had bought it from Ross Bagdasarian who did the 'Chipmunk' recordings as David Seville. Bob had owned a sporty Jaguar XKE, and I soon traded the Rolls for a black Jaguar sedan that had belonged to Desi Arnaz. In fact, the key fob was inscribed ARNAZ."

The summer of '74 was also when Bob got his flying license. He flew until 1979, during which time he owned four different Cessnas. His last was an eight-passenger, twin engine 421 with a pressurized cabin. The Ventures did fun things with Bob like flying to Reno for lunch, but the planes were never used for band work.

Bob getting ready to take-off

Between sessions for their *Carpenters* album, Bob, Don, and Dave Carr began auditioning girls in spring of 1974. They were about ready to give up when someone recommended a songstress working at an Orange County nightclub. Upon entering the club, Don and Bob immediately knew that their ninety-minute drive was not wasted. Not only was Leisha Soukary a fantastic singer with a wonderful voice, she was an absolute beauty. The guys almost fell over themselves as they hired her on the spot.

Now part of the "Ventures family," Dave Carr was also invited on the three-month Japan tour. In spite of his busy schedule, he was able to accept. Equipped with a rack of electronic keyboards, Dave brought exciting new sounds to oldies like *Pipeline*.

While Leisha rehearsed a dozen songs, Don looked for something newer to sing than *Runaway* and *Hats Off to Larry*. The three-tune *Ventures Medley* was also part of this year's show, with Bob playing the lead on Nokie's Telecaster in spite of it having no vibrato bar. He also revived *Manchurian Beat*, a favorite Ventures single from 1971. Fans may have thought Gerry played lead on that record, but on the day of the session at The Village (a popular Los Angeles studio), Gerry had called in sick. Bob saved the session by playing the lead *and* bass parts. Like many popular Ventures' recordings, the tune was given Japanese lyrics and recorded by vocalists. In this case, *Manchurian Beat* became a hit with the title, *Wandering Guitar* as sung by Rumi Koyama. [reissued in 2007 - Hotwax CDSOL-1167].

The Ventures had recently recorded *Meadowlands,* the traditional Russian folk song also known as *Song of the Steppes.* Other guitar groups had recorded *Meadowlands* some ten years earlier, including Vancouver Canada's Chessmen, and Sweden's Spotnicks. While the Swedish group had called it *Rocket Man,* The Ventures called their version *Samovar,* using it on this tour to extend Nokie's set on the electric sitar.

Arriving in Tokyo in late June, the group of six began a three-month excursion through major cities and many small towns. Once again, Yoshi Kohno performed MC duties. After flattering the beauty and charm of "Princess Leisha," Yoshi would ask her where she was born. Leisha replied; "I was born in Cairo, studied in Lebanon, Saudi Arabia, and Switzerland before spending the last twelve years in the United States." Yoshi always got a laugh as he feigned regret for asking.

Leisha Soukary

Born in Egypt as Begum Aidah Haydee Leisha Hassan Kazi El Soukary, she entertained simply as "Leisha," while simplifying her surname to "Kary."

So confident were the guys in Leisha that they gave her a pair of original songs for which they had obtained lyrics in Japanese. Leisha sang *Morning Glow* and *Alone Again Today* so well in Japanese that they recorded her in Tokyo for a single [Liberty-Japan LLR-10585].

Although the entire group now wore longer hair, Don looked even more "mod" in his stylish, oversized eyeglasses. For vocals, he selected *Pied Piper* and the aging *Jambalaya* on which he sounded much like Hank Williams himself. In faster numbers, Bob's raging bass runs sounding increasingly like lead guitar solos. Constantly adding percussive variety, Joe played hi-hat cymbal and bongos during his *Wipe Out* breaks. He appeared to be having fun, in contrast to Nokie, who, with little facial expression, expressed his joy through his fingers. When asked by Yoshi why he did not smile, Nokie always got a laugh from the audience with; "I'm saving it."

After dark, there was plenty of action in Tokyo, but in smaller centers, entertainment spots were scarce. With nothing to do after their evening meal, the group usually read or worked on music in their hotel rooms. As drummer Joe Barile was a songwriter, he spent many evenings humming and strumming a 1955 Fender Esquire that he had obtained at age eighteen.

In July, Toshiba recorded another live Ventures concert while fans ravaged Japan's record stores for Nokie's *Glorious Guitarist* album. During an August autograph session, some fans surprised The Ventures when they reported seeing Gerry McGee backing Kris Kristofferson at a Tokyo concert.

Back to sunny California, The Ventures rested, night-clubbed, and generally took it easy until the end of the year. While enjoying brisk sales of his Japanese solo albums, Nokie launched a project that took very little work. With Dave Carr and Don sorting mustaches for quite some time, Nokie decided it was his turn. It did not take long for his friends and fans to get used to the new look, and the mustache became permanent.

The first publicity photo showing Nokie with a mustache

ANOTHER STING

Leisha and The Ventures kicked off 1975 with a Mexico City nightclub job that ran for nearly two weeks. While dining at a restaurant, The Ventures heard a captivating love song with a wonderful melody. Although sung in Spanish, they learned that *Sentimientos* translated to *Feelings* and that its writer, Brazil-born Morris Albert had written English lyrics for it. It seemed perfect for Leisha, so they obtained the recording and brought it back to Hollywood. Leisha was immediately recorded singing *Feelings* and a cover of the Hues Corporation's *Miracle Maker*, but United Artists held it back, indicating they would release it strategically at just the right time. Don forged ahead, arranging a follow-up album to complement Leisha's single. What happened next harkens back to when Josie and Christian Wilde produced the Nordic Trio on *Softly, As I Leave You* while Frank Sinatra, with offices in the same building, managed to release the song first. Suddenly, Morris Albert's recording [RCA PB-10279] was in Billboard's Top Ten, and before long, *Feelings* was recorded by everyone including Andy Williams, Elvis Presley, Brenda Lee and Glen Campbell. With literally hundreds of versions recorded, *Feelings* became a lounge standard from Florida to Alaska. For Don and Leisha, there was nothing to do but curse United Artists and dream of what might have been if they had introduced the song to America.

Leisha's *Feelings* eventually appeared in America [UAXW-595X], Japan [Liberty LLR-10741], and South America [UA-1158]. Her rendition also appeared in Italy on the compilation album, *Disco Action* [Derby DBR-81082].

In Mexico City, the group met a club performer and long-time Ventures fan, Dave Dalton. Socializing after their nightly performances ended with Dave deciding to return with The Ventures to Hollywood, where Don and Bob would produce and record him. In time, not only would Dave be playing on a Ventures record, he would also perform on stage as a band member.

Dave Dalton

In spite of no American tours or a new U.S. album, 1975 was another busy year for the band. With Japan scheduled for mid June, there was little time for anything but work. First was their fifteenth anniversary album for Japan, *15 Years of Japanese Pop* [Liberty LLS-80188] with Leisha's album also in the works. Both projects were started when Toshiba requested The Ventures to drop everything and accompany a popular Japanese singer on an album to be sung in English. As Japan was the bastion of their livelihood, The Ventures agreed, and the thirty-five year-old rocker was in Los Angeles by the end of March. Since opening for The Ventures in January of 1965, Yuya Uchida had married a famous movie actress. The resulting connections brought him parts in several movies helping him to rise in the music business. Bob, Don, and Nokie barely remembered that Terry and the Blue Jeans had opened for their concerts back then, let alone Uchida being the singer. Ten years later, here was this enthusiastic, hyperactive rock 'n' roll lover ready to sing the standards with them.

Yuya knew the hit of Elvis, Chuck Berry, and Little Richard, and to the band's surprise, the southern gospel classic, "When The Saints Go Marching In!" For this one, Yuya modified the lyrics to fit a rock combo instead of a Dixieland band. He also selected a couple of numbers appearing on Ventures albums; Ricky Nelson's "Lonesome Town" and "Linda Lou" from *Bobby Vee Meets The Ventures*. Yuya had a fair grasp of English, though he sang with a heavy accent. Along with The Ventures, Jackie Kelso's sax, Dave Carr's keyboards, and Leisha's background fills provided accompaniment. Of special interest is Bob Bogle's piano playing on *When the Saints Go Marching In*. The lyrical arrangement required Yuya to introduce a solo by each instrument with lines such as "When the sax, begins to wail." For the piano's verse, as Dave Carr searched desperately for something to play, Bob walked up to the piano and said; "How about something like this?" Bob did a little riff on the keyboard, and everyone said; "Yeah, let's use that!" and so they did.

Meanwhile, Sherry Carr (Dave's wife) and Leisha, having co-written several songs with Dave, wrote the lyrics for two instrumentals written by Don and Bob. *Dance All Night* and *Goodbye Rock and Roll* were the result, with Nokie doing a superb sitar solo on the latter. The outcome was an exciting collection of good-time rock 'n' roll with some of Nokie's best guitar breaks ever. With the masters in hand, Yuya returned to Japan where he would finalize his work with producer Leo Sato.

Regarding the sessions, Don commented; "It took us two weeks to do the recording, including time for eating, discussion, rehearsals, and all the joking around that goes with friendly musicians. Yuya had many original ideas and hints for our music part, and we gave him hints and ideas for the singing part. We had perfect cooperation. Even after the recording started, if someone came up with a new idea, the arrangement was changed right there and then. Yuya really knows rock 'n' roll and he loves it. During recording sessions, he would bounce around the studio as if he was on stage. People are going in for more technicalities these days, but excitement, good singing, and playing are still necessary."

As a "Thank You," Yuya dedicated a song to The Ventures. Leisha and Sherry helped him write lyrics for *The Ventures Song*, telling how The Ventures had brought their music to Japan, making it acceptable for young people to play the electric guitar.

The album cover and a liner photo of Don, Leisha, and Yuya *[Toshiba-EMI LLS-80302]*

Excitedly, Yuya publicized his work in a wild rant in the Japanese press. However, in attempting to master American 'jive talk,' he had picked up some rather odious language. The "f" word caused little dismay in Japan, but English-speaking fans acquiring The Ventures' next souvenir tour book were somewhat shocked at Yuya's testimony reprinted in its entirety. At age 90, Josie commented; "It was gross, but I'm not such a prude that it kept me from laughing."

As Yuya and friends returned to Japan, The Ventures resumed work on the melodies chosen by Toshiba for release in June. At the same time, Don recorded Leisha for her *Feelings* album, also to be released on the tour. Simply titled *Leisha*, the LP was released in June [United Artists LA 414-G], and July in Japan [Liberty - LLS-80210].

During the recording of Leisha's album, Nokie had time for a trip home to Washington. While in Tacoma, he seized the opportunity to play alongside country music star Lefty Frizzell, whose career had peaked in 1951 when he had four hits sitting in the Top Ten at once. Then, as Japan Tour '75 grew near, Dave Carr announced that his busy career would prevent him from accompanying the band on such a lengthy tour. Fortunately, the void was quickly filled when Leisha remembered a friend. Although Phillip "Biff" Vincent was just nineteen, Leisha was sure he could fill the position admirably. Needless to say, the group was duly impressed, not only with Biff's fine keyboard work, but his ability to do a little singing.

Rehearsals began immediately, and, as Biff excelled in effects, he and Joe Barile developed a drum and synthesizer prologue for the opening number, *Fire*. Like David Carr, Biff's tasteful background playing was never too much or too loud.

Leisha's performance now included *Feelings*, it being an international hit. Don did not sing at all on the 1975 tour, giving way to Biff's vocals that included a rendition of The Ventures' original, *Goodbye Rock and Roll* from Yuya Uchida's album.

Biff Vincent

Promoting his "Hollywood" album, Yuya Uchida appeared as guest artist at The Ventures' shows in Tokyo. In keeping with his bizarre facade and behavior, Yuya appeared at one show wearing pajamas and toting an open bottle of wine. The Ventures said that if he was sober, he convinced everyone otherwise; holding a microphone in one hand while swigging on the bottle with the other during his performance of *Hound Dog*.

Yuya aside, audiences and promoters seemed pleased. It was said that The Ventures' show now packed as much variety and excitement into ninety minutes as one might expect in Las Vegas. *Caravan* remained as the finale, but this year it was different as Joe played part of his drum solo through Biff's synthesizer via a transducer called a Moogdrum. As Joe played harder, the device made a higher-pitched sound, creating a weird sci-fi effect. In all, this version of *Caravan* clocked out at over fifteen minutes!

The band had been in Japan for exactly one month when the music world received news that nearly put Nokie into shock. On July 19, less than two months after sharing the stage with Nokie, country legend Lefty Frizzell suffered a stroke and died at the age of forty-seven. Diagnosed with high blood pressure, he had refused any treatment.

SHATTERED GLASS

The 1975 Japan tour comprised seventy-seven performances, ending with an open-air concert on the island of Okinawa on September 7. The fun was not over yet, however, with two nights in Korea and three in Hong Kong before the group of six could go home. As dedicated fan, Wan Shin remembers; "It was the first time for The Ventures in Korea, and because many fans could not attend, one concert was shown on television. The Ventures came to Seoul when most of Korea was very poor. I couldn't afford to attend, but when it came on MBC TV, I recorded the sound on a cassette while watching them play in a very large hall. Nearly all of the LPs in our stores were illegal copies. Manufacturers made a lot of illegal copies and they changed artist's names, thinking no one would know the difference. Several small-scale businessmen who didn't know English well also made illegal LPs in those days. I have an album titled in English as *Christmas In Guitar Beat* by The Lotus', but on the rear of the jacket, it says in Korean, *Happy Tonight With The Ventures*. It has several songs from The Ventures' repertoire, but some that are not. This is why many Korean people believe The Ventures played *My Blue Heaven*, *Django*, and *Auld Lang Syne*."

Recordings like this can be found in used-record stores around the globe, and are considered novelty items by collectors. One such album purported to be "Ventures Live in Korea" is merely a sampling of the group's sixties studio albums. The only so-called live track is *Wipe Out* extracted from the 1965 Dolton album, *The Ventures On Stage*.

Although thousands could not afford the Seoul concerts, the hall was filled. Biff Vincent recalls; "When our limo took us to the auditorium that first night, we saw a lot of commotion outside. Later in the dressing room, we were scared out of our wits when rocks came crashing through the windows. We learned that the promoter had oversold both of our shows, so that scores of fans were left out in the cold and wanted their money back. Pretty soon a riot squad showed up, and everything quieted down. We assumed the promoters took care of the refunds, as the second night was uneventful, but that may have been because there were now so many police outside the hall."

Hong Kong was just a short hop by air from Seoul, and the concerts there were well organized. By mid-September, Leisha and The Ventures were safely home in California.

During the final week of the Japan tour, Toshiba had recorded *On Stage '75* [Liberty LLS-67067-8] at Osaka's Festival Hall. Unaware of this wonderful live recording, faithful North American fans were nevertheless rewarded. At first glance, *Now Playing* was a compilation of movie themes taken from other albums, but upon closer inspection, three new Ventures tracks appeared. *Man with the Golden Gun* and *Airport '75*, recorded in the fall of '74, had been quietly released on a single [UA XW578], but *Lawrence of Arabia* was totally new to everyone. Although the remaining cuts were recycled from the past, *Now Playing* [United Artists LA471G] was enough to keep the band alive in the minds of vigilant fans. However, as United Artists made plans for the band's next album, an unpleasant shock was in store for all Ventures enthusiasts.

DISCO FEVER

True to his word, Marco Carlieri came to Hollywood where The Ventures found him to handle lead, rhythm, and bass with equal ease. It didn't take long for Bob to put him to work. Leisha's role in Japan Tour '75 seemed to give Bob a boost of energy, or as Don recalls; "Back then, Bob was always wanting to try 'something different', just to get away from doing pure 'Ventures music'. This time he wanted to experiment with the club circuit, playing the current disco hits. He got Marco to play a lot of the lead work and Dave Dalton and Leisha for vocals. Then they worked up a lounge act using The Ventures' name in order to get bookings."

Their tour began with two successful weeks in Portland before heading towards northern California for several dates. Assigning the lead work to Marco and rhythm to Dave Dalton, Bob played bass except for a few Ventures tunes where he traded instruments with Marco. Vocals were shared between Leisha and Dave. With Joe Barile on drums, they hit the road with a repertoire of disco hits and about twenty Ventures' classics. Marco's playing was a bit "heavy" at first, and Bob recalled that it took some effort to tone him down to their straightforward style. However; "By the end of the run, we felt we were very 'tight,' and we planned to do it again."

Dave, Joe, Leisha, Marco, and Bob

As the Holiday season drew near, United Artists staff producer Denny Diante approached Don and Bob with an idea. Disco was huge, and Denny wanted to use The Ventures' name on an album aimed at the growing number of discotheques applying fantastic lighting and mammoth sound systems to the sound of recorded music. Disco finally had a white audience, which UA desired to attract. The Ventures balked at first, feeling they had come close enough to disco with 1968's *The Horse*. Being under contract made it hard to refuse, but they did gain a concession. As Don reluctantly recalls; "That *Rocky Road* album was another of those times when we were embarrassed by our record company. Disco was *in*, so they talked us into letting them hire some people that did that kind of thing to come in and do it. None of us were to play on it at all! I said, 'Well, if you do that, you're not going to say it's 'The Ventures'. They asked if they could call it *The New Ventures*, and we said that would be acceptable. I didn't know for twenty years that they put our pictures on the inside liner. When record companies do things like that to fool people, we almost feel like we should be suing them."

The foremost Ventures connection on this album was Leisha's background vocals. Also, the liner notes "in association with B&W Productions," partially credited Don and Bob for writing *The Stroke*. Along with Don, Bob, Biff, and Leisha, the inside liner pictured Dave Dalton in place of Nokie. Although *Rocky Road* [United Artists LA586G] seemed to be aimed at the western world, buyers knew nothing of Dave, Biff, or Leisha unless they were fan club members. The album sent UK club president Dave Peckett, in his words, "reeling with shock and disappointment." Many Ventures fans abandoned *Rocky Road* after finding no hint of their favorite group amid the throbbing disco. As Dave Peckett wrote in *New Gandy Dancer*, the album's list of players resembled "half the population of Los Angeles!"

Accepted by most as the best track on the album, Glenn Miller's classic *Moonlight Serenade* was issued on a single. With an assembly of top disco players in the studio, Don took the opportunity to record Leisha with them for her Japan summer single, *Moonlight Serenade* b/w *At Every End There's a Beginning* [Liberty LLR-20082].

Still steaming over *Rocky Road*, The Ventures balked at their contract renewal in May. They compromised by signing for three years instead of the normal five. Then, scorning the persistent disco phenomenon, they focused on a new project for Japan.

While recycling some tracks for *Early Sounds of The Ventures* [Liberty LLS 80512], Toshiba-EMI requested some new songs for sales insurance. In addition to Dave Carr's synthesized version of the Japanese *Susukake Street*, the album saw Nokie exhibit amazing fingering on *How High The Moon* and *The World is Waiting For the Sunrise*. In spite of his blinding licks, both tracks had sped-up guitar sequences for added Les Paul flavor. Borrowing the B side from a recent U.S. single, *Little People* became the tour theme under a new title, *Sunflower '76*. Packaging of *Early Sounds of The Ventures* was unusual in that an entire panel of the gatefold cover contained text in English. *The 15 Years of a Supergroup* was a poem submitted by ardent UK fan, Keith Gleeson. Two years later, Keith and his wife were rewarded by King Records with prime seating at a Ventures concert in Japan.

During Japan Tour '76, July saw another single [LLR-20062] recorded in Tokyo with Don singing *Beautiful Sunday*, which he performed on the tour program. The flip side, *Things Have Got to Get Better*, was written by Joe and Diana Barile, although as time progressed, things actually got worse for the couple.

After such success with Leisha, Don and Bob decided to produce a second discovery, Miss Jonell Calendar. During May rehearsals, they decided to take both girls to Japan, expanding the Ventures tour-group to an all-time high of seven.

Before the first concert, the group appeared with Chiyo Okumura and Yuko Nagisa on NHK TV's *Grand Special*. Before this Ventures season was over, The Ventures appeared four more times on television and twice on radio. Prior to leaving Hollywood, Leisha had changed her hair color to blond. Jonell being also a blond brought more than a little confusion to some of the fans seeking autographs.

Ventures '76 - Don, Nokie, Leisha, Jonell, Joe, Biff, Bob

For this 1976 tour, in addition to acoustic guitar and electric sitar, Nokie brought a six-string banjo to Japan. Music stores had recently introduced the "guitar banjo," which, like the Coral sitar, was fitted with a six-string guitar neck. Nokie did a superb job on a medley composed of *Dixie* and *Dueling Banjos*. For this portion of the show, Bob accompanied on acoustic guitar with Biff adding a bit of keyboard bass.

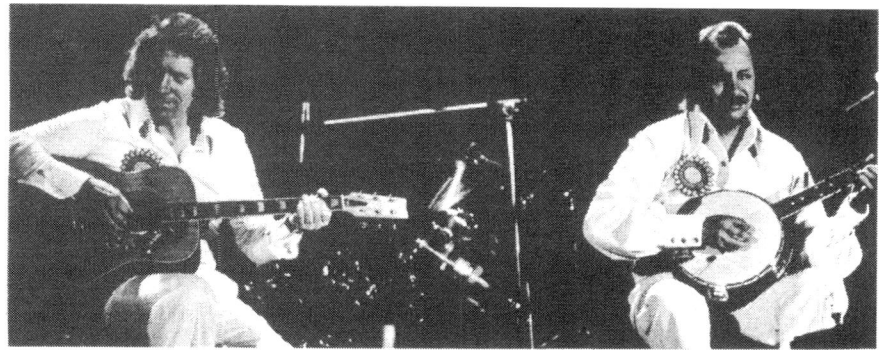

New Gandy Dancer

Near the end of the tour, Nokie had an accident with his Fender Telecaster when the strap broke at the fastening eyelet, allowing the guitar to crash first onto the stage. Recalling later, Nokie said; "I broke the fall with my toe, but a large chunk of paint was chipped from the body. I would have caught it on the second bounce, but it didn't! As soon as we got home, I sanded the paint off and left it with a natural finish."

Nokie's damaged Telecaster before he sanded the body

At the end of the tour, Kyodo Agency affirmed plans for the following year's program. Included was a request for The Ventures to revert to their original format of four pieces. The purpose was specified as nostalgic rather than economic, as the tour theme would be "The Roots of Rock 'n' Roll." However, Toshiba did seem concerned with expenses, as this year's live album was allotted only one LP disc. The ensuing package, recorded at Shibuya Public Concert Hall on September 1, omitted nine numbers, including Nokie's sitar medley and acoustic rendition of *I've Got A Woman*. Also missing was most of Yoshi Kohno's dialog, two of Leisha's vocals, and one of her two duets with Jonell. Guest singer, Michiko Tanaka was also deleted along with instrumentals such as *Keep Japan Beautiful* and *Manchurian Beat*. Even Joe's drum solo during *Caravan* was partially cut in the middle. The remnants were then sent to Hollywood, where Don and Bob did the mixing. *On Stage '76* [Liberty LLS-80716] was a great album, but fans spoiled by the double-disc LPs in the previous five years were left wishing for more.

Although Biff Vincent's career with The Ventures was cut short after only two live albums, he remained a good friend of the band. Having taken interest in the technicalities of the record business, he was soon making demo records for aspiring musicians on an eight-track console in his father's garage. In his new venture, Biff was embarking on a profession in which he would become highly in demand.

Upon returning from Japan, Don was surprised to receive a call from Semie Moseley. Since the bankruptcy, Semie had repeatedly failed to re-establish a guitar factory. After recovering the Mosrite name in 1971, distribution contracts with Kustom Electronics and Pacific Music Supply were short-lived. Semie had made a few custom guitars for famous musicians, and some Black Widow instruments for the Acoustic Company, but the work was not steady. Returning to Oklahoma, he tried spreading the Gospel through music from a used Greyhound bus. Now, in 1976, he was back in Bakersfield, having devised a guitar with frets literally embedded in a solid brass bar to generate longer sustained notes. While showing this "Brass Rail" model to music dealers, the Japanese owner of a Los Angeles store had offered backing for Semie to resume building The Ventures Model for export to Japan. As Don recalls; "Semie was asking us for the right to use The Ventures' logo on his guitars for Japan. We were still very disgusted with Moseley and didn't want anything to do with him. He had nearly broken us, and now he had the nerve to call and ask to use our name? I said, 'No, you absolutely can*not*!' He did it anyway and paid us nothing! He told his Japanese customers that he had the rights to The Ventures' name, and he went ahead and used it!"

Semie made approximately 150 guitars for Japan before being struck with colitis. After therapy and rest, he was soon building guitars in Nevada. Looking ahead, it was there in Carson City where married his second wife, Loretta, in 1980. Loretta became increasingly involved in the company, enough to qualify for the position of president.

LIMITED EDITION

In November 1976, The Ventures accepted a Pacific Northwest tour proposal, even though they had no lead guitarist. As Bob recalls; "After Japan, Nokie wasn't keen on touring right away, so I hired studio guitarist John Hunt. After two weeks of rehearsing, we had to cancel the whole thing because a project arose for a new Ventures album. When I called John with this news, he said 'Fine, just pay me for what I would have made on the tour, and we can forget about it.' When I said we couldn't pay him for work that he didn't do, he insisted because he had cancelled a lot of sessions for the tour. I told him that I'd get back to him after I talked to Don."

United Artists album coordinator John Ierardi had conceived another Ventures album, although his idea was not as original as *Rocky Road*. TV theme albums had been done before, including The Ventures' *Batman* LP. *The Ventures play T.V. Themes* would cover current crime-detective programs along with *Star Trek*, *M*A*S*H*, and *Medical Center*. Bob continues; "I told Don about John Hunt's request, and suggested using him for the new album. Don agreed, seeing as Nokie was living back in Washington and would not enjoy this type of album anyway. I called John and he was really happy with the idea, saying he would much rather earn his money if given the opportunity."

Fuzzy distortion and lengthy sustain were the order of the day, achieved with a device called a compandor, first "<u>compressing</u>" the volume, then "ex<u>panding</u>" as a note began to fade. Don and Bob produced ten tracks with Joe Barile providing first-rate percussion and Dave Carr adding synthetic strings and brass. Rhythm guitar was absent in this type of music, but when Hunt needed backing, Don and Bob assigned the work to Marco Carlieri. Bob recalls working hard on the bass parts, as the songs were fast and complicated. On the *Charlie's Angels* theme, Jonell Calendar made her second appearance on a Ventures album. *Hawaii-Five-O* and *Nadia's Theme* brought the track count up to twelve.

The Ventures -T.V. Themes [United Artists LA717G] was yet another album that did not sound like The Ventures. In February 1977, fans discovered this new LP packaged with a nice color photo that included Nokie, only to hear an unfamiliar style of lead guitar, credited in the liner notes to the unfamiliar names, Hunt and Carlieri. Later, in 1984, Capitol Records obtained the rights to the music and America saw a release of *T.V. Themes* as a Liberty budget-package with *Medical Center* and *Police Woman* omitted. The complete set finally became available on CD format in the 1990s from America's One Way Records and from See-For-Miles in England.

While working on *T.V. Themes*, The Ventures received a recording from the UK fan club containing a performance of *Walk-Don't Run* by a European vocal group called the Pistons. The version inspired a new instrumental version, and a year later, *Walk-Don't Run '77* appeared [UA - XW1100]. Although the version resembled a disco recording, with backing by Leisha, Jonelle (and Don in falsetto), fans remained receptive to this fourth arrangement of the song, now affectionately called "WDR." Younger generations might also have enjoyed the record, but once more, United Artists failed to promote it.

VENTURING NORTH

With no recording scheduled before 1977's summer Japan tour, Bob took his "New Ventures" group north through Washington and into Western Canada. By the end of February, patrons at The Cave in Vancouver, Canada, were swinging to this very different version of The Ventures. In addition to the five performers, Dave Dalton and Joe Barile brought their wives along, which made good company for Leisha. To complete a convoy of three vehicles, Bob's twenty-three-year-old son, Mike, transported the band's equipment in a van. As equipment manager, Mike had little free time, but he recalled it being the time of his life.

Bob playing "WDR" in Edmonton, Alberta

Sections of the tour entailed extensive drives such as crossing the Rocky Mountains through the Rogers Pass and trekking further north to Prince George, British Columbia. Some stops were quite relaxing, such as the resort town of Kelowna, B.C. where they played from Monday through Saturday in the first week of March at a newly renovated club called Gatsby's. The group spent another six days in Calgary, Alberta playing three one-hour sets each night at The Refinery. Here, in various interviews, Bob explained the structure of the group, relating that he and Don had always been The Ventures, hiring extra musicians as required for recording sessions and touring. George Creswick, an enthusiastic fan attending a dozen of the shows, later reported patiently waiting for "the disco stuff to end so the band could get back to Ventures music."

March 22 found the group at The Point After supper club in Edmonton, Alberta for two shows with a meal included. Inquiring about the odd name, they learned that a pro-football player owned the place. For Bob, it was a chance to meet an old acquaintance, as the opening act was Johnny Rivers.

A typical set compiled around ten instrumentals with five Leisha vocals. With Marco on lead, the new single, *Charlie's Angels*, was also promoted. A medley of fifties rock 'n' roll songs sung by either Dave or Joe sometimes included Bob singing the Larry Williams rocker, *Bony Moronie*. During each set, Bob switched instruments with Marco to play lead on a few Ventures classics. Dave Dalton played rhythm on Don's vintage Jazzmaster while Marco played a 'Les Paul' Custom with a Bigsby vibrato tailpiece. Besides backing Leisha and Joe Barile's vocals, Dave sang numbers like George Benson's *Breezin'*, and the Lou Rawls hit, *You'll Never Find Another Love Like Mine*.

Truly the most vocal period for The Ventures, it was a great show for patrons not heavily "into" the band. Conversely, longtime fans left disappointed that their favorite group had succumbed to the invasion of disco, and was now a fragment of its former being. Those inquiring about Don or Nokie were told that both were busy on other projects. If anyone asked about a fan club, Bob scribbled the address of The Ventures' Burbank office on a napkin or a ticket stub. It was, of course, the home address of Sonny Rivera, who now handled everything from bookkeeping, publishing, and royalties to promotional material and Japan tour planning. It was good news for those who asked, as domestic albums had not shown a club address since 1971's *New Testament*.

Marco, Leisha, Bob, & Dave at The Point After in Edmonton, Alberta

It was nearly May when the "new" Ventures returned to Hollywood in time for the "real" Ventures to get ready for Japan Tour '77. Rehearsals included Ventures standards plus a few oldies like *My Bonnie Lies*, *Wheels*, *Driving Guitars*, and the newly recorded *Peace Pipe*. In line with the "Roots of Rock 'n' Roll" tour theme, they retained the fifties hits from the recent Canada tour. Don added Frankie Ford's *Sea Cruise* to the Chuck Berry-Little Richard set and Bob finished the medley with his *Bony Moronie* rendition. Nokie embellished the oldies with intricate guitar solos, except for *Roll Over Beethoven*, on which Bob played lead as he had on the northern tour.

This year, a one-nighter was booked in Waikiki for Friday, June 24, allowing the band a relaxing two days in Hawaii before going on to Tokyo. As usual, the first few days in Japan were spent on interviews and TV appearances. On one of these, a pair of local groups joined in on *Let's Go* and *Wipe Out* for the grand finale. On June 28, The Ventures took the stage in front of a sold out audience. The promoters always had interesting backdrops built for transport to the various venues with the other equipment. Sometimes it was a huge logo or caricature of each band member's face. For 1977, Bob recalls several venues showing segments from *Beloved Invaders* on a large screen above the stage during intermission.

Rewarded for his roadwork in Canada, Mike Bogle accompanied The Ventures on this Japan tour. Mike had enjoyed being a roadie, but he was happy to relax now while a crew unloaded the truck and set up in advance while the band traveled by plane or train. The Ventures simply walked on stage, did their show and walked off. There were still publicity sessions, but the mob scenes of the sixties were replaced by well-organized interviews. It was not long however, before Kyodo Tokyo's new young soundman ran into difficulty and Mike was put to work on the console, balancing the feed from several microphones while carefully avoiding feedback. Thirty years later, Mike still proclaimed that touring Canada and Japan with his dad was a highlight of his life.

Nokie seated in front of Dave Carr, Bob, Don, and Joe.

Through the seventies, various Japanese companies had supplied amplifiers with names like Royal and Teisco. This year, The Ventures used mammoth Yamaha amplifiers, and through this connection, each member obtained a Yamaha electronic tuner. These accurate and timesaving devices were yet unheard of at home, but in time they became standard equipment for amateur and professionals alike.

In August, the group spent a week touring Japan's northern island, Hokkaido. A traveling day then took them to Aomori and Akita on the north end of the mainland. It was between these two concerts that The Ventures received shocking news from home. Although Elvis Presley had never performed outside the U.S.A. and Canada, his death launched a global shockwave. At forty-two, Elvis was just four months older than Nokie.

On September 2nd, two final concerts were recorded for 1977's live album in Tokyo's Sun Plaza Hall. The closing *Caravan* included great drum work by Joe, which, thanks to technology, seemed to come from a deep echo chamber. For his bass tattoo, Joe came out from behind the drums to the front of the stage.

Yoshi Kohno did not work on stage this year, but he did spend time with the group in Tokyo, especially with drummer Joe. As Bob recalls, an event arising from this friendship sadly ended in disaster; "It began when Joe ran out of his medication for chronic sinusitis, and a doctor in Tokyo supplied a prescription for nasal spray. After using it a few times, Joe said he felt a bit high from it, which led to us teasing him with jokes like 'Got your cocaine with you today?' Near the end of the tour, Yoshi told Joe that he too, had sinus trouble and would like to try the medication. As we were leaving for home, Joe gave the near-empty spray-bottle to Yoshi. When Yoshi tried the spray, he agreed that it made the user feel slightly high." Although the results of this action resemble a chapter from a cheap pocket novel, the consequences for Joe were grim and would cause major discomfort to the band.

FURY OF A WOMAN SCORNED

While The Ventures toured Japan, United Artists was busy transferring Toshiba's right-of-sale for Liberty-UA recordings to Japan's King Records. Following the transfer, King launched a string of attractive albums compiling early Ventures material on titles like *Best 20, Rock And Roll Graffiti*, and *Surfin '77*. Included in the lot was 1965's *The Ventures On Stage*, seen now for the first time in Japan.

In the days following the tour, Yoshi Kohno ended his relationship with a girlfriend. In bitter reprisal, the girl reported to police that Yoshi was using a controlled substance. Brought in for questioning, Yoshi argued that Joe's prescription had been prescribed for medicinal purposes. It should have ended there, but the Tokyo police were diligent as well as patient, and they knew that The Ventures would be back.

In November, King Records released *The Ventures - Live in Japan '77* on a brilliant ninety-minute 2-LP set. With a large centerfold showing the band in action, the gatefold cover was one of the most attractive Ventures packages ever [King GXF-9017/18].

The prolific repertoire of The Ventures contains several songs with alternate titles, but even more confusing are a pair of songs bearing the same title of *Amanda's Theme*. In the mid-sixties, Don and Bob had written a love ballad called *Haunting Memories*, which an alternate title of *Amanda's Theme*. The song was kept under wraps until it became the flip side for the North American single, *Walk-Don't Run '77*. Both titles were shown on the record, the preferred *Amanda's Theme* boldly printed above *Haunting Memories* in brackets. In Japan, *Walk-Don't Run '77* was backed with *Peace Pipe*, the latter being part of that year's tour set. Although King Records had begun re-issuing The Ventures' back catalog on 45rpm singles, they also wanted new material. The Ventures responded with Jerome Kern's *The Way You Look Tonight* plus an original named after Dave and Sherry Carr's new baby girl, Amanda. Somehow, *Amanda* arrived in Japan as *Amanda's Theme*. Many years passed before ardent collectors owned both recordings and differentiated the songs. The final resolve came in year 2000 when both cuts appeared in the See-For-Miles album, *The Ultimate Collection*, [SFM-1969-2000] presenting the original tune as *Haunting Memories*. Scarcely known elsewhere, *Amanda's Theme* made a sizeable impression in Japan, where someone wrote lyrics to be sung by Loren Nakano [United Artists CM-147].

King Records then petitioned The Ventures for an instrumental re-mix of the *Yuya Meets The Ventures* album plus an entire album of originals. Realizing the time that would take, they provided a list of Latin songs to be recorded immediately. Replacing Yuya's vocals with a lead guitar was a fairly small project. Working at California Recording Studios, Nokie laid down the lead and several harmony tracks. The taping went smoothly until it was time to record Paul Anka's *Diana*. The dynamics of this song varied so much from the soft introduction to the brass-backed chorus that it was hard for Nokie to maintain a satisfactory sound from his Telecaster *or* his acoustic guitar. After some head scratching, Bob solved the problem when he sat down and played not two, but *three* lead guitar tracks, each in a different octave. If UK fan Dave Towers had not witnessed and documented the proceedings for the fan club, these session details would likely have been forgotten.

On completion of the guitar tracks, Dave Carr added keyboards while Joe enhanced the percussion. After mixing by Don, the master tape was shipped to King Records, who had begun re-issuing the group's back catalog of albums. It was not intended that the new album be shelved, but when the complicated contract between UA and Toshiba-EMI was finalized, over four years had elapsed. By then, cobalt-modified iron oxides were in use as a base for metal film cassette tapes. Although they were costly and players required harder heads, metal tapes provided vastly superior sound. In a clever move to launch their star act on this medium, King Records issued the modified Yuya tracks as *Metal Dinamic Sound 3000* [K30W-4007] in the third week of March of 1981. Not only did the album never appear on an American label, metal- only tape made it a rare item in Japan. Luckily for fans in the rest of the world, the efforts of UK club operator Gerald Woodage culminated in this exciting "instrumentalized" album appearing on a 1996 See-For-Miles compact disc [C5HCD 636].

In the fall, having lightened his Telecaster by sanding away much of the body, Nokie mounted *two* palm-pedals on the guitar. Being able to bend four notes at once seemed like a good idea at the time, but as Nokie put it later; "Two sets was kind of an overkill. I went back to just one, and I never used it very much anyway."

Gerry McGee had also tried palm-pedals on the gold-top Gibson 'Les Paul' that he used on the 1973 tour with Mel Taylor and the Dynamics. As Gerry recalls; "It was just an experiment, and I didn't get much use out of them either."

Late in 1977, sessions began for over a dozen Latin instrumentals that had been big band hits during the Ventures' childhood years. Numbers such as *Brazil*, a number two hit in 1943 for Xavier Cugat, were older than thirty-year-old Joe Barile. Joe however, was no stranger to Latin music, quickly recommending Steve Foreman as the essential extra percussionist. Marco and Joe must have done a good job in restoring Joe's 1955 Fender Esquire, for after trying it out, Don actually played it on some of the Latin recording sessions. Soon after, Joe used the guitar to compose a new Ventures tune that would be called *Surfin' USA '78* [UA-King CM-135].

Pacing their releases carefully, King Records held the Latin package back for over a year until March 1979. With content of such worldwide appeal, it was indeed a pity that *The Ventures' Latin Album* was only available in Japan [King GP-685].

By December 1977, several instrumentals had been completed for the "originals" album requested by King Records. With rumors fueling keen anticipation among the UK fan club, members did not expect the five-year wait that lay ahead. The delay may have ensued when King discovered that nine of the fourteen tracks were tender ballads. It seemed that the band and even Dave Carr had been influenced by some romantic substance in the California air. Some songs, such as Don Craig's *Nightly News Theme*, had been picked up from friends along the way such as Joe Sousa and Dick Burns. As Don recalls; "I often ate at a restaurant called Monte Leone's where Joe Sousa was a bartender and played his songs on the piano after hours. I liked his *Warm Hearts* and *Papa* so much that I used them for guitar instrumentals on that album." Informed fans that had eagerly been waiting eventually forgot about the new songs until five years later when they surfaced on the group's *Last Album on Liberty* [King K28P318 - 1982].

As had happened in America, the main core of Japanese fans began turning attention to young families and newly launched careers. As a dedicated follower in Tokyo, Mahiro Tada relates; "By 1978, Japanese people felt that The Ventures' music was becoming 'evergreen', so their record sales became gradually less each year. Only the serious completist would sacrifice money for music already appearing several times in their collections. But a new Ventures recording was still something for us older fans to run out and buy before they were all sold." Kyodo Entertainment may also have sensed the lull, as they booked The Ventures' 1978 Japan tour to wind up in less than six weeks.

There was always a single or two released before an upcoming Japan tour, but one in particular is worth pointing out. 1977 being the year of *Star Wars* and *Close Encounters of the Third Kind*, "The World's Number One Instrumental Group" could not overlook the music from these sci-fi blockbusters. In the spring of '78, The Ventures recorded both themes for United Artists. As current disco arranging replaced the rhythm guitar with strings and horns, Don worked on producing these cuts. At the time, Gerry McGee had just finished acting a small part in *Convoy*, a movie starring Kris Kristofferson. Don and Bob considered Gerry for the session, but Marco Carlieri got the job when it was learned that Gerry was going on tour with Kristofferson and Rita Coolidge.

ROCKETS, RAIDERS, AND A DUMB CROOK

Whenever he had time, Bob Bogle jumped into his airplane and flew home to Vancouver, Washington. While there, he would drop into the Red Caboose, a nightclub owned by his friend, Dave Callaham. Having long desired to get into the music business, Dave invested with Bob in producing some albums. First, they recorded Merrilee Rush in the home studio of Alabama's Jeff Cook, in Fort Payne, Alabama. Bob played on some of the tracks, as did Merrilee's husband, Bill McCarthy. Bob considered it a good album, but their attempts to interest a record company were in vain.

They tried again early in 1978 after Dave booked Louie and the Rockets to perform at the Red Caboose. An excellent singer, Louie Fontaine's musicians had worked with Paul Revere And The Raiders. Of course, a band with such a name just *had* to record *Louie, Louie*. During the session, as Bob pondered on how to break out a new group, someone in the band suggested they appear as "The Raiders minus Paul Revere" (Paul having retired, and singer Mark Lindsay having gone solo). Bob invited Paul to the sessions while proposing that (for a percentage), the album be released by *Paul Revere's Raiders*.

Upon hearing Fontaine and the group, Revere was sufficiently impressed to start looking for outfits to fit the early Raiders' image. Subsequently, Bob took the finished tapes to Hollywood's Atlantic Records and secured an *unsigned* contract for three albums. Martie Nairbase, an attractive woman in her forties and head of Atlantic's Hollywood Atco division, told Bob that she would not sign the contract until hearing the group on stage. When Bob informed her of the group's extended booking at Lake Tahoe, she said she would get back to him. Bob and Dave then went to Tahoe to see how the group was doing. The Raiders were well received at the time, with Bill Medley of the Righteous Brothers making an admiring backstage visit. Thus, it was a shock when a few days later, Martie Nairbase called to say that the deal was off. Bob suspected something negative had occurred, but all that Marty said was; "We've decided not to get involved with an 'oldies' act." It may have been true, but Paul took the group on the road with lasting success through late summer of 1980. Meanwhile, Bob and Dave presented the album to A&M and Motown, but again, neither company was interested.

In late 1980, Paul reformed the Raiders, which kept busy for the next ten years, and Fontaine reformed Louie and the Rockets as the house band for Hawaii's posh Sheraton Waikiki for the next two years before returning to Nevada as a popular 'oldies' act.

One of Bob's memories from this period involves a burglar who ran out of luck; "I was living in Encino at the time, and one day I came home from shopping in time to see a stranger backing out of my driveway. I thought he looked suspicious, so I went to the end of the block, did a u-turn, and followed until I got his license number. Then I went home, and sure enough, there had been a break-in. The first thing I noticed was a guitar and a couple of amplifiers missing. I called the police and in less than an hour, they called back and said 'We got him!' They asked for a description of the equipment, and it wasn't long before I got it all back."

SURF'S UP!

Plans for the 1978 Japan tour having culminated in a surfing theme, rehearsals focused on Joe Barile's *Surfin' U.S.A.'78* and tunes from the past like *Surf Rider*, and *The Cruel Sea*. Yuzo Kayama's *Black Sand Beach* and *Yuhi Wa Akaku* were also revived from the sixties, the latter title being slightly mysterious. Although *Yuhi Wa Akaku* translates to "Red Sunset," the English title as printed on Japanese records consistently appears as *Blue Sunset*. Even Japanese fans are mystified as to how this came about.

Near the approaching flight date, the group went shopping for attire in keeping with the surfing theme. Colorful Hawaiian shirts and white slacks were selected, plus an item that surprised even the Japanese fans. Nokie had taken to wearing a hat made of soft brown fabric with the brim turned down and banded with silver medallions. He liked it so much that hats became part of his image for the next twenty years.

Late in June, Joe Barile and wife Diana vacationed in Hawaii for a week, and then Joe went to Japan while Diana returned home. Near month-end, Don, Bob, and Nokie crossed the Pacific to meet Joe and begin touring. Yoshi Kohno, back to being Master of Ceremonies, was slightly uneasy about the previous year's police incident, but when nothing happened in the first few days, his fears gave way to sharing Joe's interest in Championship Sumo Wrestling on television.

As usual, every concert was packed as fans enjoyed Joe Barile's newly penned *Surfin' USA'78*, played to surfers careening on a rear-projected backdrop. During the closing *Caravan*, Joe seemed increasingly inspired throughout his ten-minute drum solo. Constantly improvising, he added bongo drums to one passage, and played on Bob's bass strings for a full two minutes before an exciting stereo-echo climax. There was an irony to this triumphant performance, as it would quickly become Joe's "swan song" with The Ventures. As Bob recalls; "When the final concert ended and we returned to our hotel, the Tokyo police were waiting for Joe. His arrest took place in front of reporters who were always around whenever we performed. A sprawling headline on the morning paper boldly stated that The Ventures' drummer had been arrested, not for 'alleged' or 'suspicion of,' but for 'possession of a controlled substance.' The red-letter headline of *The Japan Times* simply stated VENTURES MEMBER ARRESTED in English above a photo of Joe. It wasn't long before the news spread all across the country. Joe was certain he could settle the matter quickly, and he insisted that the rest of us catch our flight home. We did as he asked; not yet realizing that 'innocent until proven guilty' is not a universal principle. Back then, Japanese law allowed someone to be held for twenty-one days without being formally charged. Joe was questioned repeatedly for the maximum period until he was released due to lack of evidence."

Hiroshi Yamachika - OSAKA

Recalling the ordeal, Don remarked; "I couldn't see how they could arrest Joe on nothing more than the word of Yoshi's girlfriend. Where's the justice in that? Joe was caught with absolutely nothing! Released due to lack of evidence? How could they arrest him to begin with? That uncalled-for arrest almost ended our career in Japan!"

When Joe returned to Hollywood, he related his fearful experience. Answering the same questions over and over, he had felt himself deteriorating daily, a bushy beard growing ever thicker on his face. Mr. Uchino had visited him a number of times but could not get him released. After twenty-one days, the tabloid that put Joe's arrest on its front page, buried his release in its middle pages. Shocked fans in Japan believed they would never see their "Beloved Invaders" again, even if the group survived.

At home, the incident was a dark secret. Even Josie, living in Tacoma, did not hear about it for over twenty years; "I suppose the boys didn't want to upset me; or maybe they knew that I would have written a letter or two with plenty of exclamation marks to the authorities in Japan! I would have surely tried to help Joe get free of blame."

Although Joe had been vindicated, it looked as if a return to Japan was impossible. A Japan company quickly scrapped a commercial agreement for advertising music, and a soon-to-be released TV show was suddenly cancelled. When King Records began compiling a boxed set of eight long-play platters for release by year's end, it seemed that the group that had become an important part of Japanese culture was now a part of history. After mulling over their career-damage and financial losses, Bob and Don decided that they would have to replace Joe, even though he was innocent.

THE ORIGINAL FOUR

It was not easy to dismiss the man described in *New Gandy Dancer* as The Ventures' finest drummer ever, but Joe understood and remained on good terms with the band in years to come. A drummer and songwriter of his caliber had no problem keeping busy in Los Angeles. Much of his immediate spare time was spent with Marco Carlieri, writing songs and recording demo tapes. Joe was soon doing nightclub work, backing well-known musicians like keyboard wizard Gabriel Magno, who worked with famed guitar rocker and confirmed Ventures admirer, Ted Nugent. As late as 2003, patrons of the southern California nightclub circuit could enjoy dinner and dancing to the music of Joe Barile And The Rhythm Kings.

Finding Joe's replacement was not difficult for Don and Bob, as Mel Taylor was ready to return to the throne. Following the Dynamics' break up, Mel had taken up music projects that included work in 1976 with Frankie "*Sea Cruise*" Ford's all-star band. The job lasted for several months until Ford, known widely as "The New Orleans Dynamo," returned home to Louisiana.

Mel also managed musical groups, one of which was Harrison Swift, led by singer Harvey Wicklund who also played drums and bass. One day in a coffee shop, Harvey was introduced to Mel, which led to Mel managing and recording Harrison Swift for almost three years. As Harvey recalls; "We must have got airplay somewhere, as I eventually received royalty payments for *Do You Still Love Me Girl*." [PBR 509]

Harvey soon met Mel's family, which included daughters Silvia, Rita, and son Leon. Harvey and Silvia became engaged, and while living together, Leon moved in for a while. Having finished school and learned much from his father, Leon had drummed in groups playing everything from hard rock to Ventures classics.

Mel (left) with "Harrison Swift" – Harvey Wicklund (center)

While seeking a recording contract for Harrison Swift, Mel had approached Pat Boyle, a former United Artists associate who ran a label of his own called PBR. From that meeting, Mel landed a job with PBR, put Harrison Swift on vinyl, and began signing up more groups. One of note was Jan Davis, who was ready to blend his flamenco guitar with the current disco craze. *Flamenco Dance Man* was released in 1978 [PBR-511]. Mel and Jan then re-mixed that cut and *Bolero* to produce a twelve-inch single as "The Jan Davis Guitar With The Flamenco Boogie Band" [PBR-1000].

Another group that Mel signed was Ruby, headed by Tom Fogerty, formerly of Creedence Clearwater Revival. PBR had released two Ruby albums by the time Bob and Don approached Mel to rejoin The Ventures. Bob remembers the reunion; "Mel was enthused about returning to the group, not only because he loved playing, but also because he was not satisfied with what he had been doing, financially or artistically. Before he left us, he had always done the extra legwork like finding us new stage outfits and ensuring everything ran smooth."

Fairly soon, Mel was applying his new expertise. Together with Don, he formed the production company Taylor, Wilson, and Associates. As the band became busier by the month, Mel soon realized that there wasn't enough time to operate the new production company. There was however, still some use for Taylor, Wilson, and Associates. In a gesture of commitment and faith in each other, Mel, Don, and Bob formed a three-way partnership. It should have been called something like Bogle, Wilson and Taylor, but as Bob recalls, use of the existing name was a matter of convenience; "I don't have much of an ego so it didn't matter if my name wasn't on the letterhead. The company name was already registered, and I didn't mind being the unnamed 'associate'."

Between touring with The Ventures, Nokie played in Washington nightclubs with a band called Country Justice. Mel was anxious to record again with The Ventures, but Nokie living nearly a thousand miles away made it rather inconvenient. Mel solved the problem by convincing Gerry McGee to make some Ventures recordings.

Gerry had just finished two solo albums for which he needed a label. The Ventures, while not recommending United Artists, invited Gerry to record four tracks with them. Although three of the tunes never appeared on an album, they were eventually heard when Don and Bob supplied a few unreleased tracks on tape to their fan clubs. Among several other rarities, *Dancin' Fool, Searchin'* (*for my Baby*), and *Minyo Disco North To South* finally debuted on a special UK fan club cassette called Vintage Ventures II. *Minyo Disco* (a medley of popular Japanese tunes) eventually appeared on CD releases in Japan and the UK, but it remained classified as a rare "bonus track."

The fourth song was a mellow instrumental named after Russia's Republic of Karelia, recorded in 1965 by Sweden's instrumental group, The Spotnicks. In 1966, *Karelia* had been a top hit in Japan, and although Toshiba had requested The Ventures to record it in 1975, the guys were just getting around to it. The Ventures' version surfaced in less than a year on a scarce Japanese single, and on King's *The Ventures - Rare Collections* album. David Carr was usually very busy, but for this session, he found time to arrange, produce, and embellish *Karelia* with his keyboards. Marco Carlieri also played, this being his final session with The Ventures. After two more years in Hollywood doing studio and nightclub work, Marco returned to Rome and toured for another four years. Keeping in touch with Joe Barile, he eventually reported becoming dissatisfied with his career while deciding to further his education. The next news from Marco announced that he was practicing dentistry instead of the guitar.

Once Mel was back, The Ventures hoped their business in Japan would return to normal. But, as Don recalls; "Once Joe was released and sent home, Mr. Uchino came to the States and met with Bob and myself, apparently looking to make a lot of money. He said that we were pretty much through in Japan, but that he would bring us back to do seven 'Sayonara concerts,' advertising that we were 'Never to return to Japan again.' Fortunately, we were smart enough not to bite on that one!"

Instead, the group signed with Sound Comfort, a Japanese agency that immediately arranged a six-week tour for the fall of 1979. October saw the release of *On Stage '78* [King GXF-77/78], followed closely by a fancy twenty-seven-track compilation called *Double Gold Superdisc* [GXC 9001/2]. There was only one new track in this set; the unreleased *Diana* from the de-vocalized *Hollywood Metal Dinamic 3000* album.

Before Christmas 1979, King surprised fans with a twelve-inch "live" EP [UA CML-8] extracted from the recent album. On it were three of Japan's all-time favorites, *Diamond Head* and *Slaughter on Tenth Avenue* backed with *Caravan*.

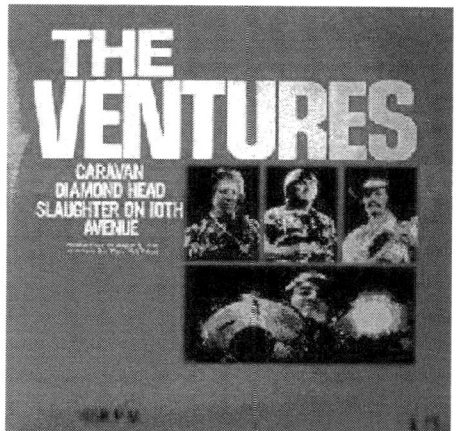 

Rare 12-inch disco recordings CML-8 and CML-9 featuring Joe Barile on drums

Response to the discofied *Star Wars/Cantina Band* and *Close Encounters of the Third Kind* single (4 and 3.5 minutes on UA CM-143) must have been higher than expected, for also in December, King released them again on a twelve-inch disc [UA CML-9] in longer (7.5 and 6.6 minute) disco versions. Although both sides are considered rare, the shorter versions did appear on the afore-mentioned *Double Gold Superdisc*.

CONTRACT POKER

In March 1979, King Records gave Japan the first of three Ventures albums with Joe Barile as drummer; namely *The Latin Album*, recorded in 1977. Perhaps a bit deviously, the cover bore a faded background image of the group showing Mel instead of Joe. When the remaining sets were released some years later, *Metal Dynamic 3000* and *Last Album on Liberty* also pictured Mel in place of Joe.

While King Records was doing its part, United Artists had begun to flounder. Beginning in April of '78, businessmen Art Mogull and Jerry Rubinstein had purchased all of the United Artists labels including Liberty, Sunset, Imperial, and Minit, along with all of the master recordings. To swing the deal, they borrowed from EMI, the parent company of Capitol Records. However, the men defaulted on their loan and in February 1979, the labels and master tapes (including everything The Ventures had recorded) became the property of EMI/Capitol. The Liberty label had been discontinued in America, but EMI eventually resurrected it for re-issuing its back-catalogs.

In Los Angeles, Don and Bob learned that Biff Vincent had set up shop in his father's garage and was recording demo records. Curious, the guys paid Biff a visit. Upon arrival at the Vincent's Costa Mesa home, the musicians were both surprised and impressed with the huge garage studio attached to the house. The walls were lined with sound absorbing material, and a utility room had been converted to a control booth. Now married and living next door, Biff had a remarkably short distance to go to work.

When The Ventures queried Biff about recording them, Biff was a little hesitant, feeling that he would need better equipment. After trying some eight-track recording, the results were so good that Don and Bob offered to finance Biff for new, twenty-four-track equipment. In turn, Biff could pay off the loan in studio time. With a bold plan in mind, Don, Bob, Mel, and Nokie told Biff that they would like to begin taping as soon as possible. Biff swung into action, and with his father's help, revamped the studio for twenty-four-track recording.

The Ventures' plan was to escape the apathy of United Artists, which they considered a major factor in their decreased record sales. The only recent Ventures' items seen at home were the nine-track budget-issues of *In Space* and *Rock & Roll Forever* on the Pickwick label. When their contract expired in August, The Ventures declined renewal, and instead, signed with Toshiba for newly recorded material only, their past masters being now owned by EMI. An important clause allowed the Ventures to self-market their new material outside of Japan. King Records, in contract with UA, retained rights to The Ventures existing material for another two years.

Toshiba contracted The Ventures to record six albums within the next two years. Although the contract covered new material only, Toshiba wished to release an "oldies" album, as most of the group's fans were now grown with jobs and families. The solution was simply to make new recordings of all the old hits. They would then compile an album and call it *The Original Four*. The Ventures agreed to start working on the project, so as to have the music in the can when the contract took effect in autumn of 1979.

GARAGE ROCK

When The Ventures walked into the garage studio in the middle of summer, Biff was elated. In just one month, he had become an expert on the twenty-four-track console. Recording began immediately so that twelve to fifteen tracks could be flown to Japan as soon as possible. As Biff was the engineer and Dave Carr was unavailable, Biff recruited Rob Cammack, a capable friend who could deliver the rich B3 organ sounds required on songs like *House of the Rising Sun*. The six men reworked hit after hit, while Biff's parents maintained a constant supply of snacks and beverages. Many rock bands tell of beginning in the backyard garage, but few if any can attest to recording a double album in a garage after twenty years in the business. Taking full advantage of the new console, Biff used six microphones just for the drums. Mel's Slingerland kit was nearly ten years old, but now included four toms, two bass drums, and a Rogers snare with several Zildjian cymbals. The list of songs grew until, by the end of the third day, there were over thirty tracks on tape that included a surprising pair of tunes from the UK's Shadows, *Dance On*, and *Wonderful Land*.

~ ~ ~

Occasionally, Don hosted parties in his beautiful Sherman Oaks home, one of which led to a lasting friendship with an aspiring musician. Through Mel and his friend Harvey Wicklund, Don met Russ Deck, a thirty-year-old singer who had been writing songs and playing guitar since the age of twelve. After hearing several songs Russ had written, Don offered to produce Russ and promote his material to other artists. Russ was soon recording in Biff Vincent's studio with backing by Harrison Swift. One of the songs penned by Russ was called *Until the End*. The material was shelved when both Russ and The Ventures were suddenly sidetracked. It was time for Japan Tour '79 with a stop in Korea on the way back home. Japan Airlines had flown The Ventures over thirty times, and now, in addition to placing full-page ads in the group's tour books, JAL had sponsored Ventures performances in four Korean cities.

Upon arrival in Tokyo, The Ventures began an exhausting schedule of seventy-nine concerts. Appropriately, the tour's theme was the return of "The Original Four," indicating the lineup that had impacted Japan in 1965. Japan welcomed Mel back with Nokie, Don, and Bob by cramming the concert halls to capacity. In line with the tour theme, the set list reflected the early albums. Nokie still played his acoustic set, but instead of *I've Got A Woman*, some audiences heard *The World Is Waiting For The Sunrise* or the beautiful McGee-Durrill number from Mel's *James Bond 007* album, *Morning Glory*. During *Caravan*, Mel now moved to the stage front for his bass tattoo, keeping his cymbals boiling during the transition to Bob's bass.

There was no live album for 1979, but Toshiba did corral the band for a studio session in mid-September. Only two songs were recorded, all that was needed to ensure hefty sales of the company's first Ventures album in over three years. For *Ventures Original Four*, the new tracks were *Movin'*, (as performed by The Astronauts on their 1965 tour with The Ventures) and *Le Dernier Train De L'espace* (The Last Space Train), a hit from The Spotnicks of Sweden.

On October 7, the "original four" packed their bags for the short flight to Seoul, South Korea. The first concert was in a huge sports venue called Chamsil Gymnasium. Sadly, the venue much too large for the amount of tickets sold. With admission prices set near that in Japan, more than half of the 20,000 seats were vacant.

From Seoul, The Ventures bussed south to perform at Kwangju before flying to the southern tip of Korea for concerts in Taegu and Pusan. It was the third week of October when Japan Airlines delivered the tired band home to Los Angeles. A week later, *Original Four* was released on Toshiba's subsidiary label, East World [EWS 81264]. The master had been cut at half-speed, giving the recording a greater feel of presence and warmth. Highlights of the album were the new tracks, but the updated versions of the old songs were also a treat. The Ventures had gained fifteen years of experience since those first recordings, and it showed.

Japanese cassette buyers were also treated to six of the revamped recordings along with some rare tracks from a previous session. Ventures' versions of *Dance On*, and *Movin'* were eventually found on various albums, but *Sun and Moon*, and *Wonderful Land* on the cassette titled *Pure Gold - Best 10* [East World ZR25-911] would be considered rarities for another twenty years.

Christmas 1979 marked two decades of fame and fortune for The Ventures, but the band had no illusions that this success would continue. The mere sight of their middle-aged audience in Japan, many of who had brought along their children, was a pleasant reminder. At this time, the band still did not imagine that these children would grow up to be another generation of Ventures fans.

As King Records concentrated on Ventures back-catalog production, they seemed to have forgotten the previously recorded "originals album." When Toshiba also showed more interest in their sixties hits than anything newly recorded, the writing was on the wall. The Ventures were now a nostalgia act. The *Original Four* concept helped The Ventures to accept this fact, and to consider presenting themselves as such on their home ground. Having placed thirty-seven albums in the Top 100, it seemed there should be plenty of mature fans in North America that would love to see Ventures music back in the stores. Furthermore, they thought; "Why not go independent, and put it on our own label? It wouldn't be the first time."

Proceedings were reminiscent of 1960 as The Ventures worked to establish a label of their own. It would have been nice to re-use their first label, but by 1970, Blue Horizon had been recycled, beginning with the early recordings of Fleetwood Mac. Reviving the name of their 1969 publishing company, The Ventures called their label TRIDEX.

East World EWS-81264 - October 1979

CHAPTER THREE
The Eighties

The Ventures began 1980 at a slow pace, with nothing definite planned until July's return to Japan. Don, acclimatized to sunny California, had spent some time in Tacoma for the Holiday season, ending up in bed an attack of pneumonia. Meanwhile, Nokie returned to Puyallup in Washington while Bob spent time with family and friends in the Portland area. A few months earlier, Larry Taylor had joined the Hollywood Fats Band, and Mel had signed this legendary blues group to PBR for its first record album, *Hollywood Fats Band* [PBR 7008]. As the festive season waned, Mel spent part of January on a promotional trip to Europe for PBR Records with his associate, Patrick Boyle.

The Ventures' album for America was still being planned when diversions delayed its progress. Having sold both of his nightclubs, Dave Callaham and Bob started a homebuilding company called Norwood Homes Development Corporation. Bob never suspected that the band would soon be involved in much more than their Tridex album.

The late seventies saw the emergence of "punk rock," an explosive musical trend based on the beat and sounds of fifties-sixties pop. For wider appeal, punk was fused with electronic synthesis to create "new wave" music. Toshiba Records decided that its star act should embrace new wave as it had with every other trend in the past two decades. In presenting the concept, Toshiba offered not only a list of Japan-composed songs with demos, but also a top Japanese musician to come over and assist with production. The custom-ordered album was agreed upon, with stipulations that while The Ventures would do exactly as asked with the music, they could include a couple of their own arrangements. Biff Vincent would be the engineer, but instead of his father's garage, the largest studio in Los Angeles was employed, California Recording Studios.

As The Ventures absorbed the sound of a dozen celebrated Japanese pop songs, Kazuhiko (Kaz) Katoh arrived from Tokyo to work with them. The project combined nine Japanese songs with Ventures' arrangements of *Goldfinger, Washington Square*, and a new version of their *Ginza Lights*. At the time, there was a revival of "ska," the modernized calypso sound from which reggae evolved. Thus, *Ginza Lights* was given a Jamaican flavor to become *Ginza Ska*. Once more, The Ventures had embraced another popular music trend. In recognition of the guys having prolonged their career with chameleon-like changes, Toshiba called the album *Chameleon*. With no apparent intention for export, Japanese titles relating to "beautiful swimming teachers" and the "beautiful flamingo" were not translated to English.

In Japan, *Chameleon* received additional tweaking as Kaz Katoh added some guitar while engaging Yu Imai on the synthesizer. In June, Japanese radio stations received promotional copies while The Ventures received short-sleeved *Chameleon* shirts printed with the album's artwork. By autumn, 15,000 Japanese fans owned a copy of the long-play album [East World EWS81332].

Back in Washington, Dave Callaham accepted the job of procuring entertainment for a fundraising banquet for the State's popular Senator, Al Henry. As Bob's business partner, it was natural for Dave to approach The Ventures to entertain for an hour following the meal. The group had not played on American soil for nearly ten years, but as a favor to Dave, they accepted the job. With less than three weeks before Japan Tour '80, it was like getting paid for a dress rehearsal. Concert highlights included Nokie's arrangements of *I've Got a Woman* and *Yesterday*. In gratitude to the Senator for his fine work in the area, The Ventures also performed Mickey Newbury's *American Trilogy*. It was the first and only time for The Ventures to play the patriotic medley, popularized eight years earlier by Elvis Presley at Madison Square Garden. If the guys were uncertain of their reception upon attempting an American comeback, audience response at this show provided an encouraging hint. Home video on television was now firmly established, allowing Dave Callaham to have The Ventures' performance recorded. Although an audio problem voided any sales of the video, illicit copies of the tape were soon being shared among fans. Even with its annoying overtone and poor quality from repeated dubbing, copies were sold or traded as if they were gold.

A special Japan issue of *Chameleon*

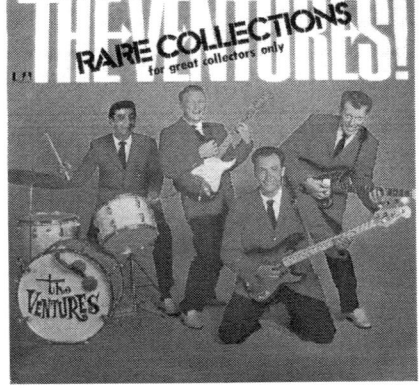
The double LP, *Rare Collections*

While Toshiba's East World division reveled in heavy sales of *Chameleon*, King Records strategically released a double album of rare oldies during this "Ventures Season." *Rare Collections* [King K18P12/13] appeared in July with an amusing bit of photo magic on its cover. On the classic pose from The Ventures' second album, Howie Johnson's face had been replaced with that of Mel Taylor. In addition to many of the early Dolton singles, the package contained several tracks that most fans had never heard, such as the *Dick Tracy* theme. Most surprising was side three of the double-disc album, containing nine of Don's rare vocals. *Karelia*, recorded by the group in 1975, finally made an appearance here, possibly because Sweden's Spotnicks (who had popularized the song in Japan), had toured there earlier in the year.

For its theme, 1980's Japan tour expounded the 20th Anniversary of *Walk-Don't Run*. Concerts opened with The Ventures' hits from the sixties; the second half featuring numbers from *Chameleon*. Near the end of the six-week run, local group Hikashu opened an outdoor concert for The Ventures, and both groups joined on some Ventures sixties hits. The combination worked so well that Hikashu was invited to appear on the last night of the tour, recorded at Tokyo's Shibuya Public Hall. At this show, bassist Kouichi Makigami stepped up to sing *Pike*. His voice was close enough to Don's that when English-speaking fans heard *Super Live '80* [East World EWS-67153/4], many thought Don had mastered the art of singing in Japanese.

Home by fall, The Ventures returned to Biff Vincent's garage. Biff rolled the tape while the foursome covered oldies like *Hey Paula, Johnny Angel, Lipstick on Your Collar,* and *Save the Last Dance for Me* along with fresh recordings of *Whittier Boulevard, Runaway, Comin' Home Baby,* and *Penetration*. They also taped a tune often requested in Japan, *One Way Ticket (to the Blues)*, it having been a hit there by Neil Sedaka. When some of Biff's young friends dropped by, they were indignant at first, hearing no power chords or "controlled feedback." Indulgence soon turned to admiration as they remarked how The Ventures' music resembled that of the "punk" bands playing the dance clubs.

In January 1981, twenty-six tracks were selected for test marketing in Portland Oregon. The band, ranging in age from forty-five to forty-eight, decided against a group photo on the cover. Instead, they selected a photo of twelve classic guitars from the collection of Norm Harris of Norman's Rare Guitars, a nationally known vintage guitar shop located near Mel's home in Reseda. A clue that suitable marketing deals were not easy to obtain came when they approached K-Tel Records. The related massive TV promotion required a much higher cash outlay than the band was willing to gamble.

At about this time, Don Lee Wilson went all the way back to 1960 for material to record for a single. Back then, Marty Wilde had made 45 in Billboard with a tune called *Bad Boy*. Don backed this single with the master from his 1964 Imperial release, *Tell Laura I Love Her*. Pressed on Tridex 101, the label was erroneously spelled "Tri-Dex."

At around this time, Sonny Rivera received an amazing call from a DJ in Pasadena. One of many fantasies harbored by Ventures fans is that of being a disc jockey able to flood the airways with Ventures music. Rodney Bingenheimer was in a position to fulfill the fantasy, and he had actually done it. Bingenheimer was a rock 'n' roll buff whose life had revolved around his collection of celebrity autographs. The humble, soft-spoken little man was trusted and even endeared by all the celebrities he met. It seemed only natural that he fell into a career in pop radio and concert promotion. Bingenheimer distinguished himself in the early seventies by bringing "Glam-rock" artists like David Bowie and T. Rex from the UK to Rodney Bingenheimer's English Disco in Hollywood. By the middle of the decade, he was popular on radio with his *Rodney on the ROQ* show at KROQ FM. As he became known as *Mayor of the Sunset Strip*, a fascinating film documenting Bingenheimer's life was released in 2003 under that title.

At a time when pop music was largely male dominated, Rodney helped popularize The Go-Go's, a promising five-girl group with a sound bridging punk and new wave. Rodney also disc jockeyed Hollywood's Starwood Club on evenings when no band was booked. Noting similarities between punk and sixties surf rock, he played Ventures' music and was thrilled to see the dance floor suddenly fill. Back at KROQ, Rodney included several Ventures hits in his play list, only to be deluged with responses from teenagers interested in this "new wave" or "instrumental punk" group. Subsequently, music stores were being asked for records by The Ventures.

Bingenheimer was calling Sonny to book The Ventures at the Starwood. Under his direction, this hard-rock club of the seventies was breaking ground by presenting local punk bands with names like The Circle Jerks, the Germs, and Quiet Riot. The Ventures were hesitant about playing to punkers and new wave fans until Rodney mentioned that less raucous groups like Paul Warren & Explorer had been well received at the Starwood. Next, Rodney introduced The Ventures to The Go-Go's. In a gesture of support for the band's U.S. revival, the girls offered their lone instrumental, *Surfin' and Spyin'*. As the generation gap narrowed, The Ventures felt more at ease with Bingenheimer's proposal. With a new double album on tap, the timing seemed right and they accepted a Wednesday night booking for December 17. Immediately, the event was publicized on KROQ with The Ventures appearing on Rodney's radio show for an interview.

As The Ventures approached yet another peak in their career, the entertainment world was shocked into disbelief on December 8 when ex-Beatle John Lennon was assassinated outside his apartment building in New York. Once again, the thought of playing in a club filled with punk rockers became unsettling for The Ventures, but it was not enough to stop them. The show would go on, just three days after millions of fans around the world participated in a ten-minute silent vigil for John Lennon.

Rodney Bingenheimer with The Ventures – notice Bob's new bass

Among the distinguishing traits of punk rock was its overly loud volume. As the Starwood date grew near, Bob worried that his powerful Peavey Mk III amp head would overdrive the speakers in his Fender Bassman cabinet. A visit to Red's Royal Amp Service in Hollywood would solve the problem, and also facilitate their meeting a long-time fan who was also a wonderful musician. As Bob and Don approached the storefront, the window displayed what appeared to be a Fender Precision bass with a curly-maple body and a gold pick-guard.

The shop's proprietor was none other than Orville "Red" Rhodes, the pedal-steel player on The Ventures' *Walk-Don't Run Vol.2* and *Theme From Shaft* albums, as well as Don and Mel's early single records. Having rheumatoid arthritis, fifty-year-old Red now devoted his time to this shop. He informed Bob that although there was a Fender decal on the headstock of the beautiful bass in the window, the instrument featured a narrow, specialty neck attached to a custom-made body from a company called Boogie Bodies. Red pointed out his own Velvet Hammer pickups and the Badass Bridge that he had installed while building the bass for a local professional. For sale on consignment, it was soon Bob's. Included in the purchase was a custom-made sound cabinet that would easily reduce the load on Bob's Bassman speakers. Red also introduced his helper, who happened to be a professional studio guitarist as well as a twenty-year Ventures fan. Through the seventies, thirty-two-year-old Jeff Baxter had been an integral part of Steely Dan and of The Doobie Brothers. Jeff quickly took the opportunity to tell Don and Bob what a big Ventures fan he had been since age twelve while living in Mexico where his father had worked. While learning to play, Jeff had been one of the first to join The Ventures' fan club. Serious about a music career, Jeff had asked for advice on purchasing a guitar. The reply recommended the Fender Jazzmaster, which Bob and

Don both played at the time. When his family returned to New York in 1964, Jeff got a job at Jimmy's Music Store and was soon the owner of a Jazzmaster. By his late teens, Jeff was an educated scholar and playing guitar in a psychedelic band called Ultimate Spinach. Around this time, Jeffrey Allen Baxter became Jeff "Skunk" Baxter. Unable to shake the label and knowing that some mystery and intrigue was good for his career, Jeff kept the nickname's origin a secret from journalists that constantly asked.

Jeff Baxter – back then   *Frank Zinn*

Jeff had recently come to California after leaving the Doobie Brothers, and, having mastered the pedal-steel guitar, made his living doing country band work, studio sessions, and guitar repair. Don and Bob found Jeff to be friendly and interesting, but as yet, had no plans for further association.

To open the evening at the Starwood, Rodney Bingenheimer had booked a popular punk group called The Plimsouls. They were good, but so different that The Ventures felt nervous as they approached the stage. The Ventures hurried through their repertoire, limiting dialog to naming each song and the usual introduction of band members. Bob stuck to the bass entirely, leaving Nokie to play lead on *Walk-Don't Run*, *Perfidia*, and the rest of the hour-long set. When it was time for *Surfin' & Spyin'*, Charlotte Caffey and Jane Wiedlin of the Go-Go's appeared, adding exclamatory shouts contained in their own rendition of the song. Continuing in Ventures' tradition, *Caravan* closed the show around Mel's powerful drum solo and bass tattoo. Thinking back, Bob recalls their reception; "It was like we had gone back in time to the sixties, except the audience was a mixture of people our age and a bunch of youngsters. But *everyone* yelled and cheered like teenagers! The floor was packed and we heard that they turned away hundreds at the door. Song after song, they just went nuts after each number. We relaxed so much that, with Christmas around the corner, we played *Sleigh Ride* and the response was just wonderful! Then we had people coming backstage to congratulate us. It was really an exciting time, and very encouraging for our new album."

To this, Don added; "There was also a contingent of punkers that got into violent slam-dancing and jumping up on stage. Our road crew took care of that, but the same bunch followed us to our next gig at Disneyland. They were harder to control there, and we felt lucky that no one got hurt."

Among the Ventures' backstage visitors were the B-52s, Rockpile's bassist Nick Lowe, Blondie's bassist Nigel Harrison, and members of Dr. Feelgood. All knew The Ventures' music, and many claimed to have been influenced by the band. Chat with the Go-Go's led to talk of The Ventures recording *Surfin' and Spyin'*, with Charlotte and Jane being invited to add their background vocalizing. Elated with the proceedings and promising to book more Ventures gigs in the New Year, Rodney Bingenheimer hinted strongly that he wanted to be involved in the *Surfin' & Spyin'*, session. He also requested that The Ventures add one of his all-time favorites to their set-list, only to be crushed when they told him that they had not performed *Lolita Ya Ya* since the 1962 recording session.

Following the Christmas holidays, Charlotte Caffey, Jane Wiedlin, and Rodney Bingenheimer met with The Ventures to record *Surfin' & Spyin'* in Biff Vincent's Costa Mesa garage studio. Rodney brought along two friends, David and Dan Kessel. Sons of big band and jazz guitarist Barney Kessel, the brothers had been hanging out with "Wall of Sound" producer Phil Spector since 1973 when they helped mix some tracks on the *John Lennon - Rock and Roll* sessions. Now, the two were eager to assist in producing the new Ventures single. The Kessel brothers also added some percussion to *Surfin' & Spyin'* while Charlotte and Jane inserted carefully timed bursts of vocal energy.

For the flip side, The Ventures had chosen Yuzo Kayama's *Black Sand Beach*, which had yet to be heard in America. Bingenheimer loved it, but suggested the title, *Showdown at Newport*, saying the tune would identify with Newports in at least twenty states as well as Newport Beach in California, plus a few Newports in Canada and the UK. At the same time, Rodney announced a booking of The Ventures *and* The Go-Go's for three nights at the end of January at the historic Roxy Theater on Sunset Boulevard.

As producers, the Kessels wanted a picture sleeve for TDX-501, and summoned their favorite L.A. photographer, Theresa Kereakes. Adhering to the "spy" theme, Theresa photographed her friend Pleasant Gehman. In an unusual move, separate pictures were selected for each side of the recording, giving Ventures fans two views of the gorgeous Miss Gehman. In the years to come, Pleasant became Hollywood's premier belly dance instructor and performer under the pseudonym, Princess Farhana.

The Kessel brothers' [*a.k.a. David Scott and Dan Phillips*] Ventures productions

Early in 1981, the Kessel brothers were impressed with tapes from The Ventures' recent Costa Mesa sessions. Acting as producers, they prepared and sent a batch of tracks to Japan, including the fresh version of *Black Sand Beach* minus the name change. Toshiba eagerly selected a dozen for immediate release on their East World label, simply titling it *60's Pop*. The company already had recordings from the first Costa

Mesa sessions, but they were being held for a big summer project that would combine them with some even newer recordings, plus selections from *Chameleon* for a three-record set titled *The Collection! Ventures Forever* [East World WTP50095/6/7].

In March, *60's Pop* [East World EWS-91012] was a big hit in Japan, providing grounds for the band to retain the Kessel brothers as producers for future sessions. Wishing to work outside the shadow of their father's reputation, David and Dan produced under the pen names, David Scott and Dan Phillips. Credit to these names was given on the *Surfin' & Spyin'* single, along with a plug for their Martian Records label.

When the Roxy dates arrived, *The Ventures Greatest Hits* was selling well in Portland while 1,000 copies of *Surfin' & Spyin'* were being pressed for packaging in the picture sleeve. A few twelve-inch singles were also pressed for use by disc jockeys in various clubs, creating another rare item for serious collectors [TEX 1245].

The Ventures opened for the Go-Go's, who witnessed fantastic crowd response to their *Surfin' & Spyin'* played live on stage by The Ventures. Before year-end, the Go-Go's released their own version of *Surfing and Spying* (sic) on a single, and later included it on their album, *Return To The Valley Of The Go-Go's* [IRS-29694].

Following rave reviews in the Los Angeles press, more Ventures dates were booked at the Roxy and Starwood, plus a midnight skulk at the Country Club in Reseda. Reviewers were consistent in their praise of the band's musicianship and the variety of sixties rock, surf, and the reggae version of *Goldfinger*. Press reviews included national exposure in Billboard, bringing inquiries for bookings from across the country. Meanwhile, Japan's Dentsu Corporation contracted a Hollywood company to video-record the Country Club show for the Japanese market. When February 20 rolled around, Myriad Media's cameramen were there for the midnight madness. The Ventures were flattered, but had little confidence that the company would end up with anything marketable. The timing was right however, as Pioneer Electronics had just introduced home players for the digital LaserDisc, a twelve-inch predecessor to the DVD. Dentsu was amazingly quick in releasing *Live in L.A.* on Pioneer's new video medium.

Pioneer disallowed a videotape release of the concert material for two years. Then, Toshiba-EMI purchased the rights for a VHS release. Simply entitled THE VENTURES, Toshiba's videotape version was actually more appealing to fans than the LaserDisc, having the L.A. freeway shots deleted in favor of missing tracks *Driving Guitars*, *Walk-Don't Run '64*, and the "member introductions."

Following the Country Club show, Nokie was invited to spend the night at Don's home as a matter of convenience. Nokie had begun feeling pain in the abdomen during the concert, and before long it worsened to the point where he required hospitalization. The diagnosis was pancreatitis, and after a few days, Nokie was released with prescription medicine and instructions to modify his diet.

Two weeks later, The Ventures returned to the Starwood. Don remembers an incident following the concert; "When we finished playing, everyone went upstairs to a reception area next to the dressing rooms. There were all kinds of people up there, and it was sort of a party atmosphere. One guy spoke to me, and like so many of our fans, he said; 'I really enjoyed the show and I have a lot of your records at home.' I thanked him, and then somebody else nudged me and asked, 'Is that who I think it is?' I said, 'I don't know him at all. Who do you think he is?' He says, 'I'm sure that's David Lee Roth!' At the time, I had no idea who David Lee Roth was, but I found out in a hurry that he was the front man for the group, Van Halen!"

With the ever-increasing publicity, it became obvious to The Ventures that a cross-country tour would be welcomed. Mel contacted Concerts West booking agency and a one-year contract was drafted, initiating a massive tour covering twenty states through the Midwest, the East Coast, and up into Canada. The band then purchased a thirty-foot Sportscoach motor home and a sixteen-foot equipment trailer. A solid-state Peavey MK III bass amplifier powered Bob's speaker cabinets, while Don stuck to vacuum-tube technology with a trusted 150-watt Sunn Spectrum top driving a JBL equipped Fender Bassman bottom. Nokie's preference combined both technologies, as Peavey's Deuce VT amplifier used integrated-circuit chips to drive a final amplifying stage employing four large vacuum tubes. Nokie also ran his guitar through a Peavey Custom that could handle the load alone if the VT should die. This amp also served as an extension at the far side of the stage. The equipment included a mixer board, two speaker stacks, and three monitor cabinets, all housed in aluminum-frame road cases on heavy-duty casters. With Mel's massive drum kit loaded, there was just enough room for guitars, mike stands, and boxes of accessories and cables. Nokie took along an Ovation thin-line guitar for his acoustic numbers, but on the road, he kept it in the motor coach.

Early '80s promotional photo

Touring in the eighties required two men to drive and handle the equipment. During a show, the "roadies" kept a watchful eye to prevent theft of equipment. Further duties included selling souvenir tapes, records, and T-shirts, plus introducing the band when a concert began. One roadie was designated "bag man," his job being to collect the band's pay before the group went on stage. There was also plenty of fun to be had, but as touring kept the men from home and family for extended periods, staff turnover was frequent. The Ventures would have many road managers in the coming years, but for now, friend and musician Russ Deck was hired along with Kent Smythe, a former roadie and bodyguard for The Go-Go's.

Night after night, the band met fans that had driven extreme distances to attend one and sometimes two shows. Following each performance, thirty to fifty-year-old devotees, with reactions ranging from a speechless daze to bubbling excitement, lined up for autographs. Besides the army of seasoned fans, The Ventures observed many new admirers. From the stage, they noticed that the "punkers" of the eighties were repeating history by crowding to the front, trying to learn the guitar licks. The first month of this triumphant touring ended on a nostalgic weekend in Anaheim California at Disneyland's "Blast From The Past." Here, The Ventures shared the stage with Jan and Dean, The Association, and The Surfaris.

In March, King Records were promoting their cassette-only release of The Ventures' *Metal Dynamic Sound 3000*, the set converted to an instrumental album four years earlier by replacing Yuya Uchida's voice with Nokie's lead tracks. Although Joe Barile was the drummer at the time, the insert pictured Mel in a 1966 photo of The Ventures. In early spring, Toshiba's request of new material for Japan's approaching "Ventures season" had The Ventures spending most of May in Biff's garage studio, now called Front Page Recording and Productions. *Surfin' & Spyin'* had hit the local airwaves, and when the *Los Angeles Weekly* pegged it at Number 4 on its new wave chart, it gave The Ventures a positive outlook on their career status. As Mel pondered to interviewers; "How could we be a nostalgia band when most of these kids weren't even born when *Walk-Don't Run* and *Diamond Head* were hits? They're not reminiscing; they're hearing our music for the first time!"

In the following weeks, the band concentrated on songs that had been popular Japanese vocals. To the delight of Russ Deck, two of his songs were also chosen and recorded as original material for Japan. As he recalls; "One song that The Ventures recorded instrumentally was *Until the End*, a song I recorded and performed on various TV shows and on a Japanese television program taped in Los Angeles. Don had introduced me to Leisha and I did a TV show that she hosted for release in Japan. One week I sang *Everyone Knows A Star*, and the next week I did *Until the End*. Around 1994, I received a letter from a gentleman named Kojo Suzuki, saying he had heard *Until the End* on a Ventures album [*Pops in Japan '81* - East World WTP 90074] and fell in love with it. Under pressure to assemble his own album, he covered the song and wrote his own lyrics. True to his word, a few weeks later I received his CD with *Until the End* on it. He was a good musician and singer, with sort of a Japanese-Elvis-country sound. Twenty years later, I still receive an occasional royalty check from Taiyo Music."

Russ Deck

A yet unnamed instrumental by Russ was sent to Japan along with *Until the End*. Russ recalls how his instrumental was finally given a name; "We were setting up one night, and Mel came rushing out of the motel and said, 'Hey Russ! Sonny got a call from Toshiba. They're pressing the album and you still haven't named that song. You have until midnight tonight to come up with a title.' Laughing, I thought 'Dang! I don't know what to call it.' I looked at the guys, then back at Mel and I said, 'by midnight tonight, huh? Ok, call back and tell them it's called *Midnight Tonight*!"

Two months later in Japan, two Ventures albums appeared, produced by the Kessel brothers (still hiding behind their pen names). There were no originals on *Tokyo Callin'* [East World WTP-90073], but *Pops in Japan '81* [WTP-90074] contained the two Russ Deck songs, *Until the End* and *Midnight Tonight*.

Near the end of the Santa Monica sessions, as Concerts West began booking dates for a Ventures winter tour in America, the guys met a guitar maker from Little Rock, Arkansas. Tony Hunt was such a big fan that he wanted to make a guitars for the band. Interested in custom instruments, Nokie gave Tony some specifications. In addition to the neck matching that of his Telecaster, including all six tuners in row, he requested a Scruggs banjo-tuner for the low E string. Measuring the neck of Nokie's guitar, Tony said he would keep in touch.

ON THE ROAD

The 1981 summer tour is one of Russ Deck's fondest memories; "There are some funny stories about the motor home and the sixteen-foot trailer we pulled behind us for those four months and 44,000 land miles. What a summer! Each of the guys had their own personalities and a distinctly different sense of humor. Don and I became best friends and often laughed until we had tears. Strangely enough, soft-spoken fact-oriented Bob Bogle was one of the funniest guys I've ever met. Mile after mile, he kept us rolling on the floor of the motor home. Not only was he a deadpan comedian, he could solve a Rubik's Cube in thirty seconds. I would twist and turn that thing until I thought no one could ever fix it, but time after time, he solved it in less than half a minute."

Closing a show with "Caravan"

"Mel was the group's business manager, and he had a more life-experienced, joking sense of humor. Nokie had his moments, but he laughed at the rest of them mostly. Mel and I played cards in the back of the motor home a lot. My initiation to the road began when it was time to get out the big hose and empty our sewage holding tank. It was during a hailstorm with driving rain. Later, when they said it was my turn to empty the sewage tank again, I knew I was being had. I said 'No way! It's Mel's turn!' Then, Mel bet me over a card game that if he lost, he would do it the next *two* times. That's when I found out how good he was. I tried the card thing over the holding tank with Mel one more time, and I ended up doing the sewage again.

"Whenever we arrived in a city, everyone else got a room, but I always slept in the motor home. It had a TV, VCR, stove, and refrigerator, everything a person could want. It was far better than some of the motel rooms. In Medford, Oregon, I met a gorgeous lady who spent some time with me in the motor home. In the morning, after coming back from breakfast, Mel asked me where the money was from the job. I looked where I had put the payroll, but it was gone! ... thousands of dollars! After about four hours on the highway, still feeling horrible because I couldn't find it, and thinking that the girl had taken the money, Mel pulled out the payroll bag and everyone laughed until their sides hurt. I was perturbed beyond words, but I got Mel's message.

"In April, we flew to Anchorage Alaska for a concert and right back after forty-eight hours. I'll never forget the twenty-four-hour sunlight and the people walking around in T-shirts and shorts when it was only forty degrees. I guess it was summer for them as soon as the snow melted. Kent, the other roadie, didn't stay with us past the West Coast trips. We hired Bill Ford for the Midwest and East Coast trips and he was tireless."

Home from Alaska, there was little time to rest, but when Bob checked *Los Angeles Weekly*, he saw their *Surfin' & Spyin'* sitting at Number 4 on the new wave chart. In the June, while doing four gigs in Texas, guitar maker Tony Hunt popped in Austin. There on business, he said that Nokie's guitar was nearly ready. By coincidence, the band was heading east after Houston, so they arranged a stop in Little Rock. Nokie was surprised, both at the size of Tony's shop, ("It wasn't much more than a shed behind the house"), and at the outstanding quality of the guitar. The body was made from two different woods that Tony had "cut from an old kitchen table that was hard as a rock." Built exactly as specified, the guitar also had Nokie's name inscribed on the headstock.

In the next few years, Tony sold over 200 guitars from the resulting publicity, but then health issues forced him to quit; "I built four guitars for Nokie and one for Don that had a discontinued Gibson 'Dirty-Fingers' pickup in it. Don asked for a couple of changes, but I never got the guitar back to him. I also started on a bass for Bob, but that was never finished either. I kept making guitars and helping Semie until 1988 when I developed allergies to everything in my shop. I got sick from walnut and maple dust plus the chemicals such as sealers and acrylics. I needed a new career, so in 1989 I went into law enforcement. In 1993 I got my Master's degree in Criminal Justice, and opened my own Private Investigation and security office."

Back to The Ventures on the road, Russ Deck continues; "That stop in Arkansas was the one of few on our *very* long trip from Houston to Disney World in Orlando, where Paul Revere and the Raiders were on the same bill. With dual tanks on the motor home, we could travel a long way without stopping. We drove 44,000 miles that summer without even one flat tire. We *did* stop for a couple of hours when I insisted on having 'Catfish and Hush Puppies' in Shreveport, Louisiana. As a child, I'd lived in Macon, Georgia where we went out on Friday nights for 'All you can eat' catfish and hush puppies with iced tea. Once when I was a slim nine-year-old, I ate over twenty catfish.

"It seemed to take hours for them to make my dinner. Having finished eating, Bill Ford and The Ventures sat and watched me fill up with catfish. When we headed out again, I was filled to the eyeballs and very happy. Bob drove, which reminds me, someone always had to stay awake when he was driving because he always drove on the edge of the road. He never completely adjusted that big vehicle, but he did alright."

Next was another long trek up the coast, with stops along the way in Chicago and Detroit before entering Canada. Russ recalls some fun in Chicago and a traumatic experience with U.S. Customs; "This is almost a 'You had to be there' story. To start off, we had a heck of a time trying to turn the motor home and trailer into the back alley behind the club on those one-lane Chicago streets with cars parked bumper to bumper. After numerous attempts and only inches to spare, we managed to get into the alley without tearing the bumper off someone's parked car. We set up in the afternoon, and then did a sound check that went great. Bill and I did a lot of the sound checks. I would pick up a guitar and play a few bars of *Walk, Don't Run, Pipeline*, or whatever struck me at the time. After the show, The Ventures were flattered when a fan came backstage and said 'You guys are the answer to world-peace! I've seen so many fights in this place, but nobody would think about fighting while listening to music like that."

Around 4:00 a.m. we packed up the equipment and I began backing the vehicle and trailer, about fifty feet in all, out of driveway. By now, more parked cars had arrived, leaving us absolutely *no* clearance to get out of the alley. A Toyota Corolla was blocking the alley exit, so, there we were, Don, Nokie, Mel, Bob, Bill Ford, and I, staring at the situation. There was only one thing to do. We circled the Toyota and began trying to lift it. After a lot of grunts, moans, and a few cries of 'NO WAY', we regrouped and gave it everything we had. Somehow, we found it within ourselves to lift this car up over the curb onto the sidewalk - and then we were off to Detroit. I would love to have seen the owner come out to go to work. It would have been a great *Candid Camera* moment.

"A few days later, we went up to Toronto to do a show at the El Mocambo, where the Rolling Stones played their first club gig in 1977. Some Ventures fans were there from Czechoslovakia with some albums to be autographed. It was a pleasurable trip except for one thing. Bob had warned me about the forms and red tape involved because of all the equipment we had, but Canada's Customs officials said 'The Ventures, eh?' and waved me right on through. When the guys woke up, I felt pretty good telling them we were already in Canada. We didn't think any more about it until returning to the States.

Live at the El Mocambo – Toronto, June 23, 1981

"We came to the Customs depot, and those U.S. Customs agents tore that trailer apart. Packed away back, behind the equipment, we had boxes of records, tapes, buttons, photos, and T-shirts that we sold at the nightclubs. When they discovered all that merchandise, we were in trouble for not declaring everything and keeping records in order to pay duty on whatever sales we made. Not only were we scolded loudly; the agent threatened us with jail for exporting undeclared merchandise. We sat on the ground for hours, pleading ignorance and apologizing while they decided what to do with us. Just as the guy was getting out the handcuffs, a nice Customs lady appeared. Like some guardian angel, she let us go without any penalty. This was just one of the memorable incidents during my life on the road with The Ventures."

WELCOME TO NEW YORK!

Returning to the States, The Ventures played a club in Albany called J.B. Scott's on the evening of June 25. Nokie had not been feeling well, and later that night he succumbed to the diet of a band on the run. Rushed to a hospital by ambulance, Nokie had immediate gallbladder surgery, which kept him from performing for several weeks.

An attempt to locate Gerry McGee revealed that he had returned with his wife to her homeland of New Zealand. Remembering the other superb guitarist on his Dynamics tour, Mel telephoned Bob Spalding in Austin, Texas. Working as a data processor, Bob played a nightclub on weekends. It was around 2:00 a.m. when he received the call. He accepted the challenge, but he did not sleep anymore that night; "I kept thinking about what I had committed to, and what to say to my employer. At the crack of dawn, I went down to IBM and told my boss that I wanted a month's leave of absence immediately. I figured my job was history, but he was very understanding, saying it would be OK. Whew! I wanted to be as comfortable as possible if I was going to stand in Nokie's shoes, so I took my favorite guitar, an Aria Pro II (Strat copy) with a natural finish. I knew that Bob played a lead guitar medley, so I even brought along my own bass.

"Upon arrival in New York, I took a cab to the hotel where The Ventures were, only to find that they had checked out. I asked if they had left a message, and sure enough, there was a note from Mel. It said, 'Bob. Get a cab and take the Holland Tunnel to the Hoboken Holiday Inn.' What a relief! I went outside to find a cab, and right there in front of the hotel, a policeman was holding a woman down with his nightstick across her throat. He looked up at me and said, 'Welcome to New Yawk!"

That evening and a few hours on Saturday were spent rehearsing in the hotel room. Russ Deck recalls; "We sat around the hotel for hours as Bob Bogle worked with Bob Spalding on the arrangements. I was totally amazed that bass-man-Bogle had all of the lead parts in his head (again...that unusual brain). The show at the Mudd Club went off without a hitch. The guys said it wasn't one of their best nights, but I'm sure they were the only ones aware of it. The kids in the audience were thrilled."

No one in the audience was more excited than New Jersey's Michael Kuhn, now age twenty-nine. Mike had kept track of the band's activities by telephoning Sonny Rivera in order to report regularly to Davy Peckett in England, who now published a bulletin dedicated solely to The Ventures. When the group appeared anywhere near New Jersey, Mike showed up; "I first met the guys in New York City on June 27, 1981. We went to a club called Bond's where they were booked, only to learn that the place was shut down. We learned that the booking had been diverted across New York City to the Mudd Club. Inside, it was packed with people much younger than us, who seemed unaware of The Ventures. It didn't matter though, because they became instant fans after the first few numbers. I was surprised to see someone I didn't recognize playing lead guitar. I then learned that Nokie had been hospitalized just two days earlier, and that Bob Spalding was in his place. Bob played amazingly well. I got another surprise when someone in the audience called my name. It was Terry Delaney, a Ventures club pen pal all the way from England. He was following the group for two full weeks of their tour.

"A few months later, I got a call from Sonny, saying the guys had been talking about the inactive fan club. They wanted to know if I would like to start it up again. Who, me? WOW! Of course I said 'Yes!' I started it with about $100, and it just grew and grew. I went to several concerts whenever The Ventures came east, and back then, they did that a lot. They were always very personable, and whenever I met them, they treated me and my family like part of their family."

As The Ventures resumed touring, Russ Deck's adulation of his employers increased; "We arrived at Long Island that Sunday to play a nice little town called Roslyn. We were supposed to open for comedian George Carlin in a club called My Father's Place, but George insisted on opening the evening because he was such a big Ventures fan. About a week later, we went back to New York City for two nights at the Lone Star. *Never* drive a twenty-eight-foot motor home with a sixteen-foot trailer through downtown New York! I can still hear the policeman screaming at me, 'Have you lost your mind?'"

"I have to say that Don had a great voice for the songs that he chose. Whenever he sang 'Runaway,' everyone loved it. He always joked with the crowd and said, 'Now you know why we're an instrumental group!' They laughed, but he got a lot of standing ovations.

"Don had some crazy ideas, but they usually turned out great. Once, he went down to the L.A. aquarium and videotaped fish swimming around for a full two hours. Then he came home and put a big glass container in front of his TV set. It was square and about an inch thick. He played the tape on the TV and everyone who came to the house thought it was a big fish tank, even while standing up close.

"Bob Spalding is another one of the nicest guys I have met. His style is nothing like Nokie's, but he's an excellent player. I was amazed how he memorized all those instrumentals in such a short time, especially since he was low on sleep. There was one song though, where he constantly hit a wrong note. It was a running joke after a while because of this one spot in *Hawaii Five-O*. I don't think he ever got it right during the rest of the tour. He used his own guitar at first, but pretty soon he was playing Nokie's Hunt guitar. He improvised on a song I wrote called *Stompers*, and later he played it with The Ventures on an album. It got a bit confusing having two Bobs in the band, but Mel fixed that when he hung the nickname Zonk on Bob Spalding. I'm not sure where that came from, but it was a quick solution to the problem."

By midsummer, news of The Ventures' U.S. revival was on the cover of *Goldmine* and heralded in *Rolling Stone,* dictating an autumn tour following Japan Tour '81. While the band rolled through New Jersey, D.C., and Massachusetts, Russ Deck received an exciting offer; "During the tour, Don began saying, 'Russ, why don't you play rhythm on the next tour?' He was very tired of the traveling, with the exception of Japan, which he loved. On Long Island, both Don *and* Bob sat me down and asked me to stand in for Don after they returned from Japan. I said YES! What a great honor to play for The Ventures, whose songs I learned on guitar so many years ago. I could hardly wait for them to complete the Japan trip so we could get back on the road together."

As Don recalls, the next stop was in Washington D.C. on July 2 at a place called the 9:30 Club; "This place had a stage about two feet high, with a little two-step stairway for access. At the end of our show, the lights were turned off just as I was walking offstage. I missed that first step and went down real hard, hitting my back on the edge of the stage. I was in real pain the next day, and I was worried about our next job, as it was a real big one. Luckily, there was a day in between without any concerts, and I was all right by the Fourth of July. I'd also been having some speaker problems, so Russ and Bill had a chance on the third to find me a new speaker cabinet."

The 4th of July concert was the annual *Spirit of America* show on the National Mall near the Washington Monument. The Mall is a long strip of green that stretches for over two miles from the Lincoln Monument to the Capitol.

Bob "Zonk" Spalding leading The Ventures in front of a half-million people

Keith Thompson, who became a radio station music director/announcer and huge Ventures fan, was a teenager then, and recalls the first time that he heard The Ventures on stage; "I was introduced to The Ventures by my father's records while growing up, beginning with the *Hawaii Five-O* album. In 1981, I was fifteen and living in Northern Virginia when I heard about them opening for the Beach Boys at the National Mall. I hadn't been listening to The Ventures a lot, since I'd worn out my Dad's old albums, and with no new album since *Rock 'n' Roll Forever*, I thought the band was broken up. When I heard they were opening the show, I assumed they were on a reunion tour or something. I just *had* to see them, so I rode the Metrobus into Washington. There was already about half a million people there, so I couldn't see much, but I sure could hear them. If Nokie wasn't there, I didn't even notice. The Ventures played for nearly an hour and then the Beach Boys came on. I really enjoyed The Ventures but the Beach Boys didn't impress me. It seemed they were having difficulty with their harmonizing. After that, I discovered the Tridex *Greatest Hits* album, and my interest picked up again, collecting more albums and attending their shows through the eighties and nineties."

The D.C. Mall show was also a highlight for Russ Deck; "On that Fourth of July, The Ventures played for more people than attended *Woodstock*! I went to the microphone and simply yelled, 'Are you *READY*?' Half a million people screaming back at me, 'YEEAAAAAAAAHHH!!' was an incredible feeling to say the least. The following day, while returning to New York City for a date at the Lone Star Café, viewers in Washington, D.C. were able to catch the show on TV's *Evening Magazine Special*."

After the next couple of club dates, Bob Spalding's month of vacation had expired. The group was very thankful, and so impressed with his work that they offered to help with production should Bob ever decide to do some recording. Bob counter-offered to help The Ventures whenever they wished.

For the half-dozen Eastern bookings left, Gerry McGee was available. Having played several different guitars in his career, Gerry had finally selected the Fender Stratocaster as his instrument of choice.

Gerry's recent activities included work with Billy Swan [*I Can Help*] in backing Rita Coolidge at the Aladdin showroom in Las Vegas. Then, when Billy went solo, he employed Gerry for his 1978 album, *Your Ok I'm Ok* [A&M 64686]. Having worked on several Kristofferson albums, Gerry was given a small part in the 1980 Kristofferson movie, *Heaven's Gate* playing alongside Joe Henry "T-Bone" Burnett. This meeting culminated in Gerry doing some fine solo work on Burnett's album, *Truth Decay*.

While recording *Truth Decay* [Takoma 7080], producer Denny Bruce was sufficiently impressed to engage Gerry for an album with Colin Winski, ex The Rockabilly Rebels. On *Rock Therapy* [Takoma 7083], Gerry worked again with long-time bassist friend, Larry Taylor. Winski's wild mimicry of Elvis, Rick Nelson, and Jerry Lee Lewis seemed almost twenty years too late, but it gave Gerry the chance to make some of the best rockabilly and fifties-style guitar sounds heard anywhere. A superb slide guitar break by Gerry also enhanced Winski's performance of *Tennessee Rock and Roll*.

A favorite project of Gerry's was the Emmylou Harris/Roy Orbison duet, *That Loving You Feeling Again* [Warner Bros. WBS 49262]. This single won a 1980 GRAMMY award.

After this Ventures tour, Gerry would join Booker T. Jones, Emmylou Harris, and a young Vince Gill to work with Rosanne Cash on her enormously successful album, *Seven Year Ache* [Columbia JC 36965].

As Gerry and The Ventures neared the tour's end, road manager Russ Deck was envisioning himself as rhythm guitarist after the upcoming Japan tour; "It seemed that everywhere we played, someone showed up with a guitar for the guys to scrawl their names on. And it was a kick when we stopped at some little gas station in the middle of nowhere and some good old country boys would come out and recognize The Ventures. The guys signed guitars, backs, arms, casts, ladies faces, paper, and a ton of albums. There was always with something happening that we least expected. What fun we had! I had my thing for catfish and hushpuppies, but with Don it was fried chicken. He simply could not pass a KFC outlet without stopping."

On the way home, the Sportscoach began showing signs of deterioration from long trips with a trailer in tow. Quick repairs were only temporary and expensive. With an agency already booking concerts for the New Year, the decision was made to replace the motor home with another vehicle once the Japan trip was over.

As Nokie had recovered and joined The Ventures in preparing for Japan, an odd request came from Toshiba/East World Records. They had a Japanese pop singer for whom they wanted Ventures backing on a commercial for Turbo 66 Petroleum. The song chosen by Turbo was (*Get Your Kicks On*) *Route 66*, written in 1946 by Bobby Troup and sung by literally dozens of artists since, from Nat "King" Cole to Depeche Mode. Uncertain of the required musical style, The Ventures hired Harvey Wicklund to sing and sent two versions of the song to Japan. As Harvey recalls; "It was exciting to work with Mel and The Ventures, singing *Route 66* in my normal rock 'n' roll style, and then again in a swinging, jazzy style. Knowing that a Japanese guy was going to overdub it, I hadn't intended to work very hard on the production, but something just happened and we really cooked! It was live and spontaneous, with only one overdub by Nokie on lead. It was a good version, and I always hoped they would do something more with it."

In Japan, Eddie Ban, the Japan-born Chinese who had opened for The Ventures in 1967 with his band, The Golden Cups, replaced Harvey's vocal track on both versions. Near the end of 1981, both versions were released on a single [East World WTP-17291]. While the Turbo Petroleum logo adorned the record's picture sleeve, reports from Japanese fans revealed that one side was also used in a Bridgestone Tire commercial.

More unusual Ventures recordings from the same sessions appeared in December, when East World released a soundtrack album from the Japanese TV movie *Kekkon Shitai Onna,* (Women wants to be married) [WTP 60433]. Although mostly instrumentals by a Japan's Tonics, three were Ventures tracks. The movie's theme (*Pipeline* by The Ventures) was not unusual, but *Karelia* from their 1978 session with Gerry McGee was a four-minute version re-titled *Kanashiki Baikal* (Sad Memories of Baikal). The third Ventures track was reminiscent of the New Vaudeville Band hit, *Winchester Cathedral*. As Don recalls, his voice on *St. Louis Memory* was filtered to sound like an antique mechanical phonograph; "We did that one at California Recorders in Hollywood, and the engineer was Del Casher, inventor of the wah-wah pedal and who's played with everyone from Lawrence Welk to Frank Zappa. It was a lot of fun recording that way."

The soundtrack album ended with The Tonics playing a magnificent instrumental version of *St. Louis Memory* that many Ventures fans wished their idols had done.

East World also released *St. Louis Memory* on a single, backed with Bob Spalding's composition of *Vicar* [WTP-17272] while adding both tracks to ten selections from the Biff Vincent sessions to call the resulting album *St. Louis Memory* [WTP 90144].

As Harvey Wicklund recalls, he was offered a job after Russ Deck was promoted to rhythm guitarist; "I wasn't really interested in becoming a roadie until Mel started listing their bookings at famous venues like New York's Lone Star Café and the Peppermint Lounge. Also, I had always wanted to see the East Coast, and this chance was too good to pass up. When The Ventures returned from Japan, I would be ready to roll."

In Japan, Festival Entertainment handled the group from August 30 to October 10. Patrons at the thirty-three concerts saw much the same show as seen in North America, including Nokie's acoustic guitar set. Enjoying heavy sales of the Country Club video, Toshiba chose not to produce a live album for Japan Tour '81. In fact, the company's indifference to live albums for the remainder of the decade led to speculation by some fans that videos had made live audio recordings obsolete.

Arriving home, The Ventures found themselves featured once more in the country's most popular guitar magazine. Back in April, freelance journalist and guitarist Dan Forte had interviewed the entire group in Palo Alto, California. Subsequently, he wrote articles for *Musician, Modern Drummer,* and *Guitar Player*. The Ventures had appeared in *Guitar Player* before, but never on the cover.

There was little time for rest before hitting the road to do thirty-five U.S. concerts in the next two months. Having been designated to play rhythm guitar, Russ Deck was suddenly devastated; "A week before the guys came home from Japan, I broke my left hand and badly mangled three fingers. In rushing out of a room, I slammed a heavy door with my hand still in it. Needless to say, it was a major frustration for me."

Saddled with a workload of producing and mixing, Don put out a call for help. Nokie had a friend who qualified, but like Bob Spalding, J.D. Hoag could only spend a month with the group. For Harvey Wicklund, it was the beginning of an exciting time; "The Ventures had bought a Dodge six-seater window van with four 'captain's chairs' and a bench seat in the back. We hooked up a U-Haul trailer, and the six of us hit the road. The other roadie was an amazing guy called Bill Ford. We could wake him up in the middle of the night in any city, and he could tell us exactly where we were. I learned that there is a lot more to being a road manager than back in the sixties when you simply lugged in a couple of amps and set up the drums. There's finicky sound equipment, security issues both backstage and in the dressing rooms, making sure the band members are not thirsty or hungry before going on stage, and collecting the money. Sometimes the winter weather caused life-threatening situations, but mostly it was a lot of fun. The Ventures really showed me what professionalism is all about. We got to this place in Ohio one time, and the gig was in a Quonset hut about five miles out of town. Some people had come on snowmobiles, but when we got inside, there was less than twenty in the audience. The club owner couldn't give us the rest of our pay because hardly anyone had showed up due to the weather. He apologized, and said he would write off the advance money he had sent. That's when Bob said 'If twenty people drove through this weather to see The Ventures play, then we're playing.' And that happened more than once when I was with them. I have nothing but respect for those guys... and I agree with Russ Deck. Don doesn't think of himself as a good singer, but I really do. I loved hearing him do *Needles and Pins*."

J.D. Hoag (signing autographs as "Jay Dee") adapted well to the group, and when it was time for a vocal, he sang a medley of Jerry Lee Lewis hits. The Ventures remember J.D. for his amazing energy both on and off the stage. Seemingly never tired, he would drive as long as they would let him. After a gig, while everyone else slept, J.D. would find an arcade machine and play Pac-man for hours.

Nokie, Bob, and Mel with J.D. Hoag on rhythm and vocals

Many of the dates were for colleges and universities, the first being Santa Barbara's University of California. The date was memorable to The Ventures after seeing themselves with top billing over "King of the Surf Guitar," Dick Dale.

On November 1, The Ventures were in New Jersey for a TV appearance on a weekly WTBS variety show hosted by popular anchorman Bill Tush. *Atlantic City Live* was broadcast from Resorts International Hotel's Stars Casino showroom. Also appearing were Herbie Mann and Lou Rawls. The Ventures opened the show with Bill Tush plugging their latest single, *Surfin' & Spyin'* along with their *Greatest Hits* album on Tridex. It was one of the few times when the band actually played live on American TV. Unfortunately, the reason for pre-recorded performances became apparent when, during the *Ventures Medley*, J.D. Hoag missed the opening four chords to *Perfidia*. It was not serious, although the intro sounded a little thin with only Bob and Mel playing. Next, the audience heard *Surfin' & Spyin*, *Hawaii Five-O*, and a few strains of *Pipeline* as the curtain descended. Vigilant Ventures fans observed that Nokie was playing yet another guitar created by Tony Hunt.

When it was time for J.D. Hoag to leave, his replacement was Chuck Effenger, as recalled by Bob Bogle; "Chuck was one of those guys who could play and sing as well as anyone, but knowing those odds, and having a family, he had chosen to remain in the work force. At the time, he lived in Vancouver, Washington and worked in our construction company. We had him fly out right away, and he played right through until the end of 1981."

Like J.D. Hoag, Effenger sang the hits of Jerry Lee Lewis, including the movie theme from *High School Confidential*. Twenty gigs and a month later, the tour was over and Christmas was near. When the band arrived in Hollywood, Don showed the group a copy of Billboard calling *The Ventures' Greatest Hits* on Tridex its "Top Album Pick." Unfortunately, the band had some bad news. A club owner had been very upset that Don was not with the band. Brandishing his signed contract, he had reduced the amount of their paycheck by a thousand dollars.

The band's next tour agent was Spotlite Enterprises, a company with offices in Hollywood and New York. For promotion to dance clubs, Spotlite had prepared a brochure comprising a dozen raving newspaper articles. The Ventures could now boast over 80 U.S. albums and 150 in Japan.

COWABUNGA

For The Ventures, 1982 was much like 1981. They toured America from January to mid July with sporadic work on a new recording project, followed by two months in Japan and more U.S. touring. Again, J.D. Hoag played rhythm while Don worked in the studio and handled the business. After three months, Harvey Wicklund expected to be finished, but the band convinced him to stay on until July when they left for Japan.

On March 5th, The Ventures were driving from Arizona to California when they learned of actor-comedian John Belushi's death due to drug abuse. Four days later, Belushi's funeral was publicized, but they paid little attention until hearing some details from Don. Apparently there had been a deal between Belushi and actor Dan Aykroyd, both of TV's *Saturday Night Live* set before teaming up as *The Blues Brothers*. While enjoying a recording of *The 2000-Pound Bee* one day, they had promised each other that whoever lived the longest would play this Ventures instrumental at the other's funeral. According to Aykroyd, he said; "Wouldn't it be great to lay this noisy, heavy tape on a church full of people?" John agreed and the pact was made.

Aykroyd attended the funeral in Massachusetts, but did not fulfill the pledge until two days later at a memorial service in New York's Cathedral of Saint John the Divine. When he held a small tape player up to the microphone and played *The 2000-Pound Bee* by The Ventures, the thousand-plus congregation went into shock for a moment, and then broke into laughter.

In 1989, a notoriously bad movie called *Wired* chronicled Belushi's precarious life and tragic death. The film was classed as a "bomb," but fastidious Ventures nuts were delighted to discover another slightly different arrangement of *The 2000-Pound Bee*.

The Ventures with J.D. Hoag - Plattsburgh, NY - 1982

In mid-March, The Ventures arrived at a small California town called Sutter Creek. Upon entering the Sutter Creek Theater, they were surprised to find journalist Dan Forte leading the opening act. As Dan recalls; "Back in high school I started learning Ventures' songs from their *Play Guitar* albums and by jamming with friends. During the punk movement, I formed a surf group that used vintage Fender amps, and we called ourselves Cowabunga. When The Ventures released *Surfin' & Spyin'* and started touring, it was a major event to us. We were pretty excited to be opening for them, but they were a little worried about us. They preferred not to have instrumental bands open for them, but I assured them that we wouldn't play any Ventures tunes. It was a memorable night, and it brought me some incredible good fortune about eighteen months later."

The Ventures were halfway through the tour when they arrived in Providence, Rhode Island to play at Lupo's Heartbreak Hotel. Mel had been coughing more than usual, and was feeling pain in the side of his chest. A local doctor diagnosed a lung infection with fear of pneumonia to follow. Along with an antibiotic prescription, he strongly advised Mel to stop smoking. Then and there, Mel gave up the harmful habit.

Arriving for their sound check, The Ventures found an eager fan waiting to meet them. Paul Huckle was from Montreal and mentioned being a drummer in a dance band. Immediately, Bob asked; "How would you like to play drums for us tonight?" Excitedly, Paul said; "Yes!" and was soon sitting at the drums playing *Walk-Don't Run*. By the end of the song, he was trembling so much that he set Mel's sticks on Nokie's guitar case and walked off the stage. Apparently, traveling to see a Ventures show and being asked to replace a member was just too much for Paul. Mel resumed the throne, but the band dropped *Wipe Out* and *Caravan* from their set list. The antibiotics allowed Mel to perform for a week, but it was soon evident that he needed bed rest. With J.D. Hoag already subbing for Don, Mel set about locating a substitute drummer. The stand-in he found was Bill Lewis, who had worked with Gerry McGee and the Cajuns in the sixties. As Mel flew home from Cleveland, Bill flew in from California. In recalling this time, Bob Bogle chuckles; "When we told Bill that he would have to play on my bass during his solo in *Caravan*, I said 'You can play anything you like, and I'll work the frets to add melody. We've done this many times so I won't let anything go wrong. Just come out from behind your drums and start playing on the E string.' It's pretty easy, but I forgot to tell him about the humorous part where I turn the volume down and Mel looks around as if trying to figure out what happened, and then I turn it up again. Our first show was in at Astair's in Olympia Washington. The minute that the bass went off during his solo in Caravan, Bill stood up, gave me a real dirty look and walked back to the drums with his hands on his hips. He looked at Don and said 'Bob turned the volume off and just left me hanging!' We laughed about it later, but at the time, he was really upset. Once I explained the whole thing, he did a great job on it."

When Mel resumed his throne almost three weeks later, he confirmed that he was a non-smoker and had kicked the habit for good.

HOOKED ON VENTURES

In order to work closer with The Ventures, Bob Spalding relocated to Fountain Valley, California. For the next few months, he spent his spare time at Don's home, where the two worked on arrangements, mixing, and composing new instrumentals. With Japan Tour '82 on the horizon, the plan was to have a second Tridex album ready by fall. Dave Carr was also on hand for the required keyboard work. When the Ventures tour paused in Hollywood for a few days, several songs were recorded at Biff Vincent's studio. Included were new versions of *Joy, Needles and Pins, When You Walk in The Room*, and (due to the recent John Belushi publicity) *The 2000-Pound Bee*. Some original tracks were also produced, including Russ Deck and Bob Spalding's *Stompers*, Bob's own *Spindrift*, and his arrangement of *Somewhere Over the Rainbow*. The preceding year (1981) had seen a series of six-minute instrumental classical medleys set to a throbbing disco beat by London's Royal Philharmonic Orchestra. *Hooked on Classics* was so popular that four successive volumes followed amid various take-offs by other artists. Having performed medleys of their own since 1965, this was a natural format for The Ventures. With Dave Carr, a medley was arranged from around ten of the band's most popular tunes, played at one tempo and beat. The five-minute mix was intended to open a Tridex album called *Hooked On Ventures*, but it was soon July, and the band was off to Japan for their twentieth visit that lasted until mid-September.

In time for Ventures Season '82, King Records had come up with an album concept. Two double albums, *The Fender Years* [K18P-256/7] and *The Mosrite Years* [K18P-254/5] were released simultaneously, summarizing The Ventures' output from 1960 to 1966. Clever artwork on *The Fender Years* reproduced the cover of their *Knock Me Out* album, but with Fender guitar headstocks shown in place of Mosrites.

An interesting side project on this trip was a recording session on which The Ventures played for a Subaru automobile commercial. Composed by Asei Kobayashi, *Ride On Try!* [East World WTP-17392] was released in September with photos of the band and a Subaru van on the colorful picture sleeve. With Bob on lead guitar, this was the last Ventures vinyl single to be released in Japan.

On September 5th, The Ventures played Tokyo's Rainbow Charity Festival in aid of a child orphaned in a traffic accident. The concert was held in a large portable band shell erected on a vacant lot where Tokyo's City Hall now stands. In the past year or so, fans had begun presenting Nokie with guitar pins. When he had around eight or ten, he put them on one of his Stetsons, and by the summer of '82, over thirty little guitars decorated the hat. At the end of the Rainbow concert, the usual autograph seekers mobbed the whole band and many took pictures of the king's guitar-jeweled crown.

After thirty shows, the group returned to Hollywood. They had intended to resume the *Hooked On Ventures* project when they learned that the cost of their *Greatest Hits* on Tridex had gone far past expectations. Studio time and mixing had been minimal compared to the publishing fees, copyright registration, pressing, and labeling. Then there was the photography, graphic art, printing of cover sleeves, and packaging. During the period when Don had remained in Hollywood, he searched for a distribution deal for the Tridex *Greatest Hits* album. Repeatedly, he was met with an exorbitant quote for the cost of the venture. With no distribution deal for this first album, it seemed pure folly to proceed with a second; that is, until Biff Vincent suggested a solution.

Mid-seventies disco clubs required singles with longer playing time than possible on a seven-inch vinyl record. Disc jockeys first solved the problem by playing identical singles in succession on side-by-side turntables. In response, record companies began making twelve-inch singles containing overly long dance versions, specifically for use in discotheques. The twelve-inch single having wider spaced grooves, provided the bonus of better bass reproduction. The superior sound quality soon made them a popular consumer item, even after disco's heyday had passed. Having appeared on one of these records for King in 1978, The Ventures asked Biff about their cost structure. He explained that the cost of a 45-RPM extended-play recording was in the range of a regular single. Under budget restrictions, the group could do its own artwork, and by keeping it simple, printing costs could also be reduced. At that, Bob Spalding indicated his wife, Artie to be a talented artist.

The title of the medley, and hence that of the package was named *Stars On Guitars*. Artie then produced a brilliant jacket with red stars and guitars on a black background. Borrowing an idea from The Ventures' East World *Original Four* album, headshots of the members were placed in each corner on the back of the jacket. At Santa Monica's Rainbo pressing plant, the twelve-inch forty-five was logically baptized TDX 1245. Enough copies were pressed to allow fans to buy the record at concerts and through the band's fan clubs. The fact that Sonny Rivera was now shipping goodly amounts of records and souvenir merchandise to the U.S.A. Fan Club ensured Mike Kuhn's address being included on the back cover of *Stars On Guitars*. Davy Peckett's UK address was also published, but ironically, many of his American subscribers were switching to the club at home, eventually forcing Davy to drop his Ventures-specific bulletin. Davy continued, however, to publish *New Gandy Dancer* with a section of *Ventures News* contained in his instrumental rock journal.

While in Japan, The Ventures learned that J.D. Hoag was unable to play the fall tour at home, having signed with another act. As Harvey Wicklund remembers; "Mel called me from Japan and asked if I would like to play rhythm guitar with them when they got home. I hesitated at first, but he said I would do fine because I had stage experience and had been traveling with them for a while. When I agreed, he said 'OK, our first job will be at the Civic Center in Galveston in thirty days. Get hold of Bob Spalding down in Orange County, and he'll run over our show with you.' "Well, for the next month, I went to Bob's place about twice a week. He charted out the show and we went over everything. He was just fantastic, and became another good friend. The only guitar I owned was an acoustic, so Bob lent me his Aria Pro II. After finishing the first tour, I bought a Jazzmaster in Los Angeles so as to get closer to Don's sound. One thing I learned about The Ventures' music was that although it sounds straightforward, it is really deceptive when you try to play it. I found that you have to know those tunes well, and you have to know the way *they* play them. I practiced on the acoustic guitar all the way to Galveston in the backseat of the van, and Bob showed me some more stuff. When we walked out on that stage, I was petrified! When it was over, people came up and were shaking my hand, and I'm thinking, 'Man, I don't even have a clue yet, and they want my autograph. I did a vocal medley of things like Little Richard's *Keep a Knockin'* and *Great Balls of Fire* by Jerry Lee Lewis. Maybe that was why they liked me."

Thus, while Don worked to complete TDX 1245, The Ventures launched their fall tour with Harvey on rhythm. Again, they crossed the country to New York, circling back through Ohio and Texas to California. The highlight of the tour was three-days in Knoxville, Tennessee for the World's Fair. To anyone checking on what kind of entertainment The Ventures provided, it was now certified. The fair's *Official Guidebook* tagged our guys as being a "nostalgia group."

Playing in the specially constructed Tennessee State Amphitheater, The Ventures entertained an estimated 10,000 people. Settling in one place for three days gave them a break from the rigors of the road, and a chance to celebrate Mel's 49th birthday. It was not the first time Mel had heard 10,000 fans yell *"Let's go!"* but it was his first to hear them yell (prompted by Bob), "Happy Birthday, Mel!"

Harvey Wicklund with The Ventures - 1982 World's Fair – Knoxville, Tennessee

Home for December, the weary travelers received good news from Don. The first distribution deal for the Tridex material had been finalized with California Record Distributors. An agreement had also been made in the UK through Mel's association with Pat Boyle of PBR records. With excellent liner notes written by Davy Peckett summarizing the band's career, the sixteen-track *The Ventures Today* [Valentine VAL-8054] appeared in UK stores in the summer of 1983.

PLAY NOW, PAY LATER

As demand for The Ventures and their records increased, Spotlite Enterprises booked more concerts across the U.S.A. With five months ahead on the road, the band decided to replace the six-seater Dodge with a motor home. In a few days, Bob and Mel traded the window-van in on a new twenty-five foot, class C mini-home, built on a Dodge van frame with a full-size bed above the open-backed cab. Slightly shorter than their first motor home, this vehicle was more powerful. New Year celebrations were only a week old when Nokie, Harvey, Bob, and Mel (along with two new roadies) hit the road with a trailer in tow behind the sparkling new coach.

Whenever a tour swung back west, the guys were booked in Los Angeles clubs like the Palomino or Music Machine, only to head back out in a few days. Before going out this time, they received a "thank you" from Fender. Bob Bogle recounts; "In 1983, the Fender factory was still in California, where we were invited for a small ceremony in the business office. They presented us with three re-issued 1962 Jazzmasters. The model had long been discontinued, and for this run they used Stratocaster necks having the narrower headstocks. They only made six, the other three going to the guys at Fender who built them. With only six in the entire world having the different necks, these were very rare instruments. I still have mine and I often play it at home. Don took his on the road as a backup for a while, and then gave it to his son, Tim. Nokie didn't play his at all. He didn't have it very long when someone stole it."

Early in March, there was a job in Tennessee that no one ever forgot, especially Phil Philips and Jeff Cox. Phil and Jeff were the new road managers, but we get this story from Nokie; "The way we worked, after being burned a few times, was to get half the money before we went on tour, and collect the rest before going on stage. We pulled into a town in Tennessee.. I think it was called Clarksville. When we got settled in a hotel, Jeff and Phil took the equipment down to the club and set it all up. As Jeff was the bag man, he went to the owner and said, 'I have to collect the rest of the money now, like it says in our contract.' The guy says 'I don't care what's in the contract. I always pay the bands with cash from the door receipts. There won't be any problem, because tonight's a sellout.' Jeff said, 'Well, The Ventures won't play unless you pay up front. We might as well load up the equipment right now and leave.' He says, 'No, you're not doing that either. They're gonna play the job or leave without the equipment. This is my town and I have my rules!' So Jeff says, 'We'll just see about that. I'm taking the equipment out of here right now!' With that, the owner pulls out a handgun and says, 'Not so fast! That stuff is on my premises and in my control. If The Ventures don't play, I'm gonna sell it to recoup my losses.' Jeff called the hotel and explained the situation to Bob, saying, 'What should I do? This guy's got a gun on me.' Bob told him, 'You guys hang tough and I'll get back to you.' Bob called Spotlite in New York and they said, 'Call the highway patrol and then you can get your equipment out of there. That guy is in breach of contract!' I think Bob even called Don back in Hollywood and got the same answer. Bob said OK, but after talking it over with Mel and the rest of us, he said, 'No good! We would need a court order to get the stuff off his premises.' He called Jeff back and said, 'It looks like we're screwed out of half our money, so we'll just have to play and cut our losses.' Once the owner saw that we were going along with his demands, he calls our room and, polite as you please, says to Mel, 'Do you guys need a ride down to the club?' Mel said, 'Well, we usually have Jeff or Phil bring the motor home back and pick us up.' Then the guy says, 'Hell no, I'll come and get you.' He drove us down there and later came in the dressing room to ask if we minded if he let some DJ's or the press in without paying. After so many tickets are sold, we revert to a percentage, and by this time we were past that point. After the concert, we got paid in full, including our percentage of the gate. We just had to do things his way and he was fine!"

Soon after that, Phil Philips and Jeff Cox quit the tour. Their replacements were Chuck Churella and Greg Rowland, who turned out to be very loyal to the job.

There was one soft touch among the eighty-plus jobs before Japan-time in July. For a whole week in April, The Ventures became a lounge act at Harrah's in Reno, Nevada. The hotel spoiled the guys for a few days, making it that much harder to resume the one-niters through Wyoming and Utah, and then east to perform in seven northeastern states and back to California through Texas and New Mexico.

The final gig was a private function outside Deming, New Mexico. It was a landmark in more than one way for Harvey Wicklund; "It was the very last job I played with The Ventures. The hosts barbecued a whole steer, and neighbors came from miles around. We put on a good show and they treated us like kings. I'll never forget it because it was the end of the tour, and thanks to Mel, it was also the day I stopped smoking cigarettes! I've stayed with music ever since, but I never went back on the road. It's a lot of fun, but it's also a very hard grind. The tours zigzagged all over the country, but The Ventures just kept on truckin'. They were tougher than any group I ever met. They taught me a lot and I love every one of them."

Mention of the barbeque concert reminded Bob of a similar job; "Those big cattle-ranch jobs were usually paid for by huge New York corporations operating on the stock exchange, but this one was for a gal near Fort Smith, Arkansas by the name of Taylor Burnett. Being quite a big Ventures fan, she had attended several of our concerts and we had gotten to know her. The story goes that after receiving a large settlement from a bad accident she suffered at work, she booked us for a private party on her ranch. Normally, we turned down something like that, but in this case, we had known her for a while and we accepted. She flew us all the way out there to play in this big barn for her and all of her friends."

Also acquainted with Taylor Burnett was fan club manager Mike Kuhn; "I met Taylor in Baltimore when she came to see The Ventures in 1984. She had lost three or four fingers in an industrial accident, and it seemed to her that many in her family were after her money. 'Taylor Burnett' was actually an alias, assumed after her monetary settlement. It must have really been something, to fly your favorite band in for a party!"

TRIDEX IN SPACE

In the early eighties, New Yorkers Aleks Rosenberg, John Fraker, and Joe Cohen ran a production company that made promotional rock videos for the bigger record companies. The videos were short clips of live footage and custom animations for groups like Foreigner and Aerosmith. After reading press reports containing testimonials by musicians having been influenced by The Ventures, the partners were inspired to create something bigger. Their masterpiece would be a television special combining a live Ventures concert with guest appearances and testimonials by popular musicians influenced by the band. In June, 1983, as The Ventures played their spring tour, the men from Rosenberg-Fraker Productions attended some concerts while finalizing the deal. With a second tour slated after their month in Japan, videotaping in New York was scheduled for the last Monday in August.

Four summer weeks in Japan were looking very attractive, but in 1983, it was not to be. Bob Bogle recalls; "One day Sonny got a call from the L5 Society, asking if we would do an album honoring NASA's twenty-fifth anniversary of space travel. Apparently NASA is not allowed to exploit itself, but there's nothing stopping outsiders from promoting their cause. So the L5 Society was formed to educate the public and promote the space program. We were honored and immediately said 'yes'. After the paperwork, NASA sent audio and video footage plus an assortment of photos for our use. The astronaut moon-mission dialog was included, and we used it. We were already committed to a heavy tour schedule here in the States, but it wasn't too late to cancel the Japan trip. We thought of re-recording our old *In Space* album, but some of those songs weren't conducive to promoting space travel. I'm sure NASA would have choked at titles like 'Exploration in Terror' and 'He Never Came Back'. We had plenty of material to pick from, so we didn't use anything from *The Ventures in Space*."

A project for the National Aeronautics and Space Administration [NASA] justified Joe Saraceno being hired for production. Also, Biff Vincent's garage was abandoned in favor of Hollywood's foremost recording plant, California Recording Studios. The band recorded fresh versions of *Journey To The Stars*, *Skylab*, *Telstar*, and *Gemini*, plus the themes from *Star Trek*, *Star Wars*, *Close Encounters*, and *2001 A Space Odyssey*. For the remainder, Dave Carr wrote *Apollo 11*; Bob Spalding added *Columbia*; and The Ventures revamped their own *Sand, Sea and Love* as *Theme for Sally* in honor of the first female astronaut, Sally K. Ride. The theme from *Return of the Jedi* completed the list.

The L5 Society having specified music of general appeal, no attempt was made to produce a "Ventures sounding" album. Digital sampling and synthesis technology allowed Dave Carr to record the bulk of the content on keyboards, with The Ventures adding their parts later. Bob Spalding did most of the guitar work, and Mel played drums when more than a synthesized disco beat was required. Listeners could only hear the sound of The Ventures by focusing on the background, where nearly every track featured Bob Bogle's throbbing bass. It wasn't enough for fans expecting an album laden with rocking guitar riffs and spanking new melodies, but the album remains to be an enjoyable listen for just about anyone.

Although Don's ideas were used in the design of the glossy gatefold cover containing thirty-four colorful photos, the crowning touch was the record itself, being pressed in clear vinyl. Only 5,000 copies were pressed, with at least fifty reserved for NASA staff and the L5 Society.

The cover on *NASA 25th Anniversary Commemorative Album* [Tridex TDX-1003], with its detailed photograph of space shuttle Columbia, is now a monument to historic tragedy. After twenty-seven space missions, Columbia's crew of seven was lost when the ship disintegrated over Texas while returning to Earth in February, 2003. During liftoff, a flying chunk of insulation had damaged the shuttle's thermal tiles.

A TAXING SITUATION

Working with The Ventures, Joe Saraceno learned how nearly two-thirds of the band's pay was eaten by taxation. Having left the music business in 1976 to become a tax advisor, Joe presented a solution, as explained by Fiona; "The way I understood it, someone investing in the arts could write off *several times* the actual investment. For example, if you paid $10,000 to license some masters, and another $10,000 to press 5,000 copies, you could write off $100,000 for tax purposes."

The Ventures simply needed some material not owned by a record company. The only recordings fitting this criterion were Mel's ten-year-old solo projects for Japan. Planning to press a quantity of records and warehouse them indefinitely, Taylor, Wilson and

Associates signed the required documents. Mel then submitted the tapes for his 1972 *James Bond 007* album and his (unreleased) 1973 live in Japan Dynamics tracks. Evidence that something had gone awry surfaced when two vinyl albums appeared as being Ventures recordings. Released by Heritage Sound Recording Distributors, *Movie Themes - The Ventures* was the *James Bond* album in its entirety (note the cute serial number, HSRD 007). In attempting to change the title of *Pearl Diver* to *Dr. Yes*, the playing order of the tracks was also changed, and a real mess ensued. *Bond Street* was called *Dr. Yes* and *Thunderball* was called *Bond Street*, resulting in *Pearl Diver* being labeled as *Thunderball*.

These LP records do NOT contain music by The Ventures

The other album was *Spotlight – The Ventures* [HSRD-010], containing ten of the twelve live tracks by the Dynamics, later released as *Roll Over Beethoven*. The Heritage albums should have stayed in the Arizona warehouse, but being a distributor, Heritage apparently could not help distributing and advertising them in *Billboard* for $6.98. Other than crediting the wrong band for the music, minimal harm was done, but later, this folly was considered just the tip of the proverbial iceberg.

I'M NO DON WILSON!

1983 was The Ventures' first year pass up Japan since 1969 when *Hawaii Five-O* had demanded heavy touring at home. This time, they were already under pressure to release the NASA album in time for Space Observance Week when another project arose. Japan's Orange Sisters were a teenage trio whose manager had arranged for Ventures backing in a Tokyo studio. Upon learning that the band was not coming to Japan, he brought "Candy, Judy, and Sandy" to Los Angeles. In high-energy harmony, the girls sprinkled Japanese "bubblegum" songs with English lyrics in the style of the Beach Boys. The driving background included first-rate solos from Nokie with Dave Carr assisting on keyboards. When *The Orange Sisters Farewell Party* [Moon 28023] was released the following year, The Ventures were heard on six tracks, the other half backed by sax, keyboards, and orchestra. Ventures fans were particularly delighted to hear the instrumental break in *Dry Martini*, containing a familiar riff from *Driving Guitars*.

Due to the immediate mixing job for the Orange Sisters album, Don missed the next scheduled tour, this one in the Rocky Mountains region for a period of two weeks.

The Orange Sisters meet The Ventures

Harvey Wicklund, Bob Spalding, and J.D. Hoag being unavailable, Mel queried Steve Soest, who in addition to being Dick Dale's bassist from 1979 to 1985 and a skilled surf guitarist, was reputed to be the best guitar repairman in Southern California. Being much too busy in his shop, Steve recommended thirty-year-old Dan Forte, with whom the Ventures were already familiar. Being invited to play on the road with a favorite group is pure fantasy for most fans, but for Dan it was a dream fulfilled; "The Ventures had only heard me play guitar once in Sutter Creek, so I was surprised when Mel called and asked if I would like to sub on rhythm. I had been with *Guitar Player* magazine from 1976 to 1978, but I was now working for Hewlett-Packard in Palo Alto [California]. Luckily, I had accrued just enough vacation time that I could leave to go on tour. The first thing Mel asked was if I had a guitar. I said I would use the '64 Jazzmaster that I played in Sutter Creek. The next thing he asked was if I could play the *Pipeline* glissando lick. Having always put a little shtick in my show, I had been putting that lick into everything I did. When I told Mel about that, he said, 'Great. You're hired. You get $500 a week and we cover your living-expenses.'

"When the time came, I put my Jazzmaster in a garment bag and flew to L.A. where I met with Don. No audition, no rehearsal, just an afternoon in his poolroom, running through the rhythm parts with our unplugged Jazzmasters. We would just get started on a song when he would stop and say 'OK, you know that one..let's try another one.' The one I found hard was *Classical Gas*. I didn't have time to memorize it, so I made a chord sheet for that and for the *Stars On Guitars* medley. We drove all the way to Pueblo, Colorado for the first gig. When we went on stage, it suddenly hit me that the very first notes that the crowd would hear would be *me* with the opening chords to *Walk-Don't Run*.

"As we wound our way through Colorado, Wyoming, Idaho, and Utah, some of the scheduled gigs were either cancelled or had failed to materialize. It occurred to me that with the expense of hotels, food, fueling the Winnebago, plus paying two roadies and myself, the whole outing might just break even. The four of us each had our own room every night, and I believe the two roadies shared one. I also surmised that some of the shows were in places where the exposure was of no value. This was after playing in an Elks Lodge somewhere, and another gig on a flatbed trailer at a rodeo in Lander, Wyoming. When I aired my thoughts, I was quickly shot down. I learned that big or small gigs, this is what The Ventures do. It later became apparent that [financially] the big shows made up for the small ones.

Dan Forte with Nokie   *Ramon Vega*

"This was my first time on the road, and I was excited to be doing it with The Ventures. I never thought they would be so enthusiastic, having done this for so many years, but Mel seemed just as pumped as I was about the tour. He had a great time on the road and he never got tired of thrilling people with his solo in *Caravan*. When we walked off the stage for Mel's solo at the Elk's Lodge show, I grabbed my camera and ran outside around the hall, came in through the front, and walked up past the seated audience. As Mel played on the strings of Bob's bass, I started taking pictures. That's when Greg, at his sound table near the front, looked at me and slowly shook his head. I got some great pictures, but I felt like such a greenhorn as I went back out, ran around to the side door and put on my Jazzmaster just in time to hit the stage.

"While traveling, I received a startling indoctrination from Mel. He kept a chart to determine who would drive the next hundred miles. On my third turn to drive, I was in the passenger's seat waiting for him to pull over and stop. Suddenly he said 'She's all yours, Dan!' and he got up and walked to the back. I couldn't believe what was happening. I leaped into the driver's seat and quickly got control of the wheel while we swerved a bit with the trailer in tow. They had a big laugh so I'm guessing they played that trick on all newcomers when they had the chance on a deserted highway. I didn't have to drive again due to another big embarrassment. After fueling up, while the Winnebago was getting up to speed, the car behind was catching up quickly. I floored the pedal and got going OK, but I heard Nokie cussing in the back. When I asked what had happened, I learned that he had just made a sandwich and poured a big glass of milk. His sandwich was all over the floor, and he, in his gray velour jacket, was covered in milk. I was already feeling bad when Greg came up and said 'Way to go, Dan. You're retired. Thanks to you, I have to drive two shifts!' Talk about humiliation!

"Our worst gig was likely the rodeo concert on that flatbed trailer. It was really hot and dry, and the cowboys were miserable because someone had forgotten to obtain the beer license. The bad part, though, was the sound. We were blasting straight into banks of wooden bleachers, and we were getting an echo as loud as our amps were putting out. The Ventures took it all in stride, having likely played under every imaginable condition, but this setup really threw me out of sync. Mel tried to help me by emphasizing the backbeat, but it just made the echo louder. So he yelled at me, 'If you can't hear me, watch me!' We laughed about it later, but I was pretty stressed at the time. With so much echo, I was even having a hard time with *Green Onions*, which was second nature to me. Flustered by then, I played the intro to *The Cruel Sea* so fast that it briefly stunned the others before they pulled it down to a reasonable tempo. I felt bad after that gig, but I felt redeemed after we went on to Crested Butte, Colorado. That was the best gig we had, although I was amazed at how small it was. I remember a huge buffalo head mounted on the wall, and Bob cracking us up with 'That buffalo must have been going pretty fast when he hit that wall.' The stage was *really* small, but they had conformed to The Ventures' contract and installed a drum riser for Mel. I stayed in the Winnebago until the last minute, waiting for the up-front money to arrive. Greg finally appeared with it, and we proceeded to this tiny stage. We were so close that we didn't need monitors. We could hear each really well, and everything just seemed to click.

"I never got tired of playing *Walk-Don't Run*. We played two shows in some places, and each one contained *Walk-Don't Run*, *Walk-Don't Run '64*, and the *Stars on Guitars* medley. This meant playing *Walk-Don't Run* six times, but it was just as exciting every time. Even now, it makes my hairs stand up when I hear it on the radio. To me it's one of the greatest records ever made. My last gig with the group was in San Francisco, and it was just great. We finally got to play a real showcase in front of a big crowd. We shared billing with the Chambers Brothers, which was also a great experience. I made sure my family and girlfriend were there for that one. By then we were playing well together -- but hey, I'm no Don Wilson. That short stint was really the pinnacle of my musical career.. to actually be part of The Ventures!"

Dan Forte soon returned to *Guitar Player* magazine, and it was then that he assumed a double identity; "I had recently written a couple of guitar articles for *Musician* magazine, so when *Guitar Player* commissioned an article from me, it was stipulated that I write under a pen name so they didn't appear to be copying from *Musician*, (even though they were)."

Subsequently, many *Guitar Player* issues presented articles by Dan Forte, as well as a zany "Off the Wall" guitar column by Teisco Del Rey, named after vintage Japanese guitars. In *Guitar Player*'s September 1996 "instrumental" issue, Dan cited The Ventures' *007-11* as one of the fifteen greatest moments in instrumental rock. As Teisco Del Rey, Dan wrote; "If there's such a thing as 'spy guitar,' this is it."

BURNING UP THE ROAD

Beginning in August, The Ventures toured from Tennessee to Virginia, Washington D.C. and the densely populated East Coast. The return path was through Louisiana and Texas to arrive in California by October. The plan was to stop in New York for the first few days in September to tape live concert footage for the Fraker-Rosenberg TV special. This meant that Don was touring again with Bob, Nokie, and Mel, plus road managers Greg Rowland and Chuck Churella. As usual, Don seized every opportunity to startle the audience with his talent for mimicry. His short quips in voices ranging from Lawrence Welk to forties western sidekick, George "Gabby" Hayes were as recognizable as they were hilarious. On August 26, after a late-night show at Kum's Nitery in Ithaca, New York, the group packed up and began an all-night trip to their next venue. The 250-mile drive took the group to a town in Maryland called California. Everyone was sleeping as Chuck Churella drove into Pennsylvania on Interstate 81. Suddenly, the motor home was full of smoke and fire. Chuck slowly brought the vehicle and heavy trailer to a stop while yelling at everyone to wake up. Bob Bogle recalls the horrifying experience; "It was about five in the morning and I was a little groggy, but I woke up fast when I saw the smoke. I was in the passenger's seat and although we were still moving, I opened my door and jumped out. Mel came off the bed over the cab and was right behind me. I couldn't believe how fast the flames were spreading. There wasn't time to put on shoes, so we were out on the road in our bare feet. Chuck finally got the outfit stopped and bailed out of the driver's door. Greg and Nokie were next, and by the time Don got out, he had to jump through really thick smoke. He landed on some rocks and I noticed him limping in pain. Then the propane tanks exploded and the whole vehicle was on fire. By the time Greg and Chuck disconnected the trailer and pushed it away, the motor home was engulfed in flames. We got the first car that came along to call 911, but by the time the fire truck arrived, the motor home was completely destroyed. All that the fire fighters could do was to call a tow truck for our trailer on their radio. We'd been stopped on the highway for almost two hours, and I started poking around the rubble while waiting for the tow truck. I was relieved as well as amazed when my little bag of personal items such as nail clippers and a little black book containing my telephone contacts turned up, a bit scorched on the edges but completely intact. An ambulance arrived, and when they saw Don's foot, they took him to a hospital."

A disaster of undetermined origin

Everyone lost clothing in the fire. It was all replaceable except for an item that Nokie lost; "The first couple of times that I tried to get up, someone jumped down from a bunk and landed on me. Don and I were the last ones out and we had to jump through smoke. It was pretty scary because flames were shooting up about fifty feet in the air. My hat got burned up and all the guitar pins just melted. That's one thing I really hated to lose. Some of the pins were real silver or gold. Anyway, people kept on giving me all kinds of pins. I got another hat and started putting the pins on it. I wore it until the late eighties and I still have it."

The ambulance took Don back across the border to a hospital in New York State. The tow truck followed later with the trailer behind and the rest of the group squeezed into the cab. They checked into a motel next to a mall, which was convenient, as they had lost all of their clothing, including shoes and their stage outfits. Also lost was a briefcase containing contracts and $5,000 from the last concert. Luckily, Bob had his wallet that contained a credit card. By the time they had breakfast, it was daylight on Saturday morning. After Mel cancelled the evening's concert at the Town Creek Marina in Maryland, the group purchased clothing at the mall. Then Bob rented two cars and a trailer hitch. When they picked up Don, his left foot was heavily bandaged due to a cracked heel. He was ordered to keep his weight off the foot for three months, and always walk with crutches.

When Don insisted he could play the Fraker-Rosenberg concert, it was back to the mall for more clothing, courtesy of Bob and his MasterCard. The band also contacted their insurance company, and learned that burned cash was only covered up to $500. The company sent an investigator to work with the fire inspector, but they were unable to determine the cause of the blaze.

It was early to bed on Saturday for The Ventures and their roadmen. On Sunday, the weary six headed for New York City to make a movie for television. After a restful night at midtown Manhattan's Milford Plaza Hotel, the project seemed more appealing.

WALK-DON'T RUN, THE MOVIE

Meeting with Fraker-Rosenberg Productions on Monday, The Ventures were taken to Studio Instrument Rentals on New York's West 25th Street. This company, also also rented rehearsal space. The reason for rehearsals became quickly apparent when The Ventures saw the list of musicians with whom they would share the stage. Along with some current acts, there were several former members of groups that were now part of rock 'n roll history. Among them were Peter Frampton and Chris Spedding from the UK, Jeff Baxter (Steely Dan, Doobie Brothers), Robbie Krieger (The Doors), David Johansen a.k.a. Buster Poindexter (New York Dolls), Rick Derringer (The McCoys), drummer Max Weinberg (Bruce Springsteen's E-Street Band before The Max Weinberg Seven on *Late Night With Conan O'Brien*), and New York City's retro-instro group, The Raybeats. Adding some glamour to the show, new wave singer Josie Cotton flew in from L.A. Known for her cover of the Go-Go's novelty single, *Johnny, Are You Queer,* Josie had recently performed in the Nicholas Cage movie, *Valley Girl.*

The performers were all splendid, but if anyone stole the show, it was Jeff Baxter with his colorful soloing in *Tequila* and his flashy pedal-steel work on *Sleepwalk.* Jeff's key change from C to D worked so well that The Ventures introduced another key change during Josie Cotton's rendition of *Secret Agent Man.* While some of the acts resorted to pretentious posturing, The Ventures appeared as always, genuinely relaxed while enjoying the contrived antics of their guests.

After rehearsing with The Ventures, each guest testified to the group's early influence on them. Tributes were also gathered from non participants including Gerry McGee, Elliot Easton (The Cars), Jeff Cook (Alabama), Mark and Joey Ramone (The Ramones) and the most surprising guest, jazz guitarist Al Dimeola. Musicians claiming Ventures influence, but who could not attend were John Geils (The J. Geils Band), Rick Neilson (Cheap Trick), and Marshall Crenshaw, who was later seen with his Ventures Model Mosrite in the Francis Ford Coppola movie, *Peggy Sue Got Married* [1986].

Although viewers of the special would not know that the band was wearing all new clothing, many noticed Don sitting on a stool for the entire production. This was unusual for Don, as he liked to move around and interact with the audience. Bob recalls the shoot; "We rehearsed for two whole days before shooting the entire performance in one day. The producers brought in an audience for atmosphere, and that made it a lot more fun. Every time we took a break, Mel would go and change his shirt. I'm not sure if he was sweating or just enjoying his new wardrobe. Don wore a black stocking stretched over the cast on his injured foot."

After taping the musical performances, the producers began adding and editing documentary material. Alabama, the most successful group in country music's history, was now at the peak of its career, forcing Jeff Cook's interview to be remotely recorded.

As president of the U.S.A. Fan Club, Mike Kuhn became involved; "The night we saw The Ventures at the Governor's Inn at Lake Hopatcong, Bob Bogle introduced me to two men who were excited about doing a special video about them. I made two trips to New York City in connection with the production. I had memorized three different lines to be taped, and two were featured on the video. On the second trip, I brought my daughter with me and John Fraker shot footage of my album covers and treated us to lunch."

Chris Spedding and Peter Frampton on the set with The Ventures

When the shooting was finished, Don flew home to let his foot heal while Bob Spalding flew out to finish the tour. However, as Bob Bogle recalls, the tour was cut short; "We were at Toad's Place at New Haven, Connecticut, and Mel could barely make it onto the stage. We played for awhile, but he couldn't carry on. The club manager was upset, but after everything that had happened, we didn't care. We got Mel on a plane for home, and we hit the highway. The next day, Fiona took Mel to the hospital, where he stayed for about two weeks recovering from pneumonia."

News of the special, then called *Walk-Don't Run*, reached the public in *Guitar World* and *Playboy*. For the next couple of years, American, UK, and Scandinavian fans watched their club bulletins in vain. Apparently, the costs had overrun the budget, followed by difficulty, as Aleks Rosenberg stated; "in finding the right distributor." After five years, Toshiba released the special as *The Ventures – 30th Anniversary Super Session* on VHS and LaserDisc, complete with Japanese subtitles.

PAUL WARREN

In the months that followed, J.D. Hoag, Bob Spalding, and Harvey Wicklund were invited to replace Don on the road, but the men were simply unable to get away from their work. Then, road manager Chuck Churella remembered a friend in Los Angeles, twenty-eight-year-old Paul Warren. Although Paul was a busy session guitarist, he was available to work with The Ventures until the end of the year.

At age twelve, Paul had cut his guitar-playing teeth on mid-sixties Ventures tunes. In the early seventies, he did session work in Detroit for the Temptations and Rare Earth before migrating to the West Coast. In Hollywood, two albums were released with Paul writing or co-writing many of the songs on which he also sang. Most recent was Paul's 1980 solo album, *One Of The Kids* [RSO RS-1-3076]. With his three-man backup group, Explorer, Paul played guitar and sang songs that he had written. Along with liner notes thanking Chuck Churella and others, the record came with an autographed photo of Paul on which he wrote, "The song 'A&R Man' is dedicated to all the unsigned bands playing the various club circuits. To those who have played for free and starved for the sake of what they believe is art, to you I say, Hats Off."

Paul Warren

Don fondly remembers Paul's talent; "He really did his homework to work with us. He played Bob's bass parts practically note-for-note on every song that we did, and like Jay Dee and Harvey, he could sing those Chuck Berry and Jerry Lee Lewis hits."

While the band toured, Don worked continued the quest for record distribution. Finally, in 1984, Canadian shoppers found the Tridex set on record racks through an agreement with A&M Records. However, this company sold the *Ventures Greatest Hits* in two separate albums subtitled *Volume One* and *Volume Two*.

Another deal involved wider of the *NASA 25* album, which had been only available in limited edition. In Baltimore, the investment firm, Award Masters Inc. had recently branched into the record business. With Hollywood's Allegiance Records handling distribution, a five-year contract for one album per year was signed with The Ventures.

After Award re-issued *NASA 25*, they released a unique twelve-inch Ventures EP. For this recording, Indigo Ranch, a fantastic studio located faraway in the Malibu hills was selected. Formerly owned by actor John Barrymore, the fifty-eight-acre hunting lodge was bought by the Moody Blues in 1974 and converted for recording. Subsequently, Moody Blues crewmember Richard Kaplan maintained the operation, outfitting the Indigo Ranch with tons of the best analog equipment available.

The Ventures' EP project was for two tracks each of *Telstar* and *Out of Limits* (four-minute "radio" versions and "dance-club" versions lasting roughly twice as long). *Out of Limits* had not appeared on the NASA album, and for this project, Leisha sang lyrics with doctored sound suggesting a visitor from outer space. Electronic keyboards were handled by Dave Carr and programming wizard Jamie Sheriff, with Mel having a great deal of fun on synthesizer drum pads while Paul Warren added some heavy guitar.

Although this clear-vinyl gem [Award EVP 8401] is the only documented Ventures project at the Indigo Ranch, Richard Kaplan thinks there were more; "I worked on several Ventures records at Indigo Ranch. It seems there were four Ventures projects from the period surrounding the *NASA* album. I don't have the records, as I lost all my possessions in a Malibu home fire. I also did the sound for The Ventures at a few Southern California concerts. I still have an Award Records butane lighter that Mel Taylor gave me at one of the sessions."

After working with The Ventures, Leisha Soukary sang for a few months with a band called Z Factor. Later, she appeared in a 1988 movie from Moonstone Pictures called *Emperor of the Bronx*. As the leading actress, Leisha was the best part of this B rated gangster picture as she fronted a club band called American Dream. Billed as Leisha "Sukary," five more titles were added to her songwriting credits.

Later on, Leisha became skilled in the art of spiritual mind treatment. On October 5, 2006 she passed away while interning as a Religious Science Practitioner near Palm Springs, California.

~ ~ ~

With Paul Warren on rhythm guitar, The Ventures wound their way to the East Coast in the fall of '83. As Bob recalls, their next motor home remained reliable up to November, but it was not immune to human attack; "We had played the night before at Deep Creek Lake [Maryland] in a hall that seemed full of lumberjacks wearing plaid shirts. It was Thanksgiving Day and we were on our way to Worcester, about forty miles west of Boston for our next job. We were down the road apiece when we noticed the engine overheating. Stopping and lifting the hood, we found several holes in the radiator that looked like they had been punched with a tire iron. We figured that the damage must have been done by a fellow at the hall who was drinking quite a lot and got upset with us when his woman paid more attention to us than she did to him. There was quite a bit of drinking water in our tank, so we kept stopping and filling the radiator until we ran out. We were stopped and looking for some water to fill our pail when another band on its way to Deep Creek stopped to see if we needed help. The drummer said he was a big Ventures fan and knew all of our songs, and then he helped us to find a store down the road that sold a product called *Stop Leak*. When we parted, he gave us his card and said to call him if we ever needed a drummer. We found the place, but the *Stop Leak* didn't work because the holes were too big. We limped into the next town and asked a waitress if there was a hotel we could stay in until we got get the motor home fixed. She said that her husband was a mechanic and could likely help us out right away. We were astounded that the fellow would work on Thanksgiving Day, but he got us fixed up and we headed down the road."

The drummer that stopped to help was Keith John, whose top-forty group was based in the Washington, D.C. area. He talked with Mel long enough to find out that they had a mutual friend in Hollywood's premier session drummer, Hal Blaine. Keith had offered his musical services to The Ventures, but he never expected to get a call from them.

MORE FIRE

Fifteen years after The Ventures stopped playing Mosrite guitars, fans worldwide still held the instrument in high regard. In Japan, album covers and tour books still carried images of the Mosrite, and demand for the guitar remained high as nostalgia gripped grownups that had been Ventures worshippers since their teens.

Three months after fire destroyed The Ventures' motor home, a guitar factory fashioned from an abandoned schoolhouse in North Carolina was reduced to ashes. Inside were nearly 700 Mosrite guitars in various stages of completion. In 1981, after meeting and getting married in less than twenty-four hours, Semie and Loretta Moseley had moved to Loretta's North Carolina home of Jonas Ridge, where they acquired an old schoolhouse to be converted to a Gospel auditorium. During the renovations, Semie was invited him to oversee the making of 500 guitars in Japan, but having extra space in the schoolhouse, he opted to start a factory there. Then, while driving to collect his $50,000 advance payment, he fell asleep. The car rolled several times, severing Semie's left leg. Surgeons reattached the limb, but three months in hospital, complicated with Crohn's disease stalled guitar production for another two years while the Japan order grew to 700 guitars. Still in a wheelchair, Semie went further into debt to equip his factory. Then, on November 22, 1983, shortly after the first six Mosrites were shipped, fire broke out and burned everything in the shop and the adjacent paint-spray booth. Loretta saved a few unfinished guitars, but being overcome by smoke, it was her turn to spend time in a hospital. The press was quick to declare this as the end of Mosrite, but as Tony Hunt recalls, there was one building that did not burn; "The only building left standing after Semie's fire was the school cafeteria. He slept upstairs and the factory was downstairs. I had worked with Semie ever since he was in Jonas Ridge. He would call for help and I would come a-running. I grew up in North Carolina, so the first time that he called, I knew exactly where to go. With all of the fumes and dust in the place, I'm surprised he lived as long as he did. It was terrible!

"Semie was one of the most unusual men I had ever met. I think the Brass Rail guitar was the best thing he ever came up with, but his *real* genius was in mass-producing hand-built guitars. He had a bit of an ego, but we got along great because I knew when to keep my mouth shut. We would work late into the night after everyone else had gone home. We had the best times then, laughing and telling jokes. Like a lot of geniuses, Semie was not a good businessman. His intentions were always honorable, never ever meaning to stiff anybody, but unfortunately, there were times throughout his life when he did. Semie had spooks that would visit him in the night, and the bills constantly followed him. I reckon the first time his ego became apparent was in the early sixties when he noticed that The Ventures' logo was bigger than the Mosrite logo. It bothered him enough to have The Ventures silkscreen reduced in size by thirty percent."

MOGUL BITES BOGLE

Near the end of 1983, there were Ventures fan clubs in the America, Sweden, Germany, and Japan. Davy Peckett announced new recordings in his UK publication, but it was nothing like his previous all-Ventures bulletin. However, there was a Thames Valley policeman in the UK who refused to watch a dedicated Ventures club vanish from existence. A staunch fan and collector, Gerald Woodage started an all-new *Ventures Resurgence* booklet. In a few years, he and friend Maurice Preece attracted members all over the globe. Quality steadily improved, as did Gerry's service, providing members with Ventures news, recordings from Japan, and souvenir merchandise.

Gerry "The Creeper" Woodage

1984 began with The Ventures having some time for rest and relaxation, broken only by a booking on the first Saturday in February at North Hollywood's Palomino club. The month-long lull in touring gave Bob a chance for some skiing fun on Mount Hood, about forty miles east of Portland. Although the course he chose was not a "mogul run," it had some mounds of snow and ice that were formed unintentionally. When Bob hit one of these, he fell and cracked three ribs on his left side. He was not disabled for long, but he missed some gigs in February and March, including a date in Walla Walla, Washington, and a special weekend in Oklahoma City. As Paul Warren was unavailable until March, Mr. Gary Woods was hired s for the February gigs. Having grown up with Ventures music, Gary had played for years in his own Los Angeles band. Of Gary, Don says; "Gary was another musician that could play great lead or bass and more. He blew us away one time when we walked into a hall that had a piano. He just sat down and played the hell out of it. He was a wonderful musician, but like so many, he found it hard to make enough money at it. He got into the movie business as a soundman, and that became his career. Fortunately, he was available for as long as we wanted him, and eventually we needed him for over a year."

Mel, Nokie, and Don with Gary Woods

Although trumpeter-bandleader, Doc Severinsen was the Pops conductor for Arizona's Phoenix Symphony Orchestra, he also owned Doc Severinsen's Music and Sports Showplace in Oklahoma City. Award Records videotaped a Ventures evening at Severinsen's Club in March, to be sold later through their Baltimore office. With endless delays in Fraker-Rosenberg project, fans would have happily embraced this video, even though Paul Warren played bass in place of Bob Bogle. Of course, with Bob missing from the line-up, The Ventures disallowed the video's release. A copy was leaked, however, and by the end of summer, many fans had a poor quality copy-of-a-copy. It was a surprise to see Nokie with his "sanded down" Telecaster again, a temporary measure until he received his third Tony Hunt guitar. The big surprise regarding this concert came twenty years later when it appeared for sale on eBay.com as a budget priced DVD from Europe, then from Korea, and later, China.

The spring tour saw the band in Washington, Montana, and Minnesota, circling back to California in April for three days at Knott's Berry Farm in Buena Park. This gave Award Records an opportunity to corner the guys for taping a video to promote the re-issued *NASA 25* album. Meeting with Dave Carr in Hollywood's Conway Studios, The

Ventures donned matching "space suit" athletic-wear for a campy quarter hour miming to their recordings of *Theme From 2001*, *Sally*, and *Telstar*. Although NASA space mission footage was added later, the guys did not take themselves too seriously. With Nokie retaining his cowboy hat and boots as part of his "space suit," more hi-jinks followed, including Bob mouthing "Hi Mom" into the camera.

The rest of 1984 was looking to be uneventful (except for a month in Japan after missing a year) when Norwood Homes contracted a property-development in Portland, forcing Bob to leave for most of the summer. This made it imperative that Don return to the road. As Paul Warren could no longer spare the time, Gary Woods was brought in again to play bass, a job he would retain through the spring of 1985. Bob still planned to go on Japan tour '84, but when he learned it was for only three weeks, he bowed out in favor of appointing Gerry McGee, who had recently accompanied Sonny Rivera and Paul Warren to a Ventures night at the Palomino. Gerry was not fond of playing bass, but he loved Japan and the pay was good. During rehearsals, Gerry and Nokie arranged several acoustic guitar duets. When fans in Japan asked why Bob was not with the group, Mel remembered Bob's accident on Mount Hood and replied; "Oh, Bob was hurt in a skiing accident." While it was not completely true, it simplified trying to explain Bob's absence. However, the rumor finally spread to the fan club bulletins.

In Japan, the world's first Ventures compact disc had been released in February. The album chosen by Toshiba/EMI was *Surfin' Deluxe* [CP35-3085], a 1981 vinyl compilation from 1981. Reproduction was incredible to anyone hearing a CD for the first time. The jacket of the album still gave homage to Mosrite, as did the ten-page CD booklet written in Japanese. Unfortunately, it would be another three years before North Americans would experience The Ventures on compact disc.

The highlight for Japan Tour '84 was Nokie and Gerry's acoustic set. The two lead guitarists entertained alone for nearly half an hour with eye-popping finger work on *Joy*, *Yesterday*, *Walk Right In*, and *Classical Gas*. Another highlight saw Nokie and Gerry trade places for six numbers. Most fans knew that Nokie had played bass in the past, but to see this in 1984 was a rare event indeed. This unique combination of The Ventures was taped for LaserDisc and videocassette. Unfortunately, the hour-long video omitted three of the Nokie-Gerry duets, one of Don's vocals, Gerry's sitar work, and the band's *Stars on Guitars* medley. As Bob was absent from this tour, the video's title *Original Member* seemed rather peculiar to avid Ventures fans.

Upon returning to America, The Ventures kept right on touring. As they headed east, Gary Woods again replaced Bob, who was still occupied with the construction project. While media reviewers praised the band's fresh sound and endless energy, fans raved in club letters about the group's generosity and openness to concertgoers. Most stops on the tour included time for autographs and chatting with enthusiastic fans. Three of the bookings were weeklong stops, first in Canada for two shows a night at Lulu's Roadhouse in Kitchener, Ontario. Next was Cajun's Wharf in Nashville Tennessee with *three* nightly shows, followed by six nights at Cajun's Wharf in Little Rock, Arkansas.

In Nashville, several celebrities dropped in to hear The Ventures. Billy Strange came in one night, and on another, David Frizzell and Shelley West came to see Nokie. One October afternoon, Don heard a knock on his hotel door; "We had played in Nashville for three or four nights when Nokie came to my room to announce that he was joining up with David Frizzell. He said he was tired of playing the songs we were doing, and he was going back to playing country. I begged him not to do it because I figured it wouldn't last. I've always had a real fondness for Nokie and I would always try to help him any way I could. I almost cried when he said he'd made up his mind already, because whenever he sets his mind to do something, he's gonna do it. I tried offering all kinds of concessions, but whatever I offered, he just said 'Nope'."

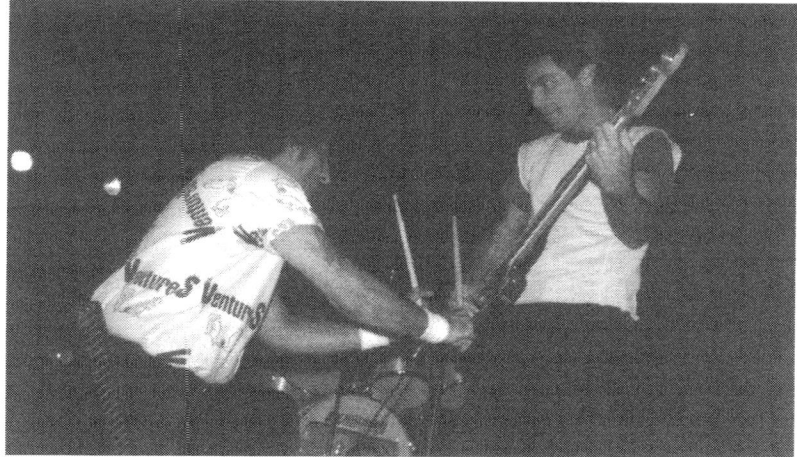

Mel and Gary Woods at Lulu's Roadhouse – Kitchener, Ontario

The warnings had been there, but no one had recognized them. For over a year, while packing up after a show, Nokie was heard to exclaim "What a hell of a way to make a living!" It occurred like clockwork, but everyone thought he was joking. After breaking the news to Don, Nokie finished the tour before taking up residence in Nashville.

With country music background, it seemed Nokie had attained a lifelong goal. He worked with David Frizzell and Shelley West for almost a year before striking out on his own once more. Although this was the end of his epoch as an official member of The Ventures, in time he would return as a "special guest" to record and tour with them.

~ ~ ~

Returning to California, The Ventures stopped taking tour dates for the New Year, but when local nightspots beckoned, Bob Spalding filled the void. Fans expecting to see Nokie and Bob Bogle were surprised to see Gary Woods or Bob Spalding on the stage. Meanwhile, Don and Mel put out a call for Gerry McGee.

Since recording with Tanya Tucker, Rosanne Cash, and *The Dukes of Hazard*'s John Schneider, studio work had been less demanding for Gerry McGee, allowing him time for more screen acting. After signing with a casting agent, he played small parts in TV episodes such as the CBS adventure series, *Simon and Simon*, as well as the full-length MGM film, *Fever Pitch*. This movie starred Ryan O'Neal in the roll of a compulsive gambler. When the screenplay called for a woeful prisoner with an old guitar, Gerry strummed *Red River Valley* while gazing through the bars of a large holding cell.

Hearing that 1985 would be The Ventures' Silver Anniversary, and that Toshiba Records was interested in new material, Gerry heartily agreed to return to the band. By mid-December, he was on stage with The Ventures at the Palomino Club, and for the first time, "Jerry" was signing his autograph as "Gerry." Up to this point, "Jerry" had appeared on everything carrying his name, including four single records, his *Dynamite Guitar Licks* book, and a dozen U.S. Ventures albums. Finally, Gerry explains; "I just decided to start insisting on my name being spelled right. I had been letting it go as 'Jerry' for too long, and if the Screen Actor's Guild could get it right, so could the music business. My fifth single had it right, but that was the only one." [*Moonlight Surfin* b/w *Cajun Guitar* - A&M 771]

Another reason for setting the name straight was to avoid confusion with the *real* Jerry McGee. This short, bald, and bespectacled actor was being seen in horror flicks with titles like *Bloodrage* and *The Burning*.

What began as a promising alliance between The Ventures and Award Records was now a thing of the past. Whatever the reasons, Award completely missed the opportunity to promote The Ventures' album when NASA celebrated its 25th anniversary on national television with Bob Hope. When The Ventures exercised their option to terminate after one year, Award Records evaporated almost immediately.

When news of Nokie's departure reached the fans, feelings were mixed. Speculation varied from this being the end of The Ventures to predictions that it was the beginning of a new era. The fact that Nokie had recently started his own fan club led to speculation that he might have been on the verge of leaving The Ventures anyway. While Nokie would be missed, fans were relieved that Gerry would again fill the position, and that the band would be intact for its Silver Anniversary.

VENTURE 25

The Ventures began 1985 with a huge spring tour and some new recordings to celebrate their 25th Anniversary. First and foremost was *Venture 25*, a smooth guitar medley combining *Wipe Out*, *Walk-Don't Run*, *Pipeline*, and *Hawaii Five-O*. The single was pressed on clear vinyl, but even more special was hearing Bob' Bogle on lead guitar for the first time since 1977. The flip side carried Bob Spalding's tasty new instrumental, *Blue Dawn* [Tridex 502].

Meanwhile, Toshiba Records was requesting eight new tunes for a special album to commemorate the Band's upcoming anniversary. Japanese lyrics would then be composed for use by local pop stars. By the time The Ventures hit the road, eight tunes with Gerry on lead guitar were in the hands of music director, Leo Sato. Although Bob Bogle managed time to record, he returned to Oregon when the sessions were over. Then, after completing some regional dates in March and April, The Ventures began their extensive spring tour on May 1, covering sixteen states in less than eleven weeks.

To avoid disputes with club owners, a new promotional photo showed Gary Woods in place of Bob. Copies were sent to the venues, as well as sold on the road beside the *Venture 25* single and other souvenir merchandise. Daily concerts in different cities allowed days off only when the traveling distance approached 1000 miles. Many of the band's Japan tours were just as long, but here, there were no comfortable busses or speedy bullet trains, and no pampering road crew.

The tour consisted mostly of fundraising events for benevolent clubs and societies throughout the country, placing the concerts in arenas, gymnasiums, or civic centers. Local bands in each city were invited to open for The Ventures, who followed on stage using the same sound system. A different system in each venue, usually with abysmal acoustics, contributed to the band's hardships. It was here that Mel and Don vowed to remedy this situation before the next tour.

After ninety days on the road, the group pulled into Los Angeles for some well-deserved rest. It was mid-July and they had also been invited to perform on Dick Clark's *Rock and Roll Summer Action*, hosted by actor Christopher Atkins (*The Blue Lagoon* - 1980). The Fender equipped band was shown before a live crowd on a windy Malibu beach, but when the show aired in August, close inspection revealed that Clark's policy on live broadcasting had not changed in twenty-five years. The guitars were unplugged as the group pantomimed their *Venture 25* medley with Gary Woods on bass and Gerry McGee on lead. Fans in the know thought it strange to hear Bob's familiar guitar style emanating from Gerry McGee. The TV taping was the end of the line for Gary Woods, as Bob was ready to rejoin the band. When September arrived, a tour schedule was ready that covered several of the states they had missed, and Bob returned to the road with a new (and very different) bass guitar.

Gerry behind Mel, Gary Woods, and Don   1985

Almost one year earlier, The Ventures had received a twenty-fifth anniversary gift of three guitars and a bass from the Tokyo Sound Company. Bearing The Ventures' logo and fourteen karat gold-plated hardware, they were specially crafted Guyatone instruments. The radically shaped guitars were identical to those used by a talented Ventures-inspired band that had enjoyed popularity in Japan for two decades...... Munetaka Inoue and his Sharp Five.

The tri-pickup guitars were finished in candy-apple red, pearl-white, and metallic-silver (Mel's guitar). The bass, fashioned from a single piece of wood, displayed a rich sunburst finish. In Japan, Don played the red guitar at several concerts following the presentation, and the instruments were then taken home. Now, back from his Norwood Homes project, Bob used his Sharp Five bass on tour in North America. It was not long before a Japanese visitor offered $15,000 for one of the guitars, but none of the instruments were for sale.

One of this group's albums is titled "Sharp Five Plays The Ventures"

THUNDER ROAD

While planning the fall tour, Don had found an engineer to conquer the band's sound problems. Coming highly recommended, Rick Darby agreed to furnish sound and lighting equipment and travel with road manager Bobby Ward as his assistant. As Don recalls, they had a four-day booking with Roy Orbison at the Club Casino in Hampton, New Hampshire; "I was excited about that show because I wanted to meet Roy Orbison. It never happened though, because he was in and out so fast you would think he was Elvis or the American President. In fact, it was *easier* to see Elvis! One time in Las Vegas I walked into the Hilton casino at around 5:00 a.m. and there he was playing a slot machine. I lived in the same hotel as Orbison for four days and never saw him once."

Touring from May into late August had taken a toll on Mel, now three weeks away from his 52nd birthday and less than one week from another ninety-day tour that would go until Christmas. As Fiona aptly observed; "Like almost everyone else at some point in the eighties, Mel got burned out on touring. He just needed a few months off."

There were not many standby drummers around, but Mel kept track of his connections. Keith John, the drummer that had helped when their motor coach had a leaking radiator in Maryland, tells the story; "I had been playing with the Starland Vocal Band [*Afternoon Delight*] and backing John Denver when I decided to move out West. Having become friends with Hal Blaine in 1983, I contacted him after my arrival, and was invited to the *We Are The World* session. That day, it seemed like I met everyone in the music business. Months later I got a call from Mel Taylor who had been talking to Hal, and Hal referred him to me. When Mel asked if I'd like to drum for The Ventures, I went 'Yow!! Are you serious?' Your songs were the first ones I ever learned! To actually play them with The Ventures would be a terrific honor! Mel told me when and where to meet them, and I drove to this rather dingy old rehearsal hall in Studio City. I set up my drums and we ran through several songs. I got a surprise when I had to play a tattoo on Bob's bass like Gene Krupa had done on *Big Noise From Winnetka*. I had played that technique before, but I wasn't used to the angle, as Bob played an electric bass.

Sometimes I missed the string and hit the body. That's when I realized why Bob used an old, beat up bass for *Caravan*. Just when I thought I was doing fairly well, they said, 'OK, now we're going to try *Wipe Out!* During my younger years, that song was requested so much that I had grown to hate it. I remembered it however, and when we were finished, the guys said to me, 'You just passed the audition and you are going to get a standing ovation every night for doing that number.' Then Don handed me a tape, saying 'Listen to these songs as much as you can, because we're leaving *tomorrow* to start a national tour.' I listened to that tape all across the United States and I made charts for the harder tunes. When I wasn't doing that, I just enjoyed being part of the group. We traded jokes from Burbank to Albuquerque before I could think of one they hadn't heard. Meanwhile, they kept me laughing for hours. As Mel was the kingpin, I really felt that I had some big shoes to fill. I had to uphold the honor of this great band, and although I took it very seriously, it was the most fun I have ever had drumming. The music that The Ventures play gives the drums a chance to thunder!

Bobby Vee and The Ventures with Keith John - Des Moines 9/27/85 *press*

"About two weeks into the tour, we played two nights on the same bill with Bobby Vee. It was sort of a reunion between Bobby and the two original Ventures, as they reminisced about touring together some twenty years back.

The road isn't for everyone. You have to be tough. We'd play every night, sometimes twice, and then travel all night and the next morning to the next town, play one or two shows, get back in the motor home and head for the next stop. I didn't really mind the grind, because The Ventures were seasoned pros and Bobby Ward was the best road manager that I had worked with in thirty-some years of touring. From mid-November to Christmas we did about five nights in Montana and ten in Texas. As we headed for home, we hit strong winds in California. From Needles to Burbank, pieces of aluminum were flying off the motor home into the desert. Anxious to get home, Don said 'Just keep going!' We were all drained, but for me, it was the end of a wonderful adventure."

Keith continued touring and recording with many different groups, including sessions with Kiss and the reincarnated Buffalo Springfield (Neil Young and Stephen Stills) before returning to the D.C. area where work was just as abundant. One admired group he worked with was called Honky Tonk Confidential, but Keith's tenure with them was short-lived, finding that western swing did not give his drums enough opportunity to "thunder."

DISSENSION IN THE RANKS

By late '85, the fan clubs buzzed with the news of Gerry's return. As some members lamented Nokie's leaving, others welcomed Gerry's style and stage presence as a breath of fresh air. Debates on the subject (never conclusive, but always interesting) have recurred in fan clubs and chat groups ever since.

The band's Silver Anniversary had been celebrated with fans at roughly 150 shows on American soil, billed as "25 Years of Rock and Roll with The Ventures." Leo Sato's album with Japanese lyrics set to the band's original melodies never developed. In fact, *Venture 25* was the beginning of a four-year drought for newly recorded material. Fans would, however, eventually enjoy unpublished tracks from the "Biff Vincent" sessions.

Gerry, Bob, and Don at the Club Casino – Hampton, NH   *R. D. Moore*

The year ended on a sad note for musicians and pop music fans in America. Rick Nelson died on December 31, en route from Alabama to a New Year's Eve show in Texas when his chartered plane crashed 130 miles short of its destination. The Ventures had only covered one hit from Rick's twenty-seven-year career [*Lonesome Town* - 1959], but as Gerry reflected, he had known Rick since 1958; "Actually, I was almost on that flight with the Stone Canyon Band. Rick's bassist got me to tour with them when their guitarist was unavailable. We toured the Midwestern States in a private plane, and I never felt comfortable in that thing. Who knows? If Bobby Neal hadn't come back on lead guitar, I might not be here today."

For The Ventures, 1986 began on a more positive note, when Nashville's Compleat Entertainment Corporation agreed to re-master, press, and market *The Ventures Greatest Hits* on double vinyl, double cassette, and 8-track cartridge. Specializing in "best of" sets for nostalgia groups ranging from Bachman Turner Overdrive to Mr. Acker Bilk, the company deemed The Ventures an excellent candidate for its *Compleat Collection Series*, except for one hitch. Knowing *Hawaii Five-0* to be the band's most recent and best-known hit in America, the company wanted this tune in the package. Although *Hawaii Five-0* had been omitted from Biff Vincent's garage sessions to avoid the expensive orchestral enhancement, it did not take long to record a new version featuring synthesized orchestral backing. Bob recalls how; "Dave Carr could do just about anything on the new keyboards. He played all the orchestra parts except for percussion. Synthetic timpani just didn't sound right, so we had someone play real ones on another track. To sound right, they have to be in tune with the song."

END OF AN ERA

After twenty-five years of dedicated work for The Ventures, Sonny Rivera was fifty-five and ready to retire. It was a sad time for the band, but not so sad for Josie; "In 1971, not long after I had moved back to Tacoma, the Riveras came to visit me, greatly enjoying the novelty of snow from a recent storm. In 1986, after Sonny closed her Ventures' office, the family decided to move here, just a few doors away from me. In their retirement, Sonny and Ray anticipated doing a lot of traveling, but it wasn't long before tragedy struck. Soon after the move, Ray became ill and passed away. For several years, Sonny worked for the school system here before retiring to Florida, not far from her mother and sister in Puerto Rico."

When Sonny left Burbank, Mel handled even more of The Ventures' business affairs. As Sonny had done, Mel set up a home office with Fiona becoming increasingly involved. At the same time, Bob became a partner in a home-remodeling enterprise in Portland known as Bogle and Donovan Construction. As the firm was less demanding than Norwood Homes, Bob didn't miss any more Ventures dates, even though he had also formed a real-estate company with his brother.

As the band began a tour that would last through the summer of 1986, April 26 became a memorable date in Ventures lore when Leon Taylor, then thirty, sat in on drums at the Palomino Club where father Mel had first sat in with the group. During *Green Onions* with Leon on drums, Mel added fills on the floor-tom. It was instantly obvious that in addition to his Iron Butterfly, Kansas, and Styx collections, Leon had spent plenty of time listening to recordings of The Ventures.

LIFE IS A BEACH

As Don had predicted, Nokie's tenure with David Frizzell did not last long. Nokie then turned to Japan, where he was still a popular attraction. Takeshi Terauchi, who had attained stardom with his black Mosrite guitar, invited Nokie to collaborate on an album and video with a follow-up tour. As Nokie had tried to re-invent himself, he found it impossible to avoid the demand for Ventures' music. His part in the Terauchi production comprised seven Ventures hits including *Walk-Don't Run*, *Slaughter on Tenth Avenue*, and *Caravan*. After this, Nokie paced regular visits to Tokyo with new solo albums (and a second set with Terauchi).

In America, The Ventures with Gerry McGee played two shows nightly along the West Coast and inland northwest states. Highlights of the tour included the Evergreen Ballroom near Olympia, Washington, which had featured The Ventures in 1960. In keeping with the nostalgia theme, several venues featured The Ventures with other sixties acts like Paul Revere and Flash Cadillac. The best of these was the *Surf City USA* spectacular on June 26 at the Great Western Forum in Los Angeles. Here, in front of 10,000 happy surf music fans, The Ventures shared billing with Jan & Dean, the Chantays, the Surfaris, and Dick Dale.

Mid-July found the group in the middle of the desert for a full week. Cactus Pete's Resort Casino in Jackpot, Nevada (fast becoming competitive with many Las Vegas casinos), provided The Ventures with easy work and luxurious accommodation for seven days. However, the next stop was in Las Vegas, and as Bob recalls, it was not as much fun as in Jackpot; "We had been booked for some kind of computer convention at Bally's Hotel and Casino. We set up and played at the poolside, and it was embarrassing because there wasn't anyone that knew who we were. As far as those young computer guys were concerned, we were just background noise. We really hated that job."

The Ventures at the Great Western Forum in Los Angeles - June 26, 1986

A few days later, The Ventures played one of the most bizarre venues of their career. Major League Rodeo producer Steve Gander had put Williamsburg, Iowa on the map with *The World's Toughest Rodeo*. Known for going 'all out' with his ideas, Steve spent three months preparing "The World's Biggest Beach Party." With no beach within hundreds of miles, he trucked in over 1,000 cubic yards of sand while paying $40,000 in advance for entertainment. Along with The Ventures, Gander booked Jan and Dean, Gary Lewis and The Playboys, Johnny Tillotson, and Tommy Roe for a two-day extravaganza. When the weekend arrived, so did music lovers with swimsuits, beach blankets, and umbrellas. Besides the music, contests were held for the best bikinis on the girls and the worst looking legs on the guys. Amid hundreds of sunbathers, surfers struggled to balance on battery powered, wheel-equipped surfboards. The scene was a major distraction to traffic on Interstate 80, as drivers gazed in disbelief at the sight of a beach in the middle of the prairie.

The end of July found The Ventures in Northern California for an engagement in Grass Valley, about seventy miles west of Reno. Ventures fan Joe Tate was a patron that night, and tells of a rumor in circulation; "The show was at the Holiday Cabaret, and when we saw Gerry McGee, we wondered aloud about Nokie. Then someone said that he was killed in Vietnam! The Ventures sounded wonderful, and it was a great night if not for that terrible news. After the show, I got to meet the band and ask questions, but I didn't have the nerve to ask about Nokie. Later, when I learned of the band's U.S. comeback some six years back, I was glad that I hadn't embarrassed myself by asking if Nokie had died in Vietnam. I was relieved and happy to find out that he was still playing, even if he was out on his own."

Heading back west, The Ventures spent the first weekend in August on the shores of a *genuine* lake in Northern California. It was a job that Don remembers; "We had a two-night booking at the Silverthorne Resort near Redding on the shore of Lake Shasta. The place was just beautiful and they gave us a houseboat to take out on the lake. We were amazed that it had a refrigerator, gas range, washer and dryer, and such comfortable furnishings that it was like a first-class hotel suite." Bob adds; "As the resort was owned by Merle Haggard, we were hoping to meet him. We also hoped for a reunion with Don Markham, whom was part of Merle's band, but they were out on tour when we arrived. Markham's wife Wanda was there and we talked with her a couple of times. Don, Mel, and the roadies stayed at a motel in Redding, about fifteen minutes away, but Gerry and I stayed right on the houseboat."

Two weeks later found The Ventures in cooler surroundings at Vancouver, British Columbia, where the World's Fair ran from May to October. "Expo '86" hosted the highest attendance record for an event in its category since New York's fair in 1939. This time, The Ventures were one of the *Legends of Rock 'n Roll* along with Paul Revere's Raiders and Merrilee Rush. Acts appearing on other days included Chuck Berry, Fabian, Frankie Avalon, Bobby Rydell, Roy Orbison, Jerry Lee Lewis, Ray Charles, and Fats Domino, along with Canada's Bobby Curtola and The Guess Who.

The Ventures at Expo '86 – Vancouver, B.C. *Jim Harrison*

Thinking back, Josie recalls her part in arranging the band's attendance; "When I heard about Expo '86 to be held in Vancouver Canada, and that a rock 'n' roll revival show was planned, my wheels began turning at once. It had been years since I was active in the music industry, but I always watched for an opportunity for The Ventures. Consequently, I wrote to the program director, saying that I felt they would be a tremendous draw for the Exposition, and I included their management office address. When a contract was signed, I happily made plans to attend. As I had predicted, The Ventures proceeded to captivate each sold-out crowd amid thunderous applause."

VENTURING IN METAL

Touring completed, and with nothing planned for Japan, the band looked for ways to sustain itself. It was a time when music video was making giant strides. As Dire Straits droned; "I want my MTV" in their gigantic hit, *Money For Nothing*, Bob Bogle presented an idea. It did not turn out as planned, but as he recalls; "Actually, the idea came from Dave Callaham, and I liked it. It involved compiling footage of accidental wipeouts ranging from racecar wrecks to spills in sporting events like skiing and surfing. They would be shown while we played an extended version of *Wipe Out*. I figured there must be thousands of these things available once we located a source. Everyone thought it was a great idea, but then, it went terribly wrong. Somehow, the project evolved into us donning ridiculous looking costumes with makeup and colored wigs to emulate a Heavy Metal band. I was really disappointed, did not want to be involved."

Gerry McGee had similar feelings; "I couldn't really get into the video because I felt the same as Bob. For the second time, I was like the 'new guy' so I went along with it, but I was disappointed when it became a Heavy Metal clown act."

Enzo Giobbé was Don's future son-in-law and a professional director of photography. Scripting the entire production, Enzo ably cast Lauri Kristian as the "blonde bombshell," with The Ventures and Rodney Bingenheimer (as the car driver) rounding out the cast. Enzo was also able to pick up a camera crew to work for little more than expenses.

Enzo Giobbé [Gerry McGee in background]   *Staci L. Wilson*

Most of the scenes were shot in Don's home or backyard, flashing between pie-in-the-face comedy routines, constant pursuit of the blonde bombshell, and an appearance of the great white "Jaws." The production centered on a pantomimed spoof depicting a zany Heavy Metal punk performance of *Wipe Out*.

Although Paul Warren was a busy session guitarist, he obligingly took time to play the wailing lead guitar for this modern version of the surf hit, and when Bob opted out, Paul played the scary looking bassist. Mel appeared with his Slingerland drums, while Gerry and Don brandished their 25th Anniversary "Sharp Five" guitars.

Eventually, Bob participated; "When it was almost finished, they asked me to do one shot with them to complete the cast credit to The Ventures. I agreed, but only if I didn't have to dress like a member of Kiss. They said 'Just go in and open a guitar case and beckon Don to look inside.' Of course, he got smacked in the face with another vanilla cream pie. That was it for me. I still think it was a waste of what could have been a huge commercial success." Bob was right, as programs closely employing his concept appeared on network television sometime later.

Nearly a year had passed before editing was completed. In spring of 1987, The Ventures' *Wipe Out* video was submitted to MTV in New York. After several weeks, a reply was received rejecting the work. Reasons were not given, but upon inquiring, Mel was told that MTV took its Heavy Metal acts seriously enough to shy away from a video making fun of them. By this time, the decade's surf revival had spawned several versions of *Wipe Out* that included an early "Rap" trio known as The Fat Boys. With Paul Warren's screaming metal lead at the fore of their new version, The Ventures envisioned another outlet for the track, but it never happened. By the time their scheduled touring was over, there were more versions of *Wipe Out* around than the market could handle, and *Wipe Out '87* was shelved.

THE COMPACT VENTURES

Compact discs and the hardware to play them were still quite expensive in 1986, and many people (remembering the fate of eight-track tapes) doubted that the small, shiny disc would replace the long-play vinyl medium. Mostly baby-boomers, North American Ventures fans had no plans to replace large vinyl collections with the latest audio fad, but in 1987, the changeover began when EMI released *The Best of The Ventures*, comprising fifteen of the band's top sixties recordings that included live performances of *Slaughter On Tenth Avenue* and *Journey to the Stars*.

EMI [CDP 7 46600 2] ~ America's first two Ventures CDs ~ GARLAND [GR2003]

Meanwhile, Don and Mel's efforts to get their newer material on compact disc soon paid off, beginning with Dunhill's Compact Classics collection on their Garland label. Soon, fans were amazed to discover a seventeen track CD with several titles recorded in Biff Vincent's garage that were not released on the Tridex/Compleat collection. *The Compact Ventures* was basically East World's *60's Pop* album from 1981, plus "Goldfinger" from *Chameleon*, "Magic Night" from Mel's *Sun, Sea and Love*, and the "Dance On," also from the Biff Vincent sessions. Adding both sides of the *Surfin' & Spyin'* single, plus the *Stars on Guitars* medley gave us a seventeen track CD. Next, Mel and Don licensed some tracks to Chris Ashford, a manager and promoter who owned the ILOKI label in Los Angeles. Knowing tunes from *Original Four* and *Chameleon* would appeal strongly to fans outside of Japan, Ashford released *Radical Guitars* [ILCD 1006] on CD, vinyl LP, and cassette tape. As a bonus, the CD included new versions of *California Dreamin'* and *Nutty*, (re-titled *Rock Nuts*).

Guitar Player magazine began 1987 with its *20TH Anniversary Issue* wherein their list of twenty essential rock albums included *Walk Don't Run*. Describing it as "the album that launched a thousand bands," the editors ranked The Ventures with Chuck Berry, Duane Eddy, The Who, Cream, Led Zeppelin, and Eddy Van Halen. Elsewhere in the issue, The Ventures were included in a list of "20 Who Mattered" along with Elvis Presley, Leo Fender, B.B. King, Jimi Hendrix, and Jerry Byrd, the steel guitarist who inspired The Ventures' versions of *Beyond the Reef*, and *Adventures in Paradise*.

Within weeks of this tribute, Dan Forte, now senior assistant editor at *Guitar Player*, recruited Mel to play on a couple of tracks for a new guitar instrumental album. As one of many guest artists, Mel sat in with Dan, bassist Steve Soest [The Torquays], and the renowned Paul Johnson [The Belairs, PJ And The Galaxies] for classic surf tracks by

Dick Dale *(The Wedge)*, and Johnson's own *Small Fry*. With fond memories, Dan recalls; "I started laying the tracks in Austin around 1984. We cut a couple more in New York in '86. The tracks with Mel were done in Los Angeles. I was very lucky to get Mel together with Paul Johnson. Mel kidded me about it being the first time in twenty years that he had to set up his own drums, but when I tried to pay him for the session later, he declined. He said he was just so grateful for that front-page story in *Guitar Player*."

Mel played on this CD

When *The Many Moods of Teisco Del Rey* [Upstart CD-007] was released, *Goldmine*'s Cub Koda declared it "the coolest instrumental album to come down the pike in a long time." *CD Review* gave it five stars, and *Roots & Rhythm* called it "one of the year's very best rockers."

The American revival of The Ventures again sparked formation of countless guitar groups, some of which made names for themselves. In California, axe-man and drummer Marty Tippens led his brothers and various friends as the MarTeens from basement rehearsals to Santa Monica dance clubs and a Pasadena recording studio. By the late nineties, the part-time group had evolved as the Fabulous Planktones, transporting the surf sound on stage and recordings into the new century. As a second generation Ventures fan, Marty recalls his discovery of the music; "I wasn't into buying records until the early seventies, so it was Jimi Hendrix and his Strat or Jimmy Page and his Les Paul that made the monster guitar impression on me. But after years of listening to those guys trying to outdo each other, I began listening to bands from the pre-distortion era and I discovered the wonderful sound of The Ventures. I really love the clean sound of those first eight albums. When I obtained their records from the Mosrite era, I was disappointed at first with the overdriven sound, but I soon developed a great appreciation for those albums as well."

At the same time, a chance meeting between a drummer and a guitarist at a Minnesota Ventures concert spawned a group that would tour with Jan and Dean and later record some wonderful surf instrumentals. Scrambling the letters in "Ventures," the boys called their group The Revtunes. Drummer Ken Dresher reminisces; "It wasn't just guitar work that influenced us. After twenty years with The Ventures, Mel Taylor had developed an enviable style and power that mesmerized me and hundreds of other young drummers."

Many bands had their so-called "Nokie clone," such as Wisconsin's Rockin' Guitars with ultra-V-fan Walt Stagner on lead guitar. The phenomenon continued with groups such as The Beloved Invaders of Boulder, Colorado finding success on stage and on compact disc. Tennessee's Straightjackets donned Mexican wrestling masks and became Los Straightjackets, gaining popularity with instrumental fans across the country with recordings, concerts, and late-night television talk show appearances.

For The Ventures, 1987 was another year of extensive touring through the States. There was nothing as harrowing as radiator vandalism or a blazing motor home, but there were some memorable positive events. The March tour through California had become almost routine, but this time the band picked up a couple of new crewmembers. A sound engineer was a must by now, and Steve Bonhag filled the position admirably, always ready to hit the road for as long as the band required. There was still plenty of work for a road manager, and Bob recalls how Joe Rosignolo came into the job; "In the mid-eighties, when we appeared in or near San Diego, Joe seemed to always show up in our dressing room. We learned that he was showing up early and helping out our equipment handlers, so when we had an opening, we asked him if he'd like to work for us. It appeared to be just what he wanted to do."

To Joe Rosignolo, this was putting it mildly. A Ventures fan since he was a child in Rochester, New York, landing a job with the band was a dream fulfilled. A guitarist himself, Joe also collected Mosrite instruments. Some six years earlier, he had met The Ventures by helping to set up their equipment. From then on, he attended whenever they played nearby. His persistence finally paid off, and he the road with The Ventures.

In May, accompanying the band through the Western States became a lifetime experience for UK fan-club president Gerald Woodage. As a one-time drummer, a massive collector and faithful fan, Gerald was in heaven for two-weeks as he followed the band on tour. A greater delight was his chance to examine Don's memorabilia and some unreleased recordings stashed away for over twenty-five years.

Gerry McGee, Gerald Woodage, Mel Taylor, Bob Bogle, Don Wilson

Gerald was with the band in Seattle on May 14 when they received some very sad news. Mr. Larry Johnson visited backstage and reported that his father, Howie had passed away on May 5 at the age of fifty-four from complications following lung cancer surgery. Howie's daughter Sherri recalls her father's last days; "Dad played the drums right up to the end. He came home after a Saturday night gig and said he didn't feel well. When he got worse, he went into the hospital and never came home. He was diagnosed with lung cancer and scheduled for surgery on April 28. When he came out of Recovery, he was informed that half of one lung had been removed. After spending the night at the hospital, we went home to get freshened up. When we returned about two hours later, we were told that Dad had turned for the worse. His lungs had stopped working and he was put on a ventilator. After seven days of Intensive Care, he passed away on the morning of May 5, 1987. He was only fifty-four years old."

1987 was a banner year for new Ventures material, the crowning jewel being Toshiba's release of The Ventures' movie, *Beloved Invaders* on videocassette and LaserDisc. Gerry McGee's instructional book, *Dynamite Guitar Licks*, also appeared in music stores again, this time from Alfred Publishing.

North American Ventures fans who watched NBC TV's *L.A. Law* were surprised one evening this year when Gerry, now a member of the Screen Actors Guild, was seen performing in an episode as a juror. He had very few lines, but in the story, Gerry had to break up a fight between two other characters.

Touring continued through fall, ending in November in the Eastern States. The highlight of the summer was in Reno, Nevada when Bally's Hotel and Casino held a *Hot August Nights Beach Party* in their parking lot for over a week. Performers included Jan and Dean, Dick Dale, The Chantays, The Surfaris, The Kingsmen, and The Challengers, but on opening night, The Ventures shared the spotlight with Chuck Berry and Frankie Avalon. An item of note during this tour was Gerry's rare use of an effects-box, kicking in a phase-shifter for *Ghost Riders In the Sky*.

Near the tour's end, The Ventures were in Washington D.C. on November 23. During their performance at a place called The Bijou, Bob and Don met George Babbitt for the first time in twenty-eight years since he had been their teenage drummer in Seattle. Having made a career in the air force, George was now stationed in D.C.

~ ~ ~

Fans learned that vinyl was not dead when a company in France released just 1,000 copies of a *Walk-Don't Run/Perfidia* "picture disc" containing color photos embedded in clear vinyl. Some fans wondered why only one side featured a classic picture of The Ventures, while the flip side showed a rare 1953 Kaiser "Dragon" sedan. Could Maybelline Records have known that Don's father had been a Kaiser automobile dealer?

The 1987 picture disc on Maybelline #44

RED DOGS

The CD explosion spawned Ventures' greatest hits discs from nearly every country in the world. Most were legal, some were bootlegs, but the worst was a set of songs that were not The Ventures at all. The first of these appeared under Europe's Black Tulip label on CD and cassette, licensed from Red Dog Express. For this reason, Don Wilson dubbed this and those that followed as "Red Dog" albums, and the odd sounding hit versions as coming from the "Red Dog sessions." Although a few of the tracks were lifted from Mel's *007 James Bond*, and others were unreleased Ventures versions, several featured piano or sax rather than guitar on plodding, but pleasing versions of *Walk-Don't Run*, *Lullaby of the Leaves*, and *Batman*. Many fans enjoyed the versions, but as Don relates, the band was not pleased; "Joe Saraceno had us record a few songs for a K-Tel package, and we signed a two-year contract with a one-year sell-off period. The record never materialized, but those songs started showing up, along with stuff we didn't do. I haven't heard them for years, but that piano version of *Slaughter on Tenth Avenue* sticks in my mind. That and a bunch more are a total embarrassment. Some years after we broke with Saraceno, he apparently gathered some musicians together and recorded some more songs that emerged as having been recorded by us for Red Dog Express. We have never received a cent in royalty payment from those records, even though some of our stuff is included on them as well as some of Mel's solo recordings. We threatened to sue the company, but it would have cost more than it may have been worth. I understand that the guy who owns Red Dog is an attorney. I have to say that I consider people who do this sort of thing to be the scum of the earth!"

Bob Bogle comments also; "We filed a lawsuit over the Red Dog stuff but it never went any further. That stopped it for a while, but the tracks started showing up again under different labels from places like East Germany and Holland and it's still going on. One CD on a label called Gold is shown as a product of Holland, pressed in France, and licensed from Puerto Rico."

While a UK compilation entitled *Apache* [Success 16135CD] did contain legitimate tracks for *Let's Go* and *Perfidia*, the 1995 release added insult to injury with liner notes declaring "only guitarist Nokie Edwards remains from the original quartet." Other Red Dog tape and disc labels include Laserlight, Evergreen, Gold, Abracadabra, Blue Jay, L.T. Series, and Tel-Star. In 1997, MasterTone Multimedia released a Ventures CD with *Bondolero* misspelled "Bandolero," and another in 1998 as "Condolero." Others give credit to Bob *Bogel* and John *Burrill*. There is also a UK disc from Digimode Entertainment with the label Life-Time (easily confused with Time-Life, as the logos are alike). Such CDs continue to appear with very attractive pricing. *The Ventures - Beached In Hawaii* [Black Cat 0107] appeared in 2004 from the Czech Republic. While it bore the plodding *Walk-Don't Run* version and a few cuts from Mel's *007* collection, *Slaughter On Tenth Avenue* was the real thing. Extending from the 1960 version of *Caravan* to 1997's *James Bond Theme*, the set stirred even higher interest with its live cuts of *La Bamba* and *Telstar* taken from an early eighties U.S. concert. Eventually, Red Dog tracks appeared in Japan, where they caused considerable confusion to Ventures enthusiasts who recognized some, but not all of the music as being from Mel's solo albums.

SHADES OF '65

By 1988, The Ventures' touring pace in America was slowing, and with Europe and Japan seemingly low on enthusiasm, the guys wondered if the end was near after twenty-seven years in the business. Australia and New Zealand were probed, but again, promoters were unwilling to gamble. The band need not have worried, for like so many times in the past, the lull was only temporary as history geared up to repeat itself. The first spark ignited when Scandinavian Ventures Club members began attending record fairs put on by Sunjay Production of Sweden. Pressure by these fans convinced Sunjay to bring The Ventures over and tour four Scandinavian countries. By year's end, details were firming up when interest was rekindled in the Far East. After nearly four years of missing one of its best customers, Japan Airlines took matters in hand. The company's first proposal was for a short Ventures tour in the spring of 1988, but by this time, a visit to Australia was pending, and dates for a massive U.S. spring tour were accumulating. Patiently, JAL rescheduled for July, engaging the services of a tour agent called M&I Company Ltd. To measure the appeal of The Ventures after Nokie's departure and the band's longest ever absence from Japan, a one-week tour was booked. While booking nightclub dates for July, M&I encountered enough enthusiasm to consult The Ventures regarding a month-long fall tour. The band was more than happy to resume touring in the land of the rising sun.

A few California bookings in early July left just enough time to prepare for Japan. Although the Japan tour was only for six days, it branched south from Tokyo to Kyoto and Osaka, and then to Sapporo on the island of Hokkaido. All eight performances were packed with fans waiting to see the band for the first time since 1984 when Nokie and Gerry had shared the stage. With no Japan tour in 1983, fans were now seeing Bob Bogle for the first time in *six* years. A warm welcome greeted the band at every show, each of which ended with a message from M&I's production agent, heralding The Ventures' return in September for a greatly extended tour.

ANOTHER COMEBACK

Meanwhile, Nokie was recording *Both Sides Of Nokie* with his friend J.D. Hoag at Seattle's Ironwood Studios. The new album featured Nokie's acoustic guitar on J.S. Bach's *Joy*, a tune usually only heard on keyboards. The remainder of the album was played entirely on acoustic except for an electrified *Lucille*. But what's this? One of the cover photos showed Nokie with a Mosrite guitar! Yes, after surviving the car accident, the factory fire, a bout of poor health and struggling nearly four years to fill custom orders, Semie Moseley was back in business. Late in 1987, after his "feeler ad" in the guitar magazines received overwhelming response, Semie and wife Loretta had started another small factory in Jonas Ridge, North Carolina. When response indicated primary interest in The Ventures Model, Semie circulated a brochure to American dealers in March. When The Ventures learned of their logo being used, their lawyer sent a letter of protest, forcing Semie to take another route. After contacting Nokie and agreeing upon a slightly wider neck, a beautiful "Nokie Model" was ready by the fall of 1988.

1988 was also the year that Nokie met lovely Judy Fetters. They settled in the country near Randle, Washington, about fifty miles south of Puyallup. Some outbuildings on the acreage allowed Nokie to raise a few quarter horses while recording an occasional album. As Judy recalls; "Just to keep the record straight, it was not horses that brought us together. It was music and the great times we shared. Nokie and I were friends first, and that blossomed into a love relationship. We started seeing each other in 1988, and moved in together the following year. As neither of us was in a rush, we had a long engagement. I started running the fan club then and began helping Nokie with the rest of his business. Believe me, being lovers and working partners is not easy. We had our ups and downs like anyone else, but it's the old-fashioned love that kept us together. The fans helped with that also. Because they are so devoted, we are also devoted to them. It's like we have this very large, worldwide family."

Judy Fetters relaxing on the stage after a Nokie show

Nokie had made his compact disc debut on a second volume of songs recorded with Terry Terauchi, and would now record a pair of solo discs in Japan for King Records with Terauchi and friends as financial backers. The assortment on Nokie's *Greatest World Hits Vol. 1* ranged from love songs and a few Ventures instrumentals to popular Madonna and Michael Jackson hits. *Volume 2* stuck to The Ventures sound on all but a mellow German love ballad entitled *Was Ich Dir Sagen Will* [What I Want to Tell You]. A subtle, tiny photo on the back liner promoted the Nokie Model by Mosrite.

Although several Nokie Models sold, demand in Japan was greater for the Ventures Model. Around this time Don Wilson received an ominous phone call; "I happened to have the band at our house for a rehearsal or a meeting. A friend called and said he knew a girl at the Corporate Registry office where trade names are registered, and that she had noticed an application to use "The Ventures" on musical instruments and related items. It didn't take long before we got Semie on the phone and asked what he knew about the application. He answered with complete shock that we would even *think* of him doing such a thing. We were mystified, so the next day we called the government agency. The clerk looked it up right away and when she said it was a guy named Semie Moseley, you could have knocked me over with a feather. He must have thought we would never find out. We put a stop to the procedure, but it didn't do much good."

Soon, Semie issued The Ventures model again, explaining that it as a "tribute to the band that made my guitars famous." Putting it mildly, The Ventures were unimpressed. They had yet to forgive Semie for dropping their endorsement, causing sales to plummet, and then choosing bankruptcy over a buyout for millions of dollars, leaving The Ventures' Mosrite Distributing no choice but to also fold.

MOVIN'

At around this time, Don and Bob received some new advice from their accountant. The band's success had put them in a tax situation that was magnified because they lived in California. The advice was to move to nearby Arizona or Nevada, where taxes were less severe. A return to Washington State was more appealing to the guys, and proved to be an equally smart tax maneuver. It didn't take Bob long to relocate to his favorite city of Vancouver, but it would be a few years before Don was able to leave his home in Sherman Oaks.

Labor Day morning of 1988 found The Ventures at Caesar's Palace in Las Vegas. A month of touring the States was ending with the band doing its part for the Muscular Dystrophy Association by performing on the *Jerry Lewis Telethon*. It only took five minutes to play *Walk-Don't Run* and *Hawaii Five-0*, but over fifty million viewers (including President Ronald Reagan and wife Nancy) watched The Ventures perform in their Hawaiian shirts and white trousers. Comedy actor/National MDA Chairman Jerry Lewis warmly introduced the band by applauding the group's sales of over eighty million records. As Josie recalls; "I didn't go to Las Vegas but I watched the show on TV. After The Ventures' performance, Jerry commented on fond memories stirred by their instrumental hits. Don told me later that Jerry was warm and friendly as he thanked them for appearing. A letter of gratitude was also received at The Ventures' office."

A week later, Don, Bob, Gerry, and Mel were speeding through Japan by bullet train. After three consecutive "dark years" it was their second trip to the country in just three months. The only changes in this tour were Mel's use of a synth drum and M&I's decision to have The Ventures do their own announcing. This curious practice baffled many fans until Bob explained; "Eliminating the salary and traveling expenses of an M.C. would amount to quite a saving, so they asked us to do our own announcing. It was no big deal, so Don just accepted the duty and the rest of us helped at times."

As the band wound its way to one beautiful concert hall after another, the guys noted that entire families, some spanning three generations, were sitting in the audience. The mild-mannered patrons, including small children, maintained an atmosphere that was a far cry from the raucous, beer-swilling mobs in the smoky cabarets at home.

Meanwhile, Sunjay agent Johnny Sandberg had arranged the Scandinavian tour. Upon arriving home during the third week of October, The Ventures were informed that early in 1989, they would visit Sweden, Norway, Finland, and Denmark.

Heartened by recent events, the band began planning an album. New ideas were scarce, but since working on the (unreleased) Fraker-Rosenberg video, the guys had maintained contact with Jeff Baxter. Jeff was happy to work with the group as producer, but with pending concerts, the Scandinavian tour, and a return to Japan in spring, work on the newest project progressed rather slowly.

Five weeks after Japan Tour '88, concerts were resumed in the Los Angeles area. It was another opportunity for UK Fan Club president Gerald Woodage to take a road trip with The Ventures. Again, his visit was a boon to fans in all of the clubs, as the band decided to release the comedy video they had hoped to air on MTV. Now over two years old, the humorous Heavy Metal spoof became known as *Wipe Out '88*. Soon, copies were in the hands of fans around the world. Eight years later, the musical skit saw its first commercial release in *California Surf Music*, a videotape compilation sold through classified ads in *DISCoveries* and *Goldmine* by guitarist Merrill Fankhauser, founder of the early sixties' surf group, The Impacts.

It may have consoled Bob Bogle to learn that twenty years later, baseball fans at Citizens Bank Park in Philadelphia were treated between innings to a 'bloopers video' set to *Wipe Out*. Ventures fan Steven Chestnut comments; "It showed guys running into each other while going for the ball, losing their bats after an out-of-control swing, etc. They entitled it *Wipe Out* and the surprise was that the music track was a live Ventures version. I couldn't tell the year of the recording, but the drums were definitely Mel Taylor, and probably Gerry McGee on lead. For me, it was the highlight of the night."

HARD ROCKING

Having booked international tours in March and May, the first half of 1989 promised to be a busy time for The Ventures. While Scandinavian and Japanese fans patiently waited, other events of interest were happening. First, Fraker-Rosenberg special, all but forgotten since 1983, was finally on the market on Beta, VHS, or twelve-inch digital LaserDisc. Although six years old, it did not matter that in Japan the show was titled *The Ventures' 30th Anniversary Super Session*, or that the American issue was called "Thirty Years of Rock and Roll." To Ventures fans, the music was timeless.

Although sales of *30th Anniversary Super Session* were reportedly high in Japan, there is no record of it being aired there on television. The reason for this was likely because the special featured Nokie as the star picker when Gerry McGee had been wowing the fans as lead guitarist for the past five years.

Broadcasts of the special were seen in North America and Europe, it being available to public television networks. Since then, the Fraker-Rosenberg Company has grown and changed its name to IVM Productions, where, as Aleks Rosenberg affirmed; "It's too bad that the period from '83 to '89 was taken up finding the right distributor, but we wanted it to be a success. Although John Fraker is not involved with IVM, we are still good friends and are co-owners of the Ventures special."

Unfortunately, home computers were soon capable of making DVD movies, and just about any Ventures video could be found on eBay.com for less than ten dollars. The band's legal advisors attempted to curb the practice, but crossing international boundaries became too expensive to pursue. In spite of the bootlegging, Toshiba-EMI forged ahead, releasing *The Ventures' 30th Anniversary Super Session* on DVD in 2006.

Another diversion before the Scandinavian tour involved the Hard Rock Café and its collection of rock memorabilia. Conceived in the UK in 1971, the chain of restaurants was quickly becoming a worldwide Mecca for fans to enjoy good food and music while exploring a stunning collection of guitars and artifacts related to their favorite musicians. The first Ventures items to appear in the collection consisted of a bass drum head and autographed Mosrite guitar in the Dallas Hard Rock following its opening in the winter of 1986. The following year, a Mosrite belonging to Nokie was purchased for the chain's San Francisco branch. When the restaurant proceeded to authenticate the claim, Nokie confirmed the serial number to match one of the guitars stolen from his home some fifteen years back. Rather than claim the guitar, Nokie and the band autographed it before it was relocated to a new café in Honolulu. The next Ventures donation was a guitar presented to the Beverly Center Hard Rock Café in Los Angeles.

Hard Rock Café – Dallas, Texas   *Jon Sievert*

Prior to Christmas, 1988, the first Hard Rock Café in the San Diego area had opened in the district known as La Jolla. As San Diego was where Joe Rosignolo made his home, the young road manager decided to combine the donating of memorabilia to the new restaurant with an attempt to rekindle an affiliation between The Ventures and Semie Moseley. Meanwhile, as Fiona recalls, a wedding was in the works; "Mel and I got married in February 1989. On the way back from our honeymoon cruise, we landed in San Diego and met the band at the opening of the Hard Rock Café in La Jolla. Road manager Joe Rosignolo managed to bring in Semie Moseley, and as I recall, it was an awkward situation for all concerned."

Nokie's 1963 Mosrite in the Honolulu Hard Rock   *Nick Sadowsky*

The La Jolla meeting took place on Sunday, February 19. During the opening ceremony, Fender Musical Instruments donated a guitar in the name of The Ventures, and the band donated a pair of its Gold Records. Nokie, having come full circle as a player of Mosrite guitars, accompanied Semie to the celebration. Upon arriving, Semie donated his personal Ventures model guitar, repainted gold for the occasion. Inscribed on the pickguard were the letters V and M, (denoting Ventures and Mosrite) and the number 25 for the years 1963 to 1988. The Ventures and Nokie signed the guitar with various colored markers.

Semie Moseley's Mosrite at the San Diego Hard Rock Café   *Gary Brown*

The big surprise came when Moseley produced a sparkling new Ventures model with a sunburst finish and white pickups. On the fingerboard were inlaid letters spelling DON. Hand written behind the headstock was inscribed "To Don from Semie Moseley." Considering past history and the recent logo licensing incident, Don was dumbfounded, but he graciously accepted the gift; "When Joe brought us to that ceremony, he didn't tell us that he had invited Semie, or we would not likely have gone along with it. We were not interested in doing anything more with Mosrite. Then Semie presents me with that guitar. I thought that maybe he had finally seen the light and built a guitar with a wider neck, but no, he'd been making them the same for thirty years and he just couldn't change. Maybe it's good that he didn't, because we were not about to go back into business with him anyway."

Stirring curiosity of the band's fans in America *and* Japan, Don used the Mosrite as his "on stage spare" for almost a year.

Back in Hollywood, Gerry McGee was helping a fifties icon with music for a cinematic biography. When Jerry Lee Lewis insisted on performing his own music for the Orion movie, *Great Balls of Fire*, his orchestral arrangers engaged studio musicians that included Mr. McGee. Ventures fans would have loved to see Gerry on the screen, but renowned blues guitarist Jimmy Vaughan was cast to "pick-sync" Gerry's solos while Dennis Quaid lip-synced to the Lewis classics. As Gerry recalls; "I was already pleased that my career had allowed me to play with Rick Nelson, the Everly Brothers, and Elvis, but to back Jerry Lee on his soundtrack was a whole new thrill. He didn't act in it, but he was a consultant and he re-recorded most of the music for it with us."

Gerry's work was easily recognizable throughout the movie, but the highlight for Ventures fans was his wailing solo during the end credits. although the credits rolled by with no mention of Gerry, he and other sidemen were given credit on the soundtrack CD - *Great Balls of Fire* [Polydor 839 516-1].

SCANDINAVIAN EASTER

As Josie recalls, The Ventures' entourage on this special excursion was a little larger than usual; "By this time, I had been married for nearly seventeen years to Don Nephew. The Ventures invited us both to go with them, and we enjoyed the trip immensely. Bob brought girlfriend, Darlene DeHerrera with him, and Jan was with Don. It was particularly wonderful for me as my mother and father were born in Sweden. I had hoped to look up some distant relatives while there, but since I had moved so many times in past years, their names and addresses had become hopelessly misplaced.

"Having traveled with The Ventures before, I had been impressed once when a customs agent, seeing us in a hurry, said 'Oh, The Ventures! Go right on through!' But this time, while boarding the trans-Atlantic flight out of New York, I got a scare when one of the officers pulled Bob and Don aside and walked them over to a bench. I was expecting next to see them opening their suitcases, but instead, the officer asked the guys for their autographs.

"While in Sweden, I was interviewed for one of their newspapers. Being born in Tacoma, I knew very little Swedish, so they interviewed me in English. They gave me a copy of it, but because it was printed in Swedish, I no longer know what I said!"

Several newspapers covered The Ventures' visit, and although they were printed in Swedish, the interviews were conducted in English. As Bob recalls, this was a pleasant surprise; "Actually, I was amazed at how so many Scandinavian fans spoke very good English. I was a relief to me, as it meant that we could introduce our songs on stage and tell the jokes that were part of our act. We hadn't been this far north since Alaska in 1981, but the reception by the Scandinavian fans made up for the chilly weather."

• Det var Don Wilson som bildade gruppen Ventures 1959 — med hjälp av mamma Josie Nephew, som blev gruppens första producent.
FOTO: Alf Raimé

• Maria Jansson — hyllad och hissad av sina idoler The Ventures, Mel taylor, Barry Mc Gee, Don Wilson och Bob Bogle.

Sweden press clippings   Arild Pettersson

Upon arriving, The Ventures met Sunjay agent Johnny Sandberg and the road crew that included sound and lighting experts. Further delight came when the band met their road manager, lovely Maria Jansson. The band played seven nights in Sweden, plus one each in Norway, Denmark, and Finland, traveling between cities in a crowded mini-van. Fan club president Arild Pettersson took two weeks' vacation from his job, allowing him to host a fan convention and display his vast collection of records and memorabilia, including Ventures concert videos set to run all day long. So impressed were The Ventures that Mel exclaimed to this writer some four years later; "Don and I thought we had big collections but you should see Arild's in Sweden."

One of many press photos showing Arild Pettersson with The Ventures

Arild was exceptionally pleased with the turnout for The Ventures in Malung, some 170 miles northwest of the country's capital, Stockholm. Reminiscing about the time spent with his idols, he reflects; "We made concert videos in Copenhagen, Gothenburg, Nyköping, and Stockholm, but in Malung, it was professionally taped by two cameras and later mixed. I was real proud of that, as it is my own hometown and we were something like 1,300 people at the concert. The response was even greater than for our own Spotnicks. With standing room only, fans were crowded up to the stage all night, waving their arms. It was the biggest crowd on the tour, and in the smallest town! Being with The Ventures, I introduced them at eight of the ten shows. It was the best two weeks of my life. We lived in the same hotels and I even managed to get Don Wilson and his wife to ride in my car between the last two gigs at Gävle (pronounced "Yavley") and Stockholm. What a thing! Here I was, driving a beloved Venture in my car and talking with him for several hours. Memories are made of this!"

A lengthy autograph session followed most of the concerts, with fans bringing records and guitars to be signed. Early on the tour, The Ventures met half a dozen fans that had flown from the UK and Germany to take in a few of the shows. Among the hard-core attendees from the UK were fanzine publishers Davy Peckett and Gerald Woodage.

Other than Gerry's Aria acoustic guitar, The Ventures were completely Fender equipped by way of Bob's red Jazz bass, Don's aging Jazzmaster, and Gerry's jet black Strat. Sunjay provided the P.A. system, guitar amps, and Mel's double bass drum kit including a set of electronic synth-pads. There were a few equipment problems, most being minor and quickly dealt with by the Sunjay crew.

Gerry found several ways to delight the audience, including an eerie effect in *Green Onions* where he modulated each plucked note with his little finger on the guitar's volume control. He also recalls an unrehearsed incident on Easter Sunday that both he and the audience found amusing; "After the big show in Malung, we went to play in Nyköping, which also had a nice audience. The stagehands got hold of a fog machine and they set it up for my acoustic piece. As I sat down and started to play *Classical Gas*, the lights dimmed and a big burst of fog came from behind and completely engulfed me. I couldn't see the audience, but I could hear them laughing. I guess it was actually pretty funny. The crew turned off the fogger, and it went really well after that."

On the subject of traveling, Josie recollects; "We enjoyed the tour of the countries immensely, along with meeting so many fans. The vans were comfortable and the highways between towns were lined with spectacular forests and lakes. One surprise was the speed at which Maria drove the bus. Motorists on the highway were polite and competent, but it seemed there was no speed limit! Maria and the roadies drove fast between each venue, but there was never any mishap. We saw welcoming signs in each city where we were booked, and one restaurant had a dish named after The Ventures. During the afternoon sound checks, we women took time for souvenir shopping and seeing the sights. The morning of April 2, after the final concert in Nyköping, Sweden, our tired but happy group left Stockholm to cross the Atlantic. Over the years, this tour became the topic of many conversations as being one of the highlights of our travels."

Home from their excursion, it was less than a month before The Ventures crossed the Pacific to Japan. From May 7 to June 21 they played thirty-two venues on the mainland and four on the island of Hokkaido. The theme for this tour celebrated thirty years since the band's formation in 1959. On the final day of the tour, The Ventures were contracted to record a tune for a television commercial. The surprising aspect was the product, whereas *No Matter What Shape* (*Your Stomach's In*) had stemmed from an Alka-Seltzer jingle, the new instrumental *Try It*, was for a stomach acid remedy called OTA.

Toshiba then released on the band's first three-inch CD single. Although *Try It* was built upon the basic structure of *Wipe Out*, The Ventures created an exciting arrangement that included some excellent ad-lib work by Gerry and a searing twelve-bar bass solo from Bob.

WALK-DON'T RUN '89

While Japan celebrated thirty years since the formation of The Ventures in Washington, the State was commemorating one-hundred years of Statehood. Months earlier, Nokie had begun a Christmas album, produced by radio DJ friend, James Michael Thomas. During the centennial planning, when Thomas was approached for names of Washington recording artists worthy of receiving recognition, he nominated Nokie and proposed that a Lifetime Achievement Award be presented. When the nod was given, a party at the Governor's Mansion was arranged to make presentations to notable Washington based musicians. Among the nominees were the former members of the group known as Heart, famed for recording *Crazy on You*, *Magic Man*, and *Barracuda*.

Prior to the presentations, a short concert was given. Together with Heart's guitarist Roger Fisher, bassist Steve Fossen, and drummer Michael Derosier, Nokie had worked up a stinging version of *Walk-Don't Run*. For three and a half minutes, Nokie poured every lick he knew over Fisher's wailing, overdriven, background guitar. The group played several numbers during the festivities, including *Pipeline*, *Telstar*, *Apache*, and *Hawaii Five-O*. The Heart men gave Nokie's a modern, "heavy" sound that pleased even the youngest members in the audience. During the festivities, Nokie received a commendation from Governor Booth Gardner and Secretary of State, Ralph Munro.

The performance was recorded for a cassette that included selections from *Both Sides Of Nokie*. Entitled *Walk-Don't Run '89*, the tape finally became available in 1991 from James Michael Thomas through an ad in *Guitar Player* magazine. At the time, Nokie's fan club was not quite organized, making the cassette a collector's rarity.

The Ventures had completed two foreign tours in 1989, but there was still a string of U.S.A. concerts to do before the next studio project for Toshiba-EMI. Meanwhile, as Fiona recalls, she and Mel were also busy; "That year, I decided to branch out on my own, so with Mel's help, we incorporated as Uniglobe Research Corporation [comprising blood bank/plasma centers] with Mel and I as corporate officers. At first, I did almost everything myself. Mel gave me moral support and continued to travel with me on business trips. Later, we hired Indira Pethebridge, who became an indispensable part of Uniglobe, allowing me time to help Mel with the business of The Ventures."

The Labor Day weekend had just begun when The Ventures arrived at Orlando, Florida. Upon checking into their hotel, Bob received news that his mother had passed away unexpectedly. In a few hours, two Roberts crossed in flight as Bob Bogle flew west to his family and Bob Spalding rushed east to pick up the red Fender Bass.

The next two nights were at Little Darlin's Rock and Roll Palace in Kissimmee, Florida on the north bank of Lake Tohopekaliga. In years past, Bob Spalding had played lead, rhythm, and bass with The Ventures, but this was his first time on stage with Gerry McGee since working with Mel Taylor and The Dynamics in 1973.

After the Kissimmee concerts, the band listened to a tape Bob Spalding had made in his home studio containing ten original instrumentals and six old favorites that included interesting arrangements of *Walk-Don't Run* and *Diamond Head*. In less than a year, the tape (*The World Is A Curious Place*) became a fundraiser cassette for the fan clubs. Some twenty years later, Venture fans convinced Bob to put it on compact disc along with some of his newer work. *Bob Spalding – The Fifth Venture* [Echo - ERCD-0310] created enough excitement in fan circles that it was soon released in Japan [M&I - MYCV-30335] and in the USA [Big Dog Little Dog - BDLD-003].

TOSHIBA'S IDEA MEN

Through the eighties, Ventures recordings appeared on U.S. labels Award, Garland, Iloki, and Tridex while the band tirelessly toured the States. While turnout for concerts was heavy in the smoky clubs and taverns, record sales in North America remained less than spectacular. Still able to fill large halls in the Far East while enjoying ample sales of new *and* old material, the band concentrated once more on Japan.

Once the new medium gained acceptance, it was not long before the Ventures' entire sixties catalog was available on compact disc. Toshiba began by offering the group's first ten albums, complete with exact replicas of the original front and back artwork. It was a simple task, the company being a subsidiary of the EMI conglomerate that owned everything the band had recorded for Dolton, Liberty, and United Artists. Before the tenth disc was released, two men at Toshiba decided that The Ventures had marketing potential for more than pure nostalgia. Hiro Kadoma and Kei Ishizaka had many ideas, beginning with entire albums covering successful Japanese pop groups, like the band had done at home in 1974 with its *Carpenters* and *Jim Croce* tributes. One act chosen by Kadoma was a veteran group known as the Southern All Stars. Formed in 1975 by Keisuke Kuwata, this prolific group had enjoyed dozens of hits in just fourteen years. Their music consisted mainly of pleasant melodies resembling American middle-of-the-road or soft rock, with the lyrics frequently alternating between Japanese and English.

The Southern All Stars

Hideyuki Nozawa, Yuko Hara, Keisuke Kuwata, Hiroshi Matsuda, Kazuyuki Sekiguchi

Another of Kadoma's favorite acts was the singing duo, Shuji Shibata and Shigeaki Miyazaki, calling themselves Chage (pronounced Cage) and Aska. After winning a songwriting contest sponsored by Yamaha in 1979, the pair established themselves throughout Southeast Asia, both as performers and composers with a dozen hit albums to their credit.

Chage & Aska

Shigeaki Miyazaki and Shuji Shibata

Having asserted their affinity for Japanese pop music, The Ventures readily accepted the idea. Hence, with three decades behind them and a five-year abstinence from album recording, the winter of 1989 found the group in a Burbank studio working with Mr. Kadoma on the hits of the Southern All Stars. In addition to Bob Spalding and David Carr, extra percussion, saxophone, and background vocalists were drafted. Although Biff Vincent's Costa Mesa studio was still in operation, The Ventures selected Red Zone Studios run by Duncan Aldrich. Not only was Red Zone able to accommodate the larger number of musicians; daily commuting to Orange County was no longer necessary.

During these Red Zone sessions, Joe Saraceno had the band make fresh recordings of *Walk-Don't Run*, *Perfidia*, *Lullaby of the Leaves*, and *Hawaii Five-O* for a K-Tel oldies compilation. Bob played lead on the three older tracks, returning to bass for *Hawaii Five-O*. The K-Tel project was never surfaced, but eventually, the recordings would.

Bob Bogle   Don Wilson   Mel Taylor   Gerry McGee

CHAPTER FOUR

The Nineties

While Toshiba-EMI welcomed the concepts put forth by Hiro Kadoma and Kei Ishizaka, the company catered to the past-hits baby-boomer market with more than sixty Ventures' compilation CDs from 1990 to 1995. Most of the discs bore twenty or more tracks, and some came in pairs or sets of three. The cream of this crop was a set of beautifully packaged 4-CD boxed sets containing eighty-eight albums and two-dozen 4-track EP releases. The set also contained many rare bonus tracks. Priced for the serious collector, and with Japanese-only documentation, few of the sets were sold outside Japan.

The first ten of many Ventures boxed sets of compact discs

As the Ventures began recording new albums for Japan, Capitol/EMI created some new Ventures interest in the English-speaking world when they commandeered renowned musical archivist Ron Furmanek and engineer Larry Walsh to re-master and remix music for its *Legendary Masters Series*. Among the artists honored were Ricky Nelson, Bobby Vee, Cher, Fats Domino, Jan and Dean, as well as The Ventures. With limited knowledge of The Ventures, Furmanek consulted friend Paul Hippensteel who referred Ron to Ventures club president Michael Kuhn. As Mike recalls; "Ron Furmanek also lived in New Jersey at the time, so I took a pile of Ventures records and books to a meeting with him. We worked on the song selection and he had a photographer take pictures of my records and memorabilia for the liner. The Ventures made quite a few changes to the list, but Paul and I still received some credit in the liner notes."

The twenty-nine-track CD contained a six-minute interview with Don and Bob from 1961 and a pair of vintage radio commercials. For collectors, *The Savage* and the rare *Dick Tracy* TV theme were heard in stereo for the first time, while Steve Kolanjian provided a comprehensive biography in place of mere liner notes. For hundreds of North American Ventures fans, *Walk-Don't Run-the best of The Ventures* was one of their first Ventures compact disc purchases. The mention of an American fan club caused membership in Mike Kuhn's U.S.A. club to virtually triple. To further promote the album, EMI issued a promotional "baseball type" card to be given away at record stores.

As club membership swelled, Mike's wife joined in the packaging and mailing of everything from photos, and guitar picks, to T-shirts, and albums, all the while keeping a home and raising a nine-year-old daughter. Letter after letter told of the writer losing track of The Ventures through the seventies and being eager to join the club.

EMI CD /cassette 93451   Mike Kuhn

Pleased with the sales, EMI commandeered Furmanek and Walsh for a similar treatment of *The Ventures' Christmas Album* [EMI 94994]. On this one however, some fans opposed Ron Furmanek's method of including a previously discarded track in which Nokie had added harmony to his melody on *Rudolph, The Red Nosed Reindeer*. In Furmanek's defense, radio programmers played this track more than any of the others during the holiday season for the next ten years.

At the same time, The Ventures self-released their *Greatest Hits* (now on CD) at concerts and by mail-order from fan clubs. Collectors were surprised and delighted to find a new version of *Hawaii Five-0* not only a full minute longer, but with spectacular percussion from Mel that included rim shots, bongos, and various sized toms. Although the Compleat and Castle Communications CD inserts had indicated this 2:42 minute version, the discs actually carried an older 1:45 version.

Meanwhile, UK fan club operator Gerry Woodage had influenced See-For-Miles Records to compile all of that country's Ventures EP records on an album. Although Ventures on vinyl was history in the U.S. and Japan, *The EP Collection* appeared in April on long-play record, cassette, and compact disc. See-For-Miles continued with CDs, presenting The Ventures' U.S. sixties material including the *Play Guitar* series, a few Japan albums, with several rare singles as bonus tracks. In his inimitable style, Gerry's liner notes adorned nearly every package.

RECOGNITION AT HOME

In 1987, ex-Seattle record dealer and disc jockey Christopher Knab founded the Northwest Area Music Association (NAMA) with assistance from Fabulous Wailers bassist John "Buck" Ormsby. At annual ceremonies, NAMA presented the area's historic achievers with Gold Record awards and induction to its Pacific Northwest Hall of Fame. In 1990, the original Ventures were summoned for the third annual Northwest Area Music Association awards. Josie was also invited; "While enjoying the awards night in Seattle, I was taken by surprise when the announcer called me up to the front. Bob Bogle came down and escorted me up on stage, and Buck Ormsby presented us with a Gold Record. Don later ordered another one from NAMA for Skip Moore, but was unable to locate him. The following year, we heard that Skip had passed away, so I placed an appeal in the classified section of *DISCoveries* magazine, hoping to locate the families of both Skip and of Howie Johnson. We located Mrs. Johnson but unfortunately, there were no answers regarding Skip Moore. I'm not sure, but it might have helped if we had known his 'real' given name."

NAMA Gold Record Award denoting induction to Pacific Northwest Hall of Fame

Among the many inductees was the "Godfather of Northwest rock," Pat O'Day. The dynamic disc jockey was honored for exceptional work in promoting the area's artists for over thirty years. The celebrities were fortunate to receive their awards, for, as Buck Ormsby recalls; "The Northwest Area Music Association folded after about five years. It seems there were just too many people on the board with conflicting agendas. By the end of 1992, it had ceased to exist. Incidentally, I remember that it was actually the huge ovation of applause for Josie that rendered her speechless that night."

1990 continued to be a year of surprises for the fans *and* for The Ventures. Two days before his 57th birthday, Don was shocked when Del Shannon ended his life with a gun following a period of depression. As Don recalls; "After working with Del at one time, and having sung his songs over and over, it was like losing someone close to me."

In April, when a short tour along the California coast landed the band at the Belly Up Tavern in Solana Beach, Don was again astonished, albeit on a more positive note. As Road manager Joe Rosignolo wrote to Mike Kuhn for publication in the fan club bulletin; "After making sure the band had food and beverages backstage, Mel and Don asked me who the pretty lady was, standing next to them. When I couldn't answer them, Mel held up a copy of their album, *Walk-Don't Run*, and asked if I now knew who she was. I think my first words were 'No way,' but it *was* Barbara Grimes, the model on The Ventures' first album cover. It turns out she ran a women's fine leather clothing shop just two doors down from that night's venue."

In contrast to Japan, concerts at home were more varied and spontaneous. Many times, American audiences heard a classic rendition of *Sleepwalk* or other tunes that Gerry had not recorded with the band. Often surprised on stage, Don recalls; "We were blown away by Gerry at nearly every concert back then, and it still happens, even now. We can do a whole tour and hear him do something different every night. He hates to repeat himself, and plays different solos all the time. He can take something as simple as *Let's Go* or *Bulldog* and turn it into a four-minute r&b masterpiece. You should hear him go on *Whittier Boulevard* when he's in the mood. He's just amazing."

Three weeks into June, the band left for Japan to play seventy-four tour dates. As 1990 marked thirty years since The Ventures had recorded *Walk-Don't Run*, they arrived in Tokyo amid a shower of commendations at Toshiba's party in honor of the band's album tribute to the Southern All Stars.

Now proficient on synthesizer drum pads, Mel installed the latest Yamaha set on his kit. Fluorescent drumsticks for his solo, and radio units for cordless guitar playing presented a hi-tech image to the audience. But, as Gerry recalls, new technology takes some getting used to; "We decided to take advantage of the wireless rigs as much as possible by moving around the stage during some numbers. I would step down from the stage and walk through the audience playing *House of the Rising Sun*. One night, as I went back up on the stage, I tripped on the top step and fell flat on my face. My guitar hit the floor and there was this loud *thud!* The audience gasped and the guys were afraid I was hurt, but I jumped up and kept on playing. There was a huge applause at the end, but it was still one of the most embarrassing moments I've ever had."

Very soon, Mel went walking through the aisles with a synthesizer drum pad and transmitter on his belt, stopping frequently to let a patron tap out a few beats. As Bob recalls, even more variety was added when he embraced his Jazzmaster for the first time on stage since 1978; "I hadn't played lead for over ten years because switching guitars and adjusting amplifiers slowed the pace of our show. It was M&I who talked me into reverting to the medley, as their crew was really efficient at getting the sound just right. I enjoyed the variety and played more lead every year, both on stage and in the studio."

For the first time since 1980, Toshiba preserved the tour on an album. *Live in Japan 1990* was the first Ventures live compact disc. A fifty-one minute video was also released on VHS and LaserDisc, and was a slight wake-up call for fifty-six-year-old Bob Bogle; "When I watched that video, I was shocked at how overweight I had become. I decided to exercise more and make some significant changes to my diet."

In addition to several album re-issues and compilation discs, the next two years brought five new albums conceived by Hiro Kadoma. While most of the music was pop from the Southern All Stars or Chage & Aska, there was material from outside of Japan. Other musicians such as David Carr and Bob Spalding contributed as usual, but when fans heard *The Ventures Play Seaside Story*, a long-term controversy began. The hard rocking guitar of Jeff Baxter was the first culture shock, and when his friend, Edgar Winter, added some heavy saxophone, the rave reviews in fan magazines soon had members flocking to order the expensive, imported album.

Each successive release varied from the last, alternately straying from Japanese Pops to the latest *Major Motion Picture* themes or an entire album [*Flyin' High*] of exciting new Ventures originals. Longtime fans were also pleased to see credits on four of the new albums to Joe Barile for extra percussion work.

Included on *Flyin' High* was a pair of earlier compositions by Don, in honor of special people in his life. While immersed in a favorite pastime of songwriting, he had written *Jackie*, dedicated to sister Jacqueline and another entitled *Janis* for his wife. When the songs were put on disc, titles with broader appeal were chosen, *Jackie* becoming *Follow Your Heart*, and *Janis* renamed *Memories of Love*. The latter had previously appeared in Japan on a three-inch single CD and on *Melody Hit in Japan*, an album also containing the tune sung in Japanese by Miss Tomoko Kashima. Subsequently, the song became the theme for a popular TV drama carried on two Japanese networks.

The Kadoma albums had lesser appeal in the western world until the arrival of the sixth and final in the series. *The Ventures Play Mega Hits* was more up-tempo and pure guitar, although the number of songs was disappointing. Toshiba had seemingly rush-released eight new tracks complemented by only three Ventures' originals to coincide with Japan tour '93. Not only was the album undersized by current standards, the three original tracks were lifted from the preceding *Flyin' High* album. The Ventures had recorded, and expected to see, *ten new* tracks on the disc until it was revealed that two tracks written by Japan's The Wands had been blocked in a contract with Toshiba.

In fan club mail, there emerged two schools of thought. While those steeped in nostalgia hoped for a return to the basic lead, rhythm, and bass format, others appreciated the synthesizer, saxophone, and organ arrangements that kept The Ventures abreast of the times. Fortunately, both groups were satisfied as the band maintained its ability to change while keeping the oldies sounding as good as ever.

AXE... AND YOU SHALL RECEIVE

If anything annoyed The Ventures, it may have been the constant questioning by interviewers regarding the Mosrite guitar. Each time, they explained not having played or endorsed the instrument since 1969. After thirty years, the group's preference for Fender instruments was fairly obvious, a fact sadly publicized on March 21, 1991, following the death of Leo Fender. As guitar magazines published everything they could find about Mr. Fender, it became widely known that Leo had credited The Ventures with popularizing the Stratocaster worldwide, years before Jimi Hendrix came along.

Another dilemma for The Ventures was the fact that, while the latest Japanese Mosrites exploited their name and logo, international lawsuits were too complicated and expensive to pursue. The band took every opportunity to state this until some of the offenders began paying attention. Having duplicated The Ventures model guitar and bass since the sixties, Japan's Arai and Company now reversed its policy with an offer to build a new line of Aria Ventures models that looked entirely different.

The 1991 Aria Ventures models

Although these guitars were very nice, Gerry and Don found them to be mediocre compared to their trusty Fenders. Confirmation came a year later during the 1992 Japan tour, when Nokie dropped in at a Ventures show and was invited to join in to play *Caravan*. Nokie borrowed an Aria Ventures model, but remarked later in the USA that he did not like it at all.

Nokie joins The Ventures for Caravan

Hibiya Music Bowl - Tokyo '92/06/21   K.Takaya

The Aria Ventures bass was something else. Bob adapted immediately, using it even after the two-year endorsement had expired. His comfort with the bass was obvious during a solo he introduced on the 1991 Japan tour. His bass work had always been spectacular, but he now stepped forward during each performance of *Wipe Out* to deliver the intense refrain from *Try It*, leaving the audience stunned in disbelief. Recalling his accomplishment; "I had always used a heavy gauge pick for bass, but around the time I got the Aria bass, I began using a thinner one. Pretty soon I was using the same medium thick pick for bass as I use for lead guitar."

In addition to material from their latest album, the band liked to give the Japanese audience something new. This year it was Gerry McGee singing the old-time country hit, *Ashes of Love*. It was his first time singing since 1965 when he recorded *Twilight Zone* and *I Wonder* for his single release on Pacemaker. Response was for Gerry to strike a deal with Tokyo's Alfa Records for an album with eighty percent vocal content.

Having business contacts in several countries, it was not uncommon for Fiona to arrange meetings so as to allow her to join The Ventures for part of a Japan tour. During this visit, Mel and Fiona found time in Tokyo to visit George Reid, the old friend and director of their Japanese movie, *Beloved Invaders*. Five days later, in August, George showed up for The Ventures' evening concert.

1991 also saw the most notorious bootleg of Ventures music ever to hit the market. While attending a birthday party for M&I tour director, Jun Ariura, The Ventures were surprised to hear themselves on a strange compact disc. A pair of zealous collectors known in Japan as "Ventures freaks" had compiled several rare singles, plus *Adventures in Paradise* from the private 1965 *White Album*. Among the collections of Miyaji-san and Kitagawa-san was a tape from the 1959 session at Joe Boles' Seattle studio that included double takes of *Cookies and Coke* and *The Real McCoy*. Adding the rare *Tarantella*, The Marksmen singles *Night Run* and *Scratch*, and a few American single versions considered rare in Japan, a collection of eighteen tracks emerged for which fans anywhere would be thrilled to own. Typical variations included *Lucille* and *The Ninth Wave* without female vocal backing and *Apache* with a firm ending instead of the fade-out. *Blue Moon* was particularly interesting to Japanese fans that had never heard this version's alternate ending. Employed as a 'CD Editor,' Miyaji was able to put the collection on compact disc [*The Rarities* - Pendleton PC-101]. In spite of several discs exported to Europe and America, the unauthorized album initially fetched in excess of $100 on eBay in the new century.

1992 began with a special trip to Japan for New Year festivities. This year, prior to club dates in Kawasaki, Nagoya, and Osaka, The Ventures made a short appearance on NHK Television's traditional New Year's Eve singing contest known as "Kohaku." Clad in tuxedos and playing their new Aria guitars, they rocked through a medley comprising *Slaughter on Tenth Avenue*, *Diamond Head*, and *Pipeline*. Although it was a happy time for Bob, having met a lovely girl named Yumi, Don was a bit disgruntled; "Contrary to my advice, the engineers ran my guitar directly into the mixing console. Just as I feared, when the show was broadcast, I came out with barely any reverb at all! Not good!"

The trip ended on a sad note when the band tried to contact filmmaker George M. Reid. After several unanswered phone calls, Mel launched an investigation. George was found in his apartment, having died roughly a month earlier of heart failure. The Ventures were in shock for a while, having seen to their former director less than five months earlier after an August concert.

Before leaving Japan, The Ventures undertook an interesting one-time project with Japan's Crown Records. The concept involved adding the voices of popular female Japanese singers to six of their instrumentals. The recording was done with The Ventures on one side of the Pacific and the singers on the other. The result was a package of lively pop rock that included Dave Carr's keyboard genius and nice guitar by Bob Spalding. As Bob recalls; "Except for the overdubbing, it was done something like the Toshiba albums we were doing around the same time. On those, we were sent demo recordings to learn the tunes, and we would then do our own arrangements."

Turning to the French language, Crown titled the singers on the project as "Bel Age" (beautiful acts). *Bel Age with The Ventures* [Panam CRCP-20044] was not rushed to market, however, being saved for the next year's Ventures tour. If instrumental purists were not excited by the Bel Age project, they soon would be when Crown re-issued the material on three separate mini discs, each containing two songs from the original in both vocal *and* instrumental format. These Karaoke versions actually contained very nice guitar solos, and included the initial release of *Midnight Lights* as an instrumental.

END OF A LEGEND

Nokie also entered the nineties with an accelerated career, largely due to his association with Semie Moseley and the beautiful signature guitar. However, as years on the road had not been good to Nokie, he was treated for a heart condition with the installation of a cardiac pulse-generating pacemaker.

The man who imported the bulk of Semie's product was musician and huge Ventures fan, Keiichi Takaya. In the fall of 1990, Nokie began annual visits to Japan, backed by the Takaya Band with Keiichi on rhythm guitar. Keiichi employed a full-time interpreter, but on stage, he sang songs like *Runaway* and *Stand By Me* in surprisingly accurate English. As Semie's importer, Takaya soon formed the *Nokie Edwards and Mosrite International Fan Club*, the title somewhat grandiose, considering the club bulletin was written in Japanese. Club merchandise was of the highest quality, ranging from T-shirts and handy accessory bags to silken tour-jackets.

Roughly half of Nokie's concerts during the Takaya years were in the big, the others being held in nightclubs, or "live houses" as they are called in Japan. Takaya owned his own club called the Hilldun, possibly derived from Hilton.

High in the mountains of North Carolina's Pisgah National Forest, Semie and Loretta Moseley fashioned Mosrite guitars in the few outbuildings that survived the fire of 1983. The stress of previous years had left Semie with health problems, but he was walking again with the aid of a cane. Searching for new markets, he had revived the side-jack Ventures model in 1987, priced at around $3,000. Although ads in U.S. guitar magazines brought low response, Japan ordered as many guitars as Semie could build. When queried, Semie reasoned that he was within his rights to build Ventures model guitars, both as a tribute to the band, and because he had re-associated with Nokie. The Moseleys were still in debt over the Jonas Ridge property and equipment, but the future was now looking good. They were producing approximately one guitar per day when another setback transpired. Following the fire, Semie had begun using a number of old sheds on the property, and also built some new ones. As each one required electrical service, Semie ran feeder lines from the house. All worked well for over seven years until fire inspectors arrived and condemned the entire operation. It looked like the end, but as always, the proverbial pendulum kept swinging for Semie.

A short time earlier, a committee in the nearby State of Arkansas was searching for an industry to occupy a vacant Wal-Mart building on highway No. 10 in the center of Booneville. Jerry Standridge, an energetic young banker and politician, made an offer to the Moseley's that included moving the entire Mosrite operation to Booneville while establishing a line of credit from the town's two banks. Semie and Loretta had been considering the move when the fire inspectors forced their decision. In March of 1991, a corporation was established, and six months later, Unified Sound Association, Inc. was operating in half of the 22,000 square-foot building. With more than enough space for a factory and offices, the west wing of the building was marked as an auditorium for presenting Gospel concerts. Through its Industrial Development Commission, the State financed an employee-training program. Semie's daughter, Dana, followed her grandmother's footsteps by specializing in the winding of Mosrite pickups. Semie also acquired Gene Haugh, a former Gretsch employee as production manager.

Although afflicted with colitis, Semie set a goal to produce ten guitars a day for Japan. There were also plans for a radio broadcast from his auditorium to minister the Gospel. In May, 1992, he and Loretta flew to Tokyo with Nokie and Judy to promote the guitars and participate on stage. One concert was preserved on CD as *Nokie Edwards - Live at Yakult Hall* [King- KICP-702]. A few days later, Nokie made his first instructional video, *How To Play Caravan*, featuring his signature Mosrite guitar.

Semie and Loretta Moseley on stage with Nokie in Japan   *press*

The future looked bright until July when Semie was diagnosed with colon cancer. On August 7, he passed away at the age of fifty-seven. When the news reached Nokie in Washington and Takaya in Japan, both flew to North Carolina for the funeral. With the modest of grave markers, Semie was laid to rest in the churchyard at Jonas Ridge.

Fulfilling Semie's wish to keep the business in the family, Loretta Moseley assumed the presidency of Unified Sound Association, assisted by Jerry Standridge as company treasurer. Once the Semie Moseley Auditorium was ready, a memorial concert was planned for April 27, 1993 to help defray Semie's accumulated hospital expenses.

The former Wal-Mart building in Booneville, Arkansas

Back in Randle, Washington, Nokie and Judy decided to move to Oregon to be closer to her family. While searching for a horse trailer to facilitate the move, Nokie received a call from Loretta to headline the memorial concert, which would include performances by Loretta and a few of her staff as well as songs by stepdaughters Michelle and Dana Moseley, and Semie's mother, Irene. Keiichi Takaya helped by bringing a party of eight Japan fan club members, most of whom ordered a guitar after a tour of the factory.

From Nashville, Andy Moseley was in attendance, along with son Mark, who gave a polished performance of country singing and picking on a unique guitar from his Uncle Semie. While there, Mark enticed Nokie to come to Nashville and record at the Moseleys' Sound Control Studio.

Backed by longtime fan, Mike Tarno on drums, Takaya on rhythm, and bassist, Tommy Watts, Nokie played a set of Ventures hits and several country pleasers like *Orange Blossom Special* and *Steel Guitar Rag*. When the audience had dispersed, Nokie bought a Finnish Landola acoustic guitar from Tommy Watts who owned a music store in Fort Smith. Lingering out-of-town fans were then treated to Nokie playing romantic ballads such as *Wind Beneath My Wings* and Yuzo Kayama's *Kimi to Itsumademo*.

Semie's Memorial Concert - Nokie, Del Halterman, Mike Tarno, and Keiichi Takaya

At around this time, Judy began assisting Nokie with the operation of a fan club. Among the problems of going solo, Nokie had found it impossible to shed the notoriety of his work with The Ventures. A work-around solution saw Nokie's performances split into two parts, beginning with nostalgic selections from his Ventures days, and closing with a set of his preferred country selections. Later, Nokie began upgrading many of his past recordings using the latest technology and a bag of new licks. By the late nineties, backed by local musicians, he was presenting very good "Ventures" concerts in the USA, Canada, Europe, and Japan.

Although Unified Sound Association was busy, sales were insufficient to cover its arrears. In 1994, offers were received from Takaya in Tokyo and Ramon Jacinto in Manila to enter partnerships, but Loretta refused both. The company operated until January 5, 1995 when it was forced to shut down. After moving to Carson City, Loretta kept the trade name alive by establishing Mosrite of California as a Nevada corporation in May of 1999. Later that year, she sold the manufacturing rights to guitar builders in Japan. The specialized shop equipment was purchased by 1980s Mosrite employee, Ed Elliott, who began to manufacture beautiful mandolins in Checotah, Oklahoma.

When The Ventures signed with Aria of Japan in 1990, a side benefit included the company's help to stop use of The Ventures' name on other Japanese products. The task took longer than Aria had estimated, but once the Fillmore Company complied, the last company found to be using the logo was a Nagano firm called Tani Gakki. It took almost two more years to accomplish, but "Mosrite of California" guitars from Japan finally ceased to be manufactured bearing The Ventures' logo.

FLYING HIGH

While news of Semie's death spread, The Ventures were on Japan Tour '92, promoted by M&I as the 30th Anniversary of Don and Bob's initial visit. The band's efforts in preparation for this massive tour added to a virtual banquet on the souvenir tables. Complementing Toshiba's eight magnificent boxed CD sets were the "all original" *Flyin' High* CD, the *Say Yes* CD, *Bel Age with The Ventures*, and Gerry McGee's first solo album, *Friends From a Distance* [Alpha ALCB-550], a country-Cajun flavored disc featuring Gerry on slide guitar, accordion, and harmonica. It really was *Friends From a Distance*, as Gerry's guests included Rita Coolidge on back-up vocals, Bobby Womack on rhythm guitar, and son Kane McGee on percussion. To promote the disc, The Ventures backed Gerry singing *Long Road*, which he had written and sung in 1977 at the Las Vegas Aladdin with Kris Kristofferson, Rita Coolidge, and Billy Swan.

On grueling tours numbering over a hundred concerts, it was not unusual for someone to get sick. It was rainy from the beginning, and after an outdoor show in the third week of June, both Don and Bob came down with severe colds. Don said that if it were not for the first-class tour management by M&I, they could never have carried on. As September 24 was a traveling day, there were no evening concerts scheduled. This allowed the band to party with the crew in celebration of Mel's 59th birthday. Two weeks later, The Ventures were home suffering jetlag and fatigue, but after only one night's sleep, they were back on stage for California's annual Grape Harvest Wine Festival.

WELCOME TO THE CLUBS

While in Japan, The Ventures had accepted the commitment of Hideki Soeda to a new and improved Ventures fan club. Hideki published a periodical called *Yellow*

Jacket, named after the band's driving rocker on *The Colorful Ventures* album. Well versed in English, Hideki had enjoyed membership in the UK club as well as his home club, which he had watched slowly fizzle due to neglect. It seemed that The Ventures would again have "all corners of the globe" covered until they met with disappointing news upon arriving home. Michael Kuhn had now given ten years to The Ventures Official U.S.A. Fan Club, and as he recalls; "Besides having our address listed in the newer CD packages, it was being published in some of the record collector and guitar magazines, resulting in the club growing bigger than we ever expected. I was working so many hours at the bank that I just could not keep up with the demands of running the club. It was a very upsetting time for me, as The Ventures were so personable whenever we met them, and they always treated us like family. Back when Kristi-Lynn was very small, the band's wives would take her shopping and buy her all kinds of goodies.

"Ironically, I was laid off from the bank four years later, and I decided to return to college. While taking classes by day, most of my time at home was spent studying, but I still kept up my collection, adding all of The Ventures' and Nokie's new music releases."

One month after the club's final newsletter, members received a letter of introduction from Mike's close friend and Ventures enthusiast, Dennis Coté. Located in Newark, Delaware, Dennis started *Ten Seconds to Heaven*, a news and music-trading periodical named after The Ventures' recording. Although Dennis could not supply records, his bulletins contained track lists, cover shots, and sources for the latest CDs and videos. Perhaps the best feature of *Ten Seconds to Heaven* was the monthly discography installments of Ventures recordings, ending with a list of over 1,000 songs that the band had recorded. However, as Dennis explains, good things don't last forever; "*Ten Seconds to Heaven* was a test of sorts. I tried it because Mike wasn't doing his letter anymore, but the research turned out to be more than I could handle. Thinking back, I probably should have published every three months. It was fun and I really didn't want to stop, but just as they had with Mike, job and family obligations got the best of me."

Although Mike Kuhn was urging club members to lobby Cleveland's Rock And Roll Hall Of Fame as early as 1988, it was during Dennis Cote's *Ten Seconds to Heaven* era that the induction campaign began in earnest. In the paradox of all time, The Ventures were being bypassed each year, possibly due to their three most successful albums. *The Ventures Play Telstar And The Lonely Bull*, *Golden Greats*, and *Hawaii Five-O* had all gone Gold with no original music content. It seemed that the Hall Of Fame's "music experts" had no appreciation for an artist's version of music written by others, although "covering" had remained a popular practice since the beginnings of the industry.

Having fallen on deaf ears, Dennis Cote's petitioning campaign ended in the spring of 1993, along with his Ventures newsletter. With no American based club, Ventures fans forgot about the Rock And Roll Hall Of Fame, but only for the time being.

Dennis Coté

Matt Burgess with "The King of Guitars"

Subscribers responding to an ad in *Ten Seconds to Heaven* received a publication by fifteen-year-old Matthew Burgess of Madera, California, who now owned his father's Ventures collection. Simply titled *The Ventures*, Matt's pamphlet addressed potential subscribers with "Hey dude! Here you have it! This booklet will come out every two months. For ten dollars, you will get stuff from this club like info, discographies, and picture letters like this one. The Ventures made over 700 albums all over the world. I am going to try to get every album, CD, 45, cassette, and EP that they made. Well dude, hope to have you as a member soon!"

It was soon obvious that Matt's club was mainly a means to contact traders and sellers to complete his record collection. He was well on his way towards that goal when he surrendered the entire collection for a chance to meet Nokie. While contacting fans in several countries, Matt had found Keiichi Takaya to be a good trading partner for recordings of Nokie and The Ventures. When Takaya asked Matt (through an interpreter) if he planned to attend the Semie Moseley Memorial Concert in Arkansas, Matt indicated that he would love to, if not for the prohibitive traveling costs and the fact that he was a minor. The conversation ended with Takaya agreeing to cover roundtrip train fare for Matthew and his grandmother in exchange for all of the records Matt had collected to date. Seeing the opportunity of a lifetime, Matt agreed. In addition to his personal luggage, Matt took two suitcases of LP and single records to Booneville.

Part of the Matt Burgess collection on the walls of the Semie Moseley Auditorium

Moseleys, Loretta (partial), Irene, Michelle, Andy, Mark – Mosrite employees in back

Ten years later, armed with a computer and eBay password, Matt resumed his quest to collect Ventures albums. At age twenty-five, he reflected; "I've been in love with The Ventures' music since my dad turned me on to it when I was five years old. What really got me going again was having the privilege in the year 2000 to see The Ventures in Santa Cruz, and finding Nokie Edwards with them! During that show, which I found really awesome, I introduced a friend to The Ventures' music, and he hasn't listened to anything else since. Like me, he is collecting everything he can get his hands on."

THE SENIOR VENTURES

1993 began with Bob turning fifty-nine in January, only to be passed by Don, who hit sixty in February. By spring, recording was in session for a CD to coincide with the next Japan tour. Although *The Ventures Play Mega Hits* was another Hiro Kadoma concept, production was now in the hands of The Ventures. As a steel guitar was desired on some numbers, the band drafted Greg Leisz, a wizard reputed to fit in with groups of every genre. As on preceding albums, Dave Carr, Bob Spalding, and Joe Barile helped fill out the sound. Don remembers a note of sadness that struck when he slipped out of the studio on April 19 to pick up some lunch; "We were recording *Mega Hits*, and I went into this deli where they had a radio playing. While I waited for our sandwiches, I heard that saxophonist Steve Douglas had just died of a heart attack during a recording session. We were saddened and shocked because he was only fifty-four, and here I was, having just turned sixty." According to Steve Douglas, the admiration had been mutual, his having pled guilty in an early eighties interview to being "a real Ventures freak."

Although booking fewer homeland concerts, The Ventures accepted occasional car shows or club jobs. The band's last real U.S. tour had been a short jaunt around the Pacific Northwest in 1991, sharing a bill with the UK's Herman's Hermits.

A few dates were booked in the spring of '93, by which time Bob had brought Yumi to America, where she saw how different a Ventures gig was, compared to the big shows in Japan. However, first impressions are not always accurate when assessing a Ventures performance in America. A one-night stand with Joe Rosignolo and Tim Wilson as crewmembers was not quite the same as hitting the road for a hectic month with soundman Steve Bonhag and crew traveling ahead to make ready for each show. Furthermore, unexpected incidents might occur, such as Mel's mishap on May 8 during an antique car club gig in the Spokane Coliseum. During Gerry's vocal performance of *What'd I Say*, Mel dropped from sight behind his massive drum kit. Playing all the while, he slowly rose up looking very annoyed as he shouted at Joe for assistance. Mel's drum-stool had collapsed, having been improperly tightened at set-up. Unnoticed by the crowd, Joe ran out and corrected the problem while Mel continued to play, never missing a beat during the entire stressful episode. Gerry, Bob, and Don had noticed the accident, but being equally cool and professional, played on as if nothing had happened.

Tim Wilson, Mel Taylor, Joe Rosignolo, and Don begin a sound check.

By the second week of June, the band was ready for Japan Tour '93. Don's beloved Jazzmaster was looking a little rough by now, but with a new bridge installed, the 1968 guitar was much preferred over the 1984 model that he carried as a spare. Mel endorsed Darwin drums at the time, but had recently discovered a quality snare made by Canopus in Japan. Loyalty to drum companies was never important to Mel, but when he gave the Canopus snare a permanent place in his kit, the company produced a Mel Taylor signature model.

As M&I had scheduled two four-day mini-tours on the island of Hokkaido, a second flight took the group from Tokyo to the island. Recalling this jaunt, Don remarked; "Traveling around Japan has become a way of life for us. We enjoy the people and the country so much, and they seem to feel the same way about us." Sharing this view, Bob adds; "The groups that play only the large cities don't know what they are missing. Every time we visit, we make many wonderful friends and enjoy more marvelous countryside. I would love to spend the rest of my life there if the Japanese government permitted foreign retirees."

The Ventures always had something new for Japan, and this year was no exception. With the freedom afforded by cordless guitars, they moved around the stage during certain numbers to play opposite one another. Mel perpetuated the excitement by touring through the crowd with a wireless drum pad during his Caravan solo, stopping here and there to let someone tap out a few notes. On September 12, Toshiba preserved the final concert for CD, LaserDisc, and videotape. The production was so popular that six years later, *'93 in Japan* became the first Ventures concert released on DVD.

RUMBLE

Musically, 1993 ended with a small tour on the American West Coast. After the final concert, Bob returned to Vancouver, Washington, and Don, in the process of relocating to Tacoma, went back to California. Josie explains; "In 1993, Don leased his Sherman Oaks home with an option to purchase. But as winter fell, the people leasing the home declined on the purchase, so for the time being, Don and Janis returned to California."

In the early hours of January 17, 1994, the strongest earthquake to ever erupt in a North American city rocked Los Angeles. Widespread damage included the collapse of freeway structures, office buildings, apartment buildings, and homes. Gerry's home escaped with minor damage, but the others were not so lucky. For Mel and Fiona, destruction of their glass and ceramic souvenirs of worldwide travel was most heartbreaking. With similar losses, Don and Jan nearly lost their Sherman Oaks home. Severed gas and electrical lines caused many homes, including the Wilsons', to catch fire. While many homes burned to the ground, the water main to Madelia Avenue remained intact, and Don extinguished the fire by climbing onto the roof with his garden hose. The house remained a terrible mess, as did thousands of neighboring structures. While waiting nearly two weeks for the utilities to be restored, Don and Jan cooked meals and heated water on their outdoor barbecue. With fifty-seven deaths, and injuries in the thousands, damage in Los Angeles was over twenty billion dollars. For Don, the loss was uninsurable, with restoration costs in the neighborhood of $200,000.

Again, Japan Tour '94 began on the island of Hokkaido. For this three-month trek, Don along a guest; "That year, my son Tim came with us. He would have been about thirty then. He was with us for less than three weeks when he said, 'I've gotta go home, Dad. I'm whipped!' And he wasn't even playing or doing any work! He was just traveling with us. I guess we are just used to this life on the road."

Celebrating another Ventures anniversary, Japan now honored the group for the thirty-five years since its 1959 formation, and also for *Ginza Lights* having recently been voted Japan's "All-time number one song."

Since Eric Clapton's 1992 *Unplugged* MTV concert, The Ventures had considered recording an album with acoustic guitars. It took a few years to happen, but the project began with an acoustic set for the 1994 Japan tour. The set included oldies *Mexico* and *Tequila*, two Japanese titles, and Bob Dylan's *Don't Think Twice*. For new material,

Maria Elena was added, the medley being crowned with Gerry's ever-evolving rendition of *Classical Gas*. Audiences savored even more diversity when Gerry sang the rockabilly standard, *Mystery Train*, and Don played lead guitar on a medley of *Rebel Rouser*, *Ghost Riders*, and *Detour*. The added variety was impressive, and, as one Japanese devotee put it; "The fans had mixed feelings of wonder and amazement!"

A ninety-minute show at Urawa Culture Center was preserved for VHS tape and LaserDisc, but Toshiba simply presented thirty minutes covering the acoustic set and medleys. This was highly irritating to the fans, all of who would have enjoyed the band's stage antics during *Wipe Out* and *Walk-Don't Run '64*, along with an exciting rendition of *Flashback* and the seldom heard *Blue Chateau*. The full concert later appeared on VHS in Japan, providing hope for a future DVD release.

~ ~ ~

Since 1982 in the John Belushi biography film *Wired*, music by The Ventures was increasingly heard in the movies. Next came 1988's *Crocodile Dundee II* ("Walk-Don't Run"), followed in 1993 by the Deniro-DeCaprio feature, *This Boy's Life* ("Perfidia") and *Wayne's World 2* ("Wipe Out"). In 1994, Miramax Films released Quentin Tarantino's groundbreaking *Pulp Fiction*, winning an Oscar award for its screenplay and a platinum award for the MCA soundtrack. The Lively Ones' version of *Surf Rider* topped off a soundtrack replete with vintage rock instrumentals. As Don recalls; "We had forgotten about that song for over thirty years when Mel called to say we were receiving a Platinum Record award because *Surf Rider* was originally a Ventures recording."

When fans wondered why The Ventures' version wasn't used for the soundtrack, Bob Bogle explained; "From what I heard, Quentin Tarantino picked the music from his personal collection of 45s. We had the song on our *Surfing* album, but it was never released on a single in America. When cassette and disc sales of the *Pulp Fiction* soundtrack exceeded three million, we received Triple Platinum awards for our composition of *Surf Rider* as played by The Lively Ones."

A damper on the 1994 holiday season arrived from Judd Hamilton with news that brother Danny had passed away. Later, Judd reported; "As reasonably matured and thankful family men, Danny and I had reunited musically. We were working on an album as The Hamilton Brothers when he fell ill with Cushing's disease. He lost a courageous struggle with it on December 23, at age forty-eight."

GUITARS, BIRTHDAY CAKES, AND WEDDING BELLS

By March of 1995, The Ventures were again recording an album for the Japanese market while preparing for the annual tour. Although the fifteen-track *Pops a La Carte* had a French title and six of the ten Japanese titles were not translated, the content would please anyone loving guitar instrumentals. His guitar growling on numbers like *Have You Ever Seen the Rain*, Gerry put his gentle touch on *Maria Elena* and the temperate Japanese pop tunes. The big surprise came from Bob, who hoisted his Jazzmaster for the surf classic, *Miserlou* and the jazz standard, *Stardust*. During sessions at Biff Vincent's Front Page Studios, Bob also led the band on *Lisa Marie* in his legendary style. Renamed *Romantic Moon*, the track remained "in the can" for another six years until being released under a third title, *Island Moon*. While rehearsing for Japan, The Ventures received an invitation to celebrate Nokie's 60th birthday at a party in Auburn, Washington, a town roughly fifty miles north of Nokie's home at Randle.

~ ~ ~

Since meeting Judy Fetters, Nokie's career on home ground had begun to accelerate. New CD releases on her U&U [Unique and Unusual] record label were promoted with a fan club quarterly and merchandise that included T-shirts, tour jackets, and *Nokie Edwards* guitar strings. While doing live performances along America's West Coast, Nokie's long-awaited Christmas album was released along with a new CD, *Nokie & Friends*. The Japan version of this album had a few bonus tracks reminiscent of Nokie's Ventures days, plus *Walk-Don't Run '94*, a surprise take of *Walk-Don't Run '89* with Roger Fisher's screaming guitar accompaniment.

While enjoying sales of the guitars made at the Arkansas Mosrite factory, Keiichi Takaya continued booking Nokie for performances in the Tokyo area. Video recordings were available to club members, and compact discs appeared on Tokyo's NMT (Nokie-Mosrite-Takaya) label. Of special interest then was a set of four *Ventures Sound Karaoke* CDs in which Nokie's part was all but eliminated, allowing the aspiring student to play lead guitar on Ventures tunes with accompaniment by the Takaya band.

10-inch yellow bumper sticker - Japan

In addition to fan club news, Judy mailed out CDs, autographed photos, Nokie ball caps, T-shirts, and guitar strings. The extra work soon forced her to cut back to a semi-annual fan publication as she organized a surprise birthday party for Nokie. Judy began planning a full year in advance to provide music, food, and fun for over 200 people. Invited guests included friends and celebrities on both sides of the Pacific, The Ventures, their families, and Nokie's entire fan club. While negotiating with hotels and campgrounds for package deals for guests, Judy sought out performers that would be honored to entertain at Nokie's 60th birthday. As she traveled with Nokie to concerts and guitar clinics at home and in Japan, and to recording sessions in Seattle, it was not easy to keep the surprise party a secret.

A month later, on May 9, people gathered in a spacious Auburn supper club for a buffet style meal with entertainment provided by no less than five musical groups. While country music dominated, surf music fans were treated to the sounds of Canada's Falcons. A Seattle filming crew had been hired to provide an opportunity for absent club members to later enjoy the evening's highlights. As Josie recalls; "I had just celebrated my 80th birthday, so I was surprised while attending Nokie's party to be presented with a bouquet of roses from The Ventures, and a special cake from Nokie. I was also delighted to hear Don and Bob perform with Nokie, having not heard them together for over ten years. My only regret was missing Gerry McGee, who had signed for some film work in Louisiana, and Mel Taylor, who was in Europe on business with Fiona."

The "film work" to which Josie referred, was to be Gerry McGee's most significant to date. Named after a spicy, Southern Louisiana side dish, *Dirty Rice* was the project of that State's award-winning documentary filmmaker, Pat Mire. In a tale of rural hardship in Cajun country, Gerry arranged and played a score of Cajun, zydeco, and blues in addition to acting the part of an ill-tempered banker. While playing an accordion, Gerry sang in French, a Cajun song written by his father.

THE GUITARMAN

Nokie received no less than three beautiful guitars for his birthday. First, Don and Bob gave him a shiny new Dobro guitar, the instrument commonly heard in country and bluegrass bands. Later, the Fender Company, having learned that Nokie's vintage '62 Jazzmaster re-issue presented in 1983 had been stolen, presented him with a beautiful new Jazzmaster. This one, however, was a standard edition, having the correct neck and headstock, whereas the special edition presented to each of The Ventures had the neck of a Stratocaster with its narrower headstock.

The third guitar gift came from Ramon Jacinto, a very special guest from Manila in the Philippines. With three pickups to provide a multitude of tones, the body of the deep red RAJ model was decorated with hand-inlaid seashell.

 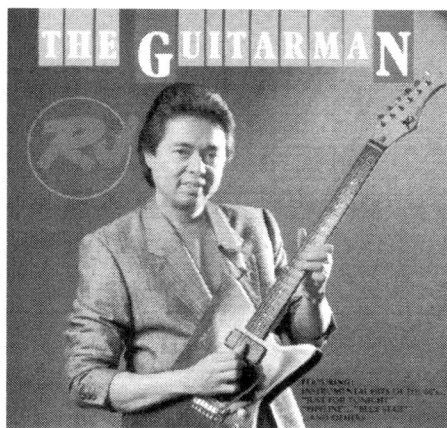

Ramon Jacinto in the '60s and the '90s

While visiting with The Ventures in Japan, Ramon Jacinto had related the tale of his survival during his country's political dictatorship, but to those at the birthday party, it was a new and fascinating story. In 1972, Ramon had been running the family steel mill corporation when President Ferdinand Marcos, in fear of losing his position, suddenly established a dictatorship. Anticipating disaster, the Jacinto family began moving its assets to foreign banks. Next, Marcos declared martial law, seizing the steel mills and Ramon's network of radio stations, but by then, Ramon and his family were out of the country and remained as exiles for the next fourteen years. In 1986, Marcos was ousted from power and Ramon returned to his home country. Within a few months, the family's steel mills and radio stations were returned. As Ramon put it; "We were very lucky. After everything was settled, we were only out about twenty-five million." At age forty-five, "RJ" plunged into business, music, and politics. In a matter of months he was operating and performing in his own popular rock 'n' roll nightspot that was soon the Mecca of the country's elite. In honor of his musical idols, Ramon named his new twin office buildings Ventures 1 and Ventures 2. He also established The Ventures Bank, which would soon boast eighteen branches in the Philippines.

Ramon's next acquisition was a small guitar repair shop that eventually became a factory. As an admirer of both Fender and Gibson instruments, RJ Guitars combined Ramon's favorite features of both. By 1991, he had recorded two fine instrumental albums in his own RJ Recording Studios. Released on his Viva-RJ label, *RJ The Guitarman* [VCD-91-005] and *RJ Guitarman II* [VCD-92-036] presented medleys of past hits by groups such as The Ventures, The Shadows, and The Fireballs. Ramon's success in music, business, and politics continued well into the twenty-first century.

During the party, so many musicians in one place gave Nokie the opportunity to do what he loved best. Jamming continued late into the night while guests either chatted at the tables or danced to every style of music imaginable. The following day, RJ planned an enormous recording project for Nokie that would take place later in the Philippines.

When the festivities ended, Nokie and Judy had little time for rest. Three days later found them in Vancouver, Canada for a NAMM type show called *Music West*. For publicity purposes, Fender's Product Training manager Peter Horsman, again presented Nokie with the new Jazzmaster, but by now, Nokie was showing more interest in several fancy Telecasters from the company's Custom Shop.

Mike Beddoes (The Falcons), Nokie, and Peter Horsman (Fender)

During this event, Nokie was careful not to miss a guitar clinic held by Australia's premiere fingerpicker, Tommy Emmanuel. In fact, no one at the clinic showed more excitement with Tommy's performance than did Nokie. Later, when the virtuosos met, Nokie heard how Tommy grew up listening and practicing to The Ventures' recordings. The two vowed to meet in the future with hopes of performing together.

The following week found Nokie and Judy touring through Montana and then on to Nashville for a recording session at Mark and Andy Moseley's Sound Control Studio. The result was a fine collection of instrumentals ranging from Dave Brubeck's *Take Five* to a Nokie original called *Mosrite Forever*. Nokie having just turned sixty, the album was titled *1995 Celebration*, but by the time the CD was released, he and Judy would have more than a birthday to celebrate. On July 17, the couple slipped off to Reno, Nevada to be married before returning to their new home in Oregon. Then, it was off to Japan for a six-week tour and honeymoon. Because *1995 Celebration* appeared in Japan *and* the USA in limited quantities, the compact disc became a rarity. In less than ten years, a copy in good condition could fetch well above $100 on eBay.

A FAN WITH A RECORD LABEL

Through the 1940s and 1950s, disc jockey Gene Norman ran a Hollywood nightclub called The Crescendo. Big bands and top jazz acts were billed "Gene Norman Presents at the Crescendo." It was this phrase from which Gene formed the name for his record label, GNP Crescendo. In the sixties, the label embraced blues, rock, and surf, recording upstart groups like the Challengers and the Renegaids (sic). With a father in the recording business, son Neil honed his musical skills to the point of becoming an active session guitarist while still in high school. By age thirty, Neil was busy with his own band, plus producing, composing, and arranging for others as GNP's A&R chief. During this time, he noticed that The Ventures' current recordings were unobtainable to Americans not members of foreign fan clubs. While assembling an ultimate compilation of sixties surf music, he thought; "Why not include something special from The Ventures?" Acquainted with David Carr, Neil was soon introduced to Mel and Fiona, and when Don and Bob returned after Nokie's birthday, a quest for something unique turned up the 1985 medley with Bob on lead unifying *Wipe Out*, *Walk-Don't Run*, *Pipeline*, and *Hawaii Five-0*. The track was distinctive, having appeared only on a vinyl single with limited distribution. It had then been called *Venture 25*, but for Neil's *Surf Crazy* CD, it was simply entitled *The Ventures Medley*.

The meeting of Neil Norman and The Ventures led to another proposal that Davy Peckett had been suggesting for years; an entire Ventures album on GNP Crescendo. Soon, a contract was signed for summer release of a thirty-track album to include a set of four live cuts from the '94 Japan tour. In line with all GNP products, the album was attractively packaged and well documented. *The Ventures SURFING* [GNPD 2246] was an important step for The Ventures, once again having high-quality product on North America's record racks containing material released only in Japan. There was more to come, but as Don remarked later; "There are a few tracks that simply do not belong on a Surf album. I mean, what's *The Lonely Bull* or *Sukiyaki* got to do with surfing?"

~ ~ ~

Arriving in Tokyo, The Ventures had their first look at a book published there in commemoration of their 35h anniversary. Although *THE VENTURES – From The Beginning To The Present* [pub. Kawade Shobo Shinsha] was written entirely in Japanese, its hefty photographic content would please Ventures' faithful in any country.

Fresh material for the '95 tour came mostly from the new *Pops a La Carte* album. In addition, Bob led the band through a medley containing no less than nine of the group's hits from the sixties, including the controversial *Lolita Ya Ya* as well as the aging Fleetwoods' classic, *Mr. Blue*. Also new was Gerry's interpretation of *Surf Rider*, owing to the recent publicity generated by the movie, *Pulp Fiction*.

While it was usual for Don and Gerry to sing, this year, the audience heard Bob step up to sing *Proud Mary*. New for Gerry were *Georgia On My Mind* and a vocal version of *Mary Jane*, heard instrumentally on *Pops a La Carte*. Hiro Tsunoda had composed this lovely Japanese tune, but with verse by lyricist Christopher Lynn, the song became *Mary Jane On My Mind*. The popular Acoustic Set was slightly modified this year, but Gerry's increasingly impressive *Classical Gas* remained as the astonishing closer.

Japan tours usually ran smoothly for The Ventures, but they were not immune to an occasional glitch. It was during a sound check roughly two weeks into the schedule, when Mel stepped off the drum-kit riser onto a box that had been provided as a stair. The box tipped and rolled, causing him to fall and land on it. Mel knew from the pain that something was broken, and when Fiona took him to a hospital, he was treated for two cracked ribs. As Bob recalls; "It wasn't easy to play without Mel, but we had to do it. We even played *Wipe Out* without a drummer. Our concerts were usually sold out, and there would have been just too many complications if we cancelled." Mel was back on stage the following night, and while his pain was considerable, fans reported that his performance was thrilling as ever. Once back home, Mel often told of how weird it felt on that night of July 7th, to be watching off stage while The Ventures played as a trio.

As happened more often as the band grew older, sad news was waiting upon their return to America. This time, it was the death in August of steel guitarist, Orville "Red" Rhodes. Although arthritis had slowed him from performing, Red had recently toured with The Monkees' Michael Nesmith before succumbing to lung disease at sixty-four.

By fall of 1995, Biff Vincent had moved his studio from Costa Mesa to Burbank in the former location of Kendun Recorders. With Neil Norman as producer, The Ventures shaped one of their most exciting albums. With seventeen sixties hits gleaned from both sides of the Atlantic, fans on either side heard old favorites mixed with unfamiliar tunes. For roughly one-third of the set, Bob played lead while Gerry handled the bass. Norman intended the disc for his GNP Crescendo label, but The Ventures were still under contract with Toshiba-EMI. *Wild Again – The Ventures Play Heavy Hitters* debuted on the Japanese label exactly one week ahead of their 1996 tour. America and the rest of the world did not see the GNP Crescendo release until Christmas '97 when *Wild Again* [GNPD 2252] hit American stores. Included were a nine-minute interview and a glossy, twelve-page booklet. If there was any question as to whether The Ventures still rocked, their treatment of *Bongo Rock* and *Wham* dispelled all doubt.

In Tokyo, the annual Yellow Jacket convention saw up to a hundred competent guitarists gather to share their talents. The Ventures were invited to these functions, but tight schedules or the Pacific Ocean had been constant barriers. Nevertheless, the invitation for December 3, 1995 was not in vain. Bob and Yumi Bogle took the time to attend, combining the event with a visit to Yumi's family. At the convention, the couple enjoyed meeting jazz guitarist Kazumi Watanabe and Yumi's homeland guitar icon, Kozo Murashita. During the concert, Bob joined in on stage to play either bass or guitar on several numbers while fulfilling a request to sing *Proud Mary*.

FENDERS KEEPERS

To Ventures fans, it seemed only fitting that Fender Musical Instruments began their 50th Anniversary celebration by introducing Ventures and Nokie signature models. The band had endorsed other brands, each time reverting to the trusty Fenders with which they began. Nokie had given the Mosrite another run, but he was more than happy to help in designing a signature Telecaster.

Built by Fender Japan, the Limited Edition models were marketed for only one year. The ash bodies and matching headstocks of The Ventures Stratocaster, Jazzmaster, and Jazz Bass were finished in a transparent "Charcoal Burst," barely showing the wood grain and fading to deep black towards the edges. A bound rosewood fretboard with pearl block inlays, a pearl pickguard, and The Ventures' logo on the headstock rounded out a classy set of instruments. Nokie's Telecaster was laminated ash, basswood, and maple, with an attractive flame maple top. All models featured pearl inlaid position markers and hardware finished in gold plate.

Design changes were made by each of the instruments' namesakes. Gerry specified the Eric Clapton model with added gold Lace-Sensor Gold pickups. The bass was simply given a heavier bridge for increased sustain, but as Bob relates; "When asked for input on the Jazzmaster, we presented some changes we had always wished for. We never used that pickup switch up high on the body, so we had it removed. We also asked for the control knobs to be mounted further away from the strings, and special Seymour Duncan JM pickups designed to produce the tones of the original Jazzmaster."

For his Telecaster, Nokie had Seymour Duncan design special humbucking pickups. For a "single-coil effect," taps were wired to a pull-switch on the tone control. In addition to his special bridge and a tilted headstock, Nokie requested an optional banjo key for tuning the low E string. A favorite Mosrite feature, the guitar boasted a zero-fret next to the "nut," ensuring uniform string height, sustain, and tone. There was, however, one feature of the L.E. Telecaster that appeared forgotten. Between various numbers, Nokie often switched between a flat pick and a thumb pick, storing one behind the pickguard. The L.E. being designed *without* a pickguard, Nokie was constantly digging into his shirt-pocket for a pick.

"VENTURES DAY"

Nokie and The Ventures began 1996 by promoting their signature guitars at the NAMM show in Los Angeles. Always a great place for getting together with other celebrated musicians, this one did not disappoint. Among those on hand to chat and renew acquaintances were Marty Stewart, Jerry Donahue, Albert Lee, James Burton, Seymour Duncan, Arlen Roth, and Steve Wariner. A highlight in conjunction with the music-merchant show was Fender's Fiftieth Anniversary concert at the Anaheim Hilton, hosted by movie icon Steven Seagal. In addition to The Ventures, the show featured country stars Bonnie Raitt and Lee Roy Parnell, rockers Ritchie Sambora (Bon Jovi), Kim Wilson (Fabulous Thunderbirds), and *Guitar Player*'s Best Overall guitarist (four years running), Eric Johnson. A surprise occurred when Manhattan's popular ska band, The Toasters, invited Don Wilson to join them for *Pipeline*. Josie was also in attendance; "After the guys had played, Bonnie Raitt came on stage. She began with, 'Hey, how about those Ventures! I just met them backstage and I got an autographed picture from them, so now I can go home happy!' Steven Seagal seemed a bit aloof, but his manager came over to The Ventures' table to congratulate them and to say that he was a fan."

With no American fan club, awareness of such proceedings was limited to the few who either joined an e-mail service called CompuServe or by maintained membership in the UK fan club. An efficient Gerry Woodage still published *Ventures Resurgence*, but events like this were usually history by press time. At this point, club members focused on the See-For-Miles compact disc series containing two Ventures albums each. The set eventually numbered over two-dozen and included some welcome Japanese material. Before the series was completed, a similar project began in America. The One Way Records collection from Capitol-EMI went a step further, filling each disc with two to five bonus tracks.

Publicity generated by the new guitars sparked several bookings for The Ventures on home ground, but Gerry McGee still found time for session work between working on a own solo album and a new Ventures project. Early in the year, he stayed late at Biff's Front Page Studio to play a unique solo in *Secret Agent Man* for New York ska legends, The Toasters. [CD title, *Hard Band For Dead* - Moon MR-083].

M&I of Japan, owner of Bad News Records, commissioned Gerry's solo project. As Gerry recalls; "Some days it was a challenge to remember whether to drive to Red Zone Studios or to Front Page Studios. I really had to watch my calendar." During the sessions for his *Born in Louisiana* project at Red Zone, Gerry occasionally picked up the accordion for a Cajun blues number. Friends Delaney and Kim Bramlett provided vocal background along with Marty Greb on keyboards, Larry Taylor on bass, and Gerry's son Kane on drums.

The evening of April 12 would kick off the first of a string of concerts at Hollywood's House of Blues, but as Don recalls, they joined Nokie further up on Sunset Strip to receive a tribute during the day; "We had been contacted by Director Dave Weiderman and invited to be inducted into Guitar Center's Rock Walk of Fame. It was a surprise and an honor to receive that recognition."

The Hollywood Rock Walk is a gallery of handprints and memorabilia museum created in honor of musicians and significant others having contributed appreciably to the evolution of rock music. Since 1985, the mega music store had collected handprints and signatures in an attractive patio display. Just in from a show in Santa Ana with The Torquays, Nokie was included in the celebrated group.

Handprints in Guitar Center's Rock Walk

Other inductees of the day included The Chantays (*Pipeline*), Jan and Dean (*The Little Old Lady From Pasadena*), and The Surfaris (*Wipe Out*), but as Josie recalls, The Ventures received a special honor; "After their friend Jeff Baxter presented The Ventures to the crowd, Los Angeles Mayor Richard Riordan proclaimed April 12, 1996 as VENTURES DAY. The band received a proclamation from him, and Don had it framed for his wall. That evening, before going to the House of Blues, the guys and I met at Don's home where the group presented *me* with a beautiful oak wall plaque with engraving on a gold plate!"

Following two opening groups at the House of Blues, The Ventures conveyed their staying power with an up-tempo ninety-minute show that also featured guest artist Jeff "Skunk" Baxter on *La Bamba* and *Tequila*. As no autograph session followed the show, only the more resourceful fans were able to congratulate their idols in the Green Room.

It was here, on Ventures Day in Hollywood, that yours truly met Josie for the first time in person. The ensuing correspondence, resumed after twenty-five years since Josie's disbanding of the fan club, sparked the creation of this book.

Although much of America remained unaware that The Ventures still existed, the band could easily sell out a thousand-ticket venue like The House of Blues. This they did, at the House of Blues and other fine concert venues. Avid followers had reached cult status, but even they could not imagine the popularity of their heroes in Japan, where a photo of The Ventures was commonly found on prepaid "phone cards," and band-member figurines were available much like America's Elvis dolls.

Amid the mass of available Ventures recordings was a string of three-inch CD singles, one featuring their *Snows of Nagano* as the theme for the '96 World Skiing Cup held in Japan. Even so, it was difficult for fans outside the Orient to imagine the band being whisked off to Tokyo for a TV special in the third week of May, knowing they must return in three weeks to begin Japan Tour '96. This happened when Fuji TV beckoned The Ventures to appear on its *Group Sounds Carnival* to be aired in early June. A Tokyo flight was quickly booked for the May 21 videotaping. Viewers of the show saw the group perform its latest super-medley known as *Surf On Guitar '96,* released that month on a three-inch CD single. On this occasion, it was Gerry instead of Bob leading the band through ten of their most requested songs.

Since 1992, Ron Furmanek and Kevin Reeves had remastered and digitally remixed The Ventures' albums *Telstar, In Space,* and *Live In Japan '65* with amazing results. Now, during the summer of 1996, Furmanek and Reeves produced the last of five special Ventures compilations. Designed to resemble an issue of *TV Guide,* the cover for *Tele-Ventures* [E2-53738] appeared to be a cheap budget item with its antiquated and reversed photo portraying the entire band to be left-handed. However, the production on this twenty-five track CD made it must-have item for the serious Ventures fan. Subtitled *The Ventures Perform The Great TV Themes*, it presented first-time stereo versions of *On the Road, Secret Agent Man,* and *Blue Star,* the latter two without the familiar background vocals. There was also the condensed version of *Dick Tracy*, intended to launch the TV episodes had the series been aired. On this, Mel opens with rolling percussion amid wailing police sirens before the band joins in and skips to ending in less than a minute. The complete stereo version of *Dick Tracy* was also included.

MEANWHILE IN NOKIE LAND

As The Ventures prepared for yet another Japan tour, Nokie spent the next few weeks in Nashville playing the NAMM show and a Chet Atkins Appreciation Society [CAAS] convention. Meeting his early idol was a great moment for Nokie, but he was disappointed that the chance to sit and talk privately with Chet consistently eluded him. While in the country music capital, Nokie appeared on TNN, known then as television's "The Nashville Network." The host on *Prime Time Country* was Bob Eubanks, known from his L.A. days as a sixties DJ, his Cinnamon Cinder teen club, and later coordinating shows like *The Newlywed Game*. Brandishing his new Limited Edition Telecaster, Nokie played *Walk-Don't Run* with the studio band before sitting down to be interviewed. The first comment by Eubanks expressed his confusion at Nokie's western garb while playing "surf music." Attired in white Stetson and cowboy boots, Nokie laughed off the host's good-natured digs. He later explained; "There was no time to rehearse with the band or I would have played *Alabama Jubilee*. I asked them what they would like to play, and they all yelled, *Walk-Don't Run!*"

Nokie with Bob Eubanks on *Prime Time Country*   TNN

    In accordance with plans made during Ramon Jacinto's visit, Nokie's next trip took him and Judy to the Philippines where they had arranged to record sixty cuts for a four-disc set. Once there, Nokie spent the end of July and nearly three weeks in August recording *seventy-five* songs for a *five*-disc set while giving three concerts and appearing on radio with Ramon's band, RJ and The Riots. Difficulties arose when both Nokie and Judy became quite ill with suspected food poisoning, putting them out of commission for a week. Having an immediate booking in Japan, their trip from Manila was an uncomfortable eight-hour flight to Tokyo on August 20. Having quickly lost forty pounds, Nokie was exhausted as he performed beside Yuzo Kayama within hours of arriving. Nightclub and fan club dates were also booked, at which time some unpleasant facts came to light. It was here that Nokie and Judy learned that NMT Records had been shorting them on CD royalties. A new representative in Japan was quickly sought, with long-time Ventures fan, Ryusuke Tomiyama picking up the reins. Nokie and Judy came home tired and weak, but there was little time to rest. Next on their agenda was a change of residence to Sweet Home, Oregon, followed by plans to create a "Nokie Land" where folks would come from as far away as Japan to enjoy an annual weekend of music and friendship.

CHAPTER FIVE

The Ventures Forever

In The Ventures' 1993 Japan Tour video, a dressing-room scene focuses on Mel Taylor as he holds up a promotional photo of the band. He says; "See that guy right there? It ain't me. That guy ain't sick. I'm sick!" The comment went almost unnoticed, but in the years to come, viewers wondered if Mel was trying to tell them something.

As revealed later, Japan Tour '96 ran smooth for over a month before anyone suspected that something was wrong. The tour had begun on June 19, and was to end on September 29. Mel had been coughing more than usual, but it had not interfered with his performance. In fact, he was now featured as a singer for the first time with The Ventures, adding *Johnny B. Goode* to an all vocal set comprising Don's *The Twomp*, Gerry singing *I've Got A Woman*, and Bob doing *The Letter*. During the sixth week, Mel called home on July 29. After talking with Fiona and agreeing to come home early on August 9, he called Dave Carr with a request to find a temporary drummer. With two months left in the tour, Mel believed that his treatment of pneumonia would not take long. Meanwhile, a physician in Tokyo ordered him to return home immediately. If the doctor indicated anything worse than pneumonia, Mel did not reveal it. Arrangements were hastily made for ex-Terry-and-the-Blue-Jeans drummer, Hisashi Takeda to fill in, and Mel flew home on August 1.

Bob, Don, and Gerry fully expected to see Mel again before tour's end, but it was still an emotional moment when they said goodbye. Ten years later, Don still had difficulty suppressing tears; "The Ventures don't socialize much between recording jobs and touring, but when we're together, we are like brothers. It's always been like that, and it's likely how we've managed to stick together so long. Mel was really upset at having to leave us, and it really bothered me to see him like that when the elevator doors closed. We didn't know it, but it was the last time we would ever see him."

Ten more days found The Ventures in Yamanashi, about sixty miles west of Tokyo. Back in California, Mel had been diagnosed with lung cancer. On the evening of Sunday, August 11, he was rushed to the Encino-Tarzana Regional Medical Center. There, the famed drummer and manager of The Ventures succumbed to cardiac failure brought on by a malignant tumor. In another six weeks he would have been sixty-three. As Fiona recalls; "We couldn't believe how fast it happened. It was less than a week since Mel told us 'I'm not giving up. I'm going to fight this.'" Bob recalls receiving the dreadful news; "About an hour before we went on stage, we were told that Mel had died of lung cancer. It was a terrible shock and it really hit us hard. It was very difficult to carry on and do our show."

A wave swept around the globe and rippled for over a year as the news reached fans of all ages. It is said that everyone in North America remembers where they were and what they were doing when they learned of the Kennedy assassination. So it is with Ventures fans when they learned of Mel's passing. The band never imagined the closeness felt by so many until one of them was taken away.

Outside the family, the last musician to talk to Mel, (having visited him on Saturday, August 10) was David Carr; "After getting the call from Japan, I obtained a video from

Bruce Gary, the original drummer for The Knack [*My Sharona* -1979]. Mel had also known him, so I thought Bruce would be a good stand-in. He had agreed to go if needed, and it was he who informed me on Monday morning that Mel had passed away. It was a complete shock, and I felt devastated, having worked with and become a good friend of the man for over twenty-five years." Bruce Gary had played drums since childhood, beginning with a surf-rock band that played Ventures music. He had played Japan twice after The Knack's *My Sharona* topped charts all over the world. The record sold three million copies in Japan alone. While Bruce was acquiring his work visa for Japan, Keith John called Fiona with condolences, and offered to be the replacement drummer.

Upon hearing from Fiona, Harvey Wicklund flew to Los Angeles to be a pallbearer. Hal Blaine, who normally avoided funerals, attended this one, citing Mel as his "first non-jazz drummer influence.", only to learn that at that very moment.

Mel was buried on Wednesday, August 14, 1996 in the Forest Lawn cemetery of Mount Sinai Memorial Park in Los Angeles. In lieu of flowers, the family requested donations to *The Boys and Girls Club of America*, a group promoting the enhancement and development of children needing adult care and supervision. Several months later, when the band was able to attend, a marker cast in bronze was unveiled.

The inscription reads, *A.J. Marik*

BELOVED HUSBAND, FATHER, GRANDFATHER

SON AND BROTHER

ALWAYS LOVING, ALWAYS LOVED

HE LOVED PEOPLE, LAUGHTER, AND MUSIC

News of Mel's death was carried in all of the guitar magazines as well as others such as *TIME* and *Billboard*. Major U.S. Newspapers also carried the report, and publications such as *Modern Drummer* printed biographical obituaries. In the trade magazines, record companies like Toshiba-EMI posted a full-page in memory of Mel. *Vintage Guitar* magazine's February '97 issue saw the beginning of a four part series entitled "Venture of the Month." The article on Mel marked the first time that the bulky guitar-collector's bible featured a drummer.

Suddenly evident from countries around the world was the great number of Ventures fans that were drummers that had been attracted to Mel's skill, technique, and power as he executed his craft. His passing especially rocked Japan, which took it as a major loss to the country's modern culture. While revealing that doctors there had been the first to diagnose Mel's cancer, a press release depicted The Ventures as being "revered almost as much as the Emperor."

The band would have come home for Mel's funeral, had the tour not made it impossible. With over thirty-five concerts left, M&I Company would have suffered dearly, as would thousands of prepaid ticket holders. In keeping with their contract, the band continued thrilling its audience in town after town, the only consolation being their knowledge that it was what Mel would have wanted.

Invasive Silence by Josie Wilson

He speaks to me in that remembered vibrant voice
I feel his gentle touch on my arm
The spontaneous laugh, breaking out unexpectedly
The little chuckle, so endearing
I hear his voice as he tells that funny little story
The little jokes he loved to tell
They always brightened my day.
He traveled his chosen path with steady footsteps
Never shy and always caring
Though there may have been a hint of a tear in his eye
He was never afraid to say "Hey, I love you guys"
Now, his love pervading everywhere
Embracing all who loved him
The road ends,
The drums are silent.

MEL TAYLOR 1933 – 1996

Hisashi Takeda performed an admirable job on *Wipe Out* and played a five-minute solo in Caravan. In respect for Mel, the drummer's trademark bass tattoo was omitted. The concerts ended with the new, five-minute *Surf-On-Guitar* medley. As Bob recalls, it was almost three weeks later when their promoters made a decision; "Near the end of August, M&I decided that a local musician acting as our drummer was unfair to our audience. They insisted we bring in an American for the final month, so we summoned Bruce Gary. He arrived in time to play with us for the month of September. He worked out fine once we convinced him that he needed to rehearse, especially on the medley. He was great on *Wipe Out,* and at the end of *Caravan* he played a terrific solo. Some in the audience said he even looked like Mel."

After winding through the country for another dozen shows, the band returned to Tokyo on September 16 to perform a memorial concert in Nakano Sun Plaza Hall. Completely sold-out, the aisles were crowded with news reporters and TV cameramen. Fiona had flown in, accompanied by Leon and wife Patti. Producer Neil Norman was also present. Soon to release *Wild Again! In* American, Neil was impressed to see The Ventures perform five of its numbers in a live environment.

At the end of the first set, professional musicians influenced by The Ventures were invited to join in the performance of *Caravan.* Responding guest artists were Ryomei Shirai, Kozo Murashita, and Hiro Tokutake, the highly skilled guitarist who led a band called Dr. K Project. The second set began with Fiona greeting the audience in Japanese and introducing Leon. The audience heard how Mel, upon learning of his terminal condition and after consulting with Leon, had expressed a desire to have his son carry on in his place. Near the end of the concert, Leon played his father's drums on *Diamond*

Head, Pipeline, Wipe Out, and the *Surf-On Guitar* medley. While Bruce Gary handled the remainder of the tour, audiences were assured of Leon's return. As the shock of losing Mel slowly waned, fans around the world rejoiced, not only because The Ventures would indeed carry on, but that the line-up remained as Bogle-Wilson-Taylor-McGee.

Bruce Gary

Leon Taylor

Home from Japan, The Ventures offered Fiona the job as their new business manager. Having worked closely with Mel for at least fifteen years, no one was more qualified than she. With the sudden void in her life, Fiona obligingly accepted.

In the coming months, a number of Japanese albums surfaced in memory of Mel. Following his sixties *In Action* album with bonus singles, came *The Dynamics Live in Japan '73* with eight more numbers than the vinyl *Roll Over Beethoven* issue. Then came *The Mel Taylor Memorial Album* with The Ventures' selections of his greatest work and a sixteen-page booklet. From Japan came *Feedback*, an uncanny two-disc Ventures tribute dedicated to Mel by the Dr. K Project. The Ventures' newest album, *Wild Again II,* was also given the subtitle, *A Tribute to Mel Taylor.*

Ten years to the month later, as Ventures fans lamented the anniversary of Mel's passing, they learned of Bruce Gary's untimely death. At the age of fifty-four, the talented drummer passed away in the same hospital where Mel had died. It was later discovered that Bruce had kept his cancer a secret for over two years.

WEB SURFING

A week after Mel's death, the first Ventures related website appeared as Hideki Soeda put Japan's Yellow Jacket fan club online. Soon to come were Paul Moraga's *Virtual Ventures* USA website, "The Fabulous Ventures" section of *Sandcastle Virgin Islands* run by Arnold Van Beverhoudt Jr., and Richard Wilson's *Legendary Ventures* website in Canada. In January 1997, University of Missouri graduate student Michael Salmons launched *Underground Fire*, an e-mail chat group that soon boasted membership from around the globe. One of the group's objectives was to get The Ventures inducted into Cleveland's Rock And Roll Hall Of Fame. The fact that the band had not been admitted long before was deemed a major travesty. Arnold Van Beverhoudt Jr. used his website to launch the campaign by garnering signatures for an untiring series of petitions. Simultaneously, Michael Kuhn began mailing letters to his former club members urging them to get online. At the same time, many Ventures fans discovered www.eBay.com, e the new global marketplace where a fan could build a collection beyond his wildest dreams if he watched for bargains or chose to bid wildly. Also luring bidders were unauthorized T-shirts, pins, bootleg recordings, and the occasional fake Gold Record award. Never before had "Buyer Beware" become so pertinent.

The next threat came when technology allowed duplication of CDs and DVDs using a home computer. Fortunately for The Ventures, the bulk of their fan base had matured with them, and had already updated their collections with legitimate purchases.

As 1996 was the year for the National Museum of American History to celebrate the electric guitar for its cultural influence on blues, country, and rock, and The Ventures were invited to headline the Smithsonian Institute's weekend of seminars and concerts in Washington D.C. Upon arriving in Washington, one of the first items on Don's agenda was to call George Babbitt, the band's first drummer, and invite him and wife Louise, to the Grand Opening cocktail party. The next day, they all met for lunch and the Babbitt's learned of Don's recent patriotic composition, "Be Strong America." A marvelous idea struck Louise Babbitt, and she requested a demo copy from Don. Within two years, her splendid plan would unfold.

While in the capital, Leon made his American debut as a Venture on November 15 at George Washington University's Lisner Auditorium. The program also included Junior Brown and his double-necked, hybrid Guit-Steel guitar. Brown had played *Walk-Don't Run*, *Pipeline*, and *Secret Agent Man* in clubs since 1966, but this year he paid homage to The Ventures in a seven-minute *Surf Medley* that combined Ventures' licks with those of Jimi Hendrix and Les Paul on the CD release, *Semi-Crazy* [Curb D2-77843].

Highlights for The Ventures included radio and television appearances; meeting Les Paul and Junior Brown; and a reunion with General George T. Babbitt. They also appeared for fifteen minutes in a program for public television called *Electrified, Amplified, and Deified: The Electric Guitar, Its Makers, and Its Players*.

Tanya & Junior Brown with The Ventures in Washington D.C. ~ Junior on Guit-Steel

By January of 1997, the Bogle's were settled in their new Washington home, but the Wilsons were not so lucky. They had moved back to the state in 1996, but until their new home was finished, they were staying with Don's brother-in-law when, on January 28, Don was rushed to hospital for emergency gall bladder removal; "I was hurting during the Japan tour but I ignored it, hoping it would pass. Eventually, the pain became unbearable. The doctors told me the operation would take an hour, but it took about two and a half. They said my gallbladder was like a piece of shoe leather! In about a month I was fully recovered in time for the move into our new home near Tacoma. Then right away, I had to return to Burbank to start recording our next album."

LEON TAYLOR

Melvin Leon Taylor was born September 23, 1955 in Johnson City, Tennessee. When he was three, the family moved to Los Angeles where Leon grew up and made his home. Leon soon began imitating his father, spending hours beating on pails and garbage cans in the family's garage. Seeing the boy's interest, Mel gave Leon a snare drum and taught him how to play it. Leon grew up to the music of Jimi Hendrix, Iron Butterfly, Styx, and Kansas, but he also had access to Mel's fine collection of Ventures records.

Two years younger than Leon, Michael began with guitar, but when the brothers started playing in bands, Michael switched to the bass. The boys played mostly at parties until the eighties when they began earning money in nightclubs. At times, father Mel would show up and be invited to sit in on a couple of numbers. As the group (known as Restless Society) evolved, the name was changed to IXL and featured various female singers. The band folded in the early nineties when Michael moved to Australia.

Michael and Leon ~ 1988   *Fiona Taylor*

While working as salesman for a video surveillance company, Leon delved deeper into the music business. When talking of retirement, Mel had hoped Leon would take his place, but no one imagined an unexpected tragedy. When the time arrived, there was suddenly a great deal of material to learn, but as Leon explains, he had a head start; "I had been playing Ventures records since I got my first drums around 1966. Even when I got my own band and started playing more progressive stuff, The Ventures' music was stored in the archives at the back of my brain. When I first joined The Ventures, I had to listen closer to my dad's fills and play the songs the way I was expected to. After a couple of years, I started phasing in my own style as well."

Leon's experience began quickly as The Ventures hit the studio in February to record *New Depths -Wild Again II* [GNP Crescendo GNPD 2259] between concerts at the Hollywood House of Blues and the Belly-Up Tavern near San Diego. Continuing with sixties classics, *New Depths* was noted for a number of guest artists. In addition to producing, Jeff Baxter performed on three of the hits. In keeping with the tribute to Mel, brother Larry played bass on one track and Bruce Gary drummed on another. Bob Spalding played his composition, *Blue Dawn*, and added rhythm on a couple of tracks. David Carr's keyboards were heard throughout, but the surprise of surprises was Mr. Duane Eddy playing lead guitar on *I Fought the Law* [which later received a GRAMMY nomination], and sharing the lead with Gerry McGee on *Spanish Armada*. The Ventures were thrilled to finally work with one of their early heroes, but Duane's remark during mixing; "rhythm guitar should be felt, not heard" caused a few raised eyebrows (especially Don's).

Another gem on *New Depths* was the band's treatment of the Freddie King classic, *Hideaway*. Gerry always excelled when interpreting the blues, but having just finished recording his own blues album, he was in excellent form.

Gerry McGee and Duane Eddy at Front Page Studios   R. Spalding

Recording for *Wild Again II* had just finished when a private booking came in from Japan's huge Takashimaya department store chain celebrating its new Osaka outlet. Money being no object, The Ventures were flown to Japan to do a one-hour show for company employees on April 20 at the luxurious New Otani Hotel.

Exactly one month later, Gerry was back in Tokyo with son Kane, Marty Greb, and Larry Taylor for the annual Japan Blues Carnival. Gerry; "It was a week-long festival with shows in various nightclubs and a couple of days outdoors in Hibaya Park. We had rain on those days, but the place was packed and everyone had a great time. We were elated to see B.B. King and Buddy Guy taking part." Billed as The Gerry McGee Blues Band, the group promoted their new CD, *Gerry McGee - Born in Louisiana* [Bad News Records BNCY-28]. Aiming square at his Japanese fans, Gerry's eight originals included his lament, *I Want to Go to Tokyo*. Cover tunes included classic blues from the likes of Robert Johnson and Arthur Crudup along with Gerry's vocal rendition of *House of the Rising Sun*. A delightful surprise at the end of the disc was Gerry's finger-snapping jazz original, *No Parking Zone*.

During the short stay in Japan, Gerry became further acquainted with Hirofumi Tokutake, also known as "Dr. K." The friendship and respect between the two guitarists produced some fine recordings a little later.

Gerry was soon back in the States, rocking with The Ventures on a California mini-tour that began with a sell-out concert at The House of Blues. For this show, Neil Norman's Cosmic Orchestra opened (with David Carr on keyboards), followed by the masked and energy packed Los Straightjackets from Nashville. When The Ventures hit the stage, Jeff Baxter, who had been heavily involved in the group's recent studio sessions, appeared as guest artist. The Ventures next appeared in Bakersfield at the Buck Owens Crystal Palace. As Buck introduced The Ventures, he acknowledged sixty-eight-year-old Gene Moles in the audience. Sold-out shows in San Diego and Costa Mesa left The Ventures in fine condition for Japan.

A NEW ERA FOR OLD FANS

Japan Tour '97 featured some new faces on stage. First, the country was now seeing Leon on drums, and later, twenty-five-year-old Michael (Leon's brother and the second son of Mel) appeared. Although primarily a bassist, Michael played lead guitar on *Pipeline* the evening of July 26. Traveling with a friend, he followed the tour for a week before going back to Australia.

The tour ended in mid-September with the final show being video recorded. One might comprehend the popularity of The Ventures in Japan if they consider that videotaped concerts were often shown on television before their commercial release.

After signing with M&I for five more years, The Ventures were home and resting. While they were in Japan, a generous helping of their old single recordings had appeared on a CD from Ace Records in the UK. A project of *Pipeline* publishers David Burke and Alan Taylor, *The Ventures in The Vaults* was purported to be a collection of rarities. To a fervent Ventures collector, there was little that was new, but as some of the tracks were Japanese-only releases, many found some pleasant surprises on the disc. Extracted from EMI's master tapes, sound quality was tops, with rarities to entice the completist such as *The Way You Look Tonight* without the stringed accompaniment heard on Japan's vinyl release. Although sales encouraged Taylor and Burke to do it again, it took them almost two years. When *Volume Two* emerged, the twenty-six rare tracks not only staggered fans, but The Ventures as well. As Bob stated later; "When we heard those tracks, it was like looking in a mirror with a huge hangover. We had thought them to be long ago discarded garbage. We hated to see such archaic material released at this point in our careers in case new fans formed their opinion of us from it."

Seasoned fans, however, rejoiced at the collection of slightly primitive performances. As Dave Burke recalls, he and Alan Taylor received enough praise to encourage more volumes; "I have come to feel vindicated, as the vast majority of fans share my view that the *Vaults 2* tracks are simply too good to be abandoned. Many have said that this has been the most important release since the sixties, and I agree. I sincerely believe that The Ventures do not truly understand the value that we, the fans, place on this material. As musicians, they have developed enormously, so when they listen, they hear only suspect notes or tiny errors. What we hear is the time and place that this wondrous music represents to each of us. It's like finding an old family photo album - it doesn't matter that they are a little browned and grainy. They evoke priceless memories of a glorious past that we all shared together."

For owners of the *Vaults 2* CD, some errors in the booklet should be noted. The voice at the end of *Stick Shift* is not Don Wilson, but a sample from Larry Verne's 1960 novelty hit, *Mr. Custer*. Also, some of the recording dates were shown to be in July '65, when the group was actually on tour in Japan [*Lites Out*, *Spanish Armada*, and *Saigon*]. Dave explains what happened; "As Liberty grew during the sixties, completed takes were compiled onto one large tape. It is sometimes the date of compilation that is logged, and not the original recording date. Unfortunately, I didn't realize this at the time."

With help from Gerald Woodage, volume three was completed in 2005 that was more like volume one, in that *Artesia*, an original from the sixties, and Bobby Goldsboro's *Honey* were the only "new" tracks to the serious collector. However, several clean recordings were presented of tunes known only from home-taped cassettes submitted previously by Don to the fan clubs. Year 2007 brought volume four, which, along with early versions of many Ventures classics and "first time on CD" singles, included at least eight completely new antiquated tracks. As always, extensive documentation accompanied the disc in the form of a fifteen-page booklet [Ace CDCHD 1176].

In November of 1997, The Ventures made a tour of America's West Coast that included Portland's historic Crystal Ballroom. Although the facility had opened during World War I, 1959 was the year in which patrons began enjoying rock entertainment on the venue's famed "floating dance floor." The end of this eight-stop tour took The Ventures to Canada's coastal cities of Victoria and Vancouver, with a ferry ride between. Then, with plenty of time before the band's next studio work, Fiona compiled a tour for the East Coast that virtually filled all of March 1998. With concert dates now posted on The Ventures' own website, good turnouts were ensured at every stop.

Leon and Don ready for an evening at Legends in Victoria B.C.

Don tops his Mesa 4-12 with a 100-watt Ampeg.

New Ventures CDs and U.S. tours stirred many old fans to pick up their guitars and look for like-minded cohorts. One was Byron Tietjen, a card-carrying fan since the early sixties near Syracuse, New York; "Our formation, which began in 1996, was more of an evolution. I had just started learning the guitar, and after several months of practicing to Ventures CDs in my basement, discovered that a fellow worker played the bass. Dave also liked The Ventures, and we started practicing together. Seeing The Ventures carry on with Leon Taylor inspired us to play more. One day at the gym, a fellow noticed my Ventures shirt. He was also a fan in addition to being a very good player. He had started with Ventures music when he was young (who didn't, right?). Anyway, I invited him to join us as a rhythm player. Before long, he got us a gig at a demolition derby. Although we were not good yet, we were unique and the crowd seemed to like us. As it turned out, there was a drummer in the audience who practically begged to play with us. Suddenly, we had a full band and we called ourselves The AdVentures. Since 1997, we have had an even better drummer (Tony), and *two* rhythm guitarists (Bjorn and Paul). We sound a hundred times better than our first gig, and the crowds still love the music. We get paid for most gigs now, but we still do a lot of benefit work. Our policy is to never let price stand in the way of performing. We don't get much cash, but we sure have a lot of fun."

In the West, Raga Raghavan renewed his interest in The Ventures. Upon discovering the Underground Fire chat group and enough like-minded locals to form his own band, he was soon selling CDs on a website. Dozens of stories surfaced, such as the one from Tom Ott, who, while developing as a proficient player, had his Ventures interest rekindled by new technology; "In 1967 when I got out of the army, I still couldn't do all the leads on those 'play guitar' records. Over the next decade, I bought all of the records I could find while The Ventures seemed to disappear from the face of the earth (I didn't know they had defected to Japan), but I never got any better on the guitar. Two decades later, when computers and the World Wide Web exposed them for me, I started buying every Ventures CD I could find and anything else that would help. The most valuable thing I have discovered is video. For the first time, I could see how and where on the guitar neck that the guys played."

THE LAST WALTZ IN AMERICA (NOT!)

Since 1988, The Ventures seldom toured locally until their eastern spring tour of 1998. There were various highlights along the way, but none so grand as the first stop in Washington D.C. As part of its *Guest Artist Series* at DAR Constitution Hall, The United States Air Force Band had invited The Ventures to play in concert with them for an audience of 3000. The band gladly accepted, and at the end of February they were rehearsing in Washington for the Sunday performance on March 1.

When the orchestra, under the baton of Commander-Colonel Lowell E. Graham was confirmed to be in tune, the silence was broken by Leon hitting the introduction to *Hawaii Five-0*. The audience contained a goodly number of Ventures fans, including Sonny Rivera, Mike Kuhn, and Byron Tietjen, who reported that if any of them could suppress tears when the orchestra joined The Ventures on one of their biggest hits, they *had* to be tough. After a vibrant opening, the pace was maintained as Don introduced *Telstar*, enhanced by choral backing in the final stanza. The applause was deafening. Later, the orchestra came on strong with trumpets and solo mandolin in *The Lonely Bull*. Bob and Gerry then traded glistening signature Fenders as Bob took the lead on *Peter Gunn*, again with rich orchestral backing.

General George Babbitt in the spotlight

Don then told of The Ventures being a duo in 1959, and of his sister's teenage neighbor who played drums on their very first record. With that, four-star General George T. Babbitt entered and sat at the drums. With Bob still on lead and Gerry on bass, George rolled the intro to *Walk-Don't Run*. He played WDR very well, displaying a wide grin throughout the performance. When The Ventures' anthem was finished, General Babbitt was given a Pacific Northwest Hall of Fame Gold Record Award.

Several more hits climaxed with *Caravan* with the orchestra adding tasteful fills. The supposed closer ended with a mesmerizing six-minute drum solo and bass tattoo by Leon, but there was one more big surprise. Two years back, when Mrs. Louise Babbitt had asked Army veteran Don for a tape of his *Be Strong America*, she had passed it on to the Air Force Band's Chief Master Sergeant, Daisy Jackson, in whose office Louise had formerly worked. Struck by Don's beautiful patriotic work, the idea was born to include The Ventures in the Guest Artist Series of concerts. Meanwhile, the piece was arranged for the band, with vocal performance by a magnificent troupe called The Singing Sergeants. *Be Strong America* was the finale, with The Ventures fronting the orchestra and chorus. When the Stars and Stripes descended from the ceiling, a rainbow of emotion swept over the audience, whose standing ovation thundered for a full two minutes. It had been a show to make every Ventures fan extremely proud.

Don's presentation to General George T. Babbitt

As Leon said later; "I found it to be a great experience, having never played with a conductor. A couple of times he motioned for me to play a little quieter, even though I was boxed in a Plexiglas® screen. I was fairly excited, and it's a bit difficult to hold back when playing Ventures' rock 'n' roll music at the best of times. The highlight for me was playing *Hawaii Five-O* with a full orchestra. It was pretty amazing."

According to Bob, even the veteran Ventures were stirred; "Being on stage with that fifty-piece orchestra was simply a magnificent experience. The sound was so moving that it nearly brought tears to my eyes." (For Ventures fans in the audience, it *did*).

The '98 tour left thousands of North American Ventures fans elated and rejuvenated. It seemed, however, the beginning of the end for such extensive excursions. With three-quarters of the group in their sixties, and Leon similarly health conscious, the noisy, smoke-filled halls and clubs were just too irritating. Around this time, Don began telling folks; "If you haven't seen The Ventures in Japan, you haven't seen The Ventures in their best light." While fans agree that the excitement and fury of The Ventures' on stage is much less evident on their studio recordings, few could afford the time and/or expense of a trip to Japan. For now, however, it seemed that fans not living in the Pacific Northwest would have to travel in order to experience The Ventures live. No one even dreamed of the day when smoking in all public places would be criminal offense.

SPICE IS NICE

In 1997, The Ventures had attended a show in Los Angeles that featured a female Japanese trio called V.I.P. With their Japan connections and having worked with such acts before, The Ventures became involved in producing *V.I.P.* Following their 1998 spring tour, The Ventures named, arranged, and re-recorded two original "Sato project" songs from the mid-eighties as *Flower of the Sun* and *Trail Blazer*. They became instrumental bonus tracks on their *Wild Again II* album, but with Japanese lyrics added, they were titled *O Game* and *Kanari Kiteru Koi* [Very Strong Love]. When the arrangements were ready, V.I.P. girls Miho Igarashi, Naho Kasai, and Yukari Sawano returned to Los Angeles to record over The Ventures' tracks. A mini CD was released in Japan during the summer, and one track was given to Neil Norman for the *Wild Again II* release in America. As mentioned earlier, this excellent GNP Crescendo release was renamed *New Depths* and given five bonus tracks, including Mel on drums in *Wipe Out 2017* from the *Wipe Out '88* video. Playing on the name of the then-popular Spice Girls, V.I.P became the "Rice Girls." To some, this seemed slightly racist, but the girls liked the name and retained it.

V.I.P. a.k.a. The Rice Girls

In the summer of 2000, the Rice Girls released a five-track CD in Japan that included instrumental versions by The Ventures and a Karaoke version of *Kiteru Koi*. On the vocals for *Kiteru Koi* and *O Game*, the backing tracks were slightly sped up, raising the key signature by a half tone.

DIRE STRAITS

In 1996, Nokie and Judy had barely recovered from food poisoning in the Philippines when Nokie's pacemaker brought serious trouble. According to Judy; "We were moving from Sweet Home to our new home in Elmira when Nokie was admitted to the hospital. They found that he had an infection in the lining of his heart and I almost lost him. Before he was released, I got everything moved real fast."

Due to the stress, Judy began suffering pneumonia attacks and a low blood cell count. 1997 was a busy year for the couple as Nokie played at various NAMM shows, the annual *Chet Atkins Appreciation Society* convention, and fundraisers such as *Muriel Anderson's All Star Guitar Night*. In August, with Mark Moseley at the console, Nokie and a host of top musicians recorded in Nashville's new Sound Control Studio. The massive project included seventy-five songs in a boxed set for Far East Island (FEI) Records in Japan. Nokie also completed ten thirty-minute videos for the company, each containing lessons for two favorite Ventures hits.

Nokie's 1997 Nashville sessions were followed by a trip to Japan in October. Once home, he was sidelined for major and long overdue dental work. While coping with the health issues and loss of various family members, Judy took care of concert bookings, the mailing of souvenir merchandise, and a fan club bulletin with color photos that rivaled anything ever seen by fans.

By early 1998, the Edwards' were indebted with medical bills as things simply got progressively worse. During tests for chest pain, Nokie was subjected to a coronary angiogram in which a catheter was inserted into his leg artery and advanced to the vessels supplying blood to his heart. Later, the artery began to swell and the doctor called for immediate surgery. The artery had been damaged, and the resultant swelling had blocked blood circulation and pinched off nerves. Doctors told Nokie how lucky he was that the artery had not burst, as he would not likely have survived the resultant internal bleeding.

Released from hospital, Nokie was thin as a rail and walked with a cane. As medical bills mounted, so did financial pressure. Bob and Don learned of the situation, and decided to help. Nokie accepted the idea of a benefit concert in which he could participate. A date in May was selected, and a young couple living in Eugene began making arrangements. Along with reduced rates for concertgoers, Springfield's Doubletree Hotel offered its ballroom and banquet facilities. Inexpensive tickets guaranteed food and an evening of music with an opening band for The Ventures. Local radio stations assisted, but at the last minute, the Springfield area was thrust into a state of shock when a Thurston High School freshman killed two students and wounded seventeen others after murdering his parents in their home. The somber mood in the community was blamed for a rather poor attendance at Nokie's benefit concert.

Within a month, Nokie was in Calgary, Canada, performing with George Tomsco of The Fireballs and Bob Clarke of Wes Dakus And The Rebels. Based in Edmonton, The Dakus band had led Canada's instrumental rock craze in the sixties with Clarke on lead guitar. The Clarke guitars he built and used were fashioned from bodies and necks obtained from Mosrite, and then fitted with electronic parts from Fender. The band's 1965 album, *Wes Dakus and the Rebels* [Capitol T-6120] contained a magnificent version of The Ventures' original, *Night Walk*. Clarke and Tomsco, having shared each other's works and played on each other's records while the two bands worked with Norman Petty in New Mexico, now enjoyed a long overdue reunion.

Calgary patrons were saddened to see Nokie walking with a cane, but it was soon obvious that his recent adversity had not affected his guitar skills. Near the end of the concert, Tomsco joked that upon returning home, he would be making his guitar into a lamp.

Nokie's next gig took him to Japan, where he worked with Yuzo Kayama to record concerts for television and a new CD. As The Ventures were doing their 1998 Japan tour, they appeared with Nokie and The Dr. K Project on Yuzo Kayama's August TV show, *Eternal Guitar Kids*.

Nokie, lean after illness, but always ready to play   *Calgary Herald*

As Nokie's health improved, he resumed his schedule of studio recording and personal appearances, sharing the stage with guitar virtuosos like Thom Bresh, Buster B. Jones, and Tommy Emmanuel. He even found time to help a very young Alexis Ebert launch a country music singing career. The assistance was not wasted, for she was soon recording, touring, and writing music for movies. By the time Alexis was thirteen years old, she had accomplished more than some good singers do in a lifetime.

On his own recordings, Nokie seemed to accept the fact that his biggest audience would always be his Ventures fans, but he continued to include the music he preferred in a skillful blend with the music that made him famous. The Ventures' reunion with Nokie had been timely, as Gerry McGee announced that, while he still loved going to Japan, he would rather not tour the smoke-filled clubs of America. He had no objection to sharing his Ventures position with Nokie, even in the studio.

Having Nokie back began paying off for The Ventures in 1999 when they signed with Japan's Blue Note nightclub chain for a weeklong tour in January. With Nokie billed as "special guest artist," the clubs were packed with fans paying the equivalent of $100 U.S. The tour became an annual event with live videos and CDs available soon after.

Broadening its horizons, Japan's M&I Company decided to expand its recording business beyond the Bad News Records label, and sell CDs by its star act, The Ventures. Capitol-EMI being outright owners of the group's vast back catalog, the solution reached was for The Ventures to re-record the best of their repertoire using the latest technology. The project was named *V-Gold*, playing on a term used in Japanese football, "V-goal." Recording began shortly after the band came back from Japan, but not before a February concert at The House of Blues in Hollywood. For this one, Johnny Rivers appeared as a guest, not only to sing *Secret Agent Man* with The Ventures, but to also to play lead guitar. Nancy Sinatra then joined the guys for *These Boots Are Made For Walkin'*, and agreed to guest on a future Ventures album.

Don Wilson, Biff Vincent, Dave Carr, Engineer Craig Nepp, and Leon Taylor

Knowing that fans were anxious to see Leon on the drums and Nokie with The Ventures again, Fiona began booking spring concerts around the band's April studio sessions. Nokie played the March shows at Santa Cruz and San Francisco, as well as the April *V-Gold* sessions at Biff Vincent's Front Page Recorders where he led the group on over thirty of the band's sixties favorites. Twenty tracks selected for the first volume included a few Japanese hits from the seventies for which Gerry played the lead. Dave Carr handled keyboards when needed, and to preserve accuracy in *Slaughter on Tenth Avenue*, the great Dino Soldo played his sax through a Leslie tone cabinet. Further exactitude included a female background trio on *Secret Agent Man* and a steel guitarist for *Hokkaido Skies*. As for drums, Leon had captured his father's style to the extent that nothing could have sounded better. Biff had retained his Hammond B3 organ for the studio, and according to Bob, it was put to good use; "Dave Carr played the organ on our new recording of *Honky Tonk*, and I saw then and there, that no matter how good the synthesizers are, they don't quite capture the true sound of the real B3. By the way, Gerry played lead on that one, but the liner showed it as being Nokie. Sometimes mistakes like that creep into the documents."

Ready in time for Japan Tour '99, *V-Gold* established the new M&I label with the number, MYCV-30001. As Don proudly remarked; "Not only was the sound quality superb, we own the masters so we have control of their release on other labels, within, of course, our contract with M&I." This referred to the condition that the recordings could not be released to another label until six months after the M&I release. Thus, fans in Europe and America were bound to buy M&I CDs unless they dared take a chance that the music would later appear on a local label. Rather than risk missing out, many bought the imported discs made available through fan clubs and Internet importers, which now included www.theventures.com.

V-Gold became a seven-disc series containing eighty freshly recorded studio tracks, a "best of" disc, and two live albums from the January '99 and 2001 Blue Note club tours. The series also introduced some Ventures originals, as *V-Gold III* contained *Bimini Bay* and *My Love For You* while volume four, *Hyper V-Gold* carried two great new songs with Bob Bogle's enchanting lead guitar style, *Open For Business* and *Island Moon*.

Packaging for the series was consistent, featuring a glossy booklet fronted by an antiquated pose of Don and Bob in their gold lamé jackets. When questioned about the cover showing only two of the musicians, Bob replied; "We didn't have anything to do with the artwork for those albums. They probably chose the picture because those jackets were 'gold,' and went along with the CD title."

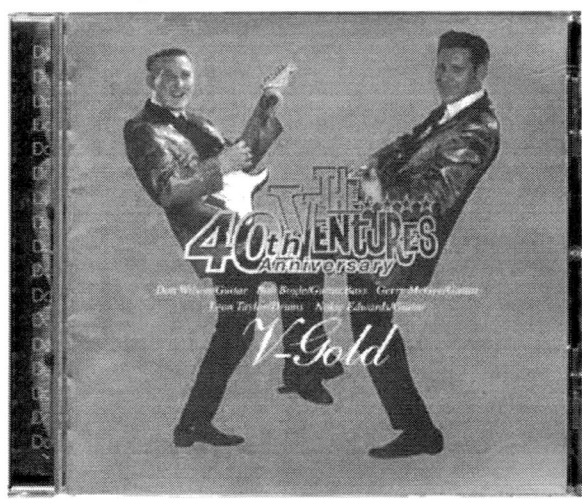

By now, a sizeable generation gap was developing in the ranks of The Ventures' fans. The thirty-five and under crowd seemed to prefer the newer albums, while the older fans professed to enjoy most everything the band had done. Although some listeners felt that the *V-Gold* recordings lacked the quaint raw magic of the originals, most were delighted with the rich, full sound. In *Pipeline Instrumental Review*, Alan Taylor and Dave Burke raved about every track in succession, their feelings being summed up in this excerpt from Dave; "…There is not a track that I do not rejoice to hear. Original arrangements are, by and large, kept the same, but the band has also brought something fresh to these tracks, be it modern technology, forty years of experience or, as I tend to believe, mostly one helluva drummer in Leon Taylor."

The *V-Gold* sessions generated seventeen new recordings slated for M&I's second release, *Walk-Don't Run 2000* [MYCV-30002]. With one exception, Gerry and Bob shared the lead guitar duties. As Bob Spalding was on hand for added rhythm, he played lead on his composition of *Spindrift* with Bob Bogle on rhythm and Gerry on bass. Several arrangements required saxophone, and for these, Dino Soldo was on the job. Nancy Sinatra also appeared on this album singing the 1966 Paul Revere hit, *Kicks*.

M&I Company was apparently not satisfied with just two CDs to promote during Japan Tour '99. Anxious for more Ventures titles on their new label, they latched onto anything they could find in time for release in June. Don helped by supplying sixteen of his vocal tracks, which the company released as *The Ventures Play Runaway: Don Wilson's Favorite Vocals* [MYCV-3005]. The album presented recordings from 1965 through the 1990s plus four fresh recordings including *Runaway* and *Keep Searchin'* with Dino Soldo on sax.

As The Ventures owned all rights to their *NASA Commemorative Album*, it was also given to M&I. After re-mastering and inclusion of Don's sped-up vocal on *Out of Limits* from the twelve-inch Tridex EP, it was dubbed *Space 2001* [MYCV-30006].

M&I next licensed twenty-two vocals by Japanese artists singing hits based on Ventures instrumentals for *Kayo Taizen* (*Cool Melodies*) [MYCV-30007]. The company also licensed *Swingin' Creepers, A Tribute to The Ventures* [Musick Recordings 0010]. This compilation of Ventures favorites by no less than twenty-three popular young bands had been released in America in recognition of The Ventures' 40th Anniversary and their outrageous omission from Cleveland's Rock And Roll Hall Of Fame.

Since Japan Tour '99 was booked near the end of June, Fiona booked five homeland concerts for the first half of that month. In Corpus Christi, Texas, "Fifth Venture" Bob Spalding made a rare performance on stage with the band.

Bogle, Edwards, Spalding, Taylor, and Wilson

In late June, Gerry McGee joined Don, Bob, and Leon on the flight to Tokyo for Japan Tour '99. Upon arriving, they learned that friend, Kozo Murashita, had died just two days earlier. After falling and striking his head at a rehearsal, he had passed away a few days later from a brain hemorrhage. A simple accident had taken the life of a wonderful musician at the age of forty-six. Kozo had professed The Ventures and Yuzo Kayama to be the most important parts of his life. Bob and Yumi Bogle attended the service.

Having recently experienced backache on stage, Bob had constructed a device made in the sixties by bassist Norm Riley, who worked with Mel in the Palomino house band. Describing his version of the device, Bob says; "I started out by installing a peg on the lower edge of my bass and connecting both ends of a waist strap to it to support the weight. It took too much time to undo when I switched to lead, so I installed a snap-lock on one end. It worked so well that I put the same thing on my guitar. With all of the weight off my shoulder, you might notice slack in the regular strap while I'm playing."

This was also the year for Leon to use new equipment in Japan; "I always take my Canopus snare with me, as the snare sound is a drummer's signature. I also bring my bass drum pedals because I'm used to them and I trust them. I had played DW [Drum Works] in Japan for the first two years until Mr. Shinichi Usuda, my friend at Canopus, began building complete drum kits. I found them to be great, and they just keep getting better. But I still use the DW kit back here in America."

In commemoration of The Ventures' 40th Anniversary, M&I Company published the most comprehensive tour book to date. One hundred giant glossy pages were packed with photos, history, and comments from The Ventures and admiring Japanese musicians. In further commemoration, Japan issued red and white Ventures Wine using the classic photo from the band's second album to label the bottles. Unfortunately for fans elsewhere, exporting was prohibited. They were compensated, however, when the band's American website offered a Belgian Chocolate Mosrite guitar in a simulated alligator case that included a Ventures guitar pick and a brief history of the band.

40th Anniversary Ventures Wine and a Chocolate guitar with case

Amazingly, there were still places in Japan that The Ventures had never played. Late in June they arrived on Miyako Island where they thrilled a sold-out audience in the thousand-seat Matida Citizen Theater. At this time, Toshiba-EMI released the first Ventures DVD, a reissue of the band's famous 1993 concert with multi-angle viewing.

As Bob recalls, their year's work ended with a special trip to China; "Late in November, we were booked by a group of businessmen that hired us for a one-hour performance at the Hong Kong Convention Center. Being mostly radio and TV moguls, the show was televised as a celebration for one of their long-time DJs. At the time, Gerry was engaged in some studio work with Emmylou Harris, so we got Nokie to play lead. We ended up playing for only half an hour, as they had also booked The Turtles and Eric Burdon and the Animals. We took our wives and flew in a couple of days early. We hadn't been to Hong Kong for about twenty-five years, but even though it's been handed over to Mainland China, there is still great shopping and wonderful sightseeing tours."

UPS 'N' DOWNS

Josie recalls that for her, 1999 was a year of tragedy, triumph, and trauma; "I was still reveling in the delight of having self-published my poetry in *If Verse Comes To Verse* in January when Don Nephew, my second husband passed away with diabetes. In April, just before my 84th birthday, I received a call from Amsterdam about a TV crew coming to America to record a half-hour program about The Ventures and their 1960 recording of *Walk-Don't Run*. They would stop first in New York to interview Bob Reisdorff, and proceed to L.A. where The Ventures were recording. Then, they were coming to Tacoma to interview me! Before they arrived on April 18, I was wondering what to say, what to wear, and how to act. As Don was in Los Angeles, I held the interview at his home, where they could film the gold records, pictures, and posters displayed on his wall. It was November before the program was shown in Holland, but I finally received a copy, which I thought was quite good."

The TV story of *Walk-Don't Run* was made for a lengthy Dutch documentary series entitled *Single Luck*. During each episode, a recording star discussed his single reaching number one on the Dutch pop charts. In this case, comments were recorded from Don, Bob, Nokie, Josie, Virginia Boles, Bob Reisdorff, as well as Gerry and Leon. Footage was also included from the 1960 Dick Clark TV production; *Beloved Invaders*; Nokie in the studio; and the recent Hollywood House of Blues concert.

Y2K - CHANGING TIDES

The year 2000 kicked off with a return to Japan for the Blue Note concerts in Fukuoka, Osaka, Nagoya, and Tokyo, again with Nokie as 'special guest'. Then it was back to Glendale for more work on the *V-Gold* series. The session was memorable to Gerry because; "It was the first time for me to record *Hawaii Five-O* with The Ventures. I'd played it with the U.S. Navy orchestra, but we had Dave Carr doing the horns and the kettledrums on a synth. Some of the other songs had Nokie or Bob on lead, and Don too. He played *Forty-Miles of Bad Road*, *Ghost Riders*, and *Rebel Rouser*." Other sidemen hired for the ongoing *V-Gold* sessions included one of the country's most recorded saxophonists, Dan Higgins.

As M&I Company was ready for yet another album, The Ventures had been looking for a new concept. Rap and grunge music were riding high on the pop charts, but it was no secret that the music was totally abhorrent to both the band *and* its fans. Inspiration struck when the group recalled Eric Clapton's *Unplugged* recordings and similar works appearing after. Thinking back to February 2000, Bob recalls how the project developed;

"At the time, our concept of an unplugged album was to record our old songs acoustically. We'd been kicking around the idea of doing our acoustic set in the studio for a while, but then friend Quince Buteau suggested that we do a whole set of songs that we'd never done before. It was a tough call, but we did it, and it worked."

A Ventures Official U.S.A. Club member some twenty years earlier, Quince Buteau was aware of the fans' craving for new material. Luckily, the band accepted his idea. Also assisting with song selection, Quince received credit as producer of *Acoustic Rock*.

About one month before their final studio booking, the band invited title suggestions from the Internet chat group, Underground Fire. As Bob recalls; "The songs were then selected by Quince. We were surprised at some of the choices, but we forged ahead and arranged the songs. Recording an entire album without amplifiers was one of the most difficult projects we had ever tackled. For variety, we used around a dozen acoustic instruments, and we never plugged in to an amplifier. We went through the [mixing] console quite a bit, as we needed some electric sounds in some of the songs. Not only was it new territory for us, the cost was almost doubled because of the new thirty-two-track digital technology. We were lucky to get one song mixed in a day. Sometimes, when listening to a recording a week after completion, we would hear something we didn't like and go back and mix it again. Sometimes we wondered if this was a curse, and if anyone but us could actually notice the difference. We had Nokie and Bob Spalding on hand as well as Dave Carr and Jeff Baxter. We wrote *Skunk Rock* and *Road Kill* especially for the album. We worked so hard and long on *Road Kill* that we were zonked by the time it was finished, so we renamed it, *Zonked*. Our engineer Craig Nepp stood by us for the entire project. Without him, we never would have made it."

The two original writings were registered under the band's new publishing company, Ventures Two Thousand Music. Simply titled *Acoustic Rock* [MYCV-30047], the album featured material from the likes of Dire Straits, The Shadows, and Eric Clapton and current hits like Ricky Martin's *Livin' La Vida Loca* and Fastball's *The Way*. Perhaps the most innovative tune was *St. James Infirmary*, a top-ten hit for Cab Calloway in 1931. The suggestion to record this blues-based classic came from a fan recalling Bob Spalding's excellent rendition on his 1990 cassette album, *The World Is A Curious Place*. Later, producer Quince Buteau humbly remarked; "It turned out quite well considering the time and budget parameters. Even if the project went over budget (they had planned four weeks and it took eight), it was miniscule compared to some that I've seen."

For the fans, "turned out quite well" was putting it mildly. They felt more like Josie, who, upon hearing the album, immediately commented; "I really think that *Acoustic Rock* may be the best thing they have ever done. This, coming from one who prefers the early albums co-produced by yours truly."

Although the fans loved the album, controversy persisted for nearly two years regarding expectations of a literally "unplugged" album. Many felt that that a guitar with a pickup under the strings is an electric guitar, regardless of the shape of the body. But as Bob explained; "We could have used pure acoustic guitars in front of the microphones, but we felt that the result would have strayed much too far from our established sound."

When the recording was done, Gerry rushed home in time for his induction to the Louisiana Hall of Fame at Lafayette. At the same time, similar honors were bestowed upon his late father, Dennis McGee.

~ ~ ~

In 1997, Microsoft billionaire Paul Allen constructed a $10,000,000 interactive museum in Seattle, dedicated to Pacific Northwest rock music, and especially to his favorite, The Jimi Hendrix Experience. The Experience Music Project [EMP] opened in late June with three days of concerts featuring stars from the past and present. As the one band to have continually performed and recorded since its 1959 inception, The Ventures were part of this celebration. During Grand Opening festivities, sixties DJ Pat O'Day introduced The Ventures, as well as The Kingsmen, Paul Revere and The Raiders, The Fabulous Wailers, The Dynamics, Merrilee Rush, Jr. Cadillac, and Gretchen Christopher of The Fleetwoods. Inside the museum, fans found a large tribute to The Ventures with a fine display of gold awards and history of Dolton records. Included was the studio log from Boles' Custom Recorders, its contents having previously been shared for the making of this book, and then contributed to the EMP by Joe's widow, Virginia.

Six days later, The Ventures were in Japan beginning their fortieth tour comprised of fifty-six concerts in eleven weeks. Aria Japan was now marketing their Ventures model 2000 Series, which the group had agreed to promote. Bob played the bass model for the duration, but Gerry stuck mostly with his Clapton Stratocaster. As Don recalls, he played the Aria for TV performances and the first part of each concert, before reverting to his primeval Jazzmaster; "There was a problem with the whammy bar, and with the guitar staying in tune. Aria was great about making changes, and they finally came up with a guitar that we could trust completely."

Aria Ventures models 2000 and 2001

Featuring active (battery-powered) circuitry, the instruments worked well, although their shape and dark brown finish seemed rather plain. Acknowledging its error, Aria quickly designed a colorful 2001 model in the shape of the Mosrite, trimmed with body binding minus the expensive onboard electronics. Also, the vibrato mechanism was redesigned to resemble a Fender model. Don found this guitar to stay perfectly in tune.

Instead of a video this year, M&I Company put the final concert on CD. With a colorful sixteen-page booklet, the double-disc package included Don and Gerry's vocals, Bob's medley, and some *Acoustic Rock* selections played on acoustic guitars. The set ended with a ten-minute *Caravan* featuring a drum solo by Leon, who introduced various numbers in Japanese; "After the first summer tour, Patti and I signed up for Japanese language classes at Pierce College in Los Angeles. It helped quite a bit, but we find if we don't practice, it's very easy to forget."

Meanwhile in Nashville, Nokie was busy with concerts and recording sessions. Following the Chet Atkins Appreciation Society convention, he had returned home to Oregon, where a meeting with Art Greenhaw and The Light Crust Doughboys led to recording two fine albums with the group. [*Adventure In Country Swing*, and *A Surf 'n' Swing/Fret 'n' String Christmas* - Art Greenhaw Records]. Next, it was a two-day Northwest Nokie Celebration at the end of July in Veneta, Oregon. In addition to Nokie performing celebrities included David Frizzell, Seymour Duncan, Gretchen Christopher of The Fleetwoods, Fireball George Tomsco, and speed-picker elite, Buster B. Jones. Happily for Judy, Nokie's new website had replaced the time-consuming club bulletins.

Although Nokie had not abandoned his signature Fender Telecaster, he was now often seen with a blue Carvin guitar. The Carvin company was happy to see him use this DC200 and an acoustic DC275 on his last two albums, and even happier when he named a song *and* one of the albums, *Carvin' It Out* [Loud Neighbors 1999]. The album was recorded in Minnesota with Nokie's friend Robert Coates, who also introduced Nokie to friend and fan, Tom "Zip" Caplan. Tom was in the midst of recording *Monsters and Heroes* featuring music from horror movies and classic TV serials. With Bob Coates on rhythm, Nokie and Tom shared lead guitar on the 1941 *Superman Cartoon Theme*.

Nokie's next album was *Pickin' It Up*, with cover artwork by engineer Jack DeFranco, a committed Ventures fan who had helped set up equipment at a 1998 Cleveland concert. After doing the same at concerts in Portland, Seattle, Corpus Christi, and Tokyo, Jack became the band's stage manager. As Josie recalls; "Don told me, 'Not only is Jack an extremely nice guy, he must also be a saint. When his company sends him around the world with first-class tickets, he takes a coach seat and donates the balance to a children's charity or the like.' When the comfort of first-class is forfeited on very long flights, it really does merit the title of Saint!"

Jack DeFranco

Jack's hidden agenda, should the job become available, had been to quit his job and manage The Ventures, but in the near future, that goal would be forgotten in lieu of a more important project.

When The Ventures returned from Japan, it was mid-September. News items waiting for them included Bob Reisdorff's move to California from New York; the destruction by fire of Washington State's historic Evergreen Ballroom; and the passing of Dick Glasser in July due to lung cancer. By now, it was becoming a common occurrence to hear of associates who had departed, but as Josie relates, no one in The Ventures' *family* was ready for the event of September 28.

"In September, I invited Sonny Rivera to come up from Florida for a visit with me in Washington State. We had a great week of catching up, shopping, and visiting. After almost a week, Sonny's left leg and lower back were hurting, so I drove her to a chiropractor who prescribed an ice bag on her lower back. That evening, we planned her 70th birthday party and then we went to bed. At seven thirty in the morning she came into my room and fell on my bed, hyperventilating and moaning 'my back, my back!' She seemed unaware of anything, all the while moaning and breathing very fast. I called my son-in-law John to come from next door, as he had worked in a hospital for over thirty years. He called 911, and in a matter of minutes paramedics were there and took her to the hospital. Shortly thereafter, Sonny died from a massive heart attack. Her wish to be cremated was carried out, and her ashes sent to Puerto Rico where her relatives live, and where husband Ray's ashes are located. She was an organ donor, and I sincerely hope her eyes allowed someone to see as many beautiful sights as Sonny Rivera had seen in her travels and in her journey through life."

TURN OF THE CENTURY

By January 2001, as Judy Edwards was recovering from back surgery performed in the fall, she stayed home while Nokie accompanied The Ventures on their third winter mini-tour in Japan. On this tour, M&I recorded a concert for the band's *V-Gold Live II* album [MYCV-30122]. The group was only home for a few days when Nokie fell on the winter ice, breaking the ball joint in one of his hips. It looked as if he would be unable to play a Seattle Ventures concert scheduled in February, but after implanting a metal pin, the doctors expressed amazement at Nokie's quick recovery. He played wonderfully at the EMP Sky Church on February 24. It was a rare occasion as American fans heard him play *Kyoto Doll* and *Paint It Black* in medley on the electric sitar.

The Ventures at Seattle's Experience Music Project

Opening for The Ventures was Los Straightjackets, the raucous group that appeared anonymous in their Mexican wrestling masks. They had opened for the band before, but this time, in their enduring homage, they presented each of The Ventures with a mask.

Internet technology provided widespread awareness for this show, attracting Underground Fire members from across the U.S. and Canada. Much of Don's family was also there, including Josie, now approaching the age of eighty-six. Many of The Ventures' long-time associates also attended, including Butch Hamblin, General George Babbitt, Christian Wilde, and Judd Hamilton.

Gen. George Babbitt,   Don, Harold "Butch" Hamblin, Bob   Christian Wilde

The Experience Music Project's Sky Church boasts the world's largest indoor video screen. Taking full advantage of this digital wonder, stage manager Jack DeFranco prepared a host of colorful visuals for the concert using Microsoft's *Power Point* software. In addition to huge logos and names of each member, dozens of album covers and flaming visuals flashed overhead throughout the concert.

Seated with Josie in the V.I.P. section was the Lieutenant Governor of Washington State, Brad Owen. Mr. Owen wore a Ventures necktie from Japan, and his wife wore earrings made from Ventures guitar picks. Well-acquainted with the couple, Josie explains their presence; "Some years back, The Ventures had played a benefit for DARE International [*Drug Abuse Resistance Education* for students]. Being then a Washington State Senator, Brad had arranged the fundraiser. Having once had a band of his own, he was also a long-time Ventures fan. Later, when Brad wrote a letter of appreciation to The Ventures, Don gave him a guitar while he was at a restaurant run by Don's son, (and my grandson) Tim. For a time, Tim had the letter framed there on the wall."

By now, the band was aware of efforts by Underground Fire to get them inducted to Cleveland's Rock And Roll Hall Of Fame. The thousands of names and letters petitioned by Arnold van Beverhoudt Jr. generated publicity in magazines, radio shows, and websites where columnists and disc jockeys expressed shock and dismay that The Ventures were not already inducted. Meanwhile, Jack DeFranco began his own mission to get The Ventures inducted by compiling a twenty-six-page book of facts that included names of no less than fifty legendary musicians or groups proclaiming to have been influenced by The Ventures or having learned from their recordings. While the booklet seemed to have little effect, Jack was just getting started.

THE HIP-HOP VENTURES

In the late nineties, a one-man British act known as The Wiseguys hit the UK charts with a Hip-Hop techno track called *Start The Commotion*. The catchy, rap-styled vocal was backed with looped samples taken from The Ventures' 1966 original composition, *Wild Child*. It wasn't long before North America heard *Start The Commotion* embedded in a TV commercial for Mitsubishi Motors, and later, in a promotion for Fox TV's *Ally McBeal* show. The Ventures were alerted to the track in August 1998 when Ventures fan Peter Malski contacted Fiona from his office at 7 Double 5 Management in the UK. As Bob recalls; "We immediately confirmed with EMI that we owned publishing rights for *Wild Child*. In the negotiations that followed, BMI awarded us two-thirds of the songwriting royalties for *Start The Commotion*. This is just another example of our sixties work paying off. Our music from that era has been, and continues to be the source for eighty percent of our income."

However, The Ventures were not yet finished with *Start The Commotion*. Royalties paid to musicians for other than record sales are known as "sync fees" where the user pays a one-time flat fee for synchronizing a piece of music to a moving picture, be it cinema, a television commercial, or even a video game. Bob continues:; "It wasn't long before we started receiving sync fees for the use of *Start The Commotion* in the movies. First it was *Gun Shy* [2000 - Buena Vista], then *Zoolander* [2001 - Paramount] and later on, *Kangaroo Jack* [Warner Bros. - 2003]. In the last few years, there have been around twenty instances where our music has found its way into TV commercials or motion pictures for which we received sync fees. Figuring that if we have done this well by accident, there must be a lot we are missing. When we engaged a fellow connected in the music business to 'shop' our sync fees, our music began doing very well in commercials and movies again. They paid well for it, but our older stuff was controlled by EMI, who are actually deal killers. Because of their high charges, we started picking public domain songs so as to get the writing and publishing royalties while remaining competitive. It's always nice to have some revenue coming in for our retirement."

How sync fee shopping began for The Ventures is an interesting tale unto itself. In early 2001, Art Ford, a friend of John Durrill, formed June Street Entertainment, a music-marketing firm that placed clients' music in films and TV. At the same time, while Nokie was negotiating with Bob's friend, Dave Callaham to produce singer Alexis Ebert, Dave introduced Bob to Art Ford regarding shopping for Ventures sync fees. Finally, as recalled by John Durrill; "I began talking to Art for exactly the same purpose, and I put a deal together for The Ventures without even knowing that they had the same intentions. When The Ventures learned of the connection, they allowed me to market their music with June Street Entertainment. June Street became the leader in licensing songs to some of the biggest advertising campaigns in the world, including Nextel, Coca-Cola, The Gap, and Old Navy leisure apparel. Their roster soon included music by Roy Orbison, LL Cool J, Aretha Franklin, Frank Sinatra, Willie Nelson, and The Ventures, to name a few, being placed in blockbuster movies and some of the biggest TV programs. One of our first successes was getting *Walk-Don't Run* played about four times in Billy Crystal's superb baseball movie, '61*.' Around that time, CBS used *Perfidia* in the TV sitcom, *King Of Queens*. Later we had The Ventures' version of *California Sun* in clothing commercials for Old Navy and *Hawaii Five-0* in the movie soundtrack for *Madagascar*."

~ ~ ~

Spring of 2001 found The Ventures back in the studio reworking their sixties Christmas album for M&I Company. Rather than let Japan mix and master their CDs, Bob and Don preferred doing it with Craig Nepp, an excellent engineer in Los Angeles. Like the *V-Gold* series, *60's Rockin' Christmas* [MYCV-30123] breathed new life into all of the well-worn tracks except for the infamous *Scrooge*. This track was replaced with not one, but *four* that included *Feliz Navidad, Winter Wonderland, The Christmas Song*, and a medley uniting *Rockin' Around The Christmas Tree* with *Here Comes Santa Claus*. In keeping with their original concept, The Ventures began each song with the intro from one of their classic sixties recordings.

The Ventures got a fun break playing for party in April at the posh Conga Room in Los Angeles. ABC TV's *Drew Carey Show* was taking its annual hiatus, and Drew was celebrating with his cast and crew. Gerry McGee and Jeff Baxter were "on duty" for the event, and after a short concert, the band presented Drew and the show's producer with autographed guitars.

While The Ventures partied with the Carey crew, Nokie headlined at North-Eastern Italy's annual Guitar Festival in Soave, known globally for its famous white wine. Other fine performers included Tom Doyle, Tommy Emmanuel, and Wayne Wesley Johnson. Meeting with Johnson led to Nokie co-performing *Walk-Don't Run*, *Venus*, and *Pipeline* on Johnson's flamenco album, *Canciones Del Alma* [Wannadu 21022D].

In June, Nokie toured through Texas and up into Canada's province of Alberta. His hip still healing, Nokie moved slowly and walked with a limp, but his performance at Edmonton's third annual Guitar Extravaganza was thrilling as ever. Life was looking brighter, but two weeks later, the passing of Chet Atkins hit the news. Nokie had finally met his mentor and become a friend of Chet, only to lose him to dreaded cancer.

~ ~ ~

Before leaving the studio, The Ventures tackled another project that produced their most bizarre recordings ever. Bob explains; "M&I asked us to write songs dedicated to the Japanese baseball players who worked with the Seattle Mariners. Ichiro Suzuki and Kazuhiro Sasaki were such national treasures that whenever a game was telecast from here, everything in Japan was pre-empted for it. Deciding to try the hip-hop approach that The Wiseguys had used on our *Wild Child* track, we did one version for Suzuki the hitter, and another for the pitcher, Sasaki. We also did one called *Let's Go Mariners* that named all the players on the team. It didn't catch on in Seattle, but we hoped it would be played on the Japanese sports stations and in their stadiums."

Oddly, even though it was a Ventures product, the disc received minimal attention in Japan. In time for the band's summer tour, M&I included a "special CD present" of *Let's Go Ichiro* [M&I MYCV-20004] glued to the centerfold of their souvenir tour book. As Bob relates, The Ventures had stepped onto a new field and struck out; "We wasted about $25,000 on that thing. It was just too far out for us. It seems that a computer is the wrong way to go, as we just got bogged down after about a month of studio time. We tried to go at it the way the hip-hoppers do, but it was a disaster. Instead of getting into all that technical stuff, I think we should have done it the way we normally record."

BE STRONG AMERICA

On July 2, 2001, The Ventures arrived in Japan armed with two new CDs, *V-Gold III* and their second dedication to the Southern All Stars, *TSUNAMI*. With fifty-four concert days and seven TV-radio appearances, their only time off was during travel between cities. As the tour got underway, they learned that their recording of *Diamond Head* was in the soundtrack of a Japanese movie called *Water Boys*. A pleasant surprise greeted Don when he was given a Canopus signature amplifier to use on the tour.

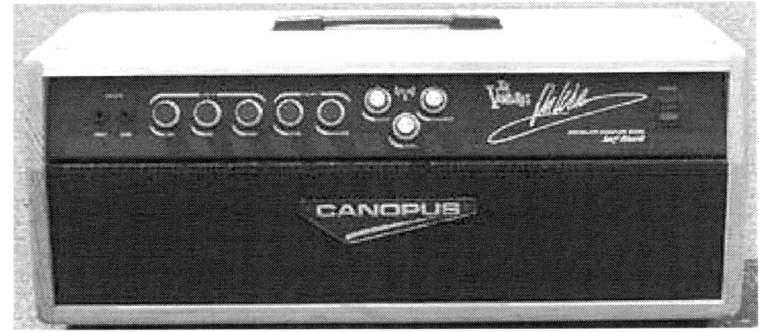

Don's first signature amp – the matching cabinet employed four ten-inch speakers

The Don Wilson Signature Amplifier was an impressive tube driven unit, but upon testing it, Don told Canopus that in America, his best tube reverb sound came from twin speakers in a Peavey cabinet driven by an Ampeg SS-150. In Japan he liked the sound he obtained from a Roland JC-120. Noting Don's preferences, and knowing the amp would sell better if Don used it in concert, Canopus went 'back to the drawing board.'

With less than two weeks remaining in the tour, a spell of fear, horror, and anger was cast upon the band and the entire world. On September 11, hijackers of commercial aircraft destroyed the twin towers of New York's World Trade Center and part of the Pentagon in Washington D.C. Another plane crashed in Pennsylvania as passengers battled to keep their hijackers from reaching a D.C. target. The thousands who perished included workers in the buildings, their rescuers, along with crews and passengers of all four Boeing airliners used as weapons by suicidal terrorists. Leon recalls the shock and disbelief felt by Gerry, Don, Bob, and himself; "We were in a hotel at Kochi in southern Japan when the news hit. When I signed onto AOL on my laptop, I saw a report of the attack on New York. It seemed impossible, so I thought it was some kind of 'what if' presentation. Just then, my wife Patti called from the USA. She told me what had happened and I was just shocked. I called Gerry, and he had just heard about it from his son. Bob and Don had also gotten calls from their wives, and Bob was reading about it on *his* laptop. The hotel staff was kind enough to bring newspapers written in English to each of our rooms. We were completely devastated, but we had to put it out of our minds and do the show that night as if nothing had happened. That was really difficult. We were a little nervous on the flight back to Tokyo. Security was very high from that point on, so our waiting to board planes was much longer than usual. A week later, we had to fly home. It's always a long trip, but that one seemed twice as long."

The first thing to cross the minds of Josie and Don was Don's daughter, who was an airline stewardess. Jill was safe, however, having not been assigned to one of the fateful flights, but she had been frightened enough to quit her job almost immediately. Knowing Jill was safe, Josie recalls her next concern; "I hurried a FAX to Don, saying, 'If ever there was a time for your song ['Be Strong America'] to be heard, that time is NOW!' It was too bad that he was not here to take care of such things himself. As he has said, it seems things that are pertinent to him always seem to happen while he is in Japan."

The day known as 9/11 brought dismay and depression as fear of the unknown gripped countries around the world. Slowly, Ventures fans returned to their Internet chat group, but the disaster topic lingered as rescue work continued and authorities sifted for evidence of the perpetrators. Then, while Underground Fire members found comfort in the posted lyrics to *Be Strong America*, Don posted the audio file on The Ventures' official website. Don had formerly hoped to sell this work, but he now gave it to the fans. The next day, searchers for Ventures items on eBay.com discovered that Be Strong America was being sold on CD for just five dollars, and that proceeds from the sale would be donated to the families of those who lost their lives at the World Trade Center, the Pentagon, and aboard the four hijacked jetliners as well as the many New York City Police Officers and Firefighters who gave their lives trying to help victims. Royalties from the sale of the disc were then directed to the New York Police and Firefighter's Relief Fund. Besides The Ventures' website, *Be Strong America* was offered on an online memorabilia store called The Rock 'n' Roll Road Show. This step was arranged by KFWB Los Angeles air personality Tammy Trujillo, who commented; "I was moved by the recording and its message so appropriate for the situation. For people not part of the tragedies of the World Trade Center and the Pentagon, it was an opportunity to contribute to the healing process."

A year earlier, Gerry McGee had returned to Louisiana to work on another project with filmmaker Pat Mire. Through Gerry, Pat had learned much about fiddler Dennis McGee and the roots of Cajun music. Also, Pat was sufficiently impressed with Gerry's talent to feature him in a related documentary. Now, with Japan tour 2001 completed, Gerry was again free to complete the filming. The musical documentary, *Forever My Love: Music From the Bayou*, followed Gerry cruising through the south of Louisiana in a Cadillac convertible, visiting and jamming with musical friends and disciples of his father, Dennis. Made for Louisiana Public Broadcasting, the hour-long video premiered in December of 2001, but owing to Gerry's humble nature, *Forever My Love: Music From the Bayou* remained virtually unknown to his Ventures-oriented fans.

BeauSoleil's Michael Doucet, Gerry McGee, Pat Mire and Sonny Landreth

While The Ventures were in Japan, Fiona had found a record label to market the band's American releases. Neil Norman's GNP Crescendo had done very good work, but as their costs escalated, contract renewals became prohibitive. California's Varèse Sarabande presented a more acceptable deal, resulting in new and attractive Ventures' recordings being available outside of Japan at reasonable prices. By fall of 2001, *The Ventures Greatest Surfin' Hits Of All Time* emerged with eighteen tracks spanning sessions from 1981's *Surfin' and Spyin'* to the latest *V-Gold* recordings. However, when Fiona heard *Hawaii Five-0*, she was unhappy with the 2000 recording, which lacked full orchestral backing. Varèse Sarabande rectified this on the next disc, *The Ventures Play The Greatest Instrumental Hits Of All-Time*. Here, the original version was presented with Mel on drums following a vibrant drum introduction by Leon.

Ventures albums on Varèse Sarabande continued at the rate of one per year, attractively packaged with eight-page booklets containing outstanding liner notes and photos. Finally, fans anywhere in the world could keep up with the group's latest work for less than a dollar per track. The seven-album series ended in 2005 with a double-disc compilation of greatest live performances called *Alive Five-0*, and the 2008 compilation, *The Ventures Play Their Greatest Hits*.

By the end of the 2001, after working hard at recording both new and old material for M&I Company, Don and Bob were becoming a bit weary. For the first time, they openly discussed retiring while admitting they had no idea what it would mean. When questioned, Bob said; "I'll just keep playing as long as my health permits. If I have to retire, I would like to spend my remaining years living alternately in Japan and the USA for three months at a time." Similarly, Don mused; "What would I do if I retired? I don't know anything about fishing or golf. Music has been my whole life, so whatever I do, it will have to involve music."

Such discussions resulted in renewing their Japan contract for just two years instead of the normal five. They also toyed with the idea that upon their retirement, Leon might want to continue The Ventures with younger musicians, to which Gerry volunteered; "I'll be sixty-five in 2002, so I'll be officially retired, but I'll still do some playing in Louisiana with my friends, and I'll work with The Ventures as long as they wish." Then Leon offered; "When Bob and Don have both retired, and if Gerry sticks around, I'd like to have Bob Spalding come in on rhythm. My brother Mike could play bass."

Year's end saw release of *60's Rockin' Christmas* [M&I MYCV-30122] and a well-needed rest. More importantly, 2002 seemed to rejuvenate the band and dispel any thoughts of retirement. The January mini-tour in Japan had now grown to seventeen performances in six different cities. Nokie resumed use of his Telecaster on stage, but as the Fender endorsement expired, murmurs were heard of a fantastic new guitar of his own design. Another rumor spread when Judy hinted of a "new baby," never imagining that it would be taken literally by fans in the UK.

NEW BABIES

In the ensuing months, rumors of The Ventures' retirement were soon forgotten. At home, Bob tried to find time for another new toy. Home DVD recorders were still unavailable in America, but in January of 2002, he had brought one home from Tokyo. He had barely begun transferring his *Columbo* collection from VHS tape to disc, when duty called. Following a March booking for Yuma's *Midnight At The Oasis* Old Car Show, they went into the studio to record the next Varèse Sarabande album. Instead of handing over the M&I Christmas demo to the company, Bob, Leon, and Bob Spalding convened with Don at his new home studio to record ten completely new Christmas tunes, including a beautiful original sung by Don called *Christmas Joy*. The new tracks also included an acoustic version of *Silent Night*. Bob Bogle played lead on this and six more, with Bob Spalding doing the honors on *We Three Kings*, *God Rest Ye Merry Gentlemen*, and *Joy To The World*. Eight more tracks were added from the M&I album, although some of the "hit-song intros" were changed completely. This allowed Gerry and Nokie to be featured also, and brought the track count for *Christmas Joy* up to eighteen.

It was time to start rehearsing for the next Japan tour, but this was put aside when The Ventures were invited back to Seattle's Experience Music Project to perform in May. Immediately, M&I Company decided to record the show for a future compact disc.

In April, when Nokie and Judy returned to Canada for Edmonton's 4th Annual Guitar Extravaganza, Nokie proudly unveiled a gleaming new guitar to his fans and co-stars Albert Lee, "Hellecaster" Will Ray, and lightning fingerpicker Buster B. Jones.

Nokie with his new baby, the HitchHiker   *Byron Tietjen*

Originally built by Jackson Guitars of California, the HitchHiker featured a headstock in the shape of a hand with an extended thumb. A neck-through-body design with laminated layers of flame maple and swamp ash enhanced the guitar's looks as well as its note sustaining capability. Gold plated hardware and diamond shaped mother-of-pearl position markers added to its beauty. A pair of Seymour Duncan tapped-coil, hum-bucking pickups fed the sound through a set of tone switches capable of twenty-one combinations. Along with Nokie's patented bridge, a zero-fret was also featured. As Nokie asserted; "This guitar has everything. It's the Rolls Royce of guitars."

Graphic designer Robert H. Sickler, Nokie's talented webmaster and also a great fan, had a hand in the development of his hero's dream guitar, and he tells how this came about; "It started as a secret project between Nokie and myself in the fall of 1998, but the real push to create a custom guitar finally came from Judy. Nokie called unexpectedly one day to request that I design a headstock based on the way he writes the script 'N' in his signature. We went through several variations until we hit upon the chosen design. Nokie mused that it looked like the thumb of a hitchhiker. He really liked it, so the design and the name were trademarked. We also went through many body variations leading to the modified classic style we all know and love. Four years later, Nokie called me to tell me that the final prototype had finally arrived. The tone and excitement in his voice said it all. Clarity, tonal variety, contour, comfort, sustain, drive, fast neck, and incredible looks...this guitar had it all. Best of all, from start to finish, it had Nokie's personal input to the design and construction. His custom builders had done an incredible job of interpreting his dream."

Is time, the HitchHiker name was also given to an acoustic electric by California's Santa Cruz Guitar Company, and a classical guitar from Canada. Later, Nokie contracted Rock Creek Guitars of Oregon to build the solid body electric, but eventually commissioned the job to overseas makers.

Within a week of his return to Oregon, Nokie received the sad news that his old friend, Gene Moles, had passed away in Bakersfield on April 28. In his last years, Gene had fought a brave but losing battle with pulmonary fibrosis that literally took his breath away at the age of seventy-three. Without his kindly support just one year earlier, several facts and quotes would be missing from these pages.

More bad news came on June 15 with the passing of Bob Reisdorff, just nine days before his 80th birthday. Following a series of strokes, Bob died of pneumonia at Modesto, California, where he had lived with a niece. The Ventures revered Bob as the man who, in the early years of their career, had ensured they received their due, in contrast to many young artists that were virtually robbed by their record companies. As with Gene Moles, had it not been for Bob Reisdorff's memories and generosity with his time, parts of this chronicle would not have been written.

In July, Gerry joined Don, Bob, and Leon for Japan Tour 2002. On this tour, Gerry had a new M&I CD to promote. *My Guitar Memories* [MYCV-30140] focused on his early Cajun roots, his time in the army, and highlights of his session work with such greats as Elvis Presley, The Monkees, and Barbara Streisand.

More new babies were seen by Japanese concertgoers as Don and Bob introduced Aria's 40th Anniversary Ventures Model guitar and bass finished in candy-apple red. In addition, Don's redesigned Canopus amplifier was presented. This time, Don was pleased; "I used it for the entire tour and found it to be one of the best amplifiers ever. Bob and Gerry were constantly checking it out and wondering when they would see their own signature models. Usuda-san said that he intended to build a complete set of

Ventures amps, so maybe that will happen. I would like to have brought it home to the States, but they wanted me to buy it, even though it had *my* name on the front. At 400,000 Yen [then $3,386 U.S.], I wasn't going to do that!"

The hybrid [transistor-tube] head is enclosed in a laminated wooden case with a matching cabinet housing two Electro-Voice EVM12L speakers.

In August, The Ventures got an unexpected six-day break when a side trip to Korea was cancelled. While Don, Bob, and Leon spent the extra time with their wives, Gerry teamed up with Hiro Tokutake to record a mini-album. Ten months later, the short but delightful CD entitled *T for Thumb* was released on M&I [MYCV-30197]. Leaving guitar lovers hungry for more, the six-track collection included two Dr. K originals, a Chi-Lites top-forty hit, *Oh Girl*, John Durrill's *Kern County Line*, and two classic country hits, *Goodtime Charlie's Got The Blues* and *Wichita Lineman*.

Gerry McGee and "Dr. K" Hirofumi Tokutake

By mid-October, Bob and Don had been home for a month and begun work on their *Live In Seattle* album. At this time, Nokie was on a plane bound for Europe, having booked appearances in the UK, Denmark, and Holland that would keep him busy through mid November. As Judy was having back therapy, Nokie was alone on this tour. In Amsterdam, he met with an excellent backing band called AdVenture before visiting his friends at Renkum, the home of Marble amplifiers. Upon receipt of a gleaming DCP-100 prototype, Nokie and AdVenture laid down studio tracks for release on Holland's Rarity Records [CD192724]. The group then flew to Surrey, near London, to headline the Instrumental Rock Guitar Festival, an event organized by Patrick Terrett, manager of rising female Welsh guitarist, Zoe McCulloch. Pat and Zoe had first met Nokie in 2001 at Muriel Anderson's All Star Guitar Night in Nashville.

Many long-time Ventures fans attended the UK's Instrumental Rock Guitar Festival, including Resurgence editor Gerald Woodage, who for the first time was enjoying a Nokie stage performance. Fans reported pure delight with Nokie's performance, but with less than 200 in attendance, the reason for The Ventures having never visited the UK seemed apparent. In fairness, October 27 saw the worst storm recorded in twelve years, which undoubtedly impacted attendance. With winds exceeding 100 miles an hour, several deaths were reported throughout the UK. Nokie told of one fan that paid the equivalent of $100 in taxi fare to attend, due to the mainline railways being shut down.

The next stop for Nokie and AdVenture was Copenhagen, Denmark. Having never met Nokie, Sweden's Arild Pettersson was another fan club president who seized the rare opportunity to meet Nokie and attend his performance.

From Denmark the group returned to The Netherlands where a concert was recorded for DVD. After holding a guitar clinic at Arnhem, and being told by AdVenture that their experience had been a dream come true, Nokie left for home. He had time to rest during the holidays, but on the first weekend of 2003, he joined with Bob, Don, and Leon for a two-week tour of Japan's Blue Note clubs.

A fan having not seen The Ventures for years and attending one of the Blue Note shows may have thought he had encountered a time warp. Not only was the old line-up of Bogle-Wilson-Edwards-Taylor on the marquee, Bob and Don's Aria models and Nokie's HitchHiker gave the impression that the band had reverted to the Mosrite guitar.

The album promoted on this trip was not a studio disc, but a compilation from The Ventures' *Experience Music Project* concerts of 2001 and 2002. Bob and Don had combined the best tracks from the two performances, and according to scores of reports, the resultant *Live in Seattle* turned out to be one of (if not the best) live Ventures albums ever recorded [M&I MYCV-30178].

SEA CRUISE – FANS IN ECSTASY!

In two weeks, the foursome was home preparing for the biggest and best event of The Ventures' career. An idea conceived by Jack DeFranco had taken shape as he and Fiona made The Ventures Cruise a reality. For over a year, excited fans around the globe had been making reservations. On February 3, over 600 fans of The Ventures and Los Straitjackets embarked on a four-day round trip from Los Angeles to Catalina Island and Ensenada Mexico, enjoying the sun, wonderful food, and music on Carnival's Cruise Ship *Ecstasy*. The *Surfin To Baja* group had exclusive entry to concerts, clinics, and meetings with the musicians in the ship's Vegas-style Starlight Lounge.

Fans hoping to see Gerry McGee were given early warning that this was unlikely as Gerry was committed to other activities, including his new album [*My Guitar Memories*]. However, in addition to Los Straitjackets (who also had their own fan base), there were plenty of guest artists to delight the ocean-bound audience.

As expected, "fifth Venture" Bob Spalding accompanied The Ventures, and when a secret guest was disclosed as being ex-Venture John Durrill, fans were elated beyond belief. As John had also been part of Mel Taylor's Dynamics, the cruise was a reunion for him and Bob Spalding. Other guests included Jeff Cook of *Alabama*, Roger Fisher, formerly of *Heart*, and *YES* drummer Alan White (also of John Lennon's *Plastic Ono Band*, and widely considered one of rock's greatest drummers).

Guitarist Zoe McCulloch and Tracy Alan Moore singing as "Elvis" provided further entertainment. Tracy claimed not to be an Elvis impersonator, but upon seeing his performance, several Elvis fans said it was the best Elvis tribute they had ever seen.

Don's "kids" Jill, Tim, and Staci – ready to cruise with Dad

For many, and especially past members of the sixties' fan club, it was also an honor to meet Josie Wilson. Daughter Sally and grandchildren Staci, Jill, and Tim accompanied Josie, who was now eighty-eight. In the midst of changing careers, successful restaurateur Tim was firming up plans for a company to import and market Ventures endorsed guitars.

The Ventures' staff included manager Fiona Taylor, activity coordinator Jack DeFranco, webmaster Kirk Schutte, and soundman Steve Bonhag. Steve operated a huge mixing console that was just part of a ton of gear hauled into the ship's lounge. The stack of instruments, amps, and PA equipment included several autographed Fender Squire guitars that were given away during evening performances. A twenty-track CD comprising Ventures originals was also issued, aptly entitled *Surfin' to Baja*.

In addition to nightly concerts and side trips to Catalina Island and Ensenada, fans were kept busy with guitar and drum clinics, an afternoon jam (fans had been invited to bring their guitars), plus the pastimes afforded all passengers; a casino, sunning on the deck, and simply exploring the huge vessel. Amongst the many food outlets to sample, wonderful evening meals in the dining room preceded each concert. Besides Americans and Canadians, fans had come from England, Scotland, Denmark, and Japan.

Each day ended with the pre-eminent evening concert as The Ventures and guests mixed polished performances with unrehearsed jamming and solos. Of special note were John Durrill's grand piano soloing, Roger Fisher's vocalizing on *House of the Rising Sun*, and the percussive spectacle of Alan White in perfect sync with Leon on *Hawaii Five-O*.

On the final day at sea, The Ventures spent an entire afternoon signing autographs for a line-up that ran half the ship's length. During this time, Los Straitjackets and Alan White conducted clinics before an impressive concert given by Zoe McCulloch.

Afternoon autograph session - Don, Bob, Nokie, Leon, and John

While some had hoped that this delightful time with their favorite band could be repeated, others felt that such a magical experience could not and should not be duplicated. An attempt to organize a second Ventures cruise *was* made, but there was simply not enough response from fans *or* the band. Those having missed out while planning to attend "the next one" were simply out of luck. A few days after *Surfin' to Baja*, Don relaxed on his 70th birthday (He had shared a cake with fans on the cruise). In less than a year, Bob would also be seventy. The future seemed to contain very few concert bookings, save for Japan, where The Ventures would receive the well-deserved pampering to which they were accustomed.

The majority of the Surfin' to Baja tour group

As the cruise neared completion, Josie was approaching her 88he birthday. With affectionate memories of the fans she had met, she proclaimed; "If it were possible to transcend time and space, I would like to shake the hands of all the Ventures fans around the world, to whom I have fondly referred to as 'our Ventures family'."

IN THE TWILIGHT

The Ventures had little time to rest after the cruise, playing less than two weeks later in Seattle at a memorial concert for Richard Dangel of The Fabulous Wailers. At the age of sixty, Rich was still an excellent guitarist when he died suddenly in December, 2002.

Next came rehearsals with Gerry McGee for the summer Japan tour while Nokie recorded, first in Dallas with The Light Crust Doughboys for *Guitars Over Texas*, and later in Nashville, where he cut *Just For Jake* and *Nokie Plays Gospel Music*. In July, Nokie hosted a festival near his home with Mason Williams as an added attraction. While The Ventures were in Japan, Nokie performed in Cleveland and Columbus, Ohio.

In Japan, The Ventures played to packed houses of 1500 to 2000 patrons despite a sagging economy. In August, Don called home in a panic, having come down with a very sore throat. Upon Don's cry for a medicine that always helped him in the past, Josie rush-shipped her own bottle of the same product to Japan.

2003 ended with excitement over a new, affordable line of Ventures Model guitars from the company known as Wilson Bros. Headed by Don's son Tim and partner James Fox, the company imported custom instruments from the Far East through Aria of Japan. Once The Ventures began using the guitars, fans were buying them faster than they could be stocked. The Mosrite styled instruments (and some in the shape of Fenders) not only looked great, but generated reports of high quality workmanship and performance capabilities by everyone who bought them. Before long, high-end instruments were added, as well as various accessories. The fact that The Ventures endorsed the units led some to believe the band to be investors in the Wilson Bros. line. As Don confirms; "They are great guitars, but our only involvement is to help my son by playing them here in the U.S.A. We can only promote them outside of Japan, as Aria has an exclusive license to use our name on guitars over there."

During the January tour of Japan's Blue Note clubs, The Ventures were informed that 2004 marked the 150th Anniversary of that country's diplomatic relationship with the U.S.A. While the government celebrated, they also wished to honor The Ventures. As the Japanese Consulate stated; "The Ventures have been actively performing rock music since the 1960s and have obtained massive popularity in Japan as well as in the U.S.A. Since 1962 they have visited Japan forty-seven times to perform, and have had a powerful influence upon the music scene in Japan. They have performed instrumental songs that have Japanese themes, and have greatly contributed to the development of Japan's rock music over a significant span of time."

A ceremony to bestow the honor took place at the Seattle Center in mid-April, but due to short notice, not everyone was available. Gerry was engaged with business in Louisiana, and Leon was visiting his brother in Australia. So, on April 16, with Fiona and Josie in attendance, Don, Bob, and Nokie received the esteemed Foreign Minister's Commendation, an accolade awarded to individuals and organizations having "significantly contributed to the advancement of bilateral relations between Japan and the United States."

Also on April 16, Bob and Nokie received documents from the Oklahoma Music Hall of Fame Foundation in which one paragraph reads;

> "Our standards require that each inductee have a solid connection with the State of Oklahoma, have excelled in a specific musical sphere, has displayed influence in the field of music for an appreciable period of time, and has had an inspirational effect on others. Candidates for induction must have recognition within the music industry or among their peers, and shall be devoted to others fostering musical development. Finally, a candidate shall have practiced the highest caliber of professional conduct, enhancing the image of themselves and Oklahoma. Obviously, you meet and exceed each of these standards."

The year 2004 was also when Bob Bogle's medical problems began to mount. He handled the July-through-September Japan tour and a few U.S. shows in the fall, but as the band readied for the January 2005 tour, Bob disclosed; "I was diagnosed with non-Hodgkins lymphoma in 1997, and it's finally reached a point where I require extended treatment. My doctor says it will take some time and that I will need a lot of rest. I do expect to recover and be back in Japan in time for the [2005] summer tour. Meanwhile, I'll keep busy with the recording and mixing of our new Ventures albums as long as I can."

Although Bob's condition forced him to give up performing, he did take part in recording a compilation of hits revived from Japan's rock 'n' roll years [*J-Rock Summer Wind: Melodies in Memories* - MYCV-30333]. However, as the 2005 Japan summer tour approached, Bob Spalding revealed; "My full-time status as bassist for The Ventures began in January while we were on a plane to the Japan winter tour. We will be moving The Ventures forward to the next 'era' and make sure the band continues."

In June, Nokie and Judy celebrated his 70th birthday by giving up their Oregon home in favor of a luxurious forty-two foot Beaver Marquis motor coach. They were soon on the road to Texas for Art Greenhaw's 3rd Annual Guitar Festival, where Art had arranged a gala evening at the Dallas Hard Rock Café.

~ ~ ~

One of the biggest pushes for Rock and Roll Hall Of Fame induction came in early 2005, one year after Japan awarded The Ventures the esteemed Foreign Minister's Commendation. Of America's fifty states, Washington seemed most aware of the band's accomplishments, and of its deserved place in the Cleveland Hall. At the same time, Tim Wilson and KBSG-FM disc jockey Mark Christopher began working hard to get The Ventures nominated.

In March of 2005, Lieutenant Governor Brad Owen invited The Ventures to appear before the Washington State Legislature to receive a resolution supporting their entry into the Rock And Roll Hall Of Fame. An introductory letter and proclamation was drafted and sent to the Hall's New York headquarters. Later, Seattle Mayor Greg Nickels and Tacoma Mayor Bill Baarsma read the proclamation on radio while designating March 12 as VENTURES DAY. In the evening, DJ Mark Christopher and Venture Bank of Washington raised awareness of the campaign by presenting The Ventures in concert featuring Lt. Governor Owen playing sax on *Tequila*, and guitar on *Johnny B. Goode*. While enjoying the music, some 1500 fans crowded Seattle's Premier Club to sign petitions to the Rock and Roll Hall of Fame.

Mark Christopher - KBSG-FM   Nokie, Bob, Lt. Gov. Brad Owen, Don, and Leon

WASHINGTON STATE SENATE

SENATE RESOLUTION
8645

By Senators Esser, Poulsen, Brown, Finkbeiner, Regala, Zarelli, Kastama, Benton, Rasmussen, Carrell, Franklin, Pridemore, Eide, Sheldon, Doumit, Benson, Kohl-Welles, Fairley, Spanel, Fraser, McAuliffe, Haugen, Johnson and Roach

WHEREAS, The Ventures were the first nationally known, popular recording group to come out of Tacoma, Washington; and

WHEREAS, The Ventures have recorded over 3000 songs and released over 250 albums, including 14 top 100 singles in the 1960s; and

WHEREAS, Having sold over 90 million albums world-wide, with such hits as "Walk Don't Run," "Perfidia," "Lullaby of the Leaves," "Diamond Head," "2,000 Pound Bee," and a version of the Hawaii Five-O theme song, the Ventures have become the world's all-time #1 rock instrumental group; and

WHEREAS, Don Wilson, Bob Bogle, Nokie Edwards, Gerry McGee, and Leon Taylor, son of long-time drummer Mel Taylor, are still entertaining millions around the world with their albums, tapes, CDs, and live performances; and

WHEREAS, The Ventures are America's ambassadors of Rock and Roll to the non-English speaking world, having sold over 40 million albums in Japan alone; and

WHEREAS, While retaining their trademark sound, the Ventures' musical stylings have adapted to shifting trends in popular music, as they experimented with blues, calypso, Latin, twist, country, pop, funk, disco, reggae, swamp, garage, TV themes, and psychedelic music; and

WHEREAS, They were willing to experiment with wildly innovative concepts, such as combining different dance crazes in one of their few vocal songs: "The Twomp." *It ain't the Twist. It ain't the Stomp. It's the Twomp!*; and

WHEREAS, Generations of guitar players have been inspired by the Ventures to twiddle with the reverb and tremolo knobs on their amplifiers; and

WHEREAS, The Ventures even had a distinctive "Ventures model" guitar and bass built for them by Mosrite; and

WHEREAS, The Ventures received the coveted "Lifetime Achievement Award" from *Guitar Player Magazine*; and

WHEREAS, The Ventures have yet to be inducted into their rightful place in the Rock and Roll Hall of Fame;

NOW, THEREFORE, BE IT RESOLVED, That the Washington State Senate honor the Ventures for their many contributions to Rock and Roll and hereby proclaim that the Ventures deserve a place in the Rock and Roll Hall of Fame; and

BE IT FURTHER RESOLVED, That copies of this resolution be immediately transmitted by the Secretary of the Senate to the members of the Ventures and to the Rock and Roll Hall of Fame.

I, Thomas Hoemann, Secretary of the Senate,
do hereby certify that this is a true and
correct copy of Senate Resolution 8645,
adopted by the Senate
March 12, 2005

THOMAS HOEMANN
Secretary of the Senate

Brad Owen
Lieutenant Governor

March 22, 2005

The Rock and Roll Hall of Fame Foundation
1290 Avenue Of The Americas, 2nd Floor
New York, NY 10104-0298

Dear Foundation Members,

Enclosed, please find an official copy of Washington State Senate Resolution 8645.

As you can see from the text, SR 8645 honors the many contributions The Ventures have made to Rock and Roll and urges their induction into the Rock and Roll Hall of Fame. I ask that you add this resolution to the thousands of letters, e-mails, proclamations and petitions you have received in support of this outstanding group.

If the purpose of your organization is to *"recognize the contributions of those who have had a significant impact over the evolution, development and perpetuation of rock and roll, by inducting them into the Hall of Fame,"* you should be hard pressed to find a more suitable candidate than the world's all-time #1 rock instrumental group. In fact, several of your own inductees site The Ventures as an influence. This list includes George Harrison, Jimmy Paige, John Fogerty, Robert Kreiger and Paul Simonon.

I thank you in advance for your positive consideration of this request

Sincerely,

Brad Owen
President of the Senate
Lieutenant Governor
State of Washington

President of the Senate
Chairman, Rules Committee

220 Legislative Building
PO Box 40400
Olympia, WA 98504-0400

Phone: (360) 786-7700
FAX: (360) 786-7749
e-mail: owen_br@leg.wa.gov

It appeared however, that petitions and letters did not affect the process by which musicians are inducted to the Cleveland institution. Still, some hope was realized when the following explanation was received from the Rock And Roll Hall Of Fame in answer to an earlier query from a disgruntled Ventures fan.

>Dear Sir:
>
>There is no doubt that rock and roll would not be what it is without the contribution of The Ventures. At the same time, you should realize that we receive literally thousands of such recommendations, many which are as worthy as yours.
>
>The Rock And Roll Hall Of Fame Foundation in New York City coordinates the entire nomination and induction process. The only criterion is that an artist's first hit record must have aged twenty-five years. First, the selection of inductees begins with an extensive panel of journalists, historians, previous inductees, industry heads, etc. In turn, the nominations are sent to a committee of more than 500 people around the world (journalists, historians, music industry management, all previous inductees, etc.) who vote. Those receiving the highest number of votes, and more than fifty percent of the votes cast, are inducted into the Hall. Usually, this means five to seven new inductees per year. As you can see, the road to being inducted is an arduous one, and completely devoid of influences or politics.
>
>On top of this, people sometimes forget that any individual brought into the circle of discussion views rock and roll and its artists in an incredibly subjective manner. As such, there is often widespread disagreement or fracturing of opinion about who is, or was important. From my perspective, time will tell. I think that all the deserving candidates will have their moment eventually. Unfortunately, it often doesn't fall into the time frame they or their fans desire. Remember too, many of the sports greats do not get into their respective Halls of Fame right away either.
>
>Peace and Soul,
>
>Terry Stewart, President
>
>Rock And Roll Hall Of Fame and Museum

On January 12, 2006, the National Academy of Recording Arts & Sciences® inducted The Ventures' 1960 single recording of "Walk-Don't Run" into its GRAMMY Hall Of Fame. A press-release from the Recording Academy® stated "Recordings also chosen this year include B.B. King's *Live At The Regal*, the O'Jays' *Love Train*, the Carter Family's *Keep On The Sunny Side*, Bob Dylan's *Bringing It All Back Home*, Bob Marley & the Wailers' *Exodus*, and Barbra Streisand's *The Barbra Streisand Album*. Other artists with selections include Jimmy Forrest, the Miracles, Anton Karas, Doc Watson, Bessie Smith, and the Jimi Hendrix Experience."

Other 2006 inductees included Doc Watson's 1964 recording of *Black Mountain Rag* and the Original Dixieland Jazz Band's 1917 recording of *The Darktown Strutters' Ball*.

THE GOLDEN YEARS – HEARTBREAK AND JOY

In addition the their regular NAMM Show performance and two trips to Japan, 2006 saw The Ventures accept bookings for a short U.S. tour. The venues included B.B. King's Blues Club [New York City], Asbury Lanes [Asbury Park, New Jersey], and the Birchmere Music Hall [Alexandria, Virginia]. The news spread quickly enough through the Internet for some fans to cross oceans in time to attend. So successful were these shows that new bookings were taken for the fall and into the next year.

The year 2007 began much like 2006, but soon took a turn for the worse. A few days after the Ventures returned from their winter Japan tour, they learned of Virginia Boles' passing on January 13th at the age of ninety five. To the end, she had remained in the Seattle home where husband Joe had first recorded The Ventures so many years earlier. Since that time, Virginia had remained a close friend of Josie and the band.

The next news was even worse, as related by Josie's daughter, Sally; "It is Mom's habit to wake around 2:00 a.m. for a cup of warm milk and a slice of toast. On Friday morning [January 19], she proceeded without her walker and tripped on a plant stand. At first she did not seem to be hurt very bad. John [Sally's husband] fixed her milk and toast and settled her in her favorite chair. After an hour, she was really hurting so we called 911. She was promptly taken to the hospital and found to have broken a rib. On January 22 she was taken to a nursing home by ambulance. When we got her checked in, she was getting so much help and attention from the staff that she soon felt more assured. She may be there for only two weeks if she works with the physical therapist."

On January 29, Sally reported; "Mom's rib is much less painful now. She is looking good and she was in great spirits yesterday! The niece of one of her care-givers did the embroidery on The Ventures' T-shirts. What a small world! It looks like we can bring her home on February 1. Her face really lit up when she heard this."

Out of the hospital, Josie recuperated at home until February 13th when Sally announced; "We've had a setback. Mom was back in hospital for a few days with a light case of pneumonia in her left lung. Weak and needing a lot of care, she has little appetite and is having trouble swallowing. We are seeking home care for her so she will not have to go back to a nursing home."

On February 19, 2007, exactly a month after her fall, Josie passed away. Although she was almost ninety-two, the news was devastating to family, friends, and devout Ventures fans around the world. After contributing to the early pages of this book, Josie followed its progress almost daily. It was absolutely heartbreaking to lose her so near to our publishing date.

Services for Josie Linnea Wilson were held on Monday, February 26 at Mountain View Funeral Home in Lakewood, just south of Tacoma. In addition to members her large family, attendees included Bob Bogle, John Durrill, Fiona Taylor, Gretchen Christopher [The Fleetwoods], Buck Ormsby and Kent Morrill [The Wailers], Lt. Governor Brad Owen and wife Linda. During the seating period, Josie's granddaughter, Sue Carroll of the Seattle Symphony soloed on the French horn. Recorded music heard during the service included Josie's early sixties production of *Softly As I Leave You* by the Nordic Trio. An historic photo slide production accompanied by a medley of mellow Ventures recordings was also presented. Josie was buried next to daughter Jacqueline, in Lakewood's Memorial Park.

STOP PRESS!

Our story was nearing its end when The Ventures received wonderful news while resting after eight weeks of touring in Japan. Within hours, fans worldwide were informed as the following message from a senior editor of *Billboard* was copied to the band's Underground Fire chat group.

> September 27, 2007, 6:45 p.m. ET
>
> Madonna, the Beastie Boys, John Mellencamp and Leonard Cohen lead a wildly disparate class of nominees for 2008 induction into the Rock and Roll Hall of Fame. They join Afrika Bambaataa, Chic, The Ventures, Donna Summer, and the Dave Clark Five on the ballot. Five acts will be inducted March 10, 2008, at New York's Waldorf Astoria Hotel.
>
> For eligibility, artists had to release their first single no later than 1982. Last year's inductees were R.E.M., Van Halen, Patti Smith, Grandmaster Flash And The Furious Five, and the Ronettes.
>
> Jonathan Cohen, N.Y.

The joy and anticipation soon spread to fans around the world, as evidenced by scores of messages on various musical Internet forums. Immediately, stage manager Jack DeFranco began studying website design. In just two weeks, he had completely revamped The Ventures' site using his experience writing technical sales presentations for Fortune 500 companies. Every page of the website was strategically designed to present Hall of Fame voters with information such as the band's current activities, accolades from well known Ventures-influenced artists, and various other facets of the band. A most effective page showed sixteen album covers, each triggering a carefully chosen music sample when clicked by the viewer.

Other than Don, few had any doubt that The Ventures would be a shoe-in. Those of a spiritual nature could not help wondering if Josie, having been departed for less than a year, had somehow engendered the long awaited nomination.

Unexpectedly, the results were announced on December 13. The Ventures were in, as were the Dave Clark Five, John Mellencamp, Madonna, and Canada's sultan of sadness, Leonard Cohen. In a press release, foundation president and CEO Joel Peresman wrote;

"From poetry to pop, these five acts demonstrate the rich diversity of rock and roll itself. We are proud to honor these artists and celebrate their contribution to rock and roll's place in our culture." Once again, it was Ventures Day in Washington, as proclaimed by Governor Chris Gregoire.

Arriving in New York early, The Ventures were invited on the New York TV show, *FOX and Friends*. Three days later, on March 10, 2008, Creedence Clearwater's John Fogerty inducted Don Wilson, Bob Bogle, Nokie Edwards, Gerry McGee, and Mel Taylor to America's Rock and Roll Hall of Fame in a ceremony at the Waldorf Astoria Hotel.

Fiona and Leon shared acceptance speeches for Mel, and As Gerry was unable to attend, John Durrill accepted his award. Sadly, due to his health, Bob Bogle could not attend. Bob "Zonk" Spalding did Bob Bogle proud on two counts; first with a heartfelt acceptance speech and then with his uncanny lead work on *Walk-Don't Run* in the style of The Ventures' original hit record on a Fender Jazzmaster owned by Jack DeFranco.

John Durrill, Don Wilson, Nokie Edwards, Leon Taylor, Bob Spalding, Fiona Taylor

The Ventures' second number was a thundering rendition of *Hawaii Five-0*, which had nearly been abandoned by music director Paul Shaffer in favor of a "fast fingers" guitar number. Shaffer gave in after Jack DeFranco cleverly sent him the *Hawaii Five-0* score used by the U.S. Air Force Band in 1998 along with a diagram of Jack's envision of the stage plot. Paul would play the woodwinds on synthesizer, while Anton Fig, drummer in Shaffer's CBS Orchestra heard on the *Letterman Late Show*, would play the essential timpani. There would be a riser for Paul's horn section and (sax man in Bob Seger's Silver Bullet Band), Alto Reed, with a huge bass sax for "added bottom end." As Jack recalls; "This was the way I wanted America to hear The Ventures, especially those who were not familiar with the group. I can tell you that the tears were streaming down my face by the time it was over, and it did my heart good to see Foundation executive Jann Wenner up on his feet and applauding. The whole thing is his show. He, along with a few others have weathered accusations of controlling the voting according to their personal wishes. The way it all turned out was better than I ever dreamed. The sound was so exciting that Tom Hanks and Chevy Chase both leaped out of their chairs when it ended. After the show, I heard so many people saying The Ventures' performance and

Tom Hanks' induction speech for The Dave Clark Five were the two big highlights of the evening. The following night on TV, Paul Shaffer reported to Dave Letterman, 'The Ventures rocked the house!'"

"Hawaii Five-0" at The Waldorf

"It's been a long wait, but Thank You, Rock & Roll Hall of Fame"

Under the care of top physicians and ever-loving wife Yumi, Bob Bogle's struggle with non-Hodgkins lymphoma continued. In 2007, a throat cancer was surgically eliminated, but on Sunday, June 14, 2009, Bob passed away at age seventy-five. The news created a shockwave around the world as fans posted hundreds of heartfelt online messages and testimonials to Bob's influence on their musical lives. The shock hit Don Wilson very hard; "I knew it was coming but I knew I was going to cry. Bob was the brother I never had, and even more. I can honestly say that in the fifty-two years we were partners, we never, ever had an argument."

It had been Bob's innovative guitar style that captured young musicians in 1960 with *Walk-Don't Run*, *Perfidia*, and *Lullabye of the Leaves*. When he switched to playing the bass, he created yet another style that was his alone. To those who knew him, Bob would also be remembered for his clever humor and obliging, relaxed personality. Our great sorrow was only consoled by knowing that he would suffer no more. On June 19 during a beautiful service in Vancouver Washington's Evergreen Memorial Gardens, friends, family, and fans listened to The Ventures' 1960 recording of *Walk-Don't Run*.

Bob and Yumi Bogle

As this chronicle closes, The Ventures celebrate their fifty-year mark in 2009 as a performing entity. An exciting new album called *Two Car Garage* was released in April that shared the anniversary with Tacoma's Fabulous Wailers on the resurrected Blue Horizon label. After a series of U.S. and Canadian concerts, it's Japan Tour 2009!

In 2010, Don expects to retire but is not making any promises. Nokie aims to keep recording and touring as long has he can, on his own or with The Ventures as needed. Meanwhile, both Bob and Don have donated their trusty Fender Jazzmasters to Cleveland's Rock and Roll Hall of Fame Museum, where the guitars will remain on display for at least two years.

In the future, other players in the "Ventures' family" may extend the legacy, but even if they do not, with 100,000,000 albums sold around the globe, there would seem to be truth in the slogan of those bumper stickers from Josie Wilson's original fan club, and with which many fans close their letters and messages. . . . .

VENTURES FOREVER!

Bob Spalding   Nokie Edwards   Don Wilson   Leon Taylor

Gerry McGee   Don Wilson   Bob Spalding   Leon Taylor

APPENDIX 1

A SAMPLING OF THE VENTURES' RECORDING SESSIONS
The musician in the left column received Session Leader Union pay rate.

22-Aug-61	Lady Of Spain	Ups 'n Downs	Opus 1 (Opus Twist?)	Opus 2 (Guitar Twist?)
Don	Bob	Nokie	Edward Hall	

6-Sep-61	Shanghied	Road Runner	Movin' n Groovin	Lady Of Spain
Don	Bob	Nokie	M C Berry	

3-Oct-61	Moon Dawg	Beatnik Fly	Ventures Stomp	40 Miles Of Bad Road
Don	Bob	Nokie	Howie	

6-Oct-61	Bongo Rock	Stick Shift	Venus	Mexico
Bob	Don	Nokie	Howie	Ramon Rivera (percussion)

10-Oct-61	Teen Beat	Driving Guitars	Bumble Bee	Bogie's tune
Don	Bob	Nokie	Howie	(Counterpoint?)

1-Feb-62	"Original" 4	"Original" 5	Bogie's tune	Besame Mucho
Don	Bob	Nokie	Mel	

5-Feb-62	Red Wing	Dark Eyes	My Bonnie Lies	Mockingbird
Don	Bob	Nokie	Mel	

21-Mar-62	Instant Mashed	Good Old Summertime	Home On The Range	
Bob	Don	Nokie	Mel	

22-May-62	Summertime	Spudnik	Country Gravy	
Nokie	Mel	Billy Strange	David Gates	Bud Coleman

23-May-62	Hot Summer	Lucille	Mashed Potato Time	
Nokie	Mel	Billy Strange	David Gates	Bud Coleman

24-May-62	Hully Gully	Wah-Watusi	Gravy	
Nokie	Mel	Billy Strange	David Gates	Bud Coleman

25-May-62	Poison Ivy	Hernando's Hideaway	Scratch	
Nokie	Mel	Billy Strange	David Gates	Bud Coleman

25-Jun-62	Lolita Ya Ya			
Bob	Mel	Billy Strange	David Gates	Hank Levine

12-Jul-62	Blue Star	Sweet and Lovely	Stranger on the Shore	Walkin' with My Angel
Bob	Mel	Billy Strange	Pat Vegas	

16-Jul-62	"Originals" 1 & 2	Mr. Moto	Come September	Limbo Rock
Don	Bob	Nokie	Mel	

Session tape audition by Dave Burke revealed Originals 1 & 2 to be "Night Drive" and "Gandy Dancer"

9-Aug-62	Ya Ya Wobble	Night Drive	The Intruder	Gandy Dancer
Bob	Mel	Billy Strange	David Gates	

4-Sep-62	Jaguar	Taboo		
Bob	Mel	Billy Strange	David Gates	James Burton

27-Sep-62	Bossa Nova			
Bob	Mel	Billy Strange	David Gates	Roy Harte (perc.)

4-Oct-62	Delicado	One Mint Julep	2000 Pound Bee - Part 1	
Don	Bob	Nokie	Mel	Billy Strange

12-Oct-62	Apache	Green Onions	2000 Pound Bee - Part 2	
Don	Bob	Nokie	Mel	

25-Oct-62	Calcutta	Never On Sunday	Let There Be Drums	Tequila
Bob	Don	Nokie	Mel	

30-Oct-62	Telstar	Last Night	Red River Rock	Percolator
Don	Bob	Mel	David Gates	Leon Russell

2-Nov-62	Last Night	The Lonely Bull	Never On Sunday	
Hank Levine	Don Bob Mel	David Gates	Frank Higgins (trumpet)	Al Porcino (trumpet)

21-Nov-62	Limbo	Cumbanchero	Windy and Warm	"Original"
Don	Bob	Nokie	Mel	

7-Dec-62	"Original"	Walk Right In		
Bob	Don	Nokie	Mel	

11-Dec-62	Matador	Walk Right In	"Original"	
David Gates	Bob	Don	Mel	Bud Coleman
	Al Porcino	Frank Higgins	Clifford Nile	

12-Dec-62	The Limbo	My True Love*		
Don	Bob	Mel	*Tommy Morgan	<= harmonica

5-Feb-63	Diamonds	Louisiana*	San Antonio Rose	
Don	Bob	Mel	*Tommy Morgan	<= harmonica

21-Feb-63	Pipeline	Surf Rider	Diamonds	Windy and Warm
Don	Bob	Nokie	Mel	

22-Feb-63	The Heavies	Damaged Goods	Ten Over	Barefoot Venture
Bob	Don	Nokie	Mel	

7-Jun-63	El Watusi	Hot Pastrami	Kansas City	
Billy Strange	Leon Russell	Ray Pohlman	Robert Morris	Hal Blaine Frank Capp

Strange, Russell, and Pohlman stayed an extra ½ hour to sweeten the sound.

18-Jun-63	More	Wipe Out		
Billy Strange	David Gates Leon Russell	Tommy Tedesco	"Bud" Ervan Coleman	Hal Blaine Frank Capp

16-Jul-63	The Lost Surfer	"Original" (Nokie)		
Mel	Bob	Don	Nokie	

22-Nov-63	Twilight Zone	Out Of Limits	One Step Beyond (Fear)	War of the Satellites
Mel	Don	Billy Strange	Leon Russell	Julius Wechter
	Red Rhodes	David Gates	William Airbard * (Bill Hinshaw)	Ray Lanbiny * (Roy Lanham)
			French horn	guitar

* These documents require real names, which sometimes differ from *professional names*.

23-Jan-64	Journey to the Stars	Walk Don't Run '64	Oriental (*Saigon?*)	
Mel	Nokie	Don Bob	Leon Russell	Steve Douglas

29-Apr-64	Pink Panther	Only The Young	Tall Cool One	
Mel	Nokie	Bob	Don	Evelyn Freeman

17-Aug-64	Peach Fuzz	House of Rising Sun	Blue Coral	Night Walk
Mel	Nokie	Bob	Don	Steve Douglas

30-Mar-65	(*On Stage album*)	Driving Guitars	Apache	Wipe Out
Mel	Bob	Don	Nokie	

31-Mar-65	Caravan	Pedal Pusher	Journey to the Stars	
Mel	Bob	Don	Nokie	

Play Guitar Vol. 2 album (Hal Blaine's session records show him on Vol. 2, 3, and 7)

29-Sep-65	Pipeline	Wipe Out	Let's Go	Out Of Limits
Rene Hall	Hal Blaine	Tommy Tedesco	Bill Pitman	Dennis Budimir

28-Sep-65	Jingle Bells	Sleigh Ride	Frosty the Snowman	Rudolph
Mel	Bob	Don	Evelyn Freeman	Red Rhodes
Nokie	Eddie Bracket Jr.*	Frank DeVito *	Julius Wechter *	* perc.

~ Jan-66	Secret Agent Man			
Nokie	Bob & Don	Mel	Jimmy Bryant	Frank DeVito

(Probably for *Guitar Freakout* album)

12-Dec-66	"Original" 1	"Original" 2	"Original" 3	"Original" 4
Nokie	Bob & Don	Mel	Evelyn Freeman	Gene Pello

(One of eight Originals on *Super Psychedelics*)

6-Feb-67	"Original"			
Bob	Nokie	Don Mel	Evelyn Freeman	Mike Deasy (sitar)

14-Feb-67	Strawberry	Fields Forever		
Bob	Nokie	Don Mel	Danny Hamilton	Red Rhodes
Gene Pello	Evelyn Freeman	James Gordon	Lincoln Mayorga	Paul Beaver (synth)

28-Sep-67	One For The Road	Torquay -	new version on *More Golden Greats* LP	
Don	Nokie	Mel	John Gallie-keyboards	

18-Oct-67	Georgy Girl	Windy	Groovin'	Music to Watch Girls By
Mel	Nokie	Don	Bob	Michel Rubini
	Bill Pitman	Red Rhodes	John Gallie	Gene Pello

23-Oct-67	Respect	To Sir With Love	Sealed With A Kiss	Yesterday
Mike Rubini	Nokie	Don	Bob	Mel
		Bill Pitman	Red Rhodes	Gene Pello

~ 1968	Soul Coaxing			
Bob	Don	Nokie	Mel	
Red Rhodes	Mike Rubini	Lincoln Mayorga	Gene Pello	Bill Pitman

28-Aug-68	Hawaii Five-0 (Sweetening session)			
	Tommy Tedesco			

Thanks to Dave Burke and Alan Taylor – *Pipeline Instrumental Review*

Appendix 2

VENTURES recordings with Alternate Titles

A Go-Go Guitar	Rim Shot
Action Plus	Teen Machine
After Midnight In Shinjuku	Suzanne [legal title]
Asian Mashed	Hot Summer
Black Sand Beach	Showdown at Newport
Blue Coral	Diamond Head
Bond Street	Dr. Yes, Without Love [legal title]
Bumble Bee [Twist]	The Wasp
Dance All Night	Dance The Night Away
Destiny	The Wind Blows East
Driving Guitars	Ventures Twist
Escape	Bullseye [original title was *Target*]
Expo Seven-O, Kyoto Doll	Streets of the City [voc.], Kyoto no Koi [Japan]
Fear	One Step Beyond
Flights of Fantasy	Psyched Out
Follow Your Heart	Kathy
Fourth Dimension	No Werewolf [The Frantics]
Ginza Lights	Ginza Ska, [new arrangement]
Guitar Twist	Raunchy Guitar
Haunting Memories	Amanda's Theme
Horse Power	Indian Pony
How Can I Help You Girl [vocal]	Soul Breeze [instrumental]
Indian Sun	Indian Summer [One-Way Records typo]
Instant Guitars	City Slicker [Chet Atkins]
Island Moon	Romantic Moon, Lisa Marie [original working title]
Jaguar	Damaged Goods
Journey To The Stars	Moon Journey, Trip To The Stars
Karelia	Sad Memories of Baikal [Japan]
Kickstand	A Go-Go Dancer
Kimi to Itsumademo [Forever with You]	Soky (*Ventures working title*)
Little People	Sunflower '76, Command Ship Earth
Lonely Heart	Dear Miss Lonely Heart [vocal]
Lonely Sea	Death of a Matador
Magic Night	Bondolero
Manchurian Beat	Wandering Guitar [Japan]
Memories of Love	Janis [original title]
Misty Night	Misty Hakone
Mockingbird (Listen to the) *	Candy Apple Racer
Monster Monkey	He Never Came Back; My True Love [vocal]
My Own True Love	Tara's Theme

* (Listen to the) Mockingbird is a 19th Century American folksong.

Nadia's Theme	Theme from The Young and Restless
Nagasaki Memories	Soft Breeze
Naruto	Thunder Cloud
Night Drive	On The Rocks [The Wailers]
Night Run [Nokie as Marksmen]	Rap City [Ventures]
Night Surfing	Atlantis
Night Stick	Shake It Easy (vocal on an old acetate disc)
Nokie's Boogie	Blues in A
Nutty	Rock Nuts
On the Road	Alka Seltzer Theme
Party in Laguna	Wild Night
Pearl Diver	Another Dawn [legal title]
Popcorn	Susukake Street
Prima Vera	You and Me
Reflections	Mirrors and Shadows
Reflections in a Palace Lake	Kyoto Bojo [Kyoto Splendor, Japan]
Sally [vocal]	Love Goddess of Venus [instrumental]
Samovar	Surf Gun
Sand, Sea, and Love	Theme For Sally
Seaside Story	Chako no Kaigan Monogatari [Japan]
Shonan Beach	Shonan Shores
Skylab	Passport To The Future
Snows of Nagano	Spool Paradise
Spindrift	Blue Horizon
Spudnik	Surf Rider
Stormy Nights	Stormy Affair
Stranger in Midosuji	Now Good-Bye [vocal]
Surfin U.S.A. '78	Hollywood Punk
Ten Seconds To Heaven	The Stranger, Paradise a Go-Go
The Chase	Scotch, Solar Race
Tight Fit	Nagoya Express
Trail Blazing	Issa's Treasure [Bob Spalding]
Tsunami	Long Boards [Bob Spalding]
Two On The Beach	Jackie [legal title]
Ventures Stomp	Gandy Dancer
What I Want to Tell You [Germany]	The Last Morning [Japan]
Wild and Wooly	Murfreesboro
Wipe Out '88	Wipe Out 2017
Yokohama Lights	Honcho
Zonked	Roadkill [working title]

The infamous 1966 Sunset album, "RUNNIN' STRONG"
(a.k.a. *Guitar Power* on 8-track cartridge)

Original Titles	*Runnin' Strong* Titles
Action Plus	Wild Action
Bird Rockers	Bird Swingers
La Bamba	Bamba
Lonely Girl	Lonely Karen
Ravin' Blue	Blue Guitar
Journey To The Stars	Moon Journey
Cruncher	Puncher
Night Stick	Cathy's Theme
Runnin' Wild	Runnin' Strong, Runnin' Fast (legal title)
Walkin' With Pluto	Dancing with Steve

Sato Project – Club Cassette Tapes

U.S. Club	U.K. Club	Legal
SP I	Painted Lady, Spider's Web [Bob Spalding CD]	
SP II	Just A Kiss And That's All [Mike Kuhn title]	
SP III	Streets Of Tokyo	
SP IV	Friends Across The Sea	
SP V	Lawrence Rides Again	
SP VI	Summer Mist, O Game [Japan vocal]	Flower Of The Sun
SP VII	Wild Northwest	Bimini Bay
SP VIII	You're The One, Strong Love [Japan]	Trailblazer

Index

A

Allison, Jerry 73,74

Allsup, Tommy 67, 73,74

Avalon, Al 137, 147, 156-7, 159

B

Babbitt, George 25, 33, 42, 288, 330, 335-6, 347, 348

Bedford, Carol 95, 99, 184

Bingenheimer, Rodney 239, 240- 242, 284

Blaine, Hal 71, 72, 79, 136, 138, 161, 271, 278, 327, 374, 375

Blocker, Don 27, 126

Bonhag, Steve   287, 313, 358

Burgess, Matthew 311, 312

Burke, Dave 72, 73, 80, 86, 107, 333, 340

Burton, James 56, 124, 137, 169-70, 181, 202, 322, 373

Buteau, Quince   344

C

Caffey, Charlotte 241-2

Callaham, Dave 228, 237-8, 283, 349

Calendar, Jonell 220, 221, 223

Campbell, Jo Ann   82, 83, 202

Caplan, Tom "ZIP"   346

Capp, Frank 68, 374

Carlieri, Marco 207, 218, 219, 223, 224, 227-228, 231-232

Carollo, Joe Frank   160, 161

Chaplain, Jack   65, 66, 99

Christiansen, Jim (Chris)   100

Christopher, Gretchen 17, 345-6, 366

Churella, Chuck   261, 266, 269

Claire, Nancy   23, 24, 25,26

Clothier, Stan   163

Coleman, Ervan "Bud"   72, 84, 372, 374

Cook, Jeff   228, 268, 357

Costa, Don   170

Coté, Dennis   311

D

Dalton, Dave 214-215, 218-219, 223-224
Davis, Jan 79, 112, 167, 232
Deck, Russ 244-247, 249-254, 247
DeFranco, Jack 346, 348, 357-8, 366, 368
Del Rey, Teisco   see Forte, Dan
DeShannon, Jackie   113
Douglas, Scott 46, 65, 75, 98, 99, 101
Douglas, Steve 112, 116, 313, 374
Dresher, Ken   125, 286

E

Effenger, Chuck   255
Engelhart, "Little" Bill   18, 33, 38, 60, 68
Ezell, Norman   189

F

Faith, George 127-128, 133
Fist, Fletcher 176
Forte, Dan 253, 256, 264-5-6, 285-6
Furmanek, Ron 301-2, 324

G

Gary, Bruce 327, 328, *329*, 331
Giobbé, Enzo   *284*
Gleeson, Keith   191, 220
Gold, Harvey 41, 151, 153
Gornicki, Sandy Lee *174-175*, 176
Gruggett, Bill   153-154
Guitar, Bonnie   17, *18*, 27, 38, 57, 107
Gursey, Don   157
Gutierrez, Mike   10, 188

H

Hall, Ed "Sharkey"   73, 372
Hall, Joe 153, 154
Hamblin, Harold "Butch" 32, 34, 49, 55, 58, 89, 347, *348*
Haskell, Jimmy   169

Hoag, J.D.   *254-55-56*, 258, 264, 269, 290
Hopkins, George   *50*, 104, 107, 145
Hunt, Tony   246-7, 255, 272-3

J

Jacinto, Ramon 81, *82*,118, 311, *317*, 325
Jackson, Grover   20-1, 32-3, 198
John, Keith   271, 278, *279*, 327
Johnson, Paul   285-286

K

Kary, Leisha   (see Soukary)
Keep, Ted   165, 178
Kelly, Roger   76, *77*
Kelso, Jackie   197, 205, 215
Kohno, Yoshi   206, 213, 221, 226, 229

L

Laboe, Art 78, 137
Lanham, Roy   100, 374
Lavinger, Allan   198
Lavinthal, Lou   17, 19
Leech, Stuart   43, 148, 158, 187, 191
Leonetti, Tommy   113
Lewis, Bill   80, 169, 257
Lilywhite, Jack   15, 26
Lincoln, Bill   202, 204
Longley, Douglas   see Douglas, Scott

M

Mandel, Harvey 192, 196, *197*, 204
Markham, Don   22, *31*, 32, 48, *49*, 63-5,   89, 282
Mayall, John   192, 196
McCulloch, Zoe 356-358
McGee, Dennis 168, 344, 352
Meadows, Larry   *101*
Mineo, Attilio "Art"   32, 33, 38
Moles, Gene   22, 63, *64*, 73-4, 89, 139, 332, 354

Moon Stones, The   103, 106, 126
Moseley, Andy 90, 105, 135, 139, 164, 309, *312*, 319
Munson, Artie   194, 196, 199
Murashita, Kozo   320, 328, 342

N

Nagisa, Yuko 184, 186, 190, 220
Naylor, Jerry   114-5
Nelson, Sandy 71, 78, 87, 137-8, 170, 188
Norman, Neil   319-20, 328, 332, 336, 352

O

O'Day, Pat 28, *29*, 33, 35-6, 110, 303, 345
Ohyan, Fifi   201
Ormsby, Buck   302-3, 366

P

Paxton, Gary   64-65, 78, 110
Peckett, David   191, 219, 249, 258-9, 272, 297, 319
Pello, Gene 136, 159, *160*, 161, 207, 375
Peterson, Ron   19
Pettersson, Arild   141, 191, *296*, 356

R

Raghavan, Chidambaram   334
Randazzo, Teddy   169-170
Reid, George M.   130, 201, 306-7
Revere, Paul   180, 228-9, 247, 281
  283, 341, 345
Reynolds, Tommy   *160*-1, 188-9
Rhodes, Orville "Red"   78, 86, 107-8 158-9, 163, 191, 211, 240, 320, 374-5
Riddle, Sam   115, 155
Rosignolo, Joe   287, 294, 303, *313*
Rowland, Greg   261, 266
Rush, Merrilee   228, 283, 345
Russell, Leon 72, 78-9, 87, 99, 102, 107, 112-116, 124, 126, 137, 148, 169, 373-4

S

Sanders, Jelly 89
Sanner, Ed 134, 163-164
Sato, Leo 215, 276, 280, 336
Savidge, Wilbur M. 126, 137
Schreiber, Susan *205*, 206
Sedacca, Chuck *50*
Shade, Bob 154
Shelton, Louie 170-1
Sinatra, Nancy 79, 140, 142, 146, 170, 192, 339, 341
Soest, Steve 264, 285
Soukary, Leisha 212-224, 245, 270-71
Standridge, Jerry 308-9
Stevens, Morton 165, 178, 186
Strange, Billy 72, 74, 84-6, 107, 113, 274, 372-374

T

Takaya, Keiichi 307-8-9-10, 312, 316
Taylor, Larry 76, 78, 80, 110, 137, 169-70, 192, 196, *197*, 237, 252, 322, 331-2

Taylor, Michael 77, 85, *331-2*
Tedesco, Tommy 72, 136, 149, 165-6, 374-5
Tietjen, Byron 334-335
Terauchi, Takeshi 120, 131, 143, 281, 291
Tippens, Marty 286

Tokutake, Hirofumi "Dr. K" 328, 332, *355*

U

Uchida, Yuya 120, 215, 217, 245

V

Vance, Charlie 65, 98, 101-104
Vegas, Pat 99, 102, *124*, 373
Versatones, 20-*24*, 25-26, 36
Vincent, Paul 71

W

Wagner, Stan 104-110, 115-122, 131-137, 142-147, 152-161, 200

Wailers, The 25-33, 45, 198, 302, 345, 359, 366, 370

Warren, Paul 239, 269, *270*-4, 284

Wiedlin, Jane 241-2

Wicklund, Harvey 231, 235, 252-255, 258-9, 261, 264, 269, 327

Wiley, Bill 20-1, 32-3, 198

Wilson, Staci Layne *357*, 358

Wilson, Tim 143, 260, *313*-4, 357-9, 361

Woods, Gary 273-4, 275-6, 278

A downloadable Ventures discography is online at

http://www.sandcastlevi.com/ventures/f_ventures.html

References

Burke, Dave Taylor, Alan
(1991-1999) Pipeline Instrumental Review - 10, 30, 34, 38, 42, 44

Kelly, Michael "Doc Rock"   (1993) Liberty Records: McFarlane

Kuhn, Michael   (1981-1992) Official USA Club Newsletter

Neely, Tim (1996) Goldmine Price Guide to 45 RPM Records: Krause

Osborne, Jerry (2002)
Official Price Guide to Records - 16th Edition: Crown/Random House

Tedesco, Tommy (1993)
Confessions of a Guitar Player - Centerstream Publishing

Peckett, David   (1976-1983) New Gandy Dancer

Vance, Charlie   Wagner, Stan   Wilson, Josie
(1962-1970) AdVentures International Bulletin

Yamachika, Hiroshi   (2000-2007) Venchans a Go-Go
        www5a.biglobe.ne.jp/~venchans

Wheeler, Tom (1992)
American Guitars Rev. and updated: HarperCollins Publishers

Whitburn, Joel (1955-1999)
Pop Annual - Sixth Edition: Billboard Publications

Woodage, Gerald   (1984-2007) Ventures Resurgence, issues 1 – 80

Printed in Great Britain
by Amazon